THE
unofficial GUIDE®
ᵀᴼLas Vegas

2008

THE *unofficial* GUIDE®
TO Las Vegas

2008

BOB SEHLINGER

with DEKE CASTLEMAN, MURIEL STEVENS,
LYNNE BACHLEDA, *and* CHRIS MOHNEY

WILEY

Please note that prices fluctuate in the course of time, and travel information changes under the impact of many factors that influence the travel industry. We therefore suggest that you write or call ahead for confirmation when making your travel plans. Every effort has been made to ensure the accuracy of information throughout this book, and the contents of this publication are believed correct at the time of printing. Nevertheless, the publishers cannot accept responsibility for errors or omissions or for changes in details given in this guide or for the consequences of any reliance on the information provided by the same. Assessments of attractions and so forth are based upon the author's own experience, and therefore, descriptions given in this guide necessarily contain an element of subjective opinion, which may not reflect the publisher's opinion or dictate a reader's own experience on another occasion. Readers are invited to write the publisher with ideas, comments, and suggestions for future editions.

Published by:
John Wiley & Sons, Inc.
111 River Street
Hoboken, NJ 07030

Produced by Menasha Ridge Press

Cover design by Michael J. Freeland

Interior design by Vertigo Design

For information on our other products and services or to obtain technical support, please contact our Customer Care Department within the United States at 800-762-2974, outside the United States at 317-572-3993, or fax 317-572-4002.

John Wiley & Sons, Inc. also publishes its books in a variety of electronic formats. Some content that appears in print may not be available in electronic formats.

ISBN 978-0-470-08962-0

Manufactured in the United States of America

5 4 3 2

CONTENTS

MAPS *and* ILLUSTRATIONS

ACKNOWLEDGMENTS

THE PEOPLE OF LAS VEGAS love their city and spare no effort to assist a writer trying to dig beneath the facade of flashing neon. It is important to them to communicate that Las Vegas is a city with depth, diversity, and substance. "Don't just write about our casinos," they demand, "take the time to get to know us."

We made every effort to do just that, enabled each step of the way by some of the most sincere and energetic folks a writer could hope to encounter. Cam Usher of the Las Vegas Convention and Visitors Authority also spared no effort in offering assistance and contacts. Thanks to Nevada expert Deke Castleman for his contributions to our entertainment, nightlife, and buffet coverage, to gambling pro Anthony Curtis for his tips on the best places to play, and to Lynne Bachleda for her work capturing the essence of Las Vegas hotels.

Restaurant critic Muriel Stevens ate her way through dozens of new restaurants but drew the line when it came to buffet duty. Jim McDonald of the Las Vegas Police Department shared his experiences and offered valuable suggestions for staying out of trouble. Larry Olmsted evaluated Las Vegas golf courses, and forest ranger Debbie Savage assisted us in developing material on wilderness recreation. New to our field research team were Jack Heffron and Howard Cohen, who reviewed shows and inspected hotels.

Purple Hearts to our field research team, who chowed down on every buffet and $2 steak in town, checked in and out of countless hotels, visited tourist attractions, and stood for hours in show lines:

Christine Testa	Grace Walton
Dawn Testa	Nathan Lott
Linda Sutton	Russell Helms
Georgia Duke	Casey Miller

Much gratitude to Steve Jones, Annie Long, Ritchey Halphen, Gabriela Oates, Maria Parker Hopkins, Johannah Paiva, Myra Merkle, and Ann Cassar, the pros who turned all this effort into a book.

INTRODUCTION

▌ ON *a* PLANE *to* LAS VEGAS

I NEVER WANTED TO GO TO LAS VEGAS. I'm not much of a gambler and have always thought of Las Vegas as a city dedicated to separating folks from their money. As it happens, however, I have some involvement with industries that hold conventions and trade shows there. For some years I was able to persuade others to go in my place. Eventually, of course, it came my turn to go, and I found myself aboard a Delta jumbo jet on my first trip to Las Vegas.

Listening to the banter of those around me, I became aware that my fellow passengers were divided into two distinct camps. Some obviously thought themselves on a nonstop flight to Nirvana and could not have been happier. Too excited to remain seated, they danced up and down the aisles, clapping one another on the back in anticipation. The other passengers, by contrast, groused and grumbled, swore under their breath, and wore expressions suggesting a steady diet of lemons. These people, as despondent as Al Capone en route to a tax audit, lamented their bad luck and cursed those who had made a trip to such a place necessary.

To my surprise, I thoroughly enjoyed Las Vegas. I had a great time without gambling and have been back many times with never a bad experience. The people are friendly, the food is good, the hotels are among the nicest in the country, it's an easy town to find your way around, and there is plenty to do (24 hours a day, if you are so inclined).

It's hard to say why so many folks have such strong feelings about Las Vegas (even those who have never been there). Among our research team, we had people willing to put their kids in boarding school for a chance to go, while others begged off to have root-canal surgery or prune their begonias. A third group wanted to go very badly but maintained the pretense of total indifference. They reminded me of people who own five TVs yet profess never to watch television; they clearly had not mustered the courage to come out of the closet.

What I discovered during my first and subsequent visits is that the nongambling public doesn't know very much about Las Vegas. Many people cannot see beyond the gambling, cannot see that there could possibly be anything of value in Las Vegas for nongamblers or those only marginally interested in gambling.

When you ask these people to describe their ideal vacation, they wax eloquent about lazy days relaxing in the sun, playing golf, enjoying the luxury of resort hotels, eating in fine restaurants, sightseeing, shopping, and going to the theater. Outdoor types speak no less enthusiastically about fishing, boating, hiking, and, in the winter, skiing. As it happens, Las Vegas offers all of this. Gambling is just the tip of the iceberg in Las Vegas, but it's all many people can see.

Las Vegas is, of course, about gambling, but there's so much more. Vegas has sunny, mild weather two-thirds of the year, some of the finest hotels and restaurants in the world, the most diversified celebrity and production-show entertainment to be found, unique shopping, internationally renowned golf courses, and numerous attractions. For the outdoor enthusiast, Red Rock Canyon National Conservation Area, Lake Mead National Recreation Area, and Toiyabe National Forest offer some of the most exotic and beautiful wilderness resources in North America.

This guide is designed for those who *want* to go to Las Vegas and for those who *have* to go to Las Vegas. If you are a recreational gambler and/or an enthusiastic vacationer, we will show you ways to have more fun, make the most of your time, and spend less money. If you are one of the skeptics, unwilling spouses or companions of gamblers, business travelers, or people who think they would rather be someplace else, we will help you discover the seven-eighths of the Las Vegas iceberg that is hidden.

—*Bob Sehlinger*

LOOKING BACK, LOOKING AHEAD

IN 1946, BUGSY SIEGEL OPENED the Flamingo Hotel, kicking off the metamorphosis that changed three miles of mostly barren desert into what is now the Las Vegas Strip. The original Flamingo was an eye-popper in its day and established a baseline that all subsequent casinos had to at least match, if not improve upon.

As new hotels appeared in the neon Valhalla, each contributed something different, and occasionally something better, raising the bar incrementally. Two properties, the Desert Inn and Caesars Palace, advanced the standard significantly, but because they catered to an exclusive clientele, their competitors chose not to follow suit.

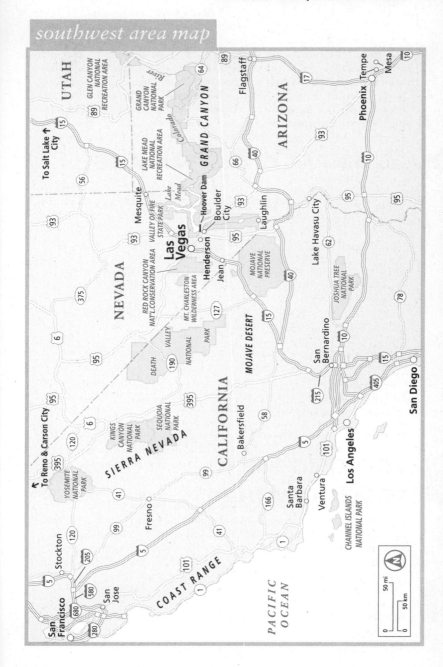

southwest area map

Then, in 1989, came the Mirage, a large hotel and casino offering the spectacle of Caesars and the refinement of the Desert Inn (almost) but, more importantly, targeting not the carriage trade but rather the average tourist. The Mirage was equal parts tourist attraction, hotel, and casino, and each part was executed with imagination and flair. Not many Las Vegas tourists could afford the Mirage's expensive guest rooms, but the place was nonetheless a must-see on every visitor's touring itinerary.

The **IMPACT** of the **MIRAGE**

THE MIRAGE'S SUCCESS DEMONSTRATED that gamblers, contrary to prevailing opinion, actually paid attention to their gaming environment and, if given a choice, preferred an interesting, dynamic, and attractive setting to the cramped, noisy, monochromatic boiler room that was the casino norm. Beyond a doubt, the Mirage was in a class by itself. Observers waited impatiently to see if any competitor would challenge the Mirage, though most believed the standard was impossibly high.

The answer was not long in coming. A veritable explosion of new developments was rushed from the drawing board to the construction zone. First was the Excalibur in 1990. It was big, plastic, gaudy, and certainly no direct competitor to the Mirage, but its Knights of the Round Table theme played exceptionally well with the blue-collar and family markets. Next came the Class of 1993, which included the pyramid-shaped Luxor, Treasure Island (sister property to the Mirage), and the MGM Grand Hotel and Theme Park. Though the MGM Grand Theme Park was a bust, the hotel and casino were immediately successful. Likewise, the Luxor and Treasure Island (T. I.), with their knockout themes, rocketed up the pop chart.

In the three years before the next wave of new hotels opened in 1996, the vital signs of the newer and older properties were monitored closely. The MGM Grand was the largest hotel-casino in the world, Excalibur was a close second, and the other new hotels offered more than 2,500 rooms each. As with the bull stock market in the late 1990s, there was endless speculation and debate about how long the building boom could last. But the preliminary data seemed to indicate that the new properties were responsible for increasing the aggregate market. Room occupancy rates remained high.

SURVIVAL of the OLDER CASINOS

THOUGH MORE VISITORS WERE COMING to Las Vegas, the lion's share of the business was going to the newer, high-profile hotels.

Older properties, including some of the Strip's most established casinos, found themselves increasingly in the margins. So too, downtown Las Vegas was in a tailspin, with gaming revenues down, or flat, year after year. The new marching orders, avoided or ignored for so long, were crystal clear: if you want to play in the big league, you have to upgrade. And upgrading meant approximating the Mirage standard.

The response of downtown Las Vegas was to combine the Fremont Street casinos into a mega–gaming venue, a new Glitter Gulch, tied together by a pedestrian plaza under the canopy of the Fremont Street Experience electric light show. Back on the Strip, older properties, including Bally's, the Desert Inn, the Flamingo, Harrah's, the Sahara, the Boardwalk, Circus Circus, and the Riviera, scrambled to upgrade. One property, Vegas World, was razed to make room for a whole new hotel-casino. The venerable Caesars Palace alone managed to stay ahead of the game, making improvements each year to maintain its position at or near the top of the Strip food chain.

HONEY, I BLEW UP
the CASINO!

IN 1991, BOB STUPAK'S QUIRKY Vegas World was demolished to make way in 1996 for the Stratosphere Hotel and Casino, which has the tallest observation tower in the United States. The fireworks had just begun. Farther south on the Strip, the Monte Carlo hit the scene, a joint venture between then–Circus Circus Enterprises and Mirage Resorts. Then, in 1997, New York–New York opened its doors. With more than 100,000 people a day visiting during its first weeks of operation, New York–New York quickly dispelled the notion that the Strip was overbuilt. In typical Las Vegas go-for-broke style, the Dunes, the Sands, El Rancho, and the Hacienda, and more recently the Boardwalk and the Stardust, were blown up to make room for yet more gargantuan gambling palaces.

The boom proceeded at warp speed, with a construction frenzy that through 2001 added a whopping 28,000 new rooms to Las Vegas's inventory (now totaling roughly 140,000). Bellagio (opened in 1998) draws its inspiration from Italy's Lake Como, adding 4,000 rooms to the MGM-Mirage galaxy and catering to the upscale market. Across the street is the 2,900-room Paris Las Vegas with its own 50-story Eiffel Tower. Just south is Planet Hollywood (formerly the Aladdin), a 2,600-room complex with an evolving Hollywood theme. On the site of the old Sands is the Venetian. An all-suite property with 3,000 suites in its first building phase and 1,013 in its second, the Venetian features a shopping complex in a Venice canal setting complete with gondola rides. At the southern end of the Strip on the old Hacienda property, the 3,300-room Mandalay Bay opened in 1999. Wynn Las Vegas opened in 2005 with 2,700 rooms.

More and more new casinos are being built around town in an effort to cater to the local population and visitors who don't want to battle the traffic of the Strip. In 2006, the Red Rock Resort opened with 400 rooms overlooking Red Rock Canyon. Also to the west of the Strip is JW Marriott, a 550-room spa and golf resort in the Summerlin area of Las Vegas that was built in 1999. To the east, the Hyatt Regency Lake Las Vegas (near Henderson) is surrounded by a man-made lake and a Jack Nicklaus–designed golf course. On the shore of the same lake, Las Vegas's first Ritz-Carlton serves the carriage clientele.

The GREAT MERGERS *and* ACQUISITIONS

THEN THERE ARE THE MERGERS and acquisitions. In 2000, Steve Wynn, the visionary behind the Mirage (and the Las Vegas transformation it started), sold the Mirage, Bellagio, T. I., Golden Nugget, and half of Monte Carlo to MGM Grand for $6.4 billion. Wynn, meanwhile, purchased the Desert Inn, where he built a 2,700-room nonthemed resort called Wynn Las Vegas, stating ironically that "themes are a thing of the past." Wynn always seems to be a step ahead of the pack and might be correct about themes. Still, it's like Dr. Spock saying that children are a thing of the past.

The Mandalay Resort Group, which owned Luxor, Mandalay Bay, Excalibur, Circus Circus, and half of the Monte Carlo, was acquired in June of 2004 by MGM Grand for a whopping $6 billion, forming MGM Mirage with control of 36,000 Strip hotel rooms. Only months earlier, Hilton's casino subsidiary, Park Place Entertainment, bought Caesars Palace and O'Shea's, adding them to a lineup that already included the Las Vegas Hilton, Bally's, Paris, and the Flamingo. In 2004, Park Place changed its name to Caesars Entertainment to reflect the prestige of its flagship properties. In an even bigger (not to mention surprising) deal, Harrah's bought Caesars Entertainment in a $9.4 billion deal, making it the largest casino-gambling company in the world. Subsequently, Harrah's also acquired the Rio, Imperial Palace, and the Barbary Coast (renamed Bill's Gambling Hall and Saloon). In 2007, before the ink was dry on the Caesars–Harrah's merger, Harrah's was acquired by Apollo Management, a private investment company.

On the Strip, Planet Hollywood and Starwood Hotels landed the financially troubled Aladdin for a bargain price. The Desert Passage Mall at the Aladdin, also on the block, was sold to a German holding company. *Sehr gut!* In one of the more curious developments, the San Remo shut down for a $130-million makeover and reopened in 2006 as the world's only Hooters Casino (as in the bosomy restaurant chain).

GLUTTONS ARE *more* LIKELY *to* CHOKE *to* DEATH

THIS FOLKSY SAYING DESCRIBES the unbridled development of the Las Vegas Strip built precariously (some would say recklessly) on a rapidly deteriorating street-and-highway infrastructure. And it's only going to get worse.

For many years there have been sizable undeveloped parcels of land along the Strip, most conspicuously between Circus Circus and the Stratosphere. In the middle of the Strip, small retailers and second-string hotels squatted on some of the planet's most valuable real estate. No more. In a development frenzy that makes the 1990s hotel crop look like home gardening, the land has been gobbled up and giant construction cranes are redefining the Strip's skyline. High-rise mania has hit Las Vegas with a vengeance. Believe it or not, this city is running out of room to develop horizontally, so it's turning vertical. Nearly 80 high-rise condominium, time-share, and condo-hotel towers have been announced in the past few years, encompassing more than 30,000 units. More than a dozen, including Turnberry Place's four luxury towers across from the Convention Center and three towers at MGM Grand, Panorama's two on the west side of I-15, the Metropolis on the Desert Inn Arterial, One Las Vegas and Trump International right on the Strip, and several downtown are either completed or about to open.

The projects underway are not just huge hotels as in the past, but veritable self-contained cities rising above every existing resort and containing hotels (yes, plural), residential condos, restaurants, entertainment, shopping, parks, and even their own road networks. Project City Center, an MGM Mirage $7.4-billion development, is the largest construction project in the United States. When finished there will be a 4,000-room casino resort, two boutique hotels, and 2,700 residences distributed among eight high-rise towers, the tallest being 57 stories. A bit to the north on the site of the old Stardust (imploded in 2007) will be Boyd's Echelon Place, similar in concept but somewhat smaller in size.

Plans for all of the combined resort and residential developments call for on-site supermarkets, pharmacies, and other services that the residents and guests will need. This is fortunate indeed because almost nothing is being done to the infrastructure to accommodate the many thousands of additional people who will live, work, and play along the Strip. We've seen model units of the condos for sale in these developments and can report that they're quite lovely, which is good, because their denizens are likely to be held hostage by surrounding traffic arteries that are already completely overwhelmed.

Sooner or later, the Strip is going to choke to death. Already the Strip is the most sclerotic traffic artery imaginable, making 45-minute slogs of a half-mile trip. Some hope of relief came in 2004 in the form of a monorail, which runs along the east side of the Strip and loops over to the Las Vegas Convention Center, then on to the Sahara. Problem is, the stations are so far removed from the Strip that only about half the riders necessary to break even are using the monorail.

Water is also a problem (look around, it's a desert out there!). Casino owners and condo and time-share developers duck the blame for spiraling water consumption by insisting that it's the expanding local population that accounts for most of the usage. This is a bit disingenuous, given that the condo–time-share building boom and the new casinos are what's driving population growth. New properties currently under construction will create almost 31,000 new jobs. That's a lot of thirsty people, dogs to bathe, and lawns to water.

WHAT *It* MEANS *to* YOU

FOR YOU, THE LAS VEGAS VISITOR, the news is mixed. The good news is that most of the hotels and casinos that opened in 2006 and 2007 are very upscale. The bad news is that most of the hotels and casinos that opened in 2006 and 2007 are very upscale. You're free to visit ritzy joints and gawk, and they will gleefully separate you from your stake, but at the end of the day it's only the fat cats who can afford a bed. For the moment you can get a luxury hotel room in Las Vegas for less than you'd pay at a lot of other places, but Vegas rooms are a bargain in only a relative sense. There's no more Courvoisier on a jug-wine budget in America's gambling mecca.

The most important development by far, however, and one that was unthinkable only a couple of years ago, is quietly taking place at these same top-of-the-line Strip properties. The Mirage demonstrated that a hotel could be positioned as a luxury product and charge accordingly. Though most Strip properties hedged their bets with various incentives to attract patrons, they learned they didn't have to offer loss-leader buffets, restaurants, and shows to get people through the door. From the establishment of the Mirage until the present, the upscale casinos and hotels have discovered, through experimenting with various pricing models, that there's apparently much less price sensitivity than previously thought. This sea change in the prevailing revenue model has paved the way for such prestigious brands as Four Seasons, Ritz-Carlton, Hyatt Regency, and JW Marriott to enter the market with luxury resorts where gaming is almost an afterthought. Facilitating the process is an upsurge in meeting, convention, and trade-show business, especially in events that can be accommodated by a single hotel.

Sales revenues from hotel rooms, food and beverages, shows and events, and ancillary sales (shopping, spa services, and such) are surpassing gaming revenues.

Though your business is welcome at any Las Vegas property, the new revenue model has created a caste system. You can play quarter slots anywhere (at least for the moment), but if you want to see a big-name show or dine at upscale hotel restaurants, you'd better be pretty well-heeled. For the other hotel-casinos, the Saharas, Rivieras, Stratospheres, Imperial Palaces, and Tropicanas, attracting guests and players requires offering bargains and discounts. If the Strip were an airliner, you could stroll up the aisle from your economy seat and see what's going on in First Class, but you won't be able to stay or eat there.

The dining scene is another plus. Buffets continue to improve as competition sharpens, and there is now a branch of seemingly every big-name restaurant in Las Vegas (Le Cirque, Aqua, Delmonico Steak House, Lawry's, Morton's, the Palm, Wolfgang Puck, and on and on). Although theme dining continues to proliferate, the public has weeded out the weak sisters. It's fine to have a theme, but patrons are appropriately voting their palate. Proprietary restaurants are holding their own, but just barely. The bad news is that, aside from buffets, it costs more to dine in Las Vegas now, especially in the new, brand-name joints. As an extreme example, the Mandalay Bay Burger Bar features a $60 hamburger! Still, compared to other cities with dynamic restaurant scenes, Las Vegas remains a relative bargain, especially if you're willing to venture away from the Strip.

Production and celebrity-headliner shows are not the bargain they once were. In fact, the average price of a ticket has increased by more than 100% in the last ten years, and more than a dozen shows now cost more than $100. On the other side of the coin, the quality of the average show has also trended up and there's more variety. Las Vegas promoters claim prices are a bargain compared to entertainment elsewhere, but that's wishful thinking. Probably half of the shows in town are overpriced. A happy development is the return of downtown shows, a species that came perilously close to extinction, and a bumper crop of afternoon shows including matinees for some of the major productions.

unofficial **TIP**
A few high-quality afternoon productions offer a bargain alternative to the mortgage-the-farm-priced shows playing the major showrooms.

The QUIET CONTENDER

A FEW YEARS BACK, the big buzz was Las Vegas as a family destination. Insiders understood, however, that all the talk was just that. At most, the family thing was a public relations exercise to make Las Vegas appear more wholesome. It was tacitly understood that the big dogs would never allow theme parks and other family-oriented attractions to actually compete with the casinos for a visitor's time. Lost in the backwash of this hollow debate, however, was the exponential burgeoning of theme shopping. Shopping is something that reached critical mass almost unnoticed and that keeps visitors out of the casinos. At present, the case can be made that shopping is almost as potent an attraction in Las Vegas as gambling. On the Strip are three huge themed shopping venues (Forum Shops, Grand Canal Shops, and Miracle Mile Shops) and a comparatively white-bread mall, but one that's buttressed with every big-name department store in North America. Not to be left in the wake, downtown launched the Las Vegas Premium Outlets complex, which features 120 stores, all flogging upmarket brands. For the first time, there is something powerful enough to suck the players right out of the casinos, and it arrived on the scene as stealthily as a Trojan horse.

A **TALE** of **TWO CITIES**

FOR AT LEAST 30 YEARS Las Vegas has been referred to as "Disneyland for Adults." At the time, this tongue-in-cheek appellation was gaining currency Las Vegas was anything but. Disneyland was systematically planned, highly polished, absolutely regimented, and totally plastic. Las Vegas by contrast grew like a weed, was raw, unrefined, and freewheeling, and was as real as a one-way ticket home on Greyhound with an empty wallet. Disneyland was a sanitized version of fantasy and history, Las Vegas the last vestige of the western frontier.

When we began covering Las Vegas less than 20 years ago, the casinos were predominantly independent. Each had a distinct identity free of the corporate veneer that blankets Las Vegas today. Personality, or the lack thereof, was defining. As with cakes at a church fund-raiser, it was what was on the inside that mattered. Now it's the icing that counts, or, expressed differently, the icon (Statue of Liberty, Sphinx, pirate ship, Eiffel Tower, Campanile . . . you choose) that sits in the casino's front yard. Inside, the product's largely the same. Four casino megacorporations now run most of Las Vegas. On the Strip it's worse. Two companies—Harrah's and MGM Mirage—own every casino except the Tropicana, Riviera, Venetian, Planet Hollywood, Stratosphere, and Sahara. Standards for restaurants, hotel rooms, entertainment, theme, and just about everything else offer all the predictability of a nice chain hotel. The maverick casinos and their rough-and-tumble owners are all but gone, and with them the gritty, boom-or-bust soul of this gambling town. Making a clichéd joke a fulfilled prophecy, Las Vegas has in fact become Disneyland.

If you'd like a taste of the old Las Vegas, now's the time. Tomorrow, or soon after, it will largely be gone. While you can, walk Glitter Gulch; enjoy a 99-cent shrimp cocktail at the Golden Gate; see *Jubilee!*, the quintessential Las Vegas Parisian revue; catch Lena Prima at the Sahara's Casbar Lounge; or play craps beneath the stained-glass canopy at the Tropicana. Linger over the porterhouse special at the Redwood Bar and Grill at the California, or the rack of lamb at the Great Moments Room in the Las Vegas Club. Make no mistake, this is not slumming; each example represents the best of Las Vegas in both a current and historical sense. And if you wait too long? Well, enjoy the new Las Vegas: systematically planned, highly polished, absolutely regimented, and totally plastic.

As most of you know, we also publish guides to Disneyland and Walt Disney World and have never for a moment doubted the overall quality of the Disney product. Comparing the new Las Vegas with Disneyland is a long way from a condemnation. Though we liked the sultry, wide-open, sinful feel of the old Vegas, we can't argue that corporate Las Vegas has built an Oz that no maverick dreamer could have envisioned. Whether the old Las Vegas or the new Las Vegas is better we'll leave you to judge.

LETTERS, COMMENTS, AND QUESTIONS FROM READERS

WE EXPECT TO LEARN FROM OUR MISTAKES, as well as from input of our readers, and to improve with each edition. Many of those who use the *Unofficial Guides* write to us to ask questions, make comments, or share their own discoveries and lessons learned in Las Vegas. We appreciate all such input, both positive and critical, and encourage our readers to continue writing. Readers' comments and observations will be frequently incorporated in revised editions of the *Unofficial Guide* and will contribute immeasurably to its improvement.

How to Write the Author:

Bob Sehlinger
The Unofficial Guide to Las Vegas
P.O. Box 43673
Birmingham, AL 35243
unofficialguides@menasharidge.com

If you write us, rest assured that we won't release your name and address to any mailing-list companies, direct-mail advertisers, or other third parties. Unless you tell us otherwise, we'll assume that you're OK with being quoted in the *Unofficial Guide*. Be sure to put your return address on both your letter and the envelope—sometimes envelopes and letters get separated. And because our work takes us out of the office for long periods of time, note that our response may be delayed.

Reader Survey

At the back of this guide, you will find a short questionnaire that you can use to express opinions concerning your Las Vegas visit. Clip the questionnaire out along the dotted line and mail it to the above address.

The *Unofficial Guide* Web Site

The Web site of the *Unofficial Guide* Travel and Lifestyle Series, providing in-depth information on all *Unofficial Guides* in print, is at **www.theunofficialguides.com.**

HOW INFORMATION IS ORGANIZED:
BY SUBJECT AND BY GEOGRAPHIC AREAS

TO GIVE YOU FAST ACCESS to information about the *best* of Las Vegas, we've organized material in several formats.

HOTELS Because most people visiting Las Vegas stay in one hotel for the duration of their vacation or business trip, we have summarized our coverage of hotels in charts, maps, ratings, and rankings that allow you to quickly focus your decision-making process. We do not ramble on for page after page describing lobbies and rooms which, in the final analysis, sound (and look) much the same. Instead, we concentrate our coverage on the specific variables that differentiate one hotel from another: location, size, room quality, services, amenities, and cost.

RESTAURANTS We give you a lot of detail when it comes to restaurants. Because you will probably eat a dozen or more restaurant meals during your stay, and because not even you can predict what kind of fare you might be in the mood for on, say, Saturday night, we provide detailed profiles of the very best restaurants Las Vegas has to offer.

ENTERTAINMENT AND NIGHTLIFE Visitors frequently try several different shows or clubs during their stay. Because shows and nightspots, like restaurants, are usually selected spontaneously after arriving in Las Vegas, we believe detailed descriptions are warranted. All continuously running stage shows, as well as celebrity showrooms, are profiled and reviewed in the entertainment section of this guide. The best nightspots and lounges in Las Vegas are profiled alphabetically under nightlife in the same section.

GEOGRAPHIC AREAS Though it's easy to get around in Las Vegas, you may not have a car or the inclination to venture far from your hotel. To help you locate the best restaurants, shows, nightspots, and attractions convenient to where you are staying, we have divided the city into geographic areas:

- South Strip and Environs
- Mid-Strip and Environs
- North Strip and Environs
- West of Strip
- Downtown Las Vegas
- Southeast Las Vegas–Henderson
- East of Strip

All profiles of hotels, restaurants, and nightspots include area names. For example, if you are staying at the Golden Nugget and are interested in Italian restaurants within walking distance, scanning the restaurant profiles for restaurants in Downtown Las Vegas will provide you with the best choices.

COMFORT ZONES Because every Las Vegas hotel-casino has its own personality and attracts a specific type of customer, for each property we have created a profile that describes the casino's patrons and gives you some sense of how it might feel to spend time there. The purpose of the comfort-zone section is to help you find the hotel-casino at which you will feel most welcome and at home. These comfort-zone descriptions begin on page 77 in Part One, Accommodations and Casinos.

▌ LAS VEGAS: *An Overview*

GATHERING INFORMATION

LAS VEGAS HAS THE BEST SELECTION of complimentary visitor guides of any American tourist destination we know. Available at the front desk or concierge table at almost every hotel, the guides provide a wealth of useful information on gaming, gambling lessons, shows, lounge entertainment, sports, buffets, meal deals, tours and sightseeing, transportation, shopping, and special events. Additionally, most of the guides contain coupons for discounts on dining, shows, attractions, and tours.

What's On is the most comprehensive of the visitor guides. *Today in Las Vegas* is also very comprehensive but is organized somewhat differently. Because both formats come in handy, we always pick up a copy of each.

A new guide, *Las Vegas Magazine,* offers much the same information but with a more upscale, high-production-values presentation.

The guides are published weekly or biweekly and are distributed on a complimentary basis in Las Vegas. If you want to see a copy before you leave home, subscriptions or single issues are available as follows:

Today in Las Vegas
4310 South Cameron Street, Suite 11
Las Vegas, NV 89103
☎ 702-385-2737
www.todayinlv.com

What's On Magazine
4425 Dean Martin Drive
Las Vegas, NV 89103
☎ 702-891-8811
www.whats-on.com

Las Vegas Magazine
2290 Corporate Circle, Suite 250
Henderson, NV 89074
☎ 702-383-7185
www.lasvegasmagazine.com

Other publications include *Las Vegas Magazine* (**www.lvshowbiz .com**), published by the *Las Vegas Sun* newspaper, and *Where Magazine of Las Vegas* (**www.wheremagazine.com**). Both have much of the same information discussed above, plus feature articles. Although all of the freebie Las Vegas visitor magazines contain valuable information, they are rah-rah rags, and their primary objective is to promote. So don't expect any critical reviews of shows, restaurants, attractions, or anything else for that matter.

The *Las Vegas Advisor* is a 12-page monthly newsletter containing some of the most useful consumer information available on gaming, dining, and entertainment, as well as deals on rooms, drinks, shows, and meals. With no advertising or promotional content, the newsletter serves its readers with objective, prescriptive, no-nonsense advice, presented with a sense of humor. The *Advisor* also operates a dynamite Web site at **www.lasvegasadvisor.com.** At a subscription rate of $50 a year, the *Las Vegas Advisor* is the best investment you can make if you plan to spend four or more days in Las Vegas each year. If you are a one-time visitor but wish to avail yourself of all this wisdom, single copies of the *Las Vegas Advisor* can be purchased for $5 at the Gambler's Book Club store at 630 South 11th Street (☎ 702-382-7555 or 800-522-1777 or visit **www.gamblersbook.com**). To speed delivery of the first issue (which includes discount coupons), send a self-addressed, legal-sized envelope with $1.06 postage along with your request. For additional information:

Las Vegas Advisor
Huntington Press
3665 South Procyon Avenue
Las Vegas, NV 89103
☎ 702-252-0655 or 800-244-2224
www.lasvegasadvisor.com

Las Vegas and the Internet

The explosive growth of Las Vegas is not only physical but also virtual. The following are the best places to go on the Web to launch yourself into Las Vegas cyberspace:

The site of the *Las Vegas Advisor,* **www.lasvegasadvisor.com,** is a great source of information on recent and future developments, dining, entertainment, and gambling. The site features a nifty trip planner as well as a miniature vacation guide.

The official Web site of the Las Vegas Convention and Visitors Authority is **www.visitlasvegas.com.** This site has hundreds of links to hotels, casinos, the airport, and area transportation, plus information on the convention center, sightseeing, and dining. To pull up the menu of categories (hotels, entertainment, etc.), click "Search."

The largest Las Vegas Web site is **www.lasvegas.com,** a travel site sponsored by the *Las Vegas Review-Journal.* The newspaper's own Web site is **www.lvrj.com.** Another big Las Vegas travel Web site, with an excellent listing of hotels and their dining and entertainment options, is **www.vegas.com.** Try *What's On* magazine's **www.ilovelasvegas.com** for shows and nightspots. Another good site for entertainment information is *Showbiz* magazine's **www.lvshowbiz.com.**

The best site for finding discounts on hotels is **www.travelaxe.com.** Travelaxe allows you to download a free software program that compares room rates offered by a wide range of discounters. You can also access Travelaxe from the *Las Vegas Advisor* site.

las vegas strip area

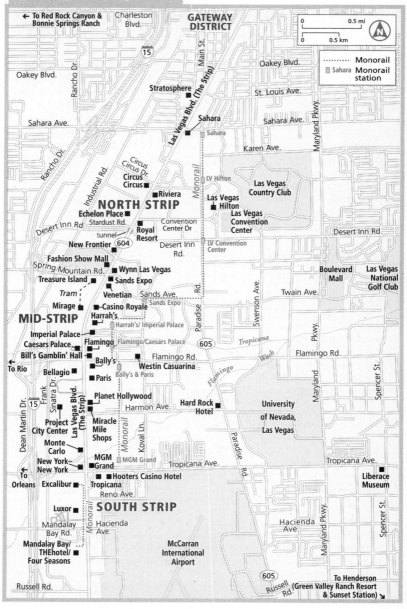

← To Red Rock Canyon &
Bonnie Springs Ranch

Charleston Blvd.

GATEWAY DISTRICT

0   0.5 mi
0   0.5 km

Oakey Blvd.

Oakey Blvd.

Rancho Dr.

Stratosphere ■

St. Louis Ave.

Sahara Ave.

Sahara ■

Sahara Ave.

Sahara Monorail station

Sahara ■

Karen Ave.

Rancho Dr.

Industrial Rd.

Circus
Circus Dr.

Circus Circus ■

LV Hilton ■

Las Vegas Country Club

Riviera ■

Las Vegas Hilton ■

NORTH STRIP

Echelon Place ■

Stardust Rd.

Convention Center Dr

Las Vegas Convention Center

Desert Inn Rd.

tunnel

Royal Resort ■

Desert Inn Rd.

Desert Inn Rd.

New Frontier ■ (604)

LV Convention Center

Fashion Show Mall ■

Spring Mountain Rd.

Wynn Las Vegas ■

Boulevard Mall

Las Vegas National Golf Club

Treasure Island ■

Sands Expo ■

Venetian ■

Sands Ave.

Tram

Sands Expo ■

Mirage ■

Casino Royale ■

MID-STRIP

Harrah's ■

Harrah's/ Imperial Palace ■

Twain Ave.

Imperial Palace ■

Caesars Palace ■

Flamingo ■

Flamingo/Caesars Palace ■

(605)

Tropicana

Bill's Gamblin' Hall ■

Bally's ■

Flamingo Rd.

To Rio

Bellagio ■

Westin Casuarina ■

Flamingo Rd.

Paris ■

Bally's & Paris ■

Planet Hollywood ■

Frank Sinatra Dr.

(15)

Harmon Ave.

Hard Rock Hotel

Project City Center ■

Miracle Mile Shops

University of Nevada, Las Vegas

Dean Martin Dr.

Monte Carlo ■

New York–New York ■

MGM Grand ■

MGM Grand ■

Tropicana Ave.

Tropicana Ave.

← To Orleans

Excalibur ■

Hooters Casino Hotel ■

Tropicana ■

Liberace Museum ■

Reno Ave.

SOUTH STRIP

Luxor ■

Hacienda Ave.

Hacienda Ave.

Spencer St.

Mandalay Bay Rd.

Mandalay Bay/ THEhotel/ Four Seasons ■

McCarran International Airport

Russell Rd.

Russell Rd.

(605)

To Henderson (Green Valley Ranch Resort & Sunset Station) ↘

Maryland Pkwy.

Swenson Ave.

Paradise Rd.

Koval Ln.

Maryland Pkwy.

Spencer St.

Las Vegas Blvd. (The Strip)

Monorail

.... Monorail
■ Sahara Monorail station

An extensive site aimed at people relocating to Las Vegas or interested in investing in Las Vegas real estate is at **www.lasvegas4sale.com**.

WHEN TO GO TO LAS VEGAS

THE BEST TIME TO GO TO LAS VEGAS is in the spring or fall, when the weather is pleasant. If you plan to spend most of your time indoors, it doesn't matter what time of year you choose. If you intend to golf, play tennis, run, hike, bike, or boat, try to go in March, April, early May, October, November, or early December.

unofficial **TIP**
The winter months in Las Vegas provide an unbeatable combination of good value and choice of activities.

Because spring and fall are the nicest times of year, they are also the most popular. The best time for special deals is December (after the National Finals Rodeo in early December and excluding the week between Christmas and New Year's), January, and during the scorching months of summer.

Weather in December, January, and February can vary incredibly. While high winds, cold, rain, and snow are not unheard of, chances are better that temperatures will be mild and the sun will shine. Though the

Las Vegas Weather and Dress Chart

MONTH	POOLS O = OPEN
January **average daytime temp. 57°F** | average evening temp. 32°F *Recommended attire:* **coats and jackets are a must.**	—
February **average daytime temp. 50°F** | average evening temp. 37°F *Recommended attire:* **dress warmly—jackets and sweaters.**	—
March **average daytime temp. 69°F** | average evening temp. 42°F *Recommended attire:* **sweaters for days, but a jacket at night.**	O
April **average daytime temp. 78°F** | average evening temp. 50°F *Recommended attire:* **still cool at night—bring a jacket.**	O
May **average daytime temp. 88°F** | average evening temp. 50°F *Recommended attire:* **sweater for evening, but days are warm.**	O
June **average daytime temp. 99°F** | average evening temp. 68°F *Recommended attire:* **days are hot; evenings are moderate.**	O
July **average daytime temp. 105°F** | average evening temp. 75°F *Recommended attire:* **bathing suits**	O
August **average daytime temp. 102°F** | average evening temp. 73°F *Recommended attire:* **dress for the heat—spend time at a pool!**	O
September **average daytime temp. 95°F** | average evening temp. 65°F *Recommended attire:* **days warm, sweater for evening.**	O
October **average daytime temp. 81°F** | average evening temp. 53°F *Recommended attire:* **bring a jacket or sweater for afternoon.**	O
November **average daytime temp. 67°F** | average evening temp. 40°F *Recommended attire:* **sweaters and jackets, coats for night.**	—
December **average daytime temp. 58°F** | average evening temp. 34°F *Recommended attire:* **coats and jackets a must—dress warmly!**	—

weather is less dependable than in spring or fall, winter months are generally well suited to outdoor activities. We talked to people who in late February water-skied on Lake Mead in the morning and snow-skied in the afternoon at Lee Canyon. From mid-May through mid-September, however, the heat is blistering. During these months, it's best to follow the example of the gambler or the lizard—stay indoors or under a rock.

Crowd Avoidance

In general, weekends are busy and weekdays are slower. The exceptions are holiday periods and when large conventions or special events are being held. Most Las Vegas hotels have a lower guest-room rate for weekdays than for weekends. Las Vegas hosts huge conventions and special events (rodeos, prize fights) that tie up hotels, restaurants, transportation, showrooms, and traffic for a week at a time. Likewise, major sporting events such as the Super Bowl, the NCAA football bowl games, the men's NCAA basketball tournament, Triple Crown horse races, the World Series, and the NBA championship fill every hotel in town on weekends. If you prefer to schedule your visit at a time when things are a little less frantic, we provide a calendar that lists the larger citywide conventions and regularly scheduled events to help you avoid the crowds. Note that two or three medium-sized conventions meeting at the same time can affect Las Vegas as much as one big citywide event.

> *unofficial* **TIP**
> For a stress-free arrival at the airport, good availability of rental cars, and a quick hotel check-in, try to arrive Monday afternoon through Thursday morning (Tuesday and Wednesday are best).

Because conventions of more than 12,000 attendees can cause problems for the lone vacationer, the list of conventions and special events on pages 24–28 will help you plan your vacation dates. Included are the convention date, the number of people expected to attend, and the convention location (with hotel headquarters, if known at the time of publication). If you would like to have a more complete convention calendar mailed to you, call the Las Vegas Convention and Visitors Authority at ☎ 702-892-0711, 702-892-7576, or 877-VISIT-LV. The convention calendar is also available online at **www.lasvegas24hours.com.**

ARRIVING *and* GETTING ORIENTED

IF YOU DRIVE, YOU WILL HAVE TO TRAVEL through the desert to reach Las Vegas. Make sure your car is in good shape. Check your spare tire and toss a couple of gallons of water in the trunk, just in case. Once en route, pay attention to your fuel and temperature gauges.

Virtually all commercial air traffic into Las Vegas uses McCarran International Airport. At McCarran, a well-designed facility with good, clear signs, you will have no problem finding your way from the gate to the baggage claim area, though it is often a long walk. Fast baggage handling is not the airport's strongest suit, so don't be surprised if you have to wait a long time on your checked luggage.

If you do not intend to rent a car, getting from the airport to your hotel is no problem. Shuttle services are available at a cost of $5 to $6 one-way and $10 to $12 round-trip. Sedans and "stretch" limousines cost about $25 to $40 one-way. Cabs charge a $3.20 trip fee with $2 per mile thereafter. Cab fare to Las Vegas Strip locations ranges from $9 to $18 one-way, plus tip. One-way taxi fares to downtown run about $15 to $20. Fares are regulated and should not vary from company to company. The limo service counters are in the hall just outside the baggage-claim area. Cabs are at the curb. Additional information concerning ground transportation is available at the McCarran International Airport Web site, **www.mccarran.com.**

TAXI OPERATORS

ABC ☎ 702-736-8444	Ace Cab Co. ☎ 702-736-8383
Henderson Taxi ☎ 702-384-2322	Nellis Cab Co. ☎ 702-248-1111
North Las Vegas Cab ☎ 702-643-1041	Western Cab ☎ 702-736-8000
Yellow Checker and Star Transportation ☎ 702-873-2000	

If you rent a car, you will need to catch the courtesy shuttle to the new consolidated McCarran Rent-A-Car Center located about two miles from the airport. The shuttle boards at the middle curb of the authorized vehicle lanes just outside terminal doors 10 and 11 on ground level. The individual car-rental companies no longer operate shuttles of any kind, so all car-rental customers use the same shuttle.

If someone is picking you up, go to ground level on the opposite side of the baggage-claim building (away from the main terminal) to the baggage-claim and arrivals curb. If the person picking you up wants to park and meet you, hook up on the ground level of the baggage-claim building near the car-rental counters where the escalators descend from the main terminal.

There are two ways to exit the airport by car. You can depart via the old route, Swenson Street, which runs north–south roughly paralleling the Strip; or you can hop on the new spur of Interstate 215. Dipping south from the airport, I-215 connects with I-15. We recommend using I-215 if you are heading downtown or to any of the hotels west of the Strip. Swenson Street is a better route if you're going to the Las Vegas Convention Center, to the University of Nevada–Las Vegas (UNLV), or to hotels on or east of the Strip.

CONVENIENCE CHART   To give you an idea of your hotel's convenience to local, popular destinations such as the Strip, downtown, the Las Vegas Convention Center, UNLV, and the airport, we have provided a section on getting around. Included in that chapter is a "convenience chart" that lists estimated times by foot and cab from each hotel to the destinations outlined on pages 42–45. In the same section are tips for avoiding traffic congestion and for commuting between the Strip and downtown.

RENTAL CARS All of the rental-car companies previously located at the airport terminal, plus a few off-site companies, have moved to the huge new McCarran Rent-A-Car Center situated two miles south of the airport. The airport provides large buses departing approximately every five minutes for the 7-to-12-minute commute to the new facility. On arriving at the Rent-A-Car Center, you'll find all of the rental-car companies listed in the chart below on the ground floor. All of the rental cars likewise are under one roof. Upon completion of your paperwork you'll be directed to a specified area of the garage to pick up your car. Having picked up your car, chances are about 95% that you'll find yourself disoriented in a part of Las Vegas you've never laid eyes on. Follow the instructions below to reach your final destination.

After you pick up your rental car, you'll exit the Rent-A-Car Center onto Gilespie Street, where you'll find signs directing you to the Strip as well as to I-15 and I-215. Unfortunately, if you follow the signs, you'll end up in a traffic jam of the first order (welcome to Las Vegas!), owing to an inadequate number of right-turn lanes and a multitude of traffic signals. The exit from the Rent-A-Car Center onto Gilespie Street forces you to turn right (south), but to avoid the traffic jams you really want to be heading in the opposite direction (north) on Gilespie. From the Rent-A-Car Center exit, this can be accomplished by working your way immediately across the southbound lanes on Gilespie to a left-turn lane and then making a U-turn. Alternatively, you can go a block or so south and then get turned around less hurriedly. Once you're headed northbound on Gilespie do the following:

TO REACH THE LAS VEGAS CONVENTION CENTER, UNLV, AND HOTELS ON THE EAST SIDE OF THE STRIP, head north on Gilespie Street and turn right onto George Crockett Road. Follow signs to the airport via the Airport Connector. You'll pass through a tunnel under the runways and pop out on Swenson Street just before the intersection with Tropicana. Use the maps in this guide to navigate to your final destination from there.

TO REACH DOWNTOWN AND HOTELS ON THE WEST SIDE OF THE STRIP VIA I-15, head north from the Rent-A-Car Center on Gilespie, cross the bridge over I-215, and turn left on Hidden Well Road. Follow Hidden Well Road to I-15 (northbound only). Use the maps in this guide to navigate to your final destination from there.

TO ACCESS I-215 NORTHWEST TOWARD RED ROCK CANYON AND SUMMERLIN, go north on Gilespie, cross the bridge over I-215, and turn left on Hidden Well Road. Follow Hidden Well Road to the I-215 westbound ramp.

The following directions do nor require going north on Gilespie:

TO ACCESS I-215 SOUTHEAST TOWARD HENDERSON, GREEN VALLEY, AND LAKE LAS VEGAS, turn right on Gilespie from the Rent-A-Car Center

las vegas weather and dress chart

Month	Average high temp.	Average low temp.	Pools (O = open)	Recommended attire
January	57°F	32°F		Coats and jackets are musts.
February	50°F	37°F		Dress warmly: jackets and sweaters.
March	69°F	42°F	O	Sweaters for days, but a jacket at night.
April	78°F	50°F	O	Still cool at night—bring a jacket.
May	88°F	50°F	O	Sweater for evenings, but days are warm.
June	99°F	68°F	O	Dress coolly for day; cover up more at night.
July	105°F	75°F	O	Bathing suits.
August	102°F	73°F	O	Dress for the heat—spend time at a pool!
September	95°F	65°F	O	See attire suggestions for June.
October	81°F	53°F	O	Bring a jacket or sweater for afternoon.
November	67°F	40°F		Sweaters and jackets, coats for night.
December	58°F	34°F		Coats and jackets musts. Dress warmly!

rental-car return and pick-up

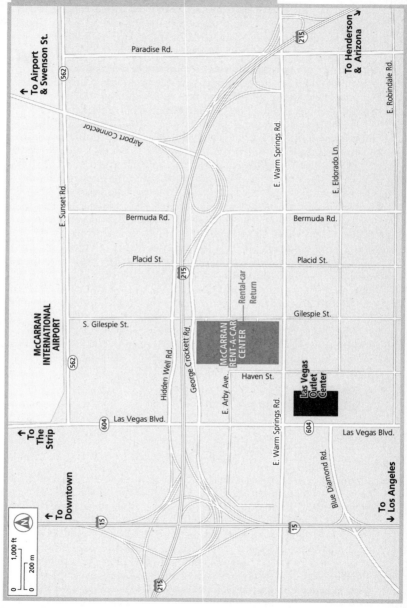

and turn left at the first traffic signal onto Warm Springs Road. Follow Warm Springs Road west to the intersection of I-215.

TO ACCESS LAS VEGAS BOULEVARD SOUTH OF THE I-15/I-215 INTERCHANGE, stay in the far-right lane on exiting the Rent-A-Car Center and turn right on Warm Springs Road. Warm Springs Road intersects Las Vegas Boulevard South.

TO ACCESS I-15 SOUTHBOUND TOWARD LAUGHLIN AND LOS ANGELES, turn right on Gilespie from the Rent-A-Car Center and then right on Warm Springs Road. After two blocks, turn south on Las Vegas Boulevard South, turning right on Blue Diamond Road. Follow the signs to I-15.

Fortunately, returning your rental car is much easier and there is little opportunity to become embroiled in a serious traffic jam in the environs of the Rent-A-Car Center. The same cannot be said, however, of I-15 and I-215, especially during rush hours. If you are coming from the east side of the Strip, take Paradise Road to the airport and follow the well-marked signs to the rental-car return. Like wise, as you come toward the airport on I-15 and I-215, follow the rental-car-return signs.

Because the Rent-A-Car Center shuttles run much more frequently than buses provided by the rental-car companies under the old system, it doesn't take any longer than before (about 20 minutes) to pick up your car or to get back to the airport once you've returned your car. En route to the Rent-A-Car Center on the shuttle from the airport it's a good idea to sit near a door so that you can be one of the first to disembark. This will ensure that you'll be ahead of your fellow bus passengers at the car-rental counter.

Although rental cars are comparatively cheap in Las Vegas, taxes and fees are not. If you rent your car at the airport (includes both terminal and off-terminal locations on airport property) here's what you can expect to pay:

State Sales Tax	7.5%
Nevada Rental Service Fee	6.0%
Airport Concession Recovery Fee	10.0%
Reimbursement of Registration and License Fee	4.0%
Total	27.5%

Had enough? Powers at the airport don't think so. In addition to the above you are charged a $3 per day Consumer Facility Charge. You can avoid the 10% fee and the three bucks per day by renting the car at a non-airport location, like your hotel. Be advised, however, that it's not unusual for agencies to bump up the rental price at such locations.

In the dollar-and-cents department, prices fluctuate so much from week to week that it's anyone's guess who will offer the best deal during your visit. Usually the best deals are on the company's Web site, but **www.expedia.com, www.travelocity.com,** and **www.orbitz.com** are often worth checking, especially if you're visiting during a particularly busy

Rental-car Agencies at the McCarran Rent-A-Car Center

Advantage/US Rent A Car	800 777-9377	www.us-rentacar.com
Alamo	800-GO-ALAMO	www.alamo.com
Avis	800-331-1212	www.avis.com
Budget	800-922-2899	www.budgetlasvegas.com
Dollar	800-800-4000	www.dollar.com
Enterprise	800-RENT-A-CAR	www.enterprise.com
Hertz	800 654-3131	www.hertz.com
National Car Rental	800-CAR-RENT	www.nationalcar.com
Payless Car Rental	800-729-5377	www.paylesscarrental.com
Savmor Car Rental	800-634-6779	www.savmorrac.com
Thrifty	800-367-2277	www.thrifty.com

time, such as during a citywide convention. On rental company Web sites, counterintuitively, you can often get a better deal if you don't indicate that you're a member of AAA, AARP, etc. After you get your quote, see if you can improve the deal by trying again, entering your organizational or age information.

Be aware that Las Vegas is a feast-or-famine city when it comes to rental-car availability. On many weekends, or when a citywide convention is in town, it may be impossible to get a rental car unless you reserved way in advance. If, on the other hand, you come to town when business is slow, the rental agencies will practically give you a car. We have been able to rent from the most expensive companies for as little as $22 a day under these circumstances. If you are visiting during a slow time, reserve a car in advance to cover yourself, and then, on arrival, ask each rental company to quote you its best price. If you can beat the price on your reserved car, go for it.

Improbably, one of the best places for rental-car deals is **www.mouse savers.com,** a site dedicated to finding deals at Disneyland and Walt Disney World. The site lists rental-car codes that you can use to get great discounts. Some of the codes are for Orlando and southern California only, but many others you can use anywhere in the United States The site also offers some great tips on how to compare different codes and deals.

unofficial **TIP**
Check out **www.mouse savers.com** for great rental-car deals in Las Vegas.

Another way to score a deal on a rental car is to bid on **www.price line.com.** We've used Priceline to get cars at less than $20 per day. Understand, however, that if your bid is accepted, the entire rental cost will be nonrefundably charged to your credit card. In other words, no backing

Conventions and Special Events Calendar

DATES	CONVENTION/EVENT	NUMBER OF ATTENDEES	LOCATION
2007			
Sept. 5–8	North American Bridal Assoc.	3,000	Sands Expo Center
Sept. 7–10	All Baby and Child/ABC Kids Expo	10,000	LVCC
Sept. 9–14	Gamestop.com	4,200	Mandalay Bay
Sept. 10–13	BISCI	2,800	MGM Grand
Sept. 11–12	PGA Fall Expo	5,000	Mandalay Bay
Sept. 12–15	Connections Convention	2,500	LV Hilton
Sept. 14–16	Las Vegas Int'l. Mariachi Festival	7,000	Planet Hollywood
Sept. 17–20	American Orthotic and Prosthetic Assoc.	2,500	Venetian
Sept. 17–20	Christian Methodist Episcopal Church	2,500	Riviera
Sept. 18–20	Memorytrends Trade Show	6,000	Sands Expo Center
Sept. 18–20	American Manufacturing Expo	5,000	LVCC
Sept. 19–21	Superzoo and Garden Market Expo	10,000	Mandalay Bay
Sept. 24–26	American Society for Industrial Security	25,000	LVCC
Sept. 26–28	Interbike Expo/Annual Fall Show	22,000	Sands Expo Center
Sept. 27–29	Amusement and Music Operators Assoc.	6,500	LVCC
Sept. 27–29	Int'l. Assoc. for the Leisure and Entertainment Industry/Fun Expo	4,000	LVCC
Sept. 27–29	Las Vegas Souvenir and Resort Show	3,000	LVCC
Sept. 27–Oct. 4	Electronic Retailing Assoc.	2,800	Venetian
Sept. 28–29	Mr. Olympia	20,000	LVCC
Sept. 28–30	Art Expo Las Vegas	10,000	Mandalay Bay
Oct. 3–5	Industrial Fabrics Assoc. Int'l.	9,000	LVCC
Oct. 3–5	Metalcon Int'l.	8,000	LVCC
Oct. 6–7	Boomers Show	10,000	Sands Expo Center
Oct. 7–10	Nat'l. Funeral Directors Assoc.	6,000	LVCC
Oct. 10–12	Hanley Wood Exhibitions	11,000	Mandalay Bay
Oct. 11–14	Automatic Transmission Rebuilders Assoc.	2,500	LV Hilton
Oct. 15–18	Pack Expo Las Vegas	30,000	LVCC
Oct. 18–19	Document Management Industries Assoc./Print Solutions Expo	3,500	LVCC
Oct. 21–25	AFLAC	3,000	Venetian
Oct. 27–29	Auto Parts Remanufacturers Assoc.	2,600	Riviera
Oct. 30–Nov. 2	Auto Aftermarket Industry Week	130,000	n/a

DATES	CONVENTION/EVENT	NUMBER OF ATTENDEES	LOCATION
2007 (CONTINUED)			
Oct. 31–Nov. 3	Int'l. Autobody Congress and Exposition	40,000	Mandalay Bay
Nov. 3–7	Int'l. Society Pharmaceutical Engineering	5,000	Caesars
Nov. 4–11	America's Community Bankers	4,200	Venetian
Nov. 6–8	Supplyside West Int'l. Trade Show and Conference	7,000	Sands Expo Center
Nov. 8–9	Blogworld	5,000	LVCC
Nov. 8–10	FireRescue	3,000	LVCC
Nov. 12–14	Nat'l. Industrial Fastener Show and Conference	6,700	Mandalay Bay
Nov. 12–16	Nat'l. Assoc. of Realtors 2007 Realtors Conference and Expo	25,000	Sands Expo Center
Nov. 13–15	Global Gaming Expo	27,000	LVCC
Nov. 15–18	Traders Expo	4,700	Mandalay Bay
Dec. 2–10	American Academy of Anti-Aging Medicine	5,000	Venetian
Dec. 6–15	NFR Cowboy Christmas Gift Show	20,000	LVCC
Dec. 10–12	Expo! Expo! IAEM's Annual Meeting and Exhibition	2,800	LVCC, Mandalay Bay
Dec. 13–15	Assoc. for Career and Technical Education	5,000	LVCC
2008			
Jan. 7–10	Int'l. CES (Consumer Electronics Show)	148,000	LVCC, Sands Expo Center
Jan. 7–10	Home Entertainment Show	4,600	St. Tropez Hotel
Jan. 9–12	Adult Entertainment Expo	37,000	Sands Expo Center
Jan. 14–18	Promotional Products Assoc. Int'l.	24,500	Mandalay Bay
Jan. 22–25	World of Concrete Exposition	85,000	LVCC
Jan. 25–Feb. 2	Guardian Building Products Group (BMA)	4,000	Paris Las Vegas
Jan. 27–30	West Coast Art and Frame Show	5,000	LV Hilton
Jan. 29–Feb. 1	Snowsports Industries America	17,000	Mandalay Bay
Jan. 31–Feb. 2	Photo Marketing Assoc. Int'l.	30,000	LVCC
Feb. 2–5	Shooting, Hunting, and Outdoor Trade Show	45,000	LVCC
Feb. 5–7	American Fence Assoc./Fencetech	10,000	Mandalay Bay
Feb. 6–11	Grand Slam Club/Ovis	3,000	Riviera

Conventions and Events Calendar (cont'd.)

DATES	CONVENTION/EVENT	NUMBER OF ATTENDEES	LOCATION
2008 (CONTINUED)			
Feb. 17–21	Western Veterinary Conference	15,000	Mandalay Bay
Feb. 19–21	Western Petroleum Marketers Assoc.	3,300	Mirage
Feb. 19–21	Power-Gen Renewable Energy	2,500	Rio
Feb. 21–24	World Shoe Assoc.	37,000	Mandalay Bay, Sands Expo Center
Feb. 21–23	Vacuum Dealers Trade Assoc.	4,000	LVCC
Feb. 22–23	Surface Fabrication and Design Expo	3,500	LVCC
Feb. 26–27	The Show	28,000	LVCC
Feb. 27–28	Digital Signage Expo	4,000	LVCC
Feb. 27–29	Int'l. Wireless Communications Expo	15,000	LVCC
Feb. 27–29	Awards and Recognition Assoc.	5,000	LVCC
Mar. 2–6	Associated Surplus Dealers/Associated Merchandise Dealers (ASD/AMD)	55,000	Mandalay Bay, Sands Expo Center
Mar. 3–6	Nat'l. Center for American Indian Enterprise Development–Reservation Economic Summit	3,250	LV Hilton
Mar. 11–15	CONEXPO–CON/AG G	135,000	LVCC
Mar. 16–18	Limousine/Chauffeured Transportation	3,300	Mandalay Bay
Mar. 16–19	Int'l Halloween Costume Show	10,000	Sands Expo Center
Mar. 17–18	Nat'l. Alliance of Certified Legal Nurse Consultants	3,000	LV Hilton
Mar. 17–19	Wedding and Portrait Photographers Int'l.	12,000	Bally's Las Vegas, Paris Las Vegas
Mar. 18–20	Automotive Oil Change Assoc.	2,500	Mandalay Bay
Mar. 24–29	Nat'l. Automatic Merchandising Assoc.	6,000	Mandalay Bay
Mar. 27–29	Nat'l. Systems Contractors Assoc.	12,000	LVCC
Apr. 1–3	Cellular Telecommunications and Internet Assoc.	40,000	LVCC
Apr. 1–3	Annual Int'l. Pizza Expo/ Nat'l. Assoc. of Pizzeria Operators	10,000	LVCC
Apr. 1–3	IPC Assoc. Connecting Electronic Industries/Printed Circuits Expo, Apex and Designers Summit	5,000	Mandalay Bay
Apr. 14–17	Nat'l. Assoc. of Broadcasters	140,000	LVCC
Apr. 27–May 1	American Planning Assoc.	6,000	Bally's Las Vegas
Apr. 27–May 2	Interop Las Vegas 2008	20,000	Mandalay Bay

DATES	CONVENTION/EVENT	NUMBER OF ATTENDEES	LOCATION
2008 (CONTINUED)			
May 6–8	Las Vegas Gourmet Housewares Show	9,000	LVCC
May 12–15	The Money Show	6,000	Mandalay Bay
May 14–15	Nat'l. Assoc. of Tobacco Outlets	4,000	LVCC
May 19–21	Int'l. Council of Shopping Centers	30,000	LVCC
May 30–Jun 3	JCK Show	40,000	LVCC
June 2–6	Nat'l. Fire Protection Assoc.	5,000	Mandalay Bay
June 9–11	SGMA: Sporting Goods Manufacturers Assoc.	10,000	Sands Expo Center
June 17–19	Nxtcomm LLLC	25,000	LVCC
June 18–20	InfoComm/Int'l. Communications Industries Assoc.	30,000	LVCC
June 18–21	Casino Chips and Gaming-Token Collectors Club	5,000	Riviera
June 25–July 1	Int'l. Esthetics Cosmetics and Spa Conference	37,000	LVCC
July 8–10	Idea Health and Fitness Assoc.	5,500	LVCC
July 13–15	Cosmoprof North America	27,500	Mandalay Bay
July 13–19	American Sportfishing Assoc.	6,000	LVCC
July 14–16	Retail Tobacco Dealers of America	6,200	Sands Expo Center
July 17–19	Natural Products Assoc.	7,500	Sands Expo Center
July 21–24	Home and Garden Party	3,000	Caesars
July 28–31	WSA Show	35,000	LVCC
July 28–Aug. 1	Nat'l. Marine Manufacturers Assoc.	2,500	LV Hilton
Aug. 9–12	Disabled American Veterans	4,000	Bally's Las Vegas
Aug. 15–23	American Poolplayers Assoc.	13,000	Riviera
Sept. 8–12	SAP Global Marketing–SAP Tech. Ed.	4,200	Venetian
Sept. 9–11	Memorytrends Trade Show	6,200	Sands Expo Center
Sept. 9–12	All Baby and Child/ABC Kids Expo	12,000	LVCC
Sept. 10–12	Amusement and Music Operators Assoc.	6,500	LVCC
Sept. 10–12	Int'l. Assoc. for the Leisure and Entertainment Industry/Fun Expo	6,500	LVCC
Sept. 20–24	Electronic Retailing Assoc.	2,700	Paris Las Vegas
Oct. 2–6	Int'l. Vision Expo	16,000	Sands Expo Center

Conventions and Events Calendar (cont'd.)

DATES	CONVENTION/EVENT	NUMBER OF ATTENDEES	LOCATION
2008 (CONTINUED)			
Oct. 16–20	Stonexpo	9,000	Mandalay Bay
Oct. 20–22	Assoc. of Records Managers and Administrators	6,000	LVCC
Oct. 21–23	Aqua Show	7,500	LVCC
Oct. 25–27	Auto Parts Remanufacturers Assoc.	2,700	Riviera
Oct. 26–29	Nat'l. Minority Supplier Development Council–Nat'l. Conference	7,000	LVCC
Oct. 26–Nov. 3	American Assoc. of Gynecologic Laparoscopists	2,500	Paris Las Vegas
Nov. 2–4	Nat'l. Industrial Fastener Show and Conference	6,700	Mandalay Bay
Nov. 10–13	Int'l. Spa Assoc.	2,500	Venetian
Nov. 18–20	G2e: Global Gaming Expo	27,000	LVCC
Nov. 18–20	Int'l. Pool and Spa Expo	16,000	Mandalay Bay
Nov. 19–22	Traders Expo	5,000	Mandalay Bay
Dec. 3–5	Nat'l. Ground Water Assoc.	5,000	LVCC

out for any reason. Before placing your bid, check our conventions and special events calendar on pages 24–28. If there's a big convention in town, demand will be high and a lowball bid might not work.

When you (or your travel agent) call to reserve a rental car, ask for the smallest, least expensive car in the company's inventory, even if you ultimately intend to rent a larger vehicle. It's possible that you will be upgraded without charge when you arrive. If not, rental agencies frequently offer on-site upgrade incentives that beat any deals you can make in advance. Always compare daily and weekly rates.

If you decline insurance coverage on the rental car because of protection provided by your credit card, be aware that the coverage provided by the credit card is secondary to your regular auto insurance policy. In most situations the credit-card coverage only reimburses you the deductible on your regular policy. Happily, most car insurance covers rental cars as well as your personal vehicle. If you're not sure about your coverage, contact your insurance agent. Also be aware that some car-rental contracts require that you drive the car only in Nevada. If you, like many tourists, visit Hoover Dam or trek out to the Grand Canyon, you will cross into Arizona. Another item to check in advance, if applicable, is whether your rental agency charges for additional drivers.

When you rent your car, make sure you understand the implications of bringing it back empty of fuel. Some companies will charge $6.50 or more per gallon if they have to fill the tank on return. At one agency, we returned a car with between a third and a half tank of gas remaining and were charged $36, the same as if we had coasted in with a completely empty tank. Also, beware of signs at the car-rental counters reading "Gas today—$2.95 per gallon" or some such. That usually applies to the price of the gas already in the car when you rent it, not the price per gallon of a fill-up should you return the car empty. The price per gallon for a fill-up on return will be somewhere in the fine print of your rental contract.

Another rental-car problem we encountered involved a pinhead-sized chip on the windshield. Understanding the fine print of rental car contracts, and because we always decline the insurance offered by the agencies, we inspect our cars thoroughly for any damage before accepting the car and leaving the lot. In this instance, as always, we inspected the car thoroughly and did not notice any windshield flaws. When we returned the car after three days, we were requested to remain at the counter to complete an "accident report." Insisting that we were unaware of any damage, we requested that the car be retrieved for our inspection. Still unable to find the alleged damage, we asked the counter agent to identify it for us. The agent who was responsible for the accident report then had to scrutinize the windshield before she could find the mark, even though she knew its exact location from the employee who checked the car in. The conclusion to be drawn here is that if you decline coverage, the rental agency may hold you responsible for even the tiniest damage, damage so slight that you may never notice it. Check your car out well before you leave. This will not inhibit them from charging you for damage sustained while the car is in your possession, but at least you will have the peace of mind of knowing that they are not putting one over on you.

unofficial **TIP**
Before you leave the lot, inspect your rental car with care, examining every inch, and have the rental agency record anything you find.

Some rental companies will charge you for "loss of use" if you have an accident that takes the car out of use. Because some car insurance policies do not pay loss-of-use charges, check your coverage with your insurance agent before you rent. Finally, if you use a credit card to pay for your rental car, be aware that Diner's Club offers the best supplemental insurance coverage.

LAS VEGAS CUSTOMS AND PROTOCOL

IN A TOWN WHERE THE MOST BIZARRE behavior imaginable is routinely tolerated, it is ironic that so many visitors obsess over what constitutes proper protocol. This mentality stems mainly from the myriad customs peculiar to gaming and the *perceived* glamour of the city itself. First-timers attach a great deal of importance to "fitting in." What makes this task difficult, at least in part, is that half of the people with whom they are trying to fit in are first-timers too.

The only hard rules for being accepted downtown or on the Strip are to have a shirt on your back, shoes on your feet, some manner of clothing below the waist, and a little money in your pocket. Concerning the latter, there is no maximum. The operational minimum is bus fare back to wherever you came from.

This notwithstanding, there are three basic areas in which Las Vegas first-timers tend to feel especially insecure:

GAMBLING The various oddities of gaming protocol are described in this book under the respective casino games in Part Three, Gambling (page 275). Despite appearances, however, gambling is very informal. While it is intelligent not to play a game when/if you do not know how, it is unwarranted to abstain because you are uncertain of the protocol. What little protocol exists (things like holding your cards above the table and keeping your hands away from your bet once play has begun) has evolved to protect the house and honest players from cheats. Dealers (a generic term for those who conduct table games) are not under orders to be unfriendly, silent, or rigid. Observe a game that interests you before you sit down. Assure yourself that the dealer is personable and polite. Never play in a casino where the staff is surly or cold; life's too short.

EATING IN FANCY RESTAURANTS Many of these are meat-and-potatoes places with fancy names, so there is no real reason to be intimidated. Others are designer, pay-big-bucks restaurants with famous chefs. In either case, service is friendly. Men will feel more comfortable in sport coats, but ties are rarely worn. Women turn up in everything from slacks and blouses to evening wear. When you sit down, a whole platoon of waiters will attend you. Do not remove your napkin from the table; only the waiters are allowed to place napkins in the laps of patrons. After the ceremonial placement of the napkin, the senior waiter will speak. When he concludes, you may order cocktails, consider the menu, sip your water, or engage in conversation. If there are women in your party, their menus will not have prices listed. If your party includes only women, a menu with prices listed will be given to the woman who looks the oldest. When you are ready to order, even if you only want a steak and fries, do not speak until the waiter has had an opportunity to recite in French from the menu. To really please your waiters, order something that can be prepared tableside with dramatic flames and explosions. If your waiters seem stuffy or aloof, ask them to grind peppercorns or grate Parmesan cheese on something. This will usually loosen them up.

There will be enough utensils on the table to perform a triple bypass. Because these items are considered expendable, use a different utensil for each dish, surrendering it to the waiter along with the empty plate at the end of the course. If there are small yellow sculptures on the table, they are probably butter.

TIPPING Because about a third of the resident population of Las Vegas are service providers in the tourist industry, there is no scarcity of people to tip. From the day you arrive until the day you depart, you will be interacting with redcaps, porters, cabbies, valet-parking attendants, bellhops, waiters, maître d's, dealers, bartenders, keno runners, housekeeping personnel, room service, and others.

Tipping is an issue that makes some travelers very uncomfortable. How much? When? To whom? Not leaving a tip when one is customary makes you feel inexperienced. Not knowing how much to tip makes you feel vulnerable and out of control. Is the tip you normally leave at home appropriate in Las Vegas?

The most important thing to bear in mind is that a tip is not automatic, nor is it an obligation. A tip is a reward for good service. The suggestions in the "Tipping Guidelines" chart below are based on traditional practices in Las Vegas.

Tipping Guidelines

Porters and Redcaps A dollar a bag.

Cab Drivers A lot depends on service and courtesy. If the fare is less than $8, give the cabbie the change and $1. In other words, on a $4.50 fare give him the 50 cents change plus a buck. If the fare is more than $8, give the cabbie the change and $2. If you are asking the cabbie to take you only a block or two, the fare will be small, but your tip should be large ($3 to $5) to make up for his wait in line and to partially compensate him for missing a better-paying fare. Add an extra dollar for a lot of luggage handling.

Valet Parking Two dollars is correct if the valet is courteous and demonstrates some hustle. A dollar will do if the service is just OK. Only pay when you take your car out, not when you leave it. Because valet attendants pool their tips, both of the individuals who assist you (coming and going) will be taken care of.

Bellmen When a bellhop greets you at your car with one of those rolling carts and handles all of your bags, $5 is about right. The more luggage you carry, of course, the less you should tip. Sometimes bellhops who handle only a small bag or two will put on a real performance when showing you your room. we had a bellhop in one Strip hotel walk into our room, crank up the air-conditioner, turn on the TV, open the blinds, flick on the lights, flush the commode, and test the water pressure in the tub. Give us a break. We tipped the same as if he had simply opened the door and put our luggage in the room.

Waiters Whether in a coffee shop, a gourmet room, or ordering from room service, the standard gratuity for acceptable service is 15% to 20% of the total tab, before sales tax. At a self-serve buffet or brunch, it is customary to leave $2 for the folks who bring your drinks and bus your dishes.

Tipping Guidelines (continued)

Cocktail waiters/bartenders   Tip by the round. For two people, $1 a round; for more than two people, $2 a round. For a large group, use your judgment: Is everyone drinking beer, or is the order long and complicated? In casinos where drinks are sometimes on the house, it is considered good form to tip the server $1 per round or per every couple of rounds.

Dealers and slot attendants   If you are winning, it is a nice gesture to tip the dealer or place a small bet for him. How much depends on your winnings and on your level of play. With slot attendants, tip when they perform a specific service or you hit a jackpot. In general, unless other services are also rendered, it is not customary to tip change makers or cashiers.

Keno runners   Tip if you have a winner or if the runner really provides fast, efficient service. How much to tip will vary with your winnings and level of play.

Showroom maître d's, captains, and servers   There is more to this than you might expect. If you are planning to take in a show, see our suggestions for tipping in Part 2, Entertainment and Nightlife (see pages 173–175).

Hotel maids   On checking out, leave $2 to $4 for each day you stayed (more if you're really messy), providing the service was good.

DOES ANYONE KNOW WHAT'S GOING ON AT HOME? (DOES ANYONE REALLY CARE?)

IF YOU'RE MORE INTERESTED in what you're missing at home than what's going on in Las Vegas, **Borders** at 2323 South Decatur Boulevard stocks Sunday newspapers from most major cities. To find out whether Borders stocks your favorite paper, call ☎ 702-258-0999.

LAS VEGAS *as a* FAMILY DESTINATION

OCCASIONALLY THE PUBLISHER SENDS me around to promote the *Unofficial Guide* on radio and television, and every year we are asked the same question: is Las Vegas a good place for a family vacation?

Las Vegas is most definitely *not* a family-friendly destination. The misconception that families are welcome is the result of a failed marketing campaign that the Las Vegas Convention and Visitors Authority (LVCVA) trotted out in the early 1990s. LVCVA's job is to fill beds and bring in trade shows and conventions. Problem is, casinos are very particular about who's occupying those beds, and the least preferred customers of all (with two exceptions) are families with children. Children can't gamble, they annoy adults who come to Las Vegas to avoid kids, and they reduce or make impossible the time their parents spend in the casino. Before LVCVA's campaign there were only two casinos that targeted the family trade: Circus Circus and Excalibur. Fifteen years and more later, guess what: Circus Circus and Excalibur remain the only two, and Excalibur is making a concerted effort to ditch the family market. Bottom line: you can't reshape the image of Las Vegas without the casinos' endorsement and cooperation.

If you don't object to being persona non grata, however, Las Vegas is a great place for a family vacation. Food and lodging are a good value for the dollar, and there are an extraordinary number of things, from swimming to rafting through the Black Canyon on the Colorado River, that the entire family can enjoy together. If you take your kids to Las Vegas *and forget gambling,* Las Vegas compares favorably with every family tourist destination in the United States. The rub, of course, is that gambling in Las Vegas is pretty hard to ignore.

TAKING YOUR CHILDREN TO LAS VEGAS TODAY

LAS VEGAS IS PREDOMINANTLY AN ADULT tourist destination. As a city (including the surrounding area), however, it has a lot to offer children. What this essentially means is that the Strip and downtown have not been developed with children in mind, but if you are willing to make the effort to venture away from the gambling areas, there are a lot of fun and wholesome things for families to do. As a rule, however, people do not go to Las Vegas to be continually absent from the casinos.

Persons under age 21 are not allowed to gamble, nor are they allowed to hang around while *you* gamble. If you are gambling, your children have to be somewhere else. On the Strip and downtown, the choices are limited. True, most Las Vegas hotels have nice swimming pools, but Las Vegas summer days are much too hot to stay out for long. While golf and tennis are possibilities, court or greens fees are routinely charged, and you still must contend with limitations imposed by the desert climate.

After a short time, you will discover that the current options for your children's recreation and amusement are as follows:

1. You can simply allow your children to hang out. Given this alternative, the kids will swim a little, watch some TV, eat as much as their (or your) funds allow, throw water balloons out of any hotel window that has not been hermetically sealed, and cruise up and down the Strip (or Fremont Street) on foot, ducking in and out of souvenir stores and casino lobbies.

2. If your children are a mature age 10 or older, you can turn them loose at the Adventuredome at Circus Circus or at the midway games at Excalibur. The kids, however, will probably cut bait and go cruising after about an hour or two.

3. You can hire a babysitter to come to your hotel room and tend your children. This works out pretty much like option 1, without the water balloons and the cruising.

4. You can abandon the casino (or whatever else you had in mind) and "do things" with your kids. Swimming and eating (as always) will figure prominently into the plan, as will excursions to places that have engaged the children's curiosity. You can bet that your kids will want to go to the Adventuredome at Circus Circus. The white tigers, dolphins, and exploding volcano at the Mirage; the pirate battle at T. I.; the MGM Grand lion habitat; the high-tech attractions at the Luxor, the Sahara, the Forum Shops, and the Las Vegas Hilton; and the Stratosphere Tower are big hits with kids. The Excalibur offers a sort of movie-ride in which you feel as if you are riding a real roller coaster. New York–New York and the Sahara each feature a real roller coaster. If you have two children and do a fraction of all this stuff in one day, you will spend $80 to $250 for the four of you, not counting meals and transportation.

If you have a car, however, there are lots of great, inexpensive places to go—enough to keep you busy for days. We recommend Red Rock Canyon and Hoover Dam for sure. On the way to Hoover Dam, you can stop for a tour of the Ethel M. Chocolate Factory.

A great day excursion (during the spring and fall) is a guided raft trip through the Black Canyon on the Colorado River. This can easily be combined with a visit to Hoover Dam. Trips to the Valley of Fire State Park (driving, biking, hiking) are also recommended during the more temperate months.

Around Las Vegas there are a number of real museums and museums–tourist attractions. The Lied Discovery Children's Museum (just north of downtown) is worthwhile, affordable, and a big favorite with kids age 14 and younger. While you are in the neighborhood, try the Natural History Museum directly across the street.

5. You can pay someone else to take your kids on excursions. Some in-room sitters (bonded and from reputable agencies) will take your kids around as long as you foot the bill. For recommendations, check with the concierge or front desk of your hotel. If your kids are over age 12, you can pack them off on one of the guided tours advertised by the handful in the various local visitor magazines.

Hotels That Solicit Family Business

As Excalibur gets out of the family trade, Circus Circus stands alone as the only casino that welcomes children. Circus Circus actively seeks the family market with carnival game midways where children and adults can try to win stuffed animals, foam-rubber dice, and other totally dispensable objects. A great setup for the casinos, the midways turn a nice profit while innocuously introducing the youngsters to games of chance. In addition, Circus Circus operates the Adventuredome theme park and offers free circus acts each evening, starring top-notch talent, including aerialists (flying trapeze artists).

Parents traveling with children are grudgingly accepted at all of the larger hotels, though certain hotels are better equipped to deal with children than others. If your children are water puppies and enjoy being in a swimming pool all day, Mandalay Bay, Venetian, Aladdin/Planet Hollywood, Flamingo, Monte Carlo, MGM Grand, Mirage, Rio, Tropicana, Caesars Palace, Wynn Las Vegas, Bella-gio, Red Rock Resort, Green Valley Ranch, and T. I. have the best pools in town. The Las Vegas Hilton, the Palms, and Hard Rock Hotel, among others, also have excellent swimming facilities.

unofficial **TIP**
Try the Green Valley Ranch for a terrific family vacation.

If your kids are older and into sports, the MGM Grand, Caesars Palace, the Las Vegas Hilton, and Bally's offer the most variety.

When it comes to child care and special programs, the Sunset Station, Orleans, Red Rock Resort, South Coast, Boulder Station, and Santa Fe provide child-care facilities.

Our personal favorite hotel for a family vacation is the Green Valley Ranch Resort, a Station casino and resort about 15 minutes southeast of the Strip. Its location is convenient to Lake Mead, Hoover Dam, the Black Canyon of the Colorado, and Red Rock Canyon, for starters. It has great swimming areas, good restaurants, and lovely guest rooms. And when you want to sneak into the casino or have an adults-only meal, the concierge will make child-care arrangements for you. Best of all, Green Valley Ranch is isolated. There's no place nearby where your kids can get into trouble (right!).

PART ONE

ACCOMMODATIONS *and* CASINOS

WHERE *to* STAY: *Basic Choices*

LAS VEGAS HAS AN ASTOUNDING INVENTORY of about 137,000 hotel rooms. Washington, D.C., by way of contrast has 31,000. Occupancy rates are over 98% on weekends and average 92% for the whole week, compared to a national average of 61%. By 2010 it's projected that the number of rooms in Las Vegas will top 170,000. As the memorable line from *Field of Dreams* suggests, "If you build it, they will come."

THE LAS VEGAS STRIP AND DOWNTOWN

FROM A VISITOR'S PERSPECTIVE, Las Vegas is more or less a small town that's fairly easy to get around. Most of the major hotels and casinos are in two areas: downtown and on Las Vegas Boulevard, known as the Strip.

The downtown hotels and casinos are often characterized as older and smaller than those on the Strip. While this is true in a general sense, there are both large and elegant hotels downtown. What really differentiates downtown is the incredible concentration of casinos and hotels in a relatively small area. Along Fremont Street, downtown's main thoroughfare, the casinos present a continuous, dazzling galaxy of neon and twinkling lights for more than four city blocks. Known as Glitter Gulch, these several dozen gambling emporiums are sandwiched together in colorful profusion in an area barely larger than a parking lot at a good-sized shopping mall.

Contrast in the size, style, elegance, and presentation of the downtown casinos provides a varied mix, combining extravagant luxury and cosmopolitan sophistication with an Old West–boomtown decadence. Though not directly comparable, downtown Las Vegas has the feel of New Orleans's Bourbon Street: alluring, exotic, wicked, sultry, foreign, and above all, diverse. It is a place where cowboy, businessperson, showgirl, and retiree mix easily. And, like Bourbon Street, it is all accessible on foot.

If downtown is the French Quarter of Las Vegas, then the Strip is Plantation Row. Here, huge resort hotel-casinos sprawl like estates along a four-mile section of South Las Vegas Boulevard. Each hotel is a vacation destination unto itself, with casino, hotel, restaurants, pools, spas, landscaped grounds, and even golf courses. While the downtown casinos are fused into a vibrant, integrated whole, the huge hotels on the Strip demand individual recognition.

While the Strip is literally a specific length of South Las Vegas Boulevard, the large surrounding area is usually included when discussing hotels, casinos, restaurants, and attractions. East and parallel to the Strip is Paradise Road, where the Las Vegas Convention Center and several hotels are located. Also included in the Strip area are hotels and casinos on streets intersecting Las Vegas Boulevard, as well as properties positioned to the immediate west of the Strip (on the far side of Interstate 15).

CHOOSING A HOTEL

THE VARIABLES THAT FIGURE MOST prominently in choosing a hotel are price, location, your itinerary, and your quality requirements. There is a wide selection of lodging with myriad combinations of price and value. Given this, your main criteria for selecting a hotel should be its location and your itinerary.

The Strip versus Downtown for Leisure Travelers

Though there are some excellent hotels on the Boulder Highway and elsewhere around town, the choice for most vacation travelers is whether to stay downtown or on (or near) the Strip. Downtown offers a good choice of hotels, restaurants, and gambling, but only a limited choice of entertainment, and fewer amenities such as swimming pools and spas. There are no golf courses and only four tennis courts downtown. If you have a car, the Strip is an 8- to 15-minute commute from downtown via I-15. If you do not have a car, public transportation from downtown to the Strip is as efficient as Las Vegas traffic allows and quite affordable.

If you stay on the Strip, you are more likely to need a car or require some sort of transportation. There are more hotels to choose from on the Strip, but they are spread over a much wider area and are often (but not always) pricier than downtown. On the Strip, one has a sense of space and elbow room, as many of the hotels are constructed on a grand scale. The selection of entertainment is both varied and extensive, and the Strip's recreational facilities rival those of the world's leading resorts.

Downtown is a multicultural, multilingual melting pot with an adventurous, raw, robust feel. Everything in this part of town seems intense and concentrated, an endless blur of action, movement, and light. Diversity and history conspire in lending vitality and excitement to this older part of Las Vegas, an essence more tangible and real than the monumental, plastic themes and fantasies of many large Strip establishments.

Though downtown caters to every class of clientele, it is less formal and, with exceptions, more of a working man's gambling town. Here, the truck driver and welder gamble alongside the secretary and the rancher. The Strip, likewise, runs the gamut but tends to attract more high rollers, middle-class suburbanites, and business travelers going to conventions.

The Fremont Street Experience

For years, downtown casinos watched from the sidelines as Strip hotels turned into veritable tourist attractions. There was nothing downtown, for example, to rival the exploding volcano at the Mirage, the theme parks at Circus Circus, the pirate battle at Treasure Island (T. I.), or the view from the Stratosphere Tower. As gambling revenue dwindled and more customers defected to the Strip, downtown casino owners finally got serious about mounting a counterattack.

The counterattack, known as the Fremont Street Experience, was launched at the end of 1995. Its basic purpose was to transform downtown into an ongoing event, a continuous party, a happening. Fremont Street through the heart of Glitter Gulch was forever closed to vehicular traffic and turned into a park, with terraces, street musicians, and landscaping. By creating an aesthetically pleasing environment, Las Vegas–style, the project united all of the casinos in a sort of diverse gambling mall.

Transformative events on the ground aside, however, the main draw of the Fremont Street Experience is up in the air. Four blocks of Fremont Street are covered by a 1,400-foot-long, 90-foot-high "space frame"—an enormous, vaulted, geodesic matrix. This futuristic structure totally canopies Fremont Street. In addition to providing nominal shade from the blistering sun, the space frame serves as the stage for a nighttime attraction that has definitely improved downtown's fortune. Set into the inner surface of the space frame are 12.5 million LEDs, which come to life in a computer-driven, multisensory show. The LEDs are augmented by 40 speakers on each block, booming symphonic sound in syncopation with the lights.

We at the *Unofficial Guide* enjoy and appreciate downtown Las Vegas, and all of us hope that the Fremont Street Experience will continue to have a beneficial effect. We are amazed and appalled, however, by the city's general lack of commitment to improving its infrastructure, particularly the traffic situation. The market, in terms of aggregate numbers of gamblers, is undeniably located out on the Strip. To create an attraction sufficiently compelling to lure this market downtown is to fight only half the battle. The other half of the battle is to make it easy for all those folks on the Strip to get downtown. There are plans to extend the monorail with a downtown station as the northern terminus. The gestation for this much-needed addition to the public transportation mix is fuzzy. Our guess is that we'll be lucky to see the monorail downtown by 2015.

If You Visit Las Vegas on Business

If you are going to Las Vegas for a trade show or convention, you will want to lodge as close as possible to the meeting site (ideally within easy walking distance), or alternatively, close to a monorail station. Many Strip hotel-casinos— including the Riviera, Flamingo, Venetian, Wynn Las Vegas, Paris, Bellagio, Mandalay Bay, Planet Hollywood, Las Vegas Hilton, MGM Grand, T. I., Tropicana, Sahara, Mirage, Caesars Palace, Harrah's, and Bally's—host meetings from 100 to 4,000 attendees, offer lodging for citywide shows and conventions held at the Las Vegas Convention Center and the Sands Expo and Convention Center, and have good track records with business travelers. Our maps should provide some assistance in determining which hotels and motels are situated near your meeting site.

unofficial **TIP**
Try to find a good deal on a room at a hotel that's not near your meeting site and commute to your meeting in a rental car. Often the savings on the room will pay for your transportation.

Because most large meetings and trade shows are headquartered at the convention center or on the Strip, lodging on the Strip is more convenient than staying downtown. Citywide conventions often provide shuttle service from the major hotels to the Las Vegas Convention Center, and, of course, cabs and the monorail are available too. Las Vegas traffic is a mess, however, particularly in the late afternoon, and there is a finite number of cabs.

LARGE HOTEL-CASINOS VERSUS SMALL HOTELS AND MOTELS

LODGING PROPERTIES IN LAS VEGAS range from tiny motels with a dozen rooms to colossal hotel-casino resort complexes of 5,000 rooms. As you might expect, there are advantages and drawbacks to staying in either a large or small hotel. Determining which size is better for you depends on how you plan to spend your time in Las Vegas.

If your leisure or business itinerary calls for a car and a lot of coming and going, the big hotels can be a real pain. At the Venetian, Excalibur, and MGM Grand, to name a few, it can take as long as 15 minutes to get from your room to your car if you use the self-parking lot. A young couple staying at the Las Vegas Hilton left their hotel room 40 minutes prior to their show reservations at the Mirage. After trooping to their van in the Hilton's distant self-parking lot, the couple discovered they had forgotten their show tickets. By the time the husband ran back to their room to retrieve the tickets and returned to the van, only five minutes remained to drive to the Mirage, park, and find the showroom. As it turned out, they missed the first 15 minutes of the performance.

Many large hotels have multistory, self-parking garages that require lengthy and dizzying drives down ramps. Post-9/11 security likewise has complicated coming and going at some large, multistory parking garages. If you plan to use the car frequently and do not want to deal with the hassle of remote parking lots, big garages, or the tipping associated with valet parking, we recommend staying in a smaller hotel or motel that provides quick and convenient access to your car.

Quiet and tranquillity can also be reasons for choosing a smaller hotel. Many Las Vegas visitors object to passing through a casino whenever they go to or leave their room. Staying in a smaller property without a casino permits an escape from the flashing lights, the never-ending clanking of coins, and the unremitting, frenetic pace of an around-the-clock gambling town. While they may not be as exciting, smaller hotels tend to be more restful and homelike.

The ease and simplicity of checking in and out of smaller properties has its own appeal. To be able to check in or pay your bill without standing in a line, or to unload and load the car directly and conveniently, significantly diminishes the stress of arriving and departing. When we visited the registration lobby of one of the larger hotels on a Friday afternoon, for example, it reminded us of Kennedy International Airport shut down by a winter storm. Guests were stacked dozens deep in the check-in lines. Others, having abandoned any hope of registering in the near future, slept curled up around their luggage or sat reading on the floor. The whole lobby was awash in suitcases, hanging bags, and people milling about. Though hotel size and check-in efficiency are not always inversely related, the sight of a registration lobby fitted out like the queuing area of Disneyland's Jungle Cruise should be enough to make a sane person think twice.

Along similar lines, a large hotel does not ensure more comfortable or more luxurious accommodations. In Las Vegas there are exceptionally posh and well-designed rooms in both large and small hotels, just as there are threadbare and poorly designed rooms in properties of every size. A large establishment does, however, usually ensure a superior range of amenities, including on-site entertainment, room service, spas or exercise rooms, concierge services, bell services, valet parking, meeting rooms, babysitting, shoe shining, dry cleaning, shopping, 24-hour restaurants, copy and fax services, check cashing, and, of course, gambling.

unofficial **TIP**
Try a local wash-and-fold service as an affordable alternative to expensive hotel-casino laundry services.

If you spill a cosmopolitan on your khakis, however, you may want to think twice before ponying up for the hotel-casino in-house laundry service. You'll pay by the piece, and you'll pay dearly. After a couple of days' laundry pile up on the bed, do like we do and take advantage of an area wash-and-fold service. Our favorite is **Wizard of Suds** (4275 Arville Street) where the courteous staff will wash and fold your dirties for cheap. At a dollar a pound, and with quick turnaround if you drop off before noon, you can't beat the Wizard; ☎ 702-873-1453.

If you plan to do most of your touring on foot or are attending a convention, a large hotel in a good location has its advantages. There will be a variety of restaurants, entertainment, shopping, and recreation close at hand. In case you are a night owl, you will be able to eat or drink at any hour, and there will always be lots going on. Many showrooms offer 11 p.m. or midnight shows, and quite a few hotels (Sam's Town, Suncoast, Gold Coast, Orleans, and Santa Fe Station) have 24-hour bowling.

For visitors who wish to immerse themselves in the atmosphere of Las Vegas, to live in the fast lane, and to be where the action is, a large hotel is recommended. These people feel they are missing something unless they stay in a big hotel-casino. For them, it is important to know that the excitement is only an elevator ride away.

GETTING AROUND:
Location and Convenience

LAS VEGAS LODGING CONVENIENCE CHART

THE FOLLOWING CHART will give you a feel for how convenient specific hotels and motels are to common Las Vegas destinations. Both walking- and cab-commuting times are figured on the conservative side. You should be able to do a little better than the times indicated, particularly by cab, unless you are traveling during rush hour or attempting to navigate the Strip on a weekend evening.

Regarding the monorail, times listed include loading and unloading as well as the actual commuting time. The Strip monorail stations are located in the far rear of the host casinos, so, for example, the walk from the Strip entrance of the MGM Grand to the station is about six to eight minutes. The MGM Grand station is the closest station to the Excalibur on the west side of the Strip. From your guest room at the Excalibur it will take about 20 to 25 minutes to walk to the MGM Grand station. In our experience, because of the walking required to reach the nearest monorail station from casinos on the Strip's west side, you might want to consider a cab if you're in a hurry. Always check traffic conditions before you hop in a cab. If the Strip is gridlocked (very common), head for the monorail.

Commuting to Downtown from the Strip

Commuting to downtown from the Strip is a snap on I-15. From the Strip you can get on or off I-15 at Tropicana Avenue, Flamingo Road, Spring Mountain Road, or Sahara Avenue. Once on I-15 heading north, stay in the right lane and follow the signs for downtown and US 95 South. Exiting onto Casino Center Boulevard, you will be right in the middle of downtown with several large parking garages

Continued on page 45

Commuting Times in Minutes

FROM	TO				
	LAS VEGAS STRIP	CONVENTION CENTER	DOWN-TOWN	McCARRAN AIRPORT	UNLV THOMAS & MACK CENTER
Alexis Park Resort and Villas	5/cab	8/cab	15/cab	5/cab	6/cab
Ambassador Strip Travelodge	3/cab	9/cab	15/cab	4/cab	6/cab
AmeriSuites	4/cab	5/walk	15/cab	10/cab	9/cab
Arizona Charlie's Boulder	12/cab	18/cab	12/cab	20/cab	22/cab
Arizona Charlie's Decatur	19/cab	18/cab	12/cab	21/cab	20/cab
Artisan Hotel and Spa	5/walk	5/cab	14/cab	14/cab	14/cab
Atrium Suites	6/cab	6/cab	15/cab	6/cab	6/cab
Bally's	on Strip	8/mono	15/cab	7/cab	7/cab
Bellagio	on Strip	11/mono	15/cab	11/cab	12/cab
Best Western Mardi Gras Inn	6/cab	10/walk	15/cab	9/cab	7/cab
Best Western McCarran Inn	6/cab	9/cab	15/cab	4/cab	7/cab
Bill's Gamblin' Hall	on Strip	7/mono	15/cab	8/cab	9/cab
Binion's Gambling Hall	14/cab	15/cab	downtown	19/cab	19/cab
Boulder Station	19/cab	18/cab	12/cab	21/cab	20/cab
Caesars Palace	on Strip	7/mono	12/cab	10/cab	10/cab
California	13/cab	15/cab	downtown	19/cab	19/cab
Candlewood Suites	5/cab	6/cab	15/cab	6/cab	6/cab
Cannery	23/cab	26/cab	20/cab	30/cab	30/cab
Casino Royale	on Strip	7/mono	14/cab	10/cab	10/cab
Circus Circus	on Strip	5/cab	13/cab	14/cab	13/cab
Clarion Hotel and Suites	5/cab	5/cab	14/cab	8/cab	10/cab
Comfort Inn Paradise Road	4/cab	5/cab	15/cab	10/cab	9/cab
Courtyard	4/cab	5/walk	15/cab	9/cab	8/cab
Courtyard Las Vegas South	4/cab	14/cab	15/cab	8/cab	12/cab
El Cortez	11/cab	15/cab	6/walk	16/cab	17/cab
Ellis Island	4/cab	6/cab	14/cab	8/cab	8/cab
Embassy Suites Convention Center	6/cab	10/walk	15/cab	9/cab	7/cab
Embassy Suites in Las Vegas	4/cab	6/cab	15/cab	6/cab	6/cab
Emerald Suites	18/cab	21/cab	15/cab	23/cab	24/cab
Excalibur	on Strip	13/cab	14/cab	7/cab	8/cab
E-Z 8 Motel	4/cab	9/cab	12/cab	9/cab	10/cab
Fairfield Inn Las Vegas Airport	5/cab	5/cab	15/cab	9/cab	8/cab

FROM	TO				
	LAS VEGAS STRIP	CONVENTION CENTER	DOWN-TOWN	McCARRAN AIRPORT	UNLV THOMAS & MACK CENTER
Fairfield Inn and Suites Las Vegas South	4/cab	14/walk	15/cab	8/cab	12/cab
Fiesta Henderson	18/cab	17/cab	19/cab	17/cab	15/cab
Fiesta Rancho	18/cab	18/cab	10/cab	22/cab	22/cab
Fitzgeralds	14/cab	15/cab	downtown	17/cab	17/cab
Flamingo	on Strip	7/mono	13/cab	8/cab	8/cab
Four Queens	15/cab	15/cab	downtown	19/cab	17/cab
Four Seasons	on Strip	14/cab	15/cab	7/cab	13/cab
Fremont	15/cab	15/cab	downtown	19/cab	17/cab
Gold Coast	4/cab	13/cab	14/cab	10/cab	10/cab
Gold Spike	14/cab	15/cab	4/walk	18/cab	17/cab
Golden Gate	14/cab	15/cab	downtown	19/cab	18/cab
Golden Nugget	14/cab	15/cab	downtown	18/cab	19/cab
Golden Palm Hotel	4/cab	14/cab	15/cab	9/cab	11/cab
Greek Isles	7/walk	5/walk	14/cab	9/cab	11/cab
Green Valley Ranch Resort and Spa	15/cab	18/cab	16/cab	15/cab	14/cab
Hampton Inn Tropicana	10/walk	6/cab	9/cab	10/cab	6/cab
Hard Rock Hotel	4/cab	6/cab	15/cab	6/cab	6/cab
Harrah's	on Strip	5/mono	15/cab	10/cab	10/cab
Hilton Garden Inn	13/cab	23/cab	26/cab	14/cab	21/cab
Holiday Inn Emerald Springs	4/cab	8/cab	15/cab	7/cab	7/cab
Holiday Inn Express	4/cab	14/cab	15/cab	8/cab	12/cab
Hooters	5/walk	11/mono	15/cab	6/cab	8/cab
Howard Johnson Airport	5/cab	7/cab	15/cab	3/cab	5/cab
Imperial Palace	on Strip	5/mono	15/cab	10/cab	10/cab
JW Marriott Las Vegas	18/cab	21/cab	15/cab	23/cab	24/cab
Key Largo/Quality Inn	5/cab	5/cab	14/cab	8/cab	10/cab
La Quinta Las Vegas Airport	5/cab	6/cab	15/cab	6/cab	6/cab
La Quinta Tropicana	5/cab	13/cab	14/cab	10/cab	10/cab
Las Vegas Club	14/cab	15/cab	downtown	19/cab	18/cab
Las Vegas Hilton	5/mono	5/walk	13/cab	10/cab	8/cab
Las Vegas Marriott Suites	14/cab	5/walk	15/cab	10/cab	9/cab

Commuting Times in Minutes (continued)

FROM	TO				
	LAS VEGAS STRIP	CONVENTION CENTER	DOWN-TOWN	McCARRAN AIRPORT	UNLV THOMAS & MACK CENTER
Loews Lake Las Vegas	45/cab	49/cab	43/cab	37/cab	46/cab
Luxor	on Strip	13/cab	15/cab	8/cab	10/cab
Main Street Station	14/cab	15/cab	downtown	19/cab	19/cab
Mandalay Bay	on Strip	14/cab	16/cab	7/cab	13/cab
Manor Suites	10/cab	17/cab	20/cab	12/cab	17/cab
Marriott Renaissance	6/mono	4/walk	13/cab	10/cab	8/cab
MGM Grand	on Strip	11/mono	15/cab	9/cab	9/cab
Mirage	on Strip	6/mono	15/cab	11/cab	10/cab
Monte Carlo	on Strip	11/mono	15/cab	11/cab	12/cab
MonteLago Village Lake Las Vegas Resort	45/cab	49/cab	43/cab	37/cab	46/cab
Motel 6 Tropicana	3/cab	12/cab	15/cab	6/cab	8/cab
Nevada Palace	21/cab	26/cab	21/cab	19/cab	18/cab
New Frontier	on Strip	8/cab	13/cab	11/cab	10/cab
New York–New York	on Strip	11/mono	15/cab	11/cab	12/cab
Orleans	4/cab	15/cab	14/cab	11/cab	11/cab
Palace Station	5/cab	10/cab	10/cab	14/cab	15/cab
Palms	5/cab	13/cab	14/cab	10/cab	10/cab
Paris	on Strip	9/mono	15/cab	8/cab	8/cab
Planet Hollywood	on Strip	8/cab	15/cab	7/cab	8/cab
Platinum Hotel	8/walk	5/cab	17/cab	7/cab	7/cab
Plaza Hotel	14/cab	15/cab	downtown	19/cab	18/cab
Quality Inn	5/walk	8/cab	15/cab	8/cab	8/cab
Red Rock Resort	18/cab	21/cab	15/cab	23/cab	24/cab
Residence Inn	4/cab	6/cab	15/cab	12/cab	12/cab
Residence Inn Las Vegas South	4/cab	14/cab	15/cab	8/cab	12/cab

conveniently at hand. Driving time to downtown Las Vegas varies from about 16 minutes from the south end of the Strip (I-15 via Tropicana Avenue) to about six minutes from the north end (I-15 via Sahara Avenue).

FROM	TO				
	LAS VEGAS STRIP	CONVENTION CENTER	DOWN-TOWN	McCARRAN AIRPORT	UNLV THOMAS & MACK CENTER
Renaissance Las Vegas	5/cab	10/walk	14/cab	9/cab	8/cab
Rio	5/cab	14/cab	13/cab	10/cab	10/cab
Ritz-Carlton Lake Las Vegas	45/cab	49/cab	43/cab	37/cab	46/cab
Riviera	on Strip	4/cab	14/cab	11/cab	10/cab
Royal Resort	3/walk	5/cab	14/cab	13/cab	11/cab
Sahara	on Strip	6/mono	13/cab	13/cab	11/cab
Sahara Westwood Inn	5/cab	10/cab	10/cab	14/cab	15/cab
St. Tropez	5/cab	6/cab	15/cab	7/cab	6/cab
Sam's Town	20/cab	25/cab	20/cab	18/cab	17/cab
Santa Fe Station	27/cab	30/cab	23/cab	33/cab	36/cab
Silverton	10/cab	17/cab	20/cab	12/cab	17/cab
South Point	16/cab	23/cab	26/cab	18/cab	23/cab
Stratosphere	3/cab	7/cab	9/cab	14/cab	14/cab
Suncoast	18/cab	21/cab	15/cab	23/cab	24/cab
Sunset Station	18/cab	17/cab	18/cab	16/cab	15/cab
Terrible's	5/cab	6/cab	15/cab	6/cab	6/cab
Texas Station	17/cab	16/cab	13/cab	22/cab	22/cab
THEhotel at Mandalay Bay	on Strip	14/cab	15/cab	7/cab	13/cab
T. I. (Treasure Island)	on Strip	6/mono	14/cab	11/cab	10/cab
Tropicana	on Strip	11/mono	15/cab	6/cab	9/cab
Tuscany	5/cab	5/cab	14/cab	8/cab	10/cab
Venetian	on Strip	6/mono	14/cab	8/cab	8/cab
Westin Casuarina	4/walk	11/mono	15/cab	7/cab	7/cab
Wild, Wild, West	3/cab	13/cab	14/cab	8/cab	11/cab
Wynn Las Vegas	on Strip	8/cab	13/cab	10/cab	9/cab

Commuting to the Strip from Downtown

If you are heading to the Strip from downtown, you can pick up US 95 North (and then I-15 South) by going north on either Fourth Street or Las Vegas Boulevard. Driving time from downtown to the Strip takes 6 to 16 minutes, depending on your destination.

Free Connections

Traffic on the Strip is so awful that the hotels, both individually and in groups, are creating new alternatives for getting around.

1. An elevated tram links the Bellagio and Monte Carlo on the west side. Farther south on the west side, a shuttle tram serves the Excalibur, Luxor, Mandalay Bay, Four Seasons, and THEhotel.

2. The Rio operates a shuttle from the Rio Visitor's Center, just south of Paris Las Vegas on the Strip, to the Rio, about half a mile west of the Strip on West Flamingo Road. Shuttles are also available linking Bill's Gamblin' Hall on the northeast corner of the Strip and the Flamingo to the Gold Coast about a mile west.

3. Free shuttle service from the nongaming Polo Towers near Planet Hollywood runs on the hour northbound to the Stratosphere and on the half hour for the southbound return from 10 a.m. until 7 p.m.

LAS VEGAS MONORAIL

THE LONG-AWAITED $650 MILLION LAS VEGAS MONORAIL began service in 2004 with nine trains running the three-mile route between the MGM Grand and the Sahara. The route parallels the Strip between Tropicana and Sands Avenue and then cuts east to the Las Vegas Convention Center and the Las Vegas Hilton before continuing to the last stop at the Sahara. Trains run approximately every 10 minutes between 7 a.m. and 2 a.m. From one end of the line to the other takes about 18 minutes and includes seven stops. The fare for a single one-way ride is $5. A better deal is a one-day fare (24 hours from first use) at $15 (summer special at $8). Other options include a ten-ride fare for $35 (with each one-way segment defined as a ride) and a three-day unlimited travel fare for $40. The monorail is a godsend to convention and trade-show attendees commuting from Strip hotels to the Las Vegas Convention Center and the Sands Exposition Center; ☎ 702-699-8200; **www.lvmonorail.com.**

unofficial **TIP**
Because monorail stations are located at the extreme rear of the casinos served, you're better off walking if you are going less than a mile.

BUSES AND TROLLEYS

LAS VEGAS'S CITIZEN'S AREA TRANSIT (CAT) provides reliable bus service at reasonable rates. Although one-way fares along the Strip are $2, one-way fares in residential areas are only $1.25. Children age 5 and under ride all routes free. All public transportation requires exact fare; transfers are free on all routes but must be used within two hours of issue. All CAT buses are equipped with wheelchair lifts and bicycle racks, both of which are provided at no extra charge. Handicapped persons requiring door-to-door service should call ahead for reservations. For general route and fare information, to request a schedule through the mail, or to make reservations for door-to-door service, call ☎ 702-228-7433, or visit **www.rtcsouthernnevada.com/cat.**

COMMONLY USED PUBLIC TRANSPORTATION ROUTES

	ROUND-TRIP FROM/TO	HOURS OF OPERATION	FREQUENCY OF SERVICE	FARE
Monorail	MGM Grand/ Sahara	7 a.m.–2 a.m.	Every 5 minutes	$5
Citizen's Area Transit Bus #301	South Strip Transfer Terminals/ Downtown Transportation Center	24 hours	Every 15 minutes	$2
Citizen's Area Transit Bus #302 (Strip Express Northbound)	South Strip Transfer Terminals/ Downtown Transportation Center	10:35 a.m.– 11:55 p.m.	Every 20 minutes	$2
Citizen's Area Transit Bus #302 (Strip Express Southbound)	South Strip Transfer Terminals/ Downtown Transportation Center	10:35 a.m.– 11:55 p.m.	Every 20 minutes	$2
Citizen's Area Transit Bus #303 (Mall Circulator)	South Strip Transfer Terminals/ Belz Factory Outlet World	8:30 a.m.– 10:30 p.m.	Every 30 minutes	$2
Las Vegas Strip Trolley Route	Mandalay Bay/ Stratosphere	9:30 a.m.– 1:30 a.m.	Every 15 minutes	$1.75

The Las Vegas Strip Trolley Company is privately owned and provides transportation along the Strip and between the Strip and downtown. These vehicles are styled to look like San Francisco cable cars, and a ride costs $1.75 (exact change). The transit runs from 9:30 a.m. to 2 a.m., making trips on the half hour. Children age 4 and under ride free. Call ☎ 702-382-1404 for more information. *Note:* Fare collection on the trolleys is inefficient; it's quicker to take a regular transit bus.

WHAT'S *in an* ADDRESS?

DOWNTOWN

THE HEART OF THE DOWNTOWN casino area is Fremont Street between Fourth Street (on the east) and Main Street (on the west). Hotel-casinos situated along this quarter-mile four-block stretch known as Glitter Gulch include the Plaza Hotel, Golden Gate, Vegas Club, Binion's Gambling Hall, Golden Nugget, Fremont, Four Queens, and Fitzgeralds. Parallel to Fremont and one block north is Ogden Avenue, where the California and the Gold Spike are located. Main Street Station is situated on Main Street at the intersection of Ogden Avenue.

All of the downtown hotel-casinos are centrally positioned and convenient to the action, with the exception of the El Cortez, which sits three blocks to the east. While there is a tremendous difference in quality and price among the downtown properties, the locations of all the hotels (except the El Cortez) are excellent. When you stay downtown, everything is within a five-minute walk. By comparison, on the Strip it takes longer to walk from the entrance of Caesars Palace to the entrance of the Mirage, next door, than to cover the whole four blocks of the casino center downtown.

THE STRIP

WHILE LOCATION IS NOT A MAJOR CONCERN when choosing from among the downtown hotels, it is of paramount importance when selecting a hotel on the Strip.

We once received a flier from a Las Vegas casino proclaiming that it was located "right on the Strip." It supported the claim with a photo showing its marquee and those of several other casinos in a neat row with their neon ablaze. What recipients of this advertisement (except those familiar with Las Vegas) never would have guessed was that the photo had been taken with a lens that eliminated all sense of distance. While the advertised casino appeared to be next door to the other casinos in the picture, it was in reality almost a mile away.

A common variation on the same pitch is "Stay Right on the Las Vegas Strip at Half the Price." Once again, the promoter is attempting to deceive by taking advantage of the recipient's ignorance of Strip geography. As it happens, the Las Vegas Strip (South Las Vegas Boulevard) starts southwest of the airport and runs all the way downtown, a distance of about seven miles. Only the four-mile section between Mandalay Bay and the Stratosphere contains the large casinos and other attractions of interest to visitors. South of Mandalay Bay "on the Strip" are the airport boundary, some small motels, discount shopping, and nice desert. North of the Stratosphere en route to downtown, the Strip runs through a commercial area sprinkled with wedding chapels, fast-food restaurants, and small motels.

The Best Locations on the Strip

Beware of hotels and motels claiming to be on the Strip but not located between Mandalay Bay and the Stratosphere. The Mandalay Bay basically anchors the south end of the Strip, about a quarter mile from the Luxor, its closest neighbor. Likewise, at the other end, the Stratosphere and the Sahara are somewhat isolated. In between, there are distinct clusters of hotels and casinos.

STRIP CLUSTER 1: THE CLUSTER OF THE GIANTS At the intersection of the Strip (South Las Vegas Boulevard) and Tropicana Avenue are five of the world's largest hotels. The MGM Grand Hotel is the largest hotel in the world. Diagonally across the intersection from the MGM Grand is the Excalibur, the sixth largest hotel in the world. The other two corners of the intersection are occupied by New York–New York and the Tropicana. Nearby to the south is the Luxor (third largest) and Mandalay Bay, the Four Seasons, and THEhotel. To the north are the

Monte Carlo and Planet Hollywood (both on the Strip). Hooters is situated on Tropicana across from the MGM Grand. From the intersection of the Strip and Tropicana, it is a half-mile walk south to Mandalay Bay and a three-tenths-mile hike north to Planet Hollywood. The next cluster of major hotels and casinos is at the intersection of Flamingo Road, one mile north. With New York–New York, Planet Hollywood, and the Monte Carlo, Strip Cluster 1

unofficial **TIP**
If you stay on the Strip, you want to be somewhere in the Mandalay Bay–Stratosphere stretch. Even there, though, some sections are more desirable than others.

challenges the status, at least in terms of appeal and diversity, of Strip Cluster 2 at the heart of the Strip. Progress always has its dark side, however; here it is the phenomenal increase of traffic and congestion on East Tropicana Avenue as it approaches the Strip.

STRIP CLUSTER 2: THE GRAND CLUSTER From Flamingo Road to Spring Mountain Road (also called Sands Avenue, and farther east, Twain Avenue) is the greatest numerical concentration of major hotels and casinos on the Strip. If you wish to stay on the Strip and prefer to walk wherever you go, this is the best location. At Flamingo Road and Las Vegas Boulevard are Bally's, Caesars Palace, Bill's Gamblin' Hall, Paris, and Bellagio. Heading east on Flamingo Road is the Westin Casuarina. Toward town on the Strip are the Flamingo, O'Shea's, Imperial Palace, Mirage, Harrah's, Casino Royale, the Venetian, and T. I. Also in this cluster are the Forum Shops and the Grand Canal Shoppes, Las Vegas's most distinctive shopping venues. A leisure traveler could stay a week in this section (without ever getting in a car or cab) and not run out of interesting sights, restaurants, or entertainment. On the negative side, for those with cars, traffic congestion at the intersection of the Strip and Flamingo Road is the worst in the city.

STRIP CLUSTER 3 Another nice section of the Strip is from Spring Mountain Road up to the New Frontier and Wynn Las Vegas. This cluster, pretty much in the center of the Strip, is distinguished by its easy

unofficial **TIP**
Try Strip Cluster 3 for convenience and to escape traffic congestion.

access. The New Frontier can be reached by two different roads, as can Wynn Las Vegas. Visitors who prefer a major hotel on the Strip but want to avoid the daily traffic snarls could not ask for a more convenient location. Though the New Frontier and Wynn Las Vegas are about a quarter mile from the nearest casino cluster in either direction, they are situated within a four-minute walk of Fashion Show Mall, one of the most diversified upscale shopping centers in the United States. There are also some very good restaurants here. Finally, this cluster is a four-minute cab ride (or a 16-minute walk) from the Las Vegas Convention Center.

STRIP CLUSTER 4 The next cluster up the Strip is between Convention Center Drive and Riviera Boulevard. Arrayed along a stretch slightly more than a half-mile long are the Riviera and Circus Circus with its Adventuredome theme park. Casinos and hotels in this cluster are considerably less upscale than those in the "grand cluster" but offer

hotel clusters

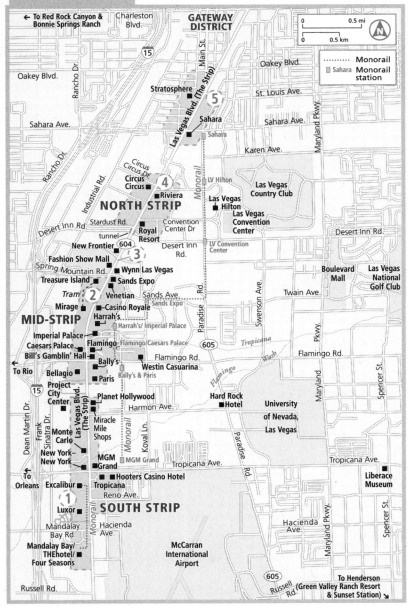

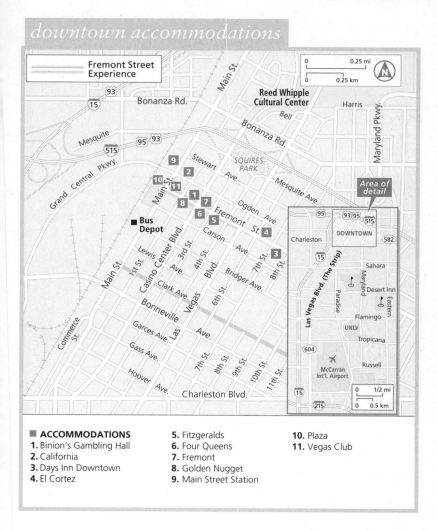

downtown accommodations

ACCOMMODATIONS
1. Binion's Gambling Hall
2. California
3. Days Inn Downtown
4. El Cortez
5. Fitzgeralds
6. Four Queens
7. Fremont
8. Golden Nugget
9. Main Street Station
10. Plaza
11. Vegas Club

acceptable selections for dining and entertainment, as well as proximity to the Las Vegas Convention Center.

STRIP CLUSTER 5 Finally, near the intersection of Las Vegas Boulevard and Sahara Avenue there is a relatively isolated hotel cluster that contains the Sahara and, about a third of a mile toward town, the Stratosphere. Though fairly isolated if you intend to walk, for visitors with cars or monorail riders this cluster provides convenient access to the Strip, the convention center, and downtown.

south strip accommodations

■ **ACCOMMODATIONS**

1. Ambassador Strip Inn Travelodge
2. America's Best Value Inn
3. Courtyard by Marriott Las Vegas South
4. Emerald Suites Tropicana
5. Excalibur
6. Fairfield Inn & Suites Las Vegas South
7. Four Seasons at Mandalay Bay
8. Golden Palm Hotel
9. Hampton Inn Tropicana
10. Hilton Garden Inn Las Vegas Strip South
11. Holiday Inn Express
12. Hooters Casino Hotel
13. Howard Johnson Airport
14. La Quinta Tropicana
15. Luxor
16. Mandalay Bay
17. Manor Suites
18. MGM Grand
19. Monte Carlo
20. New York–New York
21. Orleans
22. Residence Inn by Marriott Las Vegas South
23. Silverton
24. South Coast
25. THEhotel at Mandalay Bay (all suites)
26. Tropicana
27. Wild Wild West

JUST OFF THE STRIP

IF YOU HAVE A CAR, and if being right on the Strip is not a big deal to you, there are some excellent hotel-casinos on Paradise Road, and to the east and west of the Strip on intersecting roads. The Rio, Palms, and Gold Coast on Flamingo Road, Palace Station on Sahara Avenue, and Orleans on Tropicana Avenue offer exceptional value; they are less than a half mile west of the Strip and are situated at access ramps to I-15, five to ten minutes from downtown. To the east of the Strip are the Hard Rock on Harmon Avenue, the Tuscany on Flamingo Road, and the Las Vegas Hilton on Paradise Road, among others.

mid-strip accommodations

■ **ACCOMMODATIONS**

1. Planet Hollywood
2. Bally's
3. Bill's Gamblin' Hall
4. Bellagio
5. Caesars Palace
6. Casino Royale

7. Flamingo
8. Gold Coast
9. Harrah's
10. Imperial Palace
11. Mirage
12. Palms
13. Paris

14. Rio
15. Treasure Island
16. The Venetian
17. Westin Casuarina
18. Wynn Las Vegas

BOULDER HIGHWAY, GREEN VALLEY, SUMMERLIN, AND NORTH LAS VEGAS

TWENTY MINUTES FROM THE STRIP in North Las Vegas are Texas Station, the Fiesta Rancho, the Cannery, and, on the edge of civilization, Santa Fe Station. All four hotels have good restaurants, comfortable guest rooms, and lively, upbeat themes. Hotel-casinos on Boulder Highway southeast of town include Boulder Station, Sam's Town, Arizona Charlie's Boulder, and Nevada Palace. Also to the southeast are Sunset Station, Fiesta Henderson, and Green Valley Ranch Resort and Spa. Like the North Las Vegas trio, the Boulder Highway properties cater primarily to locals. West of town is the posh JW Marriott Las Vegas, with two upscale hotels and the Tournament Player's Club (TPC) at the Canyons Golf Course. Nearby are the Suncoast and the unique Red Rock Resort. Also northwest of the Strip is Arizona Charlie's Decatur.

north strip accommodations

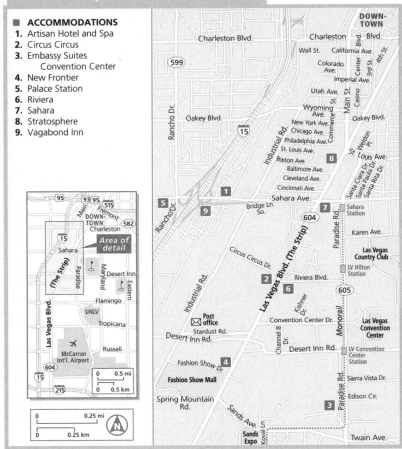

■ ACCOMMODATIONS
1. Artisan Hotel and Spa
2. Circus Circus
3. Embassy Suites
   Convention Center
4. New Frontier
5. Palace Station
6. Riviera
7. Sahara
8. Stratosphere
9. Vagabond Inn

THE LIGHTS OF LAS VEGAS: TRAFFIC ON THE STRIP

DURING THE PAST DECADE, Las Vegas has experienced exponential growth—growth that unfortunately has not been matched with the development of necessary infrastructure. If you imagine a town designed for about 300,000 people being inundated by a million or so refugees (all with cars), you will have a sense of what's happening here.

The Strip, where a huge percentage of the local population works and where more than 80% of tourists and business travelers stay, has become a clogged artery in the heart of the city. The heaviest traffic on the Strip is between Tropicana Avenue and Spring Mountain

east of strip accommodations

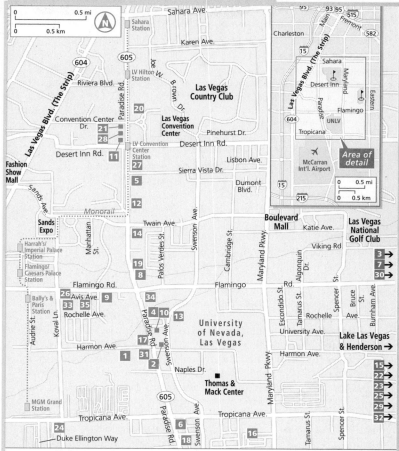

■ ACCOMMODATIONS

1. Alexis Park Resort and Villas
2. AmeriSuites
3. Arizona Charlie's Boulder
4. Atrium Suites Las Vegas
5. Best Western Mardi Gras Inn
6. Best Western McCarran Inn
7. Boulder Station
8. Candlewood Suites
9. Clarion Hotel and Suites
10. Comfort Inn Paradise Road
11. Courtyard by Marriott
12. Embassy Suites Convention Center
13. Embassy Suites in Las Vegas
14. Fairfield Inn Las Vegas Airport
15. Fiesta Henderson
16. Green Valley Ranch
17. Hard Rock Hotel
18. Howard Johnson Airport
19. La Quinta Convention Ctr.
20. Las Vegas Hilton
21. Las Vegas Marriott Suites
22. Loews Lake Las Vegas
23. MonteLago Village Resort
24. Motel 6 Tropicana
25. Nevada Palace
26. Platinum Hotel
27. Renaissance Las Vegas
28. Residence Inn by Marriott
29. Ritz-Carlton Lake Las Vegas
30. Sam's Town
31. St. Tropez
32. Sunset Station
33. Super 8
34. Terrible's
35. Tuscany

Sneak Routes—West

HOTELS ON THE WEST SIDE OF THE STRIP

Bellagio has an entrance off Flamingo Road (heading east).

Caesars Palace can be accessed from Frank Sinatra Drive.

Circus Circus can be reached via Industrial Road.

Excalibur, Luxor, and **Mandalay Bay** can be reached from east of the Strip by turning south off Tropicana Avenue onto Koval Lane and then turning right onto Reno Avenue. Reno Avenue intersects the Strip at a traffic light, allowing you to cross to Excalibur and Luxor. From west of the Strip, you can also access all three hotels via Frank Sinatra Drive.

The **Mirage** and **T. I.** are accessible by taking Industrial Road or I-15 and then turning east on Spring Mountain Road.

The **Monte Carlo** can be reached from Frank Sinatra Drive.

The **New Frontier** has an entrance off Fashion Show Drive, which connects to Industrial Road.

New York–New York can be reached via Tropicana Avenue or from Frank Sinatra Drive.

The **Stratosphere**'s self-parking garage is off Baltimore Street, which connects to Las Vegas Boulevard.

Drive, in the heart of the Strip. Throughout the day and night, local traffic combines with gawking tourists, shoppers, and cruising teenagers to create a three-mile-long, bumper-to-bumper bottleneck.

When folks discuss the "lights of Las Vegas," it used to be that they were talking about the marquees of the casinos. Today, however, the reference is to the long, multifunctional traffic lights found at virtually every intersection on the Strip. These lights, which flash a different signal for every possible turn and direction, combine with an ever-increasing number of vehicles to ensure that nobody goes anywhere. The worst snarls occur at the intersection of the Strip and Flamingo Road. Trying to cross the Strip on perpendicular east-to-west-running roads is also exceedingly difficult. Desert Inn Road, which tunnels under the Strip, is the fastest way to get from one side to the other. Unfortunately, if you're heading west, Desert Inn Road is hard to access on the east side of the Strip, especially from Paradise Road. To use the tunnel from the east side, turn west on Desert Inn Road from Swenson Street.

Strip traffic is the Achilles heel of Las Vegas development and growth. It is sheer lunacy to believe you can plop a litter of megahotels on the Strip without compounding an already horrific traffic situation. While city government and the hospitality industry dance around the issue, traffic gets worse and worse. Approximately 48,000 hotel rooms were added along the Strip during the 1990s, and about 30,000 more came on line since the millennium, with another 25,000 or more under construction or planned. The monorail along the east side of the Strip

Sneak Routes—East

HOTELS ON THE EAST SIDE OF THE STRIP

Planet Hollywood is accessible from westbound Harmon Avenue.

Bally's and **Paris** can be reached by turning north off Harmon Avenue onto an isolated section of Audrie Street.

Bill's Gamblin' Hall is the only major hotel on the east side of the Strip that is truly stuck. If you want to go to Bill's Gamblin' Hall, park somewhere else and walk over. Don't even think about arriving at or departing from Bill's parking lot between 3:30 p.m. and 8 p.m.

The **Flamingo Hilton, Harrah's Las Vegas,** the **Imperial Palace,** and **O'Shea's** each have a back entrance off Audrie Street, a small thoroughfare branching off of Flamingo Road. Audrie Street can also be reached by turning west on Albert or Ida avenues from Koval Lane.

The **MGM Grand** is accessible by heading west (toward the Strip) on Tropicana Avenue or by turning west off Koval Lane.

The **Riviera** can be reached by turning west on Riviera Boulevard from Paradise Road.

The **Sahara** has an entrance on Paradise Road.

The **Tropicana** is accessible by turning south off Tropicana Avenue onto Koval Lane and then turning right onto Reno Avenue.

The **Venetian** is accessible from Koval Lane.

Wynn Las Vegas can be reached by heading west on Convention Center Drive, then turning left onto Channel 8 Drive to the north entrance of the hotel-casino.

represents a great alternative to driving, but it has not noticeably mitigated gridlock. Also, stations are positioned so far to the rear of the casinos that walking is faster than taking the train for distances up to one mile. In another effort, I-15 between downtown and the I-215 junction to the south has been widened and the interchanges improved. While welcome, the project has done little to alleviate traffic. Interestingly, the only initiative that has really worked is the construction of elevated pedestrian bridges over the major Strip intersections. In addition to improving safety, the bridges remove pedestrians from the street, leaving the battlefield to vehicles.

Sneak Routes

Fortunately, most of the large hotels along the Strip have back entrances that allow you to avoid the insanity of the main drag. Industrial Road, Frank Sinatra Drive, and I-15 run parallel to the Strip on the west side, providing backdoor access to hotels situated on the west side of Las Vegas Boulevard. Although a better option than the Strip, traffic on Frank Sinatra between the Bellagio and the New York–New York is frequently snarled by construction at Project City

Center. Avoid this section of Frank Sinatra during shift change times at the casinos, usually from 7 to 9 a.m. and 4 to 5:30 p.m. There's also a shift change from 10 to 11 p.m. It has less impact on traffic, however, due to the lateness of the hour. Paradise Road and Koval Lane run parallel to the Strip on the east side.

A hallmark development in 2004 was the construction of Frank Sinatra Drive between and parallel to the Strip and I-15. The new road runs from south of Mandalay Bay to the intersection with Industrial Road and serves as a backdoor entrance to T. I., the Mirage, Caesars Palace, Monte Carlo, New York–New York, Excalibur, Luxor, Mandalay Bay, THEhotel, and Four Seasons. Frank Sinatra Drive also runs behind the Bellagio, but there is no access to the Bellagio's self-parking lot.

Though a real boon for those in the know, the road is primarily used by casino employees and by truckers making deliveries. It is usually congested only during the 3:30 p.m. to 6 p.m. shift-change period.

ROOM RESERVATIONS: *Getting a Good Room, Getting a Good Deal*

BECAUSE LAS VEGAS IS SO POPULAR for weekend getaways, weekend occupancy averages an astounding 92% of capacity for hotels and 70% of capacity for motels. Weekday occupancy for hotels is a respectable 83%, and for motels, 63%. What these figures mean, among other things, is that you want to nail down your lodging reservations before you leave home.

Also, consider that these occupancy percentages are averages. When a large convention is in town or when Las Vegas hosts a championship prizefight, the National Finals Rodeo, or any other major event, rooms become hard to find. If you are heading to Las Vegas purely for fun and relaxation, you may want to avoid going when the town is packed. For more information about dates to avoid, see page 60.

THE WACKY WORLD OF LAS VEGAS HOTEL RESERVATIONS

THOUGH THERE ARE ALMOST 140,000 hotel rooms in Las Vegas, getting one is not always a simple proposition. In the large hotel-casinos, there are often five or more separate departments that have responsibility for room allocation and sales. Of the total number of rooms in any given hotel, a number are at the disposal of the casino; some are administered by the reservations department at the front desk; some are allocated to independent wholesalers for group and individual travel packages; others are blocked for special events (fights, Super Bowl weekend, etc.); and still others are at the disposal of the sales and marketing department for meetings, conventions, wedding parties, and other special groups. Hotels that are part of a large chain (Holiday Inn, Hilton, etc.) have some additional rooms administered by their national reservations systems.

At most hotels, department heads meet each week and review all the room allocations. If rooms blocked for a special event, say a golf tournament, are not selling, some of those rooms will be redistributed to other departments. Since special events and large conventions are scheduled far in advance, the decision-makers have significant lead time. In most hotels, a major reallocation of rooms takes place 40 to 50 days prior to the dates for which the rooms are blocked, with minor reallocations made right up to the event in question.

If you call the reservations number at the hotel of your choice and are informed that no rooms are available for the dates that you've requested, it does not mean the hotel is sold out. What it does mean is that the front desk has no more rooms remaining in their allocation. It is a fairly safe assumption that all the rooms in a hotel have not been reserved by guests. The casino will usually hold back some rooms for high rollers, the sales department may have some rooms reserved for participants in deals they are negotiating, and some rooms will be in the hands of tour wholesalers or blocked for a citywide convention. If any of these remaining rooms are not committed by a certain date, they will be reallocated. So a second call to the reservations department may get you the room that was unavailable when you called two weeks earlier.

THE INTERNET REVOLUTION

PURCHASING TRAVEL ON THE INTERNET has revolutionized the way both consumers and hotels do business. For you it makes shopping for a hotel and finding good deals much easier. For the hotel it makes possible a system of room inventory management often referred to as "nudging." Here's how it works. Many months in advance, hotels establish rates for each day of the coming year. In developing their rate calendar, they take into consideration all of the variables that affect occupancy in their hotel as well as in Las Vegas in general. They consider weekend versus weekday demand; additional demand stimulated by holidays, major conventions, trade shows, and sporting events; and the effect of the four seasons of the year on occupancy.

After rates for each date are determined, the rates are entered into the hotel's reservation system. Then hotel management sits back to see what happens. If the bookings for a particular date are in accord with management's expectations, no rate change is necessary. If demand is greater than management's forecast for a given date, they might raise the rate to take advantage of higher than expected bookings. If demand eases off, the hotel can revert back to the original rate.

If demand is less than expected, the hotel will begin nudging, that is, incrementally decreasing the rate for the day or days in question until booking volume increases to the desired level. Though this sort of rate manipulation has been an integral part of room inventory management for decades, the Internet has made it possible to rethink and alter room rates almost at will. A hotel can theoretically adjust rates hourly on its own Web site. Major Internet travel sellers such as Travelocity, Hotels.com, and Expedia, among others, are fast and agile and quite capable of getting a special deal (that is, a lower rate) in front of travel purchasers almost instantaneously. For the hotel, this means they can manage their inventory on almost a weekly or daily basis, nudging toward full occupancy by adjusting their rates according to demand. Of course, the hotels don't depend entirely on the Internet. Lower rates and various special deals are also communicated by e-mail to preferred travel agents, and sometimes directly to consumers (especially slot club members) via e-mail, print advertisements, or direct-mail promotions.

GETTING THE BEST DEAL ON A ROOM

COMPARED TO HOTEL RATES in other destinations, lodging in Las Vegas is so relatively inexpensive that the following cost-cutting strategies may seem gratuitous. Yes, there are $400-per-night rooms, but if you are accustomed to paying $130 a night for a hotel room, you can afford 60% of the hotels in town. You may not be inclined to wade through all the options listed below to save $20 or $30 a night. If, on the other hand, you would like to obtain top value for your dollar, read on.

The Season

December and January are roller-coaster months for Las Vegas. In December, the town is empty except for National Finals Rodeo week in early December and Christmas–New Year's week. Similarly, in January, the town is packed during the Consumer Electronics Show and Super Bowl weekend, and pretty much dead the rest of the time. During the slow parts of these months, most of the hotels offer amazing deals on lodging. Also, hotels frequently offer reduced rates in July and August. While the list at upper right stands up pretty well as a general guide, one type of deal or package might beat another for a specific hotel or time of year.

Sorting Out the Sellers and the Options

To book a room in a particular hotel for any given date, there are so many different in-house departments, as well as outside tour operators and wholesalers selling rooms, that it is almost impossible to find out who is offering the best deal. This is not because the various deals are so hard to compare but, rather, because it is so difficult to identify all the sellers.

Though it is only a rough approximation, see the opposite page for a list of the types of rates and packages available, ranked from the best to the worst value.

The room-rate ranking is subject to some interpretation. A gambler's rate may, at first glance, seem to be the least expensive lodging

ROOM RATES AND PACKAGES	SOLD OR ADMINISTERED BY
1. Gambler's rate	Casino or hotel
2. December, January, and summer specials	Hotel-room reservations or marketing department
3. Wholesaler packages	Independent wholesalers
4. Tour operator packages	Tour operators
5. Reservation service discounts	Independent wholesalers and consolidators
6. Internet discounts	Internet travel vendors
7. Corporate rate	Hotel-room reservations
8. Hotel standard room rate	Hotel-room reservations
9. Convention rate	Convention sponsor

option available, next to a complimentary room. If, however, the amount of money a guest is obligated to wager (and potentially lose) is factored in, the gambler's rate might be by far the most expensive.

Complimentary and Discounted Rooms for Gamblers

Most Las Vegas visitors are at least peripherally aware that casinos provide complimentary or greatly discounted rooms to gamblers. It is not unusual, therefore, for a business traveler, a low-stakes gambler, or a nongambling tourist to attempt to take advantage of these deals. What they quickly discover is that the casino has very definite expectations of any guest whose stay is wholly or partially subsidized by the house. If you want a gambler's discount on a room, they will ask what game(s) you intend to play, the amount of your average bet, how many hours a day you usually gamble, where (at which casinos) you have played before, and how much gambling money you will have available on this trip. They may also request that you make an application for credit or provide personal information about your occupation, income, and bank account.

If you manage to bluff your way into a comp or discounted room, you can bet that your gambling (or lack thereof) will be closely monitored after you arrive. If you fail to give the casino an acceptable amount of action, you will probably be charged the nondiscounted room rate when you check out.

Even for those who expect to do a fair amount of gambling, a comp or discounted room can be a mixed blessing. By accepting the casino's hospitality, you incur a certain obligation (the more they give you, the bigger the obligation). You will be expected to do most (if not all) of your gambling in the casino where you are staying, and you will also be expected to play a certain number of hours each day. If this was your intention all along, great. On the other hand, if you thought you would like to try several casinos or take a day and run over to Hoover Dam, you may be painting yourself into a corner.

Taking Advantage of Special Deals

When you call, always ask the reservationist if the hotel has any package deals or specials. If you plan to gamble, be sure to ask about "gambling sprees" or other gaming specials. If you do not anticipate gambling enough to qualify for a gambling package, ask about other types of deals.

unofficial **TIP**
If the hotel reservationist can't help you with packages or special deals, try the sales and marketing department and ask them.

If you have a lot of lead time before your trip, write or call the hotel and ask about joining their slot club. Though only a few hotels will send you a membership application, inquiring about the slot club will get you categorized as a gambler on the hotel's mailing list. Once in Las Vegas, sign up for the slot clubs of hotel-casinos that you like. This will ensure that you receive notification of special deals that you can take advantage of on subsequent visits. Being a member of a hotel's slot club can also come in handy when rooms are scarce. Once, trying to book a room, we were told the hotel was sold out. When we mentioned that we had a slot card, the reservationist miraculously found us a room. If you are a slot club member, it is often better to phone the slot club member services desk instead of the hotel reservations desk.

If you enjoy window shopping on the Internet, log onto the home page of hotels that interest you. As far as rooms go, however, it's rare in our experience to find a deal on the hotel's Web site that's better than the ones they quote you on the phone. A reservationist on the phone knows she has a good prospect on the line and will work with you within the limits of her authority. On the Web there's no give or negotiation: it's a take-it-or-leave-it deal. Finally, most hotels, including many of the new super-properties, really haven't learned how to merchandise rooms through their Web site.

Having shopped the hotel for deals, start checking out Las Vegas vacation or weekend packages advertised in your local newspaper, and compare what you find to packages offered in the Sunday edition of the *Los Angeles Times.*

Take the better deals and packages you discover, regardless of the source, and discuss them with a travel agent. Explain which one(s) you favor and ask if he or she can do any better. After your travel agent researches the options, review the whole shooting match and select the deal that best fits your schedule, requirements, and budget.

Timing Is Everything

Timing is everything when booking a guest room in Las Vegas. If a particular hotel has only a few rooms to sell for a specific date, it will often, as we discussed earlier, bounce up the rate for those rooms as high as it thinks the market will bear. Conversely, if the hotel has many rooms available for a certain date, it will lower the rate accordingly. The practice remains operative all year, although the likelihood of hotels having a lot of rooms available is obviously greater during off-peak periods. As an example, we checked rates at an upscale non-gaming hotel during two weeks in October. Depending on the specific dates, the rate for the suite in question ranged from $75 (an incredible bargain) to $200 (significantly overpriced) per night.

Which day of the week you check in can also save or cost you some money. At some hotels a standard room runs 20% less if you check in on a Monday through Thursday (even though you may stay through the weekend). If you check into the same room on a weekend, your rate will be higher and may not change if you keep your room into the following week. A more common practice is for the hotel to charge a lower rate during the week and a higher rate on the weekend.

NO ROOM AT THE INN (FOR REAL) More frequently than you would imagine, Las Vegas hotels overbook their rooms. This happens when guests do not check out on time, when important casino customers arrive on short notice, and when the various departments handling room allocations get their signals crossed. When this occurs, guests who arrive holding reservations are told that their reservations have been canceled.

To protect yourself, always guarantee your first night with a major credit card (even if you do not plan to arrive late), send a deposit if required, and insist on a written confirmation of your reservation. When you arrive and check in, have your written confirmation handy.

Precautions notwithstanding, the hotel still might have canceled your reservation. When a hotel is overbooked, for whatever reason, it will take care of its serious gambling customers first, its prospective gambling customers (leisure travelers) second, and business travelers last. If you are informed that you have no room, demand that the hotel honor your reservation by finding you a room or by securing you a room at another hotel of comparable or better quality at the same rate. Should the desk clerk balk at doing this, demand to see the reservations manager. If the reservations manager stonewalls, go to the hotel's general manager. Whatever you do, do not leave until the issue has been resolved to your satisfaction.

Hotels understand their obligation to honor a confirmed reservation, but they often fail to take responsibility unless you hold their feet to the fire. We have seen convention-goers, stunned by the news that they have no room, simply turn around and walk out. Wrong. The hotel owns the problem, not you. You should not have to shop for another room. The hotel that confirmed your reservation should find you a room comparable to or better than the one you reserved, and for the same rate.

WHERE THE DEALS ARE

HOTEL ROOM MARKETING and sales are confusing even to travel professionals. Sellers, particularly the middlemen, or wholesalers are known by a numbing array of different and frequently ill-defined terms. Furthermore, roles overlap, making it difficult to know who, specifically, is providing a given service. Below we try to sort all of this out for you and encourage you to slog through it. Understanding the system will make you a savvy consumer and will enable you to get the best deals regardless of your destination.

Tour Operators and Wholesalers

Las Vegas hotels have always had a hard time filling their rooms from Sunday through Thursday. On the weekends, when thousands of visitors arrive from Southern California, Phoenix, and Salt Lake City, the town comes alive. But on Sunday evening, as the last of the Los Angelenos retreat over the horizon, Las Vegas lapses into the doldrums. The Las Vegas Convention and Visitors Authority, along with hotel sales departments, seek to fill the rooms on weekday nights by bringing meetings, conventions, and trade shows to town. While collectively they are successful, on many weekdays there remain a lot of empty hotel rooms.

Recognizing that an empty hotel room is a liability, various travel entrepreneurs have stepped into the breach, volunteering to sell rooms for the hotels and casinos. These entrepreneurs, who call themselves tour operators, inbound travel brokers, travel wholesalers, travel packagers, Internet retailers, or receptive operators, require as a quid pro quo that the hotels provide them a certain number of rooms at a significantly reduced nightly rate, which they in turn resell at a profit. As this arrangement extends the sales outreach of the hotels, and as the rooms might

---

TOUR OPERATORS AND TRAVEL WHOLESALERS

Some of the following businesses will deal directly with consumers; have your travel agent call the others.

A & P TOURS
East McKeesport, Pennsylvania
☎ 412-351-4800
(Deals directly with consumers)

U.S. AIRWAYS VACATIONS
Tempe, Arizona
☎ 800-235-9298
www.usairwaysvacations.com
(Deals directly with consumers)

EDISON TRAVEL
Kansas City, Kansas
☎ 913-788-7997
(Deals directly with consumers)

FUNJET VACATIONS
Milwaukee, Wisconsin
☎ 800-558-3050
Southfield, Michigan

☎ 800-669-4466
www.funjet.com
(Deals directly with consumers)

MILE HIGH TOURS
Denver, Colorado
☎ 303-288-8100
www.milehitravel.com
(Deals directly with consumers)

MLT VACATIONS
Minnetonka, Minnesota
☎ 952-474-2540 or
888-225-5658
www.mltvacations.com

SUNQUEST
Toronto, Ontario
☎ 416-485-6060
www.sunquest.ca

otherwise go unoccupied, the hotels are only too happy to cooperate with this group of independent sales agents.

TAKING ADVANTAGE OF TOUR OPERATOR AND TRAVEL WHOLESALER DEALS There are several ways for you to tap into the tour operator and wholesaler market. First, check the travel section of your Sunday paper for travel packages or tours to Las Vegas. Because Las Vegas hotels work with tour operators and wholesalers from all over the country, there will undoubtedly be someone in your city or region running packages to Las Vegas. Packages generally consist of room, transportation (bus or air), and often rental cars and shows. Sometimes the consumer can buy the package for any dates desired; other times the operator or wholesaler will specify the dates. In either event, if a particular package fits your needs, you (or your travel agent) can book it directly by calling the phone number listed in the ad.

If you cannot find any worthwhile Las Vegas packages advertised in your local paper, go to a good newsstand and buy a Sunday paper, preferably from Los Angeles, but alternatively from San Diego, Phoenix, Salt Lake City, Denver, or Chicago. These cities are hot markets for Las Vegas, and their newspapers will almost always have a nice selection of packages advertised. Because the competition among tour operators and wholesalers in these cities is so great, you will often find deals that beat the socks off anything offered in your part of the country.

*un*official **TIP**
One of the sweetest deals in travel is to buy the "land-only" part of a package at a time when the airlines are running a promotion.

Find a package that you like and call for information. Do not be surprised, however, if the advertised package is not wholly available to you. If you live in, say, Nashville, Tennessee, a tour operator or wholesaler in Los Angeles may not be able to package your round-trip air or bus to Las Vegas. This is because tour operators and wholesalers usually work with bus and air carriers on a contractual basis, limiting the transportation they sell to round-trips originating from their market area. In other words, they can take care of your transportation if you are flying from Southern California but most likely will not have a contract with an airline that permits them to fly you from Nashville. What they sometimes do, however, and what they will be delighted to do if they are sitting on some unsold rooms, is sell you the "land-only" part of the package. This means you buy the room and on-site amenities (car, shows, etc.), if any, but will take care of your own travel arrangements.

Buying the "land-only" part of a package can save big bucks because the wholesaler always has more flexibility in discounting the "land-only" part of the package than in discounting the round-trip transportation component. We combined a two-for-one air special from Delta with a "land-only" package from a wholesaler and chalked up a savings of 65% over separate quoted rates and a 22% savings over the full air-land package offered by the wholesaler.

Finding Deals on the Internet

By far the easiest way to scout room deals on the Internet is through **www.travelaxe.com.** At Travelaxe, you can download free software (only runs on PCs) that scans the better Internet sites selling discounted rooms. You enter your proposed check-in and checkout dates (required) as well as preferences concerning location and price (optional), and click "Search." The program scans a dozen or more Internet seller sites and presents the discounted rates for all hotels in a chart for comparison. The prices listed in the chart represent the *total* you'll pay for your entire stay. To determine the rate per night, divide the total by the number of nights you'll be staying. If you decide to book, you deal directly with the site offering the best price. The software doesn't scan the individual hotel Web sites, so if you have a specific hotel in mind, you should check the hotel's site and call the hotel's reservation desk to ask about specials. We've run a number of tests on the Travelaxe program and found that it usually delivers the best prices available on the Internet.

Finally, for Internet shopping, consider **www.priceline.com**. There you can tender a bid for a room. You can't bid on a specific hotel, but you can specify location ("Convention Center, UNLV Area, Las Vegas Strip Area," etc.) and the quality rating expressed in stars. If your bid is accepted, you will be assigned to a hotel consistent with your location and quality requirements, and your credit card will be charged in a non-refundable transaction for your entire stay. Notification of acceptance usually takes less than an hour. We recommend bidding $40 to $55 per night for a three-star hotel and $65 to $90 per night for a four-star. To gauge your chances of success, check to see if any major conventions or trade shows are scheduled during your preferred dates. Reduce your bid for off-season periods. Note that Priceline lists "Las Vegas Strip Area" as opposed to "Las Vegas Strip." Thus you might be booked into a hotel close to, but not on the Strip.

Reservation Services

When wholesalers and consolidators deal directly with the public, they frequently represent themselves as "reservation services." When you call, you can ask for a rate quote for a particular hotel, or alternatively, ask for their best available deal in the area where you prefer to stay. If there is a maximum amount you are willing to pay, say so.

*un*official **TIP**
Regarding hotel specials, hotel reservationists do not usually inform you of existing specials or offer them to you. In other words, you have to ask.

Chances are the service will find something that will work for you, even if they have to shave a dollar or two off their own profit.

Our experience has been that the reservation services are more useful in finding rooms in Las Vegas when availability is scarce than in obtaining deep discounts. Calling the hotels ourselves, we were often able to beat the reservation services' rates when rooms were generally available.

RESERVATION SERVICES	
Accommodations Express	☎ 800-444-7666 www.accommodationsexpress.com
Hotel Reservations Network	☎ 800-96-HOTEL www.hotelreservationsnetwork.com
National Reservations Bureau	☎ 800-805-9528; www.bookme.travel

When the city was booked, however, and we could not find a room by calling the hotels ourselves, the reservation services could almost always get us a room at a fair price.

Hotel-sponsored Packages

In addition to selling rooms through tour operators, consolidators, wholesalers, and Internet retailers, most hotels periodically offer exceptional deals of their own. Sometimes the packages are specialized, as with golf packages, or are offered only at certain times of the year, for instance December and January. Promotion of hotel specials tends to be limited to the hotel's primary markets, which for most properties is Southern California, Arizona, Utah, Colorado, Hawaii, and the Midwest. If you live in other parts of the country, you can take advantage of the packages but probably will not see them advertised in your local newspaper.

Some of the hotel packages are unbelievable deals. Once, for instance, a hotel offered three nights' free lodging, no strings attached, to any adult from Texas. On certain dates in November, December, and January, the Flamingo offered a deal that included a room for two or more nights at $35 per night (tax inclusive), with two drinks and a show thrown in for good measure. In July of 2006, 23 hotels offered rates less than $45. Look for the hotel specials in Southern California newspapers, or call the hotel and ask.

Traveler Discount Guide

A company called Traveler Discount Guide (TDG) publishes a book of discount coupons for bargain rates at hotels throughout California and Nevada. These books are available free of charge in many restaurants and motels along the main interstate highways. Since most folks make reservations prior to leaving home, picking up the coupon book en route does not help much. For $3 ($5 Canadian), however, TDG will mail you a copy (third class) before you make your reservations. Properties listed in the guide for Las Vegas are generally smaller, nongaming hotels. If you call and use a credit card, TDG will send the guide first class for an additional charge. Write or call:

Traveler Discount Guide
4205 NW Sixth Street
Gainesville, FL 32609

☎ 352-371-3948 or 800-332-3948
www.roomsaver.com or
www.travelerdiscountguide.com

HOW TO EVALUATE A TRAVEL PACKAGE

HUNDREDS OF LAS VEGAS PACKAGE TRIPS and vacations are offered to the public each year. Almost all include round-trip transportation to Las Vegas and lodging. Sometimes room tax, transportation from the airport, a rental car, shows, meals, welcome parties, and/or souvenirs are also included.

In general, because the Las Vegas market is so competitive, packages to Las Vegas are among the best travel values available. Las Vegas competes head-to-head with Atlantic City for Eastern travelers and with Reno, Lake Tahoe, Laughlin, and other Nevada destinations for Western visitors. Within Las Vegas, downtown competes with the Strip, and individual hotels go one-on-one to improve their share of the market. In addition to the fierce competition for the destination traveler, the extraordinary profitability of gambling also works on the consumer's behalf to keep Las Vegas travel economical. For a large number of hotels, amazing values in dining and lodging are used to lure visitors to the casino.

Packages should be a win–win proposition for both the buyer and the seller. The buyer (or travel agent) only has to make one phone call and deal with a single salesperson to set up the whole trip: transportation, lodging, rental car, show admissions, and even golf, tennis, and sightseeing. The seller, likewise, only has to deal with the buyer one time, eliminating the need for separate sales, confirmations, and billings. In addition to streamlining selling, processing, and administration, some packagers also buy airfares in bulk on contract like a broker playing the commodities market. Buying or guaranteeing a large number of airfares in advance allows the packager to buy them at a significant savings from posted fares. The same practice is also applied to hotel rooms. Because selling packaged trips is an efficient way of doing business, and the packager can often buy individual components (airfare, lodging) in bulk at a discount, savings in operating expenses realized by the seller are sometimes passed on to the buyer. So the package is not only convenient but an exceptional value. In any event, that is the way it is supposed to work.

In practice, the seller occasionally realizes all of the economies and passes none of the savings along to the buyer. In some instances, packages are loaded with extras that cost the packager next to nothing but run the retail price sky-high. While this is not as common with Las Vegas packages as those to other destinations, it occurs frequently enough to warrant some comparison shopping.

When considering a package, choose one that includes features you are sure to use. Whether you use all the features or not, you will most certainly pay for them. Second, if cost is of greater concern than convenience, make a few phone calls and see what the package would cost if you booked its individual components (airfare, lodging, rental car) on your own. If the package price is less than the à la carte cost, the package is a good deal. If the costs are about the same, the package is probably worth it for the convenience.

AN EXAMPLE Bob's niece and a friend were looking at a package they found with Delta Vacations. The package included round-trip airfare (on Delta) from Atlanta, four nights' lodging (Friday through Monday) at the Luxor, airport transfers (transportation to and from the airport), and about 20 "bonus features," including:

- 2-for-1 admission to Hoover Dam tours
- Free admission to the Imperial Palace Auto Collection
- 2-for-1 cocktails at New York–New York
- A free Planet Hollywood souvenir
- Discounted Lake Mead boat cruises

The price, tax included, was $548 per person, or $1,096 all together. Checking the Luxor and a number of airlines, they found the following:

Same room at the Luxor, 2 people to a room, for 4 nights with room tax included	$519
Transportation to and from the airport	$14
Subtotal	$533

Subtracting the $533 (lodging and airport transfers) from the cost of Delta's package total of $1,096, they determined that the air and "bonus features" portion of the package was worth $563 ($1,096 − $533 = $563). If they were not interested in using any of the bonus features, and they could fly to Las Vegas for less than $563, they would be better off turning down the package.

Scouting around, the lowest fare they could find was $320 per person on American Airlines with an advance purchase ticket. This piece of information completed their analysis as follows:

Option A: Delta Vacation package for 2	$1,096
Option B: Booking their own air and lodging	
Lodging, including tax	$519
Airfare on American Airlines for 2	$640
Transportation to and from hotel	$14
Total	$1,173

In this example, the package saves money and is also more convenient. Most of the two-fers and other deals bundled into the package are available through freebie Las Vegas visitor magazines, but you might not have discovered them. Be aware that it doesn't always work out this way. We analyze dozens of packages each year, and there are as many bad deals as good deals. The point is, always do your homework.

For BUSINESS TRAVELERS

CONVENTION RATES: HOW THE SYSTEM WORKS

BUSINESS TRAVELERS, PARTICULARLY THOSE attending trade shows or conventions, are almost always charged more for their rooms than leisure travelers. For big meetings, called citywide conventions, huge numbers of rooms are blocked in hotels all over town. These rooms are reserved for visitors attending the meeting in question and are usually requested and coordinated by the meeting's sponsoring organization in cooperation with the Las Vegas Convention and Visitors Authority.

Individual hotels negotiate a nightly rate with the convention sponsor, who then frequently sells the rooms through a central reservations system of its own. Because the hotels would rather have gamblers or leisure travelers than people attending conventions (who usually have limited time to gamble), the negotiated price tends to be high, often $10 to $50 per night above the rack rate.

Meeting sponsors, of course, blame convention rates on the hotels. Meanwhile the hotels maintain a stoic silence, not wishing to alienate meeting organizers.

To be fair, convention sponsors should be given some credit simply for having their meeting in Las Vegas. Even considering the inflated convention rates, meeting attendees will pay 15 to 40% less in Las Vegas for comparable lodging than in other major convention cities. As for the rest, well, let's take a look.

Sam Walton taught the average American that someone purchasing a large quantity of a particular item should be able to obtain a better price (per item) than a person buying only one or two. If anyone just walking in off the street can buy a single hotel room for $50, why then must a convention sponsor, negotiating for 900 rooms for five nights in the same hotel (4,500 room-nights in hotel jargon), settle for a rate of $60 per night?

Many Las Vegas hotels take a hard-line negotiating position with meeting sponsors because (1) every room occupied by a convention-goer is one less room available for gamblers, and (2) they figure that most business travelers are on expense accounts. In addition, timing is a critical factor in negotiating room rates. The hotels do not want business travelers occupying rooms on weekends or during the more popular times of the year. Convention sponsors who want to schedule a meeting during high season (when hotels fill their rooms no matter what) can expect to pay premium rates. In addition, and regardless of the time of year, many hotels routinely charge stiff prices to convention-goers as a sort of insurance against lost opportunity. "What if we block our rooms for a trade show one year in advance," a sales manager asked, "and then a championship prizefight is scheduled for that week? We would lose big-time."

A spokesman for the Las Vegas Convention and Visitors Authority indicated that the higher room rates for conventioneers are not unreasonable given a hotel's commitment to the sponsor to hold rooms in reserve. But reserved rooms, or room blocks as they are called, fragment a hotel's inventory of available rooms, and often make it harder, not easier, to get a room in a particular hotel. The bottom line is that convention-goers pay a premium price for the benefit of having rooms reserved for their meeting—rooms that would be cheaper, and often easier to reserve, if the sponsor had not reserved them in the first place. For a major citywide convention, it is not unusual for attendees to collectively pay in excess of $1 million for the peace of mind of having rooms reserved.

Whether room-blocking is really necessary is an interesting question. The Las Vegas Convention and Visitors Authority works with convention sponsors to ensure that there is never more than one city-wide meeting in town at a time and to make sure that sponsors do not schedule their conventions at a time when Las Vegas hotels are otherwise normally sold out (National Finals Rodeo week, Super Bowl weekend, New Year's, and so on). Unfortunately for meeting planners, some major events (prizefights, tennis matches) are occasionally scheduled in Las Vegas on short notice. If a meeting planner does not block rooms and a big fight is announced for the week the meeting is in town, the attendees may be unable to find a room. This is such a nightmare to convention sponsors that they cave in to exorbitant convention rates rather than risk not having rooms. The actual likelihood of a major event being scheduled at the same time as a large convention is small, though the specter of this worst-case scenario is a powerful weapon in the bargaining arsenal of the hotels.

On balance, meeting sponsors negate their volume-buying clout by scheduling meetings during the more popular times of year or, alternatively, by caving in to the hotels' "opportunity cost" room-pricing. Conversely, hotels play unfairly on the sponsor's fear of not having enough rooms, and they charge premium rates to cover improbable, ill-defined opportunity losses. Is there collusion here? Probably not. The more likely conclusion is that both hotels and sponsors have become comfortable with an inflexible negotiating environment, but one that permits meeting sponsors to distribute the unreasonable charges pro rata to their attendees.

Working through the Maze

If you attempt to bypass the sponsoring organization and go directly through the hotel, the hotel will either refer you to the convention's central reservations number or quote you the same high price. Even if you do not identify yourself as a convention-goer, the hotel will figure it out by the dates you request. In most instances, even if you lie and insist that you are not attending the convention in question, the hotel will make you pay the higher rate or claim to be sold out.

By way of example, we tried to get reservations at the Riviera for a major trade show in the spring, a citywide convention that draws about 30,000 attendees. The show runs six days plus one day for setting up, or seven days total, Saturday through Friday. Though this example involves the Riviera, we encountered the same scenario at every hotel we called.

When we phoned reservations at the Riviera and gave them our dates, they immediately asked if we would be attending a convention or trade show. When we answered in the affirmative, they gave us the official sponsor's central reservations phone number in New York. We called the sponsor and learned that a single room at the Riviera (one person in one room) booked through them would cost $91 per night, including room tax. The same room (we found from other sources) booked directly through the Riviera would cost $80 with tax included.

We called the Riviera back and asked for the same dates, this time disavowing any association with the trade show, and were rebuffed. Obviously skeptical of our story, the hotel informed us that they were sold out for the days we requested. Unconvinced that the hotel was fully booked, we had two different members of our research team call. One attempted to make reservations from Wednesday *of the preceding week* through Tuesday of the trade show week, while our second caller requested a room from Wednesday of the trade show week through the following Tuesday. These respective sets of dates, we reasoned, would differ sufficiently from the show dates to convince the Riviera that we were not conventioneers. In each case we were able to make reservations for the dates desired at the $80-per-night rate.

It should be stressed that a hotel treats the convention's sponsoring organization much like a wholesaler who reserves rooms in a block for a negotiated price. What the convention, in turn, charges its attendees is out of the hotel's control. Once a hotel and convention sponsor come to terms, the hotel either refers all inquiries about reservations to the sponsor or accepts bookings at whatever nightly rate the sponsor determines. Since hotels do not want to get in the way of their convention sponsors (who are very powerful customers) or, alternatively, have convention attendees buying up rooms intended for other, nonconvention customers, the hotel reservations department carefully screens any request for a room during a convention period.

Strategies for Beating Convention Rates

There are several strategies for getting around convention rates:

1. CHECK THE INTERNET Unlike packagers and wholesalers, Internet sellers serve as a communications nexus and can often point you to a hotel you had not considered that still has rooms available, or to a property that unexpectedly has some last-minute rooms because of cancellations. Try the aforementioned **www.travelaxe.com,** which facilitates comparing rates offered by more than a dozen online sellers.

2. BUY A PACKAGE FROM A TOUR OPERATOR OR A WHOLESALER This tactic makes it unnecessary to deal with the convention's central reservations office or with an individual hotel's reservations department. Many packages allow you to buy extra days at a special discounted room rate if the package dates do not coincide perfectly with your meeting dates.

Packages that use air charter services operate on a fixed, inflexible schedule. As a rule these packages run three nights (depart Thursday, return Sunday; or depart Friday, return Monday) or four nights (depart Monday, return Friday; or depart Sunday, return Thursday). Two-night, five-night, and seven-night charter packages can also be found. Charter air packages offer greater savings, but usually less flexibility, than packages that use commercial carriers.

If you are able to beat the convention rate by booking a package or getting a room from a wholesaler, don't blow your cover when you check in. If you walk up to the registration desk in a business suit and a convention ID badge, the hotel will void your package and charge you the full convention rate. If you are supposed to be a tourist, act like one, particularly when you check in and check out.

3. FIND A HOTEL THAT DOES NOT PARTICIPATE IN THE CONVENTION ROOM BLOCKS Many of the downtown, North Las Vegas, and Boulder High-way hotels, as well as a few of the Strip hotels, do not make rooms available in blocks for conventions. If you wish to avoid convention rates, obtain a list of your convention's "official" hotels from the sponsoring organization and match it against the hotels listed in this guide. Any hotel listed in this book that does not appear on the list supplied by the meeting sponsors is not participating in blocking rooms for your convention. This means you can deal with the nonparticipating hotels directly and should be able to get their regular rate.

STRIP HOTELS THAT RARELY PARTICIPATE IN ROOM BLOCKS

Circus Circus	Excalibur	Luxor

DOWNTOWN HOTELS THAT SELDOM PARTICIPATE IN ROOM BLOCKS

Binion's Gambling Hall	California	El Cortez
Fitzgeralds	Four Queens	Fremont

Most citywide trade shows and conventions are held at the Las Vegas Convention Center. Of all the nonparticipating hotels, only Circus Circus is within a 15-minute walk. If you stay at any of the other hotels, you will have to commute to the convention center by shuttle, cab, or car.

4. RESERVE LATE Thirty to sixty days prior to the opening of a citywide convention or show, the front desk room reservations staff in a given hotel will take over the management of rooms reserved for the meeting from the hotel's sales and marketing department. "Room Res," in conjunction with the general manager, is responsible for making sure that the hotel is running at peak capacity for the dates of the show. The general manager has the authority to lower the room rate from the price negotiated with the sponsor. If rooms are not being booked for the convention in accordance with the hotel's expectations, the general manager will often lower the rate for attendees and, at the same time, return a number of reserved rooms to general inventory for sale to the public. A convention-goer who books a room at the last minute might obtain a lower rate than an attendee who booked early through the sponsor's central housing service. Practically speaking, however, do not expect to find rooms available at the convention headquarters hotel or at most of the hotels within easy walking distance. As a rule of thumb, the farther from the convention center or headquarters a hotel is, the better the chances of finding a discounted room at the last minute.

THE LAS VEGAS CONVENTION CENTER

THE LAS VEGAS CONVENTION CENTER (LVCC) is the largest single-level convention and trade show facility in the United States. Almost 3.2 million square feet of exhibit space are divided into two main buildings: the brand new South Hall and the older North Hall. A pedestrian bridge over Desert Inn Road connects the halls. Trade shows that crowd facilities in Washington, San Francisco, and New York fit with ease in this immense Las Vegas complex. In addition to the exhibit areas, the Center has a new lobby and public areas, a kitchen that can cater a banquet for 12,000 people, and 144 meeting rooms. Serving as headquarters for shows and conventions drawing as many as 250,000 delegates, the convention center is on Paradise Road, one very long block off the Las Vegas Strip and three miles from the airport.

For both exhibitors and attendees, the Las Vegas Convention Center is an excellent site for a meeting or trade show. Large and small exhibitors can locate and access their exhibit sites with a minimum of effort. Numerous loading docks and huge bay doors make loading and unloading quick and simple for large displays arriving by truck. Smaller displays transported in vans and cars are unloaded on the north side of the main hall and can be carried or wheeled directly to the exhibit area without climbing stairs or using elevators. The exhibit areas and meeting rooms are well marked and easy to find. The Las Vegas Convention and Visitors Authority also operates Cashman Field Center, home of Las Vegas's AAA baseball team. In addition to a baseball stadium, the Center contains a 2,000-seat theater and 100,000 square feet of meeting and exhibit space. For more information, call ☎ 702-892-0711 or browse **www.lasvegas24hours.com.**

Lodging within Walking Distance of the Las Vegas Convention Center

Although participants in citywide conventions lodge all over town, a few hotels are within easy walking distance of the LVCC. Next door, and closest, is the huge Las Vegas Hilton, with over 3,100 rooms. The

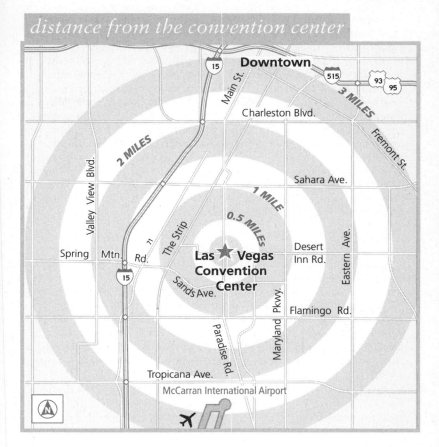

distance from the convention center

HOTELS WITHIN A 20-MINUTE WALK OF THE CONVENTION CENTER

AmeriSuites	202 suites	7-minute walk
Best Western Mardi Gras Inn	314 suites	12-minute walk
Circus Circus	3,763 rooms	15-minute walk
Courtyard (Marriott)	149 rooms	6-minute walk
Las Vegas Hilton	3,174 rooms	5-minute walk
Las Vegas Marriott Suites	278 suites	9-minute walk
New Frontier	986 rooms	20-minute walk
Renaissance Las Vegas	548 rooms	4-minute walk
Residence Inn (Marriott)	192 suites	10-minute walk
Riviera Hotel	2,075 rooms	10-minute walk

Hilton routinely serves as headquarters for meetings and shows in the convention center and provides, if needed, an additional 220,000 square feet of exhibit, ballroom, banquet, special event, and meeting room space. Many smaller conventions conduct all their meetings, including exhibits, at the Hilton. The walk from the lobby of the Hilton to the LVCC is about five minutes for most people.

Also nearby is the 548-room Marriott Renaissance, a nongaming hotel targeting business travelers. A long half-block away is the rear entrance of the 2,075-room Riviera Hotel. Like the Las Vegas Hilton, the Riviera is often the headquarters for large shows and meetings at the convention center. With 150,000 square feet of meeting and banquet space, the Riviera, like the Hilton, hosts entire meetings and provides supplemental facilities for events at the convention center. The walk from the rear (eastern) entrance of the Riviera to the convention center takes about ten minutes.

Cabs and Shuttles to the Convention Center

Large citywide conventions often provide complimentary bus service from major hotels to the convention center. If you are staying at a smaller hotel and wish to use the shuttle bus, walk to the nearest large hotel on the shuttle route. Though cabs are plentiful and efficient in Las Vegas, they are sometimes in short supply at convention or trade show opening and closing times. Public transportation—CAT buses ($2) and the Las Vegas Strip Trolley ($1.75)—is also available from the larger hotels. Exact fare is required. Your best bet is to stay within walking distance of the convention center. If you end up staying too far away to walk, a car is often less trouble than depending on cabs and shuttle buses.

Monorail to the Convention Center

If you are staying at a hotel in the section of the Strip between Tropicana and Sands (Spring Valley Road) avenues, or at the Sahara or Stratosphere, the best way to commute to the convention center is via the monorail. It's a no-brainer for guests in hotels on the east side of the Strip. For convention-goers who are lodging on the west side of the Strip, it's often a long walk to the nearest station. If traffic on the Strip isn't snarled, west-siders may want to consider taking a cab.

Lunch Alternatives for Convention and Trade-Show Attendees

The convention center's food service provides a better-than-average lunch and snack selection. As at most convention centers, however, prices are high. Outside of the convention center, but within walking distance, are the buffet and coffee shop at the Hilton, restaurants at the Marriott Renaissance, and Nippon, a Japanese restaurant and sushi bar (a ten-minute walk). The better restaurants at the Las Vegas Hilton are not open for lunch.

The restaurants mentioned above provide decent food and fast service but are bustling eateries not particularly conducive to a quiet business lunch. At 3900 Paradise Road, however, there is a small shopping center (only three minutes from the convention center by cab) that has several quiet, high-quality ethnic restaurants. Also located in the shopping center is a sandwich shop.

unofficial **TIP**
Take the monorail to Harrah's (about a five-minute ride), where you'll find dozens of fast-serve and full-service restaurants within a five-minute walk of Harrah's.

Parking at the Las Vegas Convention Center

In all, there are 5,200 parking spaces for cars in nine color-coded parking lots at the LVCC. The most convenient parking is in the Silver Lots right in front of the main entrance. The largest and third-most convenient parking is in the Gold Lots across Paradise Road north of Convention Center Drive. On the east side of the convention center are the Blue, Orange, Red, and Green lots. The Blue Lot, tucked into the northeast corner of the property, is second only to the Silver Lots in convenience, but is used extensively by convention center employees. The Orange Lot on the southeast side is likewise convenient, but is largely reserved for tractor-trailer parking during large trade shows. The Red Lot is adjacent to the new South Hall and is a good choice if the South Hall is where you'll spend most of your time. Finally, the Green Lot is the most remote of all, though more acceptable if your primary business is in the South Hall.

Though access to the exhibit floor varies from meeting to meeting, attendees are often required to enter through the convention center's main entrance off Paradise Road. If not parked in the Gold or Silver lots, convention-goers must hike around the complex in order to reach the front door, a seven- to ten-minute walk. For other meetings, attendees with proper credentials (that is, those with registration badges) are permitted to enter the exhibit halls by one of several doors along the sides of the convention center halls. As a rule, getting out is not as hard as getting in, and attendees are usually permitted to exit through the side doors.

COMFORT ZONES:
Matching Guests with Hotels

WE REMEMBER A GOOD FRIEND, a 32-year-old single woman, who, in search of a little romance, decided to take a Caribbean cruise. Thinking that one cruise was pretty much like any other, she signed up for a cruise without doing much shopping around. She ended up on a boat full of retired married folks who played bingo or bridge every evening and were usually in the sack by 10:30 p.m. Our friend mistakenly assumed, as have many others, that cruises are homogeneous products. In fact, nothing could be further from the truth. Each cruise provides a tailored experience to a specific and narrowly defined market. If our friend had done her homework, she could have booked passage on a boat full of young single people and danced and romanced into the night.

In Las Vegas, it is likewise easy to assume that all the hotels and casinos are fairly similar. True, they all have guest rooms, restaurants, and the same mix of games in the casino, but each property molds its offerings to appeal to a well-defined audience. This concerted effort to please a specific population of guests creates what we call a "comfort zone." If you are among the group a hotel strives to please, you will feel comfortable and at home and will have much in common with the other guests. However, if you fail to determine the comfort zone before you go, you may end up like our friend—on the wrong boat.

Visitors come to Las Vegas to vacation and play or to attend a meeting or convention. While these reasons for coming to Las Vegas are not mutually exclusive, there is a marked difference between a recreational visitor and a business traveler. The vacationer is likely to be older (45 years and up), retired, and from the Midwest, Southern California, Arizona, Colorado, or Hawaii. The business traveler is younger on average and comes from just about anywhere. Individual hotels and casinos pay close attention to these differences and customize their atmosphere, dining, and entertainment to satisfy a specific type of traveler.

The California Hotel, downtown, for example, targets Hawaiians and maintains a food store and restaurants that supply their clientele with snacks and dishes from the islands. On the Boulder Highway, Sam's Town is geared toward cowboys and retired travelers. Entertainment at Sam's Town consists of bowling and country-western dancing. Circus Circus on the Strip attracts the RV crowd (with its own RV park) but also offers large, low-priced rooms, buffets, free circus acts, and an amusement park to lure families. Palms, Planet Hollywood, and Hard Rock target a hip, younger audience, while the Las Vegas Hilton and the Venetian, both next door to the convention centers, go the extra mile to make business travelers feel at home.

Some hotels are posh and exclusive, while others are more spartan and intended to appeal to younger or more frugal visitors. Each property, however, from its lounge entertainment to its guest-room decor or the dishes served in its restaurants, is packaged with a certain type of guest in mind.

Because Las Vegas is basically a very informal town, you will not feel as out of place as our friend did on her cruise if you happen to end up in the wrong hotel. In any given property, there is a fairly broad range of clientele. There always will be hotels where you experience a greater comfort level than at others, however. In a place as different as Las Vegas, that added comfort can sometimes mean a lot.

DEMOCRACY IN THE CASINOS

WHILE LAS VEGAS HOTELS AND casinos continue to be characterized as appealing to "high rollers" or "grinds," the distinction has become increasingly blurred. High rollers, of course, are wealthy visitors who come to gamble in earnest, while grinds are less affluent folks who grudgingly bet their money a nickel or quarter at a time. For many years, the slot machine was symbolic of the grinds. Unable to join the action of the high-stakes table games, these gamblers would sit for hours pumping the arms of the slots. More recently, however, the slots are the symbol of casino profitability, contributing anywhere from 40 to 100% to a given casino's bottom line.

The popularity of the slot machine among gamblers of all types has democratized the casino. The casinos recognize that the silver-haired lady at the quarter slots is an extremely valuable customer and that it is good business to forgo the impression of exclusivity in order to make her comfortable. In Las Vegas there are casinos that maintain the illusion of an upper-crust clientele while quietly practicing an egalitarianism that belies any such pretense. By virtue of its economic clout, the slot machine has broadened the comfort zone of the stuffiest casinos and made Las Vegas a friendlier, more pleasant (albeit noisier) place.

THE FEEL OF THE PLACE

LAS VEGAS'S HOTEL-CASINOS have distinctly individual personalities. While all casinos contain slot machines, craps tables, and roulette wheels, the feel of each particular place is unique, a product of the combined characteristics of management, patrons, and design. This feel, or personality, determines a hotel-casino's comfort zone, the peculiar ambience that makes one guest feel totally at home while another runs for the exit.

THE AUTHOR'S BIAS OPENLY ADMITTED As you read the hotel-casino descriptions that follow, you will perhaps intuit that the author is a little claustrophobic. we do not understand why some casinos are dark, noisy, and confining; they are more like submarines than places of recreation. Why, we'd like to know, isn't there a casino in a nice, rooftop atrium where you can watch the sun set and the birds fly over? Is there a reason why we should be blinded by blinking lights or deafened by clanking coins in gloomy, red-Naugahyde-upholstered tunnels?

Apparently there is some casino marketing theory which postulates that customers will gamble longer and more aggressively if their circadian rhythms are disturbed, their natural clocks unplugged. Zoos confuse nocturnal animals this way to make them rummage around when they should be sleeping. Casino customers, like these animals, are never supposed to know if it is day or night. This is patently ridiculous, of course, because unlike bats and lemurs, almost every gambler has a watch or can tell what time it is by the type of food on the buffet.

Why do we worry about this, you ask? Isn't doubling down on any two cards and re-splitting pairs in blackjack more important than how low the ceiling is? Maybe to you, friend, but not to us. We want to gamble where we can breathe, stand up straight, and not smell the person playing at the next machine. We'd like our pupils to be the same size for more than three consecutive seconds, and we'd like to be able to conduct a conversation without using a megaphone. We'd even like to know whether or not it's raining outside. And while we're aware that it is perfectly possible to play craps in an alley, that's not why we go to Las Vegas. We've got plenty of alleys at home.

This is not to imply that we gamble in the departure concourse at the airport but to warn you about our natural bias against hotels and casinos that feel like velveteen U-boats. If, in the following descriptions, we talk about "ceiling height" a lot, we hope you'll understand.

HOTELS *with* CASINOS

HOW TO AVOID READING THE HOTEL-CASINO DESCRIPTIONS If you don't care how a place "feels" but just want to know whether it has room service and tennis courts, or when checkout time is, you can skip to the alphabetically arranged Hotel Information Chart at the end of this chapter.

Arizona Charlie's Boulder and Decatur (www.arizonacharlies.com)

PATRONIZED PRIMARILY BY LOCALS, Arizona Charlie's are working person's casinos with a southwestern ranch flavor. Everything is informal, a sort of shirtsleeves place. And it's busy. There is an energy, a three-ring circus feel of much going on at once—lots of slots, some table games, a sports book, burgers and beer, and a lounge that often features big-name (OK, medium-name) entertainment. The hotel rooms are passable, but the real reason to patronize Arizona Charlie's is the video poker—they're among the best machines in town, and considering what town you're in, this means they're among the best machines anywhere. The original Arizona Charlie's is on Decatur, west of the Strip. The newer Arizona Charlie's Boulder is on the Boulder Highway.

Bally's (www.caesars.com/ballys/lasvegas)

BALLY'S BILLS ITSELF AS "the classic Las Vegas experience." Targeted to the gamer of any age, the emphasis is clear when you step inside the main entrance from under the broad, sky-lit porte cochere. On your right, a football-field-long casino stretches beyond you. The casino is immense, open, and elegantly modern—sophisticated in a formal, understated way, like a tuxedo. Active without being claustrophobic, and classy without being stiff, Bally's captures the style of modern European casinos without sacrificing American informality. On the left of the same great room is the registration desk, along with services such as a coffee bar and newsstand conveniently located directly in the lobby area.

Originally themed for Hollywood, now Bally's doesn't bear much of a specific visual motif. This is not at all a shortcoming. Bally's simply carries itself with a certain forthrightness, with a kind of class that says "We are confident to be who we are—timeless Las Vegas." After all, Bally's has the enduring, quintessential, top-quality topless show *Jubilee!* with which it celebrated its 25th anniversary in 2006. Million-dollar sets and Bob Mackie and Pete Menefee costumes, skimpy though they may be, hark back to the days of Sinatra and gang.

A complete resort, Bally's is blessed with exceptional restaurants, one of the better buffets in Las Vegas, and a groundbreaking Sunday Champagne brunch. All of the north tower wings have been renovated, and the south tower is scheduled for renovation. Although quite spread out, Bally's is easy to navigate. Amenities include a 19,000-square-foot health club and spa and a large, diversified shopping arcade. Standard guest rooms are a generous 450 square feet and comfortable. One-bedroom grand suites have king-sized beds and a whirlpool spa. To enjoy this layout you should be physically very comfortable with your traveling partner, as most of the bathroom is exposed to the sleeping area.

For those that drive, the guest parking is all valet out front. There is limited self-parking in the back, but it is mainly for oversized vehicles. The hot tip is to park at Bally's sister property, Paris Las Vegas (the hotels are internally connected). Demonstrating legitimate concern about the traffic congestion on the Strip, Bally's joined with the MGM Grand in constructing a monorail that was the first link in the Las Vegas Monorail line. Subsequently, the monorail was extended north along the Strip all the way to the Sahara, with a loop over to the Las Vegas Convention Center and the Las Vegas Hilton. Bally's also offers airport check-in shuttle service and another free shuttle every 30 minutes to take you to Caesars, Paris, Rio, and Harrah's (all Harrah's properties). In a separate project, Bally's has built a series of moving walkways to transport guests from Las Vegas Boulevard into the casino. In a Las Vegas first, Bally's also offers moving walkways *out* of the casino. Maybe this is the only way, short of a forklift, that Bally's could get the bulk loaders out of the buffet.

Bally's caters to meetings and conventions and is one of the few hotels where you will not feel out of place in a business suit. Guests are frequently under age 40 here and come from all over, but particularly Southern California, Chicago, and elsewhere in the Midwest. Bally's also has a loyal Spanish-speaking clientele.

Bellagio (www.bellagio.com)

IT'S NO SECRET THAT STEVE WYNN established a new standard for Las Vegas hotel-casinos when he opened the Mirage in 1989. While it's doubtful that Wynn foresaw the impact the Mirage would have on Las Vegas, it's certain that he relishes his role as an instrument of change. Like an author trying to build on the success of an earlier work, Wynn took another shot at bumping up the standard in 1999. The vehicle for Wynn's aspirations this time was the Bellagio, on the site of the old Dunes hotel and golf course. Quite simply, Wynn intended for it to be the best hotel in the world, a hotel intended to rewrite the concept of hospitality. In 2000, however, in a move that took everyone by surprise, Wynn sold the Bellagio, along with his other casino properties, to MGM Grand (now MGM-MRG

[Mandalay Resort Group]) for $6.4 billion in cash. Wynn's latest attempt to rock the Las Vegas status quo is Wynn Las Vegas, opened on the site of the venerable Desert Inn. For now, though, back to the Bellagio.

With its main entrance off the Strip just south of Flamingo Road, the Bellagio is inspired by an Italian village overlooking Lake Como in the sub-Alpine north of Italy. The facade of the Bellagio will remind you somewhat of the themed architecture Wynn employed at T. I., only this time it's provincial Italian instead of Caribbean. The Bellagio village is arrayed along the west and north sides of a man-made lake, where dancing fountains provide allure and spectacle, albeit more dignified than the Mirage's exploding volcano or T. I.'s buccaneer carnage.

Rising behind the village facade in a gentle curve is the 3,933-room hotel, complete with casino, restaurants, shopping complex, spa, and pool. Added in late 2004 was a 33-story Spa Tower with 819 hotel rooms and 109 suites. Bundled with the tower are a restaurant, four shops, and additional convention space. Imported marble is featured throughout, even in the guest rooms and suites, as are original art, traditionally styled furnishings, and European antiques. Guest rooms and meeting rooms also feature large picture windows affording views of lushly landscaped grounds and formal gardens.

Surprisingly, the Italian village theme of Bellagio's lakefront facade is largely abandoned in the hotel's interior. Though a masterpiece of integrated colors, textures, and sight lines, the interior design reflects no strong sense of theme. In two steps, passing indoors, you go from a provincial village on a very human scale to a monumentally grand interior with proportions reminiscent of national libraries. You've heard it's lovely, and naturally it is, but somehow in a very different way than you might have anticipated. The vast spaces are exceedingly tasteful and unquestionably sophisticated, yet they fail to evoke the fun, whimsy, and curiosity so intrinsic to the Mirage and T. I.

Perhaps because Las Vegas has conditioned us to a plastic, carnival sort of stimulation, entering the Bellagio is like stepping from the midway into the basilica. The surroundings impress but do not engage our emotions—except, of course, for the art, and that is exactly the point. Seen as a rich, neutral backdrop for the extraordinary works of art displayed throughout Bellagio, the lapse of thematic continuity is understandable. No theme could compete, and none should.

Truly the art is everywhere, even on the ceiling of the registration lobby, where a vibrantly colorful blown-glass piece by Dale Chihuly hangs. Some wonderful works are showcased in the Bellagio's restaurants. Original Picassos, for example, are on exhibit in the restaurant of the same name. The Bellagio Gallery of Fine Art is touted as Las Vegas's premier art gallery. Each year the gallery presents world-class exhibitions of artworks and objects drawn from internationally acclaimed museums and private collections, such as an impressive body of Impressionist works and the photographs of Ansel Adams.

Architecturally, Bellagio's most creative and interesting spaces are found in its signature conservatory and botanical gardens and in its restaurants. As you walk in the main entrance the primary garden is straight ahead.

Although the opulent and oversized displays do change seasonally, there may be a new permanent resident. Rescued from a Florida development, a once-failing 100-year-old-plus banyan tree (the same kind of tree the Buddha sat under when he gained enlightenment) is a powerful and poised backdrop for the theatrical floral whimsies of the supremely accomplished botanical staff. A recent visit gave witness to fabulously monstrous flowers reminiscent of Audrey, the man-eating plant in *Little Shop of Horrors*.

If you spend time at the Bellagio, visit each of the restaurants for a moment, if only to take in their stunning design. All Bellagio's restaurants, including a Las Vegas branch of Le Cirque, feature panoramic views. Some offer both indoor and outdoor dining experiences. In addition to the restaurants, Bellagio serves one of Las Vegas's best—and not unexpectedly one of the city's most expensive—buffets. With the exception of the buffet and coffee shop, Bellagio's restaurants require reservations, preferably made a month to six weeks before you leave home.

The Bellagio's showroom hosts a production of the justly acclaimed Cirque du Soleil. Though terribly expensive, the show is one of Cirque's most challenging productions yet, featuring a one-of-a-kind set that transforms seamlessly from hard surface to water. Like Bellagio itself, the Cirque production "O" (from the pronunciation of the French word *eau*, meaning "water") lacks the essential humor and humanness of Cirque's *Mystère* at T. I. but is nonetheless heartrendingly beautiful.

Meant to be luxurious, the Bellagio seeks to establish itself as the prestige address of Las Vegas. Retailers in the shopping venue include Chanel, Hermes, Tiffany, Prada, and Giorgio Armani. Rates for guest rooms and suites are among the highest ever seen on the Strip, and its purported target market includes high rollers and discriminating business travelers who often eschew gaming properties. It's hard, however, to discuss exclusivity and personal service in the same breath with 3,933 rooms. Also, there's a lot of both new and old competition for the upscale market, including Caesars, the Venetian, and Mandalay Bay, to name a few. What's more, Bellagio guests do not have to look far to make comparisons: All north-facing guest rooms peer directly down on the stunning pool complex at Caesars Palace.

Room rates have bounced all over the place in recent years and in the future may bounce to a level that you find acceptable. If you stay at the Bellagio, you will find the same basic informality typical of the rest of the Strip, and, surprisingly, you will encounter in the hotel more people like you than super-rich. Expressed more directly, Bellagio is a friendly place to stay and gamble and not at all pretentious. We did have a funny experience, however, in one of its retail shops. For three days, we passed the same men's clothing shop and never saw a soul in it. Suspecting that it was being avoided because of the Bellagio's reputation for expensive boutique shopping, we ventured in. As a test, we chose a cotton shirt-jacket almost identical in appearance to one I had seen in a Banana Republic catalog for $68. Not finding a price tag, we inquired of the helpful salesperson and was informed that this garment sold for $1,490. When we laughed out loud, he explained in all seriousness that the shirt was made in Italy. Indeed, and no doubt hand-delivered via the *QE2*!

Bill's Gamblin' Hall and Saloon   (www.billslasvegas.com)

BILL'S GAMBLIN' HALL AND SALOON, formerly the Barbary Coast, is an old-fashioned casino for real gamblers. Appointed in dark wood embellished with murals in stained glass, this small hotel-casino serves a loyal clientele of locals and serious gamblers. With the feel of an exclusive and tasteful gentlemen's club, Bill's offerings are straightforward and simple. Table games still reign supreme in the casino, and its gourmet restaurant, Drai's, is regarded by many locals as the most dependable in town. There is no showroom, no swimming pool, no sauna or whirlpool, and most of the 200 hotel rooms (decorated in a style reminiscent of early-1900s San Francisco) are reserved for regular customers. Bill's is centrally located if you're on foot but just about the worst hotel on the Strip to get into and out of by car.

Binion's Gambling Hall   (www.binions.com)

BINION'S GAMBLING HALL IS ONE OF THE ANCHORS of Glitter Gulch. The casino is large and active, with row upon row of slots clanking noisily under a suffocatingly low ceiling. The table games are less congested, occupying an extended vertical space canopied by mirrors. With an Old West theme executed in the obligatory reds and lavenders, Binion's is dark, but not dark enough to slow the enthusiasm of the locals and "real gamblers" who hang out there. One of the city's top spots for poker and craps, Binion's Gambling Hall is famous for not having any maximum bet limitations. You can bet $1 million on a single roll of the dice if you wish.

On the lower (basement) level is the coffee shop and what may be one of the most pleasant bars in the city; it, too, is dark but for once is paneled in rich woods. Twenty or so stories up from the cellar is the Ranch Steak House restaurant and lounge, offering a great view of the city. Also offering a great view is Binion's rooftop pool.

Boulder Station   (www.boulderstation.com)

BOULDER STATION IS A CLONE OF PALACE STATION, sharing its railroad theme and emphasis on good food and lounge entertainment. Located on Boulder Highway not far from the Arizona Charlie's Boulder, Boulder Station features a roomy casino with a Western town motif (more in the image of turn-of-the-century Denver than of Dodge City). Tastefully done, with much attention to detail, the casino includes one of the nicest sports books in Las Vegas. Thirty-three big-screen, high-resolution monitors make the Boulder Station sports book a superb place for spectators. Like its sister properties, Boulder Station is an oasis for the hungry, with a great buffet, several good full-service restaurants, and possibly the best selection of fast food found in any casino. Guest rooms in the 300-room hotel tower are modest but comfortable, with good views. There is a swimming pool, but it is small and stark. Clientele consists primarily of locals and Southern Californians.

Comparing Boulder Station to Palace Station, we like the casino much better at Boulder Station but prefer the guest rooms at Palace Station's tower. The buffets and restaurants run pretty much a dead heat, but Boulder Station is less crowded.

Caesars Palace (www.harrahs.com)

IF ROME IS "THE ETERNAL CITY," then its Las Vegas legacy at Caesars is a worthy, long-lived heir. Forty years old in 2006, Caesars Palace was the first of the themed hotels and casinos to realize fully its potential, and it is among the foremost at staying fresh through constant updating and remodeling. The perennial classic that reinvents itself, Caesars is a must-see even if you don't stay there.

An exercise in whimsical fantasy and excess, Caesars' Roman theme has been executed with astounding artistry and attention to detail. Everywhere fine mosaics, handsome statuary, mythological references, famous sculptures (including a Carrera marble copy of Michelangelo's *David*—from Florence, not Rome—but let's don't quibble) delight the eye and mind. Creating an atmosphere of informality in surroundings too pretentious to believe is hard to pull off, but that is exactly what Caesars Palace has done.

If Caesars was on a small scale it would be exquisite kitsch, but it's on a grand scale that elevates you into some kind of time machine where the bustling commerce of ancient Rome lives again. Gambling at Caesars does feel a little like pitching horseshoes in the Supreme Court, but, incredibly, it works. Everywhere the vaulted ceilings, classic statuary, and graceful arches easily accommodate the legions (pun intended) of slots, activity of the pits, shopping, dining, and lolling about in opulent pools surrounded by towering gardens. Truly, here is the grandeur that was Rome with all its desirable excesses and indulgences.

Caesars Palace provides three spacious and luxurious casinos, including a poker room with celebrity events (for example, *The Sopranos*—who else?), 24 excellent restaurants and cafes, beautiful landscaping, and top celebrity entertainment. Celine Dion is a staple in the Colosseum showroom Caesars built for her, and Elton John is booked for 50 nights a year through 2008. For all of the guests who inhabit its 3,348 superb rooms, Caesars has all of the services and amenities of a world-class resort.

A couple of years ago the more intimate Apollo pool was added to the five-acre swimming complex (with two outdoor whirlpool spas), bringing the total number of pools to four. Other pools include the 10,000-square-foot pool of the Temple which is capped by a rotunda and decorated with marble and mosaics. For lusty sinews there's the Neptune pool with 5,000 square feet for lap swimmers; and for European-style (aka topless) bathers, the Venus pool is neatly tucked away within an evergreen enclave. All the pools have cabanas available for rent with stocked refrigerators, snack and beverage service, soft lounge chairs, and television so you don't have to choose between the big game or the soaps and your tan.

The lobby and guest registration area has been remodeled, too, but you don't have to spend much time in its glory if you use the airport check-in/ shuttle feature that delivers you with your room key and your luggage to the hotel for $11.50 round-trip. Or for extra ease, use the fee-based luggage concierge service that will ferry your bags from your home or office to your hotel room.

In 2003, Caesars finished a complete renovation and face-lift of its original hotel towers. The year 2004 saw the opening of the Roman Plaza, a shopping, dining, and entertainment venue reaching from Caesars' Flamingo Road entrance to the hotel lobby and casino. The 26-story luxury Augustus tower opened in 2005. Besides nine-foot ceilings, the new tower rooms feature spa tubs, televisions in the bathrooms, and great views of the Strip that include the "dancing waters" at the Bellagio or its own Garden of the Gods pool area, a sight to behold, especially from on high.

The Palace Tower, built in late 1997 and renovated in 2006, generally costs $50 to $70 more than the standard room price, beginning at $150 per night in the Forum, Roman, and Centurion towers. With a small sitting area in addition to the traditional marble bathroom, the standard room of 300 to 400 square feet—all with high-speed Internet access—is a great room for the price. Palace Tower rooms have 500 square feet or more, with many amenities, including marble dry bars. The Premiere Palace Tower rooms have his-and-her bathrooms that are connected by a large, sexy, glass walk-in shower. For another kind of grand experience, double bay suites with parlors and dining tables for entertaining are available in the Forum and Roman towers.

Some say the spa, newly remade and opened in September of 2006, is Caesars' best-kept secret. With the Roman penchant for water joys, it's logical that Caesars would have a full line of luxurious treatments and settings for men and women. Situated on the second floor of the Augustus Tower, the all-new spa has 51 therapy rooms, signature Roman baths with hot, cold, and tepid pools, and sculpted stone chaise longues submerged in heated pools and designed as pre-massage relaxers.

Caesars is on a roll with its nightlife scene, offering four hot lounges. Pure offers three luxurious rooms, including a dance club and a heated outdoor rooftop balcony overlooking the Strip. Pussycat Dolls Lounge is a clean-smelling risqué cabaret with song, dance, and girls popping out of giant Champagne glasses. At Shadow, silhouetted dancers contort to DJ-spun hip-hop. Cleopatra's Barge, a decades-old dance club on a free-floating boat, continues to rock on. Nearby is the Seahorse Lounge, where you can watch the endangered species variety drift by in the aquarium.

For the less nocturnal, there are two shopping venues. At the Appian Way (look for the *David*) you can purchase apparel, gifts, art, and jewelry, including Caesars logo items. The extensive Forum Shops is an entirely different kind of experience. Opened in 1992 and expanded in 1997 and again in 2005, the astonishing adjoining Forum Shops give Caesars Palace the distinction of offering one of the most unusual themed shopping complexes in the United States with 160 mercantile venues as well as 13 restaurants and specialty food shops. Ambling through its gently cobblestoned "streets," replete with slightly sloping gutters, the sightseer and shopper alike can be delighted and charmed by the full-scale fountains featuring Neptune and Bacchus, the building facades topped by second-story "residences," all set against the background of a sweeping Italian sky at sunset. At every turn, you find the perfect blend of old-world commerce and cutting-edge merchandise, including, of course, the famous Italians Versace and Armani. At 3:15 p.m. Monday through Friday, you can take a tour of the Atlantis Aquarium, located at the Neptune Fountain, going underneath the 50,000 gallons of saltwater to learn how the environment is maintained.

Dining at Caesars has been totally revamped with the addition of 8-0-8 (Pacific Rim cuisine), Mesa Grill, and Bradley Ogden, honored by the James Beard Foundation, that serves "fresh farm" American cuisine. A more recent addition to the lineup is Restaurant Gus Savoy overlooking the Roman Plaza. Headed by Parisian restaurateur Guy Savoy, recently named Chef of the Year in France, the restaurant offers one of the most singular dining experiences in town. Among other choices are authentic Chinese and Japanese (including a sushi bar) and steak and seafood. For casual dining, there's the 24-hour Café Lago, featuring menu service and buffet, and Cypress Street Marketplace, an all-hours gourmet deli and food court. A good antidote to the interior casino spaces, the fine buffet at Caesars is in a large sun-drenched room with a view of the pool area, also a welcome balm in counterpoint to the constant clamor of the gaming floor. Here is where you can hear the music of pianist David Osborne, who also plays at the White House (we recommend you hear him at Caesars, where he creates his own playlist rather than variations on "The Yellow Rose of Texas").

Rao's, also new, is a Las Vegas edition of the East Harlem Italian restaurant that's so popular that neither Madonna nor Bill Clinton could waggle a reservation. Dine in a replica of the New York original or choose the spacious upscale dining room overlooking the pool.

Originally designed for high-rollers, from the beginning Caesars opened its arms to the world, marketing far and wide. Enjoyed by a broad range of clientele from the East, the Midwest, and Southern California, it's also popular with Asian and Hispanic visitors. Of course, it also hosts meetings and caters to business travelers in its 240,000-square-foot conference center. No matter what the motivation for a visit, each guest—supported by a staff of 6,000—no doubt feels like Caesar.

California (www.thecal.com)

THE CALIFORNIA IS A PLEASANT, DOWNTOWN hotel-casino with excellent, moderately priced restaurants and a largely Hawaiian and Filipino clientele. It is a friendly, mellow place to stay or gamble—unpretentious, and certainly comfortable. The casino rambles but, like most downtown casinos, does not allow much elbow room. The decor is subdued and tasteful, with wood paneling and trim. For a taste of old Las Vegas, try the porterhouse steak special at the Redwood Bar and Grill. The shops, menus, and services work to make visiting Pacific Islanders feel as much at home as visitors from Kansas City or Tampa. While some hotel-casinos are spectacles or happenings, the California is simply a nice, relaxed place to spend some time.

Cannery (www.cannerycasinos.com)

FOUR MILES NORTH OF DOWNTOWN ON CRAIG ROAD, the Cannery opened in January 2003 and expanded in 2004 with the usual locals' formula: big casino, small hotel. The theme has nothing to do with Steinbeck or fish, though the industrial, 1940s-style structure of corrugated metal and steel beams would be right at home on Cannery Row. Instead, produce, specifically vegetables and fruit, take center stage with murals and paintings of colossal berries, apples, and veggies. Even the red, patterned carpet is festooned with oranges, apples, and pears.

The roomy, uncluttered casino is roughly circular, surrounding a slightly elevated lounge decorated with World War II–era, Betty Grable–style pinups. Restaurants, including a good Mexican eatery, a steak house, fast-food court, and a respectable buffet, are arrayed around the periphery. For entertainment, there's a 14-screen movie theater. A recent expansion added 15,000 square feet to the casino, including a poker room and a race and sports book. Also new are a parking garage and an Italian restaurant.

Guest rooms are smallish, with oak-finish furniture and brightly colored soft goods. Views from guest-room windows are about as uninspiring as it gets.

Casino Royale (www.casinoroyalehotel.com)

LOCATED ACROSS THE STRIP FROM THE MIRAGE, the diminutive Casino Royale has about 150 guest rooms. Small, accessible, and unpretentious, Casino Royale provides bargain lodging in the Strip's high-rent district. While the crowded and slot-heavy casino will make downtown gamblers feel right at home, the Casino Royale's second-floor Outback Steakhouse offers an affordable alternative to the Strip's pricey chophouses. The property's clientele runs the gamut from tour groups to convention-goers on a tight budget to folks who could not get rooms at other hotels on the block.

Circus Circus (www.circuscircus.com)

CIRCUS CIRCUS IS VERY LIKELY THE ONLY hotel on the Strip that has an escalator from within the casino to a McDonald's, and that tells you pretty much what you need to know. Although most hotels do not cater to families with young children, Circus Circus is a notable exception, and it was the first hotel on the Strip to actively pursue the family trade. For parents who must bring their children, it's a good alternative and a bargain to boot.

With so many swarming, milling, and mewing short people, the lobby can sometimes remind you of a day-care center. The main casino has a second level called The Midway with good reason, as it features the simple kinds of games found at a state fair venue (wham a spring-loaded chicken into a moving pot and win a prize-sort-of-thing). At the core of the Midway is a small grandstand that features very competent regular circus acts, also primarily for children. The entire casino affair is obviously designed as an easy hand-off platform for such directives as, "Here, honey, you take the kids for 45 minutes while I go play the quarter slots."

In 1993, Circus Circus launched what is now the Adventuredome, formerly Grand Slam Canyon, a desert-canyon-themed amusement park totally enclosed in a giant pink dome. Here guests can enjoy a roller coaster, a flume ride, robotic dinosaurs, and more. A detailed description of Adventuredome can be found in Part Five, Shopping and Seeing the Sights, on pages 406–407. The meandering hallway to the Adventuredome and the Skyrise Casino is lined with shops catering to the younger set as well. Maps and signs throughout the facility indicate the "Green Zone," where children are allowed to be (because the law against children lingering in the gaming areas is very strictly enforced in Las Vegas). Children can walk through the casino if they must, but the general atmosphere does not encourage this practice.

Perhaps because of price, in addition to families, Circus Circus also attracts some seniors and novice gamblers who don't mind dodging strollers and jacked-up kids in this ADD paradise. The labyrinthine casino has low ceilings and is frenetic, loud, and always busy, but sometimes in contrast to the main public spaces it can seem like an oasis of sanity. Nickel slots abound, as do table games, including dollar blackjack. The circus theme, both colorful and wholesome, is extended to every conceivable detail of the hotel's physical space and operation. The rooms are adequate, but not luxurious, a sensibility probably enhanced by the garish, raucous circus motif.

Circus Circus has a very good steak house (the only escape from the circus theme); a huge, inexpensive buffet; an RV park; and a monorail shuttle that connects the property's two main buildings. And, to give credit for great innovation, Circus Circus was the first casino to set aside a nonsmoking gaming area. A hotel tower, as well as a shopping and restaurant arcade, adjoin Adventuredome. The arcade restaurants provide Circus Circus with much-needed alternatives to the steak house and the buffet. For parents with children, Circus Circus is a great alternative, but for happily child-free others, it might feel more like a zoo.

El Cortez (www.elcortezhotelcasino.com)

SEVERAL BLOCKS EAST OF THE CENTRAL downtown casino area, El Cortez caters to seniors, motor-coach tours, and blue-collar locals. The large, rambling casino is congested and bustling; the slots are the major draw. The oldest original casino in Las Vegas, El Cortez until 2006 had the aesthetic appeal of a garment factory, with narrow aisles, low ceilings, and slot machines packed into every conceivable crevice. The crowded aisles and low ceilings remain, but El Cortez has undergone a good plussing up, including a top-to-bottom renovation of its guest rooms. It's not Mandalay Bay, but the rooms are very nice and a great bargain. Food and drink are reasonably priced and the loose slots give patrons a lot of play for their money. Also, there is considerable Las Vegas history in El Cortez; one section of the original building appears just as it did when the casino opened in 1941.

Ellis Island (www.ellisislandcasino.com)

ELLIS ISLAND, ON KOVAL LANE NEAR HARMON AVENUE just minutes from the Strip, is the most modest casino imaginable, but a treasure for those in the know. Its $4.95 complete New York Strip steak dinner has been among the best meal deals in town for years. The casino is joined at the hip to an equally modest Super 8 hotel.

Excalibur (www.excalibur.com)

THE EXCALIBUR IS a hotel in transition, attempting to chunk its family business for a more adult, middle-income market. Although it's difficult to transform a medieval casino the size of an airplane hanger, Excalibur has succeeded to a remarkable degree. The new hotel lobby, as well as the casino, are tasteful, with dark woods and stylish lighting fixtures. Gone are the cheap plastic look rendered in a Wal-Mart color palette and the ridiculous faux Knights of the Round Table artifacts. There are still vestiges of Ozzie and Harriet's decorating touch, but the Excalibur no longer assaults the senses like it did in the good olde days.

The guest rooms likewise are in the process of a makeover. Here the medieval theme has been mercilessly exorcised and replaced by surprisingly luxurious rooms replete with 42-inch plasma television, plush bedding, dark-wood furnishings, and contemporary baths (shower only). Though the windows are not huge, the views are great. About 35% of Excalibur's guest rooms will be renovated by the end of 2008.

The Excalibur's restaurants and shops are on the top floor of three levels. On the lower floor is a midway-type games arcade and the Excalibur's showroom, where jousting tournaments are featured. A primitive motion simulator (it was the worst virtual ride in Las Vegas) has been replaced with a zippy SpongeBob SquarePants 4-D ride. The cavernous middle level contains the casino.

The Excalibur is the sixth-largest hotel in the world and the fifth-largest in Las Vegas, and it certainly features the world's largest hotel parking lot (so far removed from the entrance that trams are dispatched to haul in the patrons). If you can get past the parking lot commute and the fact that most guest rooms have showers only (no tubs), and you do not object to joining the masses, there is good value to be had at the Excalibur. The food is good and economically priced, as is the entertainment. The staff is friendly and accommodating, and you won't go deaf or blind, or become claustrophobic, in the casino. A high-energy nightclub, a spa, and a workout facility round out Excalibur's product mix. If you need a change of pace, a covered walkway connects the Excalibur with the Luxor next door, pedestrian bridges provide direct access to New York–New York and the Tropicana, and an overhead train runs to Luxor and Mandalay Bay.

Fiesta Henderson (www.fiestacasino.com)

FIESTA HENDERSON WAS FORMERLY THE RESERVE, an African-safari-themed casino. In an effort to convert the property to a Mexican theme, its parent company, Station Casinos, has created a most peculiar mélange (even for Las Vegas). The casino, stripped of its stuffed monkeys and lions, is now southwestern/Mexican in flavor, but the guest rooms still sport the safari motif with African prints and dark-wood furniture. Located southeast of Las Vegas at the intersection of I-515 and West Lake Mead Drive,

Fiesta Henderson offers a 37,000-square-foot casino, four restaurants, and three up-and-coming bars. As is the case with all Station casinos, the Fiesta Henderson caters primarily to locals.

Fiesta Rancho (www.fiestacasino.com)

THE FIESTA RANCHO, WHICH OPENED IN 1994, was the first of two casinos to be situated at the intersection of Rancho Drive and Lake Mead Boulevard in North Las Vegas (the other is Texas Station). With 100 guest rooms and a video-poker-packed, 40,000-square-foot casino (including the Spin City annex), the Fiesta features an Old Mexico theme. Entertainment includes a lounge and nightclub. Restaurants specializing in southwestern food and steaks are the Fiesta's major draw. An excellent buffet features a mesquite grill. In 1997, the Fiesta finally got around to putting in a swimming pool, and in 1999, it expanded the casino and added a food court. The food court allowed them to expand the southwestern restaurant, add an oyster bar and a tequila bar (300 different margaritas—*olé*!). The Fiesta depends primarily on local clientele.

Fitzgeralds (www.fitzgeraldslasvegas.com)

LOCATED DOWNTOWN, FITZGERALDS ANCHORS the east end of the Glitter Gulch section of Fremont Street. After filing for bankruptcy in 2002, the hotel was purchased by Don Barden, which made him Nevada's first African-American casino owner. The casino is large and compartmentalized with gold press-metal ceilings, mirrored columns, and print carpet. Completely renovated, the casino has largely abandoned its signature "luck of the Irish" theme. While the new look is more consistent with the clean, polished style pioneered by the Golden Nugget, Fitzgeralds has sacrificed much of its traditional warmth and coziness.

Rooms on the upper floors of the Fitz afford some of the best views in town, and corner rooms with hot tubs are a great bargain. Recently, the Fitz added a streetside swimming pool. The Fitzgeralds's registered guests tend to be older travelers and retirees from the Midwest. In the casino, the crowd is a mixed bag of regulars and bargain hunters lured by ads for free gifts in the local visitor guides.

Flamingo (www.flamingolasvegas.com)

BUILT WITH GANGSTER MONEY in the 1940s and acquired by the Hilton Hotel chain in 1970, and more recently by Harrah's, the Flamingo is an oasis in the desert. When you're feeling the need for lush green other than the casino kind, head there. True to its name, the Flamingo's nature theme is in full play, especially in the public spaces. With a tropical panorama behind the registration desk, grass-themed bathroom stalls, and real plants lining the escalator, the Flamingo is an organic reprieve from the clanking slot machinery that runs the Strip. Its heart is a 15-acre Caribbean-style water playground adjacent to a large wildlife habitat that is home to Chilean flamingos, swans, ducks, koi, African penguins, turtles, and foliage from around the world. Maybe best of all, you don't have to be a guest to take a stroll through this sliver of paradise.

Begun by notorious "businessman" Bugsy Siegel in 1946, and once a tourist attraction in itself, this venerable hotel was the first super-resort on the Strip. Today, with its 3,500-plus rooms and suites, four towers, and prime location, it is the Queen Mother of the Strip's most prestigious block, surrounded by Bally's, Bill's Gamblin' Hall, the Imperial Palace, Caesars Palace, Harrah's, and the Bellagio. Hilton, as you might expect, curbed the excesses of the colorful previous owners and transformed the Flamingo from a Las Vegas exaggeration into a very dependable hotel. Today, owned by Harrah's, the Flamingo is flashier than Bally's (its sister property that also caters to business travelers). It is also less formal, offering an ambience comfortable to leisure and business travelers.

Bugsy would be very proud of the newly remodeled 77,000 square-foot Caribbean-style casino with more than 2,000 slot machines, 70 gaming tables, and race and sports book broadcasting results on wide-screen television. The large, bustling casino's bright neon pinks, magentas, and tangerines established the Flamingo's identity more than four decades ago, but the rooms (undergoing renovation) and services are standard Hilton. The Flamingo has consistent restaurants, a pretty good buffet, varied showroom productions, truly creative lounge entertainment—the Flamingo is home to the famed *Second City* comedy-improvisation show—in addition to boasting one of the top swimming areas in town.

The hotel's clientele comes in all colors and sizes, and from all over the country (but especially Southern California). The Flamingo actively cultivates the Japanese market and also does a strong business with tour wholesalers. Because it has one of the most diverse customer bases of any Las Vegas hotel, the Flamingo likewise has a very broad comfort zone.

Four Queens (www.fourqueens.com)

THE FOUR QUEENS, SITUATED IN THE HEART of downtown, offers good food, respectable hotel rooms, and a positively cheery casino. Joining its neighbor, the Golden Nugget, as a member of the "All Right to Be Bright Club," the Four Queens casino was among the first to abandon the standard brothel red in favor of a glistening, light decor offset by a tropical print carpet. The result, as at the Golden Nugget, is a gaming area that feels fun, upbeat, and clean. Loyal Four Queens hotel guests tend to be middle-aged or older and come from Southern California, Texas, Hawaii, and the Midwest. The Four Queens also caters to the motor-coach tour market. In the casino there is a mix of all ages and backgrounds. Locals love Hugo's Cellar restaurant, but the Four Queens' top-quality lounge has been closed by the property's new owner, a local slot bar operator.

Four Seasons (www.fourseasons.com/lasvegas)

FOUR SEASONS HOTELS AND MANDALAY RESORT GROUP (now MGM–MRG) have combined to introduce a new concept to Las Vegas: the hotel within a hotel. The Four Seasons is an exclusive, 424-room, noncasino hotel contained by the greater Mandalay Bay megaresort.

You can get to Four Seasons from within Mandalay Bay, but just barely: You walk almost behind the Mandalay Bay front desk, pass through two sets of double service doors, climb down a spiral staircase, and blunder into the Four Seasons lobby. Signs are few and small. This is the "back" entrance; Four Seasons prefers you to use the main, front, valet entrance, which is right off the Strip, a little south of Mandalay Bay's entrance.

You can access Mandalay Bay from Four Seasons by backtracking or by taking the private elevator to the casino level. You can also walk up the stairs at the Four Seasons elevator bay (the elevators are a pretty long hike from the front desk).

The lobby area has a plush feel, decorated with wood, Victorian sofas and easy chairs, a grand piano, and even a fireplace—a 1930s, New York atmosphere that's very different (and pleasingly so) from Las Vegas in the new millennium. Off the lobby is a 60-seat sitting area and a second lounge that fronts the First Floor Grill gourmet room. There's also the Verandah Café, the most exclusive coffee shop in town—giant French doors open onto the Four Seasons' private pool area, where you can also dine al fresco. The pool has lush foliage, a spa, and cabanas, which are kept cool and refreshing by misters.

Four Seasons' 424 rooms are on the 35th to 39th floors of the Mandalay Bay tower. Private express elevators deliver guests to the Four Seasons' floors. Rates start at $305 for a superior king, but if you haggle a little, you can land a moderate king for less. However, it will still come at a hefty premium over Mandalay Bay's rooms, which are nearly identical. The main difference between the two standard rooms is the Four Seasons' fully stocked "private bar" (you'll pay about $2.75 for a can of Coke, $4 for a pack of Life Savers, $6 for an airline-sized bottle of liquor, and $19 for a small bottle of wine). Clear out the beverages from the mini-refrigerator and store your own drinks and snacks. Housekeepers provide turndown service before bedtime.

Four Seasons will appeal to ultra-upscale travelers looking for a mini-oasis that insulates them from the hullabaloo of Las Vegas. But it doesn't come cheaply. You're paying for the "brandness" as much as the grandness, and plenty of better values are nearby (even in the same building).

Fremont   (www.fremontcasino.com)

THE FREMONT IS ONE OF THE LANDMARKS of downtown Las Vegas. Acquired by the Boyd family in 1985, the Fremont offers good food, budget lodging, and a robust casino. Several years ago they redecorated and considerably brightened the casino, which is noisy and crowded. The table games are roomily accommodated beneath a high ceiling ringed in neon, while the slots are crammed together along narrow aisles like turkeys on their way to market. Locals love the Fremont, as do Asians, Hawaiians, and the inevitable Southern Californians. The Fremont, like all Boyd properties, is friendly, informal, and comfortable.

Gold Coast   (www.goldcoastcasino.com)

THE GOLD COAST, A HALF MILE WEST of the strip on Flamingo, is a favorite hangout for locals. A casual inspection of the Gold Coast reveals nothing unique: no fantasy theme, no special decor or atmosphere. But the

Gold Coast does pay attention to detail and has the local market wired. The Gold Coast serves one of the best breakfast specials in town, has one of the top buffets for quality and value, provides lounge entertainment at all hours of the day, offers headliners and modest production shows in its showroom, and makes sure it has the locals' favorite kind of slots. To top things off, there is also a two-screen movie complex and a huge bowling alley. Free transportation is provided throughout the day to the casino's sister property, Bill's Gamblin' Hall, on the Strip.

Gold Spike (www.goldspikehotelcasino.com)

SITUATED DOWNTOWN AND ABOUT A four-minute walk from the heart of Fremont Street, the Gold Spike is basically a slot joint. Congested, loud, and smoky, with all the ambience of a boiler room, the Gold Spike lures customers with low minimums, cheap food, and $35 rooms.

Golden Gate (www.goldengatecasino.net)

ANOTHER DOWNTOWN CASINO DEVOTED PRIMARILY to slots, the Golden Gate is crowded and dingy but redeems itself in part by offering one of the best shrimp cocktail specials in Las Vegas. Incongruously, the Golden Gate has a piano player performing mellow standards. Although odd, his presence takes the edge off the ever-frenetic casino and shrimp cocktail bar. On the western end of Glitter Gulch on Fremont Street, the Golden Gate has 106 budget hotel rooms.

Golden Nugget (www.goldennugget.com)

THE UNDISPUTED FLAGSHIP OF THE DOWNTOWN hotels and one of the most meticulously maintained and managed properties in Las Vegas, the Golden Nugget is smack in the middle of Glitter Gulch. Celebrating its 60th birthday in 2006, the hotel offers newly renovated bright, cheery rooms, a first-rate showroom, plus lounge entertainment, excellent restaurants, a large pool, a first-rate spa, a shopping arcade, and a workout room. The casino is clean and breezy, with white enameled walls and white lights. The feel here is definitely upscale, though comfortable and informal. There is breathing room at the Golden Nugget, and an atmosphere that suggests a happy, more fun-filled approach to gambling. In 2003, previous owners sold the Golden Nugget to 30-somethings Tim Poster and Tom Breitling. The new kids on the block immediately inked a deal with the FOX Network for a 13-episode reality TV series called *The Casino* starring, who else, themselves! In 2005, the whiz kids spun off the Nugget to Landry's restaurant chain (Rainforest Café, Landry's Seafood, Joe's Stone Crab Shack).

The Golden Nugget is undergoing a $200 million renovation and expansion, the first since 1973 for the perpetual AAA Four-Diamond Award winner. Ground was broken in 2006 for a new hotel tower and a 1,200-seat showroom. Other elements of the makeover include a new covered porte cochere, a new VIP lounge, Vic and Anthony's Steakhouse, and Lillie's Noodle House specializing in Cantonese and Szechuan fare. The current showroom has been enlarged to 650 seats, and the spa and fitness center have likewise been modernized and expanded. The most intriguing touch is the reconfiguration of the swimming complex to surround a 30-foot-deep shark aquarium. Overlooking the aquarium is a revamped buffet. Integrated into the shark tank and pool is grotto, a trattoria-style Italian restaurant.

Though the Golden Nugget has always been downtown's prestige address, the new hotel tower and top-to-bottom makeover will catapult the Nugget into the rarified atmosphere of the premiere Strip resorts. More, the Golden Nugget's renovation and expansion may well be the investment gamble that triggers the metamorphosis of all of downtown Las Vegas.

If you stay or gamble at the Golden Nugget, you are likely to meet people from New York, Dallas, Chicago, Los Angeles, and San Diego, as well as visitors from Taiwan, Hong Kong, and Japan. Younger travelers (ages 28 to 39) like the Golden Nugget, as do older tourists and retirees, many of whom arrive on motor-coach tours.

Greek Isles (www.greekislesvegas.com)

THE GREEK ISLES IS LOCATED ON CONVENTION CENTER DRIVE within five to seven minutes of the Las Vegas Convention Center by foot. Originally the Paddlewheel, it was purchased by Debbie Reynolds and completely renovated. So extensive were Debbie's improvements that she couldn't pay the mortgage and sold the place to, get this, the World Wrestling Federation (now known as World Wrestling Entertainment). WWF turned out to be (big surprise) clueless about running a hotel and sold it to the current owners, who have turned it into the Greek Isles. Operating with a small, slots-only casino, a combination Greek restaurant/coffee shop, a pool, and a designed-by-Debbie showroom with bizarrely eclectic entertainment, the property offers nice guest rooms at great rates to convention and trade-show attendees.

Green Valley Ranch Resort and Spa
(www.greenvalleyranchresort.com)

IF YOU LIKE PAMPERING AND FRESH AIR along with your gambling and dining, you'll love Green Valley Ranch. This Mediterranean-Mission style indulgent retreat, perched on a hill overlooking the distant Strip and the mountains, is in an upscale residential area about 15 minutes southeast of the Strip at the intersection of Green Valley Parkway and the I-215 Beltway. The property offers a 496-room hotel, a casino with 40 table games and almost 2,500 slot and video poker machines, seven restaurants (including a buffet), a spa, and a 10-screen cinema complex. Like all Station casinos, Green Valley Ranch provides locals with high-pay slots, good dining value, an excellent slot club, and high-quality lounge entertainment.

Unlike most Station casinos, however, Green Valley Ranch is very upscale. The restaurants are trendy, featuring some of Las Vegas's best-known chefs, and the unique Whiskey Bar dance club rivals the best nightspots on the Strip. Other watering holes include the elegant Drop Bar and the raucous Fado Irish pub with live Celtic music. The hotel and its enfolding guest rooms, starting at $129 on the Web site, are truly luxurious, many with great views of the pool and spa areas and/or the desert and Strip beyond. You can get a lot of walking done traversing the many long corridors that are accented by varied lighting and ubiquitous rich textures and patterns.

The eight-acre pool complex is lovely, more resembling a country club setting than that of a Las Vegas hotel. Features include vanishing-edge pools near the spa and a large centrally located swimming pool that has a sandy beach at one end, perfect for the kids to mess around in. There is also a small grassy playground area for children.

Dining options abound. Hank's is a plush, masculine chophouse and martini bar named after a man who neither ate meat nor drank alcohol. Other fine dining options include Il Fornaio, with a menu that reads like a map of Italy, and the ultra-hip Sushi + Sake that specializes in . . . well, take a guess. The Feast Around the World Buffet is one of Las Vegas's best, and for those who like their carbs served with butter and maple syrup, there's an Original Pancake House. An informal Chinese bistro and a food court complete the culinary collage.

The newly expanded spa is a real star. The curving path from the hotel proper to the relaxation center is lined by a small vineyard offset by red roses. In addition to a wonderful array of treatments, the soothing architectural aesthetics at Green Valley do their part in providing a higher-quality experience. For example, the gym here is filled with light that pours in a window wall. On the treadmills you can meditate on the Zen sculpture arising from the three-lane lap pool or contemplate the Spring Mountains. The steam room has an outdoor view. Waterfall showers and the Jacuzzi with a waterfall complement the treatment suites with sofas, double or single massage tables, and tubs. Jivamukti yoga and movement classes for $15 are held in a perfect wood, glass, and mirrored high-ceilinged studio, and BOSU and spinning classes are also available at the same rate.

Located within easy striking distance of Lake Mead, Hoover Dam, the Black Canyon of the Colorado, and Red Rock Canyon, Green Valley Ranch offers a super option for families, the outdoor-oriented traveler, and for those who believe in the healing powers of being pampered.

Hard Rock Hotel (www.hardrockhotel.com)

LOCATED OFF THE STRIP ON HARMON AVENUE near Paradise Road, the Hard Rock is billed as the world's first rock-and-roll hotel and casino. Like the adjoining Hard Rock Café, the 668-room hotel and domed casino are loaded to the gills with rock memorabilia and artifacts. Everywhere it's rock, rock, rock, from lounge music to the casino, which features piano-shaped roulette tables and chandeliers made from gold saxophones. The guest rooms, which offer a nice view, are surprisingly tasteful, with a Danish-modern European feel. The pool area is comfortable, nicely designed, and was recently enlarged. Other strengths include five restaurants; Body English, one of the hottest dance clubs in town; and The Joint, Las Vegas's most intimate venue for live rock. With an off-Strip location, the Hard Rock is removed from the worst traffic, which makes for easy coming and going if you have a car. The Hard Rock Hotel targets baby boomers and younger folks from Southern California, the Midwest, and the big northeastern cities.

Harrah's Las Vegas (www.harrahslasvegas.com)

A LAS VEGAS STAPLE, JAZZY HARRAH'S occupies the middle of the Strip's most prestigious block and is within easy walking distance of Bally's, the Flamingo, the Mirage, Caesars Palace, Paris, Bellagio, the Venetian, and T. I. Unpretentious and upbeat, Harrah's offers newly renovated guest rooms as well as a beautiful showroom, a comedy club, above-average restaurants, a buffet alongside the casino, a hot dance club, a pool, an exercise room, and a spa.

Harrah's theme celebrating carnival and Mardi Gras is evident in the two giant gold-leaf court jesters hefting a 10-ton, 22-foot-diameter globe that first welcome you on either side of the main hotel entrance, and a gold-swirled ceiling above the registration area continues the theme. The casino is decorated with brightly colored confetti-patterned carpet, ceiling murals, and hip fiber-optic lighting. Although the theme treatment is only a few years old, it already sports a somewhat tired feeling, rather like a Mardi Gras dawn.

The L-shaped casino of 86,000-plus square feet is bright and loud beyond average. It can be entered directly from the Strip alongside an open-air lounge with very talented "show" bartenders and a stage that hosts mostly rock music. This covered amphitheater adds to the raucous, let-loose feeling of Harrah's, but might interrupt the sleep of some guests.

The staff at Harrah's, from dealers to desk clerks, is exceptionally friendly and helpful. Though it is hard to imagine anyone not feeling comfortable at Harrah's, its clientele tends to be older visitors from the Midwest and Southern California, as well as business and convention travelers.

Other enticements include a large but otherwise unremarkable swimming area where you get sound bleed from the outdoor stage, a cozy upscale steak house with a view of the Strip, and an outdoor plaza with fountains. With its "Let the good times roll" spirit, Harrah's is an interesting blend of modern and vintage Las Vegas.

Hooters Casino Hotel (www.hooterscasinohotel.com)

LET'S GET ONE THING SETTLED AT THE BEGINNING. If you like Hooters—the chain of restaurants featuring hot wings and other pub grub served by waitresses in tight T-shirts and hot pants—then you will love the Hooters Casino Hotel. If you don't like Hooters restaurants, you won't much care for this place either, as the Hooters "mystique" is omnipresent from the casino floor to the hotel rooms (the latter even replaces typical hotel chairs with Hooters-style barstools). However, if you're not constitutionally averse to the brand, you might be surprised how well the restaurateurs transformed the darkly dank San Remo into this bright, happening, and admittedly fun place. The casino floor looks remarkably like a Hooters restaurant, with the same light blonde wood, cheerful lighting, and simple orange accents. A large Hooters-like square bar greets you at the front door. At the gaming tables, rotating shifts of dealers are often attired in full Hooters uniform, right down to the orange hot pants. In addition to a pleasant lounge, coffee shop, and Dan Marino's steak and seafood restaurant, there's an actual Hooters restaurant inside as well, and it draws huge lines of eager diners at peak times. A decent-sized pool dominates the back of the hotel, complete with waterfall, pool bar, and stage for live music. The reasonable room rates, utter lack of pretension or attitude, and party-hearty atmosphere draw a mix of middle-aged patrons and college kids, with a few families thrown in for good measure. Rooms are vaguely Florida tropical and trimmed in Hooters orange, with moderate-budget amenities (bathrooms are a little on the cheap side). The debut of a Hooters-themed hotel raised a few eyebrows locally, and that's saying something in this lowbrow town. However, the Hooterites are laughing all the way to the bank, as their hotel casino has proven a breakout hit.

Imperial Palace (www.imperialpalace.com)

IMPERIAL PALACE OWNER RALPH ENGELSTAD died in November of 2003. Though most Vegas watchers expected the then 27-year-old resort to go on the auction block, Engelstad's plucky wife, Betty, not only decided to keep plugging away, but also ordered a major renovation. Though Betty's intentions were good, she sold the property to Harrah's before much of the renovation was completed.

Directly from the Strip, a common access to the Imperial Palace casino is from a shallow reception area that immediately feeds up an escalator. Although you almost have to hunt for the architectural grace amidst the large, active casino, it's still there. Massive wooden beams and carved dragons crowning the ceiling supports whisper a once-grand Eastern elegance. The Teahouse restaurant up a flight from the casino floor does a better job of carrying out the theme, and here in this casual coffeehouse you can stoke up 24-7 on breakfasts of two eggs and a meat selection for $6.99. Save this bargain staple, in general the Imperial Palace food is a decidedly sub-par compared to most neighboring hotels.

The casino has a "Geisha Bar," but the burly bartender will definitely be omitted from the memoirs. The attraction on the casino floor is the dealers who are fair to poor celebrity impersonators, including the likes of Stevie Wonder (would a blind dealer be a good thing?), Reba McEntire, Dolly Parton, Little Richard, and the perennial Elvis. It's a fun gimmick, even when it's weakly executed. These players are a nod to the excellent impersonators of *Legends in Concert,* one of the hottest shows in Las Vegas that plays nightly at the Imperial Palace's showroom. (The on-site auto museum is a first-rate tourist attraction in its own right.) The Imperial Palace casino is full of action, and the intensity of it is multiplied by the unusual number of mirrored surfaces that nearly pay homage to Orson Welles's famous classic reflection on life's enigmas, *A Touch of Evil.*

The small bank of elevators to the guest rooms is at the back of the casino, and this same relatively narrow hallway feeds the modest shopping area, monorail, and casino-level restaurant. Pity the people also trying to use the pay phones here in this traffic-jam central. The rooms are of modest but adequate size for the budget traveler, but the fluorescent overhead hallway lighting and the buzz of hairdryers and TVs imparts a college-dorm feel. High-speed wireless Internet service is available in the rooms, as is a small refrigerator, but both add to the standard room rate.

The single swimming pool and sunbathing area are large, but unremarkable by Las Vegas standards. The exercise (five treadmills, two exercise bikes, and so on) and spa spaces (two massage rooms) are small, but adequate for the traveler who wants basic service.

The ambitious renovation, on hold for the moment, calls for a new facade for the building, a sidewalk cafe, a glass-walled upscale restaurant, a pedestrian corridor for monorail passengers, and a redo of all the resort's guest rooms in a new design. Many Las Vegas insiders, however, maintain that the renovation will never happen, citing the size and value of the real estate the Imperial Palace sits on. In their opinion, the Imperial Palace's future will more likely involve a lot of dynamite.

JW Marriott Las Vegas/Rampart Casino (www.gowestmarriott.com)

THE JW MARRIOTT LAS VEGAS IS THE FIRST of several new upscale properties to offer a Scottsdale–Palm Beach resort experience as an alternative to the madness of the Strip. Situated west of town near Red Rock Canyon, the JW Marriott Las Vegas consists of two southwestern-style hotels built around the Tournament Players Club (TPC) golf course. The JW Marriott officially opened as The Resort at Summerlin in 1999, and a year or so later changed its name to The Regent Las Vegas. Marriott acquired the property in late 2001, and the name changed again. As an added twist, the classy, circular casino has yet another name, Rampart Casino (after the road on which the casino is located). The JW Marriott is operated primarily as a meeting venue with secondary emphasis on golf and the resort's exceptional spa. The casino, operated by an independent contractor, targets the local market.

Standard hotel rooms are huge at 560 square feet. In many rooms, French doors open onto a balustrade overlooking the pools and gardens (11 acres of palms and pines tower over the winding pools, waterfalls, and walkways), or better yet, the mountains to the west, a stirring alternative to the usual neon. Baths feature a whirlpool tub, separate shower, bathrobes, and telephone.

Restaurants serve Italian, continental, and beef fare. The buffet here is one of the better spreads in town. Although the lounges, including an "Irish Pub," offer live entertainment, there is no showroom. The JW Marriott is pricey, but perfect for those who come to enjoy the beauty and recreational resources of the mountains and valleys west of Las Vegas. Only minutes away are world-class hiking, rock climbing, mountain biking, and road biking.

Las Vegas Club (www.vegasclubcasino.net)

THE LAS VEGAS CLUB IS A DOWNTOWN hotel-casino with a sports theme. The corridor linking the casino with the sports bar is a veritable sports museum and has dozens of vintage photos of boxing, baseball, and basketball legends. The casino itself, with its high, mirrored ceilings, is modest but feels uncrowded. It also has some of the more player-friendly blackjack rules around. If you plan to stay at the Las Vegas Club, ask for a room in the new North Tower. The food is good and consistent, and the upscale Great Moments Room is a perfect example of the old-time Las Vegas gourmet rooms. The food? It's great. The Las Vegas Club draws from Hawaii and the Midwest, but also does a big business with bus groups and seniors.

Las Vegas Hilton (www.lv-hilton.com)

IN SOME WAYS LIKE BALLY'S, the Las Vegas Hilton bills itself as a classic, straightforward Vegas experience with comfortable lodging, very good restaurants, a strong casino, and headliner entertainment, but no exotic theme. Lacking a theme hook, the Hilton has the advantage of being adjacent to the Las Vegas Convention Center. What it lacks in convenient access to the Strip (a 10- to 12-minute walk or 5-minute monorail ride away), it makes up for in one-stop partying for the conventioneer who can go to sessions via a hall connecting the hotel and convention center. Consequently, this hotel does more meeting, trade-show, and convention business than any other hotel in town. There are days at the Hilton when it's rare to see someone not wearing a convention badge. Operating under the valid assumption that many of its guests may never leave the hotel during their Las Vegas stay (except to go to the convention center), the Hilton is an oasis of self-sufficiency. It boasts lounges, a huge pool, an exercise room, a shopping arcade, a buffet, and a coffee shop. It is also next door to a golf course.

The architecture is vintage high-rise—bland, smooth, and unmemorable, but not at all unpleasant. Renovations are underway, and these areas have been completed: the lobby, the large theater where Barry Manilow is the regular headliner, the spa and pool area, and some of the bars (the Tempo, with its small spaces for dancers and intimate parties, has a new facade). Continuing in 2007, renovations on the 3,000 rooms will be done incrementally. In the meantime, the rooms are more than adequate—accommodating, but not glitzy, providing a comfortable, neutral environment for the business clientele.

The Las Vegas Hilton has a decent buffet and some excellent fine dining options with enough ethnic and culinary variety to keep most guests happy. The showroom at the Hilton hosts big-name headliners. *Star Trek: The Experience,* an interactive video and virtual reality amusement center featuring a space-flight simulation ride and a 3-D theater presentation, is one of the top casino-based attractions in the city.

The casino is moderate in size by Las Vegas standards and, like the hotel, tastefully businesslike in its presentation, but by no means formal or intimidating. The Hilton sports book is one of the largest in Las Vegas, and perhaps in the world. It has 30,000 square feet, 300 seats and 28 giant screens, plus one "mondo" puppy for viewing that measures 15x20 feet.

If you can afford it, the Hilton is the most convenient place to stay in town if you are attending a trade show or convention at the Las Vegas Convention Center. If, however, you are in Las Vegas for pleasure, staying at the Hilton is like being in exile. Anywhere you go you will need a cab, a car, or the new monorail that drops you right inside the hotel. If you park in one of the Hilton's far-flung, self-parking lots, it will take you as long as

15 minutes to reach your car from your guest room. Inside the hotel, the public spaces are only about three minutes apart, another convenience factor for those who do elect to stay at this classic property.

Luxor (www.luxor.com)

THE LUXOR IS ON THE STRIP SOUTH OF TROPICANA AVENUE next to the Excalibur. Representing Mandalay Resort Group's (now MGM-MRG) first serious effort to attract a more upscale, less family-oriented clientele, the Luxor is among the more tasteful of Las Vegas's themed hotels. Though originally not believed to be on a par with T. I. and the MGM Grand, the Luxor may well be the most distinguished graduate of the much-publicized hotel class of 1993. While the MGM Grand is larger and T. I. more ostentatious, the Luxor demonstrates an unmatched creativity and architectural appeal.

Rising 30 stories, the Luxor is a huge pyramid with guest rooms situated around the outside perimeter from base to apex. Guest-room hallways circumscribe a hollow core containing the world's largest atrium. Inside the atrium, inclinators rise at a 39-degree angle from the pyramid's corners to access the guest floors. While the perspective from inside the pyramid is stunning, it is easy to get disoriented. Stories about hotel guests wandering around in search of their rooms are legend. After reviewing many complaints from readers, we seriously recommend carrying a small pocket compass.

The Luxor's main entrance is from the Strip via a massive sphinx. From the sphinx, guests are diverted into small entryways designed to resemble the interior passages of an actual pyramid. From these tunnels, guests emerge into the dramatic openness of the Luxor's towering atrium. Rising imposingly within the atrium is an ancient Egyptian city.

Proceeding straight ahead at ground level from the main entrance brings you into the casino. Open and attractive, the 100,000-square-foot casino is tasteful by any standard.

One level below the casino and the main entrance is the Luxor's main showroom. One floor above entry level, on a mezzanine of sorts, is an array of structures that reach high into the atrium. These dramatic elaborate buildings and facades transform the atrium. They are styled and themed to conjure up an Egyptian bazaar or town center. Here you'll find an attraction designed by Douglas Trumbull, creator of the *Back to the Future* ride at Universal Studios Florida, and an IMAX theater. In addition to the attractions, on this level are three restaurants, a huge electronic games arcade, and a collection of retail shops.

Flanking the pyramid are two hotel towers that were part of a $300-million expansion completed in 1997; the expansion included a new health spa and fitness center, and additional meeting and conference space.

The biggest surprise of all (to anyone who has ever stayed at sister properties Excalibur and Circus Circus) are the Luxor's large, tasteful guest rooms. Decorated in an understated Egyptian motif with custom-made furniture, the standard guest rooms are among the most nicely appointed in town. The only disappointment is that many of the guest rooms do not have tubs. In all, the Luxor offers 4,474 guest rooms, which makes it the second largest hotel in Las Vegas.

The Luxor's large, attractive pool complex, surrounded by private cabanas, desperately needs some additional plants and trees. Self-parking is not as much a problem at the Luxor as at most large properties. Valet parking is quick and efficient, however, and well worth the $1 or $2 tip. The Luxor is within a 5- to 12-minute walk of the Excalibur, the Tropicana, and the MGM Grand. A moving walkway connects the Luxor to the Excalibur and an overhead "cable liner" (a monorail propelled by a cable à la San Francisco cable cars) connects it with Mandalay Bay.

Main Street Station (www.mainstreetcasino.com)

SITUATED ON MAIN STREET BETWEEN OGDEN and Stewart avenues in downtown Las Vegas, Main Street Station originally opened in 1992 as a paid-admission nighttime entertainment complex with a casino on the side. Owned and managed by an Orlando, Florida, entrepreneur with no casino experience, it took Main Street Station less than a year to go belly-up. The property was acquired several years later by Boyd Gaming, which used Main Street Station's hotel to accommodate overflow guests from the California across the street. In 1997, the Boyds reopened the casino, restaurants, and shops, adding a brewpub in the process.

The casino is one of the most unusual in town (thanks largely to the concept of the original owner), with the feel of a turn-of-the-20th-century gentlemen's club. Though not as splendid now as in its original incarnation, the casino still contains enough antiques, original art, and oddities to furnish a museum. With its refurbished guest rooms, brewpub, steak house, excellent buffet, and unusual casino, Main Street Station is both interesting and fun, adding some welcome diversity to the downtown hospitality mix.

Mandalay Bay (www.mandalaybay.com)

MANDALAY BAY OPENED ON MARCH 1, 1999, on the site of the old Hacienda, imploded on New Year's Day 1998. It completes the Mandalay Bay "Miracle Mile," which stretches along the Strip south from the Bellagio and includes Project City Center, the Monte Carlo, New York–New York, the Excalibur, Luxor, and finally Mandalay Bay. A cable liner connects Excalibur, Luxor, and Mandalay Bay every 15 minutes, 24 hours a day (it stops at Luxor on the northbound leg only).

Mandalay Bay, with over 4,800 rooms (including the on-site Four Seasons Hotel and THEhotel), is a megaresort in the true sense of the overworked word. Within the sprawling complex are the 43-story, three-wing tower; a 12,000-seat arena; an 1,800-seat theater; a 1,700-seat concert venue; two dozen restaurants; an 11-acre water park; three large lounges; and the third-largest convention facility in Las Vegas. Mandalay Bay had Las Vegas's first hotel-within-a-hotel on the property: the 400-room Four Seasons. The whole schmear cost a cool billion plus. Adjoining the main casino is a second on-site hotel, THEhotel at Mandalay Bay, with 1,120 suites. Both the Four Seasons and THEhotel are profiled in this section under their own names.

But that's not the half of it, because Mandalay Bay isn't your standard megaresort. It's clear that the planners and designers set out to take a few risks and appeal to a young, hip, fun-seeking market—as opposed to Bellagio, which has targeted a more refined, sophisticated, older clientele. If Bellagio is the crowning culmination of the Las Vegas of the 20th century, Mandalay Bay might be Las Vegas's first foray into the 21st. All the different ideas jammed into Mandalay Bay might not always add up to a cohesive whole, but so many parts of the sum are unique that you can't help being intrigued.

The signature spectacle is the four-story wine tower at Manhattan celebrity chef Charlie Palmer's restaurant, Aureole. This nearly 50-foot-tall glass-and-stainless-steel structure stores nearly 10,000 bottles of wine. Lovely, athletic women dressed all in black—spandex tights, racing gloves, hard hats—manipulate the motorized cable, one on each of the four sides, that raises them up to retrieve a selected bottle and lowers them back down to deliver it.

The China Grill Café, the bar-and-grill annex to Mandalay Bay's Oriental room, China Grill, has a centerpiece 34-seat bar, which is circled by a rubber conveyor. The belt goes round and round between the bar sitters and the open kitchen, carrying plates of "Zen Sum" appetizers.

Red Square Russian restaurant has a one-of-a-kind refrigerated walk-in showcase, open to the public, which stores 150 different varieties of vodka at 15 degrees. Drinks are served on a long bar top that has a thick strip of ice running its length (basically it keeps the bottom of the glasses chilled and provides a great medium for leaving fingerprints). Red Square also has a 16-foot-tall statue of Vladimir Lenin out front; the howl of criticism over the questionable taste of such a display prompted Mandalay to lop off Lenin's head, and the statue now has a big hole at the neck. Inside, Red Square sports a curious Communist theme, a paean to the Soviet 1930s when Joe Stalin was slaughtering his nation's civilians. Huge heroic posters of Russian intellectuals and professionals carrying shovels and pipe and automatic weapons fill the walls, and plentiful hammer-and-sickles symbolize the former Soviet Union no less than a swastika represents the Third Reich.

Rumjungle, a Polynesian dining and nightclub combo, is fronted by a huge "wall of fire": 80 small gas-fed flames surround two big flames at the entrance. The House of Blues restaurant and entertainment complex serves food (Southern style and Creole/Cajun) and has the world's largest collection of Deep South folk art, as well as a strange dark bar with a crucifix theme. House of Blues also puts on a Sunday gospel brunch and holds rock and pop concerts in its 1,800-seat theater. Wolfgang Puck's Trattoria del Lupo (serving Italian fare), a Mexican restaurant, a noodle room, a coffee shop, a buffet, and ice cream and coffee counters round out the dining possibilities at Mandalay Bay. A main attraction at Mandalay Bay is Shark Reef, a 90,000-square-foot aquarium exhibit with a walk-through acrylic tunnel. The aquarium is home to about 2,000 marine species, including Nile crocodiles, moray eels, stingrays, and, of course, sharks.

J-POP is one of the largest and most interesting bars in Las Vegas. Taking up a good part of an acre of the property, J-POP is surrounded by lush tropical "foliage" (though fake, it's very effective) and has three distinct sitting areas: the 25-seat marble video-poker bar; the lounge itself, with a big stage and good enough acoustics that the bands can crank it up; and a wooden deck away from the main noise, where you sit amongst the virtual vegetation, rock waterfalls, and lily ponds.

Speaking of acreage, the casino is typically monumental, with plenty of elbowroom between machines and tables. The race and sports book boasts the largest screen in town, which is only right, since the book is so big the screen must be seen from long distances. The 80-seat (each one an oversized, velour-covered easy chair) Turf Lounge and the large poker room are connected.

The pool area is also imaginative. The 11-acre Mandalay Beach has a lazy river, a placid pool, a beachfront cafe and bar, and a wedding chapel. The centerpiece, however, is a huge wave pool. The surf can be cranked up from one to eight feet, but there seems to be a little problem with the big water—it floods the sandy beach! Apparently, even machine-made seas can get too high. For the surfing lessons, the beach area is cleared so that sunbathers don't get drenched.

Mandalay Bay's only weakness, until 2004 that is, was its miniscule number of shopping opportunities. This was corrected with the opening of the Mandalay Place Mall. In the pedestrian passage that connects Mandalay Bay with the Luxor, the mall features 40 boutiques and restaurants, including a superb wineshop, a bookstore with the best selection of titles on Las Vegas we've seen, and a burger joint where you can purchase a $60 hamburger.

All in all, Mandalay Bay accomplishes what every mega–casino-hotel sets out to do—deliver an inventive and hip experience that sets a new standard for all the megajoints that follow.

MGM Grand Hotel and Casino (www.mgmgrand.com)

WHEN STEVE WYNN OPENED THE MIRAGE, he combined the amenities of a world-class resort with the excitement and visual appeal of a tourist attraction. At the Mirage, T. I., and Bellagio, however, the attraction component is rendered in terms of nonparticipatory visual spectacle: at the Mirage, an exploding volcano; at T. I., a pirate battle; and at Bellagio, dancing fountains. The attraction is peripheral, no more or no less than a powerful and eye-popping way to generate traffic for the casino.

At Kirk Kerkorian's MGM Grand, the evolutionary combination of gambling resort and attraction was carried to the next logical stage, the development of a theme park ostensibly, if not actually, on an equal footing with the casino. This elevation of a nongaming attraction to a position of prominence signaled the first significant tourism product diversification in Las Vegas since the dawn of the luxury resort hotel-casinos in the 1950s. Make no mistake, the purpose of the theme park was to funnel patrons into the casino. But the theme park offered a recreation alternative intended to attract nongamblers as well as gamblers. As it happened, however, the highly publicized theme park was pitifully designed. In 2000, after seven years of limping along, the MGM (not so) Grand Adventures park closed. Probably, in retrospect, the park served its purpose, that is, to draw attention to the MGM Grand Hotel and Casino in its opening year.

The MGM Grand claims the distinction of being both the largest hotel in the United States (with 5,034 rooms) and the world's largest casino. Within the 112-acre complex, there is a 15,200-seat special-events arena, 380,000 square feet of convention space, an enormous swimming area, four tennis courts, a health spa, and a multilevel parking facility. There's also a small casino outside the lobby of the Mansion, MGM's ultra-upscale whale digs. Finally, a 6.6-acre pool-and-spa complex took over a chunk of the now-defunct amusement park along with the dedicated convention center.

The MGM Grand is on the northeast corner of Tropicana Avenue and the Strip. The Strip entrance passes beneath a 45-foot-tall MGM Lion atop a 25-foot pedestal, all surrounded by three immense digital displays. The lion entrance leads to a domed rotunda with table games and a Rainforest Café, and from there to the MGM Grand's four larger casinos. All of the casinos are roomy and plush, with high ceilings and a comfortable feeling of openness.

A second entrance, with a porte cochere 15 lanes wide, serves vehicular traffic from Tropicana Avenue. For all practical purposes, this is the main entrance to the MGM Grand, permitting you to go directly to the hotel lobby and its 53 check-in windows without lugging your belongings through the casinos. Just beyond the registration area is the elevator core, with 35 elevators servicing 30 guest floors.

Beyond the elevator core, a wide passageway leads toward five of the MGM Grand's eight distinct restaurants (not counting theme-park restaurants or fast food). The MGM Grand's supernova restaurant is Joël Robuchon at the Mansion, a French culinary feast of the highest quality and greatest exclusivity. Other fine dining stars in the hotel's galaxy include Craftsteak, offering beef and seafood; Nob Hill, serving California-style cuisine; Emeril's, offering Creole/Cajun dishes; SeaBlue, a Mediterranean tapas restaurant; Fiamma, an Italian trattoria; Grand Wok, featuring Asian specialties from a half-dozen countries; and Pearl, a Chinese restaurant. More informal dining is available at the Rainforest Café and the Studio Café. The MGM Grand's buffet (disappointing), and pizza kitchen adjoin the casinos between the porte cochere and lion entrances. For fast food there is a food court housing McDonald's, Mamma Ilardo's, and Hamada's Oriental Express.

There are three showrooms at the MGM Grand. The 740-seat Hollywood Theater features headliners, the larger KÀ Theatre is home to Cirque du Soleil's KÀ, and the Crazy Horse Cabaret is home to the saucy Frenchy show of the same name. Entertainment is also offered in the casino's four lounges. In addition, the MGM Grand's special-events arena can accommodate boxing, tournament tennis, rodeo, and basketball, as well as major exhibitions.

Amenities at the MGM Grand, not unexpectedly, are among the best in Las Vegas. The swimming complex is huge—23,000 square feet of pool area, with five interconnected pools graced with bridges, fountains, and waterfalls. Other highlights of the complex include an artificial stream to float in, a poolside bar, and luxury cabanas. Adjoining the swimming area are a complete health club and spa and four lighted tennis courts. For those to whom recreation means pumping quarters into a machine, there is an electronic games arcade supplemented by a "games-of-skill" midway. The most exotic addition to the entertainment mix is Lion Habitat, where you can watch live lions. In the transportation department, the MGM Grand is the southern terminus of the Las Vegas monorail.

Guest rooms at the MGM Grand are comfortable, with large baths. Almost all of the rooms have a small sitting area positioned by a large window. Rooms on the higher floors have exceptional views. Part of the old MGM Marina Hotel was incorporated into the new MGM Grand. Rooms in the old structure have been renovated but are not comparable in size or quality to the new rooms.

A rare enclave of peace and privacy are MGM Grand's Signature condo/ hotel towers, which opened in 2007. Located a five-to-seven-minute walk east of the main casino, the towers offer suite accommodations including floor-to-ceiling windows, full kitchens, plasma televisions, Jacuzzi tubs, and high-speed Internet connections. Conspicuous by its absence is on-site gambling. Signature's suites are not especially large but are beautifully appointed, and some units have private balconies. Each tower has its own pool, 24-hour concierge service, and a private entrance with valet parking. The private entrance makes for easy coming and going if you have a car.

Drawing from a wide cross-section of the leisure market, the MGM Grand gets the majority of its business from individual travelers and tour and travel groups, but with a rising percentage coming from trade-show and convention attendees. Midrange room rates make the MGM Grand accessible to a broad population. Geographically, the MGM Grand targets Southern California, Phoenix, Denver, Dallas, Houston, Chicago, and the Midwest.

Mirage (www.mirage.com)

THE MIRAGE HAS HAD AN IMPACT ON THE LAS VEGAS tourist industry that will be felt for years to come. By challenging all the old rules and setting new standards for design, ambience, and entertainment, the Mirage precipitated the development of a class of super-hotels in Las Vegas, redefining the thematic appeal and hospitality standard of hotel-casinos.

Exciting and compelling without being whimsical or silly, the Mirage has demonstrated that the public will respond enthusiastically to a well-executed concept. Blending the stateliness of marble with the exotic luxury of tropical greenery and the straightforward lines of polished bamboo, the Mirage has created a spectacular environment that artfully integrates casino, showroom, shopping, restaurants, and lounges. Both lavish and colorful, inviting and awe-inspiring, the Mirage has avoided cliché. Not designed to replicate a famous palace or be the hotel version of "Goofy Golf," the Mirage makes an original statement.

An atrium rain forest serves as a central hub from which guests can proceed to all areas of the hotel and casino. Behind the hotel's front desk, a 60-foot-long aquarium contains small sharks, stingrays, and colorful tropical fish. In the entranceway from Las Vegas Boulevard is a natural-habitat zoological display housing rare white Bengal tigers. Outside, instead of blinking neon, the Mirage has a 55-foot-tall erupting volcano that disrupts traffic on the Strip every half hour. There is also a live dolphin exhibit and a modern showroom that is among the most well designed and technologically advanced in Las Vegas.

The Mirage boasts several fine-dining opportunities, including Japonais, a concept restaurant featuring Japanese and "old style" European cuisine; Fin, serving contemporary Chinese; Kokomo's, a chop, seafood, and lobster house; STACK, an American grill; Samba, a Brazilian *churrascuria;* and Onda, one of the city's better Italian restaurants. For bulk eaters, there is an excellent and affordable buffet. *LOVE,* a Cirque du Soleil production based on the music of the Beatles, plays in one of two showrooms. Impressionist Danny Gans performs in the other. Amenities include a swimming and sunning complex with waterfalls, inlets, and an interconnected series of lagoons; a shopping arcade; and a spa with exercise equipment and aerobics instruction. The casino is huge and magnificently appointed, yet informal, with its tropical motif and piped-in Jimmy Buffett music. Guest rooms at the Mirage have been completely renovated and are now among the nicest in town.

Though registered guests pay premium prices for the privilege of staying at the Mirage, the hotel is not an exclusive retreat of the wealthy. With its indoor jungle, live tigers and sharks, and traffic-snarling volcano, the Mirage remains one of Clark County's top tourist attractions. Whether by foot, bus, trolley, cab, or bicycle, every Las Vegas visitor makes at least one pilgrimage. The Mirage has become the Strip's melting pot and hosts the most incredible variety of humanity imaginable. Visitors wander wide-eyed through the casino at all hours of the day and night.

Monte Carlo (www.montecarlo.com)

THE MONTE CARLO OPENED ON June 21, 1996. With 3,002 guest rooms, the Monte Carlo ranks as one of the larger hotels in Las Vegas. The megaresort is modeled after the Place du Casino in Monte Carlo, Monaco, with ornate arches and fountains, marble floors, and a Gothic glass registration area. If the Monte Carlo fails as a resort, the building will be a perfect place to relocate the Nevada State Capitol.

On the surface, it's yet another huge hotel in the Las Vegas Age of the Megaresort. But scratch the surface just a little and you glimpse the future of Monopoly-board Las Vegas and the gambling business in general.

The guest rooms, furnished with marble entryways and French period wall art, are mid- to upper-priced. There is an elaborate swimming complex with slides, a wave pool, and a man-made stream. There is also an exceptional health and fitness center, an interesting shopping arcade, and a brewpub with live entertainment. The casino, about a football field long and similarly shaped, is capped with simulated skylights and domes. The showroom is designed especially for illusionist Lance Burton, who signed a long-term contract to perform there. Restaurants cover the usual bases, offering steak, Italian, and Asian specialties, with the brewpub thrown in for good measure.

Compared to the powerful themes of New York–New York, T. I., and the Luxor, the Monte Carlo's turn-of-the-century Monegasque theme fails to stimulate much excitement or anticipation. Besides being beyond the average tourist's frame of reference, the theme lacks any real visceral dimension.

The word *grand* comes to mind, but more in the context of a federal courthouse or the New York Public Library. Simply put (and this may be a big plus), the Monte Carlo is an attractive hotel-casino as opposed to a crowd-jammed tourist attraction.

MonteLago Village Resort at Lake Las Vegas (www.montelagovillage.com)

PART OF THE LAKE LAS VEGAS DEVELOPMENT 17 miles east of the Strip, MonteLago Village Resort took its place in 2004 alongside the Ritz-Carlton and the Hyatt Regency. An Intrawest Resort real estate property, MonteLago Village brings a Mediterranean village ambience, with winding cobblestone streets, to complement the neighboring golf and meeting hotels. Specialty shops, galleries, small cafes, and restaurants line the plazas and narrow avenues. Como's Steakhouse, the flagship eatery when MonteLago Village opened, has since been augmented by additional restaurants. The Tuscan-inspired casino, adjacent to the village, offers the usual, plus a large number of penny, two-cent, and nickel slot machines. Tenuta, located in the casino, serves as the resort's 24-hour restaurant.

The resort offers one-, two-, and three-bedroom condominiums, all with DVD players and high-speed Internet access. Light carpets and wall colors contrast with rich burgundy upholstery and dark hardwoods in the rooms. The full kitchens offer countertop dining. Lower units provide patios, most upper units balconies. Resort amenities include a marina, a fitness center, two swimming pools, and a games room.

The New Frontier (www.frontierlv.com)

IF EVER A LAS VEGAS HOTEL HAS BEEN THROUGH the wringer, it's the Frontier . . . oops, make that the NEW Frontier. Though mostly forgotten, this is the hotel that essentially launched *Siegfried & Roy* in Las Vegas, the hotel with a super location smack in the middle of the Strip, and the hotel with owners, the Elardi family, who allowed the Frontier to get embroiled in a labor dispute and strike that lasted six and a half years. In 1998, the Elardis sold the Frontier to Phil Ruffin, who quickly settled the strike and christened the property the New Frontier. Ruffin poured a couple million dollars into repairs and improvements. Some, like the new roof, you probably won't notice, but others, such as the Mexican and steak restaurants and the addition of a Gilley's Saloon (the bar with the mechanical bull from the film *Urban Cowboy*) stand out proudly. In 2007, the Elad Group, owner of New York's Plaza Hotel, purchased the New Frontier and announced plans to bring their venerable Plaza brand to Las Vegas as part of $5-billion development that will include a Plaza hotel, private residences, a casino, and a retail and entertainment complex. The project is scheduled to open in 2011. The fate of the mechanical bull is unclear.

In the meantime, the New Frontier stands, and may yet survive for some time. It is easily accessed from Fashion Show Drive or the Strip and is within easy walking distance of some of the best shopping in town. Through the improvements, the New Frontier has retained that unpretentious feel that has made it popular with both visitors and locals for more than 40 years.

New York–New York (www.nynyhotelcasino.com)

WHEN IT OPENED IN DECEMBER 1996, this architecturally imaginative hotel-casino set a new standard for the realization of Las Vegas megaresort themes. It's a small joint by megaresort standards ("only" around 2,000 rooms), but the triumph is in the details. The guest rooms are in a series of distinct towers reminiscent of a mini–Big Apple skyline, including the Empire State, Chrysler, and Seagram's buildings. Though the buildings are connected, each offers a somewhat different decor and ambience.

A half-size Statue of Liberty and a replica of Grand Central Station lead visitors to one entrance, while the Brooklyn Bridge leads to another. The interior of the property is broken into themed areas such as Greenwich Village, Wall Street, and Times Square. The casino, one of the most visually interesting in Las Vegas, looks like an elaborate movie set. Table games and slots are sandwiched between shops, restaurants, and a jumble of street facades.

The street scenes are well executed, conveying both a sense of urban style and tough grittiness. New York–New York sacrificed much of its visual impact, however, by not putting in an imitation sky. At Sunset Station, by way of contrast, the Spanish architecture is augmented significantly by vaulted ceilings, realistically lighted and painted with clouds. This sort of finishing touch could have done wonders for New York–New York.

Like its namesake, New York–New York is congested in the extreme, awash day and night with curious sightseers. There are so many people just wandering around gawking that there's little room left for hotel guests and folks who actually came to gamble. Because aisles and indoor paths are far too narrow to accommodate the crowds, New York–New York succumbs periodically to a sort of pedestrian gridlock.

Manhattan rules, however, do not apply at New York–New York: It's OK here to make eye contact and decidedly rude to shove people out of the way to get where you want to go. If you find yourself longing for the thrill of a New York cab ride, go hop on the roller coaster. New York–New York's coaster is the fourth one on the Strip, but it's the only one where you can stand on the street and hear the riders scream.

In the entertainment department, there are two showrooms, one featuring Cirque du Soleil's *Zumanity* and one hosting famous stand-up comics. Lounges include a raucous Irish pub, a dueling pianos club, and a Coyote Ugly bar. Based on the movie of the same name, the bar features a platoon of dancing female bartenders with enough attitude to stop a real New Yorker dead in his tracks.

Guest rooms at New York–New York have been renovated and upgraded. However, the swimming area and health and fitness center are just average. Full-service restaurants are a little better than average, though Gallagher's Steakhouse, a real Big Apple import, can hold its own with any beef place, in or out of Las Vegas. Counter-service fast food is quite interesting, if not altogether authentic New York.

Nevada Palace (www.nvpalace.com)

THE NEVADA PALACE IS A SMALL, RECENTLY renovated Boulder Highway property patronized primarily by locals and by seniors who take advantage of its 168-space RV park. Pleasant, with a new pool, spa facilities, two decent restaurants, and fair room rates, the Nevada Palace is a friendly, less hectic alternative to staying downtown or on the Strip.

Orleans (www.orleanscasino.com)

OPENED IN 1997, ORLEANS IS JUST WEST of I-15 on Tropicana Avenue and owned by Coast Resorts, which also run the Suncoast and the Gold Coast. Marketed primarily to locals, Orleans has a New Orleans–bayou theme executed in a hulking cavern of a building. The casino is festive with bright carpets, high ceilings, a two-story replication of a French Quarter street flanking the table games, and a couple of nifty bars. Orleans has a celebrity showroom that is attracting great musical talent (The Doobie Brothers, Willie Nelson) and several restaurants that have little to do with the Louisiana theme. The buffet, which does serve Creole/Cajun dishes, is good but can't quite match Louisiana standards. Upstairs, over the slots and buffet area, is a 70-lane bowling complex. The Orleans arena is a 9,000-seat facility and home to the Las Vegas Wranglers pro hockey team. Two hotel towers with a total of 1,886 large guest rooms complete the package.

Orleans has expanded steadily since its first year, adding restaurants, a movie complex, more casino space, the arena, a games arcade, and a child-care center.

Palace Station (www.palacestation.com)

LOCATED FOUR MINUTES OFF THE STRIP on West Sahara Avenue, Palace Station is a local favorite that also attracts tourists. With great lounge acts, a first-rate buffet, dependable restaurants that continuously offer amazing specials, a tower of Holiday Inn–caliber guest rooms, good prices, and a location that permits access to both downtown and the Strip in less than ten minutes, Palace Station is a standard setter for locals' casinos. Decorated in a railroad theme, the casino is large and busy and places heavy emphasis on the slots (which are supposedly loose—that is, having a high rate of payoff). There is also first-rate lounge entertainment.

Palms (www.palms.com)

LOCATED WEST OF THE STRIP ON FLAMINGO ROAD, the Palms is one of the primo hangouts for well-heeled youth. Consisting of two high-rise hotel towers and a 50-story luxury hotel-condo, the Palms offers solid four-star guest rooms with floor-to-ceiling windows and some of the best views of the Strip.

Though the casino is roomy, at over 100,000 square feet, it's the Palms nightlife mix that sets the hotel apart. Atop the 55-story original tower is Ghostbar with panoramic views of the entire Las Vegas Valley. On the ground level of the same tower is Rain, a high-energy dance club with pulsing fountains and high-tech special effects. Small and intimate is Moon at the top of the newer Fantasy Tower (so called because of the tower's fantastic high-roller suites featuring such amenities as basketball courts). Like Ghostbar, Moon offers incredible views. Unlike Ghostbar, Moon has a retractable roof. One floor down from Moon is the Playboy Club, the only such club in existence and the first new Playboy Club to open in decades. The club features table games, knock-out views, and a lot of cleavage. A show lounge; a 14-screen cinema; and Pearl, a very cool concert venue, complete the mix. All of the clubs, as well as Pearl, attract a hip under-30 crowd that keeps the Palms jumping until the wee hours.

Also very cool is the two-acre pool complex featuring three bars, including one situated beneath a glass-bottom pool. Strong drinks relieve the pain of sprained necks. At the pools you can swim, of course, but mostly they're used as a party or concert venue or as an additional nightspot.

The restaurant lineup, equally impressive, leads off with Alizé, serving gourmet French cuisine; N9NE, a steak house imported from Chicago; and NOVE Italiano, an elegant room graced by topiaries in the form of classic nudes. Rounding out the dining mix are an Asian fusion restaurant, a Mexican restaurant, a good buffet, a 24-hour coffee shop, and a food court.

Palms is too far from the Strip for most guests to feel comfortable walking. For those with a car, however, the coming and going is easy, and the hotel location on West Flamingo Road facilitates accessing Strip casinos via alternate routes rather than joining the gridlock on Las Vegas Boulevard. Both in design and target market, Palms is very much like the Hard Rock Hotel. You can bet that the two will compete head-to-head for the trend-conscious, affluent, young adult market. Older guests may feel like relics at Palms' nightspots, but will otherwise find the property friendly, accessible, and convenient.

Paris Las Vegas (www.parislasvegas.com)

ON THE STRIP NEXT TO BALLY'S AND ACROSS from Bellagio, Paris trots out a French Parisian theme in much the same way New York–New York caricatures the Big Apple. Paris has its own 50-story Eiffel Tower (with a restaurant halfway up), and an Arc de Triomphe. Thrown in for good measure are the Champs-Elysées, Parc Monceau, and the Paris Opera House.

Like New York–New York, Paris presents its iconography in a whimsical way, contrasting with the more realistic Venetian or the Forum Shops at Caesars Palace. The casino resides in a parklike setting roughly arrayed around the base of the Eiffel Tower, three legs of which protrude through the roof of the casino. The video-poker schedules are lackluster, but the casino offers all of the usual table games.

Flanking the tower and branching off from the casino are dining and shopping venues designed to re-create Parisian and rural petit-village street scenes. Though spacious, the casino and other public areas at Paris are exceedingly busy, bombarding the senses with color, sound, and activity. While at the Venetian you have the sense of entering a grand space, at Paris the feeling is more of envelopment.

The hotel towers, with almost 3,000 guest rooms, rise in an L shape framing the Eiffel Tower. The rooms are quite stunning, and rank along with the dining as one of Paris's most outstanding features.

Like at the Venetian, the pool complex is on the roof. The facility is spacious but rather plain and underdeveloped in comparison with the rest of the property. One of the better spas and health clubs in Las Vegas connects both to the pool area and to the hotel.

The dining scene at Paris is a work in progress, with the homogenization mandated by the parent company, Harrah's, adversely impacting the quality of Paris's better restaurants. The flagship Eiffel Tower Restaurant is situated 11 stories above the Strip in the, of course, Eiffel Tower. Several other restaurants, closer to the ground, and including the buffet, also feature French cuisine. An Sin, presenting the flavors of the Pacific Rim; the Italian/French Le Provençal; Les Artistes Steakhouse; and what passes for a coffee shop and late-night restaurant round out the dining offerings. This last, called Mon Ami Gabi, serves until 2 a.m. on an outdoor terrace overlooking the Strip.

Back inside, there's the Rue de la Paix shopping venue, not as large or impressive as the Canal Shops or the Forum Shops, but offering exclusive boutique shopping. The showroom hosts Mel Brooks's *The Producers* of Broadway fame. Risqué, with balconies overlooking the Strip, is the happening nightspot. And, of course, if you don't mind a little waiting, you can take an elevator ride to the top of the Eiffel Tower for a knockout view of the Strip.

Planet Hollywood Resort and Casino
(www.aladdincasino.com)

PLANET HOLLYWOOD IS THE LATEST AND BEST INCARNATION of the Aladdin. The Aladdin opened in 1963 as the Tally Ho but was renamed the King's Crown in 1964. In 1966, the King's Crown was purchased by Milton Prell, who gave the property a $3-million face-lift with an Arabian Nights theme and dubbed it the Aladdin. For the next 30 years, the Aladdin changed ownership many times, which resulted in an eclectic, constantly changing identity. Each new owner of the Aladdin tacked on a wing, changed the carpeting, or removed the wall art inherited from the previous owner.

While the Aladdin was choking on its own mixed metaphors, the real estate it occupied became increasingly more valuable. In the late 1990s, the Aladdin was once more acquired and promptly blown up to make way for a brand-new Aladdin, where the exotic Arabian Nights theme could realize its full potential and where there was room for a Middle Eastern bazaar–themed mall to compete with Caesars Forum Shops and the Venetian's Grand Canal Shops. Though the vision of the new Aladdin was executed with flair and imagination, it failed to attract enough patrons to offset the considerable debt. After passing into receivership, the Aladdin was sold in 2003 to Planet Hollywood and Starwood Hotels.

From the beginning, Planet Hollywood, or PH as they bill themselves now, were committed to throwing the exhausted Arabian Nights under the bus in favor of a youthful, upscale, Hollywood look. PH, however, took their own sweet time in making the change and it wasn't until fall of 2007 that the casino and all of the public spaces were completed. Guest room renovations won't be complete for some time.

The new look, clubby and masculine with dark woods and rich textiles, is drop-dead gorgeous. Carpet patterns and stone works capture the feel and beauty of a desert canyon and integrate them into a whole that is both sophisticated and relaxing. Face it, there are dozens of casinos that awe and overwhelm the senses, but only a handful that are artful and soothing.

Placement of the hotel lobby separates quite distinctly the bustle of guests and baggage from the casino, eliminating the flow of almost all transitory traffic in the casino. The casino floor, at almost three acres, offers the usual slots and table games but feels more exclusive. In fact, the whole casino has the ambience of sequestered high-roller gaming areas in other hotels. As for theme, there are some strictly Hollywood touches, but in the public areas it's very much understated.

The new guest rooms are created around a focal object of Hollywood memorabilia and a room-long combination wardrobe and entertainment center with a flat-screen plasma television. The furniture is a little large and plentiful for the size of the room, but the distinctly masculine overall effect is one of luxury and great attention to ergonomic detail.

Planet Hollywood has three showrooms, including the 7,000-seat Theatre for the Performing Arts. An additional two showrooms in the adjoining Miracle Mile Mall (formerly Desert Passage) make PH one of the most happening entertainment venues in Las Vegas. Speaking of the shopping venue, it's owned by a German company. The jury is still out on whether its Middle Eastern Bazaar theme will be replaced by something, well, more Hollywood.

As for the rest, it's a work in progress. Retained from the Aladdin is the highly acclaimed Spice Market Buffet, but the fine-dining options won't become fully realized for about a year. Ditto for nightlife. The PH has a rooftop pool with a less-than-optimal layout, but this too is being redesigned and upgraded.

PH targets an under-50 market from the southwestern United States and is also active in the European, Asian, and Latin American markets.

Plaza (www.plazahotelcasino.com)

THE PLAZA HAS THE DISTINCTION OF BEING THE ONLY hotel in Las Vegas with its own railroad station (though the passenger trains no longer run on this stretch of track). Not too long ago, the hotel was run-down and about what you would expect for a downtown property attached to a train terminal. However, the Plaza renovated its tower rooms and now offers nice but simple accommodations at very good prices. The only downtown hotel to provide on-site tennis, the Plaza also has one of the few downtown Las Vegas showrooms featuring production shows and, periodically, live theater (invariably comedy). The property houses a domed restaurant, Center Stage, with a view straight down the middle of Glitter Gulch and the Fremont Street Experience. The view is the main attraction here, but the food has improved as of late. If you go, reserve a table by the window.

The casino's table-gaming area is dated but pleasant, with a high, dark-green ceiling punctuated by crystal chandeliers. Patrons include downtown walk-ins, attendees of small meetings and conventions, and Southern Californians.

The Plaza is not associated with the Plaza Hotel of New York, which will be building a hotel on the Strip at the site currently occupied by the New Frontier.

Red Rock Casino Resort Spa (www.redrocklasvegas.com)

THE STATION CASINOS CONTINUE THE UPSCALE evolution begun with Green Valley Ranch Resort and Spa, creating a very similar and even tonier property in the Red Rock Casino Resort Spa. Set about ten miles west of the Strip on Charleston Boulevard and isolated from any other property of similar stature, Red Rock attempts to make itself a destination worth the trip. It's an impressive place, with a low, curving, monolithic roofline meant to echo the desert landscape and slopes of the nearby Red Rock Canyon. Inside, the decor and layout represent the continuing Station mission to fuse the "wow" factor with the practical desires of their local fan base. Stone, wood, and glass predominate, more casually attractive and subtle than austere or intimidating; again, forms and colors are often meant to echo the surrounding geography. The overall impression is reminiscent of an accessible, upscale desert spa hotel, as opposed to the more glitzy palaces on the Strip. The casino's arrangement is similar to that of Green Valley Ranch—wide alleys between banks of slots and rings of table games—and the two casinos even share some of the same restaurants. Swarovski crystal is a favorite design element, with the finer restaurants and bars sporting hundreds or even thousands of individual crystals built into light fixtures or chandeliers. Several of the restaurants open onto the pool area, which while not staggeringly huge is quite elegant. Tiers of outdoor lounges and patios look over smaller wading pools and rentable cabanas, plus the inevitable pool bar. As you proceed further through the casino, the feel gets more and more "local"; the entrance on the far end is in fact specifically geared to locals, with close parking on the outside and local-friendly assortments of games right inside the door. This is also where you find the attached movie theater and Kids Quest children's complex, making it convenient to drop off the offspring en route to the casino.

Red Rock Resort takes advantage of its location by offering a number of outdoor adventure programs including guided rock climbing, hiking, and mountain biking outings, among others. The spa at Red Rock Resort can hold its own with any on the Strip, and in variety of treatments and amenities offered, surpasses most.

Rooms and suites are extremely mod in appearance and in amenities, mixing chocolate browns and other earth tones with high-tech gadgetry and high-end appointments. Best of all, however, are the guest-room views. West-facing rooms look out onto Red Rock Canyon while east-facing rooms peer down the valley to the Las Vegas Strip.

Dining at Red Rock Resort is predominantly casual, except for T-Bones Chophouse. Other options include Terra Rossa for Italian cuisine, Salt Lick BBQ, Cabo Mexican Restaurant, Tides Oyster Bar, a top-notch buffet, and several cafes and sandwich shops. In the entertainment department, Cherry Nightclub is the place for wee-hour dancing, while the Onyx Bar, the Lucky Bar, and Rocks Lounge provide stunning settings for a drink.

Finally, for the sedentary there's a 16-screen cinema, and for the more active a 72-lane bowling complex.

Finally, a navigation note. Although Red Rock Resort is located at the W. Charleston Boulevard exit off I-215, it's faster to commute to the Strip and downtown on W. Charleston. Under most circumstances it's about a 25-minute trip to either destination.

Rio (www.harrahs.com)

THE RIO IS ONE OF LAS VEGAS'S GREAT TREASURES. Vibrantly decorated in a Latin American carnival theme, the Rio offers resort luxury at local prices. The guest rooms (all plush one-room suites) offer exceptional views and can be had for the price of a regular room at many other Las Vegas hotels. The combination of view, luxury, and price makes the Rio a great choice for couples on romantic getaways or honeymoons.

On Flamingo Road, three minutes west of the Strip, the Rio also allows easy access to downtown via I-15. The Rio's dining scene is headed by fine dining at Antonio's Italian Ristorante, Buzio's Seafood Restaurant, and Café Martorano, another Italian eatery, this time under the direction of Fort Lauderdale legend Steve Martorano. Unique is Gaylord India Restaurant, the only Indian restaurant located in a casino-hotel. The VooDoo Steakhouse and the more casual All-American Bar Grille are the Rio's chophouses, and the Tilted Kilt, an Irish-American tavern, specializes in pub food. The Rio has two buffets that are perennially at the top of everyone's hit parade. The Carnival World Buffet offers 300 dishes from a dozen cuisines prepared fresh daily, while the Village Seafood Buffet stands alone as the best seafood buffet in Las Vegas.

With five showrooms plus the free *Masquerade in the Sky* pageant and a high-energy stage show in the casino, the Rio's entertainment mix is one of the most varied and extensive in Las Vegas. Long-running shows include the Penn & Teller comedy-magic show; *Tony 'n' Tina's Wedding*, an audience-participation dinner show; and the *Chippendales* beefcake revue. Nightspots include the rooftop VooDoo Lounge, one of the city's most dynamic and enduring clubs; and Lucky Strike, a combination plush bowling alley and a lounge. Factoring in an extensive shopping arcade, a workout room, and an elaborate multipool swimming area, the Rio offers exceptional quality in every respect. Festive and bright without being tacky or overdone, the casino is so large that it's easy to get disoriented.

Masquerade Village—a retail, restaurant, and specialty shopping venue that rings the casino—is home to the *Masquerade in the Sky,* a parade featuring floats and performers suspended from tracks high above the casino floor.

In a phased expansion over the past eight years, the Rio has quadrupled its guest-room inventory, doubled the size of its swimming complex, beefed up its lineup of restaurants, and in the process turned into a true destination resort.

The Rio staff ranks very high in terms of hospitality, warmth, and an eagerness to please. The Rio is one of the few casinos to successfully target both locals and out-of-towners, particularly Southern Californians.

The Ritz-Carlton, Lake Las Vegas
(www.ritzcarlton.com/resorts/lake_las_vegas)

OPENED IN EARLY 2003, this is the first Ritz-Carlton in Nevada. The Mediterranean-themed hotel is set on Lake Las Vegas across from the Hyatt Regency (accessible by boat or gondola). Both hotels are part of the larger Lake Las Vegas hotel-golf-residential-retail development, though the Ritz-Carlton is, of course, on the ritzier side. Geared primarily to golf, spa, and corporate business, this resort area is a pleasant change from the frenetic pace of the Strip. Emphasis is placed on relaxation rather than frenzied activity. The hotel's public spaces are sumptuously comfortable without being intimidatingly ornate (even though a Florentine high tea takes place in the lobby).

The hotel's 349 guest rooms include 35 suites and 64 Club Level concierge rooms. Warm colors, premium fabrics and furnishings, and oversized marble bathrooms meet and exceed the luxurious standards established by the chain at large. A decent percentage of the rooms sport terraces or balconies with views of the lake or pool area. One arm of the hotel, modeled after the Ponte Vecchio bridge in Florence, spans a corner of the lake and does in fact serve as a transit across the water (reaching a future retail development zone). The upper levels of the bridge host the Club Level rooms.

The Spa Vita di Lago offers the full-court press of pampering, including a dizzying array of massages, baths, beauty treatments, and therapies. Private spas and saunas, a state-of-the-art fitness center, and an upscale salon round out the possibilities. Resort packages are available, combining various spa regimens with local touring and excursions, golfing arrangements, or water recreation on the lake. The hotel has a sheltered pool area as well as a sand beach on the lake itself. With 33,000 square feet of reconfigurable meeting space, this property has the most meeting space per guest room of any Ritz-Carlton.

Dining options include the "elegant yet relaxed" (let's not say casual) Medici Café and Terrace, which offers Mediterranean and Italian cuisine for breakfast, lunch, dinner, and Sunday brunch. Health-oriented and "spa" cuisine can also be had poolside or in the spa. The adjacent Monte Lago Village continues the prevalent Florentine theme and decor, with shops and restaurants nestled along cobblestone streets. The Village also features a casino that is modest in size but opulent in appointments, modeled after those found in the French Riviera. Set under an Italianate bell tower and decorated to match its surroundings, the casino has the inevitable slots, plus craps, roulette, blackjack, and mini-baccarat, among other games.

Riviera (www.rivierahotel.com)

EXTENDING FROM THE STRIP HALFWAY TO PARADISE ROAD (and the Las Vegas Convention Center), the Riviera is well positioned to accommodate both leisure and business travelers. Though not isolated, the Riviera provides so much in the way of gambling, entertainment, and amenities that many guests never feel the need to leave the property. The Riviera has more long-running shows (four) than any other hotel in Las Vegas and offers a highly varied entertainment mix. These include a comedy club, a topless revue, a female-impersonator show, and celebrity entertainers and lounge acts.

Guests on the move can choose from a number of fast-food restaurants in the Food Court or go for the Riviera's buffet. More upscale restaurants round out the package and supply ethnic diversity. As for amenities, the Riviera provides a spacious pool and sunbathing area, tennis courts, a shopping arcade, and a wedding chapel. Guest rooms, particularly in the towers, are more comfortable than the public areas suggest.

The casino is large (big enough for guests to get lost in on the way to the restroom) and somewhat of a maze. There is always a lot of noise and light, and a busy, unremitting flurry of activity. Walk-in traffic mixes with convention-goers, retirees on "gambling sprees," and tourists on wholesaler packages. Asians, Asian Americans, and Southern Californians also patronize the Riviera.

Sahara (www.saharavegas.com)

THE SAHARA, SPORTING A MOROCCAN THEME after an extensive reno-vation, is at the far north end of the Strip (toward downtown). A complex of buildings and towers, the Sahara offers a casino, a convention hall, two showrooms, a decent buffet, a shopping arcade, and a swimming pool. The House of Lords restaurant is one of the few remaining old Las Vegas gourmet rooms. Dining there transports you back to the days of the Rat Pack. Fronting the building along the Strip are two attractions worth noting: Cyber Speedway, a virtual reality racecar "ride," and Speed, a roller coaster. The Sahara is a little remote for anyone who wants to walk, but if you have a car or take the Las Vegas Monorail (a station is on-site), it is nicely posi-tioned in relation to the Strip, downtown, and the convention center.

The Sahara is comfortable but not flashy. Guest rooms are modern, and the new casino, with its Moroccan styling, is both tasteful and visually appealing. The Casbar Lounge is one of the most dependable lounges in Las Vegas for great live music. Best of all, there's no cover and no minimum. For the most part, the Sahara caters to businesspeople attending meetings or con-ventions and to leisure travelers from Southern California and the Southwest.

Sam's Town (www.samstownlv.com)

ABOUT 20 MINUTES EAST OF THE STRIP on Boulder Highway, Sam's Town is a long, rambling set of connected buildings with an Old West mining-town motif. In addition to the hotel and casino, there is a bowling alley, a very good buffet, one of Las Vegas's better Mexican eateries, a steak house, a great 1950s-style diner, and two RV parks. The lounge is popular with both locals and visitors and features live country-and-western music and dancing. An events center and an 18-screen movie theater round out the mix.

Other pluses include a free-form pool, a sand volleyball court, and a spa. Joining the "let's be an attraction" movement, Sam's Town offers an atrium featuring plants, trees, footpaths, waterfalls, and even a "mountain." A waterfall in the atrium is the site of a free but very well-done fountains-and-light show (keep your eye on the robotic wolf). Frequent customers, besides the locals, include seniors and cowboys.

Santa Fe Station (www.stationcasinos.com)

SANTA FE STATION IS ABOUT 20 minutes northwest of Las Vegas, just off US 95. Like Sam's Town, the Rio, and the Suncoast, Santa Fe Station targets both locals and tourists. Bright and airy, with a warm southwestern decor, Santa Fe Station is one of the more livable hotel-casinos in Las Vegas.

Santa Fe Station offers a spacious casino with a poker room and sports book. Restaurants include the upscale Charcoal Room steak house, as well as an oyster bar, a Mexican restaurant, Salt Lick BBQ, and Station Casino's signature Feast buffet. The Chrome showroom features an eclectic mix of country and rock headliners, and there is also entertainment in the lounge. In addition to a pool, there is a bowling alley and a movie theater. Guest rooms, also decorated in a southwestern style, are nice and a good value.

Silverton (www.silvertoncasino.com)

SOUTHWEST OF LAS VEGAS AT THE Blue Diamond Road exit off I-15, Silverton opened in 1994 as Boomtown, with a nicely executed Old West mining-town theme. The casino has since removed or replaced much of the mining paraphernalia, however. The Silverton just might be the best-kept secret in Las Vegas. Its newly remodeled guest rooms feature dark hardwood furniture, leather couches, pillow-top mattresses, and tile bathrooms. Thick drapes and good soundproofing insulate the rooms from nearby highway noise. At rack rates of about $50, Silverton hotel rooms are among the best values going.

As concerns dining, the Twin Creeks Steakhouse can hold its own with any chophouse in town, and the 24-hour Sundance Grill, aside from serving excellent food, is a gorgeous room, reminiscent in decor of the celebrity chef restaurants at Bellagio or Mandalay Bay. On the quirky side is the Shady Grove Lounge, with a 1967 Airstream trailer and a couple of bowling lanes worked into the theme. There's also a Mexican restaurant and an excellent buffet. The Silverton Pavilion showroom features celebrity bands and headliners; and good lounge entertainment is a Silverton's tradition.

In 2004, the casino was doubled in size and designed around $5 million worth of freshwater and saltwater aquariums. And speaking of fish, an adjacent retail development includes a 145,000-square-foot Pro Bass Shops Outdoor World megastore with an indoor archery, a putting range, a driving range, and a stuffed specimen of every mammal on Earth. There are whales, dolphins, and game fish dangling from the ceiling, and Earthbound creatures from every continent placed fetchingly around the store. There's probably more dead stuff in the Pro Bass Shop than in many cemeteries. Even if you're not outdoorsy, this veritable natural history museum is worth a visit.

Ten minutes from the Strip, Silverton is in a great position to snag Southern Californians. Silverton also targets the RV crowd with a large, full-service RV park.

South Point (www.southpointcasino.com)

ACQUIRED BY MICHAEL GAUGHAN, THE SOUTH POINT sits almost alone in a huge desert plot off the south end of Las Vegas Boulevard, well away from the Strip. Rising up with nothing of comparable size anywhere nearby, South Point Hotel Casino looks gigantic. This isn't just a trick of perspective, as South Point holds 1,350 large rooms, an 80,000-square-foot casino, two lounges, an enormous bingo auditorium, and a unique equestrian center. The latter, already being touted as one of the better indoor horse facilities in the country, includes a 4,400-seat arena and 1,200 climate-controlled horse stalls. The equestrian center hosts a number of prestigious equestrian events each year. For those without a horse, there's a 64-lane bowling alley, a 600-seat showroom that doubles as a dance club, a spa and fitness center, and a manicured swimming pool complex complete with sand volleyball court. South Point also has a state-of-the-art child-care facility. Restaurants include Michael's, a longtime Las Vegas culinary standard setter, recently relocated from Bill's Gamblin' Hall; the Silverado steakhouse; an Italian bistro; an oyster bar; and a better-than-average buffet.

The decor of public spaces is ostensibly inspired by design accents from Southern California and the Pacific Coast, but the overriding visual theme is lots and lots and lots of yellow—deep golds to light wheats to every other shade in the crayon box. It's attractive and soothing, though not particularly memorable or impressive. Locals and regional guests are much beloved, and the roomy casino floor is a vast, open rectangle designed for their enjoyment. You only need walk along the walls to find the restaurants and lounges; the bowling alley and bingo hall are up an escalator. The South Point rooms are quite large and have nicer-than-average beds, plus a few tech treats like big LCD TVs; otherwise, they're outfitted with standard, generic hotel furnishings and decor.

Stratosphere (www.stratospherehotel.com)

THE STRATOSPHERE TOWER IS THE BRAINCHILD of Vegas World owner Bob Stupak, the quintessential Las Vegas maverick casino owner. Vegas World had been one of the last sole-proprietorship casinos in Las Vegas, but the lack of financing to complete the tower forced Stupak to sell 75% of his company to Lyle Berman and Grand Casinos of Minnesota and Mississippi (not to be confused with Las Vegas's MGM Grand). Stupak's original idea was to attach a tourist attraction (the tower) to Vegas World. Berman, however, ultimately realized that such a juxtaposition would be like locating the Washington Monument next to a Texaco station and insisted that Vegas World be bulldozed. The resort that has risen from the rubble happily combines Stupak's vision with Berman's taste.

The Stratosphere hotel-casino opened on April 30, 1996, and Las Vegas hasn't been the same since. At 1,149 feet, Stratosphere Tower is the tallest building west of the Mississippi—taller than the Eiffel Tower (the real one). It houses indoor and outdoor observation decks, a 360-seat revolving restaurant, and meeting rooms. The 360-degree view is breathtaking day (a life-size relief map of Las Vegas Valley and beyond) and night (the shimmering blaze of a billion bulbs).

Also at the top (hang on to your hats!) are three thrill rides. X Scream is a vacuous ride that essentially lifts the gondola-thingy you're in over the side of the tower and pretends it's going to drop you. A much better ride is Insanity, where you're not only dangled but also spun at speeds approaching three g's. The fourth ride, a gravity-thrill experience called The Big Shot, is a monster: It rockets you straight up the tower's needle with a force of four g's, then drops you back down with no g's. And it all happens, mind you, at 1,100 feet in the air!

Suncoast (www.suncoastcasino.com)

LIKE MOST OF THE COAST CASINOS, SUNCOAST is designed to attract locals. Located west of Las Vegas in Summerlin near some of the area's best golf courses, Suncoast offers high-return slots and video poker, a surprisingly good (for a locals joint) fitness center, 64 lanes of bowling, and a 16-screen movie complex. In the food department, there's a decent buffet as well as restaurants serving Italian, Mexican, and big slabs of meat respectively. The casino is open and uncrowded, rendered in a southwestern Mission style. A 500-seat showroom that features name bands and a pool round out the offerings. For its size (427 rooms/80,000-square-foot casino), the Suncoast offers a pretty amazing array of attractions and amenities. Perhaps the Suncoast's most extraordinary yet unheralded feature is the breathtaking view of the mountains to the west as seen through floor-to-ceiling windows in every guest room. And speaking of mountains, the Suncoast is a perfect location for anyone interested in hiking, rock climbing, mountain biking, or road biking in the nearby canyons and valleys.

Sunset Station (www.sunsetstation.com)

SUNSET STATION OPENED IN JUNE 1997, the fourth Station Casino (after Palace, Boulder, and Texas), just off I-215 in far southeast Las Vegas Valley about a 20-minute drive from the Strip (depending on traffic). Known as the "Henderson high-rise," the 21-story tower presides over a fast-growing residential neighborhood; with 457 rooms, Sunset is large for a locals' casino. It's also one of the classiest, most highly themed and architecturally realized of the Station Casinos, decorated to replicate a Spanish village. The casino's centerpiece is the Gaudí Bar; with its tiled floors and stained-glass ceilings, it reflects the eccentric vision of Barcelona architect Antoni Gaudí.

Station's formula of good food, lounge entertainment and movies, child care, and extra touches prevails. It boasts a steak house; Italian, Mexican, and Mediterranean seafood restaurants; as well as a Hooters, the Feast Buffet, a 24-hour coffee shop, and fast food galore. There's also a Kid's Quest child-care center, the 500-seat Club Madrid lounge, a 13-screen movie theater, and a $26-million bowling center—the most expensive bowling facility in the United States. The extras include a pool and plaza area featuring two sandy volleyball courts, a badminton court, and a 5,000-seat outdoor-concert amphitheater.

All in all, it's worth staying in the slightly oversized and moderately priced rooms at Sunset Station if you're visiting friends and relatives in Henderson or want to be close to Hoover Dam, Lake Mead, or Valley of Fire.

Terrible's (www.terribleherbst.com/casinos)

TERRIBLE'S IS THE PRODUCT OF A WELL-DONE $65 million renovation of the dilapidated old Continental Hotel and Casino. Located a couple of blocks off the Strip at the intersection of Paradise and Flamingo roads, Terrible's offers excellent value with totally refurbished guest rooms, a good buffet, and a casino that's clean, bright, and busy. Terrible, by the way, is a person, Terrible Herbst to be exact. The Herbst family is well known locally for their gas stations and for auto racing. Terrible's targets locals but is a good choice, by virtue of its location and easy parking, for anyone who has a car and intends to use it.

Texas Station (www.texasstation.com)

OWNED BY STATION CASINOS, WHICH ALSO OWNS and operates Palace Station, Sunset Station, Boulder Station, Green Valley Ranch, the two Fiestas, and the new Red Rock Resort, Texas Station has a single-story full-service casino with 91,000 square feet of gaming space, decorated with black carpet sporting cowboy designs such as gold, boots, ropes, revolvers, covered wagons, etc. The atmosphere is contemporary Western, a subtle blend of Texas ranch culture and Spanish architecture. This property offers seven restaurants, one of Las Vegas's better buffets, two bars, a dance hall, a 60-lane bowling center, child-care facilities, and an 18-screen theater showing first-run movies. Also, in the finest Texas tradition, Texas Station has a $40-million ice arena. Texas Station caters to locals and cowboys and is at the intersection of Rancho Drive and Lake Mead Boulevard in North Las Vegas.

THEhotel at Mandalay Bay (www.mandalaybay.com)

LIKE THE FOUR SEASONS AT MANDALAY BAY, THEhotel is another "hotel within a hotel." Situated on the west side of the main casino, THEhotel can be accessed through a connecting corridor or through a dedicated porte cochere. While the Four Seasons is designed to blend with and reinforce the general style of Mandalay Bay, THEhotel, very much a boutique property, offers a starkly contrasting experience. THEhotel is clubby and masculine with rich dark woods, modern furnishings, and a style that mixes empire, Art Deco, and Asian influences. The public areas achieve a feeling of both spaciousness and intimacy, while the suites are cozy in the way of a private library or reading room. Elegant and sophisticated—descriptors often applied indiscriminately—are words that fit THEhotel perfectly.

Though multibedroom suites are available, the standard one-bedroom suite at 725 square feet is the largest of any hotel in Las Vegas. The suites offer a separate sitting room with slate-colored walls and oversized upholstered couch and side chair. These are complemented by a polished-wood contemporary desk and side tables. The overall effect is totally congruent and extremely striking. A large plasma television, a wet bar, and simple yet arresting Asian wall art complete the picture. The bedroom is more conventional with earth-toned soft goods, but includes a dark-colored accent wall behind the bed. The bathrooms, appointed in granite, marble, and chrome, are large with separate glass-enclosed tub and shower. Because THEhotel targets business travelers, all suites are equipped with high-speed Internet connections and a fax/printer/copier.

On the top, 43rd floor of the hotel tower is Mix, offering fine dining and panoramic views of the Strip. Adjoining the restaurant is a lounge. An informal 24-hour restaurant on the ground floor rounds out the dining options. Also on the ground floor is THEbar. One floor up is a full-service spa and a fitness center.

T. I. (www.treasureisland.com)

RECENTLY, TREASURE ISLAND BECAME THE HIPPER T. I. It's one of three mega–casino resorts that opened during the fall of 1993. On the southwest corner of the Strip at Spring Mountain Road next door to the Mirage, T. I. is Caribbean in style. Management thought the original buccaneer theme was juvenile and Disneyesque, and further believed that it was responsible for luring thousands of unwanted families with children to the resort. So down came all the pirate hats, sabers, skulls, crossbones, and all the other grisly skeletal parts that were the, shall we say, backbone of the joint's decor. The new adult version is fine, but a little dull by comparison. The only vestige of the buccaneer days is the streetside battle where pirates now fight very adult, full-bosomed "sirens" instead of the frumpy English Navy. As you would expect, all the cleavage and leg ensures about twice as many kids in the audience as before. Though similar in amenities and services, T. I. targets a younger, more middle-class family clientele than the Mirage.

T. I. is an attraction as well as a hotel and casino. Crossing the Sirens' Cove from the Strip on a plank bridge, guests enter a seaside village. Colorful and detailed, the village (which serves as the main entrance to the hotel and casino) is sandwiched between rocky cliffs and landscaped with palms. Every 90 minutes a pirate ship sails into the harbor and engages the sirens in a raging battle (firing over the heads of tourists on the bridge). Exceptional special effects, pyrotechnics, and a cast of almost two dozen pirates and sirens per show ensure that any Strip traffic not snarled by the Mirage's volcano (next door) will most certainly be stopped dead by T. I.'s battle of the sexes. The pirates are always defeated, of course, but have a lot more fun losing to the sirens than they ever did beating the British.

Passing through the main sally port, you enter the commercial and residential area of the village, with shops, restaurants, and, of course, the casino. The casino continues the old Caribbean theme, with carved panels and whitewashed, beamed ceilings over a black carpet, punctuated with fuchsia, sapphire blue, and emerald green. The overall impression is one of tropical comfort: exciting, but easy on the eye and spirit. In addition to the usual slots and table games, a comfortable sports book is provided.

The main interior passageway leads to a shopping arcade, restaurants, and the buffet. Dining selections include Isla, thought by many to be the best Mexican restaurant in Las Vegas; the Italian bistro Francesco's; Social House, specializing in sushi and sake; Steak House; and Kahunaville, a sort of Parrot Head joint serving Bahamian and Caribbean dishes.

T. I. amenities include a beautifully landscaped swimming area. The Caribbean theme gives way to luxury and practicality in the well-equipped health club and spa. Larger than that of the Mirage, the facility features weight machines, free weights, a variety of aerobic workout equipment, large whirlpools, steam rooms, and saunas.

T. I. is home to Cirque du Soleil's extraordinary *Mystère,* which is performed in a custom-designed 1,500-seat theater. The hottest T. I. nightspot is Tangerine, with an indoor lounge and an outdoor deck where "seductive" barmaids augmented by "burlesque dancers" work the crowd into a hormonal frenzy for the DJ. For the less arousable, there's Kahunaville, a Jimmy Buffet Margaritaville clone, and Mist, a chic, alluring, intimate lounge where the music is usually too loud to permit conversation.

Guest rooms at T. I. are situated in a Y-shaped, coral-colored tower that rises directly behind the pirate village. Decorated in soft, earth-toned colors, the rooms provide a restful retreat from the bustling casino. Additionally, the rooms feature large windows affording a good view of the Strip or (on the east side) of the mountains and sunset. The balconies that are visible in photos of T. I. are strictly decorative and cannot be accessed from the guest rooms. Self-parking is easier at T. I. than at most Strip hotels. Valet parking is fast and efficient. An elevated tram connects T. I. to the Mirage next door.

Tropicana (www.tropicanalv.com)

AT THE SOUTHERN END OF THE STRIP, the Tropicana sits across Las Vegas Boulevard from the Excalibur and opposite MGM Grand on Tropicana Avenue. With its Paradise and Island Towers and 1,910 rooms, the Tropicana is the oldest of the four hotels at the intersection of the Strip and Tropicana. It offers a full range of services and amenities, including an exercise room, meeting and convention space, and a shopping arcade. The Tropicana is also home to one of Las Vegas's most celebrated swimming and sunbathing complexes. This facility, a system of lagoons and grottoes embellished with flowing water, is less a swimming pool than a water park.

The "Trop" was sold in 2007. It's unclear whether the new owner will renovate it or blow it up to make way for a megaresort. In either case, the Tropicana will never be the same. Check it out while you can—there's a lot of Las Vegas history there.

The Tropicana, while it lasts, has four restaurants of merit that specialize, respectively, in steak and prime rib, Italian food, and Japanese teppangrill combinations. Entertainment offerings consist of a comedy club; the *Folies Bergere,* a long-running production show; and lounge acts. The Tropicana's casino is bustling and bright, with multicolored floral carpeting and a stunning, 4,000-square-foot stained-glass canopy over the table games. Both festive and elegant, the Tropicana casino is an attraction in its own right and ranks as one of the city's more pleasant places to gamble, especially for table players.

Guest rooms in the Island Tower are furnished in an exotic, tropical bamboo motif. Guest rooms in the Paradise Tower are more conventional, with bright tropical yellow soft goods and blond furniture. Views from the upper rooms of both towers are among the best in town.

The Tropicana does a thriving business with the travel wholesalers and motor-coach tours, and also aggressively targets the Japanese and Hispanic markets. In the casino, you will find a more youthful than average clientele, including a lot of guests from the nearby Excalibur enjoying the Trop's more luxurious and sophisticated style. The Tropicana's domestic market draws, not unexpectedly, from Southern California. It is particularly popular with slot players.

Tuscany (www.tuscanylasvegas.com)

TUSCANY IS AN ITALIAN-THEMED HOTEL AND casino located on East Flamingo Road between Koval Lane and Paradise Road, just far enough from the Strip to make commuting on foot problematic. After years of railing against low-ceilinged, noisy, claustrophobic casinos and big, hyperthemed, whimsical megaresorts, you'd think the open, sedate, and tasteful Tuscany would be the answer to a travel writer's prayer. Wrong. The Tuscany is none of the things we hate, and at least physically embodies all of the features we admire, but . . . it's B-O-R-I-N-G! Wide aisles in the casino, multiple shades of decorator beige, tasteful carpet, and shiny tile floors (also beige) combine to send you yawning back to your room (more about that in a minute). It's the quietest casino we've ever experienced by far, and there's nothing—repeat, *nothing*—to excite you or even catch your eye.

The casino markets primarily to locals and has succeeded in pleasing them with its choice of slots and good video-poker schedules. Table games, like most everything else, are understated. As for restaurants, there's a nice Italian restaurant in the adjoining hotel, a coffee shop with good 24-hour steak specials, and a Mexican cantina.

Now speaking of the adjoining hotel, it's what saves the Tuscany. A beautiful exposed-beam lobby with an inviting hearth leads to a cozy lounge-showroom and the aforementioned Italian eatery. Guest rooms are large, with a plush sofa and armchair, pine-finish furniture, round dining table with chairs, wet bar, and fridge. The bath offers a separate, glass-door shower, a roomy tub, large vanity, and a private toilet enclosure. The windows are small, which is fine because there's not much of a view. Two framed prints, one of an Italian village, and the other . . . can it be? Yes, the second print is an exact copy of the first! Oh well, who notices wall art in hotel rooms anyway? Hotel parking (easy and conveniently adjoining the various guest-room buildings) coupled with comfy guest rooms make the Tuscany a nice place to stay and an easy place to leave when you want to go somewhere more exciting.

The Venetian (www.venetian.com)

ON THE SITE OF THE FABLED SANDS HOTEL across the Strip from T. I., the Venetian is a gargantuan development constructed in two phases. The first phase, the Venetian, drawing its theme from the plazas, architecture, and canals of Venice, Italy, opened in spring 1999. The second phase, including a 1,000-guest-room tower, opened in the summer of 2003. The Venetian follows the example of New York–New York, Mandalay Bay, Luxor, and Paris Las Vegas in bringing the icons of world travel to Las Vegas.

Visiting the Venetian is like taking a trip back to the artistic, architectural, and commercial center of the world in the 16th century. You cross a 585,000-gallon canal on the steep-pitched Rialto Bridge, shadowed by the Campanile Bell Tower, to enter the Doge's Palace. Inside, reproductions of famous frescoes, framed by 24-karat-gold molding, adorn the 65-foot domed ceiling at the casino entrance. The geometric design of the flat-marble lobby floor provides an M. C. Escher–like optical illusion that gives the sensation of climbing stairs—a unique and thoroughly delightful touch. Behind the front desk is a large illustrated map of the island city, complete with buildings, landmarks, gondolas, and ships. Characters in period costumes from the 12th to 17th centuries roam the public areas, singing opera, performing mime, and jesting.

Although the Venetian claims that its bread-and-butter customers are business travelers and shoppers, it hasn't neglected to include a casino in its product mix. In fact, the Venetian casino, at 116,000 square feet, is larger than that of most Strip competitors. When the Lido Casino came on line with the completion of Phase II, the overall resort topped out at more than 200,000 square feet of casino; the MGM Grand weighs in at 175,000 square feet. The Venetian casino is styled to resemble a Venetian palace with architecture and decor representative of the city's Renaissance era. Period frescoes on recessed ceilings over the table games depict Italian villas and palaces. The huge and stupefyingly ornate casino offers 110 table games and 2,100 slot machines. The perimeter of the casino houses a fast-food court, along with French, Italian, and southwestern restaurants, and what could be the fanciest coffee shop in town.

Upstairs are the Grand Canal Shoppes, with 54 stores, mostly small boutiques. The Escher-like floor design continues throughout the shopping venue, with different colors and shapes providing variations on the theme. The centerpiece of the mall is the quarter-mile Grand Canal itself, enclosed by brick walls and wrought-iron fencing and cobbled with small change. Gondolas ply the waterway, steered and powered by gondoliers who serenade their four passengers ($15 adults, $7.50 children). Passing beneath arched bridges, the canal ends at a colossal reproduction of St. Marks Square. Like The Forum Shops, the Grand Canal Shoppes are arranged beneath a vaulted ceiling painted and lighted to simulate the sky.

The Venetian's 18 restaurants, most designed by well-known chefs, provide a wide range of dining environments and culinary choice. Wolfgang Puck's Postrio, Joachim Splichal's Pinot Brasserie, Emeril Lagasse's Delmonico Steakhouse, the David Burke restaurant for modern American cuisine, Piero Selvaggio's Valentino, Thomas Keller's Bouchon, Tom Moloney's AquaKnox, and Zefferino Belloni's Zefferino are some of the culinary power-hitters represented.

An all-suite hotel, the Venetian offers guest accommodations averaging 700 square feet and divided into sleeping and adjoining sunken living areas. The living-room areas contain adequate space for meetings, work, or entertaining and feature combination fax machines–copiers with dedicated phone lines. The development plan calls for two Y-shaped hotel towers—each with 3,000 suites—that connect directly to the Sands Expo and Convention Center.

The five-pool swimming complex and spa area are situated on the roof-top over the shopping venue and are well insulated from the bustle of the Strip. One of the largest of its kind in the country, the ultra-upscale bilevel Canyon Ranch Spa offers fitness equipment and classes, therapies, and sauna and steam rooms, as well as a 40-foot indoor rock-climbing wall, medical center, beauty salon, and cafe.

The Venetian targets the convention market with its mix of high-end business lodging, power restaurants, unique shopping, and proximity to Sands Expo and Convention Center (with 1.7 million square feet, the Sands has more convention space than the Las Vegas Convention Center). The Venetian will certainly welcome tourists and gamblers, who come mostly on the weekend, but the other five days will be monopolized by the trade-show crowds.

Westin Casuarina (www.starwoodhotels.com/westin)

TALK ABOUT PHOENIX RISING. Westin acquired the old Maxim hotel, a place where business travelers reluctantly stayed when they couldn't get into Bally's, and transformed it into a high-end boutique hotel. Both the casino and showroom are modest by Las Vegas standards, and the guest rooms are exceptionally nice. The Westin caters to business travelers, so each room is equipped with dual-line telephones, a cordless phone, and high-speed Internet access by request. There is ample meeting space for small meetings and conventions. If you travel with Fido, he's welcome at the Westin (they even supply a special dog bed). Travelers with some downtime can enjoy the pool, full-service spa, and fitness center. As for dining, the Westin offers Suede, a 24-hour venue that serves an excellent breakfast buffet. Situated about a block from the heart of the Strip, the Westin is within easy walking distance of dozens of shows and hundreds of restaurants. If you have a car, the Westin has ample parking and is easy to enter and exit. Finally, in case you're interested, a casuarina is a type of tree that is native to the Cayman Islands. If you want to see one, the Cayman Islands is where you'll have to go: there are no casuarina trees at the Casuarina.

Wild Wild West (www.wwwesthotelcasino.com)

LOCATED JUST WEST OF THE STRIP AT Exit 37 off I-15 at Tropicana Avenue, Wild Wild West is a small, 261-room hotel and casino that is convenient to the Strip, downtown, and the airport. Its guest rooms are very basic but clean and comfortable. For east-facing rooms especially, however, there is a lot of road noise from I-15. The casino offers mostly slots and video poker, with a few table games and a sports book thrown in to keep up appearances. There is a lounge, a 24-hour bar and restaurant serving a half-pound burger and fries for $2.69, a pool and Jacuzzi, and in case you're packing a pig, a barbecue pit. The adjacent Wild Wild West Truck Plaza offers over 15 acres of paved and lighted parking, designated drop pads, security patrol, and easy access from I-15. Also available are diesel and unleaded fuel, a truck wash, convenience store, and weigh station. Wild Wild West markets to locals and truckers. Sometime in 2007 or early 2008, the Wild Wild West will be razed to make room for a new Station Casinos flagship hotel.

Wynn Las Vegas (www.wynnlasvegas.com)

TO ENTER THE NEW SIGNATURE WORLD OF Steve Wynn, approach the hotel's sleek, sienna-colored curving facade, a model of restraint in a city known for its design excesses, and look for the Ming lions. Within and without, a garden of delights invites you into the cool sophistication of Wynn Las Vegas. Inside, drift toward the registration desk for a view of the water wall, one of five waterfalls gracing the complex. Along the way you won't be assaulted by the money-charged energy of the casino on the other side of the conservatory, for this is a resort first and a fine casino second. If you must wait to register, take in the stunningly original, arresting floral designs by Paige Dixon. Feasting your eyes on Wynn's personal Matisse, Cezanne, and Picasso paintings that hang behind the backlit amber agate registration counter will soothe your road weariness. Matisse-inspired floral glass mosaics swirl under your feet. Rounding corridors, brightly beaded figurative folk art, quiet French garden photographs, tall sandstone Shivas, peaceful larger-than-life Buddhas, and shimmering Rajastani textiles await you. All this and more even before you reach your room.

With each property he develops on the Las Vegas Strip, Wynn's vision for the ultimate megaresort-casino becomes more sophisticated. Wynn Las Vegas opened in May 2005, and did so without whumping volcanoes, jets of water undulating to Frank Sinatra tunes, or pirate-versus-siren skirmishes. The handsome swoosh of the sunlit-copper glass facade stands in stark contrast to the immediate, raucous fun of traditional Las Vegas hotel-casinos. Up close, the building positively looms, and there's no attraction, no show, no kitsch visible to the passerby from any vantage point. That is the point. This newest megahotel-casino wasn't designed to lure visitors in from the sidewalk. Instead it is internally focused, stylish, and mysterious. It's grown-up, and it's for grown-ups in the best sense of the word.

Wynn Las Vegas is all about exclusivity—and tiers of exclusivity within exclusivity. From the sidewalk, the cards are held tight to the chest. The resort offers nothing but its stark canyon wall of a facade. Step through the main entrance as a visitor, and you're privy to perhaps three of five cards. Guests are shown all five cards, with guest-only pools, spa, golf, and lounges. But to see the dealer's hand, you must be a guest in the exclusive (and pricey) South Tower or Villa Suites, where guests have access to VIP check-in, private elevators, and a separate swimming terrace. (Guests staying in the South Tower will find the baccarat and high-limit gaming rooms conveniently located immediately adjacent to their private elevator bank.)

This appearance of exclusivity is purposeful. WLV was ostensibly designed to bring to mind the exclusive boutique hotels of New York City, but with 2,716 rooms, 233,000 square feet of meeting space, a 110,000-square-foot casino, 76,000 square feet of shopping, an 18-hole golf course, an art gallery, and 22 places to have a meal or whet your whistle, that's one hell of a boutique. The trick, and it's done well, is to create intimate spaces within the larger whole. If Wynn's Bellagio is an ocean with one sweeping vista all the way to the horizon, then Wynn Las Vegas is a mountain river with a delightful surprise and changing view around every twist and turn.

This is also the resort that bears Steve Wynn's name, and the man's flourish of a signature is on absolutely everything—from the building itself to the poker chips to the mini-bar snacks in guest rooms. (If you're a free-souvenir hunter tired of lugging around an armful of bulky slots cups or crushed matchbooks, Wynn Las Vegas is going to make you very happy indeed.) That's not the way it started, though. The original name for the resort was Le Rêve (now the name of WLV's Cirque du Soleil–style show), but it didn't resonate well with the public and was discarded. It took two years of collaboration between a New York design firm and the Wynns to come up with the branding concept, and it includes everything from color palette (warm browns, rusty reds, amber yellow, and the occasional shock of chartreuse green) to typography to the logo and crest. Every detail of the experience at Wynn Las Vegas has been thoughtfully considered, and it shows. Likewise, each detail has been approved by Steve Wynn, whose reach extends from personally testing mattresses for comfort and to designing 18 holes of golf with Tom Fazio so that no tee off faces into the sun. Longtime collaborator and interior designer Roger Thomas was on board here, too, creating with Wynn the immensely comfortable and well-appointed guest rooms.

But don't think that the exclusivity means that tourists and visitors aren't made very welcome at Wynn Las Vegas. Just the opposite. We found the staff to be one of the most courteous and helpful of any major resort on the Strip. The cocktail servers make frequent passes on the casino floor, the front desk and concierge are pleased to answer questions, and the security staff monitoring who goes where is kind and not in the least condescending.

One of the most remarkable aspects of this resort is that entering visitors aren't immediately shunted through a brain-rattling casino cavern, as is typical in most hotel-casinos. This adds to the impression that WLV is a resort first, and a casino second. From both the main entrance, off the Strip, and the south entrance, off Sands Avenue, visitors are welcomed with a spacious, verdant atrium lobby. The ceiling is a high, domed skylight above an elaborate indoor garden where balls of flowers dangle like oversize Christmas ornaments from the branches of trees overhead. In addition to these two main entrances, the South Tower entrance, reserved for guests staying in the Tower, shares a drive with the south entrance.

In the casino proper, just to the left of the lobby, ceilings are raised over aisles and walkways and lowered over the gaming tables, instead of the other way around, as is common in many casino designs. We at the *Unofficial Guide* have lamented for years the suffocating atmosphere in most casinos and are pleased as punch to find a casino that provides gamblers with natural light and room to breathe. Another gaming amenity at WLV is a poolside casino (guests only) where you can work on your tan while you empty your wallet. Of course, there is the usual run of slots and gaming tables in the casino area, a 27-table poker room, sports book, keno, baccarat, and so on. The poker area is just across from the Ferrari/Maserati dealership, should you win really, really big.

The resort is loaded with exclusive brands like Ferrari and nowhere-else-in-Vegas shopping, most positioned along the shopping Esplanade, which begins across the main entrance lobby from the casino. Boutiques include perfumier Jo Malone, couturiers Jean Paul Gaultier and Chanel, Manolo Blahnik for the serious shoe diva, and the requisite Louis Vuitton, Cartier, and many others. Then there are the shops exclusive to WLV: The Gallery Shop, where you can purchase reproductions of artwork from the gallery; Wynn & Company Jewelry; Wynn & Company Watches; Wynn Las Vegas Chocolat; and the Wynn Signature Shop. By all means check out the shopping on the Esplanade, but be aware that unlike the Forum Shops at Caesars, there aren't any retailers here you're likely to find in the mall at home. If you're prepared to drop $500 (and up) for a pair of fabulous heels, this is your place. If you need an extra pair of khakis or flip-flops for the trip, head across the street to the Fashion Show Mall.

There are many upscale options for a drink or a meal at WLV, all under the guidance of executive chef Grant MacPherson. But even at the (comparatively) modest Zoozacrackers, a Reuben sandwich runs $10.95 plus tax. Granted, it was outstanding, but it smarted to part with such a sum for a sandwich. A selection of WLV restaurants are reviewed in the dining chapter of this guide.

"Water features" are an integral part of creating intimate spaces at Wynn Las Vegas. The five different water features are keyed to various viewing areas such as registration, night clubs, and restaurants. For example, grab an outdoor table at Parasol Up/Parasol Down (before you head outside, look up and you'll see where the name comes from) to watch the nightly light-and-water show (age 21 and up only). If you can't make it by in the evening, the lake, with a 150-foot waterfall, is still mesmerizing and worth stopping for during the day. Statues placed in the water to resemble waders gaze thoughtfully at a wall of water at the far end of the lake and impart a meditative (and welcome) sense of peace.

Probably the ultimate WLV water feature is *Le Rêve*. Under the creative direction of Franco Dragone, creator of Cirque du Soleil's watery "O," *Le Rêve* is an aquatic Cirque-style show performed in the round. The claim is that no seat is more than 40 feet from the performance, which may well be true. On the Wynn Las Vegas Web site, the following warning is issued: "You will get wet in rows A through C of every section. In row A you may get soaked."

If *Le Rêve* inspires you to get wet, wade into the dog-bone shaped swimming pool, the long stretch of which will give lap swimmers just about 100 yards for stroking. The water's kept at a constant 82 degrees and the landscaping surrounding you will delight and soothe when you come up for air. The complete spa has massages beginning at $120 and more, and the gym has Cybex equipment with plenty of amenities, such as one of the best free-weight training areas we've seen.

Aim high, if you can, in your choice of rooms, for the elevators are speedy, gentle, and quiet. Your reward will be an exhaling view of the Strip, the golf course, or the mountains through your room's floor-to-ceiling window wall. When it's finally time to rest, you can leave on the gentle glow of the soft lights installed *under* the bathroom vanities—the perfect solution for a kind orientation in the middle of the night.

Unexpected pluses include the self-parking garage that is closer to the guest elevators than valet parking. There's not a large hotel in Las Vegas that matches it for convenience. An unexpected minus was the signature nightclub Tryst, where we found it impossible to get in without proffering a serious bribe to the gatekeepers.

Steve Wynn, who is back to doing what he does best—planning his next grand project—has again definitely raised the bar with WLV. Overall, critics notwithstanding, WLV delivers as promised the innovative touches the city has come to expect from Steve Wynn. It's a resort for the 21st century, and its neighbors are going to have to get busy if they intend to keep up with the Wynns.

NAVIGATING *the* LAND *of the* GIANTS

GRAND HOTELS OF LAS VEGAS are celebrated on television, in film, and, of course, in countless advertisements. These are the prestige properties in a town that counts more hotel rooms than any other city in the world. Located along the center and southern end of the Strip, these hyperthemed mammoths beckon with their glamour and luxury. Specifically we're talking about:

Bellagio	MGM Grand	Planet Hollywood
Caesars Palace	Mirage	THEhotel
Luxor	Monte Carlo	T. I.
Mandalay Bay/	New York–New York	Venetian
Four Seasons	Paris Las Vegas	Wynn Las Vegas

But can so many hotels actually mean less choice? From a certain perspective, the answer is yes. The Strip, you see, is suffering a paroxysm of homogeneity. After you've chosen your preferred icon (Statue of Liberty, Eiffel Tower, pyramid, pirate ship, volcano, etc.), you've done the heavy lifting. Aside from theme, the big new hotels are pretty much the same. First, they're all so large that walking to the self-park garage is like taking a hike. Second, there are high-quality guest rooms in all of the new properties, as well as at Caesars Palace, an older hotel that has kept pace. This is a far cry from ten years ago, say, when only a handful of hotels offered rooms comparable to what you'd find at a garden-variety Hyatt or Marriott. Third, all of the megahotels are distinguished by designer restaurants, each with its big-name chef, that are too expensive for the average guest to afford. Ditto for most of the showrooms.

So let's say you're a person of average means and you want to stay in one of the new, glitzy super-hotels. Location is not important to you as long as it's on the Strip. How do you choose? If you have a clear preference for gondolas over pirate ships, or sphinx over lions, simply select the hotel with the theme that fires your fantasies. If, however, you're pretty much indifferent when it comes to the various themes, make your selection on the basis of price. Using the Internet, your travel agent, and the resources provided in this guide, find the colossus that offers the best deal. Stay there and venture out on foot to check all the other hotels. Believe us, once you're ensconced, having the Empire State Building outside your window instead of a statue of Caesar won't make any difference.

As it happens, there are also a number of livable, but more moderately priced, hotels mixed in among the giants, specifically:

Bally's	Excalibur	Imperial Palace
Bill's Gamblin' Hall	Flamingo	Tropicana
Casino Royale	Harrah's	

Many of these hotels were the prestige addresses of the Strip before the building boom of the past decade. They are still great places, however, and properties where you can afford to eat in the restaurants and enjoy a show. Best of all, they are located right in the heart of the action. It's cool, of course, to come home and say that you stayed at Wynn Las Vegas, but you could camp at the Excalibur for a week for what a Wynn Las Vegas weekend would cost.

SUITE HOTELS

SUITES

THE TERM *SUITE* IN LAS VEGAS covers a broad range of accommodations. The vast majority of suites are studio suites consisting of a larger-than-average room with a conversation area (couch, chair, and coffee table) and a refrigerator added to the usual inventory of basic furnishings. In a one-bedroom suite, the conversation area is normally in a second room separate from the sleeping area. One-bedroom suites are not necessarily larger than studio suites in terms of square footage but are more versatile. Studio and one-bedroom suites are often available in Las Vegas for about the same rate as a standard hotel room.

Larger hotels, with or without casinos, usually offer roomier, more luxurious multiroom suites. Floor plans and rates for these premium suites can be obtained for the asking from the hotel sales and marketing department.

There are some suite hotels that do not have casinos. Patronized primarily by business travelers and nongamblers, these properties offer a quiet alternative to the glitz and frenetic pace of the casino hotels. Because there is no gambling to subsidize operations, however, suites at properties without casinos are usually (but not always) more expensive than suites at hotels with casinos.

While most hotels with casinos offer suites, only the Rio, the Tuscany, Signature at MGM Grand, THEhotel at Mandalay Bay, and the

Venetian are all-suite properties. The basic studio suite is a plush, one-room affair with a wet bar and a sitting area but no kitchen facilities. The Rio, on Flamingo Road just west of the I-15 interchange, sometimes makes its suites available at $110 per night and is one of the best lodging values in town. Suites at the Venetian average about 700 square feet, divided into a sunken living room, an adjacent sleeping area, and a bathroom. The suite configuration at the Venetian is rectangular, while the suites at the Rio and Tuscany are more square in layout. In both cases the sleeping area is open to the living area. THEhotel offers suites with a sitting room and a separate bedroom. At Signature at MGM Grand, you can choose among studio, one-bedroom, and two-bedroom suites. All feature a kitchenette or full kitchen and may offer a private balcony. In addition, Signature is by far the easiest to get in and out of if you have a car.

SUITE HOTELS *without* CASINOS

Alexis Resort and Villas (www.alexispark.com)
THE ALEXIS RESORT IS THE BEST KNOWN of the Las Vegas one- and two-room suite properties. Moderately priced by comparison, the Alexis offers most of the amenities of a large resort hotel, including lovely pools and an exercise room. Suites are upscale and plush, with a southwestern decor. The hotel's staff is extremely friendly and not at all pretentious. Alexis Resort's clientele includes executive-level business travelers and a good number of Southern California young professionals.

AmeriSuites (www.amerisuites.com)
AT PARADISE ROAD AND HARMON AVENUE, AmeriSuites offers tidy, but not luxurious, one-room suites at good prices. In addition to a small fitness center, an outdoor pool, and a few small meeting rooms, the AmeriSuites serves a complimentary breakfast buffet. By taxi, the AmeriSuites is about four minutes from the Strip and five minutes from the Las Vegas Convention Center. A complimentary shuttle is offered.

Atrium Suites (www.atriumsuiteshotel.com)
THE ATRIUM SUITES IS FOUR MINUTES by cab to both the Strip and the Las Vegas Convention Center. There is a pool and a cafe, and a fine selection of ethnic restaurants is within easy striking distance. Suites are mostly of the two-room variety and are nicely, but not luxuriously, appointed.

Best Western Mardi Gras Inn   (www.mardigrasinn.com)
THE MARDI GRAS OFFERS SPARTAN SUITES at good rates. Quiet, with a well-manicured courtyard and a pool, the Mardi Gras is only a short walk from the Las Vegas Convention Center. There is a coffee shop on the property, and a number of good restaurants are less than half a mile away. Though a sign in front of the property advertises a casino, there is only a small collection of slot machines.

Clarion Hotel and Suites Emerald Springs
(www.choicehotels.com)

LOCATED TWO BLOCKS EAST OF THE STRIP on Flamingo Road is the Clarion Hotel and Suites, offering moderately priced one- and two-room suites. Featuring pink stucco, marble, and large fountains both inside and out, the lobby, common areas, and rooms are tranquil and sedate by Las Vegas standards. The Veranda Café is the in-house coffee shop and serves a breakfast buffet. There is a lounge, heated pool, and spa.

Las Vegas Marriott Suites   (www.marriott.com)

WITH AN OUTDOOR POOL AND HOT TUB, a fitness center, a full-service restaurant, and room service, the Marriott Suites offers the amenities you would expect from a Marriott. And the small building and easy access to parking make the Marriott Suites easy to navigate. Suites are tastefully decorated, though not as plush as some Marriott properties. At the southwest corner of Desert Inn and Paradise roads, the Marriott Suites is about a five-minute walk to the convention center and a five-minute cab ride to the Strip.

Residence Inn   (www.residenceinn.com)

ACROSS FROM THE LAS VEGAS CONVENTION CENTER, the Residence Inn by Marriott offers comfortable one- and two-bedroom suites with full kitchens. Patronized primarily by business travelers on extended stays, the Residence Inn provides a more homelike atmosphere than most other suite properties. While there is no restaurant at the hotel, there is an excellent selection within a half-mile radius. Amenities include a pool, hot tubs, and a coin laundry. A second Residence Inn is about a mile away at the Hughes Center.

St. Tropez   (www.sttropezlasvegas.com)

THE ST. TROPEZ OFFERS BEAUTIFULLY DECORATED one- and two-room suites at rates often less than $100 per night. Adjoining a small shopping mall, the St. Tropez provides a heated pool, a fitness center, and a complimentary continental breakfast. The St. Tropez is within five minutes of the Strip and the airport, and about seven minutes from the convention center. Most guests are upscale business and convention travelers.

 # LAS VEGAS MOTELS

BECAUSE THEY MUST COMPETE with the huge hotel-casinos, many Las Vegas motels offer great rates or provide special amenities such as a complimentary breakfast. Like the resorts, motels often have a very specific clientele. La Quinta Inn, for instance, caters to government employees, while the Best Western on Craig Road primarily serves folks visiting Nellis Air Force Base.

For the most part, national motel chains are well represented in Las Vegas. We have included enough chain and independent motels in the following ratings-and-rankings section to give you a sense of how these properties compare with hotel-casinos and all-suite hotels.

Because chain hotels are known entities to most travelers, no descriptions are provided beyond the room-quality ratings and summary charts. After all, a Comfort Inn in Las Vegas is pretty much like a Comfort Inn in Louisville, and we are all aware by now that Motel 6 leaves the light on for you.

HOTEL-CASINOS *and* MOTELS:
Rated and Ranked

WHAT'S IN A ROOM?

EXCEPT FOR CLEANLINESS, state of repair, and decor, most travelers do not pay much attention to hotel rooms. There is, of course, a discernible standard of quality and luxury that differentiates Motel 6 from Holiday Inn, Holiday Inn from Marriott, and so on. In general, however, most hotel guests fail to appreciate that some rooms are better engineered than other rooms.

Contrary to what you might suppose, designing a hotel room is (or should be) a lot more complex than picking a bedspread to match the carpet and drapes. Making the room usable to its occupants is an art, a planning discipline that combines both form and function.

Decor and taste are important, certainly. No one wants to spend several days in a room where the furnishings are dated, garish, or even ugly. But beyond the decor, there are variables that determine how "livable" a hotel room is. In Las Vegas, for example, we have seen some beautifully appointed rooms that are simply not well designed for human habitation. The next time you stay in a hotel, pay attention to the details and design elements of your room. Even more than decor, these are the things that will make you feel comfortable and at home.

ROOM RATINGS

TO SEPARATE PROPERTIES according to the relative quality, tastefulness, state of repair, cleanliness, and size of their standard rooms, we have grouped the hotels and motels into classifications denoted by stars. Star ratings in this guide apply to Las Vegas properties only and do not necessarily correspond to ratings awarded by Mobil, AAA, or other travel critics. Because stars have little relevance when awarded in the absence of commonly recognized standards of comparison, we have tied our ratings to expected levels of quality established by specific American hotel corporations.

Star ratings apply to *room quality only* and describe the property's standard accommodations. For almost all hotels and motels, a "standard accommodation" is a hotel room with either one king bed or two queen beds. In an all-suite property, the standard accommodation is either a studio or one-bedroom suite. Also, in addition to standard accommodations, many hotels offer luxury rooms and special suites, which are not rated in this guide. Star ratings for rooms are assigned without regard to whether a property has a casino, restaurant(s), recreational facilities, entertainment, or other extras.

In addition to stars (which delineate broad categories), we also employ a numerical rating system. Our rating scale is 0 to 100, with 100 as the best possible rating and zero (0) as the worst. Numerical ratings are presented to show the difference we perceive between one property and another. Rooms at the Luxor, Monte Carlo, and Riviera, for instance, are all rated as ★★★½ (three and a half stars). In the supplemental numerical ratings, the Luxor and the Monte Carlo are rated 82 and 81, respectively, while the Riviera is rated 75. This means that within the three-and-a-half-star category, the Luxor and the Monte Carlo are comparable, and both have somewhat nicer rooms than the Riviera.

HOW THE HOTELS COMPARE

HERE IS A COMPARISON of hotel rooms in town. We've focused on room quality only and excluded any consideration of location, services, recreation, or amenities. In some instances, a one- or two-room suite can be had for the same price or less than that of a hotel room.

If you used an earlier edition of this guide, you will notice that many of the ratings and rankings have changed. These changes are occasioned by such positive developments as guest-room renovation, improved maintenance, and improved housekeeping. Failure to properly maintain guest rooms and poor housekeeping affect the ratings negatively. Finally, some ratings change as a result of enlarging our sample size. Because we cannot check every room in a hotel, we inspect a number of randomly chosen rooms. The more rooms we inspect in a particular hotel, the more representative our sample is of the property as a whole. Some of the ratings in this edition have changed as a result of extended sampling.

The guest rooms in many Las Vegas hotels can vary widely in quality. In most hotels the better rooms are situated in high-rise structures known locally as "towers." More modest accommodations, called "garden rooms," are routinely found in one- and two-story outbuildings. It is important to understand that not all rooms in a particular hotel are the same. When you make inquiries or reservations, always define the type of room you are talking about.

Finally, before you begin to shop for a hotel, take a hard look at this letter we received from a couple in Hot Springs, Arkansas:

> We canceled our room reservations to follow the advice in your book [and reserved a hotel room highly ranked by the Unofficial Guide]. We wanted inexpensive, but clean and cheerful. We got inexpensive, but [also] dirty, grim, and depressing. I really felt disappointed in your advice and the room. It was the pits. That was the

How the Hotels Compare in Las Vegas

HOTEL	STAR RATING	ROOM RATING	COST ($ = $50)	LOCATION
Ritz-Carlton Lake Las Vegas	★★★★★	97	$$$$$$	Henderson
THEhotel at Mandalay Bay (all suites)	★★★★★	96	$$$$$+	South Strip
Bellagio	★★★★½	95	$$$$$$$	Mid-Strip
Caesars Palace	★★★★½	95	$$$$	Mid-Strip
Four Seasons at Mandalay Bay	★★★★½	95	$$$$$$$$–	South Strip
JW Marriott Las Vegas	★★★★½	95	$$$$$	Summerlin
Palms (Palms Tower)	★★★★½	95	$$$+	Mid-Strip
Wynn Las Vegas	★★★★½	95	$$$$$–	Mid-Strip
The Venetian	★★★★½	94	$$$$$$$$$	Mid-Strip
Mandalay Bay	★★★★½	92	$$$$$–	South Strip
Paris	★★★★½	91	$$$–	Mid-Strip
Red Rock Resort	★★★★½	91	$$$$$–	Summerlin
Mirage	★★★★½	90	$$$$–	Mid-Strip
MonteLago Village Resort	★★★★½	90	$$$$$–	Henderson
Renaissance Las Vegas	★★★★½	90	$$$$	East of Strip
Flamingo	★★★★	89	$$$$–	Mid-Strip
Palms (Fantasy Tower)	★★★★	89	$$$+	Mid-Strip
Embassy Suites Convention Center	★★★★	88	$$$+	North Strip
Hard Rock Hotel	★★★★	88	$$$$$	East of Strip
Hyatt Regency Lake Las Vegas	★★★★	88	$$$$	Henderson
New York–New York	★★★★	88	$$$+	South Strip
Silverton	★★★★	88	$$	South of Las Vegas
St. Tropez All Suites	★★★★	88	$$–	East of Strip
Green Valley Ranch Resort and Spa	★★★★	87	$$$	Henderson
MGM Grand	★★★★	87	$$$$–	South Strip
Planet Hollywood	★★★★	87	$$$$$	Mid-Strip
Sunset Station	★★★★	87	$+	Henderson
Las Vegas Marriott Suites	★★★★	86	$$$$$–	East of Strip
Residence Inn by Marriott Las Vegas South	★★★★	86	$$$	South Strip
Rio	★★★★	86	$$$–	Mid-Strip
Bally's	★★★★	85	$$$	Mid-Strip
Las Vegas Hilton	★★★★	85	$$$$$–	East of Strip
Harrah's	★★★★	84	$$$$$$$–	Mid-Strip
Treasure Island (T. I.)	★★★★	84	$$$+	Mid-Strip

HOTEL	STAR RATING	ROOM RATING	COST ($ = $50)	LOCATION
Residence Inn by Marriott Paradise Road	★★★★	83	$$$+	East of Strip
Westin Casuarina	★★★★	83	$$$$	Mid-Strip
Hyatt Place	★★★½	82	$$$$	East of Strip
Luxor	★★★½	82	$$+	South Strip
New Frontier (tower rooms)	★★★½	82	$$−	North Strip
Suncoast	★★★½	82	$$−	Summerlin
Emerald Suites Tropicana	★★★½	81	$$−	South Strip
Monte Carlo	★★★½	81	$$$−	South Strip
Palace Station (tower rooms)	★★★½	81	$+	North Strip
South Coast	★★★½	81	$−	South of Las Vegas
Holiday Inn Express	★★★½	80	$$	South Strip
Candlewood Suites	★★★½	79	$$−	East of Strip
Circus Circus (tower rooms)	★★★½	79	$+	North Strip
Courtyard by Marriott Paradise Road	★★★½	79	$$$	East of Strip
Embassy Suites in Las Vegas	★★★½	79	$$$$−	East of Strip
Fitzgeralds	★★★½	79	$	Downtown
Manor Suites	★★★½	79	$$	South of Las Vegas
Sam's Town	★★★½	79	$	Boulder Highway
Stratosphere	★★★½	79	$−	North Strip
Golden Nugget	★★★½	78	$$−	Downtown
Main Street Station	★★★½	78	$$+	Downtown
Royal Resort	★★★½	76	$$	North Strip
Artisan Hotel and Spa	★★★½	75	$$$	North Strip
Atrium Suites Las Vegas	★★★½	75	$$$$	East of Strip
Courtyard by Marriott Las Vegas South	★★★½	75	$$$	South Strip
Fairfield Inn & Suites Las Vegas South	★★★½	75	$$$−	South Strip
New Frontier (garden rooms)	★★★½	75	$$−	North Strip
Orleans	★★★½	75	$+	South Strip
Plaza	★★★½	75	$	Downtown
Riviera	★★★½	75	$$$−	North Strip
Arizona Charlie's Boulder	★★★	74	$$$$	Boulder Highway
Clarion Hotel and Suites	★★★	74	$$	East of Strip
Palace Station (garden rooms)	★★★	74	$+	North Strip
Best Western Mardi Gras Inn	★★★	73	$$+	East of Strip

How the Hotels Compare in Las Vegas (continued

HOTEL	STAR RATING	ROOM RATING	COST ($ = $50)	LOCATION
Bill's Gamblin' Hall and Saloon	★★★	73	$$$−	Mid-Strip
Hooters Casino Hotel	★★★	73	$	South Strip
Imperial Palace	★★★	73	$$$$−	Mid-Strip
Santa Fe Station	★★★	73	$$−	Rancho Drive
Tropicana	★★★	73	$$	South Strip
Tuscany	★★★	73	$$−	East of Strip
Vegas Club (tower rooms)	★★★	73	$+	Downtown
El Cortez	★★★	72	$$	Downtown
Fairfield Inn Las Vegas Airport	★★★	72	$$$−	East of Strip
Fiesta Henderson	★★★	72	$$−	Henderson
Hampton Inn Tropicana	★★★	72	$$+	South Strip
Hilton Garden Inn Las Vegas Strip South	★★★	72	$$$$	South of Las Vegas
Alexis Park Resort and Villas	★★★	71	$$+	East of Strip
Best Western McCarran Inn	★★★	71	$$−	East of Strip
Four Queens	★★★	70	$$−	Downtown
Fremont	★★★	70	$$$$$−	Downtown
Texas Station	★★★	70	$	Rancho Drive Area
La Quinta Las Vegas Airport	★★★	69	$$$−	East of Strip
Sahara	★★★	69	$	North Strip
Comfort Inn Paradise Road	★★★	68	$$+	East of Strip
Boulder Station	★★★	67	$+	Boulder Highway
California	★★★	67	$$−	Downtown
Arizona Charlie's Decatur	★★★	66	$	West Las Vegas

one real piece of information I needed from your book! The room spoiled the holiday for me aside from our touring.

Needless to say, this letter was as unsettling to us as the bad room was to our reader. Our integrity as travel journalists, after all, is based on the quality of the information we provide to our readers. Even with the best of intentions and the most conscientious research, however, we cannot inspect every room in every hotel. What we do, in statistical terms, is take a sample: we check out several rooms selected at random in each hotel and base our ratings and rankings on those rooms. The inspections are conducted anonymously and without the knowledge of the management. Although it would be

HOTEL	STAR RATING	ROOM RATING	COST ($ = $50)	LOCATION
Excalibur	★★★	66	$$–	South Strip
Binion's Gambling Hall and Hotel (east wing)	★★½	64	$	Downtown
Cannery	★★½	64	$$–	North Las Vegas
Casino Royale	★★½	64	$+	Mid-Strip
La Quinta Tropicana	★★½	64	$$	South Strip
Terrible's	★★½	64	$	East of Strip
Fiesta Rancho	★★½	62	$$–	Rancho Drive
Circus Circus (manor rooms)	★★½	59	$	North Strip
Nevada Palace	★★½	59	$	Boulder Highway
Gold Coast	★★½	58	$+	Mid-Strip
Vegas Club (garden rooms)	★★½	58	$+	Downtown
Binion's Gambling Hall and Hotel (west wing)	★★	53	$	Downtown
Days Inn Downtown	★★	53	$	Downtown
Motel 6 Tropicana	★★	53	$	East of Strip
Howard Johnson Airport	★★	52	$–	South Strip
Super 8	★★	52	$+	East of Strip
Wild Wild West	★★	51	$	South Strip
Vagabond Inn	★★	50	$–	North Strip
Ambassador Strip Inn Travelodge	★½	43	$$$+	South Strip
America's Best Value Inn	★	33	$	South Strip
Gold Spike	★	31	$–	Downtown

unusual, it is certainly possible that the rooms we randomly inspect are not representative of the majority of rooms at a particular hotel. Another possibility is that the rooms we inspect in a given hotel are representative but that by bad luck a reader is assigned a room that is inferior. When we rechecked the hotel our reader disliked, we discovered that our rating was correctly representative, but that he and his wife had unfortunately been assigned to one of a small number of threadbare rooms scheduled for renovation.

The key to avoiding disappointment is to snoop around in advance. We recommend that you check out the hotel's Web site before you book. Be forewarned, however, that some hotel chains use the same guest room photo for all hotels in the chain; a specific guest room may not resemble the brochure photo. When you or your travel agent call, ask how old the property is and when your guest room was last renovated. If you arrive and are assigned a room inferior to that which you had been led to expect, demand to be moved to another room deserving of your expectations.

Cost estimates are based on the hotel's published rack rates for standard rooms, averaged between weekday and weekend prices. Each "$" represents $50. Thus a cost symbol of "$$$" means a room (or suite) at that hotel will cost about $150 a night.

THE TOP 30 BEST DEALS IN LAS VEGAS

HAVING LISTED THE NICEST ROOMS in town, let's reorder the list to rank the best combinations of quality and value in a room. As before, the rankings are made without consideration of location or the availability of restaurants, recreational facilities, entertainment, and/or amenities.

A reader recently complained to us that he had booked one of our top-ranked rooms in terms of value and had been very disappointed in the room. We noticed that the room the reader occupied had a quality rating of ★★½. We would remind you that the value ratings are intended to give you some sense of value received for dollars spent. A ★★½ room at $30 may have the same value rating as a ★★★★ room at $85, but that does not mean the rooms will be of comparable quality. Regardless of whether it's a good deal or not, a ★★½ room is still a ★★½ room.

Listed below are the best room buys for the money, regardless of location or star classification, based on averaged rack rates. Note that sometimes a suite can cost less than a hotel room.

WHEN ONLY THE BEST WILL DO

THE TROUBLE WITH PROFILES is that details and distinctions are sacrificed in the interest of brevity and information accessibility. For example, while dozens of properties are listed as having swimming pools, we've made no qualitative discriminations. In the alphabetized profiles, a pool is a pool.

In actuality, of course, though most pools are quite basic and ordinary, a few (Wynn Las Vegas, Mirage, Tropicana, Flamingo, Monte Carlo, MGM Grand, Planet Hollywood, Mandalay Bay, Bellagio, Venetian, JW Marriott Las Vegas, and the Rio) are pretty spectacular. To distinguish the exceptional from the average in a number of categories, we provide a best-of list on pages 142 and 143.

The Top 30 Best Deals in Las Vegas

HOTEL	STAR RATING	ROOM RATING	COST ($ = $50)	LOCATION
1. South Coast	★★★½	81	$–	South of Las Vegas
2. Stratosphere	★★★½	79	$–	North Strip
3. Sam's Town	★★★½	79	$	Boulder Highway
4. Fitzgeralds	★★★½	79	$	Downtown
5. Plaza	★★★½	75	$	Downtown
6. Sunset Station	★★★★	87	$+	Henderson
7. Circus Circus (tower rooms)	★★★½	79	$+	North Strip
8. Hooters Casino Hotel	★★★	73	$	South Strip
9. Sahara	★★★	69	$	North Strip
10. Texas Station	★★★	70	$	Rancho Drive Area
11. Arizona Charlie's Decatur	★★★	66	$	West Las Vegas
12. Palace Station (tower rooms)	★★★½	81	$+	North Strip
13. St. Tropez All Suites	★★★★	88	$$–	East of Strip
14. Palace Station (garden rooms)	★★★	74	$+	North Strip
15. Emerald Suites Tropicana	★★★½	81	$$–	South Strip
16. Silverton	★★★★	88	$$	South of Las Vegas
17. Orleans	★★★½	75	$+	South Strip
18. New Frontier (tower rooms)	★★★½	82	$$–	North Strip
19. Boulder Station	★★★	67	$+	Boulder Highway
20. Circus Circus (manor rooms)	★★½	59	$	North Strip
21. Suncoast	★★★½	82	$$–	Summerlin
22. New Frontier (garden rooms)	★★★½	75	$$–	North Strip
23. Candlewood Suites	★★★½	79	$$–	East of Strip
24. Golden Nugget	★★★½	78	$$–	Downtown
25. Vegas Club (tower rooms)	★★★	73	$+	Downtown
26. Nevada Palace	★★½	59	$	Boulder Highway
27. Paris	★★★★½	91	$$$–	Mid-Strip
28. Manor Suites	★★★½	79	$$	South of Las Vegas
29. Tuscany	★★★	73	$$–	East of Strip
30. Best Western McCarran Inn	★★★	71	$$–	East of Strip

Best Dining (Expense No Issue)

1. Wynn Las Vegas
2. Bellagio
3. Venetian
4. MGM Grand
5. Caesars Palace
6. Mandalay Bay
7. Mirage
8. Paris Las Vegas

Best Dining (For Great Value)

1. Orleans
2. Suncoast
3. Main Street Station
4. Gold Coast
5. Palace Station
6. California
7. Excalibur
8. Fiesta Rancho
9. Boulder Station
10. Sam's Town

Best Sunday Brunches

1. Sterling Brunch, Bally's
2. The Steakhouse at Circus Circus
3. Bellagio Sunday Champagne Brunch
4. Green Valley Ranch Resort and Spa
5. Rio Champagne Brunch

Best Buffets

1. Wynn Buffet
2. Bellagio Buffet
3. Paris Le Village Buffet
4. Planet Hollywood Spice Market Buffet
5. Mirage Cravings Buffet
6. Rio Carnival World
7. Red Rock Feast Buffet
8. Green Valley Ranch Feast Buffet
9. Texas Station Feast Buffet
10. Orleans French Market Buffet

Most Visually Interesting Hotels

1. Venetian
2. Caesars Palace
3. Wynn Las Vegas
4. Bellagio
5. Mandalay Bay
6. Luxor
7. Red Rock Resort
8. Mirage
9. New York–New York
10. Paris Las Vegas
11. Rio
12. Sunset Station
13. Planet Hollywood

Best for Bowling

1. Gold Coast
2. Sam's Town
3. Orleans
4. Santa Fe Station
5. Sunset Station
6. Rio

**Best Spas
(listed alphabetically)**

Bellagio
Caesars Palace
Green Valley Ranch Resort and Spa
Mandalay Bay/THEhotel/ Four Seasons
MGM Grand
Mirage
Monte Carlo
Paris Las Vegas
Red Rock Resort
T. I.
Venetian
Wynn Las Vegas

Best for Golf (listed alphabetically)

Hyatt Regency Lake Las Vegas
JW Marriott Las Vegas
Las Vegas Hilton
MonteLago Village Lake Las Vegas
Ritz-Carlton Lake Las Vegas
Wynn Las Vegas

Best for Tennis (listed alphabetically)

Bally's
Flamingo
JW Marriott Las Vegas
Las Vegas Hilton
Monte Carlo
Riviera

Best for Shopping On-site or within an Eight-minute Walk

1. Caesars Palace
2. Venetian
3. Mirage
4. Wynn Las Vegas
5. T. I.
6. Planet Hollywood
7. New Frontier

Hotel Information Chart

Alexis Park Resort and Villas ★★★
375 E. Harmon Ave.
Las Vegas, NV 89109
☎ 702-796-3300
FAX 702-796-4334
TOLL FREE 800-582-2228

RACK RATE	$$+
ROOM QUALITY	71
LOCATION	East of Strip
DISCOUNTS	Gov't., military
NO. OF ROOMS	495
CHECKOUT TIME	11
NONSMOKING	•
CONCIERGE	•
CONVENTION FACIL.	•
MEETING ROOMS	•
VALET PARKING	•
RV PARK	limited
ROOM SERVICE	•
FREE BREAKFAST	—
FINE DINING/TYPES	Continental
COFFEE SHOP	•
24-HOUR CAFE	—
BUFFET	breakfast
CASINO	—
LOUNGE	•
SHOWROOM	—
GIFTS/DRUGS/NEWS	—
POOL	•
EXERCISE ROOM	•
TENNIS & RACKET	—

Ambassador Strip Inn Travelodge ★½
5075 Koval Lane
Las Vegas, NV 89109
☎ 702-736-3600
FAX 702-736-0726
TOLL FREE 888-844-3131

RACK RATE	$$$+
ROOM QUALITY	43
LOCATION	South Strip
DISCOUNTS	AAA, senior
NO. OF ROOMS	106
CHECKOUT TIME	11
NONSMOKING	•
CONCIERGE	—
CONVENTION FACIL.	—
MEETING ROOMS	—
VALET PARKING	—
RV PARK	•
ROOM SERVICE	—
FREE BREAKFAST	•
FINE DINING/TYPES	—
COFFEE SHOP	—
24-HOUR CAFE	—
BUFFET	•
CASINO	—
LOUNGE	—
SHOWROOM	—
GIFTS/DRUGS/NEWS	—
POOL	• (heated)
EXERCISE ROOM	—
TENNIS & RACKET	—

America's Best Value Inn ★
167 E. Tropicana Ave.
Las Vegas, NV 89109
☎ 702-795-3311
FAX 702-795-7333
TOLL FREE 888-315-2378

RACK RATE	$
ROOM QUALITY	33
LOCATION	South Strip
DISCOUNTS	AAA, AARP, gov't., military, senior
NO. OF ROOMS	256
CHECKOUT TIME	Noon
NONSMOKING	—
CONCIERGE	—
CONVENTION FACIL.	—
MEETING ROOMS	—
VALET PARKING	—
RV PARK	•
ROOM SERVICE	—
FREE BREAKFAST	—
FINE DINING/TYPES	—
COFFEE SHOP	—
24-HOUR CAFE	—
BUFFET	—
CASINO	—
LOUNGE	—
SHOWROOM	—
GIFTS/DRUGS/NEWS	—
POOL	•
EXERCISE ROOM	—
TENNIS & RACKET	—

Atrium Suites Las Vegas ★★★½
4255 S. Paradise Rd.
Las Vegas, NV 89109
☎ 702-369-4400
FAX 702-369-3770
TOLL FREE 800-349-0231

RACK RATE	$$$$
ROOM QUALITY	75
LOCATION	East of Strip
DISCOUNTS	AAA, AARP, gov't., military
NO. OF ROOMS	201
CHECKOUT TIME	Noon
NONSMOKING	•
CONCIERGE	•
CONVENTION FACIL.	•
MEETING ROOMS	•
VALET PARKING	—
RV PARK	—
ROOM SERVICE	•
FREE BREAKFAST	—
FINE DINING/TYPES	American
COFFEE SHOP	—
24-HOUR CAFE	—
BUFFET	—
CASINO	—
LOUNGE	•
SHOWROOM	—
GIFTS/DRUGS/NEWS	—
POOL	•
EXERCISE ROOM	•
TENNIS & RACKET	•

Bally's ★★★★
3645 S. Las Vegas Blvd.
Las Vegas, NV 89109
☎ 702-739-4111; FAX 702-967-4405
TOLL FREE 800-634-3434

RACK RATE	$$$
ROOM QUALITY	85
LOCATION	Mid-Strip
DISCOUNTS	AAA, senior
NO. OF ROOMS	2,814
CHECKOUT TIME	11
NONSMOKING	Floors
CONCIERGE	•
CONVENTION FACIL.	•
MEETING ROOMS	•
VALET PARKING	•
RV PARK	•
ROOM SERVICE	•
FREE BREAKFAST	—
FINE DINING/TYPES	Continental, Steak, Sushi, Italian
COFFEE SHOP	•
24-HOUR CAFE	•
BUFFET	•
CASINO	•
LOUNGE	•
SHOWROOM	Production show, celebrity headliners
GIFTS/DRUGS/NEWS	•
POOL	•
EXERCISE ROOM	Health spa
TENNIS & RACKET	Tennis

Bellagio ★★★★½
3600 S. Las Vegas Blvd.
Las Vegas, NV 89177
☎ 702-693-7444
FAX 702-693-8546
TOLL FREE 888-987-6667

RACK RATE	$$$$$$
ROOM QUALITY	95
LOCATION	Mid-Strip
DISCOUNTS	AAA
NO. OF ROOMS	3,933
CHECKOUT TIME	Noon
NONSMOKING	•
CONCIERGE	•
CONVENTION FACIL.	•
MEETING ROOMS	•
VALET PARKING	•
RV PARK	•
ROOM SERVICE	•
FREE BREAKFAST	—
FINE DINING/TYPES	Continental
COFFEE SHOP	•
24-HOUR CAFE	•
BUFFET	•
CASINO	•
LOUNGE	•
SHOWROOM	Production show
GIFTS/DRUGS/NEWS	•
POOL	•
EXERCISE ROOM	Health spa
TENNIS & RACKET	—

Arizona Charlie's Boulder ★★★
4575 Boulder Hwy.
Las Vegas, NV 89121
☎ 702-951-9000
FAX 702-951-1046
TOLL FREE 800-362-4040

RACK RATE	$$$$
ROOM QUALITY	74
LOCATION	Boulder Highway
DISCOUNTS	AAA, AARP, military
NO. OF ROOMS	301
CHECKOUT TIME	11
NONSMOKING	•
CONCIERGE	•
CONVENTION FACIL.	•
MEETING ROOMS	•
VALET PARKING	—
RV PARK	—
ROOM SERVICE	•
FREE BREAKFAST	—
FINE DINING/TYPES	American, Steak
COFFEE SHOP	—
24-HOUR CAFE	•
BUFFET	•
CASINO	•
LOUNGE	•
SHOWROOM	Live music
GIFTS/DRUGS/NEWS	•
POOL	•
EXERCISE ROOM	—
TENNIS & RACKET	—

Arizona Charlie's Decatur ★★★
740 S. Decatur Blvd.
Las Vegas, NV 89107
☎ 702-258-5200
FAX 702-383-5334
TOLL FREE 800-342-2695

RACK RATE	$
ROOM QUALITY	66
LOCATION	West Las Vegas
DISCOUNTS	AAA, AARP, military
NO. OF ROOMS	258
CHECKOUT TIME	11
NONSMOKING	•
CONCIERGE	—
CONVENTION FACIL.	•
MEETING ROOMS	•
VALET PARKING	•
RV PARK	—
ROOM SERVICE	—
FREE BREAKFAST	—
FINE DINING/TYPES	Chinese, Steak
COFFEE SHOP	•
24-HOUR CAFE	•
BUFFET	•
CASINO	•
LOUNGE	•
SHOWROOM	Local bands
GIFTS/DRUGS/NEWS	•
POOL	• (seasonal)
EXERCISE ROOM	—
TENNIS & RACKET	—

Artisan Hotel and Spa ★★★½
1501 W. Sahara Ave.
Las Vegas, NV 89102
☎ 702-214-4000
FAX 702-733-1571
TOLL FREE 888-315-2378

RACK RATE	$$$
ROOM QUALITY	75
LOCATION	North Strip
DISCOUNTS	—
NO. OF ROOMS	64
CHECKOUT TIME	Noon
NONSMOKING	•
CONCIERGE	•
CONVENTION FACIL.	—
MEETING ROOMS	—
VALET PARKING	—
RV PARK	—
ROOM SERVICE	—
FREE BREAKFAST	—
FINE DINING/TYPES	Italian
COFFEE SHOP	—
24-HOUR CAFE	—
BUFFET	—
CASINO	—
LOUNGE	•
SHOWROOM	—
GIFTS/DRUGS/NEWS	—
POOL	•
EXERCISE ROOM	—
TENNIS & RACKET	—

Best Western Mardi Gras Inn ★★★
3500 Paradise Rd.
Las Vegas, NV 89109
☎ 702-731-2020
FAX 702-731-4005
TOLL FREE 800-634-6501

RACK RATE	$$+
ROOM QUALITY	73
LOCATION	East of Strip
DISCOUNTS	AAA, military, senior
NO. OF ROOMS	314
CHECKOUT TIME	11
NONSMOKING	•
CONCIERGE	—
CONVENTION FACIL.	•
MEETING ROOMS	•
VALET PARKING	—
RV PARK	—
ROOM SERVICE	•
FREE BREAKFAST	—
FINE DINING/TYPES	American
COFFEE SHOP	—
24-HOUR CAFE	•
BUFFET	—
CASINO	slots
LOUNGE	•
SHOWROOM	—
GIFTS/DRUGS/NEWS	•
POOL	•
EXERCISE ROOM	—
TENNIS & RACKET	—

Best Western McCarran Inn ★★★
4970 Paradise Rd.
Las Vegas, NV 89119
☎ 702-798-5530
FAX 702-798-7627
TOLL FREE 800-626-7575

RACK RATE	$$–
ROOM QUALITY	71
LOCATION	East of Strip
DISCOUNTS	Gov't., military, senior
NO. OF ROOMS	100
CHECKOUT TIME	Noon
NONSMOKING	•
CONCIERGE	—
CONVENTION FACIL.	—
MEETING ROOMS	—
VALET PARKING	—
RV PARK	•
ROOM SERVICE	—
FREE BREAKFAST	—
FINE DINING/TYPES	—
COFFEE SHOP	—
24-HOUR CAFE	—
BUFFET	—
CASINO	—
LOUNGE	—
SHOWROOM	—
GIFTS/DRUGS/NEWS	—
POOL	•
EXERCISE ROOM	•
TENNIS & RACKET	—

Bill's Gamblin' Hall and Saloon ★★★
3595 S. Las Vegas Blvd.
Las Vegas, NV 89109
☎ 702-737-2100
FAX 702-894-9954
TOLL FREE 888-BARBARY

RACK RATE	$$$–
ROOM QUALITY	73
LOCATION	Mid-Strip
DISCOUNTS	AAA, AARP
NO. OF ROOMS	1,885
CHECKOUT TIME	Noon
NONSMOKING	•
CONCIERGE	•
CONVENTION FACIL.	—
MEETING ROOMS	—
VALET PARKING	•
RV PARK	—
ROOM SERVICE	—
FREE BREAKFAST	—
FINE DINING/TYPES	Continental
COFFEE SHOP	•
24-HOUR CAFE	•
BUFFET	•
CASINO	•
LOUNGE	•
SHOWROOM	Live music
GIFTS/DRUGS/NEWS	—
POOL	—
EXERCISE ROOM	—
TENNIS & RACKET	—

Hotel Information Chart (continued)

Binion's Gambling Hall and Hotel ★★½/ ★★*
128 E. Fremont St.
Las Vegas, NV 89101
☎ 702-382-1600
FAX 702-384-1574
TOLL FREE 800-937-6537

RACK RATE	$
ROOM QUALITY	64/53*
LOCATION	Downtown
DISCOUNTS	AAA, AARP
NO. OF ROOMS	355/390*
CHECKOUT TIME	Noon
NONSMOKING	
CONCIERGE	—
CONVENTION FACIL.	—
MEETING ROOMS	—
VALET PARKING	•
RV PARK	—
ROOM SERVICE	—
FREE BREAKFAST	—
FINE DINING/TYPES	Steak
COFFEE SHOP	•
24-HOUR CAFE	•
BUFFET	•
CASINO	•
LOUNGE	•
SHOWROOM	—
GIFTS/DRUGS/NEWS	•
POOL	—
EXERCISE ROOM	—
TENNIS & RACKET	—

*east wing/west wing

Casino Royale ★★½
3411 S. Las Vegas Blvd.
Las Vegas, NV 89109
☎ 702-737-3500
FAX 702-650-4743
TOLL FREE 800-854-7666

RACK RATE	$+
ROOM QUALITY	64
LOCATION	Mid-Strip
DISCOUNTS	AAA
NO. OF ROOMS	132
CHECKOUT TIME	Noon
NONSMOKING	•
CONCIERGE	—
CONVENTION FACIL.	—
MEETING ROOMS	—
VALET PARKING	—
RV PARK	•
ROOM SERVICE	—
FREE BREAKFAST	—
FINE DINING/TYPES	American, Italian
COFFEE SHOP	•
24-HOUR CAFE	•
BUFFET	•
CASINO	•
LOUNGE	•
SHOWROOM	—
GIFTS/DRUGS/NEWS	•
POOL	•
EXERCISE ROOM	—
TENNIS & RACKET	—

Boulder Station ★★★
4111 Boulder Hwy.
Las Vegas, NV 89121
☎ 702-432-7777
FAX 702-432-7730
TOLL FREE 800-683-7777

RACK RATE	$+
ROOM QUALITY	67
LOCATION	Boulder Highway
DISCOUNTS	AARP
NO. OF ROOMS	300
CHECKOUT TIME	Noon
NONSMOKING	•
CONCIERGE	•
CONVENTION FACIL.	•
MEETING ROOMS	•
VALET PARKING	•
RV PARK	—
ROOM SERVICE	•
FREE BREAKFAST	—
FINE DINING/TYPES	Steak/Seafood, Italian, Mexican, Chinese
COFFEE SHOP	•
24-HOUR CAFE	•
BUFFET	•
CASINO	•
LOUNGE	•
SHOWROOM	Live music
GIFTS/DRUGS/NEWS	•
POOL	•
EXERCISE ROOM	—
TENNIS & RACKET	—

Circus Circus ★★★½/ ★★½*
2880 S. Las Vegas Blvd.
Las Vegas, NV 89109
☎ 702-734-0410; FAX 702-794-3896
TOLL FREE 800-634-3450

RACK RATE	$+/$*
ROOM QUALITY	79/59*
LOCATION	North Strip
DISCOUNTS	AAA, military, senior
NO. OF ROOMS	3,763
CHECKOUT TIME	11
NONSMOKING	Floors
CONCIERGE	—
CONVENTION FACIL.	•
MEETING ROOMS	•
VALET PARKING	•
RV PARK	•
ROOM SERVICE	•
FREE BREAKFAST	—
FINE DINING/TYPES	Steak, Italian, Mexican
COFFEE SHOP	•
24-HOUR CAFE	•
BUFFET	•
CASINO	•
LOUNGE	•
SHOWROOM	Circus acts, free theme park
GIFTS/DRUGS/NEWS	•
POOL	•
EXERCISE ROOM	—
TENNIS & RACKET	—

*tower rooms/manor rooms

Caesars Palace ★★★★½
3570 S. Las Vegas Blvd.
Las Vegas, NV 89109
☎ 702-731-7110
FAX 702-866-1700
TOLL FREE 800-634-6661

RACK RATE	$$$$
ROOM QUALITY	95
LOCATION	Mid-Strip
DISCOUNTS	AAA, senior
NO. OF ROOMS	3,348
CHECKOUT TIME	11
NONSMOKING	Floors
CONCIERGE	•
CONVENTION FACIL.	•
MEETING ROOMS	•
VALET PARKING	•
RV PARK	—
ROOM SERVICE	•
FREE BREAKFAST	—
FINE DINING/TYPES	Asian, French, Japanese, Italian, Continental, Steak
COFFEE SHOP	•
24-HOUR CAFE	•
BUFFET	•
CASINO	•
LOUNGE	•
SHOWROOM	Celebrity headliner
GIFTS/DRUGS/NEWS	•
POOL	• (heated)
EXERCISE ROOM	Health spa
TENNIS & RACKET	—

Clarion Hotel and Suites ★★★
325 E. Flamingo Rd.
Las Vegas, NV 89109
☎ 702-732-9100
FAX 702-731-9784
TOLL FREE 800-732-7889

RACK RATE	$$
ROOM QUALITY	74
LOCATION	East of Strip
DISCOUNTS	AAA, AARP, gov't., military
NO. OF ROOMS	150
CHECKOUT TIME	Noon
NONSMOKING	Floors
CONCIERGE	•
CONVENTION FACIL.	—
MEETING ROOMS	•
VALET PARKING	—
RV PARK	—
ROOM SERVICE	•
FREE BREAKFAST	—
FINE DINING/TYPES	American
COFFEE SHOP	•
24-HOUR CAFE	—
BUFFET	—
CASINO	—
LOUNGE	•
SHOWROOM	—
GIFTS/DRUGS/NEWS	•
POOL	•
EXERCISE ROOM	•
TENNIS & RACKET	—

California ★★★
12 E. Ogden Ave.
Las Vegas, NV 89101
☎ 702-385-1222
FAX 702-388-2670
TOLL FREE 800-634-6255

RACK RATE	$$–
ROOM QUALITY	67
LOCATION	Downtown
DISCOUNTS	–
NO. OF ROOMS	781
CHECKOUT TIME	Noon
NONSMOKING	–
CONCIERGE	•
CONVENTION FACIL.	–
MEETING ROOMS	•
VALET PARKING	•
RV PARK	•
ROOM SERVICE	•
FREE BREAKFAST	–
FINE DINING/TYPES	Pasta, Seafood, Steak
COFFEE SHOP	•
24-HOUR CAFE	•
BUFFET	•
CASINO	•
LOUNGE	•
SHOWROOM	–
GIFTS/DRUGS/NEWS	•
POOL	•
EXERCISE ROOM	–
TENNIS & RACKET	–

Candlewood Suites ★★★½
4034 S. Paradise Rd.
Las Vegas, NV 89109
☎ 702-836-3660
FAX 702-836-3661
TOLL FREE 800-315-2621

RACK RATE	$$–
ROOM QUALITY	79
LOCATION	East of Strip
DISCOUNTS	AAA, AARP, gov't., military
NO. OF ROOMS	276
CHECKOUT TIME	Noon
NONSMOKING	•
CONCIERGE	–
CONVENTION FACIL.	–
MEETING ROOMS	•
VALET PARKING	–
RV PARK	–
ROOM SERVICE	–
FREE BREAKFAST	–
FINE DINING/TYPES	–
COFFEE SHOP	–
24-HOUR CAFE	–
BUFFET	–
CASINO	–
LOUNGE	–
SHOWROOM	–
GIFTS/DRUGS/NEWS	–
POOL	•
EXERCISE ROOM	•
TENNIS & RACKET	–

Cannery ★★½
2121 E. Craig Rd.
Las Vegas, NV 89032
☎ 702-507-5700
FAX 702-507-5750
TOLL FREE 866-999-4899

RACK RATE	$$–
ROOM QUALITY	64
LOCATION	North Las Vegas
DISCOUNTS	AAA, AARP, gov't.
NO. OF ROOMS	200
CHECKOUT TIME	Noon
NONSMOKING	•
CONCIERGE	–
CONVENTION FACIL.	–
MEETING ROOMS	•
VALET PARKING	•
RV PARK	•
ROOM SERVICE	•
FREE BREAKFAST	–
FINE DINING/TYPES	American, Mexican, Steak
COFFEE SHOP	•
24-HOUR CAFE	•
BUFFET	•
CASINO	•
LOUNGE	•
SHOWROOM	Live music
GIFTS/DRUGS/NEWS	•
POOL	•
EXERCISE ROOM	–
TENNIS & RACKET	–

Comfort Inn Paradise Road ★★★
4350 Paradise Rd.
Las Vegas, NV 89109
☎ 702-938-2000
FAX 702-938-2001
TOLL FREE 866-847-2001

RACK RATE	$$+
ROOM QUALITY	68
LOCATION	East of Strip
DISCOUNTS	AAA, AARP, military, gov't.
NO. OF ROOMS	199
CHECKOUT TIME	Noon
NONSMOKING	•
CONCIERGE	–
CONVENTION FACIL.	–
MEETING ROOMS	•
VALET PARKING	•
RV PARK	–
ROOM SERVICE	–
FREE BREAKFAST	–
FINE DINING/TYPES	–
COFFEE SHOP	–
24-HOUR CAFE	–
BUFFET	–
CASINO	–
LOUNGE	–
SHOWROOM	–
GIFTS/DRUGS/NEWS	–
POOL	•
EXERCISE ROOM	–
TENNIS & RACKET	–

Courtyard by Marriott Las Vegas South ★★★½
5845 Dean Martin Dr.
Las Vegas, NV 89118
☎ 702-895-7519
FAX 702-895-7568
TOLL FREE 800-321-2211

RACK RATE	$$$
ROOM QUALITY	75
LOCATION	South Strip
DISCOUNTS	AAA, gov't., military
NO. OF ROOMS	146
CHECKOUT TIME	Noon
NONSMOKING	•
CONCIERGE	–
CONVENTION FACIL.	–
MEETING ROOMS	•
VALET PARKING	–
RV PARK	•
ROOM SERVICE	–
FREE BREAKFAST	–
FINE DINING/TYPES	American
COFFEE SHOP	–
24-HOUR CAFE	–
BUFFET	•
CASINO	•
LOUNGE	•
SHOWROOM	–
GIFTS/DRUGS/NEWS	–
POOL	•
EXERCISE ROOM	•
TENNIS & RACKET	–

Courtyard by Marriott Paradise Road ★★★½
3275 Paradise Rd.
Las Vegas, NV 89109
☎ 702-791-3600
FAX 702-796-7981
TOLL FREE 800-321-2211

RACK RATE	$$$
ROOM QUALITY	79
LOCATION	East of Strip
DISCOUNTS	AAA, gov't., military, senior
NO. OF ROOMS	149
CHECKOUT TIME	Noon
NONSMOKING	•
CONCIERGE	•
CONVENTION FACIL.	–
MEETING ROOMS	•
VALET PARKING	•
RV PARK	•
ROOM SERVICE	–
FREE BREAKFAST	–
FINE DINING/TYPES	–
COFFEE SHOP	•
24-HOUR CAFE	•
BUFFET	•
CASINO	–
LOUNGE	•
SHOWROOM	–
GIFTS/DRUGS/NEWS	–
POOL	• (heated)
EXERCISE ROOM	•
TENNIS & RACKET	–

Hotel Information Chart (continued)

	Days Inn Downtown ★★	El Cortez ★★★	Embassy Suites Convention Center ★★★★
	707 E. Fremont St.	600 E. Fremont St.	3600 S. Paradise Rd.
	Las Vegas, NV 89101	Las Vegas, NV 89101	Las Vegas, NV 89109
	☎ 702-388-1400	☎ 702-385-5200	☎ 702-893-8002
	FAX 702-388-9622	FAX 702-474-3726	FAX 702-893-0378
	TOLL FREE	TOLL FREE 800-634-6703	TOLL FREE 800-EMBASSY
RACK RATE	$	$$	$$$+
ROOM QUALITY	53	72	88
LOCATION	Downtown	Downtown	North Strip
DISCOUNTS	Gov't., military, senior	—	AAA, gov't., senior
NO. OF ROOMS	147	300	286
CHECKOUT TIME	Noon	Noon	Noon
NONSMOKING	•	•	•
CONCIERGE	—	•	—
CONVENTION FACIL.	—	•	•
MEETING ROOMS	—	•	•
VALET PARKING	—	•	—
RV PARK	•	•	•
ROOM SERVICE	•	•	•
FREE BREAKFAST	—	—	•
FINE DINING/TYPES	American	Family/Steak, Chinese	American
COFFEE SHOP	—	•	—
24-HOUR CAFE	—	•	—
BUFFET	—	•	—
CASINO	—	•	—
LOUNGE	•	•	•
SHOWROOM	—	—	—
GIFTS/DRUGS/NEWS	—	•	•
POOL	•	—	•
EXERCISE ROOM	—	—	•
TENNIS & RACKET	—	—	—

	Fairfield Inn & Suites Las Vegas South ★★★½	Fairfield Inn Las Vegas Airport ★★★	Fiesta Henderson ★★★
	5775 Dean Martin Dr.	3850 Paradise Rd.	777 W. Lake Mead Pkwy.
	Las Vegas, NV 89118	Las Vegas, NV 89109	Henderson, NV 89015
	☎ 702-895-9810	☎ 702-791-0899	☎ 702-558-7777
	FAX 702-895-9310	FAX 702-791-2705	FAX 702-567-7373
	TOLL FREE 800-228-2800	TOLL FREE 800-228-2800	TOLL FREE 800-844-9593
RACK RATE	$$$−	$$$−	$$−
ROOM QUALITY	75	72	72
LOCATION	South Strip	East of Strip	Henderson
DISCOUNTS	AAA, AARP, gov't., military	AAA, gov't., military	—
NO. OF ROOMS	142	129	224
CHECKOUT TIME	Noon	Noon	Noon
NONSMOKING	•	•	Floors
CONCIERGE	—	—	•
CONVENTION FACIL.	—	—	—
MEETING ROOMS	•	•	—
VALET PARKING	•	•	•
RV PARK	•	—	—
ROOM SERVICE	•	—	—
FREE BREAKFAST	•	•	—
FINE DINING/TYPES	•	•	Italian, Steak, Mexican
COFFEE SHOP	—	—	•
24-HOUR CAFE	—	—	•
BUFFET	—	—	•
CASINO	—	—	•
LOUNGE	—	—	•
SHOWROOM	—	—	Live music
GIFTS/DRUGS/NEWS	—	—	•
POOL	•	•	•
EXERCISE ROOM	•	•	—
TENNIS & RACKET	—	—	—

Embassy Suites in Las Vegas ★★★½
4315 Swenson St.
Las Vegas, NV 89119
☎ 702-795-2800
FAX 702-795-1520
TOLL FREE 800-EMBASSY

RACK RATE	$$$$–
ROOM QUALITY	79
LOCATION	East of Strip
DISCOUNTS	AAA, gov't., senior
NO. OF ROOMS	220
CHECKOUT TIME	Noon
NONSMOKING	•
CONCIERGE	•
CONVENTION FACIL.	•
MEETING ROOMS	•
VALET PARKING	—
RV PARK	—
ROOM SERVICE	•
FREE BREAKFAST	•
FINE DINING/TYPES	American
COFFEE SHOP	—
24-HOUR CAFE	—
BUFFET	—
CASINO	—
LOUNGE	—
SHOWROOM	—
GIFTS/DRUGS/NEWS	•
POOL	•
EXERCISE ROOM	•
TENNIS & RACKET	—

Emerald Suites Tropicana ★★★½
3890 Graphic Center Dr.
Las Vegas, NV 89118
☎ 702-507-9999
FAX 702-507-9998
TOLL FREE 800-847-2002

RACK RATE	$$–
ROOM QUALITY	81
LOCATION	South Strip
DISCOUNTS	AAA, gov't., military, senior
NO. OF ROOMS	225
CHECKOUT TIME	Noon
NONSMOKING	—
CONCIERGE	—
CONVENTION FACIL.	—
MEETING ROOMS	—
VALET PARKING	—
RV PARK	—
ROOM SERVICE	—
FREE BREAKFAST	—
FINE DINING/TYPES	—
COFFEE SHOP	—
24-HOUR CAFE	—
BUFFET	—
CASINO	—
LOUNGE	—
SHOWROOM	—
GIFTS/DRUGS/NEWS	—
POOL	•
EXERCISE ROOM	•
TENNIS & RACKET	—

Excalibur ★★★
3850 Las Vegas Blvd. S.; Las Vegas, NV
89109 ☎ 702-597-7777; FAX 702-
597-7163; TOLL FREE 800-937-7777

RACK RATE	$$–
ROOM QUALITY	66
LOCATION	South Strip
DISCOUNTS	AAA, AARP, military
NO. OF ROOMS	4,008
CHECKOUT TIME	11
NONSMOKING	Floors
CONCIERGE	—
CONVENTION FACIL.	•
MEETING ROOMS	•
VALET PARKING	•
RV PARK	•
ROOM SERVICE	•
FREE BREAKFAST	—
FINE DINING/TYPES	Continental, Italian, Prime Rib, Steak
COFFEE SHOP	•
24-HOUR CAFE	•
BUFFET	•
CASINO	•
LOUNGE	•
SHOWROOM	Production show, King Arthur's Tournament
GIFTS/DRUGS/NEWS	•
POOL	• (heated)
EXERCISE ROOM	•
TENNIS & RACKET	—

Fiesta Rancho ★★½
2400 N. Rancho Dr.
Las Vegas, NV 89130
☎ 702-631-7000
FAX 702-638-3605
TOLL FREE 800-731-7333

RACK RATE	$$–
ROOM QUALITY	62
LOCATION	Rancho Drive
DISCOUNTS	AAA
NO. OF ROOMS	100
CHECKOUT TIME	Noon
NONSMOKING	•
CONCIERGE	—
CONVENTION FACIL.	—
MEETING ROOMS	•
VALET PARKING	•
RV PARK	—
ROOM SERVICE	—
FREE BREAKFAST	—
FINE DINING/TYPES	Mexican, Seafood, Italian, Steak, Chinese
COFFEE SHOP	•
24-HOUR CAFE	•
BUFFET	•
CASINO	•
LOUNGE	•
SHOWROOM	—
GIFTS/DRUGS/NEWS	•
POOL	• (heated)
EXERCISE ROOM	—
TENNIS & RACKET	—

Fitzgeralds ★★★½
301 Fremont St.
Las Vegas, NV 89101
☎ 702-388-2400
FAX 702-388-2181
TOLL FREE 800-274-LUCK

RACK RATE	$
ROOM QUALITY	79
LOCATION	Downtown
DISCOUNTS	AAA, senior
NO. OF ROOMS	638
CHECKOUT TIME	Noon
NONSMOKING	Floors
CONCIERGE	—
CONVENTION FACIL.	•
MEETING ROOMS	—
VALET PARKING	•
RV PARK	—
ROOM SERVICE	—
FREE BREAKFAST	—
FINE DINING/TYPES	Steak, American, International
COFFEE SHOP	•
24-HOUR CAFE	•
BUFFET	•
CASINO	•
LOUNGE	•
SHOWROOM	•
GIFTS/DRUGS/NEWS	•
POOL	•
EXERCISE ROOM	—
TENNIS & RACKET	—

Flamingo ★★★★
3555 S. Las Vegas Blvd.
Las Vegas, NV 89109
☎ 702-733-3111; FAX 702-733-3353
TOLL FREE 800-732-2111

RACK RATE	$$$$–
ROOM QUALITY	89
LOCATION	Mid-Strip
DISCOUNTS	AAA, AARP
NO. OF ROOMS	3,642
CHECKOUT TIME	Noon
NONSMOKING	Floors/ part of casino
CONCIERGE	—
CONVENTION FACIL.	•
MEETING ROOMS	•
VALET PARKING	•
RV PARK	•
ROOM SERVICE	•
FREE BREAKFAST	—
FINE DINING/TYPES	Italian, Asian, Seafood, Continental
COFFEE SHOP	•
24-HOUR CAFE	•
BUFFET	•
CASINO	•
LOUNGE	•
SHOWROOM	Production show, musical comedy
GIFTS/DRUGS/NEWS	•
POOL	• (heated)
EXERCISE ROOM	Health spa
TENNIS & RACKET	Tennis

Hotel Information Chart *(continued)*

	Four Queens ★★★	Four Seasons at Mandalay Bay ★★★★½	Fremont ★★★
	202 Fremont St.	3960 S. Las Vegas Blvd.	200 E. Fremont St.
	Las Vegas, NV 89101	Las Vegas, NV 89119	Las Vegas, NV 89101
	☎ 702-385-4011	☎ 702-632-5000	☎ 702-385-3232
	FAX 702-387-5133	FAX 702-632-5195	FAX 702-388-2660
	TOLL FREE 800-634-6045	TOLL FREE 877-632-5000	TOLL FREE 800-634-6182
RACK RATE	$$–	$$$$$$$$–	$$$$$–
ROOM QUALITY	70	95	70
LOCATION	Downtown	South Strip	Downtown
DISCOUNTS	Senior	—	—
NO. OF ROOMS	690	424	447
CHECKOUT TIME	Noon	Noon	Noon
NONSMOKING	Floors	•	•
CONCIERGE	—	•	•
CONVENTION FACIL.	—	•	•
MEETING ROOMS	•	•	•
VALET PARKING	•	•	•
RV PARK	—	—	—
ROOM SERVICE	—	•	•
FREE BREAKFAST	—	•	—
FINE DINING/TYPES	American	American, Continental	Ribs, Chinese, American, Pacific Rim
COFFEE SHOP	•	—	•
24-HOUR CAFE	•	—	•
BUFFET	—	•	•
CASINO	•	•	•
LOUNGE	•	—	•
SHOWROOM	•	—	Headliners, Wayne Newton
GIFTS/DRUGS/NEWS	•	•	•
POOL	—	• (heated)	—
EXERCISE ROOM	—	Health and fitness spa	—
TENNIS & RACKET	—	—	—

	Green Valley Ranch Resort and Spa ★★★★	Hampton Inn Tropicana ★★★	Hard Rock Hotel ★★★★
	2300 Paseo Dr.	4975 S. Dean Martin Dr.	4455 Paradise Rd.
	Henderson, NV 89012	Las Vegas, NV 89118	Las Vegas, NV 89109
	☎ 702-617-7777	☎ 702-948-8100	☎ 702-693-5000
	FAX 702-617-7778	FAX 702-948-8101	FAX 702-693-5021
	TOLL FREE 866-782-9487	TOLL FREE 800-426-7866	TOLL FREE 800-HRD-ROCK
RACK RATE	$$$	$$+	$$$$$
ROOM QUALITY	87	72	88
LOCATION	Henderson	South Strip	East of Strip
DISCOUNTS	—	AAA, corp.	—
NO. OF ROOMS	490	320	645
CHECKOUT TIME	Noon	Noon	11
NONSMOKING	•	•	Floors
CONCIERGE	•	—	•
CONVENTION FACIL.	•	•	•
MEETING ROOMS	•	•	•
VALET PARKING	•	•	•
RV PARK	—	—	—
ROOM SERVICE	•	—	•
FREE BREAKFAST	•	•	—
FINE DINING/TYPES	Irish, Italian, Steak, Seafood, American, Asian	—	Steak, Japanese, Continental, Mexican
COFFEE SHOP	•	—	•
24-HOUR CAFE	•	—	•
BUFFET	•	—	•
CASINO	•	—	•
LOUNGE	•	—	•
SHOWROOM	Headliners	—	Live music
GIFTS/DRUGS/NEWS	•	•	•
POOL	• (heated)	•	• (heated)
EXERCISE ROOM	•	•	Health spa
TENNIS & RACKET	—	—	—

Gold Coast ★★½				Gold Spike ★				Golden Nugget ★★★½	
4000 W. Flamingo Rd.				400 E. Ogden Ave.				129 E. Fremont St.	
Las Vegas, NV 89103				Las Vegas, NV 89101				Las Vegas, NV 89101	
☎ 702-367-7111				☎ 702-384-8444				☎ 702-385-7111	
FAX 702-367-8575				FAX 702-382-5242				FAX 702-386-8244	
TOLL FREE 888-402-6278				TOLL FREE 877-467-7453				TOLL FREE 800-634-3454	
RACK RATE	$+		RACK RATE	$−		RACK RATE	$$−	
ROOM QUALITY	58		ROOM QUALITY	31		ROOM QUALITY	78	
LOCATION	Mid-Strip		LOCATION	Downtown		LOCATION	Downtown	
DISCOUNTS	AAA, senior		DISCOUNTS	−		DISCOUNTS	AAA	
NO. OF ROOMS	711		NO. OF ROOMS	110		NO. OF ROOMS	1,907	
CHECKOUT TIME	Noon		CHECKOUT TIME	Noon		CHECKOUT TIME	Noon	
NONSMOKING	Floors		NONSMOKING	•		NONSMOKING	Floors	
CONCIERGE	−		CONCIERGE	−		CONCIERGE	•	
CONVENTION FACIL.	•		CONVENTION FACIL.	−		CONVENTION FACIL.	•	
MEETING ROOMS	•		MEETING ROOMS	−		MEETING ROOMS	•	
VALET PARKING	•		VALET PARKING	−		VALET PARKING	•	
RV PARK	−		RV PARK	−		RV PARK	−	
ROOM SERVICE	•		ROOM SERVICE	−		ROOM SERVICE	•	
FREE BREAKFAST	−		FREE BREAKFAST	−		FREE BREAKFAST	−	
FINE DINING/TYPES	Steak, Italian, Seafood, Chinese		FINE DINING/TYPES	American		FINE DINING/TYPES	Italian, Chinese, Continental, Steak	
COFFEE SHOP	•		COFFEE SHOP	−		COFFEE SHOP	•	
24-HOUR CAFE	−		24-HOUR CAFE	•		24-HOUR CAFE	−	
BUFFET	•		BUFFET	−		BUFFET	•	
CASINO	•		CASINO	•		CASINO	•	
LOUNGE	•		LOUNGE	•		LOUNGE	•	
SHOWROOM	Dancing		SHOWROOM	−		SHOWROOM	Visiting headliners	
GIFTS/DRUGS/NEWS	•		GIFTS/DRUGS/NEWS	−		GIFTS/DRUGS/NEWS	•	
POOL	• (heated)		POOL	−		POOL	−	
EXERCISE ROOM	•		EXERCISE ROOM	−		EXERCISE ROOM	•	
TENNIS & RACKET	−		TENNIS & RACKET	−		TENNIS & RACKET	−	

Harrah's ★★★★				Hilton Garden Inn Las Vegas Strip South ★★★				Holiday Inn Express ★★★½	
3475 S. Las Vegas Blvd.; Las Vegas, NV				7830 S. Las Vegas Blvd.				5760 Polaris Ave.	
89109; ☎ 702-369-5000				Las Vegas, NV 89123				Las Vegas, NV 89118	
FAX 702-369-5008				☎ 702-942-8403				☎ 702-736-0098	
TOLL FREE 800-HARRAHS				FAX 702-453-7850				FAX 702-736-0084	
				TOLL FREE 877-STAY-HGI				TOLL FREE 800-288-4595	
RACK RATE	$$$$$$$$−		RACK RATE	$$$$		RACK RATE	$$	
ROOM QUALITY	84		ROOM QUALITY	72		ROOM QUALITY	80	
LOCATION	Mid-Strip		LOCATION	South of Las Vegas		LOCATION	South Strip	
DISCOUNTS	AAA, corp., senior		DISCOUNTS	AAA, corp., senior		DISCOUNTS	AAA, AARP, corp., gov't.	
NO. OF ROOMS	2,579		NO. OF ROOMS	128		NO. OF ROOMS	360	
CHECKOUT TIME	11		CHECKOUT TIME	Noon		CHECKOUT TIME	Noon	
NONSMOKING	Floors/part of casino		NONSMOKING	•		NONSMOKING	•	
			CONCIERGE	−		CONCIERGE	−	
CONCIERGE	•		CONVENTION FACIL.	−		CONVENTION FACIL.	−	
CONVENTION FACIL.	•		MEETING ROOMS	•		MEETING ROOMS	•	
MEETING ROOMS	•		VALET PARKING	•		VALET PARKING	−	
VALET PARKING	•		RV PARK	−		RV PARK	−	
RV PARK	−		ROOM SERVICE	•		ROOM SERVICE	−	
ROOM SERVICE	•		FREE BREAKFAST	−		FREE BREAKFAST	•	
FREE BREAKFAST	−		FINE DINING/TYPES	American		FINE DINING/TYPES	−	
FINE DINING/TYPES	Steak/Seafood, Italian, Asian, American		COFFEE SHOP	−		COFFEE SHOP	−	
			24-HOUR CAFE	−		24-HOUR CAFE	−	
COFFEE SHOP	•		BUFFET	•		BUFFET	−	
24-HOUR CAFE	•		CASINO	−		CASINO	−	
BUFFET	•		LOUNGE	•		LOUNGE	−	
CASINO	•		SHOWROOM	−		SHOWROOM	−	
LOUNGE	•		GIFTS/DRUGS/NEWS	•		GIFTS/DRUGS/NEWS	−	
SHOWROOM	Production show, comedy show, magic show		POOL	•		POOL	•	
			EXERCISE ROOM	•		EXERCISE ROOM	•	
GIFTS/DRUGS/NEWS	•		TENNIS & RACKET	−		TENNIS & RACKET	−	
POOL	•							
EXERCISE ROOM	Health spa							
TENNIS & RACKET	−							

Hotel Information Chart (continued)

	Hooters Casino Hotel ★★★	Howard Johnson Airport ★★	Hyatt Place ★★★½
	115 E. Tropicana Ave.	5100 Paradise Rd.	4520 Paradise Rd.
	Las Vegas, NV 89109	Las Vegas, NV 89119	Las Vegas, NV 89109
	☎ 702-739-9000	☎ 702-798-2777	☎ 702-369-3366
	FAX 702-736-1120	FAX 702-736-8295	FAX 702-369-0009
	TOLL FREE 866-LV-HOOTS	TOLL FREE 800-634-6439	TOLL FREE 888-444-0611
RACK RATE	$	$–	$$$$
ROOM QUALITY	73	52	82
LOCATION	South Strip	South Strip	East of Strip
DISCOUNTS	AAA, gov't., military	AAA, gov't., senior	AAA, gov't., military, senior
NO. OF ROOMS	713	325	202
CHECKOUT TIME	Noon	Noon	11
NONSMOKING	Floors		Floors
CONCIERGE	•	–	–
CONVENTION FACIL.	•	–	–
MEETING ROOMS	•	•	•
VALET PARKING	•	–	•
RV PARK	–	–	•
ROOM SERVICE	•	–	•
FREE BREAKFAST		coffee	•
FINE DINING/TYPES	American, Steak/Seafood, Wings	Deli	–
COFFEE SHOP	•	•	–
24-HOUR CAFE	•	•	–
BUFFET	–	•	–
CASINO	•	slots	–
LOUNGE	•	•	–
SHOWROOM	•	•	–
GIFTS/DRUGS/NEWS	•	•	–
POOL	• (heated)	•	•
EXERCISE ROOM	•	•	•
TENNIS & RACKET	–	–	–

	La Quinta Las Vegas Airport ★★★	La Quinta Tropicana ★★½	Las Vegas Hilton ★★★★
	3970 Paradise Rd.	4975 S. Valley View Blvd.	3000 Paradise Rd.
	Las Vegas, NV 89109	Las Vegas, NV 89118	Las Vegas, NV 89109
	☎ 702-796-9000	☎ 702-798-7736	☎ 702-732-5111
	FAX 702-796-3537	FAX 702-798-5951	FAX 702-262-5089
	TOLL FREE 800-NU-ROOMS	TOLL FREE 800-531-5900	TOLL FREE 888-732-7117
RACK RATE	$$$–	$$	$$$$$–
ROOM QUALITY	69	64	85
LOCATION	East of Strip	South Strip	East of Strip
DISCOUNTS	AAA, AARP, corp., gov't., senior	AAA, AARP, corp., gov't., senior	AAA, AARP, gov't., military, senior
NO. OF ROOMS	251	59	3,174
CHECKOUT TIME	Noon	Noon	Noon
NONSMOKING	•	•	•
CONCIERGE	–	–	•
CONVENTION FACIL.	–	–	•
MEETING ROOMS	•	•	•
VALET PARKING	•	–	•
RV PARK	–	–	–
ROOM SERVICE	–	–	•
FREE BREAKFAST	•	•	–
FINE DINING/TYPES	American	–	Steak, Asian, Mexican, Italian, Deli
COFFEE SHOP	–	–	•
24-HOUR CAFE	–	–	•
BUFFET	–	–	•
CASINO	–	–	•
LOUNGE	–	–	–
SHOWROOM	–	–	Production show
GIFTS/DRUGS/NEWS	–	–	•
POOL	• (heated)	• (heated)	• (heated)
EXERCISE ROOM	•	•	Health spa
TENNIS & RACKET	–	–	Tennis

Hyatt Regency Lake Las Vegas ★★★★
101 MonteLago Blvd.
Henderson, NV 89011
☎ 702-567-1234; FAX 702-567-6067
TOLL FREE 800-55-HYATT

RACK RATE	$$$$
ROOM QUALITY	88
LOCATION	Henderson
DISCOUNTS	AAA, corp., gov't., senior
NO. OF ROOMS	496
CHECKOUT TIME	Noon
NONSMOKING	•
CONCIERGE	•
CONVENTION FACIL.	•
MEETING ROOMS	•
VALET PARKING	•
RV PARK	–
ROOM SERVICE	•
FREE BREAKFAST	–
FINE DINING/TYPES	American, Pacific, Mediterranean
COFFEE SHOP	•
24-HOUR CAFE	–
BUFFET	–
CASINO	–
LOUNGE	•
SHOWROOM	–
GIFTS/DRUGS/NEWS	•
POOL	•
EXERCISE ROOM	•
TENNIS & RACKET	•

Imperial Palace ★★★
3535 S. Las Vegas Blvd.
Las Vegas, NV 89109
☎ 702-731-3311; FAX 702-735-8578
TOLL FREE 800-634-6441

RACK RATE	$$$$–
ROOM QUALITY	73
LOCATION	Mid-Strip
DISCOUNTS	Gov't., military, senior
NO. OF ROOMS	2,700
CHECKOUT TIME	11
NONSMOKING	•
CONCIERGE	•
CONVENTION FACIL.	•
MEETING ROOMS	•
VALET PARKING	•
RV PARK	–
ROOM SERVICE	•
FREE BREAKFAST	–
FINE DINING/TYPES	Steak, Seafood, Chinese, Ribs, Pizza, Southwestern
COFFEE SHOP	•
24-HOUR CAFE	•
BUFFET	•
CASINO	•
LOUNGE	•
SHOWROOM	Impersonator show
GIFTS/DRUGS/NEWS	•
POOL	•
EXERCISE ROOM	•
TENNIS & RACKET	–

JW Marriott Las Vegas ★★★★½
221 N. Rampart Blvd.
Las Vegas, NV 89128
☎ 702-869-7777 FAX 702-869-7339
TOLL FREE 877-869-8777

RACK RATE	$$$$$
ROOM QUALITY	95
LOCATION	Summerlin
DISCOUNTS	AAA, gov't., military, senior
NO. OF ROOMS	548
CHECKOUT TIME	Noon
NONSMOKING	•
CONCIERGE	•
CONVENTION FACIL.	•
MEETING ROOMS	•
VALET PARKING	•
RV PARK	–
ROOM SERVICE	•
FREE BREAKFAST	–
FINE DINING/TYPES	Health Food, Mediterranean, Irish, Japanese
COFFEE SHOP	•
24-HOUR CAFE	–
BUFFET	•
CASINO	•
LOUNGE	•
SHOWROOM	–
GIFTS/DRUGS/NEWS	•
POOL	• (heated)
EXERCISE ROOM	Health spa
TENNIS & RACKET	–

Las Vegas Marriott Suites ★★★★
325 Convention Center Dr.
Las Vegas, NV 89109
☎ 702-650-2000
FAX 702-650-9466
TOLL FREE 800-244-3364

RACK RATE	$$$$$$–
ROOM QUALITY	86
LOCATION	East of Strip
DISCOUNTS	AAA, senior
NO. OF ROOMS	278
CHECKOUT TIME	Noon
NONSMOKING	•
CONCIERGE	–
CONVENTION FACIL.	•
MEETING ROOMS	•
VALET PARKING	–
RV PARK	–
ROOM SERVICE	•
FREE BREAKFAST	–
FINE DINING/TYPES	American/ Southwestern
COFFEE SHOP	–
24-HOUR CAFE	–
BUFFET	–
CASINO	–
LOUNGE	–
SHOWROOM	–
GIFTS/DRUGS/NEWS	•
POOL	• (heated)
EXERCISE ROOM	•
TENNIS & RACKET	–

Luxor ★★★½
3900 S. Las Vegas Blvd.
Las Vegas, NV 89119
☎ 702-262-4000
FAX 702-262-4137
TOLL FREE 800-288-1000

RACK RATE	$$+
ROOM QUALITY	82
LOCATION	South Strip
DISCOUNTS	Military
NO. OF ROOMS	4,407
CHECKOUT TIME	11
NONSMOKING	•
CONCIERGE	•
CONVENTION FACIL.	•
MEETING ROOMS	•
VALET PARKING	•
RV PARK	–
ROOM SERVICE	•
FREE BREAKFAST	–
FINE DINING/TYPES	American, Seafood, Steak, Asian, Mexican
COFFEE SHOP	•
24-HOUR CAFE	•
BUFFET	•
CASINO	•
LOUNGE	•
SHOWROOM	Live entertainment, production show
GIFTS/DRUGS/NEWS	•
POOL	• (heated)
EXERCISE ROOM	Health spa
TENNIS & RACKET	–

Main St. Station ★★★½
200 N. Main St.
Las Vegas, NV 89101
☎ 702-387-1896
FAX 702-388-2660
TOLL FREE 800-465-0711

RACK RATE	$$+
ROOM QUALITY	78
LOCATION	Downtown
DISCOUNTS	–
NO. OF ROOMS	406
CHECKOUT TIME	11
NONSMOKING	•
CONCIERGE	•
CONVENTION FACIL.	•
MEETING ROOMS	•
VALET PARKING	•
RV PARK	•
ROOM SERVICE	–
FREE BREAKFAST	–
FINE DINING/TYPES	Steak, Brewery
COFFEE SHOP	–
24-HOUR CAFE	•
BUFFET	•
CASINO	•
LOUNGE	•
SHOWROOM	–
GIFTS/DRUGS/NEWS	•
POOL	•
EXERCISE ROOM	–
TENNIS & RACKET	–

Hotel Information Chart (continued)

Mandalay Bay ★★★★½	**Manor Suites** ★★★½	**MGM Grand** ★★★★
3950 S. Las Vegas Blvd.	7230 S. Las Vegas Blvd.	3799 S. Las Vegas Blvd.
Las Vegas, NV 89193	Las Vegas, NV 89119	Las Vegas, NV 89109
☎ 702-632-7777 FAX 702-632-7228	☎ 702-939-9000	☎ 702-891-1111; FAX 702-891-1030
TOLL FREE 877-632-7800	FAX 702-939-9014	TOLL FREE 800-929-1111
	TOLL FREE 800-691-7169	

Mandalay Bay		Manor Suites		MGM Grand	
RACK RATE	$$$$–	RACK RATE	$$	RACK RATE	$$$$–
ROOM QUALITY	92	ROOM QUALITY	79	ROOM QUALITY	87
LOCATION	South Strip	LOCATION	South of Las Vegas	LOCATION	South Strip
DISCOUNTS	—	DISCOUNTS	—	DISCOUNTS	—
NO. OF ROOMS	7,000	NO. OF ROOMS	258	NO. OF ROOMS	5,005
CHECKOUT TIME	11	CHECKOUT TIME	11	CHECKOUT TIME	11
NONSMOKING	Floors	NONSMOKING	•	NONSMOKING	Floors
CONCIERGE	•	CONCIERGE	—	CONCIERGE	•
CONVENTION FACIL.	•	CONVENTION FACIL.	—	CONVENTION FACIL.	•
MEETING ROOMS	•	MEETING ROOMS	—	MEETING ROOMS	•
VALET PARKING	•	VALET PARKING	—	VALET PARKING	•
RV PARK	—	RV PARK	—	RV PARK	—
ROOM SERVICE	•	ROOM SERVICE	—	ROOM SERVICE	•
FREE BREAKFAST	—	FREE BREAKFAST	—	FREE BREAKFAST	—
FINE DINING/TYPES	Cuban, Chinese, French, Southern, Italian, Mexican	FINE DINING/TYPES	—	FINE DINING/TYPES	Steak/Seafood, Cajun, Italian, Chinese, French, Mexican
COFFEE SHOP	•	COFFEE SHOP	—	COFFEE SHOP	•
24-HOUR CAFE	•	24-HOUR CAFE	—	24-HOUR CAFE	•
BUFFET	•	BUFFET	—	BUFFET	•
CASINO	•	CASINO	—	CASINO	•
LOUNGE	•	LOUNGE	—	LOUNGE	•
SHOWROOM	Headliners, live music, sports	SHOWROOM	—	SHOWROOM	Production show, visiting headliners
GIFTS/DRUGS/NEWS	•	GIFTS/DRUGS/NEWS	—	GIFTS/DRUGS/NEWS	•
POOL	• (heated)	POOL	•	POOL	• (heated)
EXERCISE ROOM	Health spa	EXERCISE ROOM	—	EXERCISE ROOM	Health spa
TENNIS & RACKET	—	TENNIS & RACKET	—	TENNIS & RACKET	—

Motel 6 Tropicana ★★	**Nevada Palace** ★★½	**New Frontier** ★★★½
195 E. Tropicana Ave.	5255 Boulder Hwy.	3120 S. Las Vegas Blvd.
Las Vegas, NV 89109	Las Vegas, NV 89122	Las Vegas, NV 89109
☎ 702-798-0728	☎ 702-458-8810	☎ 702-794-8200 FAX 702-794-8445
FAX 702-798-5657	FAX 702-458-8397	TOLL FREE 800-634-6966
TOLL FREE 800-4-MOTEL-6	TOLL FREE 800-634-6283	

Motel 6 Tropicana		Nevada Palace		New Frontier	
RACK RATE	$	RACK RATE	$	RACK RATE	$$–
ROOM QUALITY	53	ROOM QUALITY	59	ROOM QUALITY	82/75*
LOCATION	East of Strip	LOCATION	Boulder Highway	LOCATION	North Strip
DISCOUNTS	Corp., senior	DISCOUNTS	—	DISCOUNTS	Military
NO. OF ROOMS	608	NO. OF ROOMS	211	NO. OF ROOMS	986
CHECKOUT TIME	11	CHECKOUT TIME	Noon	CHECKOUT TIME	Noon
NONSMOKING	•	NONSMOKING	•	NONSMOKING	Floors
CONCIERGE	—	CONCIERGE	—	CONCIERGE	—
CONVENTION FACIL.	—	CONVENTION FACIL.	—	CONVENTION FACIL.	—
MEETING ROOMS	—	MEETING ROOMS	•	MEETING ROOMS	•
VALET PARKING	—	VALET PARKING	—	VALET PARKING	•
RV PARK	—	RV PARK	•	RV PARK	—
ROOM SERVICE	—	ROOM SERVICE	—	ROOM SERVICE	•
FREE BREAKFAST	coffee	FREE BREAKFAST	—	FREE BREAKFAST	—
FINE DINING/TYPES	—	FINE DINING/TYPES	American, Deli, Steak/Seafood	FINE DINING/TYPES	Steak, Mexican, Deli, Seafood
COFFEE SHOP	—	COFFEE SHOP	•	COFFEE SHOP	•
24-HOUR CAFE	•	24-HOUR CAFE	•	24-HOUR CAFE	•
BUFFET	—	BUFFET	•	BUFFET	•
CASINO	—	CASINO	•	CASINO	•
LOUNGE	—	LOUNGE	—	LOUNGE	•
SHOWROOM	—	SHOWROOM	—	SHOWROOM	Country-Western nightly
GIFTS/DRUGS/NEWS	—	GIFTS/DRUGS/NEWS	•	GIFTS/DRUGS/NEWS	•
POOL	•	POOL	•	POOL	• (heated)
EXERCISE ROOM	—	EXERCISE ROOM	—	EXERCISE ROOM	—
TENNIS & RACKET	—	TENNIS & RACKET	—	TENNIS & RACKET	—

*tower rooms/garden rooms

Mirage ★★★★½
3400 S. Las Vegas Blvd.
Las Vegas, NV 89109
☎ 702-791-7111; FAX 702-791-7446
TOLL FREE 800-374-9000

RACK RATE	$$$$–
ROOM QUALITY	90
LOCATION	Mid-Strip
DISCOUNTS	AAA
NO. OF ROOMS	2,763
CHECKOUT TIME	Noon
NONSMOKING	Floors
CONCIERGE	•
CONVENTION FACIL.	•
MEETING ROOMS	•
VALET PARKING	•
RV PARK	—
ROOM SERVICE	•
FREE BREAKFAST	—
FINE DINING/TYPES	French, Asian, Steak/Seafood, Italian, Brazilian
COFFEE SHOP	•
24-HOUR CAFE	•
BUFFET	•
CASINO	•
LOUNGE	•
SHOWROOM	Production show, celebrity headliner
GIFTS/DRUGS/NEWS	•
POOL	• (heated)
EXERCISE ROOM	Health spa
TENNIS & RACKET	—

Monte Carlo ★★★½
3770 S. Las Vegas Blvd.
Las Vegas, NV 89109
☎ 702-730-7777
FAX 702-730-7250
TOLL FREE 800-311-8999

RACK RATE	$$$–
ROOM QUALITY	81
LOCATION	South Strip
DISCOUNTS	AAA, military
NO. OF ROOMS	3,002
CHECKOUT TIME	11
NONSMOKING	Floors
CONCIERGE	—
CONVENTION FACIL.	•
MEETING ROOMS	•
VALET PARKING	•
RV PARK	—
ROOM SERVICE	•
FREE BREAKFAST	—
FINE DINING/TYPES	Steak, Asian, Italian, French, Seafood, American
COFFEE SHOP	•
24-HOUR CAFE	•
BUFFET	•
CASINO	•
LOUNGE	•
SHOWROOM	Magic show
GIFTS/DRUGS/NEWS	•
POOL	• (heated)
EXERCISE ROOM	Health spa
TENNIS & RACKET	—

MonteLago Village Resort ★★★★½
30 Strada di Villaggio
Henderson, NV 89118
☎ 702-564-4700
FAX 702-564-4777
TOLL FREE 866-564-4799

RACK RATE	$$$$$–
ROOM QUALITY	90
LOCATION	Henderson
DISCOUNTS	Senior
NO. OF ROOMS	177
CHECKOUT TIME	11
NONSMOKING	—
CONCIERGE	•
CONVENTION FACIL.	•
MEETING ROOMS	•
VALET PARKING	• (complimentary)
RV PARK	—
ROOM SERVICE	—
FREE BREAKFAST	—
FINE DINING/TYPES	—
COFFEE SHOP	—
24-HOUR CAFE	—
BUFFET	—
CASINO	—
LOUNGE	—
SHOWROOM	—
GIFTS/DRUGS/NEWS	•
POOL	•
EXERCISE ROOM	•
TENNIS & RACKET	—

New York–New York ★★★★
3790 S. Las Vegas Blvd.
Las Vegas, NV 89109
☎ 702-740-6969; FAX 702-740-6700
TOLL FREE 800-NY-FOR-ME

RACK RATE	$$$+
ROOM QUALITY	88
LOCATION	South Strip
DISCOUNTS	Gov't.
NO. OF ROOMS	2,035
CHECKOUT TIME	11
NONSMOKING	Floors
CONCIERGE	•
CONVENTION FACIL.	•
MEETING ROOMS	•
VALET PARKING	•
RV PARK	—
ROOM SERVICE	•
FREE BREAKFAST	—
FINE DINING/TYPES	Steak, Chinese, Italian, Mexican, Irish, Deli
COFFEE SHOP	•
24-HOUR CAFE	•
BUFFET	—
CASINO	•
LOUNGE	•
SHOWROOM	Production show, comedy
GIFTS/DRUGS/NEWS	•
POOL	• (heated)
EXERCISE ROOM	Health spa
TENNIS & RACKET	—

Orleans ★★★½
4500 W. Tropicana Ave.
Las Vegas, NV 89103
☎ 702-365-7111; FAX 702-365-7500
TOLL FREE 800-ORLEANS

RACK RATE	$+
ROOM QUALITY	75
LOCATION	South Strip
DISCOUNTS	AAA, AARP, senior
NO. OF ROOMS	1,886
CHECKOUT TIME	Noon
NONSMOKING	•
CONCIERGE	•
CONVENTION FACIL.	•
MEETING ROOMS	•
VALET PARKING	•
RV PARK	—
ROOM SERVICE	•
FREE BREAKFAST	—
FINE DINING/TYPES	Italian, Steak, Cajun, Chinese, Mexican, American
COFFEE SHOP	•
24-HOUR CAFE	—
BUFFET	•
CASINO	•
LOUNGE	pub
SHOWROOM	Celebrity headliners on weekends, sports
GIFTS/DRUGS/NEWS	•
POOL	• (heated)
EXERCISE ROOM	Health spa
TENNIS & RACKET	—

Palace Station ★★★½/★★★*
2411 W. Sahara Ave.
Las Vegas, NV 89102
☎ 702-367-2411; FAX 702-221-6510
TOLL FREE 800-634-3101

RACK RATE	$+
ROOM QUALITY	81/74*
LOCATION	North Strip
DISCOUNTS	AAA
NO. OF ROOMS	1,028
CHECKOUT TIME	Noon
NONSMOKING	Floors
CONCIERGE	•
CONVENTION FACIL.	•
MEETING ROOMS	•
VALET PARKING	•
RV PARK	—
ROOM SERVICE	•
FREE BREAKFAST	—
FINE DINING/TYPES	Seafood, Chinese, Mexican, Italian, Irish, Steak
COFFEE SHOP	•
24-HOUR CAFE	•
BUFFET	•
CASINO	•
LOUNGE	•
SHOWROOM	Live music
GIFTS/DRUGS/NEWS	•
POOL	• (heated)
EXERCISE ROOM	—
TENNIS & RACKET	—

*tower rooms/garden rooms

Hotel Information Chart (continued)

	Palms ★★★★½/★★★★★	Paris ★★★★½	Planet Hollywood ★★★★
	4321 W. Flamingo Rd. Las Vegas, NV 89103 ☎ 702-942-7777 FAX 702-942-7001 TOLL FREE 866-942-7777	3655 S. Las Vegas Blvd. Las Vegas, NV 89109 ☎ 702-946-7000 FAX 702-946-4405 TOLL FREE 888-266-5687	3667 S. Las Vegas Blvd. Las Vegas, NV 89109 ☎ 702-785-5555 FAX 702-785-5558 TOLL FREE 877-333-9474
RACK RATE	$$$+	$$$–	$$$$$
ROOM QUALITY	95/89*	91	87
LOCATION	Mid-Strip	Mid-Strip	Mid-Strip
DISCOUNTS	—	AAA, senior	—
NO. OF ROOMS	455/347*	2,916	2,567
CHECKOUT TIME	Noon	11	11
NONSMOKING	Floors	Floors	•
CONCIERGE	•	•	•
CONVENTION FACIL.	•	•	•
MEETING ROOMS	•	•	•
VALET PARKING	•	•	•
RV PARK	—	—	large
ROOM SERVICE	•	•	•
FREE BREAKFAST	—	—	—
FINE DINING/TYPES	Asian, French, Steak, Mexican, Seafood	French, American, Asian, Steak/Seafood, Caribbean	International, Steak, Tapas
COFFEE SHOP	•	•	•
24-HOUR CAFE	•	•	•
BUFFET	•	•	•
CASINO	•	•	•
LOUNGE	•	•	•
SHOWROOM	Headliners, DJs	Dancing	Headliners
GIFTS/DRUGS/NEWS	•	•	•
POOL	• (heated)	• (rooftop)	•
EXERCISE ROOM	•	Health spa	•
TENNIS & RACKET	—	—	—

	Residence Inn by Marriott Las Vegas South ★★★★	Residence Inn by Marriott Paradise Road ★★★★	Rio ★★★★
	5875 Dean Martin Dr. Las Vegas, NV 89118 ☎ 702-795-7378; FAX 702-7953288 TOLL FREE 800-331-3131	3225 Paradise Rd. Las Vegas, NV 89109 ☎ 702-796-9300 FAX 702-796-9562 TOLL FREE 800-331-3131	3700 W. Flamingo Rd. Las Vegas, NV 89103 ☎ 702-252-7777 FAX 702-967-3890 TOLL FREE 800-PLAYRIO
RACK RATE	$$$	$$$+	$$$–
ROOM QUALITY	86	83	86
LOCATION	South Strip	East of Strip	Mid-Strip
DISCOUNTS	AAA, corp., gov't., military, senior	AAA, corp., gov't., military, senior	AAA, gov't., senior
NO. OF ROOMS	160	192	2,563
CHECKOUT TIME	Noon	Noon	Noon
NONSMOKING	•	Floors	Floors
CONCIERGE	—	—	•
CONVENTION FACIL.	—	—	•
MEETING ROOMS	—	•	•
VALET PARKING	—	—	•
RV PARK	—	—	—
ROOM SERVICE	(dinner from local restaurant)	—	•
FREE BREAKFAST	•	•	—
FINE DINING/TYPES	American	—	Italian, Cajun, Chinese, Southwestern, Indian, French
COFFEE SHOP	—	—	•
24-HOUR CAFE	—	—	•
BUFFET	—	—	•
CASINO	—	—	•
LOUNGE	—	—	•
SHOWROOM	—	—	Live entertainment, headliners
GIFTS/DRUGS/NEWS	•	•	•
POOL	• (heated)	• (heated)	• (heated)
EXERCISE ROOM	•	•	Health spa
TENNIS & RACKET	Tennis	—	—

Plaza ★★★½

One Main St.
Las Vegas, NV 89101
☎ 702-386-2110
FAX 702-386-2378
TOLL FREE 800-634-6575

RACK RATE	$
ROOM QUALITY	75
LOCATION	Downtown
DISCOUNTS	—
NO. OF ROOMS	1,052
CHECKOUT TIME	Noon
NONSMOKING	Floors
CONCIERGE	•
CONVENTION FACIL.	•
MEETING ROOMS	•
VALET PARKING	•
RV PARK	—
ROOM SERVICE	•
FREE BREAKFAST	—
FINE DINING/TYPES	American, Continental
COFFEE SHOP	•
24-HOUR CAFE	•
BUFFET	•
CASINO	•
LOUNGE	•
SHOWROOM	Production show, comedy
GIFTS/DRUGS/NEWS	•
POOL	• (rooftop)
EXERCISE ROOM	•
TENNIS & RACKET	Tennis

Red Rock Resort ★★★★½

11011 W. Charleston Blvd.
Las Vegas, NV 89135
☎ 702-797-7777; FAX 702-797-7745
TOLL FREE 866-767-7773

RACK RATE	$$$$$–
ROOM QUALITY	91
LOCATION	Summerlin
DISCOUNTS	—
NO. OF ROOMS	414
CHECKOUT TIME	11
NONSMOKING	Floors
CONCIERGE	•
CONVENTION FACIL.	•
MEETING ROOMS	•
VALET PARKING	•
RV PARK	—
ROOM SERVICE	•
FREE BREAKFAST	—
FINE DINING/TYPES	American, Steak, Mexican, Italian, Barbecue
COFFEE SHOP	•
24-HOUR CAFE	•
BUFFET	•
CASINO	•
LOUNGE	•
SHOWROOM	Piano bar, live entertainment, dancing
GIFTS/DRUGS/NEWS	•
POOL	•
EXERCISE ROOM	Health spa
TENNIS & RACKET	—

Renaissance Las Vegas ★★★★½

3400 Paradise Rd.
Las Vegas, NV 89109
☎ 702-733-6533
FAX 702-735-3130
TOLL FREE 866-352-3434

RACK RATE	$$$$
ROOM QUALITY	90
LOCATION	East of Strip
DISCOUNTS	AAA, gov't., military, senior
NO. OF ROOMS	548
CHECKOUT TIME	11
NONSMOKING	Floors
CONCIERGE	•
CONVENTION FACIL.	•
MEETING ROOMS	•
VALET PARKING	•
RV PARK	—
ROOM SERVICE	•
FREE BREAKFAST	—
FINE DINING/TYPES	Steak
COFFEE SHOP	•
24-HOUR CAFE	—
BUFFET	—
CASINO	—
LOUNGE	•
SHOWROOM	—
GIFTS/DRUGS/NEWS	•
POOL	•
EXERCISE ROOM	•
TENNIS & RACKET	—

Ritz-Carlton Lake Las Vegas ★★★★★

1610 Lake Las Vegas Pkwy.
Henderson, NV 89011
☎ 702-567-4700
FAX 702-567-4777
TOLL FREE 800-241-3333

RACK RATE	$$$$$$
ROOM QUALITY	97
LOCATION	Henderson
DISCOUNTS	AAA, corp., gov't.
NO. OF ROOMS	349
CHECKOUT TIME	Noon
NONSMOKING	•
CONCIERGE	•
CONVENTION FACIL.	•
MEETING ROOMS	•
VALET PARKING	•
RV PARK	—
ROOM SERVICE	•
FREE BREAKFAST	coffee
FINE DINING/TYPES	Italian, spa fare
COFFEE SHOP	•
24-HOUR CAFE	—
BUFFET	—
CASINO	—
LOUNGE	•
SHOWROOM	—
GIFTS/DRUGS/NEWS	•
POOL	• (heated)
EXERCISE ROOM	Health spa
TENNIS & RACKET	•

Riviera ★★★½

2901 S. Las Vegas Blvd.
Las Vegas, NV 89109
☎ 702-734-5110; FAX 702-794-9451
TOLL FREE 800-634-6753

RACK RATE	$$$–
ROOM QUALITY	75
LOCATION	North Strip
DISCOUNTS	AAA
NO. OF ROOMS	2,100
CHECKOUT TIME	11
NONSMOKING	•
CONCIERGE	•
CONVENTION FACIL.	•
MEETING ROOMS	•
VALET PARKING	•
RV PARK	—
ROOM SERVICE	—
FREE BREAKFAST	—
FINE DINING/TYPES	Steak/Seafood, Chinese, Italian, Barbecue, Deli
COFFEE SHOP	•
24-HOUR CAFE	•
BUFFET	•
CASINO	•
LOUNGE	•
SHOWROOM	Production show, female impersonators, comedy club
GIFTS/DRUGS/NEWS	•
POOL	• (heated)
EXERCISE ROOM	•
TENNIS & RACKET	Tennis

Royal Resort ★★★½

99 Convention Center Dr.
Las Vegas, NV 89109
☎ 702-735-6117
FAX 702-735-2546
TOLL FREE 800-634-6118

RACK RATE	$$
ROOM QUALITY	76
LOCATION	North Strip
DISCOUNTS	AAA, AARP, corp., gov't., military
NO. OF ROOMS	191
CHECKOUT TIME	11
NONSMOKING	Floors
CONCIERGE	•
CONVENTION FACIL.	—
MEETING ROOMS	—
VALET PARKING	—
RV PARK	—
ROOM SERVICE	Breakfast and lunch
FREE BREAKFAST	—
FINE DINING/TYPES	Italian
COFFEE SHOP	—
24-HOUR CAFE	—
BUFFET	—
CASINO	—
LOUNGE	•
SHOWROOM	—
GIFTS/DRUGS/NEWS	•
POOL	• (heated)
EXERCISE ROOM	•
TENNIS & RACKET	—

Hotel Information Chart (continued)

	Sahara ★★★	**Sam's Town** ★★★½	**Santa Fe Station** ★★★
	2535 S. Las Vegas Blvd.	5111 Boulder Hwy.	4949 N. Rancho Dr.
	Las Vegas, NV 89109	Las Vegas, NV 89122	Las Vegas, NV 89130
	☎ 702-737-2111; FAX 702-791-2027	☎ 702-456-7777 FAX 702-454-8014	☎ 702-658-4900 FAX 702-658-4919
	TOLL FREE 888-696-2121	TOLL FREE 800-897-8696	TOLL FREE 800-6-STATIONS
RACK RATE	$	$	$$–
ROOM QUALITY	69	79	73
LOCATION	North Strip	Boulder Highway	Rancho Drive
DISCOUNTS	Gov't., military, senior	AAA, AARP	AAA
NO. OF ROOMS	1,720	648	200
CHECKOUT TIME	Noon	Noon	Noon
NONSMOKING	Floors	•	•
CONCIERGE	–	–	–
CONVENTION FACIL.	–	•	•
MEETING ROOMS	–	•	•
VALET PARKING	•	•	•
RV PARK	–	•	–
ROOM SERVICE	•	–	breakfast
FREE BREAKFAST	–	–	–
FINE DINING/TYPES	Steak, Mexican, American	Steak, Italian, American, Mexican	Mexican, Steak, Barbecue, Seafood, American
COFFEE SHOP	•	•	•
24-HOUR CAFE	•	•	•
BUFFET	•	•	•
CASINO	•	•	•
LOUNGE	•	•	•
SHOWROOM	Production shows, variety	Western dance hall, occasional headliners	Live music, tribute show
GIFTS/DRUGS/NEWS	•	•	•
POOL	•	•	•
EXERCISE ROOM	Health spa	Health spa	–
TENNIS & RACKET	–	–	–

	Stratosphere ★★★½	**Suncoast** ★★★½	**Sunset Station** ★★★★
	2000 S. Las Vegas Blvd.	9090 Alta Dr.	1301 Sunset Rd.
	Las Vegas, NV 89104	Las Vegas, NV 89145	Las Vegas, NV 89014
	☎ 702-380-7777 FAX 702-380-7732	☎ 702-636-7111	☎ 702-547-7777 FAX 702-547-7744
	TOLL FREE 800-998-6937	FAX 702-636-7288	TOLL FREE 888-SUNSET-9
		TOLL FREE 877-677-7111	
RACK RATE	$–	$$–	$+
ROOM QUALITY	79	82	87
LOCATION	North Strip	Summerlin	Henderson
DISCOUNTS	AAA, military, senior	AAA, senior	AAA
NO. OF ROOMS	2,444	388	457
CHECKOUT TIME	11	Noon	Noon
NONSMOKING	Floors	•	Floors
CONCIERGE	•	–	•
CONVENTION FACIL.	–	•	–
MEETING ROOMS	•	•	•
VALET PARKING	•	•	•
RV PARK	–	–	•
ROOM SERVICE	•	•	•
FREE BREAKFAST	–	–	–
FINE DINING/TYPES	Asian, Seafood, Steak, Italian, American	Italian, American, Mexican, Seafood, Chinese	American, Italian, Steak/Seafood, Mexican
COFFEE SHOP	•	•	•
24-HOUR CAFE	•	•	•
BUFFET	•	•	•
CASINO	•	•	•
LOUNGE	•	•	•
SHOWROOM	Production show	Dancing	Live entertainment, concerts
GIFTS/DRUGS/NEWS	•	•	•
POOL	• (heated)	• (heated)	• (heated)
EXERCISE ROOM	Health spa	•	•
TENNIS & RACKET	–	–	–

Silverton ★★★★
3333 Blue Diamond Rd.
Las Vegas, NV 89139
☎ 702-263-7777
FAX 702-896-5635
TOLL FREE 800-588-7711

RACK RATE	$$
ROOM QUALITY	88
LOCATION	South of Las Vegas
DISCOUNTS	AAA, AARP, military
NO. OF ROOMS	300
CHECKOUT TIME	Noon
NONSMOKING	Floors
CONCIERGE	•
CONVENTION FACIL.	—
MEETING ROOMS	•
VALET PARKING	•
RV PARK	•
ROOM SERVICE	•
FREE BREAKFAST	—
FINE DINING/TYPES	Seafood, Steak, American,
COFFEE SHOP	•
24-HOUR CAFE	•
BUFFET	•
CASINO	•
LOUNGE	•
SHOWROOM	Live music
GIFTS/DRUGS/NEWS	•
POOL	• (heated)
EXERCISE ROOM	•
TENNIS & RACKET	—

South Coast ★★★½
9777 S. Las Vegas Blvd.
Las Vegas, NV 89123
☎ 702-796-7111
FAX 702-797-8041
TOLL FREE 866-796-7111

RACK RATE	$—
ROOM QUALITY	81
LOCATION	South of Las Vegas
DISCOUNTS	Senior
NO. OF ROOMS	1,341
CHECKOUT TIME	Noon
NONSMOKING	—
CONCIERGE	—
CONVENTION FACIL.	•
MEETING ROOMS	•
VALET PARKING	•
RV PARK	•
ROOM SERVICE	•
FREE BREAKFAST	—
FINE DINING/TYPES	Italian, Mexican, Seafood, Steak
COFFEE SHOP	•
24-HOUR CAFE	•
BUFFET	•
CASINO	•
LOUNGE	•
SHOWROOM	Live music
GIFTS/DRUGS/NEWS	•
POOL	•
EXERCISE ROOM	•
TENNIS & RACKET	—

St. Tropez All Suites ★★★★
455 E. Harmon Ave.
Las Vegas, NV 89109
☎ 702-369-5400
FAX 702-369-8901
TOLL FREE 800-666-5400

RACK RATE	$$—
ROOM QUALITY	88
LOCATION	East of Strip
DISCOUNTS	AAA, AARP, gov't., military, senior
NO. OF ROOMS	150
CHECKOUT TIME	Noon
NONSMOKING	•
CONCIERGE	—
CONVENTION FACIL.	•
MEETING ROOMS	•
VALET PARKING	—
RV PARK	—
ROOM SERVICE	•
FREE BREAKFAST	•
FINE DINING/TYPES	—
COFFEE SHOP	—
24-HOUR CAFE	—
BUFFET	—
CASINO	—
LOUNGE	—
SHOWROOM	—
GIFTS/DRUGS/NEWS	—
POOL	• (heated)
EXERCISE ROOM	—
TENNIS & RACKET	—

Super 8 ★★
4250 Koval Lane
Las Vegas, NV 89109
☎ 702-794-0888
FAX 702-794-3504
TOLL FREE 800-888-8000

RACK RATE	$+
ROOM QUALITY	52
LOCATION	East of Strip
DISCOUNTS	AAA, AARP, gov't.
NO. OF ROOMS	300
CHECKOUT TIME	Noon
NONSMOKING	•
CONCIERGE	•
CONVENTION FACIL.	—
MEETING ROOMS	•
VALET PARKING	—
RV PARK	—
ROOM SERVICE	—
FREE BREAKFAST	coffee
FINE DINING/TYPES	—
COFFEE SHOP	—
24-HOUR CAFE	—
BUFFET	—
CASINO	—
LOUNGE	—
SHOWROOM	—
GIFTS/DRUGS/NEWS	—
POOL	•
EXERCISE ROOM	—
TENNIS & RACKET	—

Terrible's ★★½
4100 S. Paradise Rd.
Las Vegas, NV 89109
☎ 702-733-7000
FAX 702-691-2484
TOLL FREE 800-640-9777

RACK RATE	$
ROOM QUALITY	64
LOCATION	East of Strip
DISCOUNTS	AAA
NO. OF ROOMS	371
CHECKOUT TIME	11
NONSMOKING	•
CONCIERGE	—
CONVENTION FACIL.	—
MEETING ROOMS	—
VALET PARKING	•
RV PARK	—
ROOM SERVICE	•
FREE BREAKFAST	—
FINE DINING/TYPES	American, Chinese
COFFEE SHOP	•
24-HOUR CAFE	•
BUFFET	•
CASINO	•
LOUNGE	•
SHOWROOM	—
GIFTS/DRUGS/NEWS	•
POOL	•
EXERCISE ROOM	•
TENNIS & RACKET	—

Texas Station ★★★
2101 Texas Star Lane
Las Vegas, NV 89030
☎ 702-631-1000
FAX 702-631-8120
TOLL FREE 800-654-8888

RACK RATE	$
ROOM QUALITY	70
LOCATION	Rancho Drive Area
DISCOUNTS	AAA
NO. OF ROOMS	200
CHECKOUT TIME	Noon
NONSMOKING	Floors
CONCIERGE	—
CONVENTION FACIL.	•
MEETING ROOMS	•
VALET PARKING	•
RV PARK	—
ROOM SERVICE	•
FREE BREAKFAST	—
FINE DINING/TYPES	Seafood, Italian, Mexican, Steak
COFFEE SHOP	•
24-HOUR CAFE	•
BUFFET	•
CASINO	•
LOUNGE	•
SHOWROOM	Live entertainment nightly
GIFTS/DRUGS/NEWS	•
POOL	•
EXERCISE ROOM	—
TENNIS & RACKET	—

Hotel Information Chart (continued)

THEhotel at Mandalay Bay
(all suites) ★★★★★
3950 S. Las Vegas Blvd.
Las Vegas, NV 89118
☎ 702-632-7777 FAX 702-632-7228
TOLL FREE 877-632-7800

RACK RATE	$$$$$+
ROOM QUALITY	96
LOCATION	South Strip
DISCOUNTS	—
NO. OF ROOMS	1,117
CHECKOUT TIME	11
NONSMOKING	Floors
CONCIERGE	•
CONVENTION FACIL.	•
MEETING ROOMS	•
VALET PARKING	• (complimentary)
RV PARK	—
ROOM SERVICE	•
FREE BREAKFAST	—
FINE DINING/TYPES	French, Asian, American
COFFEE SHOP	•
24-HOUR CAFE	Nearby
BUFFET	Nearby
CASINO	Nearby
LOUNGE	•
SHOWROOM	Production show, live music
GIFTS/DRUGS/NEWS	•
POOL	•
EXERCISE ROOM	Health spa
TENNIS & RACKET	—

Treasure Island (T. I.) ★★★★
3300 S. Las Vegas Blvd.
Las Vegas, NV 89109
☎ 702-894-7111; FAX 702-894-7446
TOLL FREE 800-288-7206

RACK RATE	$$$+
ROOM QUALITY	84
LOCATION	Mid-Strip
DISCOUNTS	AAA
NO. OF ROOMS	2,900
CHECKOUT TIME	Noon
NONSMOKING	Floors
CONCIERGE	•
CONVENTION FACIL.	•
MEETING ROOMS	•
VALET PARKING	•
RV PARK	—
ROOM SERVICE	•
FREE BREAKFAST	—
FINE DINING/TYPES	Seafood/Steak, American, Caribbean, Italian, Mexican
COFFEE SHOP	•
24-HOUR CAFE	•
BUFFET	•
CASINO	•
LOUNGE	•
SHOWROOM	Production show
GIFTS/DRUGS/NEWS	•
POOL	• (heated)
EXERCISE ROOM	Health spa
TENNIS & RACKET	—

Tropicana ★★★
3801 S. Las Vegas Blvd.
Las Vegas, NV 89109
☎ 702-739-2222 FAX 702-739-3648
TOLL FREE 800-634-4000

RACK RATE	$$
ROOM QUALITY	73
LOCATION	South Strip
DISCOUNTS	—
NO. OF ROOMS	1,874
CHECKOUT TIME	11
NONSMOKING	Floors
CONCIERGE	—
CONVENTION FACIL.	—
MEETING ROOMS	•
VALET PARKING	•
RV PARK	—
ROOM SERVICE	•
FREE BREAKFAST	—
FINE DINING/TYPES	Steak, Caribbean, Japanese, Italian
COFFEE SHOP	•
24-HOUR CAFE	•
BUFFET	•
CASINO	•
LOUNGE	•
SHOWROOM	Production show, comedy club, magic
GIFTS/DRUGS/NEWS	•
POOL	• (heated)
EXERCISE ROOM	Health spa
TENNIS & RACKET	—

The Venetian ★★★★½
3355 S. Las Vegas Blvd.
Las Vegas, NV 89109
☎ 702-733-5000; FAX 702-414-1100
TOLL FREE 888-2VENICE

RACK RATE	$$$$$$$$$
ROOM QUALITY	94
LOCATION	Mid-Strip
DISCOUNTS	—
NO. OF ROOMS	4,027
CHECKOUT TIME	11
NONSMOKING	Floors
CONCIERGE	•
CONVENTION FACIL.	•
MEETING ROOMS	•
VALET PARKING	•
RV PARK	—
ROOM SERVICE	•
FREE BREAKFAST	—
FINE DINING/TYPES	Italian, Gourmet, French, Asian, Mexican
COFFEE SHOP	•
24-HOUR CAFE	•
BUFFET	—
CASINO	•
LOUNGE	•
SHOWROOM	Headliners, live music, production show
GIFTS/DRUGS/NEWS	•
POOL	• (heated)
EXERCISE ROOM	Health spa
TENNIS & RACKET	—

Westin Casuarina ★★★★
160 E. Flamingo Rd.
Las Vegas, NV 89109
☎ 702-836-9775
FAX 702-836-9776
TOLL FREE 866-716-8132

RACK RATE	$$$$
ROOM QUALITY	83
LOCATION	Mid-Strip
DISCOUNTS	AAA
NO. OF ROOMS	826
CHECKOUT TIME	11
NONSMOKING	•
CONCIERGE	•
CONVENTION FACIL.	•
MEETING ROOMS	•
VALET PARKING	•
RV PARK	—
ROOM SERVICE	•
FREE BREAKFAST	—
FINE DINING/TYPES	Californian
COFFEE SHOP	•
24-HOUR CAFE	•
BUFFET	•
CASINO	•
LOUNGE	•
SHOWROOM	—
GIFTS/DRUGS/NEWS	•
POOL	•
EXERCISE ROOM	Health spa
TENNIS & RACKET	—

Wild Wild West ★★
3330 W. Tropicana Ave.
Las Vegas, NV 89103
☎ 702-740-0000
FAX 702-736-7106
TOLL FREE 800-634-3488

RACK RATE	$
ROOM QUALITY	51
LOCATION	South Strip
DISCOUNTS	AAA
NO. OF ROOMS	262
CHECKOUT TIME	Noon
NONSMOKING	•
CONCIERGE	—
CONVENTION FACIL.	—
MEETING ROOMS	•
VALET PARKING	—
RV PARK	—
ROOM SERVICE	—
FREE BREAKFAST	—
FINE DINING/TYPES	American
COFFEE SHOP	•
24-HOUR CAFE	•
BUFFET	•
CASINO	•
LOUNGE	•
SHOWROOM	—
GIFTS/DRUGS/NEWS	•
POOL	•
EXERCISE ROOM	—
TENNIS & RACKET	—

Tuscany ★★★
255 E. Flamingo Rd.
Las Vegas, NV 89109
☎ 702-893-8933
FAX 702-947-6053
TOLL FREE 877-TUSCAN-1

RACK RATE	$$–
ROOM QUALITY	73
LOCATION	East of Strip
DISCOUNTS	AAA, AARP
NO. OF ROOMS	716
CHECKOUT TIME	Noon
NONSMOKING	Floors
CONCIERGE	•
CONVENTION FACIL.	•
MEETING ROOMS	•
VALET PARKING	•
RV PARK	–
ROOM SERVICE	•
FREE BREAKFAST	–
FINE DINING/TYPES	Italian, Mexican
COFFEE SHOP	•
24-HOUR CAFE	•
BUFFET	–
CASINO	•
LOUNGE	•
SHOWROOM	Special events
GIFTS/DRUGS/NEWS	•
POOL	•
EXERCISE ROOM	•
TENNIS & RACKET	–

Vagabond Inn ★★
2601 Westwood Dr.
Las Vegas, NV 89102
☎ 702-733-0001
FAX 702-733-1571
TOLL FREE 800-522-1555

RACK RATE	$–
ROOM QUALITY	50
LOCATION	North Strip
DISCOUNTS	AAA
NO. OF ROOMS	92
CHECKOUT TIME	11
NONSMOKING	•
CONCIERGE	–
CONVENTION FACIL.	–
MEETING ROOMS	–
VALET PARKING	–
RV PARK	–
ROOM SERVICE	–
FREE BREAKFAST	•
FINE DINING/TYPES	–
COFFEE SHOP	–
24-HOUR CAFE	–
BUFFET	–
CASINO	–
LOUNGE	–
SHOWROOM	–
GIFTS/DRUGS/NEWS	–
POOL	•
EXERCISE ROOM	–
TENNIS & RACKET	–

Vegas Club ★★★ / ★★½*
18 E. Fremont St.
Las Vegas, NV 89101
☎ 702-385-1664 FAX 702-386-2378
TOLL FREE 800-634-6532

RACK RATE	$+
ROOM QUALITY	73/58*
LOCATION	Downtown
DISCOUNTS	–
NO. OF ROOMS	410
CHECKOUT TIME	Noon
NONSMOKING	•
CONCIERGE	–
CONVENTION FACIL.	•
MEETING ROOMS	•
VALET PARKING	•
RV PARK	–
ROOM SERVICE	–
FREE BREAKFAST	–
FINE DINING/TYPES	American, Hawaiian
COFFEE SHOP	•
24-HOUR CAFE	•
BUFFET	–
CASINO	•
LOUNGE	•
SHOWROOM	Occasional lounge entertainment
GIFTS/DRUGS/NEWS	•
POOL	•
EXERCISE ROOM	•
TENNIS & RACKET	Tennis

*tower rooms/garden rooms

Wynn Las Vegas ★★★★½
3131 S. Las Vegas Blvd.
Las Vegas, NV 89109
☎ 702-770-7000
FAX 702-770-1571
TOLL FREE 888-320-WYNN

RACK RATE	$$$$–
ROOM QUALITY	95
LOCATION	Mid-Strip
DISCOUNTS	–
NO. OF ROOMS	2,700
CHECKOUT TIME	11
NONSMOKING	Floors
CONCIERGE	•
CONVENTION FACIL.	•
MEETING ROOMS	•
VALET PARKING	•
RV PARK	–
ROOM SERVICE	•
FREE BREAKFAST	–
FINE DINING/TYPES	French, Italian, Seafood, Asian, American
COFFEE SHOP	•
24-HOUR CAFE	•
BUFFET	•
CASINO	•
LOUNGE	•
SHOWROOM	Production show
GIFTS/DRUGS/NEWS	•
POOL	•
EXERCISE ROOM	Health spa
TENNIS & RACKET	–

PART TWO

ENTERTAINMENT *and* NIGHTLIFE

LAS VEGAS SHOWS *and* ENTERTAINMENT

LAS VEGAS CALLS ITSELF THE "Entertainment Capital of the World." This is arguably true, particularly in terms of the sheer number of live entertainment productions staged daily. On any given day in Las Vegas, a visitor can select from dozens of presentations, ranging from major production spectaculars to celebrity headliners, from comedy clubs to live music in lounges. The standard of professionalism and value for your entertainment dollar is very high. There is no other place where you can buy so much top-quality entertainment for so little money.

 The Second City, a comedy act at the Flamingo, is one of the best buys in town, at about $45 plus tax.

But here's the bad news: The average price of a ticket to one of the major production shows topped $68 in 2007, an 11% increase since 2006. To balance the picture, however, the standard of quality for shows has likewise soared. And variety, well, there's now literally something for everyone, from traditional Las Vegas feathers and butts to real Broadway musicals. And believe it or not, the value is still there. Maybe not in the grand showrooms and incessantly hyped productions, but in the smaller showrooms and lounges and in the main theaters of off-Strip hotels. There's more of everything now, including both overpriced shows and bargains. Regarding the former, you'll be numbed and blinded by their billboards all over town. As concerns the latter, you'll have to scout around, but you'll be rewarded with some great shows at dynamite prices. Want to see Donny Osmond, Air Supply, or the Ringling Brothers and Barnum and Bailey Circus? They're a mile from the Strip at the Orleans. Meanwhile, catch Three Dog Night at the Silverton or Loveshack at Texas Station. And there are always discount coupons floating around for productions at the downtown showrooms.

CHOICES, CHOICES, CHOICES

MOST LAS VEGAS LIVE ENTERTAINMENT offerings can be lumped into one of several broad categories:

- Celebrity headliners
- Long-term engagements
- Production shows
- Broadway and off-Broadway shows
- Impersonator shows
- Comedy clubs
- Lounge entertainment

CELEBRITY HEADLINERS As the name implies, these are concerts or shows featuring big-name entertainers on a limited-engagement basis, usually one to four weeks, but sometimes for a one-night stand. Headliners are usually backed up by a medium-sized orchestra, and the stage sets and special production effects are kept simple. Performers such as Elton John, Celine Dion, David Copperfield, and Jay Leno play Las Vegas regularly. Some even work on a rotation with other performers, returning to the same showroom for several engagements each year. Other stars, such as Barbra Streisand and Paul McCartney, play Las Vegas only rarely, transforming each appearance into a truly special event. While there are exceptions, the superstars are regularly found at the MGM Grand, Mandalay Bay, Caesars Palace, Planet Hollywood, Las Vegas Hilton, and Bally's; sometimes at the Mirage and the Riviera; and occasionally at the Hard Rock. Big-name performers in the city's top showrooms command premium admission prices. Headliners of slightly lesser stature play at various other showrooms. Many hotels, including the Venetian, Mandalay Bay, Planet Hollywood, Sam's Town, Suncoast, Sunset Station, Texas Station, Orleans, Hard Rock, and MGM Grand, have concert and special-event venues where artists ranging from John Lee Hooker to Sheryl Crow to the Rolling Stones perform.

LONG-TERM ENGAGEMENTS These are shows by the famous and once-famous who have come to Las Vegas to stay. Toni Braxton has found a long-term home at Flamingo, and comic Rita Rudner is making a go of it at Harrah's. Barry Manilow holds court at the Las Vegas Hilton. None of the long-run headliners have made a bigger splash than diva Celine Dion, who plays at the Colosseum (theater) at Caesars Palace through the end of 2007. The show features Dion's hit songs elaborately integrated into a technologically groundbreaking spectacle created by Cirque du Soleil visionary Franco Dragone. The combination of Dion's music and Dragone's sets, effects, and choreography will knock you out. So will the prices, the highest for a headliner in Las Vegas entertainment history for a long-running show.

BROADWAY AND OFF-BROADWAY SHOWS Las Vegas showrooms have dallied with Broadway shows for a long time. Some caught on, but most didn't, and many were signed for limited engagements. The tide has turned, however, and there are now a goodly number of shows that originated on Broadway or in London playing long-term engagements in Las Vegas. As of this writing, these include *Blue Man Group, Mamma Mia!, Phantom—The Las Vegas Spectacular, The Producers, Spamalot,* and *Tony 'n' Tina's Wedding.*

PRODUCTION SHOWS These are continuously running, Broadway-style theatrical and musical productions. Cast sizes run from a dozen performers to more than 100, with costumes, sets, and special effects spanning a comparable range. Costing hundreds of thousands, if not millions, to produce, the shows feature elaborate choreography and great spectacle. Sometimes playing twice a night, six or seven days a week, production shows often run for years.

Production shows generally have a central theme to which a more or less standard mix of choreography and variety acts (also called specialty acts) are added. Favorite central themes are magic and illusion—six such shows are currently running—and "best of Broadway," a theme that figures prominently in four current shows. Defying categorization, Cirque du Soleil now offers five shows.

Las Vegas puts its own distinctive imprint on all this entertainment, imparting a great deal of homogeneity and redundancy to the mix of productions. The quality of Las Vegas entertainment is quite high, even excellent, but most production shows seem to operate according to a formula that fosters a numbing sameness. Particularly pronounced in the magic/illusion shows and the Broadway-style musical productions, this sameness discourages sampling more than one show from each genre. While it is not totally accurate to say that "if you've seen one Las Vegas production or magic show, you've seen them all," the statement comes closer to the truth than one would hope.

We should mention that only two shows, *Jubilee!* at Bally's and *Folies Bergere* at the Tropicana, carry on the tradition of the Ziegfeld Follies–inspired, Las Vegas grand production show. As recently as 1990, these immense productions dominated Las Vegas showrooms. They even spawned a new genre of musical theater, the "Las Vegas–Style Musical Revue," that is alive and well in a much-scaled-down form on cruise ships and elsewhere throughout the Western world. When *Jubilee!* and *Folies Bergere* end their decades-long run, a fabled piece of Las Vegas history will die with them.

In the magic/illusion shows, the decade-long rage is to put unlikely creatures or objects into boxes and make them disappear. Some featured magicians repeat this sort of tiresome illusion more than a dozen times in a single performance, with nothing really changing except the size of the box and the object placed into it. Into these boxes go doves, ducks, turkeys, parrots, dwarfs, showgirls, lions, tigers, sheepdogs, jaguars, panthers, motorcycles (with riders), TV cameras (with cameramen), and even elephants. Sometimes the illusionist himself gets into a box and disappears, reappearing moments later in the audience. Generally the elephants and other animals don't reappear until the next performance. These box illusions are amazing the first time or two, but become less compelling after that. After they had seen all of the illusion shows in Las Vegas, our reviewers commented that they had witnessed the disappearance in a box of everything except Karl Rove. Food for thought.

The Broadway-style musical productions likewise lack differentiation, tending to merge after more than one sample into a great blur of bouncing bare breasts and fanciful, feathery costumes. It should be reiterated, however, that like the magic productions, most of the musicals are well done and extremely worthwhile. But like the magic productions, the musicals offer only slight variations of the same theme.

While they share a common format, production shows, regardless of theme, can be differentiated by the size of the cast and by the elaborateness of the production. Other discriminating factors include the creativity of the choreography, the attractiveness of the performers, the pace and continuity of the presentation, and its ability to build to a crescendo. Strength in these last-mentioned areas sometimes allows a relatively simple, lower-budget show to provide a more satisfying evening of entertainment than a lavish, long-running spectacular.

IMPERSONATOR SHOWS These are usually long-running production shows, complete with dancers, that feature the impersonation of celebrities, both living (Joan Rivers, Cher, Neil Diamond, Tina Turner, Madonna) and deceased (Marilyn Monroe, Elvis Presley, Liberace, Blues Brother John Belushi). In shows such as the Imperial Palace's *Legends in Concert*, and the Stratosphere's *American Superstars,* the emphasis is on the detail and exactness of the impersonation. In general, men impersonate male stars and women impersonate female stars (as you might expect). *An Evening at La Cage* at the Riviera, however, features males impersonating female celebrities. But no one—dead or alive, male or female—is impersonated as frequently as The King. The Las Vegas Convention and Visitors Authority says there are at least 260 Elvis impersonators locally. We'd love to see them all in the same show. Wouldn't *that* be "a hunk-a hunk-a burnin' love"!

COMEDY CLUBS Stand-up comedy has long been a tradition in Las Vegas entertainment. With the success of comedy clubs around the country and the comedy-club format on network and cable television, stand-up comedy in Las Vegas was elevated from lounges and production shows to its own specialized venue. Las Vegas comedy clubs are small- to medium-sized showrooms featuring anywhere from two to five comedians per show. As a rule, the shows change completely each week, with a new group of comics rotating in. Each showroom has its own source of talent, so there is no swapping of comics from club to club. Comedy clubs are one of the few Las Vegas entertainments that draw equally from both the tourist and local populations. While most production shows and many celebrity headliner shows are packaged for the over-40 market, comedy clubs represent a concession to youth.

Most of the comics are young, and the humor is often raw and scatological, and almost always irreverent.

LOUNGE ENTERTAINMENT Many casinos offer exceptional entertainment at all hours of the day and night in their lounges. For the most part, the lounges feature musical groups. On a given day almost any type of music, from oldies rock to country to jazz to folk, can be found in Las Vegas lounges. Unlike the production and headliner showrooms and comedy clubs, no reservations are required to take advantage of most lounge entertainment. If you like what you hear, just walk in. Sometimes there is a two-drink minimum for sitting in the lounge during a show, but just as often there are no restrictions at all. You may or may not be familiar with the lounge entertainers by name, but you can trust that they will be highly talented and very enjoyable. To find the type of music you prefer, consult one of the local visitor guides available free from the front desk or concierge at your hotel. Lounge entertainment is a great barometer of a particular casino's marketing program; bands are specifically chosen to attract a certain type of customer.

unofficial **TIP**
In general, if you find a casino with lounge entertainment that suits your tastes, you will probably be comfortable lodging, dining, and gambling there also.

As an alternative to high ticket prices in Las Vegas showrooms (almost a dozen shows now cost upwards of $100), several casinos have turned their nightclubs and lounges into alternative show venues with ticket prices in the $20 to $35 range. We've seen a number of marginal or unsuccessful clubs turned into showrooms over the years, but this is the first time we've observed highly successful nightspots converted. In the main, we don't care for this trend. True, it offers some low-price shows, but at the cost of sacrificing some of the city's best lounges and nightclubs.

THEY COME AND THEY GO

LAS VEGAS SHOWS COME AND GO all the time. Sometimes a particular production will close in one Las Vegas showroom and open weeks later in another. Some shows actually pack up and take their presentations to other cities, usually Reno/Lake Tahoe or Atlantic City. Other shows, of course, close permanently. The bottom line: it's hard to keep up with all this coming and going. Do not be surprised if some of the shows reviewed in this guide have bitten the dust before you arrive. Also do not be surprised if the enduring shows have changed or moved to another casino.

LEARN WHO IS PLAYING BEFORE YOU LEAVE HOME

ON THE INTERNET, CHECK OUT **www.vegas.com/shows.** The site also provides information and reviews on long-run headliners and production shows. The Las Vegas Convention and Visitors Authority publishes an entertainment calendar for all showrooms and many lounges. The brochure *Showguide*, organized alphabetically according to host hotel, tells who is playing, provides appearance dates, and lists information and reservation numbers.

The *Showguide* can be obtained without charge at:

Las Vegas Convention and Visitors Authority
Visitor Information Center
3150 Paradise Road
Las Vegas, NV 89109-9096
☎ 702-892-7575
www.visitlasvegas.com

SHOW PRICES AND TAXES

ADMISSION PRICES FOR LAS VEGAS shows range from around $15 all the way up to $220 per person. Usually show prices are quoted exclusive of entertainment and sales taxes. Also not included are server gratuities.

Once, there was no such thing as a reserved seat at a Las Vegas show. If you wanted to see a show, you would make a reservation (usually by phone) and then arrive well in advance to be assigned a seat by the showroom maître d'. Slipping the maître d' a nice tip ensured a better seat. Typically, the price of the show included two drinks, or there would be waitstaff service and you would pay at your table after you were served. While this arrangement is still practiced in a few showrooms, the prevailing system is reserved seating. With reserved seating, you purchase your tickets at the casino box office (or by phone in advance with your credit card). As at a concert or a Broadway play, your seats are designated and preassigned at the time of purchase, and your section, aisle, and seat number will be printed on your ticket. When you arrive at the showroom, an usher will guide you to your assigned seat. Reserved seating, also known as "hard" or "box office" seating, sometimes includes drinks but usually does not.

If there are two performances per night, the early show is often (but not always) more expensive than the late show. In addition, some shows add a surcharge on Saturdays and holidays. If you tip your server a couple of bucks and slip the maître d' or captain some currency for a good seat (in a showroom without reserved seating), you can easily end up paying $27 or more for a $20 list-price show and $63 or more for a $50 list-price show.

HOW TO SAVE BIG BUCKS ON SHOW TICKETS

THE EASIEST WAY TO SAVE is to see *Dr. Naughty X-Rated Hypnosis* instead of *Celine Dion*. OK, OK, just kidding. Here are some more practical tips:

1. Most of the high-price shows are in new, state-of-the art theaters, which often have several classifications of seats. You can see Celine Dion at Caesars Palace, for example, for $115 from a mezzanine seat. A front orchestra seat at the same show sells for $250.

2. There is a half-price-ticket outlet in the Showcase Mall just north of the MGM Grand called **Tickets2Nite.** The discounter sells tickets for same-day shows for half price plus a $4 service fee. Open noon to 9 p.m., sales are first come, first serve. Generally speaking, you won't find tickets available for top-tier productions like the Cirque du Soleil shows, Danny Gans, and Celine, because, among other reasons, they sell out every night. Many, if not most of the other shows, turn up at Tickets2Nite, some routinely, some periodically. Tickets2Nite has a Web site, **www.tickets2nite.com,** but doesn't list what shows are available on a particular day. According to Tickets2Nite, "agreements with the shows restrict us from disclosing that information except on our menu boards after 11:30 a.m. daily." So yes, that means you have to trudge over to the Tickets2Nite box office in person to see what's available. A second half-price outlet is **Tix4Tonight,** with four locations—Hawaiian Marketplace (near the MGM Grand), a booth just South of the Riviera, Fashion Show Mall, and Four Queens downtown. If you're driving, avoid the super-congested Hawaiian Marketplace location. Tix4Tonight additionally offers coupons on its Web site, **www.tix4tonight.com,** that are good for discounts on the service fee. Tix4Tonight operates in pretty much the same way as Tickets2Nite, but often offers more shows than Ticket2Nite, and charges a lower handling fee. Tix4Tonight opens at 11 a.m., with available shows posted at 10:30 a.m. If you buy tickets from Tix4Tonight make sure to ask for a VIP coupon. This will allow you access to the shorter VIP line if you come back another time.

3. Showrooms, like other Las Vegas hotel and casino operations, sometimes offer special deals. Sometimes free or discounted shows are offered with lodging packages. Likewise, coupons from complimentary local tourist magazines or casino "fun books" (see page 13) provide discounts or "two-for-one" options. Since these specials come and go, your best bet is to inquire about currently operating deals and discounts when you call for show reservations. If you plan to lodge at a hotel-casino where there is a show you want to see, ask about room-show combination specials when you make your room reservations. When you arrive in Las Vegas, pick up copies of the many visitor magazines distributed in rental-car agencies and at hotels. Scour the show ads for discount coupons.

HOW TO MAKE RESERVATIONS FOR LAS VEGAS SHOWS

ALMOST ALL SHOWROOMS take phone reservations. The process is simple and straightforward. Either call, using the reservation numbers listed in this book, or have your hotel concierge call. Most shows will accept reservations at least one day, and often several days in advance. Many will accept reservations weeks in advance.

Some shows, when you call for reservations, will take only your name and the number of people in your party. Under this arrangement, you will either pay at the box office on the day of the show or, alternatively, pay in the showroom after you are seated.

Most shows will allow you to prepurchase your admission on the phone using a credit card. If you prepay, usually you will have to pick up your tickets at the box office before the show. Also, many tickets are now available from **Ticketmaster** at ☎ 702-474-4000 or online at **www.ticketmaster.com.**

unofficial **TIP**
Avoid buying show tickets from independent brokers. They tack on extra surcharges.

Trying to See a Show without a Reservation or Ticket

On Sunday through Thursday, you have a fair shot at getting into most Las Vegas shows just by purchasing a ticket at the box office if reserved seats are sold.

On most Fridays and Saturdays, however, it is a different story. If you decide on the spur of the moment that you would like to see the show at the casino where you have been dining or gambling, do not wait in line at the entrance to the showroom to make your inquiry. Instead, go directly to the box office, maître d', or to one of the other show personnel at the entrance and ask if they have room for your party. In some instances, you may be asked to join the end of the guest line or stand by while they check for no-shows or cancellations. You will, of course, be charged the regular admission price, but an amazing percentage of the time you will be admitted. Superstar celebrity headliner shows like Celine Dion and performances of Cirque du Soleil's *Mystère, KÀ, LOVE,* and *"O," Blue Man Group, Danny Gans, Legends in Concert,* and *Tournament of Kings* are generally the most difficult shows to see on an impromptu basis.

DINNER SHOWS

SOME DINNER SHOWS REPRESENT GOOD DEALS, others less so. Be aware, however, that with all dinner shows, your drinks (if you have any) will be extra, and invariably expensive. Food quality at dinner shows varies. In general, it can be characterized as acceptable, but certainly not exceptional. What you are buying is limited-menu banquet service for 300 to 500 people. Whenever a hotel kitchen tries to feed that many people at once, it is at some cost in terms of the quality of the meal and the service.

Tournament of Kings at the Excalibur does not provide the cocktail option. At *Tournament of Kings,* all shows include dinner of Cornish hen with soup, potatoes, vegetable, dessert, and choice of nonalcoholic beverage for about $55 per person, taxes and gratuities included. *Tournament of Kings* is described in detail later in the chapter. *Tony 'n' Tina's Wedding* at the Rio integrates the meal into the unfolding story line of the show. At *Tony 'n' Tina's,* you're a wedding guest. You're sucked into the story and expected to role-play as the show demands.

Several casinos offer show-and-dinner combos where you get dinner and a show for a special price, but dinner is served in one of the casinos' restaurants instead of in the showrooms. Many restaurants provide only coffee-shop ambience, but the food is palatable and a good deal for the money. At each casino, you can eat either before or after the early show.

Early versus Late Shows

If you attend a late show, you'll have time for a leisurely dinner before the performance. For those who prefer to eat late, the early show followed by dinner works best. Both shows are identical, except that for some the early show is covered and the late show is topless. On weekdays, late shows are usually more lightly attended. On weekends, particularly at the most popular shows, the opposite is often the case.

PRACTICAL MATTERS

What to Wear to the Show

While it is by no means required, guests tend to dress up a bit when they go to a show. For a performance in the main showrooms at Bally's, Bellagio, Caesars Palace, Mandalay Bay, Wynn Las Vegas, or the Mirage, gentlemen will feel more comfortable in sport coats, with or without neckties. Women generally wear suits, dresses, skirt and blouse/sweater combinations, and even semiformal attire. That having been said, however, you'll find a third to a half of the audience at any of these casinos dressed more casually than described.

Showrooms at the Luxor, the Stratosphere, Monte Carlo, New York–New York, Treasure Island (T. I.), the MGM Grand, Harrah's, the Rio, the Flamingo, Las Vegas Hilton, Paris Las Vegas, Tropicana, Planet Hollywood, the Riviera, and the Sahara are a bit less dressy (sport coats are fine, but slacks and sweaters or sport shirts are equally acceptable for men), while showrooms at the Excalibur, the Imperial Palace, the Orleans, Sam's Town, Suncoast, Sunset Station, Texas Station, the House of Blues at Mandalay Bay, the Golden Nugget, and the Hard Rock are the least formal of all (come as you are). All of the comedy clubs are informal, though you would not feel out of place in a sport coat or, for women, a dress.

Getting to and from the Show

When you make your reservations, always ask what time you need to arrive for seating, and whether you should proceed directly to the showroom or stop first at the box office. You are normally asked to arrive one hour before the curtain rises, though a half-hour or even less will do if you already have your reserved-seat tickets (ticket will show a designated row and seat number). If you are driving to another hotel for a show and do not wish to avail yourself of valet parking, be forewarned that many casinos' self-parking lots are quite distant from the showroom. Give yourself an extra 15 minutes or more to park, walk to the casino, and find the showroom. If you decide to use valet parking, be advised that the valet service may be swamped immediately following the show.

A show with a large seating capacity in one of the major casinos can make for some no-win situations when it comes to parking. At all of the megahotels except Wynn Las Vegas, self-parking is either way off in the boonies or in a dizzying multistory garage, so your inclination may be to use valet parking. After the show, however, 1,000 to 1,650 patrons head for home, inundating the valets, particularly after a late show.

Invited Guests and Line Passes

Having arrived at the casino and found the showroom, you will normally join other show-goers waiting to be seated. If the showroom assigns reserved seats, the process is simple: Just show your tickets to an usher and you will be directed to your seats. At showrooms without reserved seating, you will normally encounter two lines. One line, usually quite long, is where you will queue up unless you are an "invited guest." There is a separate line for these privileged folks that allows them to be seated without waiting in line or coming an hour early. Most invited guests are gamblers who are staying at the host casino. Some have been provided with "comps" (complimentary admission) to the show. These are usually regular casino customers or high rollers. If you are giving the casino a lot of action, do not be shy about requesting a comp to the show.

If you are an invited guest under any circumstances, always arrive to be seated for a show at least 30 minutes early.

Gamblers or casino hotel guests of more modest means are frequently given line passes. These guests pay the same price as anyone else for the show but are admitted without waiting via the Invited Guest line. To obtain a line pass, approach a floorman or pit boss (casino supervisory personnel are usually distinguished from dealers by their suits and ties) and explain that you have been doing a fair amount of gambling in their casino. Tell him or her that you have reservations for that evening's show and ask if you can have a line pass. Particularly if you ask on Sunday through Thursday, your chances of being accommodated are good.

Reservations, Tickets, and Maître d' Seating

If, like most guests, you do not have a line pass, you will have to go through the process of entering the showroom and being seated. A dwindling number of showrooms practice what is known as maître d' seating. This means that, except in the case of certain invited guests, no seats are reserved. If you called previously and made a reservation, that will have been duly noted and the showroom will have your party listed on the reservations roster, but you will not actually be assigned a seat until you appear before the maître d'.

unofficial **TIP**
After shows, patrons flood the valets. If you encounter this situation, your best bet is to use self-parking and give yourself some extra time, or use valet parking and plan to stick around the casino for a while after the show.

At some showrooms with maître d' seating, you are asked to pay your waiter for everything (show, taxes, drinks, etc.) once you have been seated and served.

At the comedy clubs and an increasing number of major showrooms, you will be directed to a booth variously labeled "Tickets," "Reservations," "Box Office," or "Guest Services." The attendant will verify your reservation and ask you to go ahead and pay. Once paid, you will receive a ticket to show the maître d' upon entering the showroom. This arrangement eliminates any requirement for paying the tab at your table (unless drinks are not included), thus simplifying service once you are seated. The ticket does not reserve you any specific seat; you still need to see the maître d' about that. Also, the ticket does not include gratuities for your server in the showroom unless specifically stated.

As discussed earlier, most showrooms have discarded maître d' seating in favor of "box office" or "hard" seating. Specific reserved-seat assignments are printed on each ticket sold, as at a football game or on Broadway.

Most showrooms that issue hard (reserved-seat) tickets will allow you to charge your tickets over the phone using your credit card. If you charge your tickets over the phone, however, the quality of your seat assignments is at the mercy of the box office. On the other hand, if you take the trouble to buy your tickets in person at the hotel box office, you can review the seating chart and pick your seats from all seats available.

Where to Sit

When it comes to show seating, there are two primary considerations: visibility and comfort. The newer main showrooms at Caesars Palace, Mandalay Bay, Bellagio, the Mirage, T. I., MGM Grand, Paris, Luxor, Wynn Las Vegas, Planet Hollywood, Monte Carlo, New York–New York, Stratosphere, and the Las Vegas Hilton provide plush theater seats, many with drink holders in the arms. The best accommodations in older showrooms are roomy booths, which provide an unencumbered view of the show. The vast majority of seats in these showrooms, however, and all in some, will be at banquet tables—a euphemism for very long, narrow tables where a dozen or more guests are squeezed together so tightly they can hardly move. When the show starts, guests seated at the banquet tables must turn their chairs around in order to see. This requires no small degree of timing and cooperation, since every person on the same side of the table must move in unison.

Showrooms generally will have banquet table seating right in front of the stage. Next, on a tier that rises a step or two, will be a row of plush booths. These booths are often reserved for the casino's best customers (and sometimes for big tippers). Many maître d's would rather see these booths go unoccupied than have high rollers come to the door at the last minute and not be able to give them good seats.

Behind the booths but on the same level will be more banquet tables. Moving away from the stage and up additional levels, the configuration of booths and banquet tables is repeated on each tier.

For a big production show on a wide stage like *Jubilee!* Cirque du Soleil shows, the *Folies Bergere,* or Celine Dion, you want to sit in the middle and back a little. Being too close makes it difficult to see everything without wagging your head back and forth as if you were at a tennis match. Likewise, at a concert by a band or musical celebrity headliner (such as Tom Jones, Al Jarreau, or B. B. King), partway back and in the center is best. This positioning provides good visibility and removes you from the direct line of fire of amplifiers and lights. This advice, of course, does not apply to avid fans who want to fling their underwear or room keys at the star. For smaller production shows on medium-sized stages (*Lance Burton, Legends in Concert,* etc.), right up front is great. This is also true for headliners like Rita Rudner and David Copperfield. For female impersonators (*La Cage*), the illusion is more effective if you are back a little bit.

 Be aware that comedians often single out unwary guests sitting down front for harassment, or worse, incorporate them into the act.

At comedy clubs and smaller shows, there are really no bad seats, though the Comedy Stop at the Tropicana has some columns in the showroom you want to avoid.

Getting a Good Seat at Showrooms with Maître d' Seating

1. ARRIVE EARLY No maître d' can assign you a seat that's already taken. This is particularly important for Friday and Saturday shows. We have seen comped invited guests (the casino's better customers) get lousy seats because they waited until the last minute to show up.

2. TRY TO GO ON AN OFF NIGHT (that is, Sunday through Thursday) Your chances of getting a good seat are always better on weeknights, when there is less demand. If a citywide convention is in town, weekdays also may be crowded.

3. TRY TO KNOW WHERE (as precisely as possible) you would like to sit. In showrooms with maître d' seating, it is always to your advantage to specifically state your seating preferences.

4. UNDERSTAND YOUR TIPPING ALTERNATIVES Basically, you have three options:
- Don't tip.
- Tip the maître d'.
- Tip the captain instead of the maître d'.

DON'T TIP Politely request a good seat instead of tipping. This option actually works better than you would imagine in all but a few showrooms, particularly Sunday through Thursday. If the showroom is not sold out and you arrive early, simply request a seat in a certain area. Tell the maître d', "We would like something down front in the center." Then allow the captain (the showroom staff person who actually takes you to your seat) to show you the seats the maître d' has assigned. If the assigned seat is not to your liking, ask to be seated somewhere else of your choosing. The captain almost always has the authority to make the seat assignment change without consulting the maître d'.

On slower nights, the maître d' will often "dress the showroom." This means that the maître d', not expecting a full house, will distribute patrons pretty equally throughout the showroom, especially nearer the stage. This procedure, which makes the audience look larger than it really is, is done for the morale of the performers and for various practical reasons, such as ensuring a near-equal number of guests at each server station. On these nights, you have a pretty good shot at getting the seats you want simply by asking.

TIP THE MAÎTRE D' When you tip the maître d', it is helpful to know with whom you are dealing. First, the maître d' is the man or woman in charge of the showroom. The showrooms are their domain, and they rule as surely as battalion commanders. Maître d's in the better showrooms are powerful and wealthy people, with some maître d's taking in as much as $1,650 a night. Even though these tips are pooled and shared in some proportion with the captains, it's still a lot of money.

When you tip a maître d', especially in the better showrooms, you can assume it will take a fairly hefty tip to impress him, especially on a busy night. The bottom line, however, is that you are not out to impress anyone; you just want a good seat. Somebody has to sit in the good seats, and those who do not tip, or tip small, have to be seated regardless. So, if you arrive early and tip $15 to $20 (for a couple) in the major showrooms, and $5 to $10 in the smaller rooms, you should get decent seats. If it is a weekend or you know the show is extremely popular or sold out, bump the tip up a little. If you arrive late on a busy night, ask the maître d' if there are any good seats left before you proffer the tip.

Have your tip in hand when you reach the maître d'. Don't fool around with your wallet or purse as if you are buying hot dogs and beer at the ball park. Fold the money and hold it in the palm of your hand, arranged so that the maître d' can see exactly how big the tip is without unfolding and counting the bills. State your preference for seating at the same time you inconspicuously place the bills in the palm of his hand. If you think all this protocol is pretty ridiculous, we agree. But style counts, and observing the local customs may help get you a better seat.

A variation is to tip with some appropriate denomination of the casino's own chips. Chips are as good as currency to the maître d' and implicitly suggest that you have been gambling with that denomination of chips in his casino. This single gesture, which costs you nothing more than your cash tip, makes you an insider and a more valued customer in the eyes of the maître d'.

Many maître d's are warm and friendly and treat you in a way that shows they appreciate your business. These maître d's are approachable and reasonable, and they will go out of their way to make you comfortable. There are also a number of maître d's and captains, unfortunately, who are extremely cold, formal, and arrogant. Mostly older men dressed in tuxedos, they usually have gray hair and an imperious bearing and can seem rather imposing or hostile. Do not be awed or intimidated. Be forthright and, if necessary, assertive; you will usually be accommodated.

TIP THE CAPTAIN Using this strategy, tell the maître d' where you would like to sit, but do not offer a tip. Then follow the captain to your assigned seats. If your seats are good, you have not spent an extra nickel. If the assigned seats are less than satisfactory, slip the captain a tip and ask if there might be something better. If you see seats you would like to have that are unoccupied, point them out to the captain. Remember, however, that the first row of booths is usually held in reserve.

Before the Show Begins

Some showrooms serve drinks, while others offer self-service. A few of the variations you will encounter: there will be a cash bar and no table service; if you want a drink before the show, you walk to the bar and buy it. At some showrooms, drinks are included, but there is no table service. You take a receipt stub to the bar and exchange it for drinks. In most other showrooms there is table service where you can obtain drinks from a server.

In showrooms where there is table service, the servers run around like crazy trying to get everybody served before the show. Because all the people at a given table are not necessarily seated at the same time, the server responsible for that table may make five or more passes before everyone is taken care of. If your party is one of the last to be seated at a table, stay cool. You *will* be noticed and you *will* be served.

BLADDER MATTERS Be forewarned that in most showrooms there is no restroom, and that the nearest restroom is invariably a long way off, reachable only via a convoluted trail through the casino. Since the majority of show-goers arrive early and consume drinks, it is not uncommon to start feeling a little pressure on the bladder minutes before showtime. If you assume that you can slip out to the restroom and come right back, think again. If you are at the Las Vegas Hilton or the Tropicana, give yourself more than ten minutes for the round trip, and prepare for a quest. If you get to the can and back without getting lost, consider yourself lucky.

At most other showrooms, restrooms are somewhat closer but certainly not convenient. The Riviera, the Imperial Palace, Luxor, Harrah's, New York–New York, the MGM Grand, Stratosphere, Venetian, Wynn Las Vegas, and the Mirage, however, seem to have considered that show guests may not wish to combine emptying their bladders with a five-mile hike. Showrooms in these casinos are situated in close and much-appreciated proximity to the restrooms.

SELECTING *a* SHOW

SELECTING A LAS VEGAS SHOW is a matter of timing, budget, taste, and schedule. Celebrity headliners are booked long in advance but may play only for a couple of days or weeks. If seeing Elton John or Jerry Seinfeld in concert is a big priority for your Las Vegas trip, you will have to schedule your visit to coincide with their appearances. If the timing of your visit is not flexible, as in the case of conventioneers, you will be relegated to picking from those stars playing when you are in town. To find out which shows and headliners are playing before you leave home, call the Las Vegas Convention and Visitors Authority at ☎ 702-892-7576 (**www.lvcva.com**) and ask them to mail you a Las Vegas *Showguide*. On the Internet, log on to **www.visitlasvegas.com.**

Older visitors are often more affluent than younger visitors. It is no accident that most celebrity headliners are chosen, and most production shows created, to appeal to the 40-and-over crowd. If we say a Las Vegas production show is designed for a mature audience, we mean that the theme, music, variety acts, and humor appeal primarily to older guests. Most Las Vegas production shows target patrons 40 to 50 years old and up, while a few appeal to audiences 55 years of age and older.

As the post–World War II baby boomers have moved into middle age and comparative affluence, they have become a primary market for Las Vegas. Stars from the "golden days" of rock and roll, as well as folk singers from the 1960s, are turning up in the main showrooms all across town. On one occasion, Paul Revere and the Raiders, the Four Seasons, the Mamas and the Papas, the Temptations, the Four Tops, B. J. Thomas, and Arlo Guthrie were playing in different showrooms on the same night.

The most hip, avant-garde shows in town are *Blue Man Group* (Luxor) and *Stomp Out Loud* (Planet Hollywood), which target younger audiences and are wild, loud, and conceptually quite different from anything else in Las Vegas.

If you are younger than 35 you will also enjoy the Las Vegas production shows, though for you their cultural orientation (and usually their music) will seem a generation or two removed. Several production shows, however, have broken the mold, in the process achieving a more youthful presentation while maintaining the loyalty of older patrons. Cirque du Soleil's *Mystère* (T. I.) is an uproarious yet poignant odyssey in the European tradition, brimming over with unforgettable characters. Ditto for Cirque's *"O"* at the Bellagio, *KÀ* at the MGM Grand, *LOVE* at the Mirage, and *Zumanity* at New York–New York. *Lance Burton* (Monte Carlo) is a smaller production but is extremely creative and works well for all ages. And, again, the comedy clubs have a more youthful orientation.

LAS VEGAS SHOWS FOR THE UNDER-21 CROWD

AN EVER-INCREASING NUMBER OF SHOWROOMS offer productions appropriate for younger viewers. Circus Circus provides complimentary, high-quality circus acts about once every half hour, and *Tournament of Kings* at the Excalibur is a family dinner show featuring jousting and other benign medieval entertainments. Other family candidates include *Legends in Concert,* a celebrity impersonation show at the Imperial Palace; *Lance Burton* at the Monte Carlo; Cirque du Soleil's *Mystère* at T. I., *LOVE* at the Mirage, and *"O"* at Bellagio.

Many of the celebrity headliner shows, including Celine Dion's, are fine for children, and a few of the production shows offer a covered early show to accommodate families. Of the topless production shows, some operate on the basis of parental discretion while others do not admit anyone under age 21. Comedy clubs and comedy theater usually will admit teenage children accompanied by an adult. All continuously running shows are profiled later in this section. The profile will tell you whether the show is topless or particularly racy. If you have a question about a given showroom's policy for those under age 21, call the showroom's reservation and information number listed in the profile.

CELEBRITY-HEADLINER ROOMS

CHOOSING WHICH CELEBRITY HEADLINER to see is a matter of personal taste, though stars like Elton John and Celine Dion seem to have the ability to rev up any audience. We talked to people who, under duress, were essentially dragged along by a friend or family member to see Wayne Newton. Many of these folks walked into the showroom prepared to hate Wayne Newton. Yet despite their negative attitude, Newton delighted and amazed them.

Our point is not to hype Wayne Newton but to suggest that the talent, presence, drive, and showmanship of many Las Vegas headliners often exceed all expectations, and that adhering to the limitations of your preferences may prevent you from seeing many truly extraordinary performers. Las Vegas is about gambling, after all. Do not be reluctant to take a chance on a headliner who is not familiar to you.

Most of the major headliners play at a relatively small number of showrooms. Profiles of the major celebrity showrooms and their regular headliners follow. The list is not intended to be all-inclusive but rather to give you an idea of where to call if you are interested in a certain headliner. Long-running (i.e., a year or more) celebrity headliner shows, including *Celine Dion, Barry Manilow, Rita Rudner, Elton John, Danny Gans,* etc., are reviewed in depth in our coverage of continuously running production shows later in this chapter.

Hard Rock Hotel—The Joint

RESERVATIONS AND INFORMATION ☎ 702-693-5066; www.hardrockhotel.com

Frequent headliners Top current and oldies rock, pop, blues, folk, and world music stars. **Usual showtimes** 8 p.m. **Dark** Varies. **Approximate admission price** $15–$180. **Drinks included** None. **Showroom size** 1,800 persons.

DESCRIPTION AND COMMENTS Have you ever been to a major rock concert in a facility so large that you needed binoculars to see the band? And did you wish that just once you could enjoy that band in a smaller, more intimate setting? Hard Rock Hotel's The Joint is that setting—a medium-sized, two-level venue for rock-and-roll concerts hosting the likes of Bob Dylan, the Black Crowes, Melissa Etheridge, the Eagles, and Seal. True, seeing Bob Dylan in an 1,800-person showroom is not as cozy as having him in your living room, but it sure beats Yankee Stadium. Because most performers playing The Joint are booked for short engagements, each show is a special event.

On the floor, the tightly packed audience sits on folding chairs and barstools around small tables; there are 1,000 of these reserved seats. The stage is high and the floor is on an incline, so visibility is good. Acoustics are excellent, especially in the middle of the floor and in front of the balcony.

CONSUMER TIPS When the reserved seats are sold out (or if someone wants to stand), 400 or so "standing-room" tickets are sold. These entitle patrons to a spot toward the back of the floor (by the bar), the back of the balcony, or in "the pit." Visibility from a standing-room position on the balcony is limited (except from the first few rows, which are reserved). And stageside at The Joint, be prepared for ear-splitting, head-pounding acoustics, not to mention being hemmed in by the crowd. If you don't want to be put in balcony Siberia where you can hear well enough but see nothing, or pinned against the stage for the whole show by a crush of sweaty rowdies, don't buy standing-room tickets. Book early for reserved seating—or shrug and say, "Oh well."

The Hard Rock Hotel box office sells reserved seats to shows at The Joint. You can purchase tickets via phone using your credit card or in person at the box office. Shows at The Joint are hot tickets in Las Vegas and sell out quickly, so buy your tickets as far in advance as possible.

Mandalay Bay—House of Blues

RESERVATIONS AND INFORMATION ☎ 702-632-7600 or 877-632-7400; www.hob.com

Frequent headliners Current and former pop, rock, R&B, reggae, folk, and country stars. **Usual showtimes** 8 p.m. **Dark** Varies. **Approximate admission price** $13–$85. **Drinks included** None. **Showroom size** 1,800 seats.

DESCRIPTION AND COMMENTS House of Blues is a newer Las Vegas concert hall, very different from The Joint at the Hard Rock, with which it competes head-on for performers and concertgoers. The House of Blues is more like an opera house than the high school–gym Joint: low-ceilinged, multi-tiered, and split-leveled, which gets the audience as close to the act as possible. To that end, the acoustics are much better than the Joint's, but the House of Blues can get claustrophobic; the more crowded, the less comfortable it is. Also, the sight-lines are highly variable, even bizarre, especially for a new room—it's almost as if the designers were modifying an old theater rather than opening a new one. And it doesn't seem to have much to do with how much you pay for a seat: some bad seats (in the nosebleed section and on the sides of the stage) don't cost much less than the best seats or much more than the cheapest tickets.

Live music is presented almost every night of the year. Major headliners, with tickets going for $30 to $100, appear once or twice a week at 8 p.m.; for these shows you must be 21 to attend. Recent performers have included Ted Nugent, Rusted Root, Violent Femmes, Al Green, and Frank Zappa. Filling in the booking gaps are minor shows, with tickets in the $12 to $30 range; check the hotline and Web site. You must be 18 or over for most of them (the few others are designated "all ages").

CONSUMER TIPS House of Blues ticket agents are very difficult to get by telephone; to save yourself an exorbitant phone bill, use the toll-free number listed above (and press 4). The box office is open 9 a.m. to 11 p.m.; the best time to call is right at 9 a.m. Once you have the operator (there's probably only one!) on the line, you'll often hear more bad news. The headliner shows sell out extremely fast, though you can usually pick up standing-room-only tickets, where you'll be sardined in front of the stage (watch your wallet). If money is no object, try to get a VIP seat front and center in the balcony (the first ten rows are prime). If you can't, you might as well just opt for the cheap standing room, as the upper balcony and many of the loge seats aren't worth the extra money. Indeed, many people give up their bad reserved seats to move down to the floor where they can see the whole stage!

MGM Grand—Grand Garden Arena

RESERVATIONS AND INFORMATION ☎ **702-891-7777 or 800-929-1111;**
www.mgmgrand.com

Frequent headliners National acts, superstars, televised boxing, wrestling, and other sporting events. Usual showtimes Varies. Dark Varies. Approximate admission price $20–$800. Drinks included None. Showroom size 16,800 seats.

DESCRIPTION AND COMMENTS This 275,000-square-foot special-events center is designed to accommodate everything from sporting events and concerts to major trade exhibitions. The venue also offers auxiliary meeting rooms and ballrooms adjacent to the entertainment center. Barbra Streisand christened this venue with her first concert in more than 20 years on New Year's Eve 1993. Championship boxing events are favorite attractions at the Grand Garden Arena, as are the many big-name musical concerts.

CONSUMER TIPS Reserved-seat tickets can be purchased one to two months in advance with your credit card by calling the MGM Grand main reservations number or Ticketmaster outlets, for most but not all shows (☎ 702-474-4000). If you are not staying at the MGM Grand, either arrive by cab or give yourself plenty of extra time to park and make your way to the arena.

MGM Grand—Hollywood Theatre

RESERVATIONS AND INFORMATION ☎ **702-891-7777 or 800-929-1111; www.mgmgrand.com**

Frequent headliners David Copperfield, Howie Mandel, Tom Jones, Don Rickles, and George Carlin. **Usual showtimes** Varies. **Dark** Varies. **Approximate admission price** $40–$100. **Drinks included** None. **Showroom size** 740 seats.

DESCRIPTION AND COMMENTS A modern and comfortable showroom, with all front-facing seats, the Hollywood Theater hosts a wide range of musical and celebrity headliner productions for one- to three-week engagements.

CONSUMER TIPS Reserved-seat tickets can be purchased one to two months in advance with your credit card by calling the MGM Grand's main reservations number. Children are allowed at most presentations (check first). If you are not staying at the MGM Grand, either arrive by cab or give yourself plenty of extra time to park and make your way to the showroom.

Orleans—Orleans Showroom

RESERVATIONS AND INFORMATION ☎ **702-365-7075 or 888-365-7111; www.orleanscasino.com**

Frequent headliners Roberta Flack, Neil Sedaka, Air Supply, and Engelbert Humperdinck. **Usual showtimes** Varies. **Dark** Varies. **Approximate admission price** $35–$40. **Drinks included** None. **Showroom size** 800 seats.

DESCRIPTION AND COMMENTS This small but comfortable showroom offers tiered theater seats arranged in a crescent around the stage. Designed for solo performers and bands, the Orleans Showroom is an intimate venue for concerts with good visibility from anywhere in the house. The star lineup runs the gamut with a concentration in country-and-western singer celebrities.

CONSUMER TIPS This showroom features some great talent at bargain prices. All seats are reserved. Tickets can be purchased at the box office to the left of the showroom or over the phone using your credit card.

PRODUCTION SHOWS

LAS VEGAS PREMIER PRODUCTION SHOWS: COMPARING APPLES AND ORANGES

WHILE WE ACKNOWLEDGE THAT LAS VEGAS production shows are difficult to compare and that audiences of differing tastes and ages have different preferences, we have nevertheless ranked the continuously running shows to give you an idea of our favorites. This is definitely an apples-and-oranges comparison (how can you compare *Zumanity* to Blue Man Group?), but one based on each show's impact, vitality, originality, pace, continuity, crescendo, and ability to entertain.

We would hasten to add that even the continuously running shows change acts and revise their focus periodically. Expect our list, therefore, to change from year to year. Also, be comforted by the knowledge that while some shows are better than others, there are only one or two real dogs. The quality of entertainment among the continuously running production shows is exceptional. By way of analogy, we could rank baseball players according to their performance in a given All-Star game, but the entire list, from top to bottom, would still be All-Stars. You get the idea.

A Word about Small Showrooms

During the past couple of years, we have seen a number of casinos convert their lounge into a small showroom. Though the stage in these showrooms is routinely about the size of a beach towel, productions are mounted that include complex choreography, animal acts, and, in one notable case, an illusionist catching bullets in his teeth. In the case of musical revues, as many as four very thin or three average-sized hula dancers can fit comfortably on the stage at one time.

A real problem with some smaller shows is that they often cost as much as productions in Las Vegas's major showrooms. We once reviewed *Hell on Heels* at the now defunct Maxim, for instance, and paid about $21, including tax and tip. Though *Hell on Heels* was a decent show and professionally performed, it could not compare in scope, talent, and spectacle to the lavish *Folies Bergere* at the Tropicana, available at the time for only a few extra dollars.

Another problem is that small shows often play to even smaller crowds. We saw a performance of *That's Magic* at O'Shea's where the cast outnumbered the audience. Though the show featured talented illusionists, a good ventriloquist, and some dancers, the small facility made the production seem amateurish. It was heartrending to see professional entertainers work so hard for such a tiny audience. We felt self-conscious and uncomfortable ourselves, as well as embarrassed for the performers.

When it comes to smaller showrooms, simpler is better. That's why *The Second City* and *Crazy Girls* work so well: both shows take a minimalist approach. Additionally, both shows play in casinos large enough to draw an audience. Little showrooms in smaller casinos that attempt to mount big productions create only parody and end up looking foolish. Better that they revert to offering lounge shows.

We've given up trying to cover the productions that play in these small showrooms, mostly because the shows are very short-lived. If a small-showroom production is exceptionally good and demonstrates staying power, however, we sometimes review it right along with the full-scale shows. In this edition, for example, we provide full reviews of seven small-room productions. (This discussion, by the way, does not apply to comedy clubs, which work best in small rooms.)

Gotta Keep on Movin'

If every player in major-league baseball were a free agent, the willy-nilly team-hopping would bear a close resemblance to the Las Vegas entertainment scene. If, after reading our show reviews, you discover that your preferred performer or production has disappeared from the listed showroom, don't despair. Chances are good that the show has moved to a different venue. Melinda, "The First Lady of Magic" (now retired after years of being impaled nightly on the giant screw of death), holds the all-time record, having played at almost a dozen different casinos during her career.

LAS VEGAS SHOW HIT PARADE

SIMPLY BASED ON EXCELLENCE, here's how we rank the continuously running productions playing the showrooms of Las Vegas. We have apples, oranges, artichokes, and even pomegranates here, so we're not making any direct comparisons. For each show listed, all we're saying is that, in our opinion, that show is a better night's entertainment than those ranking below it.

Excluded from the list are short-run engagements. Falling into this category are limited-engagement celebrity headliners and hypnosis shows. We also exclude comedy clubs (because the comedians change nightly) and afternoon shows, though both are covered in some detail later in this section. We further decided to rank the straight-up skin shows, for both men and women, separately (see lower right).

Las Vegas Show Hit Parade

SHOW	LOCATION
1. Cirque du Soleil's *Mystère*	Treasure Island
2. Cirque du Soleil's *LOVE*	Mirage
3. Cirque du Soleil's *KÀ*	MGM Grand
4. Cirque du Soleil's *"O"*	Bellagio
5. *Celine Dion—A New Day . . .*	Caesars Palace
6. Blue Man Group	Venetian
7. *Monty Python's Spamalot*	Wynn Las Vegas
8. *Stomp Out Loud*	Planet Hollywood
9. *The Producers*	Paris
10. *Phantom: Las Vegas Spectacular*	Venetian
11. Cirque du Soleil's *Zumanity*	New York—New York
12. *Le Rêve*	Wynn Las Vegas
13. *Mamma Mia!*	Mandalay Bay
14. *Elton John and the Red Piano*	Caesars Palace
15. *Menopause: The Musical*	Las Vegas Hilton
16. Lance Burton	Monte Carlo
17. *Jubilee!*	Bally's
18. Danny Gans	Mirage
19. Penn & Teller	Rio
20. The Amazing Jonathan	Sahara
21. *Barry Manilow: Music and Passion*	Las Vegas Hilton

Las Vegas Show Hit Parade (continued)

SHOW	LOCATION
22. Fashionistas	Empire Ballroom
23. The Second City	Flamingo
24. Folies Bergere	Tropicana
25. Gordie Brown	Venetian
26. Ice: Direct From Russia	Riviera
26. American Superstars	Stratosphere
27. Legends in Concert	Imperial Palace
28. The Rat Pack Is Back	Greek Isles
29. The World's Greatest Magic Show	Greek Isles
30. Rita Rudner	Flamingo
31. George Wallace	Flamingo
32. Louie Anderson	Excalibur
33. V: The Ultimate Variety Show	Miracle Mile Shops
34. The Magic of Rick Thomas	Orleans
35. Steve Wyrick: Real Magic	Miracle Mile Shops
36. Tony 'n' Tina's Wedding	Rio
37. Toni Braxton: Revealed	Flamingo
38. The Platters, Coasters, and Drifters	Sahara
39. Barbra and Frank—The Concert That Never Was	Riviera
40. Carrot Top	Luxor
41. Tournament of Kings	Excalibur
42. Hans Klok: The Beauty of Magic	Planet Hollywood
43. Fab Four Mania	Miracle Mile Shops
44. Hello Dere!	Gold Coast
45. An Evening at La Cage	Riviera
46. America's Neil Diamond Tribute	Riviera

TOPLESS REVUES*

1. Crazy Horse Paris	MGM Grand
2. Bite	Sahara
3. Crazy Girls	Riviera
4. Fantasy (best for couples)	Luxor
5. X Burlesque	Flamingo

* Does not include major production shows such as *Jubilee!* and *Folies Bergere* that are also topless but are targeted at a more general audience.

MALE STRIPPER SHOWS

1. Chippendales	Rio
2. Thunder from Down Under	Excalibur
3. American Storm	Riviera

HYPNOSIS SHOWS

IN HYPNOSIS SHOWS, volunteers from the audience are invited onto the stage to be hypnotized. The volunteers really do get hypnotized. We have had medical clinicians who use hypnosis in their practice review the shows and verify the authenticity of the trance. Folks that fake being under hypnosis or for whom the hypnotic state is marginal are quickly identified by the hypnotist and returned to their seats. To the best of our knowledge, there are no plants or ringers.

Most if not all of the Las Vegas hypnosis shows are very blue. In practice, this means that volunteers may end up doing things which after the fact may embarrass them immensely. We've seen volunteers attempt to have sex with a folding chair, perform fellatio on imaginary objects, enjoy orgasms, wear bras and underpants over their clothes, and audition for a job as an exotic dancer. One fellow was induced to have an erection every time a certain word was mentioned. We should make it clear that the contestants do all of this fully clothed. Most showrooms video each performance.

The quality(?) and relative outrageousness of any given performance depends on the number of volunteers and their susceptibility to hypnosis. So if you prefer to be a voyeur instead of a volunteer, your best chance for a really wild spectacle is to choose a show in a big hotel where the size of the audience is likely to be large. We profile only the Anthony Cools hypnosis show at Planet Hollywood, but his review is pretty representative of the genre.

LAS VEGAS SHOW PROFILES

FOLLOWING IS A PROFILE OF EACH of the continuously running production shows, listed alphabetically by the name of the show. If you are not sure of the name of a show, consult the previous section. Comedy clubs, afternoon shows, and limited-engagement celebrity-headliner showrooms are profiled in separate sections. Prices are approximate and fluctuate about as often as you brush your teeth.

The Amazing Jonathan ★★★★

APPEAL BY AGE	UNDER 21 −	21–37 ★★★★	38–50 ★★★★	51+ ★★★½

HOST CASINO AND SHOWROOM **Sahara—Congo Room; ☎ 702-737-2515; www.saharavegas.com**

Type of show Comedy. **Admission** $54.95. **Cast size** 2. **Night of lowest attendance** Tuesday. **Usual showtimes** Friday–Tuesday, 10 p.m. **Dark** Wednesday and Thursday. **Special comments** No one under 18 admitted. **Topless** No. **Duration of presentation** 1 hour and 30 minutes.

SPECIAL NOTE The Amazing Jonathan, known as John Szeles to his family, is one of Las Vegas entertainment's great characters. Szeles will be taking a long sabbatical from performing when his contract with the Sahara ends in December 2007. If you have an opportunity to catch his show before then, you'll be glad you did.

DESCRIPTION AND COMMENTS The Amazing Jonathan is very blue, a sort of George Carlin of inept magicians. He's also incredibly funny. Playing to a sold-out house every night, Jonathan went from a trial-balloon production to a fixture at the Golden Nugget in less than half a year before moving to the Sahara. As a character, Jonathan is eerily appealing and totally frightening (if you're conscripted from the audience to help out on stage, you'll know what we mean). Naturally, he's supposed to do some tricks, but most are never completed, and in any case the magic merely serves as the glue that binds the gags. Jonathan has an assistant, a lovable ditzy blond, who almost steals the show. The two of them in combination are a comedic tour de force unparalleled in our view by any two comics that we've seen in Las Vegas for 15 years. If you can stand some rough language and blue humor (or if you can suspend your moral rectitude and political correctness for just 90 minutes), this show is a must-see.

CONSUMER TIPS If you're looking for magic and illusion, forget Jonathan. If you want a PG version of *Jonathan,* the closest thing is Mac King at Harrah's. If you decide to go, buy your admission in advance: tickets to Jonathan are among the hottest in town. To avoid being part of the show, ask for seats a row or two back.

American Storm ★★★

APPEAL BY AGE   UNDER 21 ★★★★★   21–37 ★★★★   38–50 ★★★   51+ ★★★

HOST CASINO AND SHOWROOM Riviera—Le Bistro Theatre; ☎ 702-492-3960 or 866-80-SHOWS; www.rivierahotel.com or www.american-storm.com

Type of show Stud-puppy strip show. **Admission** $54.95. **Cast size** 6. **Night of lowest attendance** Wednesday. **Usual showtimes** Nightly, 10:30 p.m. **Dark** Monday. **Topless** Buff pecs. **Duration of presentation** 1 hour and 30 minutes.

DESCRIPTION AND COMMENTS Judging by audience reaction, *American Storm* might well be called *The Mighty Clouds of Joy.* Although this oiled-up male-nudity show doesn't offer the "full Monty" (by law no Las Vegas establishment can show complete nudity and serve alcohol), that didn't seem to matter to the howling, whooping, screaming audience made up of almost entirely women. Anyone who is laboring under the notion that women are dainty creatures, foresworn of raucous sexuality, should be a fly on the wall for the nearly 90 minutes of *American Storm,* where piercing chants of "Touch it!" can sometimes be heard over the fray.

The half-dozen men, roughly 25 years old, are gorgeous, with rippling physiques, and they are fair dancers, too. Their choreography in lightly themed numbers featuring cowboys, gangsters, soldiers, and the like, however, definitely takes a back seat to general prancing, gyrating, grinding, and skipping about on stage and through the audience. Several women of various body types and ages were drafted to mount the stage to participate in transparently configured sex acts, which makes the evening sound lurid, but it seemed to be great fun for all involved. The cast members, selected from the VH1 reality show *Strip Search,* have an almost embarrassed sweetness about them, which makes the show seem even more like innocent, albeit wild, excess.

Any seat in the small cabaret-style house will give you a good view, and no seat will protect you from being invited on stage, but you can always decline. The lighting isn't as bright on the left side so if you're trying to be visible and participate, sit on the right side, but the guys do a good job of getting around to all the ladies and tables. *American Storm's* men were approved in part by *Thunder from Down Under* creator Billy Cross, so the shows are relatively comparable. Drinks are served tableside, and guests ages 18 to 20 must be accompanied by an adult 21 or over. No one under age 18 is admitted.

CONSUMER TIPS Arrive early to get in line and sit in the front. The outfits are not creative so don't expect dazzling costumes. During the show, there is quite a bit of dancing and it actually takes these guys a while to get their clothes off. If the typical routine was anywhere from seven to ten minutes, you're looking at a good five minutes of dancing before the guys even start stripping. After the show, everyone is invited to pose for a free Polaroid with the cast.

American Superstars ★ ★ ★

APPEAL BY AGE	UNDER 21 ★ ★ ★	21–37 ★ ★ ★ ½	38–50 ★ ★ ★ ★	51+ ★ ★ ★ ½

HOST CASINO AND SHOWROOM **Stratosphere—Star Showroom;**
☎ **702-382-4446 (reservations necessary); www.stratospherehotel.com**

Type of show Celebrity impersonator production show. **Admission** $30.95 (ages 5–12); $41.75 (adults). **Cast size** Approximately 24. **Nights of lowest attendance** Sunday, Monday. **Usual showtimes** Sunday–Tuesday, 7 p.m.; Wednesday, Friday, and Saturday, 6:30 and 8:30 p.m. **Dark** Thursday. **Special comments** Much enhanced on the larger stage. **Topless** No. **Duration of presentation** 1 hour and 30 minutes.

DESCRIPTION AND COMMENTS *American Superstars* is a celebrity-impersonator show similar to *Legends in Concert* (Imperial Palace). Impersonated stars, which change from time to time, include Britney Spears, Michael Jackson, Christina Aguilera, Tim McGraw, and the ever-present Elvis. The impersonators, who do their own singing, are supported by a live band and (frequently upstaged) by an energetic troupe of dancers.

American Superstars is a fun, upbeat show. While the impersonations are, in general, not as crisp or realistic as those of *Legends in Concert,* the show exhibits a lot of drive and is a great night's entertainment.

CONSUMER TIPS The Stratosphere's main showroom has allowed the production to improve and become truly competitive with *Legends in Concert.* Though tickets must be purchased in advance, seat assignment is at the discretion of the maître d'. Drinks are not included, but can be purchased at a bar outside the showroom. The showroom is situated at the end of the shopping arcade near the elevator bank for the Stratosphere Tower. *Note:* A $50 package is available, including the show, drinks, buffet dinner, and tickets to the Tower.

America's Tribute to Neil Diamond ★★

APPEAL BY AGE	UNDER 21 ★	21–37 ★½	38–50 ★★★	51+ ★★½

HOST CASINO AND SHOWROOM **Riviera—Le Bistro Theatre; ☎ 877-892-7469; www.rivierahotel.com**

Type of show Impersonator and band cover Neil Diamond's many hits. **Admission** $49.95. **Cast size** 6. **Night of lowest attendance** Tuesday. **Usual showtimes** Sunday–Thursday, 7 p.m. **Dark** Friday and Saturday. **Topless** No. **Duration of presentation** 1 hour.

DESCRIPTION AND COMMENTS Despite their idol's long career and army of hit singles, Neil Diamond impersonators aren't nearly as common as those who imitate Elvis, the Rat Pack, the Beatles, or other such worthies. It may be the cheese factor, as Diamond's overwrought balladeering hasn't aged as well as some. Still, Jay White is far and away the best Neil Diamond impersonator in Vegas, with a pretty close physical resemblance and dead-on vocals. This is definitely a niche show, but those who love Neil will go nuts. White's band is tight and professional, and though the onstage patter is on the lame side, who cares? Neilophiles in our audience leaped from their seats and danced in the aisles.

CONSUMER TIPS The Le Bistro Theatre's small stage is ringed by lounge tables and chairs, with circular booths making up the outside border. However, since the showroom is actually just a curtained alcove off the main gambling floor, casino noise inevitably filters in to the booths. Even so, the room is small enough that there are no bad sight lines.

Anthony Cools ★★★½

APPEAL BY AGE	UNDER 21 –	21–37 ★★★★	38–50 ★★	51+ ★

HOST CASINO AND SHOWROOM **Paris—Anthony Cools Theater; ☎ 702-946-7000 or 800-828-3830; www.parislasvegas.com or www.anthonycools.com**

Type of show Uncensored hypnosis comedy. **Admission** $53 and $75. **Cast size** 3 (+12 volunteers). **Night of lowest attendance** Monday. **Usual showtimes** 9 p.m. **Dark** Wednesday. **Topless** No. **Special comments** Must be 21 or older to attend. **Duration of presentation** 1 hour and 30 minutes.

DESCRIPTION AND COMMENTS If you must see a hypnotist show—and you don't mind incessant cursing and dirty talking—then this is the hypnotist show. Unlike his thematic predecessor, the late and unlamented "Dr. Naughty," Anthony Cools is a slick, adroit manipulator and a truly devious creator of setups for his hypnotized zombie minions. As with any hypnotist show, you (and the audience, and the volunteers) have to buy into the idea that the volunteers really are hypnotized and unconsciously abiding by the bizarre suggestions implanted by Cools. But that suspension of disbelief gets easier when the skits devised by Cools are so funny—his volunteers are afflicted with burning nether regions, must deal with uncontrollably vocal genitals, or make sweet love (or not so sweet love) to a chair, among other torments. The young and enthusiastic crowd really gets into it, and that juice motivates the performing volunteers to greater heights of debauchery. Ultimately, you really won't care if they're hypnotized or not, as long as the hot chick on stage is really good at screaming out fake orgasms.

CONSUMER TIPS Obviously, this is not a show for the easily offended or intimidated. Salacious humor is the order of the day, and it's one of the bawdiest productions in town. Get in early if you want a seat near the front, and feel free to volunteer (or volunteer your friends) if you'd like to get into the hypnosis thing. Note that taking photos during the show is encouraged; also, an instantly produced DVD of the show you just saw is available after it's over. Grade A blackmail material.

Barbra and Frank: The Concert that Never Was   ★ ★ ★ ½

| APPEAL BY AGE | UNDER 21 ★ ★ | 21–37 ★ ★ ★ | 38–50 ★ ★ ★ ½ | 51+ ★ ★ ★ ½ |

HOST CASINO AND SHOWROOM **Riviera—Le Bistro Theater; ☎ 702-794-9433; www.rivierahotel.com**

Type of show Celebrity impersonator. Admission $39.95, $49.95. Cast size 3. Night of lowest attendance Thursday. Usual showtimes 8:30 p.m. Dark Monday and Tuesday. Topless No. Duration of presentation 1 hour and 15 minutes.

DESCRIPTION AND COMMENTS This is the kind of production that makes reviewing shows fun. Tired from reviewing several shows each night, we are seated in a diminutive showroom separated from the casino and adjoining bar only by curtains. We look at our watches and think about how we can duck out early if the show is bad. The presentation begins slowly with a film about Sinatra and Streisand that traces their careers and establishes that they never worked together except for a taped duet that they recorded in separate studios. Barbra was willing to share a stage, Frank was not. Hence "the Concert that Never Was."

Sinatra is impersonated by Sebastian Anzaldo, who has Sinatra's general build but otherwise doesn't bear much of a resemblance. When you close you eyes and listen, though, Anzaldo has nailed the voice. Ditto for mannerisms when you start observing again. Sharon Owens is a young phenom who has so completely captured Streisand's personality, voice, and quirky stage presence that you wonder what's she's doing in a lounge showroom at the Riviera. Oh yeah, did we mention that she really looks like Barbra?

Playing off each other beautifully with good-natured kidding and some caustic banter when Streisand reacts to Sinatra's curt, chauvinistic comments, Anzaldo and Owens are very convincing. Accompanied by a pianist, they each perform a few songs solo and then come together for some really sweet duets. The pleasure this modest production bestows transcends its venue and in the end you've not only been reunited with Frank and Barbra but you've fallen in love with Sharon and Sebastian, too.

CONSUMER TIPS Le Bistro Theatre is located on the ground floor toward the front of the casino near the food court. VIP seats are available for $10 extra but gain you very little in such a small intimate theater. Discount coupons are frequently available, and half-price tickets can be had from Tickets2Nite and Tix4Tonight (see page 168).

Barry Manilow: Music and Passion ★★★½

APPEAL BY AGE   UNDER 21 ★★   21–37 ★★★   38–50 ★★★½   51+ ★★★½

HOST CASINO AND SHOWROOM **Las Vegas Hilton—Hilton Theater;** ☎ **702-732-5755; www.lvhilton.com**

Type of show Celebrity headliner. **Admission cost** $110.50–$198. **Cast size** 13. **Night of lowest attendance** Wednesday. **Usual showtimes** 8 p.m. **Dark** Thursday. **Topless** No. **Special comments** Must be 18 or older to attend. **Duration of presentation** 1 hour and 30 minutes.

DESCRIPTION AND COMMENTS Long-standing pop icon Barry Manilow, supported by excellent backup vocalists and a ten-piece band, delivers 90 well-paced minutes of the music that made him famous. The staging is creative and incorporates some high-tech gimmicks, including an elevated catwalk that springs out of the stage to elevate Manilow above the audience for the finale. The show really doesn't have a weakness, BUT, it definitely helps to be a Barry Manilow fan.

    While Elton John or Gladys Knight can effortlessly turn on an audience who has little knowledge of their music, Manilow tends to stall for the uninitiated. Fortunately for Manilow, most of his audience are fans, and gushing fans at that. Like Celine Dion's fans, their gestalt is cloying and overwhelmingly saccharine, adding to the discomfort of those not in the fold.

CONSUMER TIPS The Hilton Theater is a perfect size for celebrity headliners, offering exceptional intimacy for a large showroom, and excellent lines of site. Because the stage is quite wide, we recommend requesting seats at least eight rows or more from the front. Valet parking works better than the self-parking garage if you drive, but the best bet if you're coming from the Strip is to take the Las Vegas Monorail.

Bette Midler *(not open at press time)*

HOST CASINO AND SHOWROOM **Caesars Palace—Colosseum;** ☎**702-731-7333; www.caesars.com**

Type of show Celebrity headliner. **Admission** $117–$272. **Night of lowest attendance** Wednesday. **Usual showtimes** Tuesday, Wednesday, and Friday–Sunday, 7:30 p.m. for all. **Dark** Monday and Thursday. **Special comments** No age restrictions. **Topless** No. **Duration of presentation** 1 hour and 30 minutes.

DESCRIPTION AND COMMENTS In a diva switch, Midler will replace Celine Dion at Caesars Colosseum showroom on February 20, 2008. Although there are no age restrictions, the show is designed for a mature audience. A drink coupon is included in the price of admission.

CONSUMER TIPS Because you must pass through a metal detector to enter the showroom, plan to arrive 15 minutes earlier than usual. Use the adjacent Forum Shops valet parking—Caesars' valet service will be inundated after the show.

Bite ★★★

HOST CASINO AND SHOWROOM **Stratosphere—Stratosphere Theater;**
☎ **702-382-4446 or 800-998-6937; www.stratospherehotel.com**

Type of show Erotic rock 'n' roll vampires. **Admission** $40.95. **Cast size** 12. **Night of lowest attendance** Wednesday. **Usual showtimes** 10:30 p.m. **Dark** Thursday. **Topless** Yes. **Special comments** Must be 18 or older to attend. **Duration of presentation** 1 hour and 20 minutes.

DESCRIPTION AND COMMENTS *Bite,* a skin revue featuring buff women with really weird dentition, has a big kahuna vampire, played by Mike Tyson (just kidding), on the prowl for his long-lost and now reincarnated lover. The plot, such as it is, is told through rock music of the 1970s, 1980s, and 1990s, and gets in the way as much as it binds the show together. The music, on the other hand, drives the show with a vengeance. The pace is furious, the choreography above average, and the showgirls hardworking and easy on the eye. The vampire thing doesn't add much to the show, but every production has to have its gimmick.

Your reaction to *Bite* will revolve around one factor: your ability to take vampires seriously when they groove to classic rock. Perhaps we've been culturally indoctrinated to think bloodsuckers either like orchestral dirges or dark goth punk, but it's still weird to see the Vampire Lord mooning around to the strains of the Eagles' "Desperado." Thankfully, there are no speaking parts, other than an occasional voice-over. The dancing, singing, and performing talent on display is mostly genuine, but the hokey quotient is very high.

CONSUMER TIPS This is edgier than most of the other T&A revues, with a dance style more at home in a strip club than in a casino showroom. Ziegfeld it ain't. Also, it really helps to like Guns N' Roses, ZZ Top, and Ted Nugent. Seats on the extreme left-front and right-front by the stage are too severe an angle to afford much of a view.

Blue Man Group ★★★★½

HOST CASINO AND SHOWROOM **Venetian—Blue Man Group Theatre;** ☎ **702-414-7469 or 800-BLUE-MAN; www.blueman.com or www.venetian.com**

Type of show Performance-art production show. **Admission** $65, $85, $110. **Cast size** 3 plus a 15-piece band. **Nights of lowest attendance** Sunday and Monday. **Usual showtimes** Daily, 7:30 p.m. with a second 10:30 p.m. show on Saturday. **Dark** None. **Topless** No. **Special comments** Teenagers will really like this show, but the blue guys, loud music, and dark colors could scare small children (5 years minimum age). **Duration of presentation** 1 hour and 45 minutes.

DESCRIPTION AND COMMENTS What could demonstrate more mainstream cultural success than your own custom-designed 1,760-seat theater in Las Vegas? What could be more hip than to be a mystical, magical, and mute hero and clown and be blue? If you watch Blue Man Group at their Venetian venue with its immense stage area, you may well come up with the answer that nothing is more befuddlingly mainstream or more cool.

Blue Man Group gives Las Vegas its first large-scale introduction to that nebulous genre called "performance art." If you're from Mars and the designation "performance art" confuses you, relax—it won't hurt a bit. Blue Man Group serves up a stunning show that can be appreciated by all kinds of folks ages 8 to 80. Younger children may be frightened by the silent, wide-eyed, blue characters.

The three blue men are just that—blue—and bald and mute. Wearing black clothing and skullcaps slathered with bright-blue greasepaint, their fast-paced show uses music (mostly percussion) and multimedia effects to make light of contemporary art and life in the information age. The Vegas act is just one expression of a franchise that started with three friends in New York's East Village. Now you can catch their zany, wacky, smart stuff in New York, Boston, Chicago, Berlin, and Toronto.

Funny, sometimes poignant, and always compelling, *Blue Man Group* hooks the audience even before the show begins with digital messages that ultimately spin performers and audience alike into a mutual act of joyous complicity. The trio pounds out vital, visceral tribal rhythms on complex instruments (made of PVC pipes) that could pass for industrial intestines, and makes seemingly spontaneous eruptions of visual art rendered with marshmallows and a mysterious goo. Their weekly supplies include 25.5 pounds of Cap'n Crunch, 60 Twinkies, 75 gallons of Jell-O, 996 marshmallows, 9.5 gallons of paint, and 185 miles, yes, miles, of rolled recycled paper. If all this sounds silly, it is, but it's also strangely thought-provoking about such various topics as the value of modern art, DNA, the persistence of vision, the way rock music moves you, and how we are all connected. (Hint: It's not the Internet.)

A 15-piece percussion band backs the Blue Man Group with a relentless and totally engrossing industrial dance riff. The band resides in long dark alcoves above the stage. At just the right moments, their lofts are lit to reveal a group of neon-colored pulsating skeletons.

Audience participation completes the Blue Man experience. The blue men often move into the audience to bring audience members on stage. At the end of the show, the entire audience is involved in an effort to move a sea of paper across the theater. And a lot of folks can't help standing up to dance—and laugh. Magicians for the creative spirit that resides in us all, the Blue Man Group makes everyone a coconspirator in a culminating joyous explosion.

CONSUMER TIPS This show is decidedly different and requires an open mind to be appreciated. It also helps to be a little loose, because everybody gets sucked into the production, and leaves the theater a little bit lighter in spirit because of it, judging by the rousing standing ovations. If you don't want to be pulled onstage to become a part of the improvisation, don't sit in the first half dozen or so rows. If you drive, give yourself lots of extra time to park and make it to the showroom. The Venetian showrooms are toward the rear of the property around the corner from the V Bar nightspot.

Carrot Top ★★★

HOST CASINO AND SHOWROOM **Luxor—Atrium Showroom; ☎ 702-262-4900; www.luxor.com**

Type of show Stand-up comedy. **Admission** $54.95–$65.95. **Cast size** 1. **Night of lowest attendance** Thursday. **Usual showtimes** 8 p.m. on Sunday, Monday, Wednesday, Thursday, Friday; 7 and 9 p.m. on Saturday. **Dark** Tuesday. **Topless** Only Carrot Top. **Duration of presentation** 1 hour 40 minutes.

DESCRIPTION AND COMMENTS   Fans of comedian Carrot Top will love this fast-paced, high-energy, quick-spurting comedy orgy that strikes many mature themes. The redhead makes extensive use of the special effects (including fog, smoke, and strobe), lighting, and sound capabilities of the room. These heighten the experience far beyond the boundaries of standard nightclub stand-up fare. Pulling from large crates and even a washing machine, Carrot Top relies heavily on "homemade" props. He even makes jokes about their construction, cracking one-liners about having to shop for dildos, wigs, and the like. His basic routine runs to "look at this" as he pulls strange thing after strange thing from the containers.

His humor is highly topical: rednecks, rock musicians, NASCAR, etc. Many of his quips are tasteless and offensive to various groups and persuasions, but the delivery is so fast and so brief that it's hard to take offense. In fact, his full-tilt boogie onslaught makes it difficult to stay with him, and you find yourself tuning out just to give your brain a respite. The pacing may prompt recall of the comedic delirium of Robin Williams. But whereas Williams explores our common humanity, Carrot Top fires bullets past the head that never touch the heart. His routines could be described as quick-witted, but not brainy. The 1:40 minute show includes a 15-minute opening act with another comedian. Dedicated fans will be delighted, but the uninitiated may find that Carrot Top's comedy degenerates too quickly to the bottom drawer.

CONSUMER TIPS   Alcohol is not served in the theater and you must be 18 years of age or older for admittance. The theater is tiered and seats, all with good sight lines, are preassigned. Bring along a couple of aspirins—you'll need them for your headache after the show.

Celine Dion—A New Day . . . ★★★★½

HOST CASINO AND SHOWROOM **Caesars Palace—Colosseum; ☎ 702-731-7333 or 877-4-CELINE; www.caesars.com**

Type of show Celebrity headliner. **Admission** $87.50–$225 depending on location of seat. **Cast size** 74, including musicians and dancers. **Night of lowest attendance** Thursday. **Usual showtimes** Wednesday–Sunday, 8:30 p.m. **Dark** Monday and Tuesday. **Special comments** No age restrictions. **Topless** No. **Duration of presentation** 1 hour and 30 minutes.

DESCRIPTION AND COMMENTS   The name of the show is *A New Day*, but it could just as easily be *Road-Weary Diva Joins Circus*. Er, make that joins Cirque du Soleil. Celine Dion's Las Vegas tour de force was created by Cirque du Soleil visionary Franco Dragone. In it he masterfully blends a whopping 22 of Dion's songs with the surreal characters, imagery, and athletic (often acrobatic) choreography that distinguishes Cirque du Soleil. *A New Day* is more superficial than Cirque's *Mystère* or *"O,"* but in its best moments it approximates their power and depth. Dragone augments *A New Day's* amazing costumes and sets with an enormous LED screen, the largest in the world, that wraps around the entire rear of the stage in a sweeping half circle. Displayed on it are razor-sharp moving images, both powerful and hypnotic, that add haunting texture and context to what is happening on stage. The cast alone could carry *A New Day*, but the incorporation of this technological marvel exponentially leverages their considerable talent, wowing audiences in the same way that the introduction of sound or color once amazed moviegoers. *A New Day* is not just another Las Vegas spectacle, though as a production show it's truly groundbreaking in its special effects and choreography. What makes it transcendent is a diva who has the chutzpah to share the stage with such technology and talent. There are times, literally, when the dancing and LED images (everything from Times Square to a passing storm) are so compelling that you momentarily forget Celine Dion is singing. But when you refocus your attention on her, you begin to understand the seamless way the elements of this production are integrated.

The show has two weaknesses. First, the stage and showroom are so large that it's impossible to establish the intimacy that drives the better headliner shows. The second weakness (perhaps an attempt to mitigate the first) is the seemingly inevitable compunction of all headliners, including Celine Dion, to speak personally to the audience. Celine emotes about her husband, child, world peace (or lack thereof), and myriad other topics of interest to her but not necessarily to the audience. Of course Celine's fans (who are legion) eat this up. For the rest, these syrupy interludes are somewhat uncomfortable (in addition to disrupting the flow of the production). To compound matters, all this "sharing" is punctuated by individual fans hollering, "We love you, Celine!" from every corner of the theater. Lest we overstate the case, however, there's not all that much time for "getting to know each other" (read: "getting to know me") when the performer has almost two dozen songs to belt out before the curtain comes down.

CONSUMER TIPS   The big question hanging over Celine Dion's show is whether it's worth the not-inconsiderable price. Although it's a great show by any standard, the cost is infinitely easier to swallow if you're a Celine fan. If you're neutral or you just don't know much about Celine, the question is iffier, and the answer really comes down to how much money you're comfortable spending.

A New Day is a hot ticket. Even with record-breaking prices for a continuously running show, it's advisable to purchase tickets as far in advance as possible. Concerning seat selection, there are good sight lines from every seat in the new, well-designed Coliseum theater. Plus, the enormity of the stage and the scope of the production make sitting close to the stage less than desirable unless you desire to consult with Celine on international monetary policy or some such. If you drive to Caesars, use the valet parking at the adjoining Forum Shops rather than the hotel-casino valet service at Caesars' main entrance. There is also valet parking and self-parking at the garages to the rear of the hotel, with an entrance convenient to the theater. Give yourself lots of extra time to process through the metal detectors and bag-and-purse search at the entrance to the theater.

Chippendales ★★★★

APPEAL BY AGE   18–20 ★★★★   21–37 ★★★★   38–50 ★★★★   51+ ★★★½

HOST CASINO AND SHOWROOM **Rio—The Chippendales Theater;**
☎ **702-777-7776 or 888-746-7784; www.riolasvegas.com**

Type of show Male revue. **Admission** $34.95–$75. **Cast size** 12. **Night of lowest attendance** Monday. **Usual showtimes** Sunday–Tuesday and Thursday, 8 p.m.; Friday and Saturday, 8:30 and 10:30 p.m. **Dark** Wednesday. **Topless** Yes (male). **Duration of presentation** 1 hour and 15 minutes.

DESCRIPTION AND COMMENTS *Chippendales* strives to be the ultimate ladies' night out and succeeds. The show, which originated in Los Angeles and celebrated its 25th anniversary in 2003, is a mesmerizing erotic exploration of female fantasies. Performed by a cast of one dozen flawless model types, the men of *Chippendales* exude sex appeal while acting out a sequence of 11 vignettes. Most of the tightly synchronized dance routines are performed to contemporary R&B slow jams, creating a seductive and sensual atmosphere. Unlike the comparatively tame *Thunder from Down Under*, the *Chippendales* dancers feign sex acts and remove their G-strings entirely at several times during the show (albeit only when the guys have their backs turned to the audience). Large video screens surround the 600 or more person showroom, offering a close-up view of the dancers, who can be difficult to see at times from the general-admission seating. The dancers also venture out into the audience at various points throughout the performance, although not as much as the *Thunder* cast. After the show, the men of *Chippendales* host a meet-and-greet session for an extended close-up look.

CONSUMER TIPS No smoking is allowed during the show. On weekends, tables are removed from the VIP/floor section to provide more seating, requiring guests to hold their drinks (which can be pricey, so be careful not to spill). Drink prices and types vary greatly, from $2.50 for soda to $335 for a bottle of Louis Roederer Cristal Champagne. Other choices include: beer, $4.50 to $5.50; wine by the glass, $6; frozen drinks, $7; and mixed drinks, $6 to $9.50. The bathroom is located next to the Masquerade Bar, diagonally across the casino. Paying extra for floor seats is well worth it for ladies seeking the best view. Hold on to your ticket stub, which includes a free entry to Club Rio Thursday through Saturday (up to a $20 value for men on Friday and Saturday nights).

CIRQUE DU SOLEIL SHOWS

CIRQUE DU SOLEIL HAS TAKEN LAS VEGAS by frontal assault. There are now five Cirque du Soleil productions playing Las Vegas showrooms. First to open was *Mystère* at T. I., followed some years later by "*O*" at the Bellagio. The third show to premier was *Zumanity* at New York–New York, with *KÀ* at the MGM Grand following close on its heels in 2005. Cirque's latest production, *LOVE*, based on the music of the Beatles, opened in June of 2006.

KÀ, *Mystère*, *LOVE*, and "*O*" are representative of Cirque shows everywhere, albeit on a grand scale, and are appropriate for all ages. *Zumanity*, an in-your-face celebration of everything sexual, is much different from the other productions. All Cirque shows provide an awe-inspiring evening of entertainment, so you really can't go wrong (assuming in the case of *Zumanity* that you're comfortable with the sexual content).

If you've never seen a Cirque du Soleil show, we suggest you start with *KÀ* or *Mystère*. Tickets for *Mystère* sell at $25 to $45 less than for *KÀ* and "*O*," making *Mystère* by far the best value. Below you will find reviews of all the Las Vegas Cirque du Soleil shows. This information will help you make your choice of productions.

Cirque du Soleil's *KÀ* ★★★★½

APPEAL BY AGE   **UNDER 21** ★★★★   **21–37** ★★★★★   **38–50** ★★★★★   **51+** ★★★★★

HOST CASINO AND SHOWROOM   **MGM Grand—KÀ Theater; ☎ 877-264-1844; www.mgmgrand.com/ka**

Type of show Fearsome ballet as epic journey. **Admission cost** $99, $125, $150, $175, $199 (no tax or fees included). *Note:* Wheelchair-accessible seating available at all ticket levels. **Cast size** 80. **Night of lowest attendance** Wednesday. **Usual showtimes** 7:30 and 10:30 p.m. **Dark** Sunday and Monday. **Topless** No. **Special comments** Guests age 18 and under permitted only if accompanied by an adult; no children under age 5. **Duration of presentation** 1 hour and 30 minutes.

DESCRIPTION AND COMMENTS   *KÀ*, at the MGM Grand, is a departure for Cirque du Soleil in many ways. Most striking is the menacing atmosphere of *KÀ* theater. It has the look of an enchanted Asian foundry from space complete with 30-foot bursts of flame, performers hanging batlike from girders and scampering along catwalks, and industrial clangs reverberating as you find your seat. You are shown to your seat by one of many hair-raising Gatekeepers, who also serve as security during the show. (This reviewer would not advise breaking theater rules; it will be a Gatekeeper who sees to your punishment.) At the center of the theater, a gaping pit lurks where the stage would rightfully be. The overall effect, while chilling, isn't off-putting, but the proscription against very young children makes good sense.

KÀ is also unique in that it is the first Cirque production that attempts to tell a linear story. That story follows twins who have been separated and must each make a journey to meet their destiny. That journey is the focus of the show, and the twins travel through beaches, mountains, forests, and blizzards, face warriors and whimsical sea and forest creatures, and witness remarkable feats of strength and agility. All these, of course, completely overshadow the storytelling and relegate the story to something you're vaguely conscious of from time to time, but nothing more.

If there is a single star of *KÀ*, it is the gantry stage. From the pit emerges a large deck, supported by a boom, that is manipulated with computer precision to spin, tilt, raise and lower throughout the show, all with surprising fluidity and speed. Not to knock the performers, who are as lithe and powerful as any cast of humans has a right to be, but the stage is an incredible industrial achievement. In one of the most breathtaking scenes, the stage tilts fully vertical as warriors loose arrows toward it and their intended victims scramble to find purchase. The arrows appear to stick in the stage, giving the "attacked" performers the handholds they need to dance and spin and flip their way up the vertical wall. As the performers ascend the wall, the "arrows" (which are actually 80 retractable pegs built into the stage) retract and the stage appears to shrug off the performers like so much detritus—an effect that is both unforgettable and disturbing.

In short, *KÀ* is a spectacle, and arguably the most technologically complex show in Las Vegas. The story line fails, but the production as a whole doesn't suffer from the loss. *KÀ* is a new breed of Cirque show, though it still contains the elements of all Cirque productions: elaborate costumes, haunting scores, physical prowess and beauty, and acrobatic feats. If you've already fallen, and fallen hard, for *Mystère*, *KÀ* may not be quite what you expect of a Cirque performance. While *KÀ* does display some of the whimsy of *Mystère*, the overall impression of *Mystère* is of a dreamed existence shaded with dark humor and lighthearted playfulness, and the overall impression of *KÀ* is shock, awe, and menacing power. If you are in a show-going mood, you can easily see both *KÀ* and *Mystère* in a single vacation without feeling over-Cirqued. In fact, we recommend it. *KÀ* is a fearsome production, and an elegant foil for the playful *Mystère*.

CONSUMER TIPS *KÀ* is not only the gold standard for over-the-top technological productions in a town that's all about over-the-top, it also joins sister production *"O"* in demanding over-the-top ticket prices. It's a fine show—as virile and stirring as anything on the Strip—but the tariff is steep at $99 to $150. Comparatively, though, the $99 seats are a better deal than similar seats at *"O,"* because *KÀ* Theater was thoughtfully designed without "limited visibility" seats. Also of note, there are wheelchair-accessible seats in all three of the theater's ticketed sections.

If you do see *KÀ* and if you can manage to remember this tip with menacing creatures dangling overhead, arrows zipping at the performers and a stage that's come shouldering to life in front of you, try to spot the three "performers" on stage who are actually technicians in costume.

Cirque du Soleil's *LOVE* ★★★★½

APPEAL BY AGE   UNDER 21 ★★★   21–37 ★★★★   38–50 ★★★★   51+ ★★★★★

HOST CASINO AND SHOWROOM **Mirage—*LOVE* Theater;** ☎ **702-791-4111 or 800-963-9634; www.mirage.com or www.cirquedusoleil.com**

Type of show Circus based on music of the Beatles. **Admission** $69 (upper level), $99 (upper-mid), $125 (midlevel), $150 (floor level). **Cast size** 60. **Night of lowest attendance** Monday. **Usual showtimes** Thursday–Monday, 7:30 and 10:30 p.m. **Dark** Tuesday and Wednesday. **Topless** No. **Duration of presentation** 1 hour and 30 minutes.

DESCRIPTION AND COMMENTS *LOVE*, like most Cirque du Soleil shows, is nothing if not an overwhelming spectacle. But this latest Cirque extravaganza is a definite departure from what might be loosely called the norm. First, it's heavily multimedia, combining extensive video effects projected onto a variety of screens with dancers, acrobats, and aerialists in outlandish costumes and bizarre props, all driven by the most powerful soundtrack ever, perhaps, produced. And because music, especially familiar music, is the force behind the visuals and theatrics, *LOVE* is grounded in a reality that the audience shares, which renders this show unified and accessible in a way that *Mystère* approximates, but that *"O"* and even *KÀ* with its loose plot line, can never be.

That's not to imply, however, that *LOVE* doesn't have its extreme flights of fancy. The teaming of Cirque and the Beatles is, simply put, a marriage made in psychedelic heaven. Only Cirque could so effectively choreograph, costume, and showcase the characters, images, themes, humor, whimsicality, and all-around 1960s optimism, exuberance, and magic that the Beatles continue, 40 years later, to embody.

The show opens with a rousing rendition of "Get Back." Then it flashes back to begin a loose retrospective based on the Beatles' meteoric rise to become the most influential rock 'n' roll band in history. "Eleanor Rigby" is set to video and theatrical scenes of the devastation that World War II wrought on the Beatles' Liverpool. "I Want to Hold Your Hand" introduces the collective planetary hysteria of Beatlemania. By now you know what you're in for. The stage, in pieces controlled by individual hydraulics, rises and falls as necessary. The visuals range from actual Beatles concerts and appearances to paisleys and spirals guaranteed to give (some of) you flashbacks. The music, which has been digitized and remixed by Sir George Martin (the fifth Beatle) and his son Giles, isn't exactly the same as on the LPs, as you might expect, and it's fun to listen for the little differences. The soundtrack consists of full songs, medleys, snippets of tunes down to a bar or two that disappear as soon as you recognize them, along with Beatles banter and fragments from recording sessions, plus suitably surreal transitions holding it all together. One thing's for sure: The acoustics are outstanding. More than 6,000 speakers surround you, with one installed in the backrest of every seat in the house.

Song after timeless song parades by. "Something in the Way She Moves" is accompanied by an aerial ballet; "Lucy in the Sky with Diamonds" is similar. "Mr. Kite" is set to an epic three-ring circus; Henry the Horse dances the waltz on Rollerblades. The skit around "Blackbird" is hilarious, with spastic birds learning to fly. For "Strawberry Fields," big bubbles are blown from the top of a grand piano. "Octopus's Garden" has airborne squids and anemones. If you pay close attention, you'll catch new lyrics at the end of "While My Guitar Gently Weeps." Four skaters perform amazing acrobatics on steep ramps to "Help!" "Lady Madonna," "Here Comes the Sun," "Come Together," "Revolution Number Nine," "Back in the USSR," and "Day in the Life"—ultimately, *LOVE* passes the true test of psychedelia: it doesn't matter if your eyes are open or closed.

For the finale, umbrellas spread confetti all over the room to "Hey Jude" and predictably, the show ends on "Sgt. Pepper's Lonely Hearts Club Band": We hope you have enjoyed the show and we're sorry but it's time to go. The audience is sorry too.

CONSUMER TIPS *LOVE* plays in the space where Siegfried and Roy used to perform, but the new theater underwent a mere $120 million worth of renovations. There's not a bad seat in the new 2,000-seat theater-in-the-round, but the top $150 ticket might be too close. Since all the action occurs on the elevated stages and above, the eye-level $99 and $125 seats are better. You can't see *LOVE* anywhere else on the planet, folks, so be sure to buy your tickets by phone or online (**www.cirque dusoleil.com**) as far in advance as possible. The concession stand sells bottled water ($2.75), beer ($3.75 and $7), and popcorn ($5 and $6), plus wine, mixed drinks, and Champagne ($7 to $16).

Cirque du Soleil's *Mystère* ★★★★★

APPEAL BY AGE UNDER 21 ★★★★ 21–37 ★★★★★ 38–50 ★★★★★ 51+ ★★★★½

HOST CASINO AND SHOWROOM **T. I.—*Mystère* Theater; ☎ 702-894-7722 or 800-392-1999; www.treasureisland.com**

Type of show Circus as theater. **Admission** $60, $75, $95, limited seats. **Cast size** 75. **Night of lowest attendance** Thursday. **Usual showtimes** Wednesday–Saturday, 7:30 and 10:30 p.m.; Sunday, 4:30 and 7:30 p.m. **Dark** Monday and Tuesday. **Special comments** No table service (no tables!). **Topless** No. **Duration of presentation** 1 hour and 30 minutes.

DESCRIPTION AND COMMENTS *Mystère* is a far cry from a traditional circus but retains all of the fun and excitement. It is whimsical, mystical, and sophisticated, yet pleasing to all ages. The action takes place on an elaborate stage that incorporates almost every part of the theater. The original musical score is exotic, like the show.

Note: In the following paragraph, we get into how the show *feels* and why it's special. If you don't care how it feels, or if you are not up to slogging through a boxcar of adjectives, the bottom line is simple: *Mystère* is great. See it.

Mystère is the most difficult show in Las Vegas to describe. To categorize it as a circus does not begin to cover its depth, though its performers could perform with distinction in any circus on earth. Cirque du Soleil is more, much more, than a circus. It combines elements of classic Greek theater, mime, the English morality play, Dali surrealism, Fellini characterization, and Chaplin comedy. *Mystère* is at once an odyssey, a symphony, and an exploration of human emotions. The show pivots on its humor, which is sometimes black, and engages the audience with its unforgettable characters. Though light and uplifting, it is also poignant and dark.

Simple in its presentation, it is at the same time extraordinarily intricate, always operating on multiple levels of meaning. As you laugh and watch the amazingly talented cast, you become aware that your mind has entered a dimension seldom encountered in a waking state. The presentation begins to register in your consciousness more as a seamless dream than as a stage production. You are moved, lulled, and soothed as well as excited and entertained. The sensitive, the imaginative, the literate, and those who love good theater and art will find no show in Las Vegas that compares with *Mystère* except Cirque's sister productions, *KÀ* at the MGM Grand, *"O"* at the Bellagio, and *Zumanity* at New York–New York.

CONSUMER TIPS Be forewarned that the audience is an integral part of *Mystère* and that at almost any time you might be plucked from your seat to participate. Our advice is to loosen up and roll with it. If you are too rigid, repressed, hungover, or whatever to get involved, politely but firmly decline to be conscripted.

Because *Mystère* is presented in its own customized showroom, there are no tables and, consequently, no drink service. In keeping with the show's circus theme, however, spectators may purchase refreshments at nearby concession stands. Tickets for reserved seats can be purchased seven days in advance at the Cirque's box office or over the phone, using your credit card.

Cirque du Soleil's "O" ★★★★

APPEAL BY AGE UNDER 21 ★★★★ 21–37 ★★★★★ 38–50 ★★★★★ 51+★★★★½

HOST CASINO AND SHOWROOM Bellagio—"O" Theater; ☎ 702-693-7722 or 888-488-7111; www.bellagio.com

Type of show Circus and aquatic ballet as theater. **Admission** $94–$150. **Cast size** 74. **Night of lowest attendance** Sunday. **Usual showtimes** Wednesday–Sunday, 7:30 and 10:30 p.m. **Dark** Monday and Tuesday. **Topless** No. **Duration of presentation** 1 hour and 45 minutes.

DESCRIPTION AND COMMENTS We read an article a while back in which Cirque du Soleil was described as "a circus without animals," a description so woefully inadequate that it really ticked us off. Truly, the writer who penned those words has the sensitivity of a slug. Cirque is not the sum of various tricks and stunts; rather, it is an artistic theatrical collage replete with life and all of its meaning, emotion, and color. If a performer swings from rope or juggles a hoop it is as incidental, yet as integral, as a single dollop of paint on a Rembrandt canvas. It's not the single trick that matters, it's the context.

The title "O" is a play on words derived from the concept of infinity, with 0 (zero) as its purest expression, and from the phonetic pronunciation of *eau,* the French word for "water." Both symbols are appropriate, for the production (like all Cirque shows) creates a timeless dream state and (for the first time in a Cirque show) also incorporates an aquatic dimension that figuratively and literally evokes all of the meanings, from baptism to boat passage, that water holds for us. The foundation for the spectacle that is "O" resides in a set (more properly an aquatic theater) that is no less than a technological triumph. Before your eyes, in mere seconds, the hard, varnished surface of the stage transforms seamlessly into anything from a fountain to a puddle to a vast pool. Where only moments ago acrobats tumbled, now graceful water ballerinas surface and make way for divers somersaulting down from above. The combined effect of artists and environment is so complete and yet so transforming that it's almost impossible to focus on specific characters, details, or movements. Rather there is a global impact that envelops you and holds you suspended. In the end you have a definite sense that you *felt* what transpired rather than having merely seen it.

Though *"O"* is brilliant by any standard and pregnant with beauty and expression, it lacks just a bit of the humor, accessibility, and poignancy of Cirque's *Mystère* at sister casino T. I. Where *"O"* crashes over you like a breaking wave, *Mystère* is more personal, like a lover's arrow to the heart. If you enjoyed *Mystère*, however, you will also like *"O,"* and vice versa. What's more, the productions, while sharing stylistic similarities, are quite different. Though you might not want (or be able to afford) to see them both on the same Las Vegas visit, you wouldn't feel like you saw the same show twice if you did. Cirque du Soleil's *KÀ* at the MGM Grand is as grand as *"O"* and as haunting as *Mystère*, but much darker.

CONSUMER TIPS   If you've never seen any of the Las Vegas Cirque du Soleil productions, we recommend catching *Mystère* or *KÀ* first. *Mystère* is more representative of Cirque du Soleil's hallmark presentation and tradition, while *KÀ* is a brilliant example of the Cirque concept evolved to full fruition.

If you want to go, buy tickets via credit card over the phone before you leave home. If you decide to see *"O"* at the spur of the moment, try the box office about 30 minutes before showtime. Sometimes seats reserved for comped gamblers will be released for sale.

Cirque du Soleil's *Zumanity*   ★★★★

APPEAL BY AGE	UNDER 21—	21–37 ★★★★	38–50 ★★★★	51+ ★★★½

HOST CASINO AND SHOWROOM   **New York–New York–*Zumanity* Theatre;**
☎ **702-740-6815 or 866-606-7111; www.nynyhotelcasino.com or**
www.zumanity.com

Type of show A risqué Cirque du Soleil. **Admission** $65–$125 depending on choice of seat. **Cast size** 50. **Night of lowest attendance** Monday. **Usual showtimes** Friday–Tuesday, 7:30 and 10:30 p.m. **Dark** Wednesday and Thursday. **Topless** Yes. **Duration of presentation** 1 hour and 30 minutes.

DESCRIPTION AND COMMENTS   *Zumanity* is about love, emotional and physical, in all its unrequited, sated, comedic, tender, and lunatic dimensions. It is also the first Cirque production to chart a decidedly adult course. Cirque spokespersons tell us that "flirtatious performers and musicians reach out to take the audience on a 90-minute encounter, awakening the most primal urges to a new form of eroticism blending movement, style, acrobatics, skimpy costumes, and beautiful bodies with the sensual caress of the human voice and the insistent pulse of exotic rhythms. This production is an intense visit to a world where human inhibitions are both unveiled and discarded, where style and intense sensual passion share an uncommon stage." *Gulp.* As it turns out, Cirque does love and sex as well as it does everything else, and *Zumanity* is a hell of a ride.

Zumanity is zany, raucous, and decidedly outrageous. It is lovable in its humor and insightful in its understanding of sex. The visually rich production blends its challenging theme with Cirque du Soleil's signature music, color, acrobatics, and dance. *Zumanity* is sometimes very tender but at other moments hard-edged. It urges us to look at how we define human beauty and makes a plea for the acceptance of differences. *Zumanity* delivers a powerful message.

Like all Cirque productions, *Zumanity* is hauntingly dreamlike. But where other Cirque shows operate on multiple levels of meaning and interpretation, *Zumanity* tells us in unambiguous terms that sex is amazing, infinitely varied, and wonderful. As the production unfolds, you witness an artful sequence of sexual vignettes celebrating heterosexual sex, gay sex, masturbation, sex between obese lovers, sex with midgets, group sex, sadomasochistic sex, and sex enjoyed by the very old. As the name *Zumanity* implies, sex (and the varied emotions we bring to it) is a defining element of our humanity. Sex is happy, sex is sad, sex is of the moment, sex is transcendent, sex is funny, sex is bewildering. And as *Zumanity* so ably demonstrates, sex is a window into our essential being.

Now, after digesting the above, you might be thinking that's one window you're uncomfortable peering into, that you really don't need to know all that much about our essential being. But there's also this nagging impulse to take a little peek. You might even want to take a big peek, but aren't sure it's a good idea with your wife, mother, or father-in-law sitting beside you. That's the genius of *Zumanity:* it forces you to confront your own sexuality, including your hangups—all in the presence of your friends, family, and possibly your own lover (plus, of course, 2,000 strangers). For some it's very disquieting, even frightening. Tension is palpable. Some shift continuously in their seats. They laugh a bit too loud at the jokes, try to appear unaffected by the orgasmic groaning, pretend they're quite accustomed to leather and whips, and attempt to will themselves not to be aroused. Most people, however, will find *Zumanity* to be exhilarating, and more than a few find it absolutely liberating.

CONSUMER TIPS *Zumanity* is brilliant, but clearly not for everyone. Certainly, it's not for prudes, the sexually repressed (probably half of America), the sexually phobic, or for the self-righteous who seek to impose their sexual mores on the rest of us. Equally, it's not for the "gentlemen's club" set. *Zumanity* is altogether too complex, cerebral, and theatrical for their taste.

The production is staged in a 1,256-custom-seat, custom-designed showroom that facilitates a performer–audience intimacy remarkable for a theater so large and for a production of *Zumanity*'s scope. With the exception of some first-floor seats (under the balcony outcropping) that make viewing aerial acts impossible, sight lines are excellent. The best seats are on the lower-floor center and about 12 rows or more back. As with all Cirque du Soleil shows, audience members are at risk of being hauled into the performance.

Crazy Girls ★★★½

HOST CASINO AND SHOWROOM **Riviera—Crazy Girls Showroom;**
☎ **702-794-9301 or 800-634-3420; www.rivierahotel.com**

Type of show Erotic dance and adult comedy. Admission $35, $62. Cast size 8. Nights of lowest attendance Wednesday and Monday. Usual showtimes Wednesday–Monday, 9:30 p.m. Dark Tuesday. Topless Yes. Duration of presentation 1 hour and 15 minutes.

DESCRIPTION AND COMMENTS *Crazy Girls* gets right to the point. This is a nononsense show for men who do not want to sit through jugglers, magicians, and half the score from *Oklahoma!* before they see naked women. The focus is on eight engaging, talented, and athletically built young ladies who bump and grind through an hour of exotic dance and comedy. The choreography (for anyone who cares) is pretty creative, and the whole performance is highly charged and quickly paced, though most vocals are lipsynched. The dancers are supported by a zany comedienne who doesn't shy away from X-rated humor. Solo routines (which may be dancing or just sexy writhing) are shown in close-up on large video screens, but the videos are from previous performances, creating an odd disconnect when the video and the onstage performer get out of sync.

CONSUMER TIPS The show is not really as risqué as the Riviera would lead you to believe, and the nudity does not go beyond topless and G-strings (how could it?). While designed for men, there is not much of anything in the show that would make women or couples uncomfortable. Men looking for total nudity should try the Palomino Club in North Las Vegas.

Ticket and box-office information is the same as for *An Evening at La Cage* (see Consumer Tips under that show's profile, page 205). Upclose VIP seating, available for old farts who forgot their glasses, includes a line pass. A few columns in the middle section can obstruct the views from back-center seats.

Crazy Horse Paris ★★★★

HOST CASINO AND SHOWROOM **MGM Grand—*Crazy Horse* Cabaret;**
☎ **702-891-7777 or 877-880-0880; www.mgmgrand.com**

Type of show Artsy topless dance performance from France. Admission $64.90. Cast size 12. Night of lowest attendance Sunday. Usual showtimes Wednesday–Monday, 8 and 10:30 p.m. Dark Tuesday. Topless Yes. Duration of presentation 1 hour and 15 minutes.

DESCRIPTION AND COMMENTS Imported from the legendary Crazy Horse club in Paris, *Crazy Horse Paris* is something of an oddity. The showroom is quite beautiful, done up in plush reds that call to mind an upscale bordello. All the dancers are Parisian imports as well, and they must not only be in excellent physical condition—they also are not allowed surgical enhancements. So what you see is au naturel. There's a wide variety of musical and dance numbers, and these are mixed with the odd comedy interlude or a bit of historical footage from the original Crazy Horse. The show's erotic routines are decidedly European, relying on arty lighting, sensuous music, and a lot of writhing. There's not anything else like it in Vegas (certainly not the *Folies Bergere,* also originally a French show). On the whole, *Crazy Horse Paris* is diverting, cool, and sexy.

CONSUMER TIPS The stage for *Crazy Horse Paris* is very small for such a large room, so seats in the rear may result in eyestrain. The show is general admission with usher seating, so arrive as early as possible in order to get the best spot.

Danny Gans ★★★★

APPEAL BY AGE   UNDER 21 ★★★   21–37 ★★★½   38–50 ★★★★   51+ ★★★★

HOST CASINO AND SHOWROOM **Mirage—Danny Gans Theatre; ☎ 702-791-7111 or 800-963-9634; www.mirage.com or www.dannygans.com**

Type of show Impressions and variety. **Admission** $100. **Cast size** Approximately 6. **Night of lowest attendance** Wednesday. **Usual showtimes** 8 p.m. **Dark** Sunday, Monday and Thursday. **Topless** No. **Duration of presentation** 1 hour and 30 minutes.

DESCRIPTION AND COMMENTS Danny Gans was well on his way to a promising career in major-league baseball when he suffered a career-ending injury. Baseball's loss is Las Vegas entertainment's gain. This "man of many voices" is a monster talent. He does upwards of 100 impressions during the show: Michael Jackson; Willie Nelson; James Stewart; Kermit the Frog; Pee-wee Herman; John Travolta; Peter Falk; Garth Brooks; Sammy, Frank, and Dino; Walter Cronkite with Presidents Clinton, Bush, Reagan, Carter, and Ford; Billy Joel; Bruce Springsteen; Stevie Wonder; Ray Charles; Sylvester Stallone; Homer and Marge Simpson talking to Dr. Ruth's answering machine; Henry Fonda and Katharine Hepburn doing *On Golden Pond;* Paul Lynde; Wayne Newton; Neil Diamond; Sammy Davis Jr.; Natalie and Nat King Cole; Sarah Vaughan; Prince; Bill Cosby; and, of course, Elvis. And that's a *short* list. At the end, he even does Danny Gans—typically a selection from his Christian-pop album.

Gans not only does impressions, but also expressions. He captures his characters' faces, postures, and moves; he gets maximum effect from minimal props; he even plays a mean trumpet (for the Louis Armstrong bit). But that's not all. This is perhaps the tightest show in Las Vegas. Gans, his band, and the lighting are in perfect sync every note of the night. Great for Vegas, tough luck for baseball.

In case you're wondering, Danny Gans is the best of the solo impressionists working Las Vegas showrooms. We rank André-Philippe Gagnon (limited engagements at Paris) second and Bill Acosta third.

CONSUMER TIPS Gans's show is outstanding and a reasonable buy for the $100 seats. In any event, the show is more of an auditory than a visual experience. The Mirage is a bustling place in the evenings, so allow yourself an extra 15 minutes to park and get to the showroom.

Elton John and the Red Piano ★★★★

HOST CASINO AND SHOWROOM **Caesars Palace—The Colosseum;**
☎ **888-435-8665; www.caesars.com**

Type of show Celebrity headliner. **Admission cost** $100, $125, $175, $250. **Cast size** 10. **Night of lowest attendance** Wednesday. **Usual showtimes** 8 p.m. **Dark** Monday and Thursday. **Topless** Not exactly (see below). **Duration of presentation** 1 hour and 30 minutes.

DESCRIPTION AND COMMENTS Elton John has always been a spectacle unto himself. In *Red Piano,* the legendary eccentric uses the not inconsiderable technical marvels of Caesars Colosseum showroom to achieve a level of hyperbole hardly imaginable. The basic ingredients for the cake are Elton, a red piano, and his band. The icing, supplied courtesy of Celine Dion (for whom the theater was designed), is a huge stage backstopped by the largest LED screens in America. Always edgy, images on the screen amplify the content of the music. Ranging from hilarious to stupefying to poignant, we see shots of Elton through the years, Pamela Anderson on a stripper pole, and for the hit "Daniel," a dying soldier in Vietnam. As if the LED effects aren't enough, a range of wild props and inflatables makes sure the production goes over the top and stays there. Take for example a blatantly suggestive inflatable banana rising from a flaccid state to about 20 feet tall (the banana is flanked at its base by two large cherries for those who fail to grasp the symbolism). Other near-dirigible-size blow-ups include a huge pair of women's legs, a lipstick case, a hot dog, and, lest phallic symbols run away with the show, a giant pair of inflated female breasts.

Aside from all the wacky stuff, there are two things that distinguish this production. First, the *Red Piano* operates on several planes with the images and music being evocative of both pop art and history, the latter registering with more impact if you're over 50. Second, the choice of music is somewhat surprising. Far from trotting out a greatest hits litany, John's choice of songs supports the theatricality of the production. Mood, message, and spectacle drive the music selection. In the end, you feel like you've experienced a wild romp through the entire spectrum of human emotion.

CONSUMER TIPS The Colosseum is currently the only theater in Las Vegas where bag checks are conducted and where you must pass through metal detectors, so it's smart to give yourself a little extra time. If you decide to use valet parking, the most convenient and fastest is to use the adjoining Forum Shops' valet service rather than Caesars'. There is a full bar in the showroom lobby if all the security has left you with a dry mouth.

An Evening at La Cage ★★★

HOST CASINO AND SHOWROOM **Riviera—*La Cage* Theater;** ☎ **702-794-9433 or 800-634-3420; www.rivierahotel.com**

Type of show Female-impersonator revue. **Admission** $55. **Cast size** Approximately 20. **Nights of lowest attendance** Sunday and Monday. **Usual showtimes** Wednesday–Monday, 7:30 p.m. **Dark** Tuesday. **Topless** No. **Duration of presentation** 1 hour and 30 minutes.

DESCRIPTION AND COMMENTS *An Evening at La Cage* re-creates the female-impersonator revue made famous by productions of the same name in New York and Los Angeles. A high-tempo show with a great sense of humor, *La Cage* is at once outrageous, lusty, weird, and sensitive. All the performers, of course, are men. The celebrities impersonated include Joan Rivers, Tina Turner, Cher, Carol Channing, Shirley MacLaine, Bette Midler, and Madonna. A crew of dancers (also men impersonating women) give the presentation the feel of a quirky production show.

Some of the impersonators are convincing and pretty enough to fool just about anyone. Their costumes reveal slender, feminine arms and legs and hourglass figures. Others look just like what they are—men in drag. The cast performs with great self-effacement and gives the impression that nobody is expected to take things too seriously. As one impersonator quipped, "This is a hell of a way for a 40-year-old man to be earning a living."

La Cage is kinky yet solid entertainment. It is also very popular and plays to appreciative heterosexual audiences. If you are curious, broad-minded, and interested in something different, give it a try. If the idea of a bunch of guys traipsing around in fishnet stockings and feather boas gives you the willies, opt for something more conventional.

CONSUMER TIPS In addition to *La Cage,* you can see the production show *Ice: Direct from Russia*, which plays in the Riviera's Versailles Theatre (see page 211). Shows can be purchased in conjunction with a meal, usually the buffet. The food on the show-dinner combos won't knock you out, but it's a pretty good deal for the money. Also, it's quick and convenient. There is usually plenty of time to eat between shows.

Tickets for *La Cage* and the other Riviera shows may be reserved up to 21 days in advance at the Riviera box office, or over the phone using your credit card up to ten days in advance. Seating is by the maître d'. Once seated, you can fetch your own drinks from the bar.

Fab Four Mania ★★★

APPEAL BY AGE	UNDER 21 ★★	21–37 ★★★	38–50 ★★★½	51+ ★★★½

HOST CASINO AND SHOWROOM **Miracle Mile Shops at Planet Hollywood—V Theater; ☎ 702-932-1818; www.thefabfour.net**

Type of show Musical impressionist and tribute act. **Admission** $22 age 12 and under general admission; $49 adult general admission; $59 VIP with line pass. **Cast size** 5 (4 Beatles, 1 Ed Sullivan impersonator). **Nights of lowest attendance** Tuesday and Wednesday. **Usual showtimes** Saturday–Thursday, 6 p.m. **Dark** Friday. **Topless** No. **Duration of presentation** 1 hour and 30 minutes.

DESCRIPTION AND COMMENTS The Fab Four are a Beatles tribute group, and it's immediately obvious they've honed their craft to confident expertise. The chief draw here is the music itself, as the four artists actually play all their own instruments on stage—no backing tapes or synthesized tracks. Vocally they are dead-on, and the audience gets especially charged up and rowdy during sing-alongs like "Twist and Shout." The costumes and musical selections follow the Beatles' career, from the early 1960s through psychedelia and into the 1970s. Film clips of fans from relevant eras form interludes, and "John" and "Paul" each get a chance to solo. The Beatlesque mannerisms and speech patterns are there, even if the physical resemblance falls more into the category we call the "haircut impression." Fans of the lads from Liverpool and their music will have an absolute blast.

CONSUMER TIPS The V Theater is buried deep within the Miracle Mile Shops, so be prepared for a trek to get there. Valet park at the mall's entrance if you can, rather than at the casino valet. Lines of sight can be tricky here, as seats are not elevated; if you're short, sit near the front (or behind someone shorter). As with everything else in the Aladdin, this show is subject to variation or elimination as the property changes over to Planet Hollywood in 2006.

Fantasy ★★★

APPEAL BY AGE	UNDER 21 –	21–37 ★★★	38–50 ★★★	51+ ★★★

HOST CASINO AND SHOWROOM **Luxor—Atrium Showroom; ☎ 702-262-4900; www.luxor.com**

Type of show Topless-dance and comedy revue. **Admission cost** $58.50–$64. **Cast size** 12. **Night of lowest attendance** Tuesday. **Usual showtimes** Sunday, Monday, Wednesday, and Friday, 10:30 p.m.; Tuesday, 8 and 10:30 p.m.; Saturday, 11 p.m. **Dark** Thursday. **Topless** Yes. **Duration of presentation** 1 hour and 30 minutes.

DESCRIPTION AND COMMENTS Speculate on the anthropological reasons why the American appetite for female breasts is a cultural staple. *Fantasy*, possibly the Strip's most artistic topless show, satisfies this hunger in a tasteful, glamorous way in this 70-minute smorgasbord of sexual scenarios. Jennifer Ross is the dark-haired beauty featured among the cast of eight very adept dancers, one male singer, and one comedian who very ably channels Tina Turner, Sammy Davis Jr., and James Brown to happy effect. Rubber bondage, dominatrix office-politics, and light lesbianism are a few of the erotic offerings, none of which ever reach raunchy, which is perhaps why the audience includes many women. Breasts are indeed revealed early on in the show, but not every number is topless. The office scene, for example, is performed chiefly in men's business suits. The Vegas feeling of high production values with sets, lights, smoke, and bass-filled sound is certainly there to support the well-executed Bob Fosse–style choreography. While the sexually suggestive theme runs strongly throughout, most of the numbers could stand on their own without the topless element.

CONSUMER TIPS Staged in the same fairly intimate house as Carrot Top's show, you can be pulled on stage if you are a man sitting in the first row or two. Row D offers the most leg room.

Fashionistas ★★★★½

HOST SHOWROOM **Empire Ballroom, 3765 South Las Vegas Boulevard;**
☎ **702-836-0833; www.fashionistastheshow.com**

Type of show Sexually charged fetish-fashion dance drama. **Admission** $54.95 reserved seating; $65.95 VIP; $76.95 VIP package. **Cast size** 21. **Nights of lowest attendance** Monday, Tuesday. **Usual showtimes** Thursday–Tuesday, 11 p.m. **Dark** Wednesday. **Topless** Technically, no, but clothing (what there is of it) and dancing are extremely sexual. **Special comments** Dinner packages available: general $79.95, VIP $101.95, cabana $112.95; all prices include show and dinner. **Duration of presentation** 1 hour and 30 minutes.

DESCRIPTION AND COMMENTS   Look out, Maude, this ain't the Vegas you grew up with. The fact that *Fashionistas* isn't topless should by no means imply that this production doesn't have sex on the brain (and every other part of the body). The performers heave their way through a dizzying series of costume changes, and there's enough creatively crafted leather and latex to account for a herd of cattle and a forest of rubber trees. So let's make this clear: If you are bothered by overtly sexual themes, sexual dancing, and above all sexual clothing—all of which stray well into outrageously farcical territory in terms of fetishes and fashion—this is not the show for you.

If you're still interested, you'll be treated to one of the most unusual shows Vegas has seen in a while. Created by adult-film mogul John Stagliano, it's obviously a labor of "love." Stagliano has lavished a great deal of money on *Fashionistas,* so production values are surprisingly high. The story involves fetish fashion, a love triangle, and hidden DVD tracks (no, really), but you'd never get any of that if you didn't read the synopsis in the program. That's OK, because you don't have to understand the story to appreciate the show. And as if to accept this reality, the creators made a decision we enthusiastically applaud: no dialogue. This has the welcome effect of giving the whole affair a certain ballet-like atmosphere at times, if you can believe it.

The music, while still overfamiliar to anyone who listens to dance music or dance-inflected pop, is a cut above the usual soundtrack for an adult Vegas show. We have to admit that we went into *Fashionistas* with pretty low expectations, and who knows how long this kind of production can be sustained. But like a lot of other people (the show has won numerous choreography awards), we were pleasantly surprised.

CONSUMER TIPS   *Fashionistas* moved from the Krave Nightclub adjacent to the Miracle Mile Shops to the Empire Ballroom, located on the Strip just north of the MGM Grand and behind Walgreens. This is an exceedingly congested part of the Strip, so give yourself plenty of extra time if you're driving. If you take the Las Vegas Monorail, get off at the MGM Grand, proceed to the Strip, and head north. The walk will take about 12 to 15 minutes. Self-parking and valet parking are available at the venue.

Folies Bergere (The Best of)   ★★★

APPEAL BY AGE	UNDER 21 ★★	21–37 ★★★	38–50 ★★★	51+ ★★★★

HOST CASINO AND SHOWROOM **Tropicana—Tiffany Theatre; ☎ 702-739-2411 or 800-829-9034; www.tropicanalv.com**

Type of show Music, dance, and variety production show. **Admission** $59–$69. **Cast size** Approximately 90. **Nights of lowest attendance** Monday, Tuesday, and Sunday. **Usual showtimes** Tuesday and Friday, 8:30 p.m; Monday, Wednesday, Thursday, and Saturday, 7:30 and 10 p.m. **Dark** Sunday. **Topless** 8:30 and 10 p.m. shows only. **Duration of presentation** 1 hour and 30 minutes.

DESCRIPTION AND COMMENTS   The *Folies Bergere,* a Las Vegas tradition modeled on the bawdy Parisian revue of the same name, has been playing at the Tropicana on and off since 1959. The show, which changes almost every year, is a classy dance and musical variety production with a large cast.

The *Folies Bergere* is pretty much what you would expect: exotically clad (or unclad) showgirls and cancan dancers, chorus lines, singers, and music with a fin-de-siècle French cabaret feel. The show runs through about 14 different scenes, celebrating the music and dance traditions of Paris, Hollywood, and Las Vegas from the 1860s to the 1960s. The *Folies Bergere* is elaborate and colorful but not particularly compelling. The singing and dancing are competent and professional but, with one or two exceptions, not creative or exciting. The *Folies* has been successful for over 45 years, so it is understandable that the producers would be reluctant to tamper with the formula. The ante for competing in the big leagues, however, has gone up. The production innovations of Siegfried and Roy and the energy of Cirque du Soleil established new standards for action, tempo, and creativity in Las Vegas production shows. The *Folies Bergere* has failed to keep pace.

In fairness, the *Folies* change and update various elements of the show every year. Recent changes make the show more appealing to the baby-boomer generation who cut their teeth on rock (music, that is). Updated or not, however, the *Folies* has become a sort of treasured relic, a nostalgic symbol of Las Vegas in those heady early days of the Strip.

Given the music and style of the *Folies,* you will be more likely to appreciate the production if you are over age 50. Younger patrons will fail to identify with the nostalgic music and dance of *la belle epoque,* or find much spontaneity in the overall *Folies* theme; the *Lion King* finale, for example, is strange and overwrought. But imaginative sets and costumes, elaborate staging, a diverse soundtrack, and the contemporary choreography that revs up near the end give this show some pop.

CONSUMER TIPS   The *Folies* is presented on a wide stage in the nicely designed Tiffany Theatre. There is a lot more booth seating than in most showrooms and a good view from practically every seat in the house. Dinner is no longer offered in the showroom, though there's a buffet show package for a few dollars extra. No drinks come with the price of the show. If you need to use the distant restroom before the show, allow yourself plenty of time.

Reservations can be made up to a month in advance, and all seats are reserved, so you can show up five minutes before showtime and your seats will be waiting.

George Wallace ★★★½

HOST CASINO AND SHOWROOM **Flamingo—Flamingo Showroom;**
☎ **702-733-3333; www.flamingolasvegas.com**

Type of show Stand-up comedy. **Admission** $69.80–$86.35. **Cast size** 2. **Night of lowest attendance** Tuesday. **Usual showtimes** Tuesday–Saturday, 10 p.m. **Dark** Sunday and Monday. **Topless** No. **Duration of presentation** 1 hour and 30 minutes.

Description and comments   George Wallace is a big man in his 50s with a gruff, acerbic, Redd Foxx–style stage persona. Following a warm-up comic, Wallace grouses and rails through 80 minutes of first-rate stand-up comedy. Unlike Rita Rudner, who presents as sweet and empathetic, Wallace stakes out his turf as the only sensible person in a world of idiots. Working the room with ease, Wallace moves from one topic to the next on a current of sharp one-liners delivered at a furious pace. Slipping in and out of Ebonics ("I be thinkin' "), he lampoons both black and white stereotypes en route to settling down to such favorite subjects as young people and Las Vegas traffic.

CONSUMER TIPS Wallace plays equally well across age and color lines. He keeps things moving and connects with his audience, and his commanding stage presence tells you immediately that you're in the hands of a pro. As the only black stand-up comic playing a major showroom, he delivers edgy, race-related humor and a certain hipness that's largely absent elsewhere. The Flamingo Showroom, with maître d' seating, is not the most efficient in the world. Plan on waiting in line awhile before being seated. Table service is available.

Gordie Brown ★★★½

HOST CASINO AND SHOWROOM **Venetian—Old Palazzo Ballroom;**
☎ **702-414-7469; www.venetian.com**

Type of show Impressions with music and comedy. **Admission** Not available at press time. **Cast size** 5. **Night of lowest attendance** Tuesday. **Usual showtimes** Friday–Tuesday. **Dark** Wednesday and Thursday. **Topless** No. **Duration of presentation** 1 hour and 15 minutes.

DESCRIPTION AND COMMENTS   Impressionists are almost as ubiquitous as showgirls in Las Vegas, so we weren't expecting anything special from Gordie Brown. *Wrong!* His is the sleeper show of Las Vegas. Brown sets the house on fire with his impressions, musicianship, and humor. Backed by a turbo-energized live band consisting of lead guitar, bass, two keyboard players, two drummers, and sax, Brown moves along at a gallop impersonating such artists as Travis Tritt, Roy Orbison, Willie Nelson, Paul Simon, Billy Joel, Henry Fonda, MC Hammer, and Frank Sinatra. Aside from nailing the voices and mannerisms of his celebrity subjects, Brown has an uncanny chameleon-like ability to change his countenance to actually look like them. Brown is at his best when he's moving quickly. Unfortunately, he has a pronounced tendency, particularly with his comedy, to drive a routine into the ground. As you would expect, trying to ride a horse that's been dead for ten minutes isn't good for a show's momentum. Sooner or later though, Brown will plug the holes in his act, and when he does, watch out, Danny Gans.

CONSUMER TIPS Gordie Brown earned his stripes at the Golden Nugget downtown where he played an intimate showroom. In the Old Palazzo Ballroom at the Venetian, a lot more elbowroom has enabled Brown to ramp up his production. The Old Palazzo Ballroom is near the Blue Man Group Theater toward the rear of the property. If you drive, give yourself lots of extra time to park and make it to the showroom.

Hans Klok: The Beauty of Magic ★★

APPEAL BY AGE	UNDER 21 ★★★	21–37 ★	38–50 ★★	51+ ★★

HOST CASINO AND SHOWROOM **Planet Hollywood—Planet Hollywood Theatre for the Performing Arts; ☎702-736-7114 or 877-333-9474; www.planethollywoodresort.com**

Type of show Illusion with dancers. Admission $39.90, $71.40, $113.40. Cast size 20. Nights of lowest attendance Thursday. Usual showtimes Thursday–Saturday, 7 and 10 p.m. Dark Sunday–Wednesday. Special comments No drinks included. Topless No. Duration of presentation 1 hour and 40 minutes.

DESCRIPTION AND COMMENTS Though relatively unknown in the States, Klok, who hails from the Netherlands and has been performing magic since his preteens, is renowned in Europe and Asia for being the world's fastest magician. In addition, tabloid bombshell Pamela Anderson costars with Klok. And with the fine Planet Hollywood Theatre for the Performing Arts as the venue, all the elements would seem to be in place.

They're not. The whole thing, in fact, is melodramatic, repetitious, and clichéd, with every trick in the illusion book done to death. Ostensibly tied together by an autobiographical theme, the show has a young blond Hans (portrayed by a wide-eyed 13-year-old boy) and his old gray father traveling the world in search of mystery, magic, and a receptive audience. Their appearances, along with a background video travelogue and underwhelming production numbers, are so much filler.

As for the illusions, you've seen them all before: Klok runs swords, flaming spears, and razor-sharp disks through girls in various boxes; he reads the mind of a random audience member; he submits to a guillotine; he levitates lightbulbs; he does sleight-of-hand with cards, candles, and scarves; and he switches places with various girl assistants in a parade of chambers. To be fair, Klok is amazingly fast; the ol' switcheroos occur at lightning speed and do leave you wondering how it can happen so quickly. But the "wows" come with too much downtime in between.

Meanwhile, you keep waiting for Pamela Anderson to pop from a chamber and finally, about three-quarters of the way through, out she flounces, full of saline and collagen. There's not much point to her presence other than the obvious poster appeal, and she vamps at Klok's side as if even she's wondering what in the world she's doing there.

Whatever. In the end, it doesn't really matter, because we predict this show won't be around by the time the 2008 guide gets printed.

CONSUMER TIPS Two video screens on either side of the stage project images from the focal points of the show. But if you really want to see all the action, you'll need to sit pretty close, video screen notwithstanding. Problem is, sitting through this show will be doubly depressing if you've paid for the expensive seats.

Hello Dere! ★★★

APPEAL BY AGE   UNDER 21 ★★   21–37 ★★   38–50 ★★★   51+ ★★★

HOST CASINO AND SHOWROOM **Gold Coast—Gold Showroom; ☎ 702-251-3574; www.goldcoastcasino.com**

Type of show Stand-up comedy and music. **Admission** $30 plus tax and fees. **Cast size** 2. **Nights of lowest attendance** Thursday. **Usual showtimes** 7:30 p.m. **Dark** Monday–Wednesday. **Topless** No. **Duration of presentation** 1 hour and 20 minutes.

DESCRIPTION AND COMMENTS Talk about a blast from the past. We haven't reviewed a Marty Allen show in Las Vegas since 1994, when the stand-up comic was still working with his career-long partner and straight man, Steve Rossi. Allen and Rossi became famous in the early 1960s after bringing down the house on the Ed Sullivan TV show. Allen is 85 now and works with his much younger and multitalented wife, Karon Kate, known to those of us who have been covering Las Vegas for a while as Katie Blackwell.

Allen and Blackwell clown their way through a quickly moving 80-minute show. Both performers are immensely enthusiastic and always seem to be having great fun while they work. Blackwell often gets so tickled by Allen's extraordinary expressions and grimaces that she is unable to deliver her lines. The merriment is generally infectious and spreads rapidly to their appreciative audience. Blackwell, a knock-out singer, provides the show with a musical dimension that adds variety to the production and helps maintain the pace. Overall, *Hello Dere!* is lively and fun and, for Las Vegas, surprisingly clean. The format is unusual, combining elements of celebrity headliner, comedy club, and variety musical productions.

CONSUMER TIPS At $30 plus tax this show is great value. The Gold Coast showroom is set up nightclub-style with round tables and chairs. The high stage ensures good lines of sight even though the showroom floor is not tiered, and the configuration of the seating creates a surprising sense of intimacy for so large a room. The best tables are about 25 feet back from the stage.

Ice: Direct from Russia ★★★

APPEAL BY AGE   UNDER 21 ★★★   21–37 ★★★   38–50 ★★★   51+ ★★★

HOST CASINO AND SHOWROOM **Riviera—Versailles Theatre; ☎ 800-634-3420 or 702-794-9433; www.rivierahotel.com**

Type of show Combination circus and ice-skating review. **Admission** $60 and $70. **Cast size** 26. **Nights of lowest attendance** Tuesday and Wednesday. **Usual showtimes** Saturday–Thursday, 8 p.m.; Tuesday–Thursday and Saturday, 10 p.m. **Dark** Friday. **Topless** No. **Duration of presentation** 90 minutes.

DESCRIPTION AND COMMENTS Directed by Debra Brown, who choreographed *Mystère* and *"O"* for Cirque do Soleil, *Ice* is a classy, visually rich production and a vast improvement over *Splash,* which played at the Riviera's Versailles Theatre for 20 years. In *Ice,* Brown combines the Moscow Ice Circus with the moods and ethereal sets of Cirque du Soleil. Though the ice rink is small and doesn't allow the range of movement associated with the Ice Capades or competition skating, the cast of expert skaters takes advantage of every square inch. Virtually every performer, including jugglers, stilt walkers, springboard acrobats, and even musicians, is on skates, and the eclectic music (rock, funk, New Age, Celtic, etc.) and athletic choreography weave a rich thread through the fabric of the production. Unfortunately, however, the moderately sized venue is too small for a fully realized Cirque-like presentation, and in any event, "Cirque-like" is not Cirque. *Ice* naturally invites comparisons with the five (soon to be six) Las Vegas Cirque du Soleil shows and proves wanting. Slow to get in gear and proceeding somewhat ponderously, *Ice* fails to engage the audience until late in the game, and the stunts fail to break any new ground apart from the fact they are performed on skates. *Ice* can be described as tasteful or even as elegant, but generally not as compelling. It would make a pretty good traveling show, but in Las Vegas where the standard for any show professing to incorporate Cirque production values is so high, *Ice* is but a puppy trying unsuccessfully to run with the big dogs.

CONSUMER TIPS If you're really into ice skating, *Ice* offers the best in town, and the Russians have always been leaders in the circus arts. We reviewed *Ice* soon after it opened, so its problems with pace and audience involvement eventually may be resolved. In the interim, warts and all, it's a good night's entertainment. Just don't expect it to be in the same league as Cirque du Soleil.

Jubilee! ★★★★

APPEAL BY AGE	UNDER 21 –	21–37 ★★★	38–50 ★★★½	51+ ★★★★

HOST CASINO AND SHOWROOM **Bally's–*Jubilee!* Theater; ☎ 702-967-4567 or 800-237-SHOW; www.ballys.com**

Type of show Grand-scale musical and variety production show. **Admission** $65–$89 ($6 extra on credit-card purchase). **Cast size** 100. **Nights of lowest attendance** Sunday, Thursday. **Usual showtimes** Saturday–Thursday, 7:30 and 10:30 p.m. **Dark** Friday. **Topless** Yes. **Duration of presentation** 1 hour and 45 minutes.

DESCRIPTION AND COMMENTS *Jubilee!* is the quintessential, traditional Las Vegas production show. Faithfully following a successful decades-old formula, *Jubilee!* has elaborate musical production numbers, extravagant sets, beautiful topless showgirls, and quality variety acts. In *Jubilee!* you get what you expect—and then some.

With a cast of 100, an enormous stage, and some of the most colossal and extraordinary sets found in theater anywhere, *Jubilee!* is much larger than life. Running one hour and 30 minutes each performance, the show is lavish, sexy, and well performed, but redundant to the point of numbness.

Two multiscene production extravaganzas top the list of *Jubilee!* highlights. The first is the sultry saga of Samson and Delilah, climaxing with Samson's destruction of the temple. Not exactly biblical, but certainly awe-inspiring. The second super-drama is the story of the *Titanic,* from launch to sinking. Once again, sets and special effects on a grand scale combine with nicely integrated music and choreography to provide an incredible spectacle.

Jubilee!'s opening act kicks things off in a big way. Based on a popular song by Jerry Herman, *Hundreds of Girls,* it showcases 75 singers, dancers, and showgirls multiplied by gargantuan mirrors. The opening is said to have cost $3 million to produce. The above-average specialty acts include an illusionist executing big-stage tricks, a juggler-acrobat couple whose main prop is a giant aluminum cube, and a strongman who performs mostly upside-down. The production concludes with "The Jubilee Walk," a parade of elaborately costumed showgirls patterned after the grand finale of the *Ziegfeld Follies.*

CONSUMER TIPS The 1,035-seat Jubilee Theater, with its high, wide stage and multitiered auditorium, is one of the best-designed showrooms in town. It underwent a complete $2.5 million renovation in the late 1990s. It now consists of seating at banquet tables at the foot of the stage (too close and cramped); a row of booths above the tables (more expensive but worth it); and 789 theater-style seats. The table and booth seats come with cocktail service; the theater-seat audience has to carry in their own drinks.

Reserved seats for *Jubilee!* can be purchased over the phone with a credit card up to six weeks in advance. Tickets also can be purchased in person at the Bally's box office. The price of a ticket covers admission and taxes.

Lance Burton ★★★★

APPEAL BY AGE UNDER 21 ★★★★ 21–37 ★★★★ 38–50 ★★★★ 51+ ★★★★

HOST CASINO AND SHOWROOM **Monte Carlo—Lance Burton Theatre;**
☎ **702-730-7160 or 877-386-8224; www.montecarlo.com or**
www.lanceburton.com

Type of show Magical illusion with dancing and specialty acts. Admission $66.50, $72.55. Cast size 14. Nights of lowest attendance Thursday, Friday. Usual showtimes Tuesday and Saturday, 7 and 10 p.m.; Wednesday, Thursday, and Friday, 7 p.m. Dark Sunday and Monday. Special comments No drinks included. Topless No. Duration of presentation 1 hour and 30 minutes.

DESCRIPTION AND COMMENTS In a showroom designed especially for him, Lance Burton stars in an innovative and iconoclastic magic show, one of only two magic production shows in town to escape the curse of redundancy. Performing in tight-fitting clothing with rolled-up sleeves (nothing can be concealed), Burton displays some extraordinary sleight of hand in a repertoire of illusions that cannot be seen in other showrooms. Augmented by comely assistants, a comedic juggler, and a talented dance troupe, *Lance Burton* delivers quality entertainment.

CONSUMER TIPS The Lance Burton Theatre is an opulent imitation of a Parisian opera house and is both beautiful and comfortable. Theater seats ensure that no one gets wedged sideways at cramped banquet tables. On the down side, the venue is so large that it's hard to appreciate Burton's exquisite and subtle sleight of hand if you are seated in the boonies. Also, some illusions are difficult to see from the balcony seats. Try to get seats on the main floor close to the stage. *Lance Burton* tickets can be purchased over the phone or at the Monte Carlo box office up to two months in advance.

Le Rêve ★★★★

APPEAL BY AGE   UNDER 21 ★★★   21–37 ★★★★   38–50 ★★★★   51+ ★★★★

HOST CASINO AND SHOWROOM **Wynn Las Vegas—Wynn Theater;**
☎ **702-770-9966 or 888-320-7110; www.wynnlasvegas.com/le_reve**

Type of show Aquatic theater in the round. **Admission** $112–$178. **Cast size** More than 70. **Nights of lowest attendance** Sunday and Monday. **Usual showtimes** Saturday–Wednesday, 7:30 and 10:30 p.m. **Dark** Thursday and Friday. **Topless** One act. **Special comments** No seat is more than 42 feet from the stage. **Duration of presentation** 1 hour and 30 minutes.

DESCRIPTION AND COMMENTS Imagine a wet concoction of someone else's dreams. The anchoring image is a nocturnal voyager in a red dress who explores from her own bed of dreams. Her journey recalls images from the swirling dark psychology of the fantastical movie *Brazil;* Busby Berkeley's dance routines; swamp things with long tails; the rescuing flights from *Angels in America;* "Baby Elephant Walk" from *Daktari;* dancing flowers from *Fantasia;* the deft touch of Gene Kelly's *Singin' in the Rain,* with a setting undercurrent of *Mad Max: Beyond Thunderdome.* All this is a taste of the theatrical pastiche of Frank Dragone's specialty production *Le Rêve* at Wynn Las Vegas.

The collaboration of hands-on Steve Wynn and Belgian Dragone, who logged ten years with Cirque du Soleil including designing their watery world of *"O"* (from *eau,* the French word for "water") was highly anticipated. *Le Rêve* (French for "the dream") requires a specially constructed amphitheater seating 2,100 where no seat is more than 42 feet from the action (and the front rows are given water protective clothing and a discounted price of $80 versus the maximum of $110). Performed in the round, the cast of more than 70 internationally assembled gymnasts, acrobats, synchronized swimmers, and dancers execute their impressive routines within an expansive, mysterious tank of water. Mechanical lifts hoist various configurations of the stage out of the seemingly bottomless reservoir. The set is heightened by fire, smoke, and dripping skin. At times the performers are atop a rising column, and at other times they appear to walk on water with the "beach" platform, as they call it, just below the water's surface. Sometimes they are hoisted straight up into the dome's opening. Sometimes they swing on trapezes, their exquisitely strong and athletically defined bodies shimmering in the show lights, or they dangle in suspended contortions like a Michelangelo version of Hell. Yet none of these descriptions can do justice to the physical display that arises everywhere before your eyes.

Roman in its level of spectacle and operatic in its reach, *Le Rêve* is indeed long on sensuality and short on narrative. Perhaps its only defense of weak, illogical storytelling is its very title, for who can make true sense of another's dream? Another criticism is that the water and Cirque-style elements have been seen before and done better in "*O.*" *Le Rêve* does continue to adjust its story line and execution, so it seems that some of that criticism is justified. But as with the comparable Cirque du Soleil shows, the concepts and especially the physical feats invite a thinking person to reconsider the possibilities of what it is to be human. While some may have a definite preference for "*O,*" *Le Rêve* is a lingering, inspiring treat for the eye and ear.

CONSUMER TIPS Parking in Wynn's self-parking garage is more convenient than using valet parking if you drive. In our opinion, the first 15 rows are too close and too low to take in the whole of this expansive production that makes use of the entire theater.

Legends in Concert ★★★★

APPEAL BY AGE   UNDER 21 ★★★   21–37 ★★★½   38–50 ★★★★   51+ ★★★★

HOST CASINO AND SHOWROOM **Imperial Palace—Imperial Theatre;**
☎ **888-777-7664; www.imperialpalace.com**

Type of show Celebrity-impersonator and musical-production show. **Admission** $49.95, $59.95. **Cast size** Approximately 20. **Nights of lowest attendance** Wednesday and Thursday. **Usual showtimes** Monday–Saturday, 7:30 and 10 p.m. **Dark** Sunday. **Topless** No. **Duration of presentation** 1 hour and 30 minutes.

DESCRIPTION AND COMMENTS *Legends in Concert* is a musical production show featuring a highly talented cast of impersonators who re-create the stage performances of such celebrities as Elvis, Richie Valens, Prince, Cher, Rod Stewart, the Four Tops, and Gloria Estefan. Impersonators actually sing and/or play their own instruments, so there's no lip-synching or faking. In addition to the Las Vegas production, *Legends in Concert* also fields a road show. The second show makes possible a continuing exchange of performers between the productions, so that the shows are always changing. In addition to the impersonators, *Legends* features an unusually hot and creative company of dancers, much in the style of TV's *Solid Gold* dancers of old. There are no variety acts.

The show is a barn burner and possibly, minute-for-minute, the fastest-moving show in town. The impersonations are extremely effective, replicating the physical appearances, costumes, mannerisms, and voices of the celebrities with remarkable likeness. While each show features the work of about eight stars, with a roster that ensures something for patrons of every age, certain celebrities (most notably Elvis) are always included. Regardless of the stars impersonated, *Legends in Concert* is fun, happy, and upbeat. It's a show that establishes rapport with the audience—a show that makes you feel good.

CONSUMER TIPS Admission includes two drinks. Payment must be made at the box office any time prior to the show. Arrive 40 minutes before showtime for seating by the maître d'. If you drive to the Imperial Palace and intend to use the self-parking, give yourself a little extra time. Since *Legends* is very popular and almost always plays to a full house on weekends, be sure to make your reservations early. If you are trying choose between *Legends in Concert* and *American Superstars* at the Stratosphere, your age is probably a good barometer. If you're 50 or older you'll probably like *Legends* better, if you're 40 or under try *American Superstars*. Forty-somethings could go either way.

Louie Anderson ★★★

APPEAL BY AGE	UNDER 21 ★★	21–37 ★★★	38–50 ★★★½	51+ ★★★★

HOST CASINO AND SHOWROOM **Excalibur—Merlin's Theater; ☎ 702-597-7600 or 800-933-1334; www.excalibur.com**

Type of show Stand-up comedy. **Admission** $45. **Cast size** 1. **Night of lowest attendance** Wednesday. **Usual showtimes** 7 p.m. **Dark** Friday. **Topless** No. **Special comments** Must be 18 or older to attend. **Duration of presentation** 1 hour.

DESCRIPTION AND COMMENTS Louie Anderson is a seasoned stand-up comedy pro, and his genial, aw-shucks demeanor belies his talent as a confident crowd-pleaser. Anderson can win over an audience almost instantly, and he can spin personal details culled from the crowd into a chain of truly funny improv. In fact, he seems most comfortable interacting with the audience and riffing on their answers to his questions, falling back on routine material only when the first strategy dries up. Otherwise, Anderson covers familiar stand-up ground with bits about his crazy family, the Midwest, Vegas jokes, and so on. Some of the funniest moments are when he gets a little mischievous, relishing awkward pauses or his own embarrassment.

CONSUMER TIPS A few seats in the back of the theater have obstructed views due to columns. Though you must be 18 to attend the show, Anderson's comedy is almost entirely wholesome—no sex chat, and barely any cursing.

The Magic of Rick Thomas ★★★★

APPEAL BY AGE	UNDER 21 ★★★★	21–37 ★★★★	38–50 ★★★★	51+ ★★★★

HOST CASINO AND SHOWROOM **Orleans—The Showroom; ☎ 702-365-7075; www.orleanscasino.com and www.rickthomas.com**

Type of show Magic and illusion. **Admission** Reserve seating, $27.50 and $33. **Cast size** 4. **Days of lowest attendance** Monday and Tuesday. **Usual showtimes** Monday–Thursday, 4 and 7 p.m.; Friday, 4 p.m.; Saturday, 2 and 4 p.m. **Dark** Sunday. **Topless** No. **Duration of presentation** 1 hour.

DESCRIPTION AND COMMENTS Thomas is one of the better illusionists to have played Las Vegas. About a decade ago, he gave up the nightly grind of the big showrooms and began working exclusively in the afternoon. Now he's back playing both evenings and afternoons. Like Siegfried and Roy, Thomas has stunning white tigers and cutting-edge big-stage illusions as his trademarks. Unlike Siegfried and Roy, Thomas is also a master of close work. His sleight-of-hand routine with birds is one of the best in the business. A couple of his illusions, thanks to the contribution of his lovely showgirls, are surprisingly steamy for the afternoon show but not too sensual for young viewers. Like Mac King and Lance Burton, Rick Thomas is a natural when it comes to connecting to his audience.

CONSUMER TIPS For afternoon magic and illusion, Rick Thomas is King, and the Orleans Showroom is a perfect venue. If you self-park, try to find a spot on the east side of the resort.

Mamma Mia! ★★★★

APPEAL BY AGE UNDER 21 ★★★½ 21–37 ★★★★ 38–50 ★★★★ 51+ ★★★★

HOST CASINO AND SHOWROOM **Mandalay Bay—Mandalay Bay Theatre;**
☎ **702-632-7580 or 877-632-7400; www.mandalaybay.com or www.mamma-mia.com**

Type of show Musical comedy. **Admission** $49.50, $82.50, $110. **Cast size** 36, including musicians. **Night of lowest attendance** Thursday. **Usual showtimes** Sunday–Thursday, 7:30 p.m.; Saturday, 6 and 10 p.m. **Dark** Friday. **Topless** No. **Duration of presentation** 2 hours and 15 minutes (with intermission).

DESCRIPTION AND COMMENTS *Mamma Mia!* is a musical comedy featuring the music of the Swedish pop group ABBA. Active from 1974 to 1982, ABBA was once the world's best-selling band, scoring ten top-20 hits worldwide. With more than 350 million records sold to date, ABBA's music continues to attract new fans.

Mamma Mia! was launched in London in 1999 and became a huge hit there before being exported to the United States. The story takes place on a Greek isle where three fellows wooed and slept with, in short order, the same woman. The woman became pregnant and had a little girl, Sophie, whom she raised without ever establishing the identity of the father. Now engaged to be married, Sophie contrives to use the occasion of her wedding to find her unknown father. After discovering three possible candidates in her mother's diary, she invites them to her wedding without, of course, telling Mom. You get the idea.

In the creation of most musicals, the script is written first and then the music developed to support the story line. *Mamma Mia!* is an anomaly in that the script was developed to fit ABBA's music. Amazingly, this "square peg in a round hole" approach produced a plot–music relationship as congruent as that of most musicals produced in the traditional way. There are a couple of the whopping 22 ABBA songs included that are a pretty loose fit, but in general the music integrates very nicely. Even at two and a half hours (with a 20-minute intermission), *Mamma Mia!* is fast paced, with a clever script and engaging characters. What's really refreshing, however, is *Mamma Mia!*'s essential lightness and simplicity. It's sweet, upbeat, humorous, and just for fun.

CONSUMER TIPS Though there are really no bad seats in the Mandalay Bay Theatre, it's probably worth the money to spring for closer, more expensive seats. Self-parking at Mandalay Bay is relatively convenient to the showroom. From the entrance to the casino, bear left past several restaurants and then continue left, passing the sports book en route. Although there are restrooms just outside the theater and a bar in the theater lobby, you'll save time, especially during intermission, by using restroom and bar facilities in the main casino. Hold on to your ticket stub—you'll need it to get back in the showroom.

Menopause: The Musical   ★★★★½

APPEAL BY AGE   UNDER 21 ★★   21–37 ★★★   38–50 ★★★★★   51+ ★★★★★

HOST CASINO AND SHOWROOM **Las Vegas Hilton— Shimmer Cabaret;**
☎ **702-732-5755; www.lvhilton.com or www.menopausethemusical.com**

Type of show Off-Broadway musical comedy. **Admission** $49.50. **Cast size** 4. **Night of lowest attendance** Wednesday. **Usual showtimes** 7 p.m. with matinees Wednesday, Thursday, and Sunday at 2 p.m. and on Saturday at 4 p.m. **Dark** Monday. **Topless** No. **Duration of presentation** 1 hour and 30 minutes.

DESCRIPTION AND COMMENTS This cabaret-style jewel was first launched in a 76-seat theater in Orlando in 2001. Only five years later it is a rollicking frolic, packing in people in 15 major American cities, plus in Canada, Italy, Korea, and Australia. Yes, it really is about "the change," and, yes, about 10% of the audience were unabashed men who were also having an uproariously good time. But hands down and hot flashes up, this is a show for anyone approaching, in, or past menopause. Doors open one hour before showtime, and you should arrive at least 30 minutes before showtime for a decent seat.

Many of the heads in the audience are silver, but the punch of estrogen is still palpable upon entering the theater. There was a preponderance of red and purple clothing in the house, perhaps because members of the Red Hat Society, the Red Hot Mamas, Heart Truth, and Minnie Pauz frequently attend the show in groups. Creator Jeanie Linders summed up the crux of the production: "Four women meet at a Bloomingdale's lingerie sale with nothing in common but a black lace bra, hot flashes, night sweats, memory loss, chocolate binges, not enough sex, too much sex, and more." The soap star, the earth mama, the power woman, and the Iowa housewife are each skillfully drawn and wonderfully executed. It would be hard to imagine how to improve upon the show we saw—the cast was perfect in physical style, comedic timing, and song-and-dance delivery.

The 90-minute production moves along by lyrically parodying 24 wonderful songs of the past, especially of the 1960s. For example, Aretha Franklin's "Chain of Fools" becomes "Change, Change, Change":

> *I told it to leave me alone*
> *Ignore it 'til the signs are all gone*

My doctor said take some Prozac
But these moods swings are way too strong

It's just a part of
Change, change, change.
Change, change, change
Change, change, change
Change of life.

Irving Berlin's "Heat Wave" become "Tropical Hot Flash" and "Looking for Love in all the Wrong Places" becomes "Looking for Food...," with a chorus that begins "Now I'm packin' on pounds where I don't have spaces, / Looking for food in too many places...." You get the idea.

You must be 14 years of age to attend, for some of the content is deemed "mature." It's basically a clean, if anatomically forthright show, but if the idea of mechanical "Good Vibrations" paired with "What's Love Got to Do with It?" bothers you, maybe it's time to hit the nickel slots again instead. That would be something of a shame, however, because *Menopause: The Musical* is clever, tons of fun, and very self-affirming. The synergy cycling in the room between the cast and the audience is a jubilant intoxicant that you shouldn't miss imbibing.

Finally for men, this show is a total hoot, especially if you've been married or close to a menopausal woman.

CONSUMER TIPS With maître'd seating it's necessary to arrive at least a half hour in advance. The best seats are at the front of the first raised tier of tables near the stage. Tipping the male captains (ushers) immediately seems to be necessary to get a good seat. Female captains, conversely, will offer you the best seats available without the tip (though this good service should be acknowledged—$5 is about right).

Beverages are served tableside during the show and your ticket is also a chance to attend a wine-and-cheese tasting with cast members. Until you actually see this production you can visit **www.menopause themusical.com** where you can support the spin-off W4W Foundation that provides grant support to and through qualified women's service organizations for women over 40.

Monty Python's Spamalot ★★★★

APPEAL BY AGE   UNDER 21 ★★★★   21–37 ★★★★   38–50 ★★★★½   51+ ★★★★

HOST CASINO AND SHOWROOM **Wynn Las Vegas— The Grail Theatre;**
☎ **702-770-9966 or 888-320-WYNN; www.wynnlasvegas.com or www.montypythonsspamalot.com**

Type of show Musical comedy. **Cast size** 9. **Admission** $79.85, $101.85, $112.85. **Usual showtimes** Monday, Wednesday, Sunday, 8 p.m; Tuesday, Friday, Saturday, 7 and 10 p.m. **Dark** Thursday. **Topless** No. **Duration of presentation** 1 hour and 30 minutes.

DESCRIPTION AND COMMENTS Coconuts, killer rabbits, and flatulent Frenchmen have found their way to Wynn's Broadway Theatre in *Monty Python's Spamalot*. Spun from the 1975 cult classic *Monty Python and the*

Holy Grail, Spamalot captures the lowbrow, mindless humor so beloved in the original movie. Eric Idle, one of the original Pythoners, and composer John Du Prez wind new dialogue and songs with the well-loved scenes from the movie. If you like *Monty Python,* you'll love this show. If you're not familiar with *Monty Python* but enjoy the Brits' unique brand of silly humor, you too will enjoy *Spamalot.*

Spamalot is, to put it rather vaguely, the story of King Arthur and the quest for the Holy Grail. For those unfamiliar with the original movie or the TV episodes, imagine the tale of Camelot told by someone on LSD, or in this case, by Eric Idle. Fans of the *Holy Grail* will enjoy their favorite knights battling eccentric and sometimes rather bizarre enemies, such as the legless knight.

CONSUMER TIPS *Spamalot* is one of three London or Broadway musicals that opened in Las Vegas in late 2006 or early 2007. If you go, the Wynn Las Vegas self-parking lot is more convenient than using the valet service. The Broadway Theatre is a state-of-the-art venue with good lines of sight from every seat. Drinks are not included in the ticket price but are available from the bar in the theater's lobby.

Penn & Teller   ★★★½

APPEAL BY AGE   UNDER 21 ★★★½   21–37 ★★★½   38–50 ★★★★   51+ ★★★★

HOST CASINO AND SHOWROOM **Rio—Penn & Teller Theater; ☎ 888-746-7784; www.riolasvegas.com or www.pennandteller.com**

Type of show Magic and comedy. **Admission** $75 plus tax. **Cast size** 4. **Night of lowest attendance** Wednesday. **Usual showtimes** Wednesday–Monday, 9 p.m. **Dark** Tuesday. **Topless** No. **Special comments** Sometimes they reveal secrets to their tricks. **Duration of presentation** 1 hour and 30 minutes.

DESCRIPTION AND COMMENTS OK, for starters, Penn is the big, loud one and Teller is the cute, passive little guy. They've been together for more than 30 years. The show is great fun, but long on talk (Penn's endless digressions tend to numb after 5 minutes or so), and short on magic. Well, not short actually. It's just that the setup for every illusion takes so much time that only a handful of tricks will fit in the allocated 90 minutes. But that's part of the show and provides the backdrop for Penn & Teller's playful tension and hallmark onstage chemistry. The illusions vary from the simple to the elaborate, with Penn & Teller sometimes sharing magician secrets of the trade along the way. Though most of the stuff, including Penn's occasionally blue monologues and the majority of the magic, is old hat to Penn & Teller followers, it works fine for the uninitiated. Plus, the duo always offer an illusion or two that you won't see in any of the other magic shows around town.

CONSUMER TIPS Strictly speaking, this show is about two parts comedy to one part magic. If you're hot primarily for magic, you'll be happier at Lance Burton or one of the other magic productions in town. Penn & Teller don't perform any illusions on the order of Siegfried and Roy or Steve Wyrick, so sitting up front is fine. Be aware that Penn & Teller are the whole show. There are no showgirls, singing, dancing, or warm-up acts: just the big guy and the little guy.

Phantom—The Las Vegas Spectacular ★★★★

HOST CASINO AND SHOWROOM **Venetian—Phantom Theatre; ☎ 702-414-7469; www.venetian.com or www.phantomlasvegas.com**

Type of show Adapted Broadway musical. **Admission cost** $61–$107. **Night of lowest attendance** Thursday. **Usual showtime** 7 p.m. Wednesday–Monday; 9:30 p.m. Wednesday and Saturday. **Dark** Sunday. **Topless** No. **Duration of presentation** 1 hour and 35 minutes.

DESCRIPTION AND COMMENTS The longest-running show in Broadway history has finally descended upon Las Vegas, but with a face-lift. The show has been shortened to a mere 95 minutes, but *Phantom* fans need not be too alarmed. Andrew Lloyd Webber and Hal Prince have personally revamped the show; and all of Webber's songs are sung and the story line remains the same. The Venetian built a custom theater to house the show, and enhanced illusions, expanded set designs, and more spectacular effects differentiate the Las Vegas version from its Broadway cousin.

Phantom—The Las Vegas Spectacular is based on the novel *Le Fantôme de l'Opéra* by Gaston Leroux. The Paris Opera House is haunted not by a ghost, but by a masked man residing beneath the catacombs of the Opera House. While spreading havoc and terror over all those associated with the Opera House, the Phantom falls madly in love with the soprano singer Christine and vows to transform her into a star. The fusion of all aspects of the musical, from the costumes to the haunting lyrics by Webber, will tug at your imagination and your emotions.

CONSUMER TIPS If you drive, give yourself lots of extra time to park and make it to the showroom.

The Platters, Cornell Gunter's Coasters, and Beary Hobb's Drifters ★★★½

HOST CASINO AND SHOWROOM **Sahara—Congo Room; ☎ 702-737-2515; www.sahara.com**

Type of show 1950s and '60s oldies. **Admission** $41.95 and $47.45. **Cast size** 13 singers plus backup band. **Nights of lowest attendance** Tuesday and Wednesday. **Usual showtimes** Nightly, 7:30 p.m. **Topless** No. **Duration of presentation** 1 hour and 30 minutes.

DESCRIPTION AND COMMENTS This show is inspired by the music of legendary vocal groups: the Platters, the Coasters, and the Drifters. We say "inspired" because there's not one original member of any of the groups in the production. Cornell Gunter was a bona fide Coaster and Beary Hobb an original Drifter, but they just lend their names to the acts. Does it really matter? Not if you're there just for the music. Sure, it's always fun to see the original groups still rockin' 'n' rollin', but most of all you want the music to be right. In this show you can close your eyes and believe you're listening to the original groups. It's that perfect. And with your eyes open, well, about half the performers are old enough to have been originals, so they look right. Regardless of age, they've got the moves and the choreography nailed. The only shortcoming is that Dave Backers's band, which provides the instrumental accompaniment, doesn't have a sax. Anyone who knows their oldies will tell you that covering the Coasters without a sax is like covering Jerry Lee Lewis without a piano.

CONSUMER TIPS The Congo Room is an old-fashioned maître d'—seating showroom, plenty big enough for 20 performers to be on stage at once (as in the finale of this show) but small enough to provide a very intimate concert experience. There's a cash bar outside the showroom. If you use the self-parking facility or the valet parking off Paradise, be forewarned that it's an eight- to ten-minute hike to the showroom.

The Producers ★★★★

APPEAL BY AGE   UNDER 21 ★★★½   21–37 ★★★★   38–50 ★★★★   51+ ★★★★

HOST CASINO AND SHOWROOM **Paris Las Vegas—Le Théâtre des Arts;**
☎ **877-796-2096; www.parislasvegas.com**

Type of show Musical comedy. **Admission** $69–$143. **Cast size** 38. **Nights of lowest attendance** Monday. **Usual showtimes** 8 p.m. **Dark** Sunday. **Topless** No. **Duration of presentation** 90 minutes.

DESCRIPTION AND COMMENTS This Broadway musical comedy—the winner of a record-breaking 12 Tony Awards—opened at the Paris's Théâtre des Arts in 2007. Mel Brooks once again flaunts his comic genius with the musical stage adaptation of his 1968 film of the same name. With lyrics and music by Brooks and a book by Brooks and Tom Meehan, it's a delightful evening of hilarious dialogue and memorable songs.

The story line concerns Max Bialystock, a struggling producer, and Leo Bloom, a mousy accountant, who together scheme to produce the worst musical to ever hit Broadway, raise more money than needed, and then pocket the difference when the musical inevitably bombs. They decide upon the play *Springtime for Hitler: A Gay Romp with Adolf and Eva in Berchtesgaden,* written by the neo-Nazi Franz Liebkind, believing it will offend all audiences. However, the plan backfires when the play is taken as a hilarious satire and becomes a great hit.

The production is a great evening entertainment and a show well received by all age groups. Fast paced, brilliantly written, and superbly cast, *The Producers* can be both subtle and outrageous. It's one of those shows you could see ten times and still discover things you previously missed. As in the movie and Broadway renditions, the real climax is the staging of *Springtime for Hitler,* so riotous it leaves you almost weak-kneed. The plot continues, of course, and is cleverly brought to a satisfying end. But it is the almost inconceivable hyperbole and over-the-top production of *Springtime for Hitler* that you'll remember when you get home.

CONSUMER TIPS If you are staying at a hotel on the monorail line, the monorail is your best bet for accessing Paris Las Vegas (get off at the Bally's/ Paris Las Vegas station). Le Théâtre des Arts is a stunning venue with super acoustics, plush tiered seating, and great lines of sight.

The Rat Pack Is Back   ★★★½

APPEAL BY AGE	UNDER 21 –	21–37 ★★★	38–50 ★★★½	51+ ★★★½

HOST CASINO AND SHOWROOM **Greek Isles—Star Theatre; ☎ 800-633-1777; www.greekislesvegas.com or www.ratpackvegas.com**

Type of show Celebrity impersonation. **Admission** $51.50, show only; $65.50, dinner show; $68.25, VIP show only; $82 VIP dinner show. **Cast size** 17, including 12-piece band. **Night of lowest attendance** Wednesday. **Usual showtimes** Saturday–Thursday, 8:15 p.m., 6 p.m. seating for dinner. **Dark** Friday. **Topless** No. **Duration of presentation** 1 hour and 15 minutes.

DESCRIPTION AND COMMENTS The heart and soul of the original Rat Pack were crooners Frank Sinatra, Dean Martin, and Sammy Davis Jr., and comedian Joey Bishop. They all worked the Las Vegas showrooms of the 1960s, sometimes dropping in on each other's shows and sometimes working together. Their late-night antics at the old Sands, particularly, are among the richest of Las Vegas showroom legends.

The Rat Pack Is Back re-creates a night when the acerbic Bishop and hard-drinking Martin team up with Davis and Sinatra. Backed by piano, bass, drums, along with, get this, a nine-piece horn section, four talented impersonators take you back to a night at the Sands Copa Room in 1963. The impressionists are excellent: each impersonator captures his character's voice, singing style, and body language. The performers playing Bishop and Davis bear strong physical resemblances to the originals, and the Sinatra impressionist more or less squeaks by, but the Martin character looks more like an Elvis impersonator.

The casual interplay among the four effectively transports you back to the 1960s, and what you see is pretty much how it was. The humor was racist, sexist, and politically incorrect, the showroom packed and smoky, and the music, well . . . drop-dead brilliant.

CONSUMER TIPS The showroom, designed by Debbie Reynolds and modeled on the Crystal Room at the Desert Inn, is perfect for this production. Banquet-table seating, however, is pretty cramped, especially if you get the dinner-show package. Speaking of which, the food is pretty good and at only $10 more than the show alone, represents a good value. Self-parking is a breeze and the casino so small that it takes barely three minutes to walk from your car to the showroom. There are usually discount coupons for *The Rat Pack Is Back* in the local tourists mags.

Rita Rudner   ★★★½

APPEAL BY AGE	UNDER 21 ★★	21–37 ★★★★	38–50 ★★★★	51+ ★★★★

HOST CASINO AND SHOWROOM **Flamingo—Flamingo Showroom; ☎ 702-733-3333 or 800-221-7299; www.flamingolasvegas.com**

Type of show Stand-up comedy. **Admission** $55. **Cast size** 1. **Night of lowest attendance** Wednesday. **Usual showtimes** Saturday–Thursday, 8 p.m.; Friday, 9 p.m. **Dark** Sunday. **Topless** No. **Duration of presentation** 1 hour and 30 minutes.

DESCRIPTION AND COMMENTS Rita Rudner walks onto the stage and holds forth for almost 90 minutes. No band, no singers or dancers, just Rita. And even if you've never heard of Rita Rudner, those 90 minutes will seem like 10. Her topics—male–female relationships, shopping, Las Vegas—are worn, but her perspective is fresh and her humor is sharp, very sharp. Like a good elementary-school teacher, she monitors her room, stopping to connect personally with a look, a smile, or even a question. In the end, we're all Miss Rudner's students and we find ourselves trying to file away some of her stories and zippy one-liners to repeat later to friends. But they come too fast, so finally we just go with it and enjoy.

CONSUMER TIPS Rita Rudner has to be the cleanest stand-up comic working in Las Vegas. You forget that it's possible to be uproarious in PG mode.

The Scintas ★★★

| APPEAL BY AGE | UNDER 21 ★★ | 21–37 ★★★ | 38–50 ★★★½ | 51+ ★★★½ |

Type of show Musical and comedy revue. **Cast size** 4. **Topless** No. **Duration of presentation** 1 hour and 15 minutes.

DESCRIPTION AND COMMENTS The Scintas wrapped up their long-running engagement at the Sahara in May 2007. They're such an entertainment-scene fixture, however, that we're pretty sure they'll resurface in another Las Vegas showroom soon. Hence, we've decided to keep their show's review in this year's *Unofficial Guide.*

Though the Scintas are also billed as a comedy troupe, they shine most when playing music. With a heavy emphasis on God and patriotism, the show would likely be more at home in Branson, Missouri.

The cast includes siblings Frankie, Joe, and Chrissi Scinta. Frankie provides much of the comedy and plays a variety of instruments, including keyboards. But his passion is the banjo. Joe is a stereotypically dry bass player and sometime comedian. Baby sister Chrissi sings a few numbers throughout the show, but isn't a constant stage presence. Italian pride notwithstanding, the group's drummer is handsome Irishman Peter O'Donnell.

The Scintas enjoy performing comedy, some of which can be trite; the routines include Frankie Scinta covering Tom Jones songs with socks stuffed down his pants. Some of the comedy has mildly racist and sexist undertones, which might have played well 20 years ago but now seem unnecessary—not to mention odd juxtaposed with all of the God-and-country stuff.

On the other hand, music is delivered with a great deal of warmth and skill. The set list includes typical Las Vegas fare such as Dean Martin and Elvis covers. But the Scintas also cover Billy Joel and Joe Cocker. Many songs are performed as parts of seamless medleys. With a versatile and pleasant voice, Frankie Scinta does most of the singing. Sister Chrissi sings louder and longer than her brothers, delivering a patriotic medley as well as an emotional "I Will Always Love You" (penned by Dolly Parton and made a megahit by Whitney Houston).

The Second City ★★★★

HOST CASINO AND SHOWROOM **Flamingo—*Second City* Theatre;**
☎ **702-733-3333; www.flamingolasvegas.com**

Type of show Sketch comedy. **Admission** $34.95. **Cast size** 5. **Night of lowest attendance** Tuesday. **Usual showtimes** 8 p.m.; Thursday, Saturday, and Sunday, 8 and 10 p.m. **Dark** Wednesday. **Topless** No. **Duration of presentation** 1 hour and 15 minutes.

DESCRIPTION AND COMMENTS *The Second City* comprises a team of improvisational comedians, one of several franchised groups of comics playing around the country under the same name. The difference between an improvisational group and the typical stand-up entertainers who work the Las Vegas comedy clubs is that the improv groups specialize in skits and songs as opposed to monologues. *The Second City* group is an amazingly talented lot individually and complement and balance each other well as a team. They do a crack job on the improvisational stuff, taking their cues from audience suggestions, but it's their set pieces that really demonstrate their genius.

CONSUMER TIPS The production venue is really an enclosed lounge—small and intimate, perfect for acts like *The Second City*. A maître d' handles the seating. but because there really aren't any bad seats, tipping is a waste of money unless you want to be right next to the stage. Sitting next to the stage at a comedy venue, however, is always risky because you might suddenly find yourself part of the show.

Steve Wyrick: Real Magic ★★★½

HOST CASINO AND SHOWROOM **Miracle Mile Shops at Planet Hollywood— Steve Wyrick Theater;** ☎ **702-777-9974**

Type of show Magic and illusion production show. **Admission** $60–$80. **Cast size** 6. **Nights of lowest attendance** Monday and Tuesday. **Usual showtimes** 7 and 9 p.m. **Dark** Friday. **Special comments** No drinks included. **Topless** Late show only. **Duration of presentation** 1 hour and 30 minutes.

DESCRIPTION AND COMMENTS *Steve Wyrick: Real Magic* is the Las Vegas show scene's version of "We try harder." With five or six magic-themed production shows playing in town at any given time, it takes a fair amount of creativity to be different. Steve Wyrick digs deep and delivers some great illusion and sleight of hand that you won't see in other showrooms. While his style and presentation, particularly his ability to connect with his audience, are reminiscent of Lance Burton, each illusion has a special twist that makes it unique. The Steve Wyrick Theater is small enough for sleight of hand to be effective, but large enough for Wyrick to pull off some vintage Siegfried and Roy–style eye-poppers. If you go for the magic you won't be disappointed. Expect lots of flash and thunder—pyrotechnics, roaring engines, and a pounding soundtrack.

CONSUMER TIPS The Steve Wyrick Theater is located in the Miracle Mile Shops adjoining Planet Hollywood. If you have a car, use Planet Hollywood's self-parking garage, which leads directly into the Miracle Mile Shops near the theater. Don't confuse the Steve Wyrick Theater with the V Theater, also at the Miracle Mile Shops. The Steve Wyrick box office is usually staffed by only one or two persons, so give yourself a little extra time to purchase or pick up tickets.

Stomp Out Loud ★★★★

APPEAL BY AGE   UNDER 21 ★★★★   21–37 ★★★★   38–50 ★★★★   51+ ★★★★

HOST CASINO AND SHOWROOM **Planet Hollywood—The Showroom at Planet Hollywood; ☎ 702-785-5000 or 877-333-9474; www.planethollywoodresort.com**

Type of show Musical tour de force. **Admission** Orchestra seating, $50–$110; mezzanine seating, $50–$75. **Cast size** 24. **Night of lowest attendance** Monday. **Usual showtimes** Monday, 6 and 9 p.m.; Tuesday and Thursday–Sunday, 7 p.m.; Saturday, 10 p.m. **Dark** Wednesday. **Topless** No. **Duration of presentation** 1 hour and 25 minutes.

DESCRIPTION AND COMMENTS *Stomp* runs with the big dogs. It's one of the best productions in Las Vegas, but we hate the way it's promoted. Video and print ads depict grungy dressed guys walking on oil barrels and clanging garbage can lids. You think, "What a perfect recipe for a migraine headache—who can sit through 90 minutes of that?"

But *Stomp Out Loud* is about the complexity of rhythm, not about noise. It's powerful but not loud, engaging the senses rather than assaulting them. And it's infinitely clever, in a class with Blue Man Group and Cirque du Soleil. In its most elemental distillation, *Stomp* combines terrific, wildly athletic choreography with masterful percussion played on everyday items like washboards, pots, pipes, boxes, and barrels. Even such items as cigarette lighters and long-handled brooms are brought into play to lay down the groove. To be sure, it's physical, comedic theater, but you're as much drawn to its subtlety and astounding precision as to its exuberant potency.

Each of the individual cast members is a memorable character. There's the avuncular Cam Newlin, an Everyman whose build and age belie his athleticism; and Coralissa Gines Delaforce, who may be the most intense human being on the planet; and so on with the entire cast. Within minutes you find yourself singling out the individuals who most pique your curiosity. But the production, while showcasing individual personalities, is ultimately about perfect group coordination. When all 24 cast members are onstage at once, *Stomp Out Loud* is like a tidal wave.

CONSUMER TIPS The Showroom at Planet Hollywood is to the left of the escalators on the mezzanine level of the casino. The only bad seats in the house are in the first four rows where there is little rise. For unobstructed views, select seats in rows E and higher.

Thunder from Down Under ★★★

HOST CASINO AND SHOWROOM **Excalibur—Thunder from Down Under Showroom; ☎ 702-597-7600; www.excalibur.com or www.thunderfromdownunder.com**

Type of show Male revue. **Admission** $39.95–$49.95. **Cast size** 10. **Night of lowest attendance** Monday. **Usual showtimes** Nightly, 9 and 11 p.m. **Dark** No. **Topless** Yes (male). **Duration of presentation** 1 hour and 15 minutes.

DESCRIPTION AND COMMENTS *Thunder from Down Under* offers a naughty night of ladies' fun for the bachelorette, recently divorced, and 21st-birthday crowd—a girls' night out that won't cause complete embarrassment for the conservative set. These Aussies are the guys next door—friendly and cute, but not the *Chippendales* dancers. *Thunder* is suggestive but not explicit, much tamer, in fact, than its American-based competitor. The scantily clad cast performs upbeat dance, acrobatics, and martial-arts routines, with a few comedy sketches tossed in (including one done in drag). Acts are performed to a varied soundtrack, resulting in a fast-paced, high-energy—but not always sexy—show.

There's lots of audience interaction as the Thundermen constantly pull girls out of the crowd and onto the stage. If you're shy and want to remain inconspicuous, try sitting in the back, where the lighting is also softer (our reviewer experienced light-blindness a few times from harsh overheads above her front-center seat in the 400-person showroom). After the show, cast members stick around to mingle with guests and offer photo opportunities.

Although there's lots of teasing and suggestion, the Thundermen never fully remove their G-strings (unlike the *Chippendales* guys). *Thunder* seemingly presumes that women can't appreciate blatantly risqué entertainment. Our female reviewer also got the distinct impression that the guys of *Thunder* would be more interested in each other than any of the hundreds of girls in the audience, which for some may take away from the show's sex appeal.

CONSUMER TIPS No smoking is allowed in Thunder from Down Under Showroom, located on the "Medieval" level, above the casino. Conveniently, there's a bathroom within the showroom. Drinks must be purchased directly from the bar (no at-the-table cocktail service) and range from $4.50 for soda, bottled water, or juice to $10.95 for frozen or mixed drinks in a 22-ounce souvenir glass. Bottled beer ranges from $4.75 to $5.50 and house wine is $4.50 per glass.

Toni Braxton: Revealed ★★★

HOST CASINO AND SHOWROOM **Flamingo Hotel—Flamingo Showroom; ☎ 702-733-3333 or 800-221-7299; www.harrahs.com**

Type of show Celebrity headliner. **Admission** $69–$109 plus tax/fees. **Cast size** 20.

Night of lowest attendance Wednesday. **Usual showtimes** 7:30 p.m. **Dark** Sunday and Monday. **Topless** No. **Duration of presentation** 1 hour and 10 minutes.

DESCRIPTION AND COMMENTS   Now that Celine Dion is packing it up after a successful five-year fun, the race is on to see who will be the Strip's next name performer to score big with an extended engagement. Enter Toni Braxton, six-time Grammy award winner with her new show *Revealed.* The show is billed as a look at who Braxton is and how she got where she is now. Other than a few "growin' up" stories, bringing her son onstage, and running her original audition video (complete with *giant* 1990s hair and the nose she was born with) for producer Kenny Edmonds, the show really isn't that revealing. The same can't be said for Braxton's outfits in as many as eight costume changes during the show, the first a blink-and-you-miss-it tear-away at centerstage during the first song. Later, playing the diva card to the crowd's delight, Braxton asks for a new microphone. What she gets is a uniformed guard with a briefcase handcuffed to his wrist and a bejeweled mike, reportedly worth $1 million and encrusted with 10,000 diamonds. (She finds this much more to her liking and uses it for the rest of the show.) The stage is flanked by two huge video screens and a central staircase that is big enough for a crack eight-piece band, two backup singers (her real-life sisters), six male and five female dancers, and Toni. Even with all this, however, the set is small enough to maintain the intimacy for which the show is striving. On the downside, audience members accustomed to a well-paced spectacle peppered with showstoppers may be left wanting. Also, her stage patter is flat and formulaic—Joey Bishop she ain't. Braxton is no belter, but longtime Braxton fans will love how she coos, hums, and vamps through her hits, including "Un-Break My Heart" and "You're Making Me High."

CONSUMER TIPS   From booth, banquette, or balcony, the sight lines in the theater are terrific from any angle and the sound system is excellent. If you're a big Braxton fan, get seats near the front and cross your fingers— the show finishes with Toni coming into the crowd and sitting on the lucky laps of many men (and women!).

Tony 'n' Tina's Wedding   ★★★½

APPEAL BY AGE	UNDER 21 ★	21–37 ★★★½	38–50 ★★★½	51+ ★★★

HOST CASINO AND SHOWROOM   **Rio—Calypso Room; ☎ 888-746-7784 or 702-777-7776; www.riolasvegas.com or www.tonylovestina.com**

Type of show Interactive dinner theater. **Admission** $78.95, $125 VIP. **Cast size** 20. **Night of lowest attendance** Monday. **Usual showtimes** Nightly, 7 p.m. **Topless** No. **Duration of presentation** 2 hours.

DESCRIPTION AND COMMENTS   Have you ever been to a wedding or wedding reception where you really didn't know anyone? Well, that's the premise for *Tony 'n' Tina's Wedding.* You're a wedding guest, welcomed into a large banquet hall and seated at a dinner table with total strangers. There you sit befuddled and somewhat uncomfortable as members of the bride's family (actors) stop to say hello and reminisce about Tony and Tina. And this is just the beginning. If you thought you could sit passively and watch a show, you're quite mistaken. During the course of a panicky few minutes, you become acutely aware that you are being sucked into the cast of this strange piece of theater, or if you can suspend your disbelief, this wedding. First there's the ceremony, then obligatory toasts, then dancing, then dinner followed by more toasts, and the tossing of the bouquet and the garter. As it unfolds, you are taken back to all those weddings in your life where one of the bridesmaids gets drunk, where an uninvited guests makes a five-minute toast, and where the best man wants to sing with the band. Inevitably it's you that the inebriated bridesmaid wants to spin around the dance floor, you who are pushed into the conga line, and you who are pulled into the throng to vie for the bouquet or garter.

There's a story line, of course, plus enough subplots to give Robert Ludlum a run for his money. The families don't get along well, and each in its own way tries to monopolize the reception. The strain is almost too much for the happy couple and for a while their minutes-old marriage hangs in the balance.

CONSUMER TIPS Is this fun? At the show we attended, we observed a pretty diverse range of audience reaction (if you can call it that). Some really got into it, danced to every tune, and role-played right along with cast. Others kept as much as possible to themselves, refusing to the extent possible to be drawn in. With some difficulty, we warmed to the proceedings but nonetheless kept a wary lookout for the sloshed bridesmaid. It was impossible not to admire how exactly the production nailed every wedding cliché, and how, if you weren't familiar with the family members as individuals, you had met their characters at similar events dozens of times in real life. If it helps you make up your mind, we'll tell you that the dinner was passable, sort of a pasta buffet, and that you had one chance to go through the line and load up your plate. The only alcohol served was a splash of Champagne for one of the toasts, though there was a cash bar (where we spent a goodly sum trying to improve our attitude).

Tournament of Kings ★★★

APPEAL BY AGE   UNDER 21 ★★★★   21–37 ★★★★   38–50 ★★★★   51+ ★★★★

HOST CASINO AND SHOWROOM **Excalibur—King Arthur's Arena;**
☎ **702-597-7600; www.excalibur.com**

Type of show Jousting and medieval pageant. **Admission** $49.95, includes dinner. **Cast size** 35 (with 38 horses). **Night of lowest attendance** Monday. **Usual showtimes** Wednesday–Monday, 6 and 8:30 p.m. **Dark** Tuesday. **Topless** No. **Duration of presentation** 1 hour and 15 minutes.

DESCRIPTION AND COMMENTS *Tournament of Kings* is a retooled version of *King Arthur's Tournament,* which logged 6,000 performances (from Excalibur's opening night in June 1990 till late 1998). It's basically the same show, with a slightly different plot twist. If you saw one, the other will come as no surprise.

The idea is that Arthur summons the kings of eight European countries to a sporting competition in honor of his son Christopher. Guests view the arena from dinner tables divided into sections; a king is desig-nated to represent each section in the competition. Ladies-in-waiting and various court attendants double as cheerleaders, doing their best to whip the audience into a frenzy of cheering for their section's king. The audience, which doesn't require much encouragement, responds by hooting, huzzahing, and pounding on the dinner tables. Watch your drinks—all the pounding can knock them over.

Soup is served to the strains of the opening march. The kings enter on horseback. Precisely when the King of Hungary is introduced, dinner arrives (big Cornish hen, small twice-baked potato, bush of broccoli, dinner roll, and dessert turnover). The kings engage in contests with flags, dummy heads, javelins, swords, and maces and shields and joust a while, too. The horse work, fighting, and especially the jousting are exciting, and the music (by a three-man band) and sound effects are well executed.

Right on cue, Mordred the Evil One crashes the party, accompanied by his Dragon Enforcers. Arthur is mortally slain and all the kings are knocked out, leaving Christopher to battle the forces of evil and emerge—surprise!—victorious in the end.

Except that . . . it's not over. The coronation is the culmination, after some acrobatics and human-tower stunts from a specialty act. Finally, the handsome new king goes out in a (literal) blaze of glory. It's a bit anticlimactic and bogged down, which helps hurry you out so the crew can quickly set up for the second show or clean up and go home.

CONSUMER TIPS One of the few Las Vegas shows suitable for the whole fam-ily, and one of the fewer dinner shows, *Tournament of Kings* enjoys great popularity and often plays to a full house. Reserved seats can be pur-chased with a credit card up to five days in advance by calling the number listed on the previous page (there's an extra $2 charge if you order by phone). Or you can show up at the Excalibur box office, which opens at 8 a.m., up to five days ahead.

No matter where you sit, you're close to the action—and the dust and stage smoke. The air-conditioning system is steroidal, so you might consider bringing a wrap. Seating is reserved, so you can walk in at the last minute and don't have to tip any greeters or seaters.

Dinner is served without utensils and eaten with the hands, so you might want to wash up beforehand. Eating a big meal is a bit awkward with the show going on and all the cheering duties, so you might con-sider bringing some aluminum foil and a bag to take out the leftover bird. Beverage is limited to soda with dinner, but the food server will bring you water, and a cocktail waitress will bring you anything else. Ser-vice is adequate; no one tips, so you'll be a hero if you do.

V: The Ultimate Variety Show ★★★★

APPEAL BY AGE   UNDER 21 ★★½   21–37 ★★★   38–50 ★★★   51+ ★★½

HOST CASINO AND SHOWROOM **Miracle Mile Shops at Planet Hollywood— V Theatre; ☎ 702-892-7790; www.vtheshow.com**

Type of show A hodgepodge of variety acts. **Admission** $81 VIP, $70 general. **Cast size** About 12 (varies). **Nights of lowest attendance** Monday and Wednesday. **Usual showtimes** Nightly, 7:30 and 9 p.m. **Special comments** Some of Las Vegas's quirkiest acts; great fun. **Topless** No. **Duration of presentation** 1 hour and 15 minutes.

DESCRIPTION AND COMMENTS In quite a few headlining Las Vegas shows, old and new, intermissions are handled by variety acts—comics, jugglers, acrobats, magicians, ventriloquists, and more. And in several of these cases (particularly the older ones), these variety acts become more entertaining than the headliners. The advantage of *V* is that the cast consists of a rotating stable of variety acts culled from Vegas and elsewhere. This means that no act lasts longer than a few minutes; it's the show for the short-attention-span set. Most of the acts are quite good. The emcee is a hilariously flamboyant and aggressive comic-magician, and when we visited, there was also an amusingly abusive juggler, a few species of acrobats, and a bizarre ventriloquist who uses audience volunteers as his "dummies," among others. Some of the acts are admittedly hit or miss, but as we said, nobody's on stage for long.

CONSUMER TIPS The V Theatre is located in the Miracle Mile Shops at Planet Hollywood. Self-parking at Planet Hollywood funnels you directly into the Miracle Mile Shops not far from the theater. Because there are only a couple of windows at the box office, arrive 40 minutes or more before showtime if you are buying or picking up tickets, or redeeming ticket vouchers. The split-level showroom has a bar on a mezzanine floor and most seating on ground level. Because the V Theatre is a multifunctional facility, there's no vertical rise from front to back for the seating. If you sit behind someone tall, in other words, your line of sight will be majorly obstructed. Also be aware that the available restrooms are totally inadequate for the size of the audience.

The World's Greatest Magic Show ★★★½

HOST CASINO AND SHOWROOM **Greek Isles—Star Theatre; ☎ 800-633-1777; www.greekislesvegas.com**

Type of show Magic variety show with assortment of performers. **Admission** $63.75 general; $74.75 VIP (includes dinner); free for children 12 and under. **Cast size** About 20. **Nights of lowest attendance** Tuesday and Wednesday. **Usual showtimes** Saturday–Thursday, 6 p.m.; Friday, 8:15 p.m. **Topless** No. **Duration of presentation** 1 hour and 30 minutes.

DESCRIPTION AND COMMENTS Merging a magic show with the variety show revival, the creators of *The World's Greatest Magic Show* have hit on a winner. Like the successful incarnations of other variety shows, the best thing here is that if one act bores you, there's always something else coming up in a few minutes. But what's surprising is the high standard of talent, plus, there truly is a considerable variety in class and style. When we attended, the show was hosted by a rowdy emcee who specialized in both sleight-of-hand and big-boom illusions, and the gallery of magicians included (but was not limited to) a wonderfully strange prop magician, a suave European classical illusionist, a bizarre younger fellow with an inclination for amputation, and a leather-clad Valkyrie who whipped the gentlemen into a frenzy. That last entry notwithstanding, this show was also a standout for being pointedly family friendly, with children invited to participate in several of the acts.

CONSUMER TIPS It appears that the rotating lineup of magicians goes periodically through a reshuffling, so buyer beware. The price is relatively similar to big-name solo magic acts like *Lance Burton,* so be sure you're into the variety aspect rather than a single marquee performer.

X Burlesque ★★★

APPEAL BY AGE	UNDER 21 –	21–37 ★★	38–50 ★★½	51+ ★★½

HOST CASINO AND SHOWROOM **Flamingo–Second City Theater; ☎ 702-492-3960 or 866-80-SHOWS**

Type of show Topless revue. **Admission** Reserve seating, $53.80; VIP seating, $65.80. **Cast size** 8. **Night of lowest attendance** Tuesday. **Usual showtimes** 10 p.m. **Dark** Sunday and Thursday. **Topless** Yes. **Duration of presentation** 1 hour and 30 minutes.

DESCRIPTION AND COMMENTS Less erotic than athletic, *X Burlesque* presents a half-dozen skilled dancers performing highly choreographed routines to songs ranging from Broadway standards to techno. Some numbers feature all the dancers, while others involve only one or two. The dancers wear tops as often as not, and their bodies are lithe and toned rather than top-heavy, so guys looking for a hot and juicy T&A show may want to look elsewhere. Those seeking more subtle eroticism won't be disappointed. The audience sits at round tables, nightclub-style, and the comely dancers strut on and off the stage and through the tables, sometimes taking a swing on a pole near the back of the room. The variety of music, the lights and costumes, and the sensual images flashing on large screens at either side of the small stage give the show a charged energy that captures the crowd. Given the general tone of the show, the appearance of the rotund stand-up comic Pudgy constitutes a real interruption. We've seen a lot of Pudgy over the years (there's *a lot* to see), and though she's quick and funny, she overstays her welcome and is definitely not what the crowd came to see. In *X's* defense, however, it should be pointed out that a bit of stand-up comedy is pretty routine in topless revues as well as in many strip joints.

CONSUMER TIPS The *Second City* Theater is small, giving the show an appropriate intimacy, and most of the tables are set up near the stage. The music is loud, the images bright and quick, and the choreography often frenetic, so expect a full sensory experience.

▌█ AFTERNOON SHOWS

AFTERNOON SHOWS HAVE BECOME an affordable alternative to the high-priced productions playing in the major showrooms at night.

AFTERNOON SHOWS

RANK AND SHOW	LOCATION
1. *The Mac King Comedy Magic Show*	Harrah's
2. *The Price Is Right—Live!*	Bally's
3. *The Magic of Rick Thomas*	Orleans
4. *Xtreme Magic Starring Dirk Arthur*	Tropicana
5. *The Ronn Lucas Show*	Planet Hollywood—Miracle Mile Shops
6. *Gregory Popovich Comedy Pet Theater*	Planet Hollywood—Miracle Mile Shops
7. *Nathan Burton Comedy Magic*	Planet Hollywood—Miracle Mile Shops

Most cost under $35 (sometimes including a drink) and many can be enjoyed for even less by taking advantage of coupons and special offers found in the local freebie visitor magazines. Here is a list of the profiled afternoon shows, ranked in terms of overall excellence. There's been a numbing proliferation of afternoon shows recently, and as you might expect, the shows vary immensely in quality. Finding the good ones and avoiding the bad ones is not unlike threading your way through a mine-field. The good ones are better than a lot of the high-ticket productions holding down stages around town at night. But the bad ones, oh, the bad ones: Heaven help us. From fat ladies making whoopee-cushion noises with their armpits to magicians sucking raw eggs out of the shell with their nose to Elvis impersonators who sweat like Elvis but sing like Alvin the Chipmunk, there is a dismal parade of frustrated humanity intent on torturing us.

Unfortunately, because afternoon shows erupt like wildflowers (or weeds) and disappear just as fast, we can't cover all of them in the *Unofficial Guide*. What we can do, however, is to provide a short pro-file of those afternoon shows that have demonstrated staying power. Showtimes for specific afternoon productions are usually in the 2-to-4:30-p.m. range but change almost weekly. Call the information and reservations number provided for performance times during your visit. The following profiles are arranged alphabetically.

Gregory Popovich Comedy Pet Theater   ★★★

APPEAL BY AGE   UNDER 21 ★★★★   21–37 ★★★   38–50 ★★★   51+ ★★★★

HOST CASINO AND SHOWROOM **Planet Hollywood—V Theatre; ☎ 702-932-1818; www.comedypet.com**

Type of show Family-oriented variety and animal act. **Admission** $15–$69. **Cast size** 6 humans, many animals. **Usual showtimes** Saturday–Thursday, 3:30 p.m. **Dark** Friday. **Appropriate for children** Yes. **Duration of presentation** 1 hour.

DESCRIPTION AND COMMENTS Since Cirque de Soleil changed the face of the modern circus, this show is almost so old it's new again. The act draws upon the old Russian and European circus traditions with a mix of fun animal acts, juggling, clowning, and tumbling. Popovich is a seasoned circus veteran and the son of Russian circus performers. He spent years with the Moscow Circus before coming to the States, first with Ringling Bros./Barnum & Bailey Circus and then to the Strip, where he performed for several years at Circus Circus. The show is aimed at families and kids who ooh and aah every time a doggie or a kitty appears on stage. At one point, Popovich and his talented and versatile cast of five manage to maintain order with 15 cats on stage. Another skit features nine dogs, all from the dog pound, and others showcase mice and birds. Popovich keeps the family tradition going by enlisting the help of his daughter, Anastasia, an accomplished trainer and entertainer herself. A story line keeps the show moving forward briskly and allows for a lot of variety, keeping the youngsters riveted and the adults entertained. To close the show, Popovich addresses the crowd and explains how all the animals in the act have been rescued and asks audience members to consider rescuing animals as pets themselves.

CONSUMER TIPS This is a great way to spend the afternoon with the family away from the noise and bustle of the casinos. The chairs are a little stiff but the fun on stage will keep the little ones amused for the show's duration. Some of the higher-priced tickets include a lunch deal. If you have children (or short adults) in your party, arrive early. The theater is not tiered so the only way height-challenged patrons can see is if they're close to the front.

The Mac King Comedy Magic Show   ★★★★

APPEAL BY AGE   UNDER 21 ★★★★   21–37 ★★★★   38–50 ★★★★   51+ ★★★★

HOST CASINO AND SHOWROOM **Harrah's—Harrah's Theater; ☎ 702-369-5111; www.harrahs.com or www.mackingshow.com**

Type of show Mostly comedy with some magic thrown in. **Admission** $24.95. **Cast size** 1. **Usual showtimes** Tuesday–Saturday, 1 and 3 p.m. **Dark** Sunday and Monday. **Appropriate for children** Yes. **Duration of presentation** 1 hour.

DESCRIPTION AND COMMENTS Our pick for the best afternoon show in town, Mac King uses magic and illusion as a platform for his unique brand of comedy. His humor pokes fun at Las Vegas, other Vegas magicians, and at himself. The presentation is fresh and imaginative, and the illusions are good. But it's King's ability to work an audience, coupled with his sheer insanity, that keeps audiences rolling. If it's really magic you crave (as opposed to comedy), then *Rick Thomas*, also described in this section, is a better choice.

CONSUMER TIPS Harrah's runs two-fer and discount specials on *Mac King*, but they come and go. Unique among afternoon shows, *Mac King* frequently sells out. So purchase tickets in advance if possible.

The Magic of Rick Thomas   ★★★★

APPEAL BY AGE   UNDER 21 ★★★★   21–37 ★★★★   38–50 ★★★★   51+ ★★★★

HOST CASINO AND SHOWROOM **Orleans—The Showroom, ☎ 702-365-7075; www.orleanscasino.com and www.rickthomas.com**

Type of show Magic and illusion. **Admission** Reserve seating, $27.50 and $33. **Cast size** 4. **Days of lowest attendance** Monday and Tuesday. **Usual showtimes** Monday–Thursday, 4 and 7 p.m.; Friday, 4 p.m.; Saturday, 2 and 4 p.m. **Dark** Sunday. **Appropriate for children** Yes. **Duration of presentation** 1 hour.

DESCRIPTION AND COMMENTS See full profile on page 216.

Nathan Burton Comedy Magic ★★★

APPEAL BY AGE UNDER 21 ★★½ 21–37 ★★★ 38–50 ★★★ 51+ ★★★

HOST CASINO AND SHOWROOM **Planet Hollywood–V Theatre;**
☎ **702-932-1818; www.comedypet.com**

Type of show Comedy magic (duh!). **Admission cost** Children under age 12, $15; adults, $36–$42. **Cast size** 6. **Usual showtimes** Saturday–Thursday, 2 p.m.; Friday, 6 p.m. **Appropriate for children** Yes. **Duration of presentation** 1 hour.

DESCRIPTION AND COMMENTS The show begins with a collection of video clips on two large video screens flanking the stage (you may recognize Burton from his appearance on TV's *America's Got Talent,* which brought him a lot of attention). From there, he runs the magical gamut from some baffling gimmick illusions to classic magic tricks. Burton doesn't break any new ground, but his illusions are current and represent the genre well. With a nod to magic's history, he performs Houdini's straightjacket escape with a modern twist—it's completely see through—and a levitation trick with what must be the world's largest hair dryer. High-energy (and very loud) music augments the upbeat pace of the show. Burton smiles his way through a production that is longer on magic than on comedy, but still, it all works well. If your primary interest is magic and illusion, Nathan Burton does a good job. If it's more comedy you crave, try Mac King at Harrah's.

CONSUMER TIPS The seats are close together, so you may end up getting chummy with the folks sitting nearby. If you have children (or short adults) in your party, arrive early. The theater is not tiered, so the only way height-challenged patrons can see is if they're close to the front.

The Price Is Right—Live! ★★★½

APPEAL BY AGE UNDER 21 ★★½ 21–37 ★★★½ 38–50 ★★★★ 51+ ★★★★

HOST CASINO AND SHOWROOM **Bally's—*Jubilee!* Theater; ☎ 702-967-4567 or 877-374-7469; www.ballyslasvegas.com**

Type of show Game show with prizes. **Admission cost** $49.50. **Cast size** 7. **Night of lowest attendance** Wednesday. **Usual showtimes** Tuesday–Thursday and Saturday and Sunday, 2:30 p.m.; Friday, 8 p.m. **Dark** Monday. **Appropriate for children** Yes. **Duration of presentation** 1 hour and 45 minutes.

DESCRIPTION AND COMMENTS This is a reprise of the classic TV game show. Contestants, who must be 21 or older, compete for thousands of dollars in cash and prizes. Interactive keypads attached to seats allow audience members to vie for a chance to be the next contestant. *The Price Is Right* draws the largest and most excitable audiences of any afternoon show we've ever reviewed. For the uninitiated, it's like going to a cheerleader camp. In fact, the first 20 minutes of the show are devoted to teaching the audience how to scream, applaud, and jump around. You're even instructed in the art of ooh-ing and aah-ing when the prizes are shown, as well as sighing "Awww!" when a contestant goes down in flames. If you're called upon to "come on down," you are pressed to hurl yourself down the aisle with the greatest weirdness you can manage. Videos of bizarre contestants from the TV show "coming on down" are shown to inspire you and give you an idea of what's expected. Roger Lodge from *The Dating Game* serves as host. The audience is so lathered up when he's introduced, you'd think the angel Gabriel had just arrived on a lightning bolt. Whatever the hoopla, however, the prizes are very good, ranging from cash to cruise vacations and cars.

CONSUMER TIPS Before entering, you must check in at the registration desk just to the right of the theater entrance. Here, your seat number will be recorded and you'll be issued a giant name tag. This process gets you listed in the show computer, from which contestant names are chosen at random. *Jubilee!* Theater is one of the grand dames of the Las Vegas show scene. For a glimpse of Las Vegas history, come back in the evening and see *Jubilee!*

The Ronn Lucas Show ★★★½

APPEAL BY AGE	UNDER 21 ★★★★	21–37 ★★★½	38–50 ★★★½	51+ ★★★

HOST CASINO AND SHOWROOM **Planet Hollywood Resort and Casino—Steve Wyrick Theater; ☎ 702-777-9974; www.vegas.com**

Type of show Ventriloquist/comedy. Admission cost Reserve seating, $29.95; VIP seating, $34.95. Cast size 1. Day of lowest attendance Wednesday. Usual showtimes Daily, 3 p.m. Dark Friday. Appropriate for children Yes. Duration of presentation 1 hour and 15 minutes.

DESCRIPTION AND COMMENTS Ronn Lucas has been called "The World's Best Ventriloquist," and it's tough to imagine how anyone could be better. You have to keep reminding yourself that he's the one talking for his partners. He also can throw his voice and even continues to gab while simultaneously blowing up a balloon. His show focuses mostly on Lucas verbally sparring with several irascible puppets, in particular Scorch, a green dragon, and Buffalo Billy, who wears a cowboy outfit and a mop of red hair. The comedy is pretty standard fare, but it's light and pleasant, and Lucas keeps things moving along. He's a seasoned pro and works the audience with a masterful congeniality. The afternoon time slot, the level of humor, and the engaging puppetry make this a great show for the family.

CONSUMER TIPS The Steve Wyrick Theater has a large, high stage that can be seen easily from any seat in the house. Lucas sets up front and center and rarely moves elsewhere. His puppets like to interact with the audience, so grab a seat up front at your own risk.

Xtreme Magic Starring Dirk Arthur   ★ ★ ★

APPEAL BY AGE   UNDER 21 ★ ★ ★ ½   21–37 ★ ★ ★ ½   38–50 ★ ★ ★   51+ ★ ★ ★

HOST CASINO AND SHOWROOM **Tropicana–Tiffany Theatre; ☎ 800-829-9034; www.tropicanalv.com**

Type of show Magic and illusion. **Admission** $31–$34. **Cast size** 5. **Usual show-times** Saturday–Thursday, 2 p.m. and 4 p.m. **Dark** Friday. **Appropriate for children** Yes. **Duration of presentation** 1 hour and 20 minutes.

DESCRIPTION AND COMMENTS Dirk Arthur is an excellent illusionist specializing (like rival Steve Wyrick) in making big things disappear and appear (cars, tigers, helicopters, etc.). There's nothing cutting edge here, and there's a dependence on gimmicks, devices, and technology, but it's a good show.

Dirk Arthur's show doesn't have the ensemble that augments Lance Burton's show, but is a great value if you're primarily interested in magic and illusion.

CONSUMER TIPS Be aware that the Tiffany Theatre has its own box office adjacent to the showroom. Many folks spend a long time in line at the Tropicana's main box office by mistake.

▌ COMEDY CLUBS

THERE IS A LOT OF STAND-UP COMEDY in Las Vegas, and several of the large production shows feature comedians as specialty acts. In addition, there is usually at least one comedy headliner playing in town. Big names who regularly play Las Vegas include Jerry Seinfeld, Rita Rudner, Tim Conway, the Smothers Brothers, Joan Rivers, Don Rickles, and Rich Little. Finally, there are the comedy clubs.

A comedy club is usually a smaller showroom with a simple stage and two to five stand-up comics. In most Las Vegas comedy show-rooms, a new show with different comedians rotates in each week. There are three bona fide Las Vegas comedy clubs:

> Harrah's: The Improv
>
> Riviera: Riviera Comedy Club
>
> Tropicana: Comedy Stop

The comedy clubs, unlike the production showrooms, are almost never dark. There are usually two shows each night, seven days a week. The humor at the comedy clubs, as well as the audience, tends to be young and irreverent. A favorite and affordable entertainment for locals as well as for tourists, comedy clubs enjoy great popularity in Las Vegas.

The comedy-club format is simple and straightforward. Come-dians perform sequentially, and what you get depends on who is performing. The range of humor runs from slapstick to obscene to ethnic to topical to just about anything. Some comics are better than others, but all of the talent is solid and professional. There is no way to predict which club will have the best show in a given week. In fact, there may not be a "best" show, since response to comedy is a matter of individual sense of humor.

Comedy Stop

HOST CASINO AND SHOWROOM **Tropicana—Comedy Stop Showroom;**
☎ **702-739-2714; www.tropicanalv.com**

Type of show Stand-up comedy. **Admission** $19.95. **Cast size** Usually 3 comedians. **Nights of lowest attendance** Monday–Wednesday. **Usual showtimes** 8 p.m. (nonsmoking) and 10:30 p.m. (smoking). **Duration of presentation** 1 hour and 20 minutes.

DESCRIPTION AND COMMENTS To reach the Comedy Stop Showroom, take the elevator between the main casino and the shopping arcade up one floor. The 400-person showroom is rectangular, with the stage on the long side. All seating is at banquet tables. Tickets may be purchased up to two weeks in advance by phone with a credit card, or admission can be pre-paid at the Comedy Stop guest desk near the showroom entrance. After being seated, patrons trade their ticket stubs at a self-service bar for one drink. If you use the Trop's self-parking lot, allow an extra ten minutes to get to the showroom.

The Improv

HOST CASINO AND SHOWROOM **Harrah's—The Improv; ☎ 702-369-5111;**
www.harrahs.com

Type of show Stand-up comedy. **Admission** $31.95. **Cast size** 3–4 comedians. **Nights of lowest attendance** Wednesday and Thursday. **Usual showtimes** Tuesday–Sunday, 8:30 and 10:30 p.m. **Dark** Monday. **Duration of presentation** 1 hour and 10 minutes.

DESCRIPTION AND COMMENTS Drinks are not included, but there is a cash bar. The showroom is on the second floor at the top of the escalator from the main casino. Reserved seats may be purchased by phone or in person up to 30 days in advance.

Riviera Comedy Club

HOST CASINO AND SHOWROOM **Riviera—Mardi Gras Showrooms, second floor;**
☎ **702-794-9433; www.rivierahotel.com**

Type of show Stand-up comedy. **Admission** $19.95. **Cast size** Approximately 4. **Nights of lowest attendance** Sunday–Wednesday. **Usual showtimes** Nightly, 8:30 and 10:30 p.m. **Duration of presentation** 1 hour and 15 minutes.

DESCRIPTION AND COMMENTS Venues for the Riviera Comedy Club and the *Crazy Girls* and *La Cage* shows are on the second and third floors above the Riviera casino in what are called the Mardi Gras Showrooms. In addition, the production show *Ice: Direct from Russia* plays in the Versailles Theatre. It is not possible to schedule different shows back to back unless there is a minimum of an hour and 30 minutes between performances. Show tickets can also be purchased as a package with the Riviera's buffet. The food with the show-dinner combo is a good deal for the money but is not exactly a culinary breakthrough. The buffet is fast and convenient, however, and there is usually plenty of time to eat between shows.

Tickets for the Comedy Club may be purchased 21 days in advance at the Riviera box office located in the front center of the casino or by phone with a credit card. Seating is by the maître d'. There is no table service. After you are seated, proceed to the bar and turn in your ticket stub for drinks. Drinks are included even with the dinner combos.

LOUNGE SHOWS

LAS VEGAS ENTERTAINMENT pro Rick Kanfer has long been an advocate of free lounge entertainment, citing not only its great value but also its outstanding quality. Below, Rick shares his picks of the best lounges and lounge acts in Las Vegas.

Not so long ago, lounges were as large a draw for casinos as the productions in their showrooms. Many top performers, people you knew by name, played lounges where no admission was required. Less than a decade ago, for example, you could enjoy Keely Smith in the lounge at the Desert Inn without even being required to buy a drink. Today, with multi-thousand-seat showrooms and high-cover-charge nightclubs, the traditional Las Vegas lounge has become a dying breed. In the past several years alone, dozens have been replaced by small-productions showrooms, fancy "ultralounges," Starbucks stores, or slot machines.

Before they disappear, however, we want to offer you a chance to experience the lounges that survive, many of which are in casinos that probably aren't on your must-see list. In addition to a nostalgic taste of old Las Vegas, you'll be on your way to a great night out. The lounges listed were selected because they always showcase dynamite talent. The entertainment is so good, in fact, that you need not bother to check who's playing: just go. Later on, we turn the tables and list some longtime Las Vegas lounge acts that will knock you out. In this case it doesn't matter where they're performing: they're well worth seeing wherever they are.

THE LOUNGES

Mandalay Bay—House of Blues
☎ 702-632-7600; www.mandalaybay.com or www.hob.com **High energy**

Longtime Vegas club band Boogie Knights packs 'em in every Saturday from 11 p.m. to 3 a.m. This is the hottest dance party in town, with all the great disco hits from the 1970s. The act is hysterically staged and choreographed and performed to some of the best digital tracks we've ever heard. The giant afros, bell-bottom pants, and John Travolta drummer (in the white suit) will keep you entertained all night.

On Monday nights, it's "Rock Star Live Karaoke" beginning at 10 p.m. Drop your inhibitions and get up on stage with a live rock band. Drummer, bass player, and screaming guitar player (who looks just like Steven Tyler of Aerosmith) will help you pick your favorite song. The words are displayed on a television screen sitting right in front of you about waist high. The band plays live and sings backup (or with you if you need the help). If you're with a group, you can be the Temptations. Monday and Tuesday nights are always free, and usually women can get in free on the other nights.

The Orleans—Brendan's Irish Pub
☎ 702-365-7111; www.orleanscasino.com High-energy

"Brendan's Irish Pub" is a slight misnomer. The better acts are a quasi-impersonator show called *Rock This Town* on Tuesdays at 9:30 p.m. and *Blues Zydeco with Pete Contino* on Wednesdays at 9:30 p.m. *Rock This Town* features long-time Buddy Holly impersonator George Trullinger, who is just great on stage. He throws in impersonations of Ed Sullivan, Mick Jagger, and other comedic send-ups as the host of the show. There is an above-average Elvis who comes across with charm and warmth, and the keyboard player is Frankie Moreno.

The blues-zydeco combo of Pete Contino's group is totally infectious. And it fits the dark-wood-paneled room to a T. This is a zydeco band on steroids *and* a rockin' blues band that may be the best in town. It's not unusual to hear Lynyrd Skynyrd's "Sweet Home Alabama," Jimi Hendrix's "All Along the Watchtower," and Hank Williams's "Jambalaya" back to back.

The room is quite large and is totally separate from the casino, built more with the look of a walk-in restaurant than a lounge.

Sahara—Casbar Theatre Lounge
☎ 702-737-2111; www.saharavegas.com Relaxing

The Casbar is perhaps the quintessential example of a 1970s casino lounge. Separated from the casino by only a curtain, the venue is round and dark. Service is spotty, but on the other hand, no one's constantly bugging you to buy a drink. Seating consists of bar stools surrounding cocktail tables: they're not the most comfortable but offer good lines of sight. You can enjoy some of Vegas's best performers here. Lena Prima (daughter of the famed Louis) belts out jazz classics, the sultry and gorgeous Candace Davis Martin is a torch singer extraordinaire, and platinum recording artists The Checkmates are the original group that have been performing in Las Vegas for 41 years—they opened for Sinatra and bring energy and excitement to every performance.

Suncoast—Showroom
☎ 702-636-7111 High energy

Suncoast is far off the beaten path and mostly a locals' hangout, but the showroom features another one of the brilliant acts created by Perfect World Entertainment (other acts at the House of Blues), The Spazzmatics. Complete with plaid pants worn short to expose their white socks, they are a great send-up of a 1980s band. They play along with digital tracks so perfectly (created by John Williams, former musical director) you don't even know the music is mostly on tape. And they pack 'em in to standing-room-only every Wednesday night from 10:30 p.m. to 1:30 a.m.

ENTERTAINERS

THE FOLLOWING ARE LOUNGE ACTS that are worth tracking down. Check the local visitor magazines, find out where they're playing, and go see them. Satisfaction guaranteed.

Jimmy Hopper

Former male-vocalist winner of Ed McMahon's $100,000 *Star Search,* Hopper sings everything from Sinatra to U2 with his four-octave voice. He sometimes appears at the Fontana Bar at Bellagio; **www.jimmyhopper.com.**

Cook E. Jarr

Hilarious combination of Tom Jones, Elvis, and Led Zeppelin front man Robert Plant, Jarr performs covers of the same, accompanied by his band, The Crumbs (actually an electronic drum machine and digital tracks). He usually appears at Harrah's Carnival Court but could turn up anywhere. A staple of Las Vegas lounges, Jarr has been performing his creative brand of musical humor for more than 20 years. Think Wayne Newton meets Alice Cooper.

Eric Martin and Carmen Romano as The Blues Brothers

Another longtime staple of *Legends in Concert,* Martin and Romano have this act nailed perfectly. They can often be found at the House of Blues at Mandalay Bay.

Art Vargas

Having performed for years as Bobby Darin in the hit show *Legends in Concert,* Vargas now plays free lounges all over town. He's cool, has swagger, and dresses in silk suits right out of the 1950s. One of the hippest acts in town with a spectacular voice and great stage presence; **www.artvargas.com.**

▌ LAS VEGAS NIGHTLIFE

WHEN IT COMES TO NIGHTSPOTS, visitors and locals tend to go in different directions. With the exception of patronizing the comedy clubs, locals stay away from the Strip; visitors, conversely, almost never leave it. Both groups are missing out on some great nightlife.

LAS VEGAS NIGHTLIFE BESTIARY

If you're not a regular club-hopper, the bewildering menu of nightlife choices available in Las Vegas may seem confusing. Here's a brief, half-serious guide to the evening buffet and who goes where, with examples of each nightlife type.

CASINO BAR These rectangular bars scattered about every casino floor serve mainly as the pick-up point for waitresses serving gamblers, but you can certainly pick up a drink there yourself. Patrons gathered here are either plunking away at video poker displays, or downing one last round before they hit the tables or hit the road.

Examples: Throw a rock, and you'll hit one. Every casino has a bar, and most have several.

LOUNGE A step up (sometimes literally) from the casino bar, lounges are separated from the casino floor—sometimes by little more than a curtain or railing—and are given some individual decor and a name. They usually feature light entertainment, from a piano player to dancers to an occasional DJ. Lounges tend to be closed in mornings, but they open in early evening and stay up late. Most customers are hotel guests, casino players on break, or nightlifers enjoying their first beverage before setting out.

Examples: Cleopatra's Barge and Shadow Bar (Caesars Palace); Mist (Treasure Island); Zuri (MGM Grand).

ULTRALOUNGE This was a specious marketing term invented by Vegas promoters a few years back, but "ultralounge" serves as well as anything to describe high-end venues that charge dearly both at the door and at the bar. Such places are immaculately designed and furnished, staffed with gorgeous servers (and ogrelike security), and policed to ensure compliance with a snappy dress code. "Bottle service"—that is, paying hundreds of dollars for a bottle of booze—is typically the only way to reserve a table. Clientele tends toward the well-heeled and super-cool, though if you don't mind standing, even the modestly loaded can pay the cover and drink à la carte.

Examples: Forty Deuce (Mandalay Bay), Ghostbar (Palms), Light (Bellagio), Lure (Wynn Las Vegas), Mix (Mandalay Bay), Risque (Paris), Tabu (MGM Grand).

MUSIC BOX Vegas is huge with musical headliners in the big showrooms, but finding reliably good live bar tunes convenient for visitors requires a bit more digging. Most tend to specialize, and there's a perhaps surprising amount of good jazz and blues to be heard. Call ahead to see who's playing; expect to pay a substantially higher cover/admission for name acts or regional favorites. Casual clubgoers will fill up musical bars too, and they may be quite willing to shout over your favorite song if they're just out to drink and party down. Get there early to secure the best seats and sight lines.

Examples: House of Blues (Mandalay Bay), Nine Fine Irishmen (New York–New York), Sand Dollar Blues Lounge and VooDoo Lounge (Rio), Casbar Lounge (Sahara).

DANCE PALACE Straight-ahead dance clubs (as opposed to smaller clubs with dance floors) have always struggled in Vegas. They've turned the corner lately, though, as massive rooms with overpowering sound have finally caught on. (The old-school dance hall is also one of the last local refuges of the country bar.) Rock/pop dance clubs draw heavily on the Los Angeles crowd and their style, so most patrons will be dressed to move; expect high style and bare flesh.

These joints are either dead vacant or packed to the gills, and the change can happen with alarming speed. The music and mob will eliminate conversation and make regular trips to the bar impractical, so only go if the dance party is your main mission.

Examples: Dylan's Saloon & Dance Hall, Gilley's Saloon (New Frontier); OPM (Caesars Palace); Rain (Palms); rumjungle (Mandalay Bay); Studio 54 (MGM Grand); Tangerine (Treasure Island); Tryst (Wynn Las Vegas).

MEGACLUB One way that Vegas gets around the unreliable popularity of dance clubs is by creating giant venues that feature a huge dance floor as part of a multiroomed experience. These sprawling labyrinths may cover several floors and include the dance room(s), side lounges, bars, a restaurant, and uncountable VIP rooms. They may even have separate entrances depending on which place you want to start. Count on long lines at every entrance regardless; more than anything else, the success of megaclubs have brought the era of door bribes to Vegas. Palm $20 (per person in your party) to the doorman, and you'll find your names appearing mysteriously (and invisibly) on his list. Otherwise, expect to wait an hour or more to get in, if ever. Inside, you'll find massive crowds of beautiful people, dressed to the nines and ready to party, plus a half-dozen ways to entertain yourself—DJs, dance troupes, novelty performers, live "mannequins," you name it. The time and expense effectively kills the idea of club-hopping, but with all this on offer, you probably won't need anything else—unless it's a cup of coffee at dawn.

Examples: Ice, JET (Mirage); Pure (Caesars Palace); Tao (Venetian).

Listed alphabetically below are profiles of the better nightspots in town. Celebrity-headliner shows, production shows, and comedy clubs are detailed in the preceding section. Striptease shows (for men and women) are described in "Las Vegas below the Belt" (see page 270). Microbreweries also offer a fine choice for an evening of entertainment. Check out "The Best Brewpubs" section in Part Four, Dining and Restaurants (see page 336).

▌ NIGHTCLUB PROFILES

Aurora

PLACE TO DECOMPRESS

Luxor Las Vegas, 3900 South Las Vegas Boulevard; ☎ 702-262-4591; www.luxor.com **South Strip and Environs**

Cover None. **Minimum** None. **Mixed drinks** $8 and up. **Wine** $7 and up. **Beer** $4.75 domestic, $5.50 import. **Dress** Casual. **Food available** None. **Hours** 24/7.

WHO GOES THERE 21 and older. Broad mix of ages, tends 30+. With little to make it a destination spot, it attracts mostly guests at the Luxor, Excalibur, and Mandalay Bay.

Las Vegas Nightclubs

CLUB	TYPE OF CLUB
Aurora	Place to decompress
The Bar at Times Square	Top 40, show tunes, sing-along
The Beach	Dance music of the 1970s, 1980s, and 1990s
Body English	1990s and current music dance club
Club Rio	Top 40 music
Coyote Ugly	Drink-slinging barmaids stomp and holler above the crowd
Dylan's Saloon & Dance Hall	Recorded country music
Forty Deuce	High-roller burlesque in upscale cabaret cave
Freakin' Frog	Beer snobs and whiskey nerds find a common haven
Ghostbar	Otherworldly lounge high above the Strip
Gilley's Saloon	Live country and rock-and-roll
House of Blues	Blues, R&B
Ice	Metaclub—boom, boom, boom
JET	Latest new club from the owners of Light, Fix, and Stack
Light	New York club chic, Vegas-style
Lucky Strike Lanes	Chic bowling
Lure	Cool lounge refuge
Mix Lounge	Vegas's most beautiful room
Moon	Open-air night club
Nine Fine Irishmen	Live Celtic music pub

WHAT GOES ON Opened in March of 2007, Aurora provides a break from the Egyptian theme at the Luxor. Named to evoke the Aurora Borealis or Northern Lights, it's decorated in rich blues and greens and has a hip-yet-casual elegance. Aurora offers European bottle and wine service as well as tableside martinis. Though not stuffy, it's not a party place either. It's where you go to start or end your evening or to take a break from shopping or the casinos.

SETTING AND ATMOSPHERE From the rich colors and comfortable chairs to the smooth jazz on the sound system, Aurora offers a mellow, sophisticated atmosphere. The tables are black marble and cherry wood, the bar highlighted with icicles of glass hanging above. With a capacity of more than 150 customers, it's spacious—easily enough room between tables to allow privacy and relaxation. Though the lounge juts into the main walking area, it's raised a couple of steps above the passersby, giving it a self-contained ambience.

CLUB	TYPE OF CLUB
Octane	Sanitized biker dive
OPM	Multiroom dance club
Playboy Club	Cleavage and nostalgia
Pure Nightclub	Massive, expensive, upscale nightclub
Pussycat Dolls Lounge	Hollywood burlesque show goes upscale
Rain Las Vegas	Mondo dance orgy with fire-spewing lighting rig
Revolution Lounge	Beatles music
Risque	Euro-style club and meat market
Rockhouse Bar and Nightclub	Punk, metal, and go-go dancers
rumjungle	Dance, techno, industrial, rap music
Sand Dollar Blues Lounge	Rhythm and blues
Shimmer Cabaret	Top 40/show combination
Studio 54	Dance, top 40
Tabu	Über-lounge
Tangerine	Burlesque beach-bar thing
Tao	Super-giant-mega-club, restaurant, and lounge
Tommy Rocker's Cantina and Grill	Top 40 and Jimmy Buffett–style music
Tryst	Techno-sexy dance party
VooDoo Lounge	Live music with best view of the Strip

IF YOU GO There's not enough here to warrant hanging out for long, and the crowd seems to turn over regularly, so there's no need to hit the scene early to beat the rush.

The Bar at Times Square

TOP 40, SHOW TUNES, SING-ALONG

New York–New York, 3790 South Las Vegas Boulevard;
☎ **702-740-6969; www.nynyhotelcasino.com** South Strip and Environs

Cover Friday and Saturday, $10 (kicks in at 7 p.m.). **Minimum** None. **Mixed drinks** $7–$8. **Wine** $4–$5 and up. **Beer** $4–$5 and up. **Dress** Anything goes. **Specials** None. **Food available** In casino. **Hours** Daily, 11 a.m.–4 a.m. (24 hours on weekends); shows 8 p.m.–2 a.m.

WHO GOES THERE 21–45; college students, tourists.

WHAT GOES ON   The Bar at Times Square is to karaoke night at the corner pub what the Boston Pops on July 4 is to a kiddie chorus at the corner kindergarten. This joint, in other words, has muscle. Two pianos face each other in the middle of the room, at which dueling piano players (often a guy and a girl) pound out top-40 tunes ("Walk This Way," "Build Me Up Buttercup," "Me and Bobby McGee," and such) or show tunes, and engage in witty repartee with each other and the crowd. Most people get into it and sing along (though it gets so loud that the bartenders wear cotton in both ears); many patrons walk up to the pianos and write down requests on yellow sheets of paper.

SETTING AND ATMOSPHERE   The room is plainly decorated like an old New York City licensed premises, with polished-wood floors and historical photos of the Big Apple on the walls. The pianos divide the room in half. At the end is the bar, in front of which the often standing-room-only crowd hangs around with drinks in their hands, singing their heads off in each others' ears. On the other side are a couple dozen tables; it's a bit less raucous over here, though no less crowded—you have to arrive early to get a seat.

IF YOU GO   If you have a headache, you won't care for this scene. But if you're in the mood to exercise your lungs and lend your voice to a rowdy chorus, you'll have a good time. A couple of drinks help the cause, and luckily, they're reasonably priced. But if you just want to see what goes on, or listen to the music, join the small crowd milling around outside the front doors, avoiding the cover charge and the subway-at-rush-hour claustrophobia.

The Beach

DANCE MUSIC OF THE 1970s, 1980s, AND 1990s

365 Convention Center (corner of Paradise and Convention Center, across from the Convention Center); ☎ 702-731-1925; www.beachlv.com
North Strip and Environs

Cover   Local males free before midnight; ladies free except for special events; Sunday–Thursday, $10 (after midnight, $5); Friday and Saturday, $15 (after midnight, $10). Minimum None. Mixed drinks $4.50 and up. Wine $7 and up. Beer $4 and up. Dress Very specific and strict (call for restrictions). Specials Tuesday, Sabotage Rock tribute band; Thursday, College Night; Saturday, free comedy show at 8 p.m.; Sunday, Monday, and Wednesday, ladies night. Food available In sports bar. Hours Varies according to entertainment. Sports bar, open 24 hours; dance bar open 10 p.m.–4 a.m., Sunday–Thursday and until 6 a.m. Friday and Saturday.

WHO GOES THERE   21–40+; locals, visitors, conventioneers (cosmopolitan mix).

WHAT GOES ON   These beach lovers don't miss the sand or the surf, because all the action is indoors. On the main floor, singles, couples, and new friends alike dance, drink, eat, and laugh the night away in this "locals' favorite" party club. The fun is so contagious that even the bartenders and cocktail waitresses join in the dancing. From the second-floor sports bar, patrons watch games on more than 60 TVs (including five big screens); play slots, video poker, or pool; and view the action on the main floor. The Beach is an unpretentious and fun-loving spot that radiates positive energy and good vibes.

SETTING AND ATMOSPHERE Neon beer lights, palms, coconuts, surfboards, and brightly painted murals give the club a beach flavor without adding salt or sand. The wood walls offer excellent acoustics for live performances and the DJ's music. The main floor has five bars, high-table seating, and a dance area. Adjacent to the upstairs sports bar is a room available for private parties or extra party space. ATM machines are on each floor.

IF YOU GO Long lines begin at 9 p.m. and continue well past 2 a.m. on weekends. Also, please note that the four-story garage is reserved for valet on weekends, so use the Convention Center parking lot across the street. Plan to arrive very early or take a cab. Smoke can be heavy in some corners of the club. Women on their own can expect to find company. Call ahead for special-events information.

Body English

SHINE YOUR BELT BUCKLE ON THE JAMMED DANCE FLOOR

Hard Rock Casino, 4455 Paradise Road; ☎ 702-693-4000; www.bodyenglish.com; South Strip and Environs

Cover $30 for gentlemen, $20 for ladies; local ladies are free. Minimum None. Mixed drinks $8 and up. Wine $7 and up. Beer $5 and up. Dress Upscale. Food available None. Hours Friday–Sunday, 10:30 p.m.–4 a.m.

WHO GOES THERE 21-40; young, beautiful people who want to be ogled and make the scene.

WHAT GOES ON Purportedly designed to look like a British rock star's mansion, Body English oozes icy black coolness. Many patrons high-five and whoop with self-congratulatory excitement just for getting in! A large staircase splits the club in two. The bar upstairs is definitely for observing the action on the surprisingly small, densely populated dance floor below. On ground level, a long bar keeps the movers and shakers from getting too dry as several tons of beefy security men look on. DJ Dig Dug moves from the surprisingly old-school (Prince, Sheila E., Parliament/Funkadelic, and INXS) to more-contemporary artists such as Gnarls Barkley. Heavy emphasis on reserved tables and bottle service with 11 banquettes downstairs, plus a VIP section behind the velvet ropes with eight booths downstairs and five upstairs near the club entrance.

SETTING AND ATMOSPHERE Walls, floors, and pillars are black, accented with black-marble bars and counters, brass railings, and elegant chandeliers, one of which morphs into a disco ball above the dance floor.

IF YOU GO Air-conditioning is set to polar so the place stays chilly—ahem, *cool*. Dress for it if you're not going to work up a sweat on the dance floor. Don't expect to hang out on the staircase or the bottom landing for more than a moment—you will be moved along by security with biceps like canned hams.

Club Rio

NIGHTCLUB—TOP-40 MUSIC

Rio Hotel, 3700 West Flamingo Road; ☎ 702-777-7977; www.riolasvegas.com Mid-Strip and Environs

Cover Local ladies, free; men, $20; out-of-state ladies, $10. **Minimum** None. **Mixed drinks** $5 and up. **Wine** $4.25 and up. **Beer** $3.75 and up. **Dress** Collared shirts for men; no jeans, shorts, tennis shoes, or sandals. **Specials** Thursday, Latin Libido night; Friday and Saturday, DJ music. **Food available** Restaurants on property. **Hours** Thursday, 11 p.m.–4 a.m.; Friday and Saturday, 11:30 p.m.–4 a.m.

WHO GOES THERE 25–35 professionals; locals and visitors.

WHAT GOES ON Sexy and stylish, Club Rio is a hot nightclub for successful singles and the chic well-to-do. Dancers fill the spacious dance floor. Couples snuggle in the showroom's comfy booths, while others search for and mingle with potential partners. Although the music is loud and pulsating, there's little trouble conversing with new friends or ordering drinks from the attractive cocktail waitresses.

SETTING AND ATMOSPHERE After the last show, the showroom at Club Rio is transformed into a cosmopolitan nightclub with table lamps, mosaic laser lights, and giant video panels. Selected sections of booth seating are reserved for casino players. The sound system is clean, clear, and loud, but not too loud.

IF YOU GO Arrive early to avoid the long lines after 11 p.m. The dress code encourages stylish attire (jackets for the men and dresses for the women). Watch your step along the showroom's terraced levels as you make your way to and from the dance floor. The club is located off the new Masquerade Village.

Coyote Ugly

DRINK-SLINGING BARMAIDS STOMP AND HOLLER ABOVE THE CROWD

New York–New York, 3790 South Las Vegas Boulevard; ☎ 702-212-8804; www.coyoteuglysaloon.com/vegas or www.nynylasvegas.com South Strip and Environs

Cover $10 (after 9 p.m.). **Minimum** None. **Mixed drinks** $5 and up. **Wine** $5 and up. **Beer** $4 and up. **Dress** Casual. **Specials** Too many to list, some of which will be poured directly into your mouth. **Food available** None. **Hours** Daily, 6 p.m.–4 a.m.

WHO GOES THERE 21–35; curious passersby and booze-crazed barflies.

WHAT GOES ON An imported concept from New York City (and made famous by the eponymous movie), Coyote Ugly is a rootin'-tootin' saloon whose main attractions are the slinky female bartenders who leap atop the bars and stomp, clog, sing, dance, and generally whip the crowd into a drunken frenzy (sometimes literally pouring shots into the mouths of the howling masses). The crowd is an almost immobile press, broken only by the occasional scuffle as the security thugs eject a too-rowdy patron. A small back room offers some relief, but you have to force your way through the mob in order to get there.

SETTING AND ATMOSPHERE Vaguely reminiscent of a wood-floored honky-tonk, the surprisingly small room has two bars on opposite walls. That's where you'll find the strutting barmaids doing their stuff. If you can make it through the packed gawkers, an even smaller room in back is only slightly more subdued.

IF YOU GO Forget having a conversation and get ready for some serious, protracted yee-haws. If ogling the barmaids and standing in a crowd are not your bag, you should probably go elsewhere for the evening.

Dylan's Saloon & Dance Hall

RECORDED COUNTRY MUSIC

4660 South Boulder Highway; ☎ 702-451-4006 Southeast Las Vegas

Cover None. **Minimum** None. **Mixed drinks** $4 and up. **Wine** $5 and up. **Beer** $3.50 and up. **Dress** Jeans and cowboy hats. **Specials** Line-dance lessons, Friday and Saturday, 7:30–9 p.m. **Food available** Typical bar fare. **Hours** Friday and Saturday, 7 p.m. till dawn

WHO GOES THERE 25–50; urban and rodeo cowboys.

WHAT GOES ON Whether it's doing the two-step, shooting a game of pool, or enjoying a warm summer evening under the star-filled sky, the young and lively crowd whoops it up on the weekends. From ballads to rockabilly, the DJ mixes the music to the crowd's delight. Seating around the dance floor is at a premium as singles look to meet new partners.

SETTING AND ATMOSPHERE This dance hall has a spacious, 2,400-square-foot, silky smooth dance floor, two bars, friendly folks, and the usual rodeo decor. The party flows onto the patio and, on busy nights, the chain-linked, flood-lit, dirt area adjacent to the parking lot. As the night parties on, the odors of beer and cigarette smoke get thicker.

IF YOU GO The attitude is looser and hipper than at Sam's Town Dance Hall. Arrive early for good seating. Because the parking lot is quite dark in areas, women on their own are advised to ask for an escort to their car.

Forty Deuce

HIGH-ROLLER BURLESQUE IN UPSCALE CABARET CAVE

Mandalay Bay, 3950 South Las Vegas Boulevard; ☎ 702-632-9442; www.mandalaybay.com or www.fortydeuce.com South Strip and Environs

Cover $20. **Minimum** None. **Mixed drinks** $10 and up. **Wine** $7 and up. **Beer** $6 and up. **Dress** Upscale club wear; no jeans or sneakers. **Specials** None. **Food available** None. **Hours** Thursday–Monday, 10:30 p.m.–until.

WHO GOES THERE 21–50; lounge lizards, beautiful people, would-be hepcats.

WHAT GOES ON Super-cool club entrepreneur Ivan Kane launched a version of Forty Deuce in Vegas to match his club of the same name in Los Angeles. Other Mandalay Bay clubs are larger and even egalitarian, while this smaller room attracts a serious velvet-rope crowd. If you don't see any celebs, you'll at least rub elbows with a lot of very attractive and immaculately groomed people who could pass for a quality entourage. Periodically throughout the evening (though starting late), a small band will strike up some hot jazz, and a few scantily clad burlesque dancers will shimmy out onto the bars, tables, or slow-moving patrons. No nudity, though it's about as close as modern lingerie technology allows.

SETTING AND ATMOSPHERE For all the hype, Forty Deuce is surprisingly small, and maybe even cramped. The goal is to represent a back-alley speakeasy vibe, but speakeasies were cramped because they had to be concealed from the coppers—not because the management and patrons were fans of cellar-bound nightlife, particularly. The room is very attractive and interestingly curvy, tiered among several microscopic cocktail tables and VIP holding pens. The mood is red, dark, velvety, sexy, and intimate—very, very intimate if it's a busy night.

IF YOU GO Forty Deuce's entrance is tucked away just inside the Mandalay Place shops, next to RM Seafood. Dress sharp, as pleasant-but-firm doorman attitude comes with the territory in a place like this.

Freakin' Frog

> BEER SNOBS AND WHISKEY NERDS FIND A COMMON HAVEN

4700 South Maryland Parkway; ☎ 702-597-9702; www.freakinfrog.com
East of Strip

Cover None. **Minimum** None. **Mixed drinks** $8 and up. **Wine** $7 and up. **Beer** $4 and up. **Dress** Casual Joe College. **Specials** Variety of special brews, tasting menus, whiskeys. **Food available** Full menu of pub grub and sandwiches. **Hours** Nightly, 5 p.m.–2 a.m.

WHO GOES THERE 21–40; college kids, locals, hipsters, alcohol enthusiasts, hippies.

WHAT GOES ON Downstairs it's all about the beer—10 taps that change almost daily, plus 500 more vintages in the phone book o' bottle brands. Obscure beverages from all over the world may be had, though some may be out at any given time. Upstairs in the Whiskey Attic, which has a huge selection of fine whiskeys. Both levels draw a mix of easygoing UNLV students, locals, hippies, and hipsters. The overall vibe is relaxed, sociable, and a little bohemian.

SETTING AND ATMOSPHERE Bare bones. The downstairs bar has all the charm of a decommissioned cafeteria, while the Whiskey Attic upstairs dresses up with a few covered chairs and wooden paneling. The emphasis is on friends and fluids.

IF YOU GO Feel free to ask for suggestions from the helpful staff, who are always eager to evangelize about their favorite beers or liquors. Definitely don't go looking for fancy cocktails or luxurious surroundings. This is a place for relishing fine drink and enjoying the company of others who do the same.

Ghostbar

Palms Hotel, 4321 West Flamingo Road; ☎ 702-942-7777; www.palms.com or www.n9negroup.com Mid-Strip and Environs

Cover Sunday–Thursday $10; Friday and Saturday $25; free for local ladies with ID. **Minimum** None. **Mixed drinks** $8 and up. **Wine** $6 and up. **Beer** $5 and up. **Dress** "Stylish nightlife attire"; no jeans or tennis shoes. **Specials** None. **Food available** Light pub fare. **Hours** Nightly, 8 p.m. until.

WHO GOES THERE 21–40; the super-glitzy and clubgoing elite.

WHAT GOES ON All cool lines and chilly shades of white and blue, Ghostbar is a scenester's dream. Models of both sexes float about the main lounge space, occasionally alighting on a puffy chair or delicately sipping a translucent drink. Perched on the Palms' 55th floor, Ghostbar is like a butterfly preserve for the beautiful people. Patrons waft out onto the patio, then waft back in for another circuit of the lounge. The place doesn't vibe meat market—rather, it's a spot to clinically evaluate who's hot, what they're wearing, and if they'll come with you to someplace a bit more rowdy.

SETTING AND ATMOSPHERE The beautiful main room is chic to the max, though the icy lighting and color schemes make the place feel like a giant display case (appropriately enough). The room is sparsely populated with a few chairs, benches, and cocktail tables. The outdoor patio has great views of the Strip, not to mention a large square of glass in the floor that's great for evaluating your fear of heights.

IF YOU GO Consider the perambulations of the salon-tanned and surgically enhanced, and definitely walk a few steps on the scary glass square. If you'd rather be dancing, check out the always-frenetic Rain on the ground floor of the Palms.

Gilley's Saloon, Dance Hall, and Barbecue

New Frontier, 3120 South Las Vegas Boulevard; ☎ 702-794-8434; www.frontierlv.com/gilleys.htm North Strip

Cover Wednesday–Saturday after 10 p.m., $10; valid NV ID-holders, free. **Minimum** None. **Mixed drinks** $5.75 and up. **Beer** and **Wine** $4 and up. **Dress** Come as you are; in jeans, boots, and a big hat you'll feel right at home. **Specials** Free line, swing, and two-step dance lessons, Thursday–Saturday, 8:30 p.m.; Sunday 4–6 p.m. **Food available** Full menu of chuckwagon fare, 4–10 p.m. Nightly, Angus steak with fixin's, $10. **Hours** Daily, 4 p.m. until; dinner 4–10 p.m.

WHO GOES THERE 21–55; real and urban cowboys, locals and tourists.

WHAT GOES ON Gilley's house band starts at 4 p.m. Tuesday through Saturday; a DJ spins the tunes on Wednesday, Friday, and Saturday. The band plays two-minute country tunes, complete with pedal-steel guitar and fiddle, during the late dinner sets, then cranks up the tempo later in the evening. The big dance floor gets crowded with two-steppers and line dancers.

Watchers sit at bar tables munching free peanuts from galvanized buckets. If the beer screws up your courage, you can attempt to ride Gilley's signature mechanical bull. Good luck.

SETTING AND ATMOSPHERE The smell of beer-battered onion rings, rotisserie chicken, and hickory-smoked pork permeates the place from the kitchen on one end. On the other end are the two bars. In between are the dance floor, eating areas, and mechanical bronc. Bales of hay, a Mickey Gilley logo counter, and peanut shells on the floor complete the scene. The atmosphere is as heavily country as anywhere else in town—the heaviest on the Strip.

IF YOU GO As long as it stands, the price is right no matter what mood you're in, but it helps to either be in, or ready for, cowboy hats, silver buckles, and fringed blouses. The joint is sedate till late, when everyone's finished eating, but then gets rocking and fun. Round about 11 p.m. (except on Mondays, when it closes at midnight), Gilley's loses its barbecue feel and lives up to the rest of its handle: saloon and dance hall.

House of Blues

RHYTHM AND BLUES

Mandalay Bay, 3950 South Las Vegas Boulevard; ☎ 702-632-7600; www.hob.com or www.mandalaybay.com South Strip and Environs

Cover Varies per venue. **Minimum** None. **Mixed drinks** $8–$10 and up. **Wine** $7 and up. **Beer** $7 and up. **Dress** Clothes. **Specials** Monday nights, Rockstar Karaoke at 10 p.m. (free admission with drink specials); Friday nights, Flashback Fridays with music from the 1970s, 1980s, and 1990s; Saturday nights, 1970s disco; Thursday nights, Unplugged. **Food available** Daily lunch and dinner, and Sunday Gospel Brunch; Creole/Cajun and Southern favorites (fried catfish, ribs); entrees $10–$17. **Hours** Sunday–Thursday, 8 a.m.–midnight, Friday and Saturday, 8 a.m.–1 a.m. (event nights till 2 a.m.).

WHO GOES THERE 21–60; locals, tourists, music lovers.

WHAT GOES ON First things first. House of Blues sports two venues: the 1,800-seat concert auditorium downstairs and the restaurant-bar upstairs (casino level). In this review, we're talking about the live music that takes place in the restaurant Thursday through Saturday from 10:30 p.m. to 1 a.m, when blues and R&B performers take the stage under lights that spell out "Have Mercy, Las Vegas." Three- and four-piece bands serenade the restaurant-bar patrons—some people eating, some people drinking, some people dancing, with waiters and waitresses weaving among them. It's a cool, casual, and not-too-cacophonous scene, with an eclectic audience mix all grooving to some hot licks.

SETTING AND ATMOSPHERE The House of Blues is one of the more evocative dining rooms in town, set to resemble an outdoor courtyard in the middle of a small bayou village, with a huge tree in the middle and tables on a stone floor under and around it, as well as up on patio-type wooden decks. Wrought-iron railings, stone walls, etched and stained glass, and the facades of swamp shacks extend the theme, all under dim lighting.

(They also account for the good acoustics.) The bar itself is decorated with Catholic iconography, mostly crosses made from bottle caps; Voodoo folk art and symbology round out the decor. The only incongruity is the collection of TV monitors on various walls throughout.

IF YOU GO Anything seems to go here during the music: big tables of beer-drinking college kids; couples (and singles) dancing all around the room; unreconstructed barefoot hippies in peasant blouses and patchouli perfume praising the Lord; lead singers or guitarists roaming the room wireless and interacting directly with the audience. It's best on Thursday nights when there's no concert downstairs and only those in the know are upstairs, enjoying some of the best bargain (free) entertainment in town.

Ice

METACLUB—BOOM, BOOM, BOOM

**200 East Harmon Avenue; ☎ 702-699-5528 for VIP reservations;
☎ 702-699-9888 for information; www.icelasvegas.com**
South Strip and Environs

Cover $20. **Minimum** None. **Mixed drinks** $7 and up. **Wine** $5 and up. **Beer** $5 and up. **Dress** Officially it's business/casual, but if you're really hot, wear what you want; tight, revealing jeans OK for ladies only. **Specials** DJ battles on Thursday, ladies drink free 11 p.m.–1 a.m. Service-industry night on Sunday. **Food available** Olives. **Hours** Tuesday, Thursday, 11 p.m.–5 a.m.; Friday and Saturday, 10:30 p.m.–5 a.m.

WHO GOES THERE 21–35 professionals; locals and visitors.

WHAT GOES ON Amid the techno thunder of 100,000 watts of nail-pounding beats, sassy and classy men and ladies in their prime stand around, gyrate, and occasionally sit down, while being buffeted by 100-mph sound blasts. The club keeps a jumping calendar, which can be viewed at their Web site.

SETTING AND ATMOSPHERE Featuring six microenvironments spread across 17,000 square feet of club space, walking around inside Ice is like walking around a stranger's fabulous house. Unless you're a regular, the curiosity to take the tour and continue wandering about is more urgent than to stay put and dance. Our favorite retreat is the cozy upstairs lounge, replete with cushy couches and fat pillows. From the railing you can watch the crowd, and the DJs feed off one another.

IF YOU GO Valet parking is de rigueur here unless you head down the street and park behind the shiny, silver club. It's residential back there, but it's free. If you're alone, you probably want the valet option.

JET

LATEST NEW CLUB FROM THE OWNERS OF LIGHT, FIX, AND STACK

**Mirage, 3400 South Las Vegas Boulevard; ☎ 702-492-3960;
www.mirage.com** Mid-Strip and Environs

Cover Men $30, women $20, locals free on Monday; front-of-line pass: men $50, women $40 (includes passing line and admission). **Minimum** None. **Mixed**

drinks $11 and up. **Wine** $10 and up. **Beer** $9 and up. **Dress** Casual chic. No tank tops, athletic wear, track suits, jeans, or shorts. Fashionable sneakers will be allowed. Dress code enforced. **Specials** Monday is Service Industry Night. **Food available** None. **Hours** Friday, Saturday, and Monday, 10:30 p.m.–4 a.m.

WHO GOES THERE   21 and up. Everyone who was a regular at Light: celebs, dancers, service-industry professionals.

WHAT GOES ON   JET is the newest Las Vegas hot spot backed by the Light Group. It's all about who you are and what you're wearing. This mammoth club hosts several different parties each week. The guys are there to scope out the young, hot ladies in this mosh of Palms and Hard Rock clientele. Since JET hosts a different party each weekend, your chances of running into a celeb or seeing action on the dance floor are plenty. The three distinct rooms make for a mix in the crowd, but it's always a beautiful-people place with a great sound system and even better atmosphere.

SETTING AND ATMOSPHERE   Three different rooms play three different sounds in this mammoth 15,000-square-foot nightclub. JET packs the house with some of the world's legendary DJs. The club also boasts a state-of-the-art light system, cryogenic effects, and sound design that can make the club very bright and loud all at once. The main room plays a mix of hip-hop, rock, and dance, while the other two rooms play house music and a mix of different world music, respectively. JET's four bars are located on multiple levels so you're not confined to one area within the club. The decor is a mix of wood, stone, and archlike steel placed strategically throughout the club.

IF YOU GO   If you're going with a large group, reservations are the way to go. Because the club does get really packed, you'll lose your party if you don't all have a central place. JET makes that easy, as there is seating and bottle service available in each room of the club. If you're driving to JET, make sure to park near the north hotel valet for an easy entrance. As always, when clubbing in Las Vegas and if you are thinking of going to JET, make sure that you are dressed in fashionable attire. While the dress code isn't as strict at JET as it is in some clubs, if you don't look like you just walked off the red carpet, chances are you won't be getting in until the wee later hours. This is another venue where you can go online and buy tickets prior to going, but JET's own "front of the line" passes work just as well and may even be cheaper than going to another site and purchasing.

Light

NEW YORK CLUB CHIC, VEGAS-STYLE

Bellagio Hotel, 3600 South Las Vegas Boulevard; ☎ 702-693-8300; www.bellagio.com or www.lightlv.com Mid-Strip and Environs

Cover $30 (local ladies free). **Minimum** None. **Mixed drinks** $7 and up. **Wine** $6 and up. **Beer** $4.50 and up. **Dress** Stylish and formal; no sneakers or sandals, jeans discouraged **Specials** None. **Food available** None. **Hours** Lounge, 5 p.m.–4 a.m; Thursday–Sunday, nightclub, 10:30 p.m.–4 a.m.

WHO GOES THERE 25–45; the well-to-do and sedentary.

WHAT GOES ON Light caters to those who can spring for a bottle of wine, which is what gets you a "reservation" at one of the tables. The prices for this bottle service are all on the high side—$200 or more—though they vary by vintage and the number of people in your party. The vibe is one of privileged membership in the elite set, and the emphasis is on relaxation rather than partying hearty. It's definitely a laid-back, low-energy place.

SETTING AND ATMOSPHERE Light is reached via escalator from the casino floor, so you get your first taste of ascending to Shangri-La before you even cross the threshold. The windowless room is red, plush, and dark, though not particularly distinctive. The rarely full dance floor is bordered by reservation-only tables. Stools face the dance floor from the outside and also run the length of the bar, making up the only free seats in the house. Another tier of reservable tables cluster near the entrance.

IF YOU GO Given how limited non-reservation seating is at Light, those not interested in shelling out for the reserved spaces should probably go elsewhere. Tables fill up on weekends, so a bottle service reservation in advance is recommended.

Lucky Strike Lanes

HIGHFALUTIN BOWLING ALLEY: A CLUB FOR THE REST OF US

Rio Hotel, 3700 West Flamingo Road; ☎ 702-777-7999; www.riolasvegas.com Mid-Strip and Environs

Cover None. **Minimum** None. **Mixed drinks** $6 and up. **Wine** $7 and up. **Beer** $4.50 and up. **Dress** Club casual; no torn jeans, sandals, or T-shirts. **Food available** Full-service restaurant. **Hours** 11 a.m.–3 a.m.; after 9 p.m., only age 21 and up.

WHO GOES THERE 21–45; eclectic mix of locals and hotel guests.

WHAT GOES ON At 9 p.m. each night, Lucky Strike Lanes is transformed from a modest ten-lane bowling alley to a very hip night spot that dishes up high-energy music with bowling on the side. Bowling costs $8 per game or $75 an hour. Shoe rentals run about $4.

SETTING AND ATMOSPHERE A 25-foot mahogany bar as well as an impressive neon-lit, script-lettered Las Vegas sign over the lanes dominate the scene. The bowling alley replaces traditional lane seating with oversized, plush couches, and retro bowling photographs both inside and outside the club add a touch of whimsy and nostalgia. Five projection screens, descending from a wave-patterned white ceiling, allow bowlers to view sports in addition to serving as a scorecard. A digital jukebox and, on the weekends, live DJ entertainment complete the mix. In addition to bowling, Lucky Strike Lanes offers a variety of sandwiches, burgers, pizza, and salads along with house-specialty mac-and-cheese balls and Buffalo chicken crisps.

IF YOU GO Arrive earlier rather than later if you want to bowl. If bowling's not your thing, spectating is fun, or you can watch sports and other stuff on four flat-screen plasma televisions.

Lure

COOL LOUNGE REFUGE

Wynn Las Vegas, 3131 South Las Vegas Boulevard; ☎ 702-770-7000; www.wynnlasvegas.com North Strip and Environs

Cover None–$20. **Minimum** None. **Mixed drinks** $12 and up. **Wine** $10 and up. **Beer** $7. **Dress** Upscale casual, no sneakers. **Specials** None. **Food available** None. **Hours** Sunday–Thursday, 8 p.m.–3 a.m.; Friday and Saturday, 7 p.m.–3 a.m.

WHO GOES THERE 21–50; Upscale nightlifers and clubland refugees.

WHAT GOES ON Lure is a great place to start an evening, as there's not much to it, yet it opens relatively early. Most nights, no cover will be charged before 10 p.m.; as crowds increase, cover gets charged and goes up until the peak of the night. Ladies can usually schmooze their way in for free, though. Lure sees a surge in traffic when the absurdly popular Tryst opens at the other end of the Wynn, as clubgoers thwarted by Tryst's tight door policy seek other venues.

SETTING AND ATMOSPHERE Dark and high-ceilinged with sensuously billowing drapes and low couches, the main room at Lure is a welcome change from the claustrophobia of other lounges. This feeling is furthered by a court-yard at the back that's open during warmer nights. Occasional glowing whites and sexy dancing waitresses accentuate the sultry vibe.

IF YOU GO Get there early to skip the cover and secure sitting or lounging space. As is now the case everywhere, tables are reserved for pricey bottle service, but you can usually hang out until the reserving party arrives. If you arrive late, it's not uncommon for the line at Lure's door to cause serious waits.

Mix Lounge

DRINK IN THE VIEW FROM VEGAS'S MOST BEAUTIFUL ROOM

THEhotel, Mandalay Bay, 3950 South Las Vegas Boulevard; ☎ 702-632-7777; www.mandalaybay.com South Strip and Environs

Cover $20–$25 after 10 p.m. **Minimum** None. **Mixed drinks** $10 and up. **Wine** $8 and up. **Beer** $7 and up. **Dress** The best clothes you've got. **Specials** None. **Food available** None. **Hours** Sunday–Thursday, 5 p.m.–3 a.m.; Friday and Satur-day, 5 p.m.–4 a.m.

WHO GOES THERE 21–60; the moneyed, the curious, design aficionados.

WHAT GOES ON A glass elevator in the passage connecting THEhotel to the rest of Mandalay Bay elevates guests to Mix, the lounge attached to the Alain Ducasse restaurant of the same name. Once there, prepare to spend about half an hour gaping at the stunning view of the Strip, directly north over the point of the Luxor pyramid. Then spend some time gaping at the room itself. Then go gape at the restaurant next door, with its 15,000-glass-bulb, half-million-dollar chandelier. Then realize that you're sur-rounded by a youngish but still loungey crowd intent on conversation, cocktails, and periodic stares out the windows. If there's a better place in Vegas to start your night, we're not aware of it. As far as ending your night here—or never leaving—you could do a lot worse.

SETTING AND ATMOSPHERE Did we mention the view? About 15 feet of floor-to-ceiling glass sheathes Mix on both sides of the lounge. There's an outdoor observation area railed with clear glass, as well. Inside, it's all deep reds and sleek blacks. An oversized main bar dominates, with two ranks of tables facing the windows. A smaller extra bar can be brought online to service crowds. Don't forget to check out the south view, by the way, as it's equally cool to watch the lines of jets taking off and landing at the airport. DJs play light house and pop on busy nights, but it's not intrusive—this is a lounge, after all, not a club.

IF YOU GO The lounge opens earlier than other high-end nightspots, and you can sometimes get a break on the cover charge if they're looking to fill up the room a bit. Also an obvious choice for drinks before or after a meal at the attached restaurant, though bring your gold card.

Moon

OPEN-AIR NIGHTCLUB ATOP THE PALMS

Palms Hotel, 4321 West Flamingo Road; ☎702-942-7777; www.palms.com Mid-Strip and Environs

Cover Thursday and Sunday, $20; Friday and Saturday, $4. **Minimum** None. **Mixed drinks** $11 and up. **Wine** $6 and up. **Beer** $6 and up. **Dress** Stylish nightlife attire; no tank tops, shorts, athletic wear, baseball hats, tennis shoes, or flip-flops. **Food available** Snacks. **Hours** Thursday–Sunday, 8 p.m. until.

WHO GOES THERE 21–35; ritzy, glitzy, and ditzy; celebs and wannabes.

WHAT GOES ON Every night's a full moon at Moon, with celestial bodies inside and out. This is the hippest venue in the hippest casino in Las Vegas, so half the club-goers are there to make the scene, while the other half are there to see it. To be among the former, either reserve (and pay big bucks for) a VIP table or just grab someone and step onto the large rectangular dance floor. But whether you're a leader or a follower, the setting is so spectacular that it almost doesn't make a difference. Moon is attached to the Playboy Club casino-lounge one floor down, so men (there to ogle the dealers and bunnies) generally outnumber women (good for the women).

SETTING AND ATMOSPHERE Moon, located on top of the new Fantasy Tower, is aptly named—you're halfway into orbit when you walk in, closer yet when you ascend the steel-and-glass spiral staircase that leads to the VIP balcony and patio. This place will definitely put you in a lunar frame of mind, with its color-changing glass floor tiles, laser beams flitting hither and yon, and space-age metallic waitress and dancer outfits. The boogie floor is surrounded by large VIP booths; it gets a little more intimate in the semisecluded Moon lounge. The roof—35 feet above the dance floor—retracts, allowing the mingling of stars inside and out; when it's closed, the ceiling serves as a giant screen that projects images from the cameras focused on the action. But no matter where you go or what you do, you'll always get your money's worth from the view out the floor-to-ceiling windows or outside on the patio behind the main bar.

IF YOU GO You queue up for the elevator on the ground floor in a rather haphazard and confused line. The play is to keep asking people if they're waiting and whom to talk to in order to get in; you'll keep moving forward that way. Then there's the elevator up and down. However, unlike many other clubs in Las Vegas, the bouncers here aren't on a power trip and the bartenders and cocktail runners are uniformly friendly and professional. You can access the Playboy Club below on the escalator; your admission fee covers both. If you eat at Nove, the Italian restaurant below the Playboy Club, you still have to pay the fee, but you can enter the clubs from there, which avoids the ground-floor line.

Nine Fine Irishmen

IRISH PUB AND RESTAURANT WITH LIVE CELTIC MUSIC

New York–New York, 3790 South Las Vegas Boulevard;
☎ **702-740-6463; www.nynylasvegas.com or www.ninefineirishmen.com**
South Strip and Environs

Cover Wednesday and Thursday, $5. Minimum None. Mixed drinks $10 and up. Wine $7.50 and up. Beer $6.50 and up (English pint). Dress Anything goes. Specials Guinness Stout and Irish whiskeys. Food available Traditional Irish fare. Hours Sunday–Thursday, 11 a.m.–2:30 a.m.; Friday and Saturday, 11 a.m.–3:30 a.m.

WHO GOES THERE Visitors and locals of all ages.

WHAT GOES ON Located on the casino level of New York–New York, Nine Fine Irishmen nightly offers live Celtic music and dancing, a large selection of draft beers, and a totally upbeat experience that appeals to all age groups.

SETTING AND ATMOSPHERE Built in Ireland and shipped to America, the two-story pub is wood paneled throughout, with bars on both levels. A bandstand on the lower level is home to talented Celtic singers, dancers, and bands. The bandstand is visible from the stairway and the upper level. No hidden agendas here, Nine Fine Irishmen is just for fun.

Octane

SANITIZED BIKER DIVE

Excalibur Hotel and Casino, 3131 South Las Vegas Boulevard;
☎ **702-597-7777 or 877-750-5464** South Strip and Environs

Cover None. Minimum None. Mixed drinks $7.50 and up. Wine $7 and up. Beer $4.50 and up. Dress Casual. Food available None. Hours Sunday–Thursday, 5 p.m.–2 a.m. ; Friday and Saturday, 6 p.m.–3 a.m.

WHO GOES THERE 21 and older; broad mix of ages but tends to 35 and up.

WHAT GOES ON The theme at Octane is motorcycles, from the three classic Phantoms on display to the black-leather attire on the bartenders and servers. But this is a biker bar Brady Bunch–style. It's all good clean fun. The servers perform dance routines and whip up the patrons, which can make for a good time. But the biker theme seems too bland to generate much octane. The lounge also is located too close to hotel and casino foot traffic to assert much atmosphere. If you're a fan of motorcycles, you'll want to stop by for a drink. If you're looking to jump-start your adrenal glands, you might be disappointed.

SETTING AND ATMOSPHERE Octane has a clean, varnished look, with plenty of dark woods and steel tabletops. The motorcycle theme is carried throughout, from a few classic bikes on display to gear chains hanging above the bar.

IF YOU GO Located near the Merlin Theater, Excalibur's premier room, Octane provides a nice place to have a drink before or after a show. It only holds 100, so it can be crowded at these times. Most of the tables seat two, so a bigger party may find it difficult to sit together.

OPM

MULTIROOM DANCE CLUB ABOVE THE FORUM SHOPS

Caesars Palace, 3500 South Las Vegas Boulevard; ☎ 702-387-3840; www.caesars.com or www.o-pm.com/lv Mid-Strip and Environs

Cover $20–$30. **Minimum** None. **Mixed drinks** $8 and up. **Wine** $8–$12. **Beer** $4–$6. **Dress** Hip, trendy, sexy; no jeans or sneakers. **Specials** Thirst Thursdays, $1.25 drinks; Flirt Fridays, no covers for ladies and free roses and chocolate-covered strawberries; Sugar Saturdays, free chocolate martinis to all ladies until midnight and free chocolate catered by Chocolate Swan at Mandalay Bay. **Food available** Limited from downstairs restaurant. **Hours** Thursday–Sunday, 10 p.m.–dawn.

WHO GOES THERE 21–35; early clubbers.

WHAT GOES ON Tucked away deep in The Forum Shops above Chinois restaurant, OPM seems to attract early clubgoers who start out their evening here and move on. Crowds arrive early but don't get too pressing, and there's a lot of turnover. The meandering layout, plentiful bar space, and long gallery of cocktail tables make this an easy place to find your own vibe.

SETTING AND ATMOSPHERE The main room has two bars, a large dance floor, impressive lighting and sound, and the de rigueur stacks of video monitors projecting trippy light shows. Music tends toward pounding dance-pop mixes. The adjacent chill-out room has big, poofy chairs and couches that can swallow you whole; it has its own bar, and a separate DJ plays more downbeat light trance or house mixes. A slim gallery wanders out and over The Forum Shops, with small tables lining the walls and a final small bar at the tail end.

IF YOU GO Dress well, as the no-jeans rule is strictly enforced. A lot of clubgoers tend to filter in and out despite the high cover, so patience will let you scam a table if you prefer to sit out the dance party. Waitstaff in the chill-out lounge are tolerant of customers sitting at reservation-only tables until paying clients arrive.

Playboy Club

TABLE-GAME GAMBLING AND ADMIRING THE VIEW INSIDE AND OUT

Palms Hotel, 4321 West Flamingo Road; ☎ 702-942-7777; www.palms.com Mid-Strip and Environs

Cover Monday–Thursday, $20; Friday–Sunday, $40. **Minimum** None. **Mixed drinks** $8 and up. **Wine** $7 and up. **Beer** $5 and up. **Dress** Upscale. **Food available** None. **Hours** Daily, 8 p.m. until late.

WHO GOES THERE   Beautiful under-40s and graying Playboy nostalgics.

WHAT GOES ON   Admiring the views of Las Vegas, and table-game gambling dealt by the queens of cleavage Playboy Bunnies (and you thought they were extinct).

SETTING AND ATMOSPHERE   Situated one floor below the Moon rooftop nightclub in the Fantasy Tower of the Palms, the Playboy Club is an intimate venue with floor-to-ceiling windows on three sides and, on the fourth, cushy lounge seating beneath a display of vintage *Playboy* covers and memorabilia. In the middle of the club, and taking up most of the floor space, are the gaming tables. A cozy backroom (to the left as you enter the club) features leather chairs and a chic modern gas-fed hearth but no views.

IF YOU GO   Your cover charge includes admission to Moon, one floor up, with its retractable roof and stunning views of the Las Vegas Valley. If you eat at Nove, the Italian restaurant below the Playboy Club, you can enter the clubs from there. You'll still have to cough up the cover, but you'll avoid the ground-floor line.

Pure Nightclub

MASSIVE, EXPENSIVE, UPSCALE NIGHTCLUB

Caesars Palace, 3570 South Las Vegas Boulevard; ☎ 702-731-7873; www.caesars.com or www.purethenightclub.com Mid-Strip and Environs

Cover $20. **Minimum** None. **Mixed drinks** $8 and up. **Wine** $8 and up. **Beer** $6 and up. **Dress** Stylish to impress. **Specials** Events every Tuesday. **Food available** None. **Hours** Friday, Saturday, and Tuesday, 10 p.m. to close.

WHO GOES THERE   Under 40s, high rollers, wannabes.

WHAT GOES ON   Dancing to recorded music is the main gig, but many go for the rooftop view of the Strip. Then there's the exclusivity thing, the celebrity thing, the impress-or-be-impressed thing, the we're-here-and-you're-not thing, and the curiosity thing. You get the idea.

SETTING AND ATMOSPHERE   Basically three clubs within a club—the Main Room decorated in shades of white, the VIP Red Room decorated (obviously) in red with upholstered walls and private booths, and the Terrace, up one floor with fabulous outdoor views of the Strip. Each area has its own bars, decor, dance floor, and music, so you can experience completely different atmospheres in each.

We particularly enjoyed the Terrace (largest outdoor nightclub venue in Las Vegas), with its waterfalls, fire, and views of the club and the Strip. The feeling of being outside, dancing and partying, is exhilarating.

IF YOU GO   Lines are extremely long, so reservations are a must, and you have to buy a very expensive bottle of wine to obtain the reservation. Valet parking at The Forum Shops makes for much easier arrival and departure (be sure to check how late they will be parking cars). A good second choice is Caesars' self-parking garage.

Pussycat Dolls Lounge

Caesars Palace, 3570 South Las Vegas Boulevard; ☎ 702-731-7873; www.caesars.com Mid-Strip and Environs

Cover $0–$20 (varies). **Minimum** None. **Mixed drinks** $8 and up. **Wine** $8 and up. **Beer** $5 and up. **Dress** Stylish. **Specials** None. **Food available** None. **Hours** Tuesday–Saturday, 8 p.m. to close; performances begin at 10:30 p.m. each night.

WHO GOES THERE Tourists, elbow rubbers, the curious.

WHAT GOES ON The Dolls, in their finest 1940s fashions—fishnets, high-heeled boots, bras, and so on—perform very short (three- to five-minute) sets about every half hour. They appear on different stages all over the small room and sometimes hang from the ceiling or perform in a bathtub. Between performances, a DJ plays house music.

SETTING AND ATMOSPHERE Directly connected to Pure, Pussycat offers a more subdued atmosphere, with red walls backing portraits of such beauties as Paris Hilton, Charlize Theron, Christina Aguilera, Carmen Electra, and Christina Applegate. Patrons hope to see one of them on stage, or maybe just in the crowd.

IF YOU GO Get there early (before the shows start) and you will get a good spot and won't need a reservation; go late and you may have to buy that very expensive bottle of wine to reserve a table.

Rain Las Vegas

Palms Hotel, 4321 West Flamingo Road; ☎ 702-940-RAIN; www.palms.com or www.n9negroup.com Mid-Strip and Environs

Cover $10 Thursdays; $25 Friday and Saturday; local ladies free. **Minimum** None. **Mixed drinks** $8 and up. **Wine** $6 and up. **Beer** $5 and up. **Dress** Stylish and sexy; jeans and sneakers discouraged but forgivable if you're a hottie; no sandals on men. **Specials** None **Food available** In VIP areas. **Hours** Thursday–Saturday, 11 p.m.–5 a.m.

WHO GOES THERE 21–35; dancing fiends and VIP wannabes.

WHAT GOES ON A truly assaultive spectacle of a dance club, Rain is a marvel of gleeful excess. There's booming dance music on tap at all times, the only exception being when Rain hosts headlining rock and hip-hop acts. The crowds fling themselves into the beat, barely restrained by armies of security thugs. Three hierarchic levels of 19 VIP areas create a complicated class system (militantly enforced by said thugs). Patrons are dressed to dance and seduce, with *sexy, clingy,* and *revealing* being the watchwords.

SETTING AND ATMOSPHERE The large, tiered room focuses on an elevated dance floor, which is also the focus of numerous fountains, fog machines, and a huge, spidery lighting rig that periodically shoots jets of flame. Nondancers can enjoy primo people-watching and even climb to the upper tiers for a good vantage, but the best roosting spots are cordoned off by the dreaded velvet ropes.

IF YOU GO Hurl yourself into the mob with abandon. Just be prepared to navigate a serious crush at the bars whenever you need to rehydrate. If you're really in the mood to splurge, you can reserve a VIP area to serve as home base—anything from a booth with water-filled leather banquettes ($300) to your own private skybox ($1,000).

Revolution Lounge

MEMORY-LANE PUB CRAWL WITH THE BEATLES

Mirage, 3400 South Las Vegas Boulevard; ☎ 702-693-8383; www.thebeatlesrevolutionlounge.com Mid-Strip and Environs

Cover None. **Minimum** None. **Mixed drinks** $7.50 and up. **Wine** $7 and up. **Beer** $4.50 and up. **Dress** Mature club style: no sportswear, hats, or sneakers. **Food available** None. **Hours** The Abbey Road bar is open noon–4 a.m. daily; Revolution Lounge is open 6 p.m.–4 a.m. nightly.

WHO GOES THERE 21–60; Beatles fans, showgoers coming from or going to see *LOVE*, Cirque de Soleil troupe members.

WHAT GOES ON What do you get when you take a Beatles theme and cross it with the exotic vision of Cirque de Soleil? The Beatles Revolution Lounge was opened shortly after Cirque's Beatles-inspired show, *LOVE*, opened in 2005. More Magical Mystery tour than mop top era, the decor looks like Austin Power Swinging London pad meets *A Clockwork Orange*—white molded plastic stools and vinyl booths with black striped floors said to resemble the Abbey Road studios. Some nights it's nothing but Beatles music; on other nights, Britpop, Top 40, or house music bounce off the psychedelic walls. Just outside the main entrance is the Abbey Road Bar, a smaller, full-service bar that's perfect for a quick drink or just to hang out. The tie dye–clad staff is very attentive, and the ceiling is adorned with diamond-shaped crystals that bounce light throughout the bar á la "Lucy in the Sky with Diamonds." Beatles fans will delight in all the subtle (and not so subtle) Fab Four touches throughout the Revolution Lounge.

SETTING AND ATMOSPHERE This is ultralounge by way of Sergeant Pepper. Sleek and innovative, the club has most-amazing features, such as interactive tabletops where customers can create their own electronic graffiti that is then projected onto a large column in the middle of the bar.

IF YOU GO Stake out your place at the Abbey Road Bar to avoid lines into Revolution before it opens. More laid-back than a lot of the "see and be seen" clubs on the Strip.

Risqué

EURO-STYLE COOL

Paris, 3655 South Las Vegas Boulevard; ☎ 702-946-4589; www.parislasvegas.com or www.risquelv.com Mid-Strip and Environs

Cover $20; local ladies free. **Minimum** None. **Mixed drinks** $8 and up. **Wine** $7 and up. **Beer** $5 and up. **Dress** Classy, cool, and hip. **Specials** None. **Food available** Dessert case stocked by Ah Sin restaurant downstairs. **Hours** Friday–Sunday, 10:30 p.m.–4 a.m.

WHO GOES THERE 21–30; club kids, beautiful babies.

WHAT GOES ON Set upstairs near the front of the Paris casino, Risqué has as its main advantage a row of little balconies overlooking the Strip. If you can get there soon enough to claim this prime real estate, you'd be well advised to keep it all night (send deputies to retrieve drinks). Otherwise, join the crowds grooving on the dance floor in the main room or hover at the perimeter, eyeballing the mating games in full swing.

SETTING AND ATMOSPHERE Risqué has a smallish dance floor and main lounge area with a long bar. There's also a nearby chill-out room with its own bar and a DJ playing more downbeat tracks; when we visited, a large plasma-screen TV displayed a continuous loop of NASA space footage. The high-ceilinged rooms are sparsely decorated with that breed of European furnishings that somehow manages to look eclectic and generic at the same time.

IF YOU GO Hit the place early and grab a balcony spot. Though nice, the rest of Risqué is not enough to warrant hanging around for long, despite its "ultralounge" billing.

Rockhouse Bar and Nightclub

PUNK, METAL, GO-GO DANCERS, AND SHIN SPLINTS

Imperial Palace Hotel, 3535 South Las Vegas Boulevard; ☎ 702-731-9683; www.therockhousebar.com Mid-Strip and Environs

Cover $30 for gentlemen, $20 for ladies; free for local ladies. **Minimum** None. **Mixed drinks** $6 and up. **Wine** $5 and up. **Beer** $4–$8. **Dress** Casual. **Food available** None. **Hours** Friday, Saturday, and Sunday, 10:30 p.m.–4 a.m.

WHO GOES THERE Rockers, metalheads, punks, live-music enthusiasts, skateboarding rats.

WHAT GOES ON Rockhouse opened in early 2007 and is trying to establish itself as the destination to RAWK right on the Strip, but is getting little support from the Imperial Palace. Still, it has a "little engine that could" philosophy. Advertising the "cheapest bottle service in town" and "world-famous daiquiris," Rockhouse tries to lure Strip walkers and gawkers with free shots poured by the Rockhouse Go-Go Dancers. On busy nights, eight to ten of these lovely ladies (fully though provocatively clothed) gyrate suggestively on each end of the worn wooden bar, on poles behind some of the booths, and in a metal cage suspended above the dance floor. DJs spin contemporary rap and dance tunes synced with video screens, while other nights feature live bands. A small retail space selling Rockhouse gear is situated next to the Strip entrance. Every other Thursday, local graffiti artists redecorate the walls with spray-can art.

SETTING AND ATMOSPHERE Old posters from rock shows and guitars line the walls, and a curtain of chains hangs behind the bar and the giant video screen. The bar staff is capable though not overly friendly. We saw one beautiful but bored bar-top dancer stop to check her cell phone. Whaddya want? It's rock 'n' roll!

IF YOU GO   The dance floor is poured concrete so a night hitting the dance floor hard could result in shin splints the next morning. Seating is limited so be prepared to either stand or dance with your drink in hand.

rumjungle

DANCE, TECHNO, INDUSTRIAL, RAP MUSIC

Mandalay Bay, 3950 South Las Vegas Boulevard; ☎ 702-632-7408; www.mandalaybay.com South Strip and Environs

Cover $20–$25; local ladies free. **Minimum** None. **Mixed drinks** $6.50–$11.50. **Wine** $7–$12. **Beer** $5–$10. **Dress** Club attire is strictly enforced: no tennis shoes or work boots; no ripped, oversized, or baggy jeans; no hats, tank tops, or sports attire; collared shirts. **Specials** None. **Food available** Dinner served (5–11:30 p.m.; rodizio-style with meat and fish on skewers). Dinner prices $18–$36. **Hours** Tuesday–Thursday, Sunday, 11 a.m.-2 a.m.; Friday, Saturday, Monday, 11 a.m.-4 a.m.

WHO GOES THERE   21–35; locals, tourists, scene makers.

WHAT GOES ON   White-bikinied go-go dancers writhe and squirm under black lights on platforms above the bar, in cages above the tables, and along the catwalk above the spacious concrete dance floor at the rear of the club and up a flight of stairs. The dancing is presided over by dueling percussionists riffing off of the deafening and mind-numbing recorded rap and disco music, which gets the young bodies bumping and grinding against each other—the only practical form of communication in a place where the audio volume long ago blew out the decibel meter.

SETTING AND ATMOSPHERE   A "wall of fire" greets you outside rumjungle, then you walk in (after paying a masochistic $20) where water falls down eight big vertical sheets of glass, enhancing the jungle setting. The central bar is huge and elongated, with a colorfully backlit bar top and a dozen shelves containing more than 100 bottles of rum rising almost to the high ceiling. Oh-so-aloof bartenders pour rum drinks ($6.50 to $32; try the Painkiller #4) while grim-faced bouncers circulate continually, hoping for trouble. Of course, rumjungle is so dark that trouble would be hard to see even if it did start.

IF YOU GO   If you're not old enough to care about your hearing or you're not a woman who gets in free, or you're not with a group of friends to party with, you might consider forsaking rumjungle in favor of Mandalay Bay's Island Lounge (rock), Orchid Lounge (jazz), Coral Reef Lounge (disco), or House of Blues (R&B), all of which are lighter, quieter, more conducive to conversation, and free.

Sand Dollar Blues Lounge

RHYTHM AND BLUES

3355 Spring Mountain Road (at Polaris); ☎ 702-871-6651; www.sanddollarblues.com West of Strip

Cover $5, Tuesday–Saturday. **Minimum** None. **Mixed drinks** $4 and up. **Wine** $3.50 and up. **Beer** $3 and up. **Dress** Casual. **Specials** Drink specials and prices depend on the event. **Food available** Packaged snack food—no kitchen. **Hours** Open 24 hours; music starts at 10 p.m. nightly.

WHO GOES THERE   Bikers to yuppies.

WHAT GOES ON   Everyone from attorneys to bikers sit back for an evening full of moody and marvelous blues by popular Las Vegas or out-of-town bands. It's standing-room only on Friday, Saturday, and special-event nights. Strip musicians gather for various jam sessions. In the back, pool players croon to the blues.

SETTING AND ATMOSPHERE   The exterior is nondescript. Both the interior and the patrons are earthy and full of character. The low ceiling keeps the lounge quite smoky. The U-shaped bar separates the dance floor from the pool tables. Nautical rope, worn wood pilings, small fishing nets, and sand dollars add to the bar's salty character. Neon beer signs and handwritten flyers dot the walls.

IF YOU GO   The club's unshaven appearance may deter some solo ladies from experiencing a night of great blues. The regulars make sure everything stays cool. The Sand Dollar is hard to spot at night, so arrive early or come by cab.

Shimmer Cabaret

TOP 40/SHOW COMBINATION

Las Vegas Hilton, 3000 Paradise Road; ☎ 702-732-5755; www.lv-hilton.com East of Strip

Cover None. **Minimum** None. **Mixed drinks** $5–$6.75. **Wine** $4.50 and up. **Beer** $3.50 and up. **Dress** Upscale casual. **Specials** Live entertainment start times vary. **Food available** In casino. **Hours** Sunday, 10 p.m.–12:30 a.m.; Monday–Thursday, 9 p.m.–12:45 a.m.; Friday and Saturday, 10 p.m.–2 a.m.

WHO GOES THERE   30–50; visitors, locals, conventioneers/businesspeople.

WHAT GOES ON   Couples and friends boogie to good live renditions of pop music on the small, curvy dance floor. Others are content to watch the leather-clad dancers on stage cavorting with the musicians. Meanwhile, onlookers admire the whole scene. Singles can either sit back and enjoy the show or meet new friends.

SETTING AND ATMOSPHERE   A combination of a Las Vegas showroom and a New York dance club, Shimmer Cabaret is a trendy Art Deco hot spot. The bar, situated in the rear of the 450-seat lounge, serves up libations and hosts more intimate conversation. On the wall to the left of the stage is a mutely painted mural of a cityscape. The second floor provides a bird's-eye view of the band and offers a bit more seating space. On some nights a reserved ticket show is performed in the venue. At the conclusion of the show, the dance club cranks up.

IF YOU GO   Arrive early for choice seating. Cocktail service tends to be relaxed in this no-pressure environment. Because of the long hike from the public parking areas, take a cab or use valet for convenience.

Studio 54

DANCE, TOP 40

MGM Grand, 3799 South Las Vegas Boulevard; ☎ 702-891-7254;
www.mgmgrand.com or www.studio54lv.com South Strip and Environs

Cover $10–$20, ladies free. **Minimum** None. **Mixed drinks** $5–$8. **Wine** $5 and up. **Beer** $4–$5.50. **Dress** Club attire is enforced; collared shirt or sports coat for men; no baggy jeans, shorts, flannel shirts, T-shirts, work boots, sandals, or sneakers. **Specials** Tuesday night is Eden—ladies get in free and local men get in at half price. **Food available** In casino. **Hours** Tuesday–Saturday, 10 p.m.–5 a.m.

WHO GOES THERE   25–40; locals, tourists, and trendy people.

WHAT GOES ON   The New York club that set the standard during disco's heyday in the 1970s comes to Las Vegas. Stylish, beautiful people gather for a night of high energy, music, dance, and socializing.

SETTING AND ATMOSPHERE   It's three stories tall with dance floors, bars, and conversation areas on each level. The black-girder-and-steel-grate flooring and exposed elevator lifts give the club an industrial, high-tech feel. Black-and-white photographs of celebrities and trendsetters visiting the New York Studio 54 line the walls on the second floor.

IF YOU GO   If you love a club with an attitude, then Studio 54 is for you. If you prefer a bit more fun and friendliness, try Club Rio. Studio 54 is located at the Tropicana and Las Vegas Boulevard entrance—it's a long walk from both valet and the parking garages.

Tabu

SUPER-COOL LOUNGE WHERE THE LOADED GET LOADED

MGM Grand, 3799 South Las Vegas Boulevard; ☎ 702-891-7183;
www.mgmgrand.com or www.tabulv.com South Strip and Environs

Cover $20. **Minimum** None. **Mixed drinks** $7 and up. **Wine** $7 and up. **Beer** $5 and up. **Dress** Sexy chic. **Specials** None **Food available** None. **Hours** Tuesday–Sunday, 10 p.m. until.

WHO GOES THERE   21–40; high rollers and young hotties of all persuasions.

WHAT GOES ON   Hyped as an ultralounge, Tabu may come close to whatever that means. If you can get past the crush at the door, you'll be rewarded with some excellent eye candy via both the space and its inhabitants. The staff are dressed to kill and seem to be cloned from a diverse assortment of supermodels and porn stars; the patrons do their best to rise to that standard. If you've had a great day in the casino and want to really test your meat-market mettle, this is the place.

SETTING AND ATMOSPHERE   The main room is plushly decorated with frosted glass and subtle lighting, and there are plenty of tables and chairs for the daring (since all are reservable, you'll be sitting on borrowed time unless you ante up). Two tables in the main room project images on their surface that ripple or change color in reaction to your presence or body heat. There's a second, smaller room off to the side that's a little more intimate, and it has its own bar as well. Last is the oval Tundra Room (usually called "the egg"), done up in appropriate whites, carpets, and cushions.

IF YOU GO There was no organized line to get in when we first visited; rather, would-be patrons formed a mob around the bouncers, and a Darwinian process dictated who fought their way inside. When we came back early on another night, we walked in without even paying a cover. In addition, early birds can often sit at reserved VIP tables until kicked out by those who have paid for the space (check with waitstaff or the VIP hostess about which tables to avoid).

Tangerine

ISLAND BURLESQUE SPEAKEASY NIGHTCLUB BEACH BAR THING

Treasure Island, 3300 South Las Vegas Boulevard; ☎ 866-286-3809; www.treasureisland.com Mid-Strip and Environs

Cover $20 men, $40 line pass, $10 women. Minimum None. Mixed drinks $8 and up. Wine $6 and up. Beer $6 and up. Dress Casual chic, jeans OK, no sneakers or athletic wear. Specials None. Food available None. Hours Tuesday–Saturday, 10 p.m.–4 a.m. (patio open from 5:30 p.m. daily).

WHO GOES THERE 21–50; club kids, tourists, Strip crawlers, girls gone wild.

WHAT GOES ON Replacing the "arrr, matey" ambience of the Buccaneer Bar is Tangerine, an expansive nightclub space with a singular "waterside" patio and great views of the pirate battle . . . uh, we mean, great views of the Sirens of T. I. This place has become a surprise hit, and it gets congested early, probably because it's so visible from the Strip. Crowds can pack the place tight as a sardine can, so either reconcile yourself to knowing your neighbor, or stake out space on the patio to maintain your oxygen supply. Periodic non-nude "burlesque" dancers are tossed into the mix for no reason we can fathom other than a little T&A, and few people in attendance pay much attention unless a dancer happens to pop up right in front of or on top of them.

SETTING AND ATMOSPHERE The decor is done in nondescript fruity colors, vaguely tropical and modern club–ish. Music is bass-pounding hip-hop or dance, and the majority of the floorspace is given over to rump-shakin'. The outside patio offers an excellent way to cool off, but you'll have to fight your way there—the club's entrance line dumps you squarely in the midst of the dance floor, equidistant from bars, restrooms, or exits. Two bars inside and one outside are large but get permanently log-jammed with desperate would-be drinkers.

IF YOU GO Go at opening time or be prepared to wait in a long, long line. The chaos is definitely high-octane fun, but there is no escaping it. Especially if you have to endure the line, be sure that this kind of madness is what you bargained for.

Tao

SUPER-GIANT-MEGA-CLUB, RESTAURANT, AND LOUNGE

Venetian, 3355 South Las Vegas Boulevard; ☎ 702-388-8588; www.venetian.com Mid-Strip and Environs

Cover $20. **Minimum** None. **Mixed drinks** $9 and up. **Wine** $10 and up. **Beer** $8. **Dress** Upscale chic; no sneakers. **Specials** None. **Food available** None. **Hours** Thursday–Saturday, 10 p.m.–until.

WHO GOES THERE 21–45; Hard-core clubcrawlers, pretty people, sexpots, scantily clad, hedonists.

WHAT GOES ON The Venetian finally hit the jackpot with Tao, after misfiring with several nightlife venues since the property opened. A huge combination of restaurant, lounge, and nightclub, Tao offers highly sought-after dinner reservations, a cool lounge space, and a labyrinthine club that packs 'em in from the moment the velvet rope drops. Hordes of casino patrons and Strip-walkers swarm all of Tao's parts, so it's good thing the place is so large. The music is keyed to the hottest dance mixes, and meant to move the most flesh as quickly as possible, en masse. It's meat market central for the young, sweaty, and on the make.

SETTING AND ATMOSPHERE The pretty but minimally decorated lounge serves mainly as an airlock and chill-out space for the upstairs club space, which includes several bars, two levels of VIP cells, a recessed dance floor, several dancer showcase platforms, and a tiny bit of Stripside balcony. Various Buddhas sit in nooks and crannies or in placid groups, while barely clad living models do the "human statue" thing in gauzy boudoirs. Vaguely exotic and certainly sexy, Tao's look and feel is downright aphrodisiacal when the crowd is right.

IF YOU GO Go early, or go with your celebrity friends. The line will be long, but it does move, and everyone really does get a chance to get in eventually. Front-of-line passes available from various Web sites or other sources would be well used here, and if you have (or are) a group of attractive females, your chances of skipping the line or portions thereof will be dramatically improved.

Tommy Rocker's Cantina and Grill

TOP 40 AND JIMMY BUFFETT–STYLE MUSIC

4275 Dean Martin Drive; ☎ 702-261-6688; www.tommyrocker.com Mid-Strip and Environs

Cover None. **Minimum** None. **Mixed drinks** $3–$4; wide selection of tequilas and rums. **Wine** $2.75 and up. **Beer** $3–$5; many microbrew draft selections. **Dress** Casual to sporty. **Specials** Happy hour 5–7 p.m., with $1 off all drinks and appetizers, 50¢ off imports and domestic drafts. It is also the official Jimmy Buffett fan-club location—call for special-event information. **Food available** Sports bar–type food. **Hours** Open 24 hours.

WHO GOES THERE 25–30; professionals and career starters.

WHAT GOES ON Singles and couples gather to check out the music and gregarious repartee of Tommy Rocker, the club's owner and professional musician, when he's in town. Otherwise, they enjoy meeting new friends, singing Jimmy Buffett songs, shooting a friendly game of pool, cheering their favorite team on the big-screen TV, and indulging in the tasty libations and food fare.

SETTING AND ATMOSPHERE An eclectic mix of Indian petroglyph images, palm trees, parrots, and neon gives Tommy Rocker's Cantina and Grill a refreshing twist to the beach-style bar scene. In addition to the big-screen TV and two pool tables, the club offers a small dance floor and a standard center bar.

IF YOU GO Voted best live-music club in a local survey, Tommy Rocker's offers plenty of parking, friendly yet professional security, and a great attitude. The music is loud but not deafening, allowing for conversation. Come early for best seating.

Tryst

HOT DANCING BY COOL WATERFALL; WHERE TO HAVE YOUR PEDIGREE TESTED

Wynn Las Vegas, 3131 South Las Vegas Boulevard; ☎ 702-770-7000; www.wynnlasvegas.com Mid-Strip and Environs

Cover Locals, no charge; others, varies nightly. **Minimum** None. **Mixed drinks** $10 and up. **Wine** $10 and up; bottle service available. **Beer** $7 and up. **Dress** Casual chic; no sneakers, baggy pants, jeans, hats, or athletic wear. **Food available** None. **Hours** Thursday–Sunday, 10 p.m.–4 a.m.

WHO GOES THERE 21–45; scenesters, celebs, local celebs, gorgeous girls, and a variety of out-of-towners.

WHAT GOES ON One of the hottest clubs in Vegas, Tryst attracts a crowd in part because Tryst attracts a crowd. Though it holds more than 1,200 customers, the line outside usually includes as many customers as the club. The club is packed every night and buzzes with the energy of being one of the places to be. A small dance floor in front of the lagoon is always full, and the club pulses with a variety of musical styles, from Top 40 to hip-hop to urban contemporary standards. There are lots of pretty young things on the open-air dance floor working it out to some of the best music mixes and DJs around.

SETTING AND ATMOSPHERE The velvet-lined hallways and marble staircases make for a great entrance, but the kicker to this 12,000-square-foot venue is the 94-foot waterfall as the backdrop that extends from inside the club to 15 feet over the water of the hotel's lake. The club's interior consists of various red, black, and brown hues, which definitely put some in the mood to stay up all night and gives off a sultry and luxurious feel. There is a VIP area, a library-like ultralounge, and a stripper's pole for all the sexy ladies who want to give it a whirl. The staff is almost too good-looking, and the service is absolutely top-notch. Tryst is widely known as one of the best places to spot celebs in town.

IF YOU GO Make sure you are dressed to the nines. Like most places, the door will size you up and then accordingly let you and your gang in, so if you want in, make sure you look good. The lines are usually long, but if you get there early, you may not have to pay the cover and will be swept into the opulence that's known as Tryst. You can also check out certain sites that will get you and your party a discount for the evening (*do not* use the VIP passes from any cab driver). Obviously, if you are a group of young men without any young ladies in your party, the best thing to do would be to call and make reservations for bottle service, thus cementing your entry into the club. If you arrive without reservations after a line has formed at the club entrance, you may find that it's necessary to offer the gatekeepers a hefty bribe to gain admittance.

VooDoo Lounge

LIVE MUSIC WITH BEST VIEW OF THE STRIP

Rio Hotel, 3700 West Flamingo Road; ☎ 702-247-7923; www.riolasvegas.com Mid-Strip and Environs

Cover $10 after 8 p.m. **Minimum** None. **Mixed drinks** $6 and up. **Wine** $5 and up. **Beer** $4.25 and up. **Dress** Business casual; no torn jeans, tennis shoes, sandals, or T-shirts. **Specials** None. **Food available** Downstairs in VooDoo Café. **Hours** Nightly, 5 p.m.–until.

WHO GOES THERE 21–35; visitors and chic clubgoers.

WHAT GOES ON The cozy darkness of the VooDoo Lounge is only broken by the doors to the outside patio, which floats on the 51st floor of the Rio and offers great views of the Strip. Dexterous bartenders flip bottles and glasses around while the lady customers swoon, and live bands play cool-cat jazz and R&B most nights. There's a small dance floor, but patrons are mostly content to chill out in the ample multilevel seating.

SETTING AND ATMOSPHERE The room is dim, but there's plenty to see. Comfy chairs and sofas cluster around intimate cocktail tables, providing views of the stage, bar, and the tinted windows on two walls. The patio has some tables of its own, but the gorgeous view and cool night air make these premium real estate—grab one if you can. The vibe is hip and relaxed.

IF YOU GO Enjoy the band if the night's music is to your liking, but you must spend at least some time on the patio. It would be a crime to miss this literally stellar view. If you want a different take on the same concept (and don't mind shelling out another cover charge), stop by Ghostbar at the nearby Palms.

LAS VEGAS *below the* BELT

DON'T WORRY, BE HAPPY

IN MANY WAYS, LAS VEGAS IS A BASTION of hedonism. Simply being there contributes to a loosening of inhibitions and a partial discarding of the rules that apply at home. Las Vegas exults in its permissiveness and makes every effort to live up to its image and to bestow upon its visitors the freedom to have fun. Las Vegas has a steaminess, a sophisticated cosmopolitan excitement born of super-abundance, an aura of risk and reward, a sense of libertine excess. The rules are different here; it's all right to let go.

Behind the illusion, however, is a community, and more particularly, a police department that puts a lot of effort into making it safe for visitors to experience the liberation of Las Vegas. It is hard to imagine another city where travelers can carry such large sums of money so safely. A tourist can get robbed or worked over in Las Vegas, but it is comparatively rare, and more often than not is due to the visitor's own carelessness or naivete. The Strip and downtown, especially, are well patrolled, and most hotels have very professional in-house security forces.

In general, a tourist who stays either on the Strip or downtown will be very safe. Police patrol in cars, on foot, and, interestingly, on mountain bikes. The bikes allow the police to quickly catch pickpockets or purse snatchers attempting to make their escape down sidewalks or through parking lots. Cross-streets that connect the Strip with Paradise Road and the Las Vegas Convention Center are also lighted and safe. When tourists get robbed, they are commonly far from downtown or the Strip and often in pursuit of drugs or sex.

ORGANIZED CRIME AND CHEATING

VERY FEW VISITORS WALK THROUGH a casino without wondering if the games are rigged or if the place is owned by the Mafia. During the early days of legalized gambling, few people outside of organized crime had any real experience in managing gaming operations. Hence, a fair number of characters fresh from Eastern gangs and crime families came to work in Nevada. Since they constituted the resource pool for experienced gambling operators, the state suffered their presence as a necessary evil. In 1950, Tennessee senator Estes Kefauver initiated an attack on organized crime that led (indirectly) to the formation of the Nevada Gaming Commission and the State Gaming Control Board. These agencies, in conjunction with federal efforts, were ultimately able to purge organized crime from Las Vegas. This ouster, coupled with the Nevada Corporate Gaming Acts of 1967 and 1969 (allowing publicly held corporations such as Hilton, Holiday Inn, Bally, and MGM to own casinos), at last brought a mantle of respectability to Las Vegas gambling.

Today the Gaming Control Board oversees the activities of all Nevada gaming establishments, maintaining tight control through frequent unannounced inspections of gambling personnel and equipment. If you ever have reason to doubt the activity or clout of the Gaming Control Board, try walking around the Strip or downtown in a dark business suit and plain black shoes. You will attract more attention from the casino management than if you entered with a parrot on your head.

Ostensibly, cheating exists in Las Vegas gambling to a limited degree. But a case of a Nevada casino cheating customers hasn't been publicized for decades. In fact, "gaffing" the games is seldom perpetrated by the house itself. In fact, most cheating is done at the expense of the house, though honest players at the cheater's table may also get burned. Sometimes a dealer, working alone or with an accomplice (posing as a player), will cheat, and there are always con artists, grab-and-run rip-off artists, and rail thieves ready to take advantage of the house and legitimate players.

SKIN GAMES—SEX IN LAS VEGAS Though nudity, prostitution, and pornography are regulated more tightly in Las Vegas than in many Bible Belt cities, the town exudes an air of sexual freedom and promiscuity. Las Vegas offers a near-perfect environment for marketing sex. More than 50% of all visitors are men, most between the ages of 21 and 59. Some come to party, and many, particularly convention-goers, are alone and ready for action. Almost all have time and money on their hands.

Las Vegas evolved as a gambler's city, projecting the image of a trail town where a man could be comfortable and just about anything could be had for a price. It was not until strong competition developed for the gambling dollar that hotels sought to enlarge their market by targeting women and families. Today, though there is something for everyone in Las Vegas, its male orientation remains unusually strong.

Las Vegas, perhaps more than any other American city, has objectified women. A number of Las Vegas production shows continue to feature topless showgirls and erotic dance, even though audiences are mostly couples. Lounge servers and keno runners are almost exclusively women, invariably attired in revealing outfits. Video marquees, highway billboards, taxi banners, magazine ads, and tabloids in curbside newspaper vending machines all tout naked women to some degree. Showroom comedians, after 30 years, persist in describing Las Vegas as an adult Disneyland.

STRIPPING ON THE STRIP Compared to the live adult entertainment in many cities, "girlie" (and "boy-ie") shows in Las Vegas, both downtown and on the Las Vegas Strip, are fairly tame. In some of the larger showrooms, this is an accommodation to the ever-growing percentage of women in the audience. More often, however, it is a matter of economics rather than taste, the result of a curious City of Las Vegas law that stipulates that you can offer totally nude entertainment or you can serve alcoholic beverages, but not both.

Up until only a few years ago, topless showgirls were a mere embellishment to a production that featured song, dance, and variety acts. For the most part, the partial nudity was incidental and unimportant. Of course, a half-dozen veteran large-production shows included one or more steamy, highly erotic dance numbers, which allowed the publicists—and hotel photographers—to play up the naughtiness of the entertainment scene. But over the last few years, sex has exploded in Las Vegas showrooms, with such crossover shows as *Crazy Horse Paris,* a dirtied-up *Crazy Girls, Bite,* and several others that now emphasize mostly naked women instead of using them merely to dress up a show.

If you want to see stunning topless showgirls and dancers, the most erotic of the continuously running productions are *Crazy Horse Paris* at MGM Grand, *Crazy Girls* at the Riviera, *Bite* at the Stratosphere, and *Zumanity* at New York–New York, followed by *Jubilee!* at Bally's. *Crazy Horse Paris* is as risqué as a Las Vegas production show is allowed to be. *Crazy Girls* is a steamy topless revue, as is *Bite,* only sillier. *Jubilee!* is a production spectacular that has prettier-than-average showgirls and sultrier-than-average dance numbers. *Zumanity* is a Cirque du Soleil production celebrating sex.

MALE STRIPPERS Economics and the market have begun to redress (or undress) the inequality of women's erotic entertainment in Las Vegas. Spearheaded by the Rio, which features (*Chippendales*) male strippers for lengthy engagements, and empowered by the ever-growing number of professional women visiting Las Vegas for trade shows and conventions, the rules for sexual objectification are being rewritten. Today in Las Vegas, if watching a young stud flex his buns is a woman's idea of a good time, that experience is usually available. In addition to the Rio, male strippers perform at the Olympic Gardens nightclub. *Thunder from Down Under,* the Australian male revue, plays at the Excalibur and *American Storm* is at the Riviera.

WHERE THE GIRLS ARE

BELOW WE DESCRIBE A FEW of the better-known strip joints. If you want the whole scoop, however, try **www.stripclubreview.com.** The site offers reviews of the clubs and rates the attractiveness of the dancers, among other things. A similar site, **www.vegas-after-dark.com,** is more current and provides links to the individual club Web sites. Both sites offer discussion boards where visitors discuss such topics as the relative merits of fully nude vs. topless clubs. One poster thought topless clubs superior because, as he put it, "I've never had anything contagious leap off a boobie at me." All righty, then.

THE PALOMINO CLUB (☎ 702-642-2984) In North Las Vegas, a separate jurisdiction, there is no prohibition against nude entertainment and alcoholic beverages under the same roof. At the Palomino Club, ten minutes from downtown, the customer can have it all. The Palomino Club is not inexpensive, but at least they're up front about what they're selling. There is a $30 cover charge without a Nevada ID, and a $15 cover charge with a Nevada ID and a one-drink minimum. To get one of the better seats, you should arrive before 10 p.m. and tip the maître d'. Once you've purchased your drink, you can stay as long as you can stand it—all night, if you wish.

An average of seven professionals dance every night, performing in rotation and stripping nude. The pros are supplemented by four or more alleged amateurs who compete for prize money and tips in a strip contest held nightly at 11 p.m. All of the women are attractive and athletic. A stand-up comic rounds out the entertainment. The Palomino is without pretense. It delivers some of the best erotic dancing in town for about the same cost as a production show on the Strip.

TOPLESS BARS The main difference between a topless bar and a totally nude nightclub (aside from the alcohol regulations) is a G-string. Unless you're a gynecology intern, you might be satisfied with a topless bar. If you have more than a few drinks, the topless bars aren't less expensive than the Palomino but are often more conveniently located. Downtown, on Fremont Street, is the **Girls of Glitter Gulch** (☎ 702-385-4774; **www. glittergulchlv.com**). There's no cover charge, but drinks average a stiff (no pun intended) $7 to $9 each, with a two-drink minimum. A U-shaped stage-runway ensures a good view from most seats.

Seamless (4740 Arville Street; ☎ 702-227-5200; **www.seamless club.com**) is a trendy new $20-million topless bar that doubles as an after-hours club. Starting at 4 a.m., the area in front of the stage turns into a dance floor with a DJ spinning house music. Girls from the other jiggle joints come here to hang out (with their clothes on) in the wee hours. It's $20 admission, free for local ladies, $10 for local guys; Heinekens, $9.

An upscale topless bar, catering to a professional clientele, high rollers, and conventioneer, is **Club Paradise,** not far from the Strip (4416 Paradise Road; ☎ 702-734-7990). The cover charge is $30 and there is a two-drink minimum, unless you elect to sit in the VIP section, where you are obligated to consume at least $80 worth of drinks. Fortunately, because drinks go for $4.75 and up, this is not difficult.

The **Sapphire Club** (**www.sapphirelasvegas.com**) claims 6,000 women in its lineup of strippers (insiders say it's closer to 2,000, which is still plenty). By observation, the later you arrive in the evening, the better-looking the dancers. Though the club is the largest of its kind in the world, much of the space is allocated to private rooms and VIP areas. For the average patron, Sapphire is upscale but doesn't seem all that big.

An equally upscale venue is the **Olympic Garden** at 1531 South Las Vegas Boulevard; **www.ogvegas.com.** Considered by locals and connoisseurs to be the best topless club in town, the Olympic Garden is the only club that also features male strippers for its female customers (in a separate showroom). Olympic Garden charges a $20 cover, but the price includes two drinks.

PART THREE

GAMBLING

The **WAY IT IS**

GAMBLING IS THE REASON LAS VEGAS (in its modern incarnation) exists. It is the industry that fuels the local economy, paves the roads, and gives the city its identity. To visitors and tourists, gambling may be a game. To those who derive their livelihood from gambling, however, it is serious business.

There is an extraordinary and interesting dichotomy in the ways gambling is perceived. To the tourist and the gambler, gambling is all about luck. To those in the business, gambling is about mathematics. To the visitor, gambling is a few hours a day, while to the casinos, gambling is 24 hours a day, every day. The gambler *hopes* to walk away with a fortune, but the casinos *know* that in the long run that fortune will belong to the house. To visitors, gambling is recreation combined with risk and chance. To the casinos, gambling is business combined with near-certainty.

The casino takes no risk in the games themselves. In almost all cases, in the long run the house will always win. The games, the odds, and the payoffs are all carefully designed to ensure this outcome. Yet the casino does take a chance and is at risk. The casino's bet is this: that it can entice enough people to play.

Imagine a casino costing hundreds of millions of dollars, with a staff numbering in the thousands. Before a nickel of profit can be set aside, all the bills must be paid, and the payroll must be met. Regardless of its overwhelming advantage at the tables, the house cannot stay in business unless a lot of people come to play. The larger the casino, the more gamblers are required. If the casino can fill the tables with players, the operation will succeed and be profitable, perhaps spectacularly so. On the other hand, if the tables sit empty, the casino will fail.

The gambling business is competition personified. All casinos sell the exact same product. Every owner knows how absolutely critical

ustomers (gamblers) through the door. It is literally the
n: no players, no profit. The casinos are aggressive and
en it comes to luring customers, offering low-cost buffets,
mp cocktails, stage shows, lounge entertainment, free
nbling tournaments, and slot clubs.

The most common tactic for getting customers through the door is
to package the casino as a tourist attraction in its own right. Take the
Mirage. There are exploding volcanoes in the front yard, white tigers
in the entrance hall, palm trees in the living room, and live sharks in
the parlor. Who, after all, wants to sip their free drink in a dingy, red-
Naugahyde-upholstered catacomb when they can be luxuriating in
such a resplendent tropical atrium?

THE SHORT RUN

ASK A MATHEMATICIAN OR A CASINO OWNER if you can win gambling in a casino, and the truthful answer is yes, but almost always
only in the short run. Unless you're a professional player who only
plays with the long-term edge on your side, the longer you play, the
more certain it is that you will lose.

I (Bob here) learned about the short run (and the long run) on a road
trip when I was in the fifth grade. My family lived in Kentucky, and
every year we were fortunate enough to take a vacation to Florida. This
particular year I was allowed to invite a schoolmate, Glenn, along.

As the long drive progressed, we became fidgety and bored. To
pass the time, we began counting cars traveling in the opposite direction. Before many miles had passed, our counting evolved into a
betting game. We each selected a color and counted the cars of that
color. Whoever counted the most cars of his chosen color would win.

Glenn chose blue as his color. I was considering red (my favorite),
when I recalled a conversation between my mother and a car salesman. The salesman told my mother that white was by far the most
popular color "these days." If this were true, I reasoned, there should
be more white cars on the road than blue cars. I chose white.

As we rumbled through the hilly Kentucky countryside between
Bowling Green and Elizabethtown, my friend edged ahead. This puz-
zled me and I began to doubt the word of the car salesman. By the
time we made it to Bowling Green, Glenn was ahead by seven cars.
Because I was losing, I offered to call it quits and pay up (a nickel for
each car he was ahead). Glenn, not unexpectedly, was having a high
time and insisted we continue playing.

By the time we crossed the Tennessee line I had pulled even. Once
again I suggested we quit. Glenn would have none of it. Gloating enor-
mously, he regained a three-car lead halfway to Nashville. Slowly, however, I overtook him, and by Nashville I was ahead by four cars. Tired
of the game, I tried once more to end it. Since he was behind, Glenn
adamantly demanded that we play all the way to Atlanta. We did, and
by the time we got there, Glenn owed me almost $4.

After a night in Atlanta and a great deal of sulking on Glenn's part, we resumed our travels. To my amazement, Glenn insisted— demanded, in fact—the opportunity to win back his previous day's losses. There would be one great "do-or-die battle, blues against whites," he said, all the way to our destination (St. Augustine, Florida). As we drove south, I went ahead by a couple of cars, and then Glenn regained the lead by a small margin. By the time we reached St. Augustine, however, Glenn owed me another $5.40.

Outraged (and broke), Glenn exercised the only option remaining— he complained to my parents. Shaking his head, my father said, "Give Glenn his money back. Everybody knows that there are more white cars than blue cars." Not so. Glenn didn't.

While Glenn's behavior is not particularly unusual for a preado- lescent, you would assume that adults have better sense. Everybody knows there are more white cars than blue cars, remember? In Las Vegas, however, the casinos are full of Glenns, all over age 21, and all betting on blue cars.

I nailed Glenn on the cars because I knew something that he didn't. In casino games, patrons either do not understand what they are up against, or alternatively (and more intelligently), they do understand, but chalk up their losses as a fair price to pay for an evening's entertainment. Besides, in the short run, there's a chance they might actually win.

Glenn's actions on our trip mirrored almost exactly the behavior of many unfortunate casino gamblers:

1. He did not understand that the game was biased against him.
2. He did not take his winnings and quit when he was ahead in the short run.
3. On losing, he continued playing and redoubled his efforts to pull even or win, ultimately (in the long run) compounding his losses.

EAGLES AND ROBINS

IF ON OUR DRIVE I HAD SAID, "Let's count birds. You take eagles and I'll take robins," Glenn would have laughed in my face, instantly recognizing that the likelihood of spotting an eagle was insanely remote. While the casinos will not offer a fair game (like betting even money on the flip of a coin), they do offer something a bit more equi- table than eagles and robins.

I had another friend growing up who was big for his age. Whenever I went to his house to play, he would beat me up. I was not a masochist, so I finally stopped going to his house. After a few days, however, he asked me to come back, offering me ice cream and other incentives. After righteously spurning his overtures for a time, I gave in and resumed playing at his house. True to his word, he gave me ice cream and generously shared his best toys, and from that time for- ward he beat me up only once a week.

This is exactly how the casinos operate, and why they give you a better deal than eagles versus robins. The casinos know that if they hammer you every time you come to play, sooner or later you will quit coming. Better to offer you little incentives and let you win every once in a while. Like with my big friend, they still get to beat you up, but not as often.

THE BATTLE AND THE WAR

IN CASINO GAMBLING, the short run is like a battle, and either player or casino can win. However, the casino almost always wins the war. The American Indians never had a chance against the continuing encroachment of white settlers. There were just too many settlers and too few Indians for the outcome ever to be in doubt. Losing the war, however, did not keep the Indians from winning a few big battles. So it goes in casino gambling. The player struggles in the face of overwhelming odds. If he keeps slugging it out, he is certain to lose. If, on the other hand, he hits and runs, he may come away a winner.

Gambling is like a commando raid: the gambler must get in, do some damage, and get out. Hanging around too long in the presence of superior forces can be fatal.

To say that this takes discipline is an understatement. It's hard to withdraw when you are winning, and maybe even harder to call it quits when you are losing. Glenn couldn't do either, and a lot of gamblers are just like Glenn.

THE HOUSE ADVANTAGE

IF CASINOS DID ENGAGE IN FAIR BETS, they would win about half the bets and lose about half the bets. In other words, the casino (and you), on average, would break even, or at least come close to breaking even. While this arrangement would be more equitable, it would not, as a rule, generate enough money for the casino to pay its mortgage, much less foot the bill for the white tigers, pirate battles, lounge shows, $5 steaks, and free drinks.

To ensure sufficient income to meet their obligations and show a profit, casinos establish rules and payoffs for each game to give the house

HOUSE ADVANTAGES

Baccarat	1.17% on bank bets, 1.36% on player bets
Blackjack	0.5% to 5.9% for most games
Craps	1.4% to almost 17%, depending on the bet
Keno	20% to 35%
Roulette	5.26% to 7.89%, depending on the bet
Slots	2% to 25% (average 4% to 14%)
Video poker	1% to 12% (average 4% to 8%)
Wheel of fortune	11% to 24%

an advantage. While the house advantage is not strictly fair, it is what makes bargain rates on guest rooms, meals, and entertainment possible.

There are three basic ways in which the house establishes its advantage:

1. THE RULES OF THE GAME ARE TAILORED TO THE HOUSE'S ADVANTAGE

In blackjack, for instance, the dealer by rule always plays his own hand last. If any player busts (attains a point total over 21), the dealer wins by default before having to play out his hand.

2. THE HOUSE PAYS OFF AT LESS THAN THE ACTUAL ODDS

Imagine a carnival wheel with ten numbers. When the wheel is spun, each number has an equal chance of coming up. If you bet a dollar on number six, there is a one in ten chance that you will win and a nine in ten chance that you will lose. Gamblers express odds by comparing the likelihood of losing to the likelihood of winning. In this case, nine chances to lose and one to win, or nine to one. If the game paid off at the correct odds, you would get $9 every time you won (plus the dollar you bet). Each time you lost you would lose a dollar.

Let's say you start with $10 and do not win until your tenth try, betting your last dollar. If the game paid off at the correct odds, you would break even. Starting with $10, you would lose a dollar on each of your first nine attempts. In other words, you would be down $9. Betting your one remaining dollar, you win. At nine to one, you would receive $9 and get to keep the dollar you bet. You would have exactly the $10 you started with.

As we have seen, there is no way for a casino to play you even-up and still pay the bills. If, therefore, a casino owner decided to install a wheel with ten numbers, he would decrease the payoff. Instead of paying at the correct odds (nine to one), he might pay at eight to one. If you won on your last bet and got paid at eight to one (instead of nine to one), you would have lost $1 overall. Starting with $10, you lose your first nine bets (so you are out $9) and on your last winning bet you receive $8 and get to keep the dollar you bet. Having played ten times at the eight-to-one payoff, you have $9 left, for a total loss of $1. Thus the house's advantage in this game is 10% (one-tenth).

The house advantage for actual casino games ranges from less than 1% for certain betting situations in blackjack and craps to in excess of 27% on keno. Although 1% doesn't sound like much of an advantage, it will get you if you play long enough. Plus, for the house it adds up.

Because of variations in game rules, the house advantage for a particular game in one casino may be greater than the house advantage for the same game in another casino. In most Las Vegas casinos, for instance, the house has a 5.26% advantage in roulette. At Stratosphere, however, because of the elimination of 00 (double zero) on certain roulette wheels, the house advantage is pared down to about 2.7%.

The rule variations in blackjack swing the house advantage from almost zero in single-deck games (surrender, doubling on any number of cards, dealer stands on soft 17, etc.) to more than 6% in multiple-deck games with draconian rules, such as a recent wrinkle at blackjack, where a natural 21 pays off at 6 to 5 rather than the age-old 3 to 2. Quite a few mathematicians have taken a crack at computing the house's advantage in blackjack. Some suggest that the player can actually gain an advantage over the house in single-deck games by keeping track of cards played. Others claim that without counting cards, a player utilizing a decision guide known as "basic strategy" can play the house nearly even. The reality for 95% of all blackjack players, however, is a house advantage of between 0.5% and 5.9%, depending on rule variations and the number of decks used.

Getting to the meat of the matter: blackjack played competently, baccarat, and certain bets in craps minimize the house advantage and give the player the best opportunity to win. Keno and wheel of fortune are outright sucker games. Slots, some video poker, and roulette are only marginally better.

How the house advantage works in practice causes much misunderstanding. In most roulette bets, for example, the house holds a 5.26% advantage. If you place a dollar on black each time the wheel is spun, the house advantage predicts that, on average, you will lose 5.26 cents per dollar bet. Now, in actual play you will either lose one whole dollar or win one whole dollar, so it's not like somebody is making small change or keeping track of fractional losses. The longer you play, however, the greater the likelihood that the percentage of your losses will approximate the house advantage. If you played for a couple of hours and bet $1,000, your expected loss would be about $53.

All right, you think, that doesn't sound too bad. Plus, you're thinking: I would never bet as much as $1,000. Oh, yeah? If you approach the table with $200 and make 20 consecutive $10 bets, it is not very likely that you will lose every bet. When you take money from your winning bets and wager it, you are adding to your original stake. This is known as "action" in gambling parlance, and it is very different from bankroll. Money that you win is just as much yours as the stake with which you began. When you choose to risk your winnings by making additional bets, you are giving the house a crack at a much larger amount than your original $200. If you start with $200, win some and lose some, and keep playing your winnings in addition to your original stake until you have lost everything, you will have given the house (on average) about $3,800 worth of action. You may want to believe you only lost $200, but every penny of that $3,800 was yours.

3. THE HOUSE TAKES A COMMISSION In all casino poker games and in certain betting situations in table games, the house will collect a commission on a player's winnings.

Sometimes the house combines its various advantages. In baccarat, for instance, rules favor the house; payoffs are less than the true odds; and in certain betting situations, the house collects a commission on the player's winnings.

GAMES OF CHANCE AND THE LAW OF AVERAGES

PEOPLE GET FUNNY IDEAS ABOUT the way gambling works. In casinos there are games of chance (roulette, craps, keno, bingo, wheel of fortune, slots, baccarat) and games of chance *and* skill (poker, blackjack, and video poker).

A game of chance is like flipping a coin or spinning a wheel with ten numbers. What happens is what happens. A player can guess what the outcome will be but cannot influence it. Games of chance operate according to the law of averages. If you have a fair coin and flip it ten times, the law of averages leads you to expect that approximately half of the tosses will come up heads and the other half tails. If a roulette wheel has 38 slots, the law of averages suggests that the ball will fall into a particular slot one time in 38 spins.

The coin, the roulette ball, and the dice, however, have no memory. They just keep doing their thing. If you toss a coin and come up with heads nine times in a row, what are your chances of getting heads on the tenth toss? The answer is 50%, the same chance as getting heads on any toss. Each toss is completely independent of any other toss. When the coin goes up in the air that tenth time, it doesn't know that tails has not come up for a while, and certainly has no obligation to try to get the law of averages back into whack.

Though most gamblers are familiar with the law of averages, not all of them understand how it works. The operative word, as it turns out, is "averages," not "law." If you flip a coin a million times, there is nothing that says you will get 500,000 heads and 500,000 tails, no more than there is any assurance you will get five heads and five tails if you flip a coin ten times. What the law of averages *does* say is that, *in percentage terms,* the more times you toss the coin, the closer you will come to approximating the predicted average.

If you tossed a coin ten times, for example, you would not be surprised to get six tails and four heads. Six tails is only one flip off the five tails and five heads that the law of averages tells you is the probable outcome. By percentage, however, tails came up 60% (six of ten) of the time, while heads only came up 40% (four of ten) of the time. If you continued flipping the coin for a million tries, would you be surprised to get 503,750 tails and only 496,250 heads, a difference of 7,500 more tails than heads? The law of averages stipulates that the more we toss (and a million tosses are certainly a lot more than ten tosses) the closer we should come to approximating the average, but here we are with a huge difference of 7,500 more tails. What went wrong?

Nothing went wrong. True, after ten flips, we had only two more tails than heads, while after a million flips we had 7,500 more tails than heads. But in terms of percentage, 503,750 tails is 50.375% of one million, only about one-third of a measly percent from what the law of averages predicts. The law of averages is about percentages. Gambling is about dollars out of your pocket. If you had bet a dollar on heads each toss, you would have lost $2 after ten flips. After a million flips you would have lost $7,500. The law of averages behaved just as mathematical theory predicted.

Games of Chance and Skill

Blackjack, poker, and video poker are games of chance and skill, meaning that the knowledge, experience, and skill of the player can have some influence on the outcome. All avid poker players or bridge players can recall nights when they played for hours without being dealt a good hand. That's the chance part. In order to win, you need good cards. There is usually not much you can do if you are dealt a bad hand. As the Nevada mule drivers say, "You can't polish a turd."

If you are dealt something to work with, however, you can bring your skill into play and try to make your good hand even better. In casino poker, players compete against each other in the same way they do at Uncle Bert's house back home. The only difference is that in the casino the house takes a small percentage of each winning pot as compensation for hosting the game (are you listening, Uncle Bert?). Although not every casino poker player is an expert, your chances of coming up against an expert in a particular game are good.

Our advice on casino poker: if you're not a tough fish, better not try to swim with the sharks.

Blackjack likewise combines chance and skill. In blackjack, however, players compete against the house (the dealer). Players have certain choices and options in blackjack, but the dealer's play is completely bound by rules. Much has been written about winning at blackjack. It's been said that by keeping track of cards played (and thereby knowing which cards remain undealt in the deck), a player can raise his or her bets when the deck contains a higher-than-usual percentage of aces, tens, and picture cards. In practice, however, the casino confounds efforts to count cards by combining several decks together, "burning" cards (removing undisclosed cards from play), and keeping the game moving at a fast pace. If an experienced gambler with extraordinary memory and power of concentration is able to overcome these obstacles, the casino will simply throw this person out.

In blackjack, as in every other casino game, it is ludicrous to suggest that the house is going to surrender its advantage. Incidentally, a super-gambler playing flawlessly in a single-deck game and keeping track of every card will gain only a nominal and temporary advantage over the house. On top of playing perfectly and being dealt good cards, the super-gambler must also disguise his play and camouflage his betting so the house won't know what he's up to. It's not impossible, but very few players who try ever pull it off successfully.

The Intelligence Test

If you have been paying attention, here is what you should understand by now:

1. That all gambling games are designed to favor the house, and that in the long run the house will always win.

2. That it costs a lot to build, staff, and operate a casino, and that a casino must attract many players in order to pay the bills and still make a profit.

3. That casinos compete fiercely for available customers and offer incentives ranging from 99-cent hot dogs to free guest rooms to get the right customers to their gaming tables.

Question: Given the above, what kind of customer gets the best deal?

Answer: The person who takes advantage of all the incentives without gambling.

Question: What kind of customer gets the next best deal?

Answer: The customer who sees gambling as recreation, gambles knowledgeably, makes sensible bets, sets limits on the amount he or she is prepared to wager, and enjoys all of the perks and amenities, but stays in control.

Question: What kind of customer gets the worst deal?

Answer: The person who thinks he or she can win. This person will foot the bill for everyone else.

Playing It Smart

Experienced, noncompulsive, recreational gamblers typically play in a very disciplined and structured manner. Here's what they recommend:

1. **Never gamble when you are** tired, depressed, or sick. Also, watch the drinking. Alcohol impairs judgment (you play badly) and lowers inhibitions (you exceed prudent limits).

2. **Set a limit before you leave home** on the total amount you are willing to lose gambling. No matter what happens, do not exceed this limit.

3. **Decide which game(s) interest you and get the rules down before you play.** If you are a first-timer at craps or baccarat, take lessons (offered free at the casinos most days). If you are a virgin blackjack player, buy a good book and learn basic strategy. For all three games, spend an hour or two observing games in progress before buying in. Stay away from games like keno and wheel of fortune, in which the house advantage is overwhelming.

4. **Decide how long you want to play** and work out a gambling itinerary consistent with the funds you set aside for wagering. Let's say you plan to be in Las Vegas for two days and want to play about five hours each day. If you have $500 in gambling money available for the trip, that's $250 a day. Dividing the $250 a day by five hours, you come up with $50 an hour.

Now, forget time. Think of your gambling in terms of playing individual sessions instead of hours. You are going to play five sessions a day with $50 available to wager at each session.

5. **Observe a strategy for winning and losing.** On buying in, place your session allocation by your left hand. Play your allotted session money only once during a given session. Anytime you win, return your original bet to the session-allocation stack (left hand), and place your winnings in a stack by your right hand. Never play any chips or coins you have won. When you have gone through your original allocation once, pick up the chips or coins in your winning stack (right hand) and quit. The difference between your original allocation and what you walk away with is your net win or loss for the session.

During the session, bet consistently. If you have been making $1 bets and have lost $10, do not chase your losses by upping your bets to $10 in an effort to get even in a hurry.

If you were fortunate and doubled your allocated stake during the session (in this case, walked away with $100 or more), take everything in excess of $100 and put it aside as winnings, not to be touched for the remainder of your trip. If you won, but did not double your money, or if you had a net loss (quit with less than $50 in your win stack), use this money in your next playing session.

6. **Take a break between sessions.** Relax for a while after each session. Grab a bite to eat, enjoy a nap, or go for a swim.

7. **When you complete** the number of sessions scheduled for the day, stop gambling. **Period.**

GAMING INSTRUCTION AND RESOURCES

MOST CASINO GAMES ARE ACTUALLY FAIRLY SIMPLE once you know what's going on. A great way to replace inexperience and awkwardness with knowledge and confidence is to take advantage of the free gaming lessons offered by the casinos. Going slowly and easily, the instructors take you step by step through the play and the betting without you actually wagering any money. Many casinos feature low-minimum-bet "live games" following the instruction. We also recommend the lessons to nonplaying companions of gamblers. For folks who usually spend a fair amount of time as spectators, casino games, like all other games, are more interesting if you know what is going on.

We highly recommend the free gaming lessons offered by casinos. They introduce you not only to the rules but also to the customs and etiquette of the respective games.

No matter how many books you have read, take a lesson in craps before you try to play in a casino. You don't need to know much to play baccarat, but *understanding* it is a different story. Once again, we strongly recommend lessons. Though you can learn to play blackjack by reading a book and practicing at home, lessons will make you feel more comfortable.

When "new games" are added to the traditional selection, casinos often offer instruction for a limited time. The latest rages are poker and a whole bunch of poker derivatives: Texas Hold 'Em, Let It Ride, Caribbean Stud, Three Card poker, Crazy 4 poker, 3-5-7 poker, along with Casino War, and, owing to the increasing number of Asian gamblers, Pai Gow and Pai Gow poker. Lessons are also available in traditional poker. For information on gaming lessons, inquire at your hotel or check the gaming section of one of the local visitor freebie magazines like *What's On*.

WRITTEN REFERENCES AND THE GAMBLER'S BOOK CLUB Most libraries and bookstores offer basic reference works on casino gambling. If you cannot find what you need at home, call the Gambler's Book Club at ☎ 800-522-1777 for a free catalog. If you would like to stop in and browse while you are in Las Vegas, the club's store is located at 630 South 11th Street, just off East Charleston Boulevard. The local phone is ☎ 702-382-7555. Gambler's Book Club, incidentally, sells single issues of the *Las Vegas Advisor,* quoted above.

WHERE TO PLAY

WE RECEIVE A LOT OF MAIL FROM READERS asking which casino has the loosest slots, the most favorable rules for blackjack, and the best odds on craps. We directed the questions to veteran gambler and tournament player Anthony Curtis, publisher of the *Las Vegas Advisor.* Here's Anthony's reply:

> *Where's the best casino in Las Vegas to play blackjack, video poker, and the rest of the gambling games? It could be almost anyplace on any given day due to spot promotions and changing management philosophies. A few casinos, however, have established reliable track records in specific areas. Absent a special promotion or change in policy, I recommend the casinos in the chart on pages 288–289 as the best places for the games listed.*

CHANGES IN ATTITUDE, CHANGES IN LATITUDE

MOST PEOPLE WHO LOVE TO GAMBLE are not motivated solely by greed. Usually it is the tension, excitement, and anticipation of the game that they enjoy. Misunderstanding this reality has led many naive and innocent people into the nightmare of addictive gambling.

Ed was attending a convention on his first visit to Las Vegas. One evening, he decided to try his luck at roulette. Approaching the table, Ed expected to lose ("I'm not stupid, after all"). His intentions were typical. He wanted to "try" gambling while in Nevada, and he was looking for an adventure, a new experience. What Ed never anticipated was the emotional impact gambling would have on him. It transcended winning and losing. In fact, it wasn't about winning or losing at all. It was the *playing* that mattered. The "action" made him feel alive, involved, and terribly sophisticated. It also made him crazy.

The "high" described by the compulsive gambler closely parallels the experience of drug and alcohol abusers. In fact, there is a tendency for chemical addiction and gambling compulsion to overlap. The compulsive gambler attempts to use "the action" as a cure for a variety of ills, in much the same way that people use alcohol and drugs to lift them out of depression, stem anxiety or boredom, and make them feel more "in control."

Some people cannot handle gambling, just as some people cannot handle alcohol. The problem, unfortunately, is compounded by the attitude of our society. As we profess to admire the drinker who can "hold his liquor," we reinforce the gambler who beats the odds in Las Vegas. By glamorizing these behaviors we enable afflicted individuals to remain in denial about the destructive nature of their problem. The compulsive gambler blames circumstances and other people for the suffering occasioned by his or her affliction. One may hear excuses like: "I didn't get enough sleep; I couldn't concentrate with all the noise; I lost track of the time; I'm jinxed at this casino."

If this sounds like you or someone you love, get help. In Las Vegas there is a meeting of Gamblers Anonymous almost every night. Call ☎ 888-442-2110 or check the Web at **www.gamblersanonymous.org**. If, like Ed, you catch something in Las Vegas and take it home with you, Gamblers Anonymous is listed in your local *White Pages*.

RULES *of the* GAMES

SLOT MACHINES

SLOT MACHINES, INCLUDING VIDEO POKER, have eclipsed table games in patron popularity. Few Las Vegas casinos remain that have not allocated more than half of their available floor space to various types of slot machines.

The popularity of slots is not difficult to understand. First, slots allow a person to enjoy casino gambling at low or high stakes. In downtown Las Vegas and at local casinos around the valley, you can play the slots for a penny a pop. Nickel slots, meanwhile, can be found in virtually every casino in town. Quarter slots are the most popular and the most common. Higher-stakes players can find machines that accept bets of $1 to $500 (high-stakes slots use special tokens instead of coins).

Second, many people like the slots because no human interaction is required. Absent in slot play is the adversarial atmosphere of the table games. Machines are less intimidating—at least more neutral—than dealers and pit bosses. A patron can sit at a machine for as long as his stamina and money last and never be bothered by a soul.

Finally, slot machines are simple, or at least ostensibly so. Although there are a number of things you should know before you play the slots, the only thing you have to know is how to put money into the machine (sometimes coins, but more often bills) and press the spin button (most slot machines no longer have handles).

What You Need to Know before You Play Slot Machines

Starting at the beginning: All slot machines have a slot for inserting either coins, bills, or machine tickets, a button to push (most machines no longer have handles) to activate the machine, a visual display where you can see the reels spin and stop or video symbols line up on each play, and a coin tray or machine-ticket dispenser that you hope some winnings will come out of. Today, almost all slot machines are essentially computers attached to a monitor. Gone are the mechanical reels, replaced by an electronic depiction of reels or other symbols illustrated on the monitor.

While slot machines used to have three mechanical reels, most today have been replaced by either three or four electronic reels or video screens with up to 12 depictions of reels. Each reel has some number of "stops," positions where the reel can come to rest. Reels with 20, 25, or 32 stops are the most common. On each reel at each stop (or resting position) is a single slot symbol (a cherry, orange, bar, plum, etc.). What you hope will happen (when the video reels stop spinning) is that three or more of the same symbol will line up on the pay line. If this happens, you win some number of coins or credits based on the particular symbols. With the old slot machines things were pretty simple. There was one coin slot, one handle to pull, and a display with one pay line. Symbols either lined up or they didn't. The newer machines are much more complex. Almost all modern machines accept more than one coin per play (usually three to five but up to 250). No matter how many coins the machine will take, it only requires one to play.

If you put in additional coins (bet more), you will buy one of the following benefits:

1. **Payoff schedules** On a certain type of machine, two, three, four, or five different payoff schedules are posted on the front of the machine above the reel display. If you study these schedules you will notice that by playing extra coins you can increase your payoff should you win the grand jackpot. Usually there is a straightforward increase. If you play two coins, you will win twice as much as if you play one coin. If you play three coins, you will win three times as much as if you play one coin, and so on. Some machines, however, have a grand jackpot that will pay off only if you have played the maximum number of coins. If you line up the symbols for the grand jackpot but have not played the maximum number of coins, you will not win the maximum amount possible. Always read the payoff schedule for a machine before you play, and make sure you understand it. If you do not, ask an attendant or find a simpler machine.

   Though most casino slot machines are kept in good working order, watch to make sure the machine credits you for every coin you play and for every winning round you play. If you are playing a machine with a multiple-payoff schedule, lights on the screen or buttons on the console

Anthony's Recommended Best Places to Play

BLACKJACK EL CORTEZ

The El Cortez is one of the few casinos in Las Vegas that still deals single-deck games that pay 3-2 for naturals (most other hand-helds and almost all single decks now pay the deadly 6-5), making this the best game in town for low stakes.

QUARTER SLOTS RED ROCK RESORT

Since you can't tell definitively whose slots are paying best (they can't be analyzed like video poker machines), picking a strong slot club is a good barometer, and Station Casinos has one of the best. The floor of Station's flagship casino, Red Rock Resort, has all the latest slot games in low denoms.

DOLLAR SLOTS PALMS

Evidence still points to the Palms as being loosest for slots in general. Lots of promotions and a good slot club make them the best of the bunch and the pick at the dollar level.

CRAPS CASINO ROYALE

It's the only casino in Las Vegas that still offers 100X odds. Also low limits on the line and the propositions. There's an excellent fun book for new slot club members.

QUARTER VIDEO POKER SILVERTON

Video poker expert Bob Dancer now teaches his how-to-play classes out of the Silverton, and the casino supported him by installing dozens of machines with full-pay schedules. Silverton is also known for its progressive games, many of them in bar-top machines.

DOLLAR VIDEO POKER FIESTA RANCHO

Plenty of machines (100%-plus) and a good players' club make this the top pick for dollar play.

ROULETTE NEVADA PALACE

Deals a single-zero game with a 10¢ minimum bet on the inside numbers ($1 aggregate required). The Nevada Palace is due to be replaced by an east-side Cannery but will remain open until the new casino is completely built.

should illuminate, indicating the number of payoffs you're betting on. If you put in multiple coins without the appropriate lights coming on, do not play until you check things out with an attendant.

2. **Multiple pay lines** When you play your first coin, you buy the usual pay line, right in the center of the display. By playing more coins, you can buy additional pay lines.

Each pay line you purchase gives you another way of winning. Instead of being limited to the center line, the machine will pay off on the top, center, or bottom lines, and five-coin machines will pay winners on diagonal lines. Video slots, also known as Australian machines, can pay off on a dozen lines or more, criss-crossing symbols all over the screen.

BACCARAT PALACE STATION

Action around the clock at oversized mini baccarat tables. Minimums are low.

KENO EL CORTEZ

Good schedules on the $1.15 tickets return from 84% to 87%, as opposed to the industry average of about 70%.

BINGO RED ROCK RESORT

The big bingo room at the Red Rock Resort is one of the swankiest in town. The room is divided (and partitioned) for smokers and nonsmokers. Look for frequent promotions.

POKER BELLAGIO

As poker continues its meteoric rise in popularity, casinos are opening poker rooms one after another. The big room, though, is still at Bellagio.

RACE AND SPORTS BETTING ORLEANS

Coast Casinos sports books are among the best in Las Vegas for limits, reduced odds, and promotions. Look for reduced-juice betting opportunities on big games, such as the Super Bowl.

LET IT RIDE HILTON

Not much separates one Let It Ride game from another, but the Hilton runs periodic LIR tournaments that you may qualify for in the course of normal play. You have to make the bad "Bonus Buck" bet to qualify, but it's mathematically worth doing if you plan on playing the tourney.

CARIBBEAN STUD GOLDEN NUGGET

Usually a couple of tables in operation with fatter-than-normal meters on the progressive, which means the bonus jackpot has a better chance to move into positive-return territory.

PAI GOW POKER GOLD COAST

A favorite casino of local pai gow players, so there's constant action and low minimums.

If you play machines with multiple pay lines, make sure that each pay line you buy is acknowledged by a light before you push the button.

An irritating feature of many multiple-line machines are "blanks" or "ghosts." A blank is nothing more than an empty stop on the reel—a place where you would expect a symbol to be but where there is nothing. As you have probably surmised, you cannot hit a winner by lining up blanks.

NONPROGRESSIVE VERSUS PROGRESSIVE SLOT MACHINES Nonprogressive slot machines have fixed payoffs. You can read the payoff schedules posted on the machine and determine exactly how much you will get for each winning combination for any number of coins played.

A second type of machine, known as a progressive, has a grand jackpot that grows and grows until somebody hits it. After the grand jackpot has been won, the jackpot is reset and starts to grow. While individual machines can offer modest progressive grand jackpots, the really big jackpots (several thousand to tens of millions of dollars) are possible only on machines linked in a system to other machines. Sometimes an "island," "carousel," or "bank" of machines in a given casino is hooked up to create a progressive system. The more these machines are played, the faster the progressive jackpot grows. The largest progressive jackpots come from huge multicasino systems that sometimes cover the entire state. Players have won more than $30 million by hitting these jackpots.

While nothing is certain in slot play, it is generally accepted that nonprogressives pay more small jackpots. Progressives, on the other hand, offer an opportunity to strike it really rich, but they give up fewer interim wins.

The nonprogressive machine is for the player who likes plenty of action, who gets bored when coins aren't clanking into the tray every four or five pulls. The progressive machine is for the player who is willing to forgo frequent small payouts for the chance of hitting a really big one.

How Slot Machines Work

Almost all slot machines used in casinos today are controlled by microprocessors. This means the machines can be programmed and are more like computers than mechanical boxes composed of gears and wheels. During the evolution of the modern slot machine, manufacturers eliminated the traditional spinning reels in favor of a video display, and replaced the pull handle with a button. Inside the newer machines, there is a device that computer people call a "random number generator" and that we refer to as a "black box." What the black box does is spit out hundreds of numbers each second, selected randomly (that is, in no predetermined sequence). The black box has about four billion different numbers to choose from, so it's very unusual (but not impossible) for the same number to come up twice in a short time.

The numbers the black box selects are programmed to trigger a certain set of symbols on the display, determining where the reels stop. What most players don't realize, however, is that the black box pumps out numbers continuously, regardless of whether the machine is being played or not. If you are playing a machine, the black box will call up hundreds or thousands of numbers in the few seconds between plays while you sip your drink, put some money in the slot, and push the button.

Why is this important? Try this scenario: Mary has played the same quarter machine for hours, pumping an untold amount of money into it. She cashes out and gets up to stretch her legs for a few minutes, thinking she'll come back afterwards and keep playing. In the meantime, someone walks up to Mary's machine and wins the grand jackpot. Mary is livid. "That's my jackpot!" she screams. Not

slot-machine pay lines

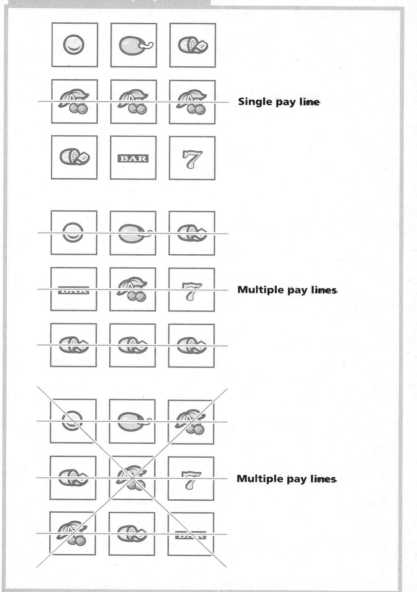

Single pay line

Multiple pay lines

Multiple pay lines

so. While Mary took her walk, thousands of numbers and possible symbol combinations were generated by the black box. The only way Mary could have hit the jackpot (even if the man had not come along) would have been to activate the machine at that same exact moment in time, right down to a fraction of a millisecond.

There is no such thing as a machine that is "overdue to hit." Each spin of the reels on a slot machine is an independent event, just like flipping a coin. The only way to hit a jackpot is to activate the machine at the exact moment that the black box randomly coughs up a winning number. If you play a slot machine as fast as you can, jamming in coins and pushing the button like a maniac, the black box will still spew out more numbers (and possible jackpots) between each try than you will have pulls in a whole day of playing.

CHERRY, CHERRY, ORANGE The house advantage is known for every casino game except slots. With slot machines, the house advantage is whatever the casino programs it to be. In Atlantic City the maximum legal house advantage is 17%. Nevada's limit for slot machines is a hold of 75%. This means that Nevada slot machines can have a house advantage of up to 25%. In theory, a casino could program a machine to keep 50% of all the coins played. Interviews with ex–casino employees suggest, however, that the house advantage on casino slots in Las Vegas ranges from about 2.5% to 25%, with most machines giving the house an edge of between 4% and 14%.

Casinos advertise their slots in terms of payout or return rate. If a casino states that its slots return up to 97%, that's another way of saying that the house has a 3% advantage. Some casinos advertise machines that pay up to 98%, and one casino even claims to offer slots paying 101%!

SLOT QUEST A slot machine that withholds only a small percentage of the money played is referred to as "loose," while a machine that retains most of the coins it takes in is called "tight." "Loose" and "tight" are figurative descriptions and have nothing to do with the condition of the machine. Because return rates vary from casino to casino, and because machines in a given casino are programmed to withhold vastly differing percentages of the coins played, some slot players devote much time and energy to finding the best casinos and the loosest machines. Exactly how to go about this is the subject of much discussion.

In terms of choosing a casino, there are several theories that have at least a marginal ring of truth. Competition among casinos is often a general indicator for finding loose slots. Some say that smaller casinos, which compete against large neighbors, must program their slots to provide a higher return. Alternatively, some folks will play slots only in casinos patronized predominantly by locals (Gold Coast, Palace Station, Boulder Station, Fiesta, Suncoast, Orleans, Texas Station, El Cortez, Gold Spike, Sam's Town, Arizona Charlie's, and Santa Fe Station, among others). The reasoning here is that these casinos vie for regular customers on a continuing basis and must therefore offer extremely competitive win rates. Downtown Las Vegas is likewise cast in the "we try harder" role, because smaller downtown casinos must go head-to-head with the Strip to attract patrons.

Extending the logic, machines located in supermarkets, restaurants, convenience stores, airports, and lounges are purported to be very tight. In these places, some argue, there is little incentive for management to provide good returns, because the patrons will play regardless (out of boredom or simply because the machine is there).

Veteran slot players have many theories when it comes to finding the loose machines in a particular casino. Some will tell you to play the machines by the door or in the waiting area outside the showroom. By placing the loose machines in these locations, the theory goes, the casino can demonstrate to passersby and show patrons that the house has loose slots. A more labor-intensive suggestion for sniffing out the loose machines is to hang around the casino during the wee hours of the morning when the machines are being emptied. Supposedly machines with the least number of coins in the hopper have been paying off more frequently. Or maybe these machines have just been played less often.

I have had a slot manager admit to me that his nickel machines are tighter than his quarter machines and that his dollar and five-dollar machines are the loosest of all. Tight or loose, however, all slots are programmed to give the casino a certain profit over the long run. It is very unlikely, in any event, that you will play a machine long enough to experience the theoretical payoff rate. What you are concerned about is the short run. In the short run anything can happen, including winning.

MAXIMIZING YOUR CHANCES OF WINNING ON THE SLOTS If you play less than the maximum number of coins on a progressive, you are simply contributing to a jackpot that you have no chance of winning. If you don't want to place a maximum bet, play a nonprogressive machine.

Slot Machine Etiquette and Common Sense

Regardless of whether you are playing a one-armed bandit, a video-poker machine, or any other type of coin-operated slot machine, there are some things you need to know:

1. Realize that avid slot players sometimes play more than one machine at a time. Do not assume that a machine is not in use simply because nobody is standing or sitting in front of it. Slot players can be fanatically territorial.

2. Before you start to play, check out the people around you. Do you feel safe and comfortable among them?

3. Read and understand the payout schedule of any machine you play.

4. Almost all machines have credit meters; be sure to cash out your credits before you abandon the machine.

5. If the casino has a slot club, join (this usually takes less than five minutes on-site, but can be accomplished through the mail prior to your trip). Use the club card whenever you play. When you quit, don't forget to take your club card with you.

6. Never play more machines than you can watch carefully. Be particularly vigilant when playing machines near exits and corridors. If you are asleep at the switch, a thief can dip into your coin tray or bucket and be out the door in seconds.

7. Keep your purse and your money in sight at all times. Never put your purse on the floor behind you or to the side.

8. If you line up a winner and nothing happens, don't leave the machine. Sometimes large jackpots exceed the coin capacity of the machine and must be paid directly by the casino cashier. Call immediately for an attendant but do not wander off looking for one. While you wait, refrain from further play on the machine in question.

9. If the appropriate payout sections or pay lines fail to illuminate when playing multiple coins, do not leave or activate the machine (push the button) until you have consulted an attendant.

Slot/Frequent-Player Clubs

Most Las Vegas casinos now have slot or frequent-player clubs. The purpose of these clubs is to foster increased customer loyalty among gambling patrons by providing incentives.

You can join a club by signing up at the casino or (at some casinos) by applying through the mail. There is neither a direct cost associated with joining nor any dues. You are given a plastic membership card that resembles a credit card. This card can be inserted into a slot on any gambling machine in the casino. As long as your card is in the slot, you are credited for the amount of action you put through that machine. Programs at different casinos vary, but in general, you are awarded "points" based on how long you play and how much you wager. Though almost all clubs award points only for slot play, some use the card at the tables to input hours played and average bets into the player-tracking database. As in an airline frequent-flyer program, accumulated points can ultimately be redeemed for awards. Awards range from casino logo apparel to discounts (or comps) on meals, shows, and rooms.

The good thing about slot clubs is that they provide a mechanism for slot players to obtain some of the comps, perks, and extras that have always been available to table players. The bad thing about a slot club is that it confines your play. In other words, you must give most of your business to one or two casinos in order to accumulate enough points to reap rewards. If you are a footloose player and enjoy gambling all around town, you may never accrue enough points in any one casino to redeem a prize.

Even if you never redeem any points, however, it's still a good idea to join. If you travel to Las Vegas regularly on business, join your hotel's slot club. Membership might make you eligible for deals on rooms and food that would otherwise not be available to you.

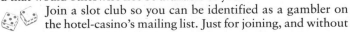 Join a slot club so you can be identified as a gambler on the hotel-casino's mailing list. Just for joining, and without

gambling that first quarter, you will be offered discounts on rooms and a variety of other special deals.

VIDEO POKER

NEVER IN THE HISTORY OF CASINO GAMBLING has a game become so popular so quickly. What's the allure of video poker? More people are familiar with poker than with any other casino game. The video version affords average folks an opportunity to play a game of chance and skill without going up against professional gamblers.

In video poker you are not playing against anyone. Rather, you are trying to make the best possible five-card-draw poker hand. In the most common rendition, you insert your coin(s) and push a button marked "deal." Your original five cards are displayed on the screen. Below the screen and under each of the cards pictured are "hold" buttons. After evaluating your hand and planning your strategy, designate the cards you want to keep by pressing the appropriate hold button(s). If you hit the wrong button or change your mind, simply "unhold" your choices by pushing the buttons again. If you do not want to draw any cards (you like your hand as dealt), press all five hold buttons. When you press the hold button for a particular card, the word "hold" will appear over or under that card on the display. Always double-check the screen to make certain the cards you intend to hold are marked before proceeding to the draw.

When you are ready, press the button marked "draw" (on many machines it is the same button as the deal button). Any cards you have not designated to be held will be replaced. As in live draw poker, the five cards in your possession after the draw are your final hand. If the hand is a winner (a pair of jacks or better on most non-wild-card machines), you will be credited the appropriate winnings on a credit meter on the video display. These are actual winnings that can be retrieved in coins by pressing the "cash-out" button. If you choose to leave your winnings on the credit meter, you may use them to bet, eliminating the need to physically insert coins in the machine. When you are ready to quit, simply press the cash-out button and collect your coins from the tray or a ticket from the dispenser.

You do not have to know much about poker to play video poker. All of the winning hands with their respective payoffs are posted on or above the video display. As with other slot machines, you can increase your payoffs and become eligible for bonus jackpots by playing the maximum number of coins. Note that some machines have jackpots listed in dollars, while others are specified in coins. Obviously, there is a big difference between $4,000 and 4,000 nickels.

To play video poker well, you need two skills: selecting the right machine and playing the proper strategy. The first skill requires the ability to decipher the pay schedules posted prominently on the faceplates of every machine. Some machines have a high payback percentage, even higher than 100%, while others pay less. You're looking for the highest paying schedules within each variation of video poker—and there are dozens of variations. Luckily, you have to know only a few of them.

These include Jacks or Better (JoB) and Double Bonus. The highest paying version of JoB is called 9/6, meaning it pays 9-for-1 per coin played when you hit a full house, and 6-for-1 when you hit a flush. When you check the payout schedule for a single coin played, it could read 8 for a full house and 5 for a flush, even 7 or 6 for a full house. But unless you're returned 9 for the full house and 6 for the flush, you're better off playing any random slot machine. The payback percentage for 9/6 JoB is 99.5%, almost break-even.

The other schedule to look for is 10/7 Double Bonus. Again, this means 10-for-1 on a full house and 7-for-1 on a flush. You'll see lower paybacks, but it's only 10/7 that we play, which pays back 100.7%, a positive game.

Other payback schedules are also playable, such as Deuces Wild and Joker Wild. But you have to recognize the highest-paying versions, which you can learn easily and quickly. Read a few pages of a good gambling primer, such as *The Frugal Gambler* or *More Frugal Gambling* by Jean Scott, and you'll be locating the beatable machines like a pro.

Learning the proper playing strategies requires a bit more work. Luckily, the tools are readily available, inexpensive, easy to use, and completely effective. In fact, the first tool, the computer tutorial, is also fun. These software programs, such as *Frugal Video Poker* and *WinPoker,* teach you "computer-perfect strategy" by alerting you to and correcting strategy mistakes as you play on your home or office computer. Programming yourself with the proper plays takes only four or five enjoyable hours; this is time extremely well spent for preparing to take on the casino with real money.

Problem is, you can't take the computer into the casino. That's where strategy cards come into play—the best video-poker aids of all. These $6.95 handy-dandy tri-fold pocket-size color-coded laminated cards use a sort of shorthand to list every decision by which you can possibly be confronted at a machine; they pay for themselves in one playing session with the saving gained by avoiding costly mistakes. And the best thing is, other than spending a few minutes deciphering the code when you first receive them, you don't have to do anything with them, except remember to put them in your pocket and refer to them while you play.

The edge at video poker ranges from more than 10% on the worst schedules up to positive 1% (a player advantage) on the best.

A computer tutorial and handy strategy cards will give you an edge in video poker.

An Example of Video-poker Strategy

Each hand in a video-poker game is dealt from a fresh 52-card deck. Each hand consists of ten cards, with a random number generator or "black box" selecting the cards dealt. When you hit the deal button, the first five cards are displayed face up on the screen. Cards six through ten are held in reserve to be dealt as replacements for cards you discard when you draw. Each replacement card is dealt in order off the top of the electronic deck. The microprocessor "shuffles" the deck for each new game. Thus on the next play, you will be dealt five new and randomly selected initial cards, and five new and randomly selected draw cards to back them up. In other words, you will not be dealt any unused cards from the previous hand.

THE POWER OF THE ROYAL FLUSH In video poker, the biggest payout is usually for a royal flush. This fact influences strategy for playing the game. Simply put, you play differently than you would in a live poker game. If in Jacks or Better video poker you are dealt

      A ♣   Q ♣   10 ♣   A ♠   J ♣,

you would discard the ace of spades (giving up a sure straight) to go for the royal flush. Likewise, if you are dealt

      5 ♠   A ♠   K ♠   Q ♠   J ♠,

you would discard the 5 of spades (sacrificing a sure spade flush) in an attempt to make the royal by drawing the 10 of spades. If you are dealt

      J ♥   Q ♥   K ♥   4 ♥   6 ♣,

draw two cards for the royal flush as opposed to one card for the flush. If you are initially dealt the following straight:

      7 ♥   8 ♥   9 ♥   10 ♥   J ♥,

keep it on a Jacks or Better machine. This particular hand occasions much debate among video-poker veterans. The 6 of clubs or the jack of clubs would give you a straight flush, while any other club would give you a flush. Your chances of improving this hand are 9 in 47, with a 5 in 47 chance of recapturing your straight with a drawn non-club 6 or jack. It's a close call, but keeping the sure straight gets the nod (with an expected win of four coins for standing versus two and three-fourths coins for drawing). If the same situation comes up on a nickel machine, however, take the gamble and draw.

The payoff for the royal flush is so great that it is worth risking a sure winning hand. The payoff for a straight flush, however, does not warrant risking a pat flush or straight.

OTHER SITUATIONS If you are dealt

      Q ♦   A ♣   4 ♥   J ♠   4 ♣,

hold the small pair except when you have a chance at making a royal flush by drawing one or two cards.

But if you are dealt

      K ♦   A ♣   4 ♥   J ♣   3 ♠,

hold the ace of clubs and the jack of clubs to give yourself a long shot at a royal flush. Similarly, if you are dealt *Continued on next page*

       K ♣   A ♣   4 ♥   J ♣   3 ♠,

hold the ace of clubs, king of clubs, and jack of clubs.

STRAIGHT POKER If you are playing straight poker (no wild cards), with a pair of jacks or better required to win, observe the following:

1. Hold a jacks-or-better pair, even if you pass up the chance of drawing to an open-end straight or to a flush. If you have

      Q ♣   4 ♠   6 ♠   2 ♠   Q ♠
   or
      Q ♥   9 ♦   10 ♣   J ♠   Q ♣,

in each case keep the pair of queens and draw three cards.

2. Split a low pair to go for a flush. If you are dealt

      2 ♦   4 ♣   4 ♦   8 ♦   10 ♦,

discard the 4 of clubs and draw one card to try and make the flush.

3. Hold a low pair rather than drawing to an inside or open-end straight.

4. A "kicker" is a face card or an ace you might be tempted to hang onto along with a high pair, low pair, or three-of-a-kind. If you are dealt, for example,

      5 ♣   5 ♦   8 ♠   10 ♠   A ♥
   or
      5 ♣   5 ♦   8 ♠   10 ♠   A ♥
   or
      2 ♣   2 ♣   2 ♥   8 ♠   A ♥,

hold the pair or the three-of-a-kind, but discard the kicker (the ace).

BLACKJACK

MANY BOOKS HAVE BEEN PUBLISHED about the game of blackjack. The serious gamblers who write these books will tell you that blackjack is a game of skill and chance in which a player's ability can actually turn the odds of winning in his favor. While we want to believe that, we also know the casinos wouldn't keep the tables open if they were taking a beating.

The methods of playing blackjack skillfully involve being able to count all the cards played and flawlessly manage your own hand, while mentally blocking the bustle and distraction of the casino. The ability to master the prerequisite tactics and to play under casino conditions is so far beyond the average (never mind beginning) player that any attempt to track cards is, except for a talented and disciplined few, exhausting and futile.

This doesn't mean that you should not try blackjack. It is a fun, fast-paced game that is easy to understand, and you can play at low-minimum-wager tables without feeling intimidated by the level of play. Moreover, most people already have an understanding of the game from playing "21" at home. The casino version is largely the same, only with more bells and whistles.

In a game of blackjack, the number cards are worth their spots (a 2 of clubs is worth two). All face cards are worth ten. The ace, on the other hand, is worth either 1 point or 11, whichever you choose. In this manner, an ace and a 5 could be worth 6 (hard count) or 16 (soft count). The object of the game is to get as close to 21 as you can without going over (called "busting"). You play only against the dealer, and the hand closest to 21 wins the game.

The dealer will deal you a two-card hand, then give you the option of taking another card (called a "hit") or stopping with the two cards you have been dealt (called "standing"). For example, if your first two cards are a 10 and a 3, your total would be 13, and you would normally ask for another card to get closer to 21. If the next card dealt to you was a 7, you would have a total of 20 points and you would "stand" with 20 (that is, not ask for another card).

It makes no difference what the other players are dealt, or what they choose to do with their hands. Your hand will win or lose only in comparison to the hand that the dealer holds.

The dealer plays his hand last. This is his biggest advantage. All the players that go over 21 points, or bust, will immediately lose their cards and their bet before the dealer's turn to play. What this means in terms of casino advantage is that while the player has to play to win, the only thing the dealer has to do is not lose. Every time you bust, the casino wins. This sequence of play ensures a profit for the casino from the blackjack tables.

Take time to observe a few hands before you play blackjack. This will give you the opportunity to find a friendly, personable dealer and to check out the minimum-bet signs posted at each table.

Be sure to check out the minimum-bet signs posted at each table. They will say something like: "Minimum bet $2 to $500." This means that the minimum wager is $2, and the maximum wager is $500. If you sit down at a blackjack table and begin to bet with insufficient cash or the wrong denomination chip, the dealer will inform you of the correct minimum wager, whereupon you may either conform or excuse yourself.

A blackjack table is shaped like a half circle, with the dealer inside the circle and room for five to seven players around the outside. Facing the dealer, the chair on the far right is called "first base." The chair on the far left is called "third base." The dealer deals the cards from first base to third, and each player plays out his hand in the same order.

If you can, try to sit at third base or as close to it as you can get. This gives you the advantage of watching the other players play out their hands before you play.

To buy in, find an empty seat at a table with an agreeable minimum wager and wait until the hand in progress is concluded. Though you can bet cash, most players prefer to convert their currency to chips. This is done by placing your money on the table *above* the bettor's box. Because blackjack is one of the many games in the casino in which the dealer is allowed to accept cash bets, he will assume that any money placed in the bettor's box is a wager.

Your dealer will take the cash, count out your chips, and push the money through a slot cut in the top of the table. Because he cannot give you change in cash, the total amount you place on the table will be converted to chips. You may at any time, however, redeem your chips for cash from the casino cashier. Once you have been given chips and have bet, you will be included in the next deal.

To confound a player attempting to count cards, many casinos deal blackjack with four to eight (two-hand held) decks shuffled together. This huge stack of cards is rendered manageable by dealing from a special container known as a shoe.

The dealer will shuffle the decks and may offer the cards to you to cut. The dealer offers you a plastic card stop. Place the card stop halfway or so into the deck, leaving the stop sticking out. The dealer will cut the deck at that point and put it into the shoe.

After he cuts a single deck, or puts the multiple deck into the shoe, the dealer will "burn" one or more cards by taking them off the top and putting them into the discard pile. This is yet another tactic to inhibit players from keeping track of cards dealt. Also to the advantage of the casino is the dealer's right to shuffle the cards whenever he pleases. Usually the dealer will deal from the shoe until he reaches the plastic stop card and then he will "break the deck," which means reshuffle and re-cut before dealing the next hand. In a single-deck game, the dealer will usually reshuffle about three-quarters through the deck.

Because the dealer always plays his hand last, you must develop your strategy by comparing your card count to what you assume (based on his visible card) the dealer has. The rule of thumb for most situations is to play your hand as if the dealer's down card has a value of ten. The principles governing when or when not to take a hit are

BASIC STRATEGY*

The Dealer Is Showing:		2	3	4	5	6	7	8	9	10	Ace
Your Total is:	4–11	H	H	H	H	H	H	H	H	H	H
	12	H	H	S	S	S	H	H	H	H	H
	13	S	S	S	S	S	H	H	H	H	H
	14	S	S	S	S	S	H	H	H	H	H
	15	S	S	S	S	S	H	H	H	H	H
	16	S	S	S	S	S	H	H	H	H	H

S=Stand H=Hit

*The correct term for the spots on playing cards is "pips."

the blackjack table

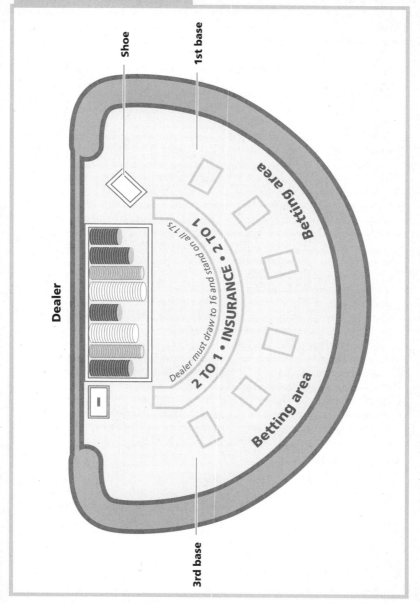

Shoe

1st base

Dealer

Betting area

2 TO 1 • INSURANCE • 2 TO 1

Dealer must draw to 16 and stand on all 17s

Betting area

3rd base

known as "basic strategy" (see chart on page 300). If you elect to take a hit and go over 21 (bust), you lose. If you stand with your original two cards or take a number of hits without going over 21, you can sit back and relax for a few seconds while the dealer continues on around the table, repeating the same process with the other players. When the other players finish, the dealer exposes his "down" card and plays out his hand according to strict rules. He must take a hit on any total of 16 or less, and he must stand on any total of 17 or more. When he finishes his hand, the dealer goes from third base to first, paying off each winning player and collecting chips from the losers who didn't bust.

If you're closer to 21 than the dealer, you win. If he is closer (or if you busted), he wins. If there is a tie, neither hand wins. When you tie, the dealer will knock on the table above your bet to indicate that the hand is a tie, or a "push." You may leave your bet on the table for the next hand, or change it.

There is a way for you to win automatically, and that is to be dealt exactly 21 in the first two cards. This can be done with an ace and any ten-value card. Called a blackjack, or a natural, this hand is an automatic winner, and you should turn your cards face up immediately. The dealer will look to see if he ties you with a blackjack of his own; this is one of the only times a dealer will look at his cards before all the players have played. If the dealer does not have a blackjack, he will pay you immediately at three-to-two odds (or a punitive six-to-five payoff in most Strip single-deck or Super Fun 21 games), so your $5 bet pays off $7.50 and you keep your original wager. If the dealer has a blackjack too, then only you and any other players at the table with a natural will tie him. The rest lose their bets, and the next round will begin.

Nothing beats a natural. If the dealer has a 4 and a 6, then draws an ace, his 21 will not beat your blackjack. A blackjack wins over everything and pays the highest of any bet in the game. Just as you can win automatically, you may lose just as fast. When your count goes over 21 and you bust, you must turn your cards over. The dealer will collect your cards and your bet before moving on to the next player.

Hitting and Standing

When dealing, whether from the shoe or from a single deck in his hand, the dealer will give two cards to each player. Most casinos will deal both cards facedown, though some casinos, especially those that use large multiple decks, will deal both cards faceup. There is no advantage to either method. Most players are more comfortable with the secrecy of the facedown deal, but the outcome will not be affected either way. Starting with the player at first base, the dealer will give you cards to play out your hand. After the initial deal, you have two basic options: either stand or take a hit. If you are satisfied with your deal, then you elect to stand. If your cards were dealt facedown, slide them under the chips in the bettor's box with one hand, being careful not to touch your

SOFT-HAND STRATEGY*

The dealer is showing:		2	3	4	5	6	7	8	9	10	Ace
You have:	Ace, 9	S	S	S	S	S	S	S	S	S	S, H
	Ace, 8	S	S	S	S	S	S	S	S	S	S
	Ace, 7	S	D	D	D	D	S	S	H	H	S
	Ace, 6	H	D	D	D	D	S	H	H	H	H
	Ace, 5	H	H	D	D	D	H	H	H	H	H
	Ace, 4	H	H	D	D	D	H	H	H	H	H
	Ace, 3	H	H	H	D	D	H	H	H	H	H
	Ace, 2	H	H	H	D	D	H	H	H	H	H

S = Stand H = Hit D = Double down

*The charts reflect basic strategy for multiple-deck games. For single-deck games, a slightly different strategy prevails for doubling and splitting.

chips or conceal them from the dealer. If the cards were dealt faceup, wave your hand over the top, palm down, in a negative fashion, to signal the dealer not to give you another card.

Sometimes you will improve your hand by asking for another card. You signal for a hit by scratching the bottom of your cards toward you on the felt surface of the table. In a faceup game, scratch your fingers toward you in the same fashion. You may say, "Hit me," or "I'll take a hit," depending on the mood at your table, but use the hand gestures also. Because of noise and distractions, the dealer may misinterpret your verbal request.

The card you request will be dealt faceup, and you may take as many hits as you like. When you want to show that you do not want another card, use the signals for standing. If you bust, turn your cards faceup right away so the dealer can collect your cards and chips. He will then go to the next player. There are times when the dealer stands a good chance of busting. At these times, it is a good idea to stand on your first two cards even though your total count may seem very low. The accompanying basic strategy chart shows when to stand and when to take a hit. It is easy to follow and simple to memorize. The decision to stand or take a hit is made on the value of your hand and, once again, the dealer's up card, and is based on the probability of his busting. Although following basic strategy won't win every hand, it will improve your odds and take the guesswork out of some confusing situations.

Basic strategy is effective because the dealer is bound by the rules of the game. He must take a hit on 16 and stand on 17. These rules are printed right on the table so that there can be no misunderstanding. Even if you are the only player at the table and stand with a total of 14 points, the dealer with what would be a winning hand of 16 points *must* take another card.

There is one exception to the rule: Some casinos require a dealer to take a hit on a hand with an ace and a 6 (called a "soft 17"). Since the ace can become a 1, it is to the casino's advantage for the dealer to be allowed to hit a soft 17.

Bells and Whistles

Now that you understand the basic game, let's look at a few rules in the casino version of blackjack that are probably different from the way you play at home.

DOUBLING DOWN When you have received two cards and think that they will win with the addition of one and *only* one more card, then double your bet. This "doubling down" bet should be made if your two-card total is 11, since drawing the highest possible card, a 10, will not push your total over 21. In some casinos you may double down on ten, and some places will let you double down on any two-card hand.

To show the dealer that you want to double down, place your two cards touching each other faceup on the dealer's side of the betting box. Then place chips in the box that equal your original bet. Now, as at all other times, don't touch your chips once the bet is made.

DOUBLING DOWN

The dealer is showing:		2	3	4	5	6	7	8	9	10	Ace
Your total is:	11	D	D	D	D	D	D	D	D	D	H
	10	D	D	D	D	D	D	D	D	H	H
	9	H	D	D	D	D	H	H	H	H	H

H = Hit D = Double down

SPLITTING Any time you are dealt two cards of the same value, you may split the cards and start two separate hands. Even aces may be

SPLITTING STRATEGY

The dealer is showing:		2	3	4	5	6	7	8	9	10	Ace
You have:	2, 2	H	H	SP	SP	SP	SP	H	H	H	H
	3, 3	H	H	SP	SP	SP	SP	H	H	H	H
	4, 4	H	H	H	H	H	H	H	H	H	H
	5, 5	D	D	D	D	D	D	D	D	H	H
	6, 6	H	SP	SP	SP	SP	H	H	H	H	H
	7, 7	SP	SP	SP	SP	SP	SP	H	H	H	H
	8, 8	SP	SP	SP	SP	SP	SP	SP	SP	SP	SP
	9, 9	SP	SP	SP	SP	SP	S	SP	SP	S	S
	10, 10	S	S	S	S	S	S	S	S	S	S
	Ace, Ace	SP	SP	SP	SP	SP	SP	SP	SP	SP	SP

S = Stand H = Hit SP = Split D = Double down

split, though when you play them, they will each be dealt only one additional card. If you should happen to get a blackjack after splitting aces, it will be treated as 21; that is, paid off at one to one and not three to two or six to five.

Any other pair is played exactly as you would if you were playing two consecutive hands, and all the rules will apply. Place the two cards *apart from each other* and above the betting box, so the dealer won't confuse this with doubling down. Then add a stack of chips equal to the original bet to cover the additional hand. Your two hands will be played out one at a time, cards dealt faceup.

You will be allowed to split a third card if it is the same as the first two, but not if it shows up as a later hit. Always split a pair of eights, since they total 16 points, the worst total. *Never* split two face cards or tens, since they total 20 and are a probably winning hand.

Some casinos will let you double down after splitting a hand, but if you're unsure, ask the dealer. Not all blackjack rules are posted, and they can vary from casino to casino, and even from table to table in the same casino.

INSURANCE When the dealer deals himself an ace as his second, faceup card, he will stop play and ask, "Insurance, anyone?" Don't be fooled. You're not insuring anything. All he's asking for is a side bet that he has a natural. He must make the insurance bets before he can look at his cards, so he doesn't know if he has won or not when he asks for your insurance bets.

The insurance wager can be up to half the amount of your original bet. Place the chips in the large semicircle marked "insurance." As it says, it pays off two to one. If your original bet was $10 and you bet $5 that the dealer had a natural, you would be paid $10 if he actually did. Depending on your cards, you would probably lose your original $10 bet, but break even on the hand. If the dealer does not have a ten-value card, you lose your $5 insurance bet, but your $10 bet still can win.

This sounds deceptively easy, but you will lose this bet more often than you will win it, though the dealer may suggest it to you as a smart move. The dealer might also tell you to insure your own blackjack, though this should never be done. The odds are always against the insurance bet. When you insure your blackjack, you can be paid off for it at one to one, as if it were 21, instead of the three to two or six to five that you would normally be paid for the blackjack. Even though you may occasionally tie with the dealer, you will more than make up for it with the three-to-two or six-to-five payoffs on the blackjacks you don't insure.

Insurance is a bad move for the basic-strategy player, because the odds are against the dealer actually having a natural.

Avoiding Common Pitfalls

1. Always check the minimum bets allowed at your table before you sit down. Flipping a $5 chip into a $25-minimum game can be humiliating.

If you make this mistake, simply excuse yourself and leave. It happens all the time.

2. Keep your bet in a neat stack, with the largest value chips on the bottom and the smallest on top. A mess of chips can be confusing should you want to double down, and your dealer will get huffy if he has to ask you to stack your chips.

3. Never touch the chips once the bet is down. Cheaters do this, and your dealer may assume you're cheating. It's too easy for a player to secretly up his bet once he's seen his cards or lower it if the cards are bad. Do not stack a double-down bet or split bets on top of the original bet Place them beside the original bet and then keep your hands away.

4. Along the same lines, don't touch a hand if the cards are dealt faceup. Use the hand signals to tell the dealer that you stand or that you want a hit. Never move your cards below the level of the table, where the dealer can't see them. When you brush your cards for a hit, do so lightly so that the dealer won't think that you are trying to mark them by bending them.

5. Take your time and count your cards correctly. The pace of the game in the casino can pick up to a speed that is difficult for a beginner. It's perfectly all right to take your time and recount after a hit. One hint: count aces as 1 first, then add 10 to your total. An ace and a 4 is equal to 5 or 15. Once you have this notion in your head, you won't make a mistake and refrain from hitting a soft hand. If you throw down an ace, a 10, and a 9 in disgust, for example, many dealers will simply pick up your cards and your bet, even though your 20 might have been a winning hand. If you are confused about your total, do not be embarrassed to ask for help.

6. Know the denomination of the chips that you are betting. Stack them according to denomination, and read the face value every play until you know for sure which chips are which color. Otherwise you might think you are betting $5 when you are actually throwing out a $25 chip on every hand.

7. Be obvious with your hand signals to the dealer. The casinos are loud and busy, and the dealer may be distracted with another player. Don't leave any room for misinterpretation. If some problem does arise, stop the game immediately; the dealer will summon a boss to mediate.

8. If cards fly off the table during the deal, pick them up slowly using two fingers. See number four, above.

9. Tip the dealer at your discretion if he or she has been friendly and helpful. One of the better ways to tip the dealer is to bet a chip for him on your next hand and say, "This one is for you." If you win, so does he. Never tip when a dealer has been rude or cost you money by being uncooperative. Then you should finish your hand and leave. Period.

CRAPS

OF ALL THE GAMES OFFERED IN CASINOS, craps is by far the fastest and, to many, the most exciting. It is a game in which large amounts of money can be won or lost in a short amount of time. The craps table is a circus of sound and movement. Yelling and screaming are allowed—

even encouraged—here, and the frenetic betting is bewildering to the uninitiated. Don't be intimidated, however; the basic game of craps is easy to understand. The confusion and insanity of craps have more to do with the pace of the game and the amazing number of betting possibilities than with the complexity of the game itself.

The Basic Game

Because it is so easy to become confused at a crowded and noisy craps table, we highly recommend that beginning players study this section, read a more detailed book, and take advantage of the free lessons offered by most of the casinos. Once you understand the game, you will be able to make the most favorable bets and ignore the rest.

In craps, one player at a time controls the dice, but all players will eventually have an opportunity to roll or refuse the dice. Players take turns in a clockwise rotation. If you don't want the dice, shake your head, and the dealer will offer them to the next player.

All the players around the table are wagering either with or against the shooter, so the numbers he throws will determine the amount won or lost by every other player. The casino is covering all bets, and the players are not allowed to bet among themselves. Four casino employees run the craps table. The boxman in the middle is in charge of the game. His job is to oversee the other dealers, monitor the play, and examine the dice if they are thrown off the table.

There are two dealers, one placed on each side of the boxman. They pay off the winners and collect the chips from the losers. Each dealer is in charge of half of the table.

The fourth employee is the stickman, so called because of a flexible stick he uses after each roll to retrieve the dice. His job, among other things, is to supply dice to the shooter and to regulate the pace of the game. When all bets are down, the stickman pushes several sets of dice toward the shooter. The shooter selects two dice, and the stickman removes the others from the table. Occasionally the stickman and boxman check the dice for signs of tampering.

The shooter then throws the dice hard enough to cause them to bounce off the wall at the far end of the table. This bounce ensures that each number on each die has an equal probability of coming up.

THE PLAY When it is your turn to throw the dice, pick out two and return the other to the stickman. After making a bet (required), you may throw the dice. You retain control of the dice until you throw a 7 ("seven out") or relinquish the dice voluntarily.

Your first roll, called the come-out roll, is the most important. If you roll a 7 or an 11 on your come-out roll, you are an immediate winner. In this case, you collect your winnings and retain possession of the dice. If your come-out roll is a 4, 5, 6, 8, 9, or 10, that number becomes "the point." A marker (called a puck or buck) is placed in the correspondingly numbered box on the layout to identify the point

the craps table

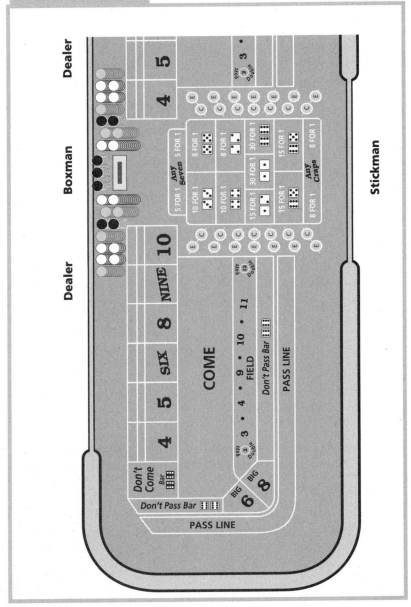

ACTUAL-ODDS CHART		
Number	Ways to roll	Odds against repeat
4	3	2–1
5	4	3–2
6	5	6–5
8	5	6–5
9	4	3–2
10	3	2–1

for all players at the table. In order to win the game, this number (the point) will have to be rolled again before you roll a 7.

Thus, if you roll a 5 on your first roll, the number five becomes your point. It doesn't matter how long it takes you to roll another 5, as long as you don't roll a 7 first. As soon as you roll a 7, you lose, and the dice are passed to another player.

Let's say 5 is your point, and your second roll is a 4, your third roll is a 9, and then you roll another 5. You win because you rolled a 5 again without rolling a 7. Because you have not yet rolled a 7, you retain possession of the dice, and after making a bet, you may initiate a new game.

Your next roll is, once again, a come-out roll. Just as 7 or 11 are immediate winners on a come-out roll, there are immediate losers, too. A roll of 2, 3, or 12 (all called "craps") will lose. You lose your chips, but you keep the dice because you have not yet rolled a 7.

If your first roll is 2, for example, it's craps, and you lose your bet. You place another bet and roll to come-out again. This time you roll a 5, so 5 becomes your point. Your second roll is a 4, your third is a 9, and then you roll a 7. The roll of 7 means that you lose and the dice will be passed to the next player.

This is the basic game of craps. The confounding blur of activity is nothing more than players placing various types of bets with or against the shooter, or betting that a certain number will or will not come up on the next roll of the dice.

THE BETTING Of the dozens of bets that can be made at a dice table, only two or three should even be considered by a novice crap player. Keeping your bets simple makes it easier to understand what's going on, while at the same time minimizing the house advantage. Exotic, long-shot bets, offering payoffs as high as 30 to 1, are sucker bets and should be avoided.

The line bets: pass and don't pass Pass and don't pass bets combine simplicity with one of the smallest house advantages of any casino game, about 1.4%. If you bet pass, you are betting that the first roll will be a 7 or 11 or a point number, and that the shooter will make the point again before he rolls a 7. If you bet don't pass, you are betting that the first roll will be a 2, 3, or 12, or, if a point is established, that the shooter

---

HOW NOT TO SHOOT CRAPS

On a recent visit to a downtown casino, one *Unofficial Guide* researcher pleaded with a Las Vegas friend to teach her how to play craps. Our Vegas friend not only outlined the basics, he also rattled off descriptions of all the various side bets and offered advice on when each was appropriate. By the time the lady was handed the dice, she was so apprehensive about remembering the rules that she forgot to pay attention to her throw. She hurled the dice with all her might right into a stack of chips in front of the boxman, scattering the house chips all over the table. The boxman and dealers sighed in annoyance but didn't complain as they put the table back in order. The other players were not pleased, however. And it only got worse when the flustered lady threw again, this time so worried about the boxman that she overthrew the table entirely, striking another player in the chest with the dice. Shortly after that, it was decided that she'd best stick with slot machines.

---

will seven out and throw a 7 before he rolls his point number again. The 2 and 3 are immediate losers, and the casino will collect the chips of anyone betting pass. A roll of 12, however, is considered a standoff ("push") where the shooter "craps out" but no chips change hands for the "don't" bettor. Almost 90% of casino crap players confine their betting to the pass and don't-pass line.

Come and don't come Come and don't-come bets are just like pass and don't-pass bets, except that they are placed *after* the point has been established on the come-out roll. Pass and don't-pass bets must be placed before the first roll of the dice, but come and don't-come bets may be placed before any roll of the dice *except* come-out rolls. On his come-out roll, let's say, the shooter rolls a 9. Nine becomes the shooter's point. If at this time you place your chips in the come box on the table, the next roll of the dice will determine your "come number." If the shooter throws a 6, for example, your chips are placed in the box marked with the large 6. The dealer will move your chips and will keep track of your bet. If the shooter rolls another 6 before he rolls a 7, your bet pays off. If the shooter sevens out before he rolls a 6, then you lose. If the shooter makes his point (that is, rolls another 9), your come bet is retained on the layout.

If you win a come bet, the dealer will place your chips from the numbered box back into the come space and set your winnings beside it. You may leave your chips there for the next roll or you may remove them entirely. If you fail to remove your winnings before the next roll, they may become a bet that you didn't want to make.

Don't-come bets are the opposite of come bets. A 7 or 11 loses, and a 2 or 3 wins. The 12 is again a push. The don't-come bettor puts his chips in the don't-come space on the table and waits for the next roll to determine his number. His chips are placed *above* the numbered box to differentiate it from a come bet. If the shooter rolls his point number before he rolls your number, your don't-come bet is retained on the layout. You are betting against the shooter; that is, that he will roll a 7 first. When he rolls 7, you win. If he rolls your don't-come number before he sevens out, you lose.

The come and don't-come bets have a house advantage of about 1.4% and are among the better bets in craps once you understand them.

Odds bets When you bet the pass/don't pass or the come/don't come, you may place an odds bet *in addition* to your original bet.

Once it is established that the come-out roll is not a 7 or 11, or craps, the bettor may place a bet that will be paid off according to the actual odds of a particular number being thrown.

Note that the Actual-odds Chart shows the chances against a number made by two dice being thrown. For example, the odds of making a 9 are three to two. If you place an odds bet (in addition to your original bet) on a come number of 9, your original come bet will pay off at even money, but your odds bet will pay off at three to two.

Because this would make a $7.50 payoff for a $5 bet, and the tables don't carry 50-cent chips, you are allowed to place a $6 bet as an odds bet. This is a very good bet to make, and betting the extra dollar is to your advantage.

To place an odds bet on a line bet, bet the pass line. When (and if) the point is established, put your additional bet behind the pass line and say, "Odds."

To place an odds bet on a come bet, wait for the dealer to move your chips to the come number box, then hand him more chips and say, "Odds." He will set these chips half on and half off the other pile so that he can see at a glance that it's an odds bet.

Etiquette of Craps

When you arrive at a table, find an open space and put your cash down in front of you. When the dealer sees it, he will pick it up and hand it to the boxman. The boxman will count out the correct chips and give them to the dealer, who will pass them to you.

A craps table holds from 12 to 20 players and can get very crowded. Keep your place at the table. Your chips are in front of you, in the rail and on the table, and it is your responsibility to watch them.

After you place your bets, your hands must come off the table. It is very bad form to leave your hands on the table when the dice are rolling.

Stick to the good bets listed here, and don't be tempted by bets that you don't understand. The box in the middle of the layout, for example, offers a number of sucker bets.

BACCARAT

ORIGINALLY AN ITALIAN CARD GAME, baccarat (bah-kah-rah) is the French pronunciation of the Italian word for "zero," which refers to the value of all the face cards in the game.

Because baccarat involves no player decisions, it is an easy game to play, yet a very difficult game to understand. Each player must decide to make a bet on either the bank or the player. That's it. There are no more

BACCARAT RULES

Player

When first two cards total

1, 2, 3, 4, 5, or 10	*Draws a card*
6 or 7	*Stands*
8 or 9	*A natural—stands*

Banker

Having	Draws when player's third card is	Does not draw when player's third card is
3	1, 2, 3, 4, 5, 6, 7, 9, 10	8
4	2, 3, 4, 5, 6, 7	1, 8, 9, 10
5	4, 5, 6, 7	1, 2, 3, 8, 9, 10
6	6, 7	1, 2, 3, 4, 5, 8, 9, 10
7	*Stands*	*Stands*
8 or 9	*Stands*	*Stands*

decisions until the next hand is dealt. The rules of playing out the hands are ridiculously intricate, but beginning players need not concern themselves with them, because all plays are predetermined by the rules, and the dealer will tell you exactly what happened.

All cards, ace through 9, are worth their spots (the 3 of clubs is worth three). The 10, jack, queen, and king are worth zero. The easiest way to count at baccarat is to add all card totals in the hand, then take only the number in the ones column.

If you have been dealt a 6 and a 5, then your total is 11, and taking only the ones column, your hand is worth 1 point. If you hold a 10 and a king, your hand is worth zero. If you have an 8 and a 7, your point total is 15, and taking the ones column, your hand is worth 5. It doesn't get any simpler than this.

In baccarat, regardless of the number of bettors at the table, only two hands are dealt: One to the player and one to the bank. The object of the game is to be dealt or draw a hand closest to nine without going over. If the first two cards dealt equal nine (a 5 and a 4, for example), then you have a natural and an automatic winner. Two cards worth eight are the second best hand and will also be called a natural. If the other hand is not equal to or higher than eight, this hand wins automatically. Ties are pushes, and neither bank nor player wins, though a longshot bet on the tie (the third wager at baccarat) does.

If the hands equal any total except nine or eight, the rules are consulted. These rules are printed and available at the baccarat table. The hands will be played out by the dealer whether you understand the rules or not.

The rules for the player's hand are simple. If a natural is not dealt to either hand, and if the player holds one, two, three, four, five, or

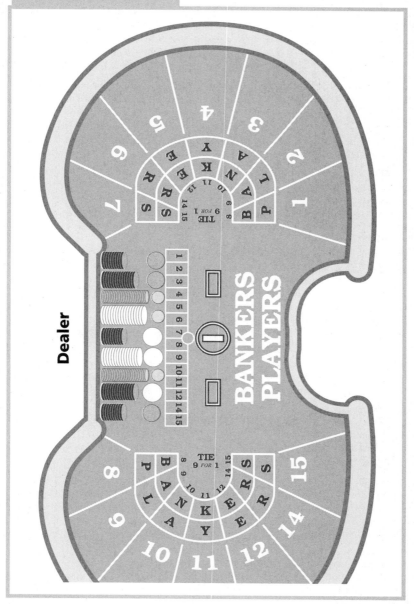

ten (zero), he will always draw a card. He will stand on a total of six or seven. A total of eight or nine, of course, will be a natural.

The bank hand is more complicated and is partially determined by the third card drawn by the player's hand. Though the rules don't say so, the bank will always draw on zero, one, or two. When the hand is worth three or more, it is subject to the printed rules.

If you study a few hands, the method of play will be clear:

FIRST HAND The player's hand is worth three, and the bank's is worth four. The player always goes first. Looking at the rules for the player, we see that a hand worth three points draws a card. This time he draws a 9, for a new total of 12 points, which has a value of two. The bank, having four points, must stand when a player draws a 9. The bank wins four to two.

SECOND HAND The player's hand is worth six points, and the bank has two queens, for a total of zero. The player must stand with six points, while the bank must draw with zero. The bank gets another card, a 4. Player wins, six to four.

The Atmosphere

The casinos try to attract players by making baccarat seem sophisticated. The section is roped off from the main casino, and the dealers are often dressed in tuxedos instead of the usual dealer's uniforms. Don't be put off by glamorous airs; everyone is welcome to play.

Because the house wants baccarat to be appealing to what they consider to be their upper-crust clientele, the table minimums are usually very high in baccarat—usually $100 to $15,000. This means that the minimum bet is $100, and the maximum bet is $15,000.

Even the shuffle and deal of the deck is designed to perpetuate the feeling of the exotic. Elaborately cut and mixed by all three dealers, the cards are cut by one player and marked with the plastic card stop. The dealer will then separate the cards at the stop, turn the top card over, and discard, or burn, the number of cards equal to the face value of the upturned card. The cards are then placed in a large holder called the shoe.

THE PLAY If the game has just begun, the shoe will be passed to the player in seat number one, who is then called the bank. Thereafter, whenever the bank hand loses, the shoe is passed counterclockwise to the next player, until it reaches seat number 15, where it is passed to seat number one again.

When all bets are down, one of the three dealers will nod to the holder of the shoe, who will then deal out four cards in alternating fashion—two for the player and two for the bank.

The player's hand is passed (still facedown) to the bettor who has wagered the most money on the player's hand. He looks at the cards and passes them back to the dealer. The dealer then turns both hands faceup and plays out the game according to the rules.

THE BETTING In baccarat, you must back either the player or the bank. You do this by putting your chips in the box in front of you marked "player" or "bank." Once the bets are down, the deal will begin.

The house advantage on baccarat is quite low: 1.36% on player wagers and 1.17% on bank bets. Because the bank bet has such an obvious advantage, the house extracts a commission when you win a bank bet. This is not collected with each hand, but must be paid before you leave the table.

MINIBACCARAT Some casinos offer a version of baccarat in the main pit, usually near the blackjack games. The tables are smaller and lower than normal baccarat tables, with each table seating seven players. The dealers dress in the standard casino floor uniform and the table minimums (and maximums) are much lower than the more common high stakes version. It's the same game with the same house advantage, except that in minibaccarat, the shoe is never passed. In fact, the dealer places the cards right-side-up on the table and the players never touch them at all. Also, the dealer is always the banker.

All of the rules of baccarat apply to the mini version: eight decks are used; face cards and 10s count as zero and aces count as one; the casino collects a 5% commission on a winning banker hand (when the player is ready to leave). The minimum bet is $10, though sometimes you can find $5 minimums. However, since there's much less ritual and fewer players, the speed of the game is very fast, so often more is bet at a $10 minibaccarat table than a $25 baccarat table.

Some experts believe that because minibaccarat lacks the atmosphere of the big table, the game loses its charm and becomes redundant and boring. That could explain why minibaccarat is one of the least popular table games in the casino.

TEXAS HOLD 'EM

POKER IS TAKING THE GAMBLING WORLD by storm, and Texas Hold 'Em is the favorite game, both in ring games (a "live" poker game where actual money is in play) and tournaments (buy-ins for tournament chips). The combination of procedures, strategy and tactics, and psychology can take a lifetime to perfect, but the rules of the game can be learned from an hour of study and another hour of practice.

We recommend studying the game, then playing the free games online at poker sites such as **www.partypoker.com** and **www.ultimate bet.com.** You should also take a lesson offered by most casino poker rooms where you play with free chips. Then, when you're ready for a live game, look for one with the lowest betting limits, such as $1 to $2 and $2 to $4. As your skills improve, you can move up in denomination, all the way to no-limit hold 'em and $25,000 buy-in tournaments. If you're just playing for fun, you'll have little to worry about in low-limit games.

The following are the basic steps in a round of Texas Hold 'Em:

There are two types of bets: blinds and antes. Antes are rare in hold 'em ring games, but they're usually imposed in the later rounds of tournaments. Blinds, a forced bet that one or more players, typically to the left of the dealer, make before any cards are dealt are always used. This starts the action on the first round of betting.

The game starts when the two players to the left of the dealer make initial bets, also known as "posting the blinds." The player to the immediate left of the dealer is the small blind; he puts up a bet equal to half the minimum limit. The player two to the left of the dealer is the big blind; his bet is equal to the lower limit. If it's a $10–$20 game, the small blind bets $5 and the big blind bets $10.

Each player is dealt two cards face down, known as hole (or pocket) cards. The first round of betting, "pre-flop," begins with the player to the left of the big blind. The betting structures can get a bit complicated, but to keep it simple, in our $10–$20 game, you'll bet $10 at a time pre-flop. You can bet four times *per betting round:* the initial bet can be "raised" by $10 three times. So if you initially bet $10, to stay in the pre-flop round, you might have to put up $30 more. "Checking" means you don't bet, but keep open your options of "calling" (betting an equal amount; not raising), raising, or folding later in the betting round. You can also "fold," which means throwing in your cards and ending your participation in the round.

At the end of the pre-flop betting rounds, the dealer "burns" (discards) the top card, then deals three cards face up on the table: "the flop." These three cards are combined with each player's two hole cards to form the initial five-card poker hand. Then there's another round of betting, starting with the player to the left of the dealer.

At the end of the post-flop betting, the dealer burns the top card, then deals one card face up on the table: "the turn." Players can now use this sixth card to improve their five-card poker hand. Another round of betting ensues. Often, this is where the betting limit doubles. So in our $10–$20 game, initial bets can be $20.

At the end of the turn betting, the dealer burns the top card, then deals one card face up on the table: "the river." Players can now combine any of the five community cards with his two pocket cards to make the best five-card hand. One more round of betting ensues, again beginning with the player to the left of the dealer.

Finally, the "showdown" occurs, when players reveal their hands. The player with the best hand wins the pot. The dealer rakes the house's cut (in a ring game), collects the cards, and another round begins.

It might sound simple, like a cousin of 7-Card Stud, but there's a lot of protocol and jargon to poker. Again, we highly recommend reading up on the game, then participating in the free tournaments at poker Web sites, before taking a lesson in a casino poker room. These steps can (and probably will) save you a certain amount of grief when you start playing for real money, even in the lowest-limit games.

KENO

KENO IS AN ANCIENT CHINESE GAME. It was used to raise money for national defense, including, some say, building the Great Wall. Keno was brought to America by the thousands of workers who came from the Far East to work on the railroads during the 1800s. It is one of the most popular games in the Nevada casinos, though it is outlawed in Atlantic City.

This game has a house advantage between 15% and 35% or more, depending on the casino—higher than any other game in Las Vegas. Too high, in fact, for serious gamblers. If you're down to your last dollar and you have to bet to save the ranch, don't go to the keno lounge.

While keno is similar to bingo, the betting options are reminiscent of exacta horse-race betting. It is like bingo in that a ticket, called a blank, is marked off and numbers are randomly selected to determine a winner. And it is similar to exacta betting because any number of fascinating betting combinations can be played in each game. The biggest difference between keno and bingo and exactas is that in the latter two, there's always a winner. In keno, hours can go by before anyone wins a substantial amount. The main excitement in keno lies in the possibility that large amounts of money can be won on a small bet.

Playing the Game

In each casino there is a keno lounge that usually resembles a college lecture hall. The casino staff sit in front while players relax in chairs with writing tables built into the arms. It is not necessary to sit in the keno lounge to play. In fact, one of the best things about keno is that it can be played almost anywhere in the casino, including the bars and restaurants. As in bingo, it is acceptable to strike up a conversation with your neighbor during a game, and because the winning numbers are posted all over the place, keno also offers the opportunity to gamble while absent from the casino floor.

Keno is one of the easiest games to understand. The keno blank can be picked up almost anywhere in any Nevada casino. On the blank are two large boxes containing 80 numbers: the top box with 1 to 40, and the bottom box with 41 to 80. Simply use one of the crayons provided with the blanks to mark between 1 and 15 (sometimes 20) numbers on the blank, decide how much you want to bet, and turn the blank in to a keno writer. The keno writer records your wager, keeping your original, and gives you a duplicate, which you are responsible for checking. The keno writer can be found at the front of the keno lounge. The keno runner is even easier to spot: she is usually a woman in a short skirt with a hand full of blanks and crayons. She will place your bets, cash in your blanks, and bring you your winnings. Of course, you are expected to tip her for this service.

The drawing of the winning numbers takes place in the keno lounge. When the keno caller has determined that the bets are in for the current round, he will close the betting just like the steward does at the racetrack. Then the caller uses a machine similar to those employed by state lotteries: a blower with numbered Ping-Pong balls. Ten balls are blown into each of two tubes. These 20 balls bear the numbers that will be called for the current round. The numbers, as called out, are posted on electronic keno boards around the casino. If any of the lighted numbers are numbers that you marked on your card, you "caught" those numbers. Catching four or more numbers will usually win something, depending on how many numbers you marked on your card. The payoffs are complicated, but the more numbers you guess correctly and the more money you bet, the greater your jackpot. Suffice it to say, however, that you are not paid at anything even approaching true odds.

If by some amazing quirk of fate you win in keno, you must claim your winnings before the next round starts, or forfeit.

THE ODDS A "straight" or basic ticket is one where the player simply selects and marks a minimum of one number to a maximum of 8 to 15 numbers, depending on the casino. The ways to combine keno bets are endless and understandable only to astrophysicists. Any number can be played with any other number, making "combination" tickets. Groups of numbers can be combined with other groups of numbers, making "way" tickets. Individual numbers can be combined with groups of numbers, making "king" tickets. Then there is the "house" ticket, called different things at each casino, which offers a shot at the big jackpot for a smaller investment, though the odds won't be any better.

All of these options and the amounts that you are allowed to bet (usually from 70 cents up per ticket) are listed in the keno brochures, which are almost as ubiquitous as the blanks. The payoffs are listed for each type of bet and for the amount wagered. Keno runners and keno lounge personnel will show you how to mark your ticket if you are confused, but they cannot mark it for you.

If you want to play keno for fun (and that is the only rational reason to play), then understand that one bet is about as bad as another. Filling out a complicated combination ticket won't increase your chances of winning. If by some miracle you do win, accept the congratulations and the winnings, and then run, do not walk, to the nearest exit.

The best strategy for winning at keno is to avoid it since the house has an unbeatable advantage.

ROULETTE

A QUIET GAME WHERE WINNERS MERELY SMILE over a big win and losers suffer in silence, roulette is very easy to understand. The dealer spins the wheel, drops the ball, and waits for it to fall into one of the numbered slots on the wheel. The numbers run from zero to 36, with a zero and double zero thrown in for good measure. You may bet on each individual number, on combinations of numbers, on all black numbers, all red numbers, and many more. All possible bets are laid out on the table.

the roulette table

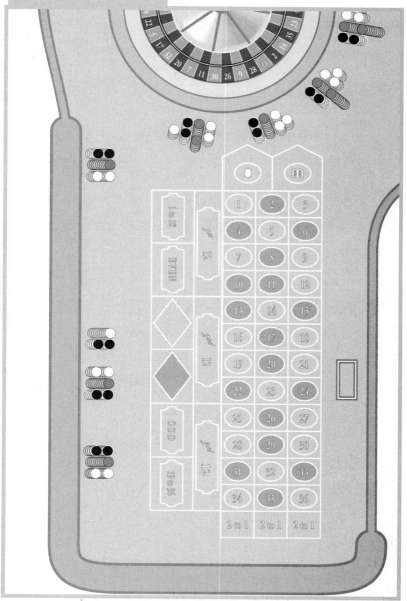

ROULETTE BET AND PAYOFF CHART

Bet	Payoff	Bet	Payoff
Single number	35 to 1	12 numbers (column)	2 to 1
Two numbers	17 to 1	1st 12, 2nd 12, 3rd 12	2 to 1
Three numbers	11 to 1	1–18 or 19–36	1 to 1
Four numbers	8 to 1	Odd or even	1 to 1
Five numbers	6 to 1	Red or black	1 to 1
Six numbers	5 to 1		

Special chips are used for roulette, with each bettor at the table playing a different color. To buy in, convert cash or the casino's house chips to roulette chips. When you are ready to cash out, the dealer will convert your special roulette chips back to house chips. If you want cash, you must then take your house chips to a casino cashier.

To place a bet, put your chips inside a numbered square or choose one of the squares off to the side. A chip placed in "1st 12," for example, will pay off if the ball drops into any number from 1 to 12. The box marked "odd" is not for eccentrics—it pays when the ball drops into an odd-numbered slot.

Roulette is fun to play, but expect to pay! The house advantage on most bets is a whopping 5.26%, and on some wagers it can be 7%.

PART FOUR

DINING *and* RESTAURANTS

DINING *in* LAS VEGAS

LAS VEGAS IS STILL "THE CITY THAT NEVER SLEEPS," but it's also the city that never stops eating. Vegas satisfies all tastes, whether simple or sophisticated. The latest trend is ethnic.

Tapas, originally the name for a wide variety of appetizers in Spanish cuisine, has been adopted conceptually by restaurants of almost every ethnicity. "The world's our oyster," proclaim such tapas stops as **Firefly** on Paradise Road and **Diego** Mexican restaurant inside the MGM Grand.

Ambience Bakery and Bistro is a French bistro that serves onion soup in a regular shouldered soup bowl, not the traditional coupe or crock. It's not billed as French onion soup and it isn't the classic, but it's OK; needs some salt and pepper to zip it up. The croissants are real, shipped in frozen containers and baked as needed. The miniature versions are super.

If you hit megabucks, try **David Burke**'s Modern American cuisine in the Venetian on restaurant row; it's terrific. Among the fun foods is a cheesecake lollipop tree. (Pass on the bubblegum whipped cream unless you're a fan of that flavor.)

The **Venetian**'s restaurant row keeps growing. Close by AquaKnox Seafood eatery is **Mario Batali.** A second Batali can be found at the Grand Canal Shoppes. Eventually Batali will open a grand dining room in the Venetian's Palazzo hotel.

Valley Cheese and Wine in Henderson is an excellent source for wine, cheese, and other delicacies. Featured are hard-to-find vintages, artisanal cheeses, a charcuterie, and wine accessories. Free wine tastings every Friday and Saturday; call ☎ 702-341-8191 for tasting times.

Macanese fare has made its way to Las Vegas via **Little Macau.** Interesting concept. Off the Strip, this 24-hour bar is connected to the adjacent Asian restaurant, **DJK Tofu,** which is open daily for lunch and dinner service.

South Point Resort is now the home of **Michael's,** previously at Barbary Coast. Same menu, same fine service. This throwback to "Old Las Vegas" is posh and plush. Decor is the same, and the Dover sole is the real thing.

The venerable **Mayflower Cuisinier** on the west side will close shortly and will become a pivotal part of the Venetian's shoppes at the Palazzo. A new name, Woo, is being considered. A January 2008 opening is anticipated. Owner Ming See Woo is touring Hong Kong in search of new ideas. As always, she'll create her own recipes.

Wolfgang Puck's Fine Dining Group will re-create his Beverly Hills steak house **Cut** in the Venetian's Palazzo wing. This is another coup for Palazzo. Better than ever...

Hugo's Cellar in the Four Queens downtown has been spruced up and looks great. Prices remain the same. Same general manager and wine director. The salad cart still comes to the table.

SO MANY RESTAURANTS, SO LITTLE TIME

DINING OPTIONS IN LAS VEGAS, as noted above, have been shaped by the marketing strategies of the casinos. Before a gambler can wager any money, the casino has to get him through the front door. If what it takes are $5 steaks, buffets, and $1 shrimp cocktails, that's what the casino does. For those more attracted to eating than to gambling, this is a great boon to mankind.

unofficial **TIP**
Locals and visitors are making their way to Red Rock Resort owned by Station Casinos. Chow down here at the pricey **T-Bones Chop House; The Salt Lick,** a genuine Texas barbecue; an Italian restaurant; a smashing buffet; and a terrific 24/7 cafe. The Creole-styled oyster bar, **Tides,** is already a locals hangout.

Although there are hundreds of restaurants in Las Vegas, you will be able to sample only a handful during your stay. But which ones? Our objective in this section is to point you to specific restaurants that meet your requirements in terms of quality, price, location, and environment. No beating around the bush.

BUFFETS

BUFFETS, USED BY THE CASINOS TO LURE customers, have become a Las Vegas institution. Like everything else, they come, go, and are upgraded or remodeled, but on average there are around 40 to choose from. The majority of casinos operate their buffets at close to cost or at a slight loss. A few casinos, mostly those with a more captive clientele (like the Las Vegas Hilton, Excalibur, and Green Valley Ranch), and the new breed of upscale spreads (Bellagio, Paris, Planet Hollywood, Wynn Las Vegas) probably make money on their buffets. **Café Lago,** the 24-hour "resort café" located in Caesars Palace ("coffee shop" is no longer hip), also serves up a small buffet.

Cravings, the buffet concept at the Mirage, was designed by Adam Tihany. He counts among his credits Charlie Palmers' Aureole at Mandalay Bay, with its eight-story wine tower. Cravings transcends

Buffet-speak

Action format	Food cooked to order in full view of the patrons
Gluttony	A Las Vegas buffet tradition that carries no moral stigma
Groaning board	Synonym for a buffet; a table so full that it groans
Island	Individual serving area for a particular cuisine or specialty (salad island, dessert island, Mexican island, etc.)
Shovelizer	Diner who prefers quantity over quality
Fork lift	A device used to remove shovelizers
Sneeze guards	The plastic barriers between you and the food

typical buffet ambience, with marble counters and stations that are self-contained "mini-restaurants," with chefs that cook food to order. Prices are midrange. **The Buffet** at Wynn Las Vegas and **The Buffet** at T. I. are similar.

Almost all of the buffets serve breakfast, lunch, and dinner, changing their menus to some extent every day. Prices for breakfast range from less than $5 (Terrible's) to $18 (Wynn). Lunch goes for $7 (Arizona Charlie's) to $22 (Wynn), with dinner ranging between $9 (Palace Station) and $36 (Bellagio). Because most buffets operate as an extension of sales and marketing, there is not necessarily any relationship between price and quality.

At breakfast, relatively speaking, there is not much difference between one buffet and the next (exceptions are the standout breakfast buffets at the **Orleans, Paris, Bellagio, The Mirage,** and **Wynn Las Vegas**). If your hotel has a breakfast buffet, it is probably not worth the effort to go somewhere else. When it comes to lunch and dinner, however, some buffets do a significantly better job than others.

If you are looking for upscale gourmet-quality food and a large variety to choose from, head straight for our top four buffets. If you're hankering for well-seasoned meats and vegetables, ethnic variety, and culinary activity, the other six will suffice nicely.

Our top choice of Las Vegas buffets is The Buffet at Wynn Las Vegas. The Wynn is also the most expensive, at $18 for breakfast, $22 for lunch, and $34 for dinner. But it's worth it. The dining area is expansive and separated into alcoves, so it's almost quiet, unlike the din at most buffets. And the food is as fresh as possible, with upscale selections such as tuna poke, octopus, pasta with Kobe meatballs, big bowls of berries, rack of lamb, king crab, and steaks.

The Red Rock Feast is the newest in town. It is a cut above the usual local super buffet, with excellent sushi and scooped ice cream.

The **Spice Market Buffet** drops a few notches, a victim of the switchover from Aladdin to Planet Hollywood. Still, it blends quality, variety, and a surprisingly attractive and cozy setting. There are Italian, Mexican, American, Middle Eastern (grape leaves, hummus, couscous, and carved

LAS VEGAS'S TEN BEST BUFFETS

RANK	BUFFET	QUALITY RATING	LAST YEAR'S RATING
1.	Wynn Buffet	99	2
2.	Bellagio Buffet	98	3
3.	Paris Le Village Buffet	97	4
4.	Planet Hollywood Spice Market Buffet	95	1
5.	Mirage Cravings Buffet	94	8
6.	Rio Carnival World Buffet	93	5
7.	Red Rock Feast	92	7
8.	Green Valley Ranch Feast	91	6
9.	Texas Station Feast	88	9
10.	Orleans French Market Buffet	87	10

unofficial **TIP**
Dishes Buffet at T. I. has changed its name to **The Buffet at T. I.** The Saturday and Sunday Champagne Brunch is a great value.

lamb), and seafood (cold king crab is the specialty) serving stations, plus salads, desserts, and breads. Everything is fresh, tasty, and well stocked. The **Planet Hollywood** buffet is also a couple of bucks less expensive than the gourmet spread at the Bellagio and $9 less than at the Wynn.

Texas Station's Feast Around the World Buffet is the best of the "bargain super buffets." The room is spacious and efficient, the choices are manifold, and the prices are among the lowest in town. In addition to the Planet Hollywood and Texas Station, **Paris, Rio, Gold Coast, Sunset Station, Green Valley Ranch, Main Street Station, Fiesta Rancho, Fiesta Henderson, Harrah's, Orleans, Cannery, Mirage,** and **Bellagio** all have the new-style "super buffets." The Rio started the craze in 1993 with its huge room, action cooking, and separate serving islands for a vast variety of ethnic choices: American, Italian, Chinese, Mexican, and Mongolian barbecue, along with sushi, fish-and-chips, pizza, burgers, salads, and desserts. The Rio completely remodeled and upgraded **The Carnival World** in 2004. **Planet Hollywood** has an excellent Middle Eastern station; the Palms' one is decent.

The **Fiesta Rancho Festival Buffet** is not as sprawling and various as the Rio's, but it has a monster rotisserie for barbecuing every kind of flesh known to man, specialty Cajun and Hawaiian selections, and the first and only coffee bar in a Las Vegas buffet, serving espresso, cappuccino, and latte. **Texas Station** introduced a chili bar with nine selections and cooked-to-order fajitas; it also has good barbecue, Chinese, Italian, and lots of pizza. **Paris** has a made-to-order crepe station, and the **Rio** has an Asian soup station.

Now that the **Wynn** is on the scene, **Bellagio** is the second-most-expensive super buffet—but it too is worth every penny. The quality, quantity, and variety of food are unsurpassed in Las Vegas history. Seafood galore, bread warm from the oven, creative salads, gourmet entrees, perfect vegetables—this joint has it all. Even at $15 for breakfast, $20 for lunch, and $28 for dinner ($36 Friday and Saturday), the Bellagio buffet barely breaks even. For the money, we like lunch here better than dinner.

Main Street Station is the only super buffet downtown, served in one of the most aesthetically pleasing buffet rooms in town. Its cuisine has a distinct Hawaiian emphasis, which is where most of its patrons come from.

Harrah's buffet gets an A for effort, a B for quality, and a C for value. **Mandalay Bay**'s buffet is expensive and odd; it's small, congested, and slow—there's something off about it. But **Boulder Station, Green Valley Ranch,** and **Sunset Station,** along with **MGM Grand** and **Luxor,** are tried-and-true; you won't go wrong at any of these.

The buffet at **Paris** has an interesting setup. The different stations represent different regions of France, and the dining room has several intimate dining nooks and a view as well. Best of all, there's virtually no waiting. You check in with the host or hostess, they tell you when a table will be available, take your name, and you are free to explore until the designated time. When you return, a table is actually ready.

As a footnote, **Bellagio, Main Street Station, Paris, Planet Hollywood, Sam's Town,** the **Flamingo, Caesars Palace,** the **Mirage, Fiesta Henderson,** the **Golden Nugget, Sunset Station,** the **MGM Grand,** and **T. I.** provide the most attractive settings for their buffets. The buffets at the **Rio, Fiesta Rancho, Arizona Charlie's Decatur,** and **Texas, Palace, Sunset,** and **Boulder Stations** are the favorites of Las Vegas locals.

Seafood Buffets

Several casinos feature seafood buffets on Friday and sometimes on other days. The best of the seafood buffets is **Rio's Village Seafood Buffet** (daily). The **Orleans**'s seafood night is Monday, the **Fremont**'s is on Sunday, Tuesday, and Friday, and **Main Street Station**'s is on Friday and Saturday. The **Golden Nugget**'s good one is on Friday, Saturday, and Sunday. Other worthwhile ocean spreads include those at the **Cannery** (Thursday), **Rampart** (Thursday), and **Suncoast** (Friday).

Rio's Village Seafood Buffet is the most expensive buffet, at $37, but the quality and variety of this piscatory repast are unbelievable, even for Las Vegas. Check it out: small lobster tails (dinner), peel-and-eat shrimp, Dungeness crab legs, Manila steamers, and oysters on the half shell; seafood salads, chowders, and Mongolian grill; plus Italian, Mexican, and Chinese dishes, along with fried, grilled, broiled, breaded, blackened, beer-battered, and barbecued preparations. And if you have even a millimeter of stomach space left after the main courses, the dessert selection is outstanding.

Buffet-line Strategy

Popular buffets develop long lines. The best way to avoid the crowds is to go Sunday through Thursday and get in line before 6 p.m. or after 9 p.m. If you go to a buffet on a weekend, arrive extra early or extra late. If a large trade show or convention is in town, you will be better off any day hitting the buffets of casinos that do not do a big convention business. Good choices among the highly ranked buffets include **Texas Station,** the two **Fiestas, Main Street Station, Boulder Station, Gold Coast, Orleans, Suncoast,** and the **Fremont.**

Some restaurants now use pagers to let diners know when their table is available. This gives you a bit more freedom to roam around while you wait, but many pagers have a fairly small range.

CHAMPAGNE BRUNCHES

UPSCALE, EXPENSIVE SUNDAY CHAMPAGNE BRUNCHES with reserved tables, imported Champagne, sushi, and seafood are making an impact on the local brunch scene. Although there are a plethora of value-priced Champagne brunches, the big-ticket feasts attract diners who are happy to pay a higher tab for fancy food and service at a place that takes reservations so they can avoid a wait. In general, the higher the price of the brunch, the better the Champagne served. **Bally's, Circus Circus,** and the **MGM** serve decent French Champagne; California sparkling wine is the norm at the others. Reservations are accepted at all of the following:

- **Broiler Brunch** Boulder Station; ☎ 702-432-7777
  Brunch at The Broiler restaurant at Boulder Station has been a sleeper for years. Here, you order your entree (eggs Benedict, crab cakes, shrimp, prime rib, lamb) off the menu, which a server brings to the table, then help yourself to buffet offerings, such as salads, cold crab legs, ham, and prime rib, and made-to-order omelets and potato pancakes. $19.99 adults, $14.99 children ages 3 to 12. Available Saturday and Sunday, 10 a.m. to 2:30 p.m.; Monday to Friday, 11:30 a.m. to 2 p.m.

- **Gospel Brunch** House of Blues, Mandalay Bay; ☎ 702-632-7777
  "Praise the Lord and pass the biscuits!" This is the most raucous and joyous Sunday brunch in town. A five-member group belts out the gospel tunes, and the food is soulful as well: fried chicken, skillet cornbread, jambalaya, turnip greens, made-to-order omelets, ham and prime rib, bagels and lox, smoked salmon, and banana-bread pudding. Purchase tickets at The House of Blues box office: adults, $40 advance, $42 in person; children ages 3 to 11, $21. Available 10 a.m. to 1 p.m.

- **The Steak House** Circus Circus; ☎ 702-794-3767
  Elaborate ice carvings and decorative food displays are a tribute to the chef's cruise-line background. Featured are many breakfast items, steak and seafood, entrees, and salads. Adults, $33 (all-inclusive); children ages 6 to 14, $20. Three seatings: 9 a.m., 11:30 a.m., and 1:30 p.m.

- **Sterling Brunch** Bally's Steakhouse; ☎ 702-967-7999
  The Sterling Brunch was the first of its kind. At $65 per person, plus tax (children ages 5 to 8, $32.50 plus tax), it's also the most costly, but there's no shortage of diners who love it, even at more than double its original price. The lavish selection of foods includes a host of breakfast items, freshly made sushi, real lobster salad, raw and cooked seafood, caviar, and French Champagne. Pheasant and rack of lamb appear regu-

larly. The dessert selection is awesome. Entree selections change weekly. Available 9:30 a.m. to 2:30 p.m.; reservations are required.

Bally's Sterling Brunch, though quite expensive, is by far the best brunch in town and, in our opinion, a fair value for the money if you are a big eater. Other good brunches include **Bellagio, Mirage, Planet Hollywood, Gold Coast,** and **Main Street Station** (the best bargain brunch at $10).

MEAL DEALS

IN ADDITION TO BUFFETS, MANY CASINOS offer special dining deals, including New York strip, T-bone, and porterhouse steaks, prime rib, crab legs, shrimp cocktails, and combinations of the foregoing, all available at giveaway prices. There are also breakfast specials.

While the meal deals generally deliver what they promise in the way of an entree, many of the extras that contribute to a quality dining experience are missing. With a couple of notable exceptions, the specials are served in big, bustling restaurants with the atmosphere of a high-school cafeteria. Eating at closely packed Formica tables under lighting bright enough for brain surgery, it's difficult to pretend that you're engaged in fine dining.

Our biggest complaint, however, concerns the lack of attention paid to the meal as a whole. We have had nice pieces of meat served with tired, droopy salads, stale bread, mealy microwaved potatoes, and unseasoned canned vegetables. How can you get excited about your prime rib when it is surrounded by the ruins of Pompeii?

Deke Castleman, coauthor of this book and writer for the *Las Vegas Advisor,* doesn't believe that discount dining is about food at all. He writes:

Of course you're entitled to your opinion, and I'll fight to the death for your right to express it. But 'quality dining experience' is not really what Las Vegas visitors, IMHO, are looking for when they pursue a $3 steak, a $5 prime rib, or a $10 lobster. To me what they're after is twofold: A very cheap steak, prime rib, or lobster, and damn the salad, vegetable, and Formica; and to take home a cool story about all the rock-bottom prices they paid for food.

Finally, it's hard to take advantage of many of the specials. They are offered only in the middle of the night, or alternatively you must stand in line for an hour waiting for a table, or eat your evening meal at 3:30 in the afternoon. In restaurants all over town, in and out of the casinos, there is plenty of good food served in pleasant surroundings at extremely reasonable prices. In our opinion, saving $5 on a meal is not worth all the hassle.

Because Las Vegas meal deals often come and go, it is impossible to cover them adequately in a book that is revised annually. If you want to stay abreast of special dinner offerings, your best bet is to subscribe to the *Las Vegas Advisor,* a monthly newsletter that provides independent, critical evaluations of meal deals, buffets, brunches, and drink specials.

The *Las Vegas Advisor* can be purchased by calling ☎ 800-244-2224. If you are already in town and want to pick up the latest edition, single copies are available at the **Gamblers Book Club** store at 630 South 11th Street, ☎ 702-382-7555 or 800-522-1777; **www.gamblersbook.com.**

STEAK Though specials constantly change, there are a few that have weathered the test of time. Our favorite is the 16-ounce porterhouse steak dinner at the **Redwood Bar & Grill** in the California, ☎ 702-385-1222. A complete dinner, including relish plate, soup or salad, and steak with excellent accompanying potatoes and vegetables, can be had for about $18, excluding drinks, taxes, and tips. What's more, it is served in one of the most attractive dining rooms in Las Vegas. The porterhouse special, incidentally, does not appear on the menu. You must ask for it.

There's a great 16-ounce T-bone served in the coffee shop of the Gold Coast 24 hours a day for $11, ☎ 702-367-7111. This big slab is accompanied by soup or salad, potatoes, onion rings, baked beans, garlic bread, and a glass of draft beer. For $11 this would be a deal *without* the steak.

Ellis Island, attached to the Super 8 motel on Koval Lane near East Flamingo Road, serves an excellent $5 steak dinner complete with rolls, salad, baked potato, and vegetable. It's available 24 hours, but it's not on the menu, so you have to ask for it. **The Hard Rock Hotel** has a steak-and-shrimp "Gambler's Special," served 24 hours in the coffee shop for $7.77, ☎ 702-693-5000.

PRIME RIB One of the best prime-rib specials in a town full of prime-rib specials is available at the **California** downtown, where you can get a good cut of meat between 5 p.m. and 11 p.m. for $7; it comes with an all-you-can eat salad bar and cherries jubilee for dessert.

For $22 more you can dine in comparative luxury with much less effort at **Sir Galahad's** at the Excalibur, ☎ 702-597-7448. The prime rib is excellent and served tableside in huge slabs, accompanied by fresh salad or soup and excellent side dishes, including Yorkshire pudding. There is no hassle about getting a table if you arrive by 6:30 p.m.

Jerry's Nugget on Las Vegas Boulevard in North Las Vegas has a trio of prime-rib meal deals for $9, $15, and $30 (for the biggest piece of beef you've ever seen), ☎ 702-399-3000.

LOBSTER AND CRAB LEGS Lobster-and-steak (surf-and-turf) combos and crab-leg deals appear regularly on casino marquees around Las Vegas. **Pasta Pirate** at the California serves the best all-around shellfish specials, ☎ 702-385-1222. Unfortunately, they are on-again, off-again. When on, they alternately feature a steak and lobster combo, a lobster dinner, or a king crab dinner, all for $12 to $22, not including tax or gratuity. Entrees are served with soup or salad, pasta, veggies, garlic bread, and wine. The setting is relaxed and pleasant. Reservations are accepted.

Lobster and crab leg meal deals, though common in the past, are now few and far between. The best place for king crab legs is at the gourmet buffets. **Planet Hollywood, Wynn Las Vegas,** and **Bellagio** serve all-you-can-eat cold king crab nightly; at Bellagio, you can make up a plate and ask a server to heat up the legs in a warmer in the kitchen.

Beware lobster deals. The lobster is almost always rubbery or mushy or just plain bad. Cheap lobsters in Las Vegas are history.

SHRIMP COCKTAILS Shrimp cocktails at nominal prices are frequently used to lure gamblers into the casinos. Usually the shrimp are small (bay shrimp) and are served in cocktail sauce in a tulip glass. The best and cheapest (99 cents) shrimp cocktail can be found at the **Golden Gate,** a small downtown casino, which has been serving this special for nearly 50 years. Other contenders are the **Four Queens, Arizona Charlie's,** and the **Riviera.**

PASTA AND PIZZA The **Pasta Pirate** at the California offers some of the best designer pasta dishes in town. The best play is to hit up pizza "satellite" outlets (fast-food counters attached to the Italian restaurants) at Boulder Station and Sunset Station for a quickie slice. You can also get a good slice of New York–style pizza at **Sports Kitchen** at the Rio. At the Palms fast-food court is **Famiglia,** well known in New York. And the Red Rock food court has **Villa Pizza,** a locals' favorite.

BREAKFAST SPECIALS The two best ham-and-eggs specials are found at the **Gold Coast** and **Arizona Charlie's Decatur** and **Boulder.** All are the best ham-and-eggs breakfasts you'll ever eat, even at three times the price. Arizona Charlie's Decatur also has a decent steak-and-eggs deal for $2.99. The little **Wild Wild West** casino at Tropicana and Dean Martin Drive (formerly Industrial Road) has the best $1.99 bacon and eggs. Other worthwhile breakfast deals include the buffets at **Sam's Town,** the **Orleans,** and the **Rio.**

THE RESTAURANTS

OUR FAVORITE LAS VEGAS RESTAURANTS

WE HAVE DEVELOPED DETAILED PROFILES for the best restaurants (in our opinion) in town. Each profile features an easily scanned heading that allows you, in just a second, to check out the restaurant's name, cuisine, Overall Rating, cost category, Quality Rating, and Value Rating.

OVERALL RATING The Overall Rating encompasses the entire dining experience, including style, service, and ambiance, in addition to taste, presentation, and food quality. Five stars is the highest rating possible and connotes the best of everything. Four-star restaurants are exceptional, and three-star restaurants are well above average. Two-star restaurants are good. One star is used to denote an average restaurant that demonstrates an unusual capability in some area of specialization—for example, an otherwise immemorable place that has great barbecued chicken.

The Best Las Vegas Restaurants

NAME	OVERALL RATING	PRICE RATING	QUALITY RATING	VALUE RATING
ADVENTURES IN DINING				
8-0-8 (Hawaiian/French)	★★★½	Expensive	★★★★	★★½
Emeril's (New Orleans)	★★★½	Expensive	★★★½	★★★½
Marrakech (Moroccan)	★★½	Moderate	★★★½	★★★½
AMERICAN				
Craftsteak	★★★★½	Expensive	★★★★½	★★★
Aureole	★★★★½	Very Exp	★★★★½	★★½
Bradley Ogden	★★★★	Expensive	★★★★½	★★½
David Burke	★★★★	Mod/Exp	★★★★½	★★★½
Simon Kitchen & Bar	★★★★	Moderate	★★★★½	★★½
Spago	★★★★	Mod/Exp	★★★★½	★★½
Wolfgang Puck Bar & Grill	★★★★	Mod/Exp	★★★★	★★★★½
Rosemary's Restaurant	★★★★	Expensive	★★★★	★★½
Lucille's Smokehouse Bar-B-Que	★★★½	Moderate	★★★★	★★★★½
Olives	★★★½	Mod/Exp	★★★★	★★★½
Neros	★★★½	Expensive	★★★★	★★½
Redwood Bar & Grill	★★★½	Moderate	★★★½	★★★★½
Table 34	★★★½	Moderate	★★★½	★★★½
Lawry's The Prime Rib	★★★½	Expensive	★★★½	★★½
Grape Street Café	★★★	Moderate	★★★½	★★★½
Hugo's Cellar	★★★	Expensive	★★★½	★★★½
Red Square	★★★	Mod/Exp	★★★½	★★½
Top of the World	★★★	Expensive	★★★	★★½
Kathy's Southern Cooking	★★½	Moderate	★★★½	★★★★½
ASIAN/PACIFIC RIM				
Ah Sin	★★★½	Moderate	★★★★½	★★★½
China Spice	★★★½	Mod/Exp	★★★★	★★★★½
China Grill	★★★½	Mod/Exp	★★★½	★★★½
BARBECUE				
Lucille's Smokehouse	★★★½	Mod/Exp	★★★★	★★★★½
Memphis Championship Barbecue	★★★	Inexpensive	★★★½	★★★★½
Sam Woo Bar-B-Q	★★★	Inexp/Mod	★★★	★★★★★

NAME	OVERALL RATING	PRICE RATING	QUALITY RATING	VALUE RATING
BRAZILIAN				
Samba Brazilian Steakhouse	★★★½	Mod/Exp	★★★★	★★★½
rumjungle	★★★	Mod/Exp	★★★½	★★½
CHINESE (SEE ALSO DIM SUM)				
Mayflower Cuisinier	★★★★	Moderate	★★★★	★★★★½
Pearl	★★★★	Expensive	★★★★	★★½
China Spice	★★★½	Moderate	★★★★	★★★★½
Little Buddha	★★★½	Mod/Exp	★★★★	★★★
168 Shanghai Restaurant	★★★½	Moderate	★★★½	★★★★
Noodles	★★★	Moderate	★★★★	★★★½
CHINESE/FRENCH				
Mayflower Cuisinier	★★★★	Moderate	★★★★	★★★★½
Chinois	★★★	Moderate	★★★½	★★★½
CONTINENTAL/FRENCH				
Bouchon	★★★★½	Moderate	★★★★	★★★★
Picasso	★★★★½	Very Exp	★★★★	★★½
Alizé	★★★★	Expensive	★★★★★	★★½
Marché Bacchus/Bacchus Bistro	★★★★	Moderate	★★★★	★★★★
Andre's	★★★★	Expensive	★★★★	★★½
Mon Ami Gabi	★★★½	Mod/Exp	★★★★	★★★½
8-0-8	★★★½	Expensive	★★★★	★★½
Michael's	★★★½	Very Exp	★★★★	★★½
Fiore	★★★½	Expensive	★★★½	★★½
Pamplemousse	★★★	Moderate	★★★½	★★½
Pinot Brasserie	★★★	Moderate	★★★½	★★½
Bonjour French Restaurant	★★★	Mod/Exp	★★★	★★½
CREOLE/CAJUN				
VooDoo Steak	★★★	Expensive	★★★½	★★½
CUBAN				
Florida Café	★★★	Inexp/Mod	★★★½	★★★★½
GERMAN				
Hofbräuhaus	★★★	Moderate	★★★½	★★★★½
Café Heidelberg	★★★	Moderate	★★½	★★★½

The Best Las Vegas Restaurants (continued)

NAME	OVERALL RATING	PRICE RATING	QUALITY RATING	VALUE RATING
HAWAIIAN				
8-0-8	★★★½	Expensive	★★★★	★★½
INDIAN				
Gaylord	★★½	Mod/Exp	★★★	★½
ITALIAN				
Medici Café	★★★★	Expensive	★★★★½	★★★½
Circo	★★★★	Mod/Exp	★★★★½	★★½
Fiamma Trattoria	★★★★	Mod/Exp	★★★★	★★★½
Piero's	★★★★	Expensive	★★★★	★★½
Panevino Ristorante/ Gourmet Deli	★★★½	Mod/Exp	★★★★½	★★★½
Antonio's	★★★½	Mod/Exp	★★★★	★★★½
JR's Italian Kitchen	★★★½	Moderate	★★★½	★★★★
Trattoria del Lupo	★★★½	Mod/Exp	★★★★	★★½
Ventano	★★★½	Moderate	★★★½	★★★★½
Anna Bella	★★★½	Moderate	★★★½	★★★½
Il Fornaio	★★★½	Moderate	★★★½	★★★½
The Bootlegger Bistro	★★★	Mod/Exp	★★★½	★★★★½
Fellini's	★★★	Moderate	★★★½	★★★★½
Sazio	★★★	Moderate	★★★½	★★★★½
La Scala	★★★	Moderate	★★★	★★½
Mama Jo's	★★½	Inexp/Mod	★★★	★★½
JAPANESE (SEE ALSO SUSHI)				
Koto	★★★★	Inexp/Mod	★★★★½	★★★★★
Ah Sin	★★★½	Moderate	★★★★½	★★★½
Makino Sushi Restaurant	★★★½	Moderate	★★★★	★★★★½
Noodles	★★★	Moderate	★★★★	★★★½
Fuji	★★½	Inexp/Mod	★★★½	★★★½
Tokyo	★★½	Moderate	★★★	★★★½
KOREAN				
Koreana	★★½	Moderate	★★★★	★★½

NAME	OVERALL RATING	PRICE RATING	QUALITY RATING	VALUE RATING
LOBSTER				
Alan Albert's	★★★	Expensive	★★★½	★★½
Rosewood Grille	★★★	Mod/Exp	★★★½	★★½
MEDITERRANEAN				
Olives	★★★½	Mod/Exp	★★★★	★★★½
MEXICAN				
Isla	★★★★½	Inexpensive	★★★★	★★★★½
Lindo Michoacan	★★★½	Inexp/Mod	★★★★	★★★★
Garduño's of Mexico	★★★½	Inexp/Mod	★★★½	★★★½
Garduño's at the Palms	★★★	Inexp/Mod	★★★½	★★★½
MOROCCAN				
Marrakech	★★½	Moderate	★★★½	★★★½
PERSIAN				
Habib's	★★★	Moderate	★★★½	★★½
PRIME RIB				
Redwood Bar & Grill	★★★½	Moderate	★★★½	★★★★½
Lawry's The Prime Rib	★★★½	Expensive	★★★½	★★½
Sir Galahad's	★★★	Mod/Exp	★★★½	★★★★½
SEAFOOD				
Joe's Seafood, Prime Steak & Stone Crab	★★★★½	Expensive	★★★★½	★★★½
SeaBlue	★★★★	Mod/Exp	★★★★	★★★½
Buzios	★★★½	Mod/Exp	★★★★	★★½
Kokomo's	★★★½	Very Exp	★★★★	★★½
Emeril's New Orleans Fish House	★★★½	Expensive	★★★½	★★★½
Pasta Pirate	★★★	Mod/Exp	★★★½	★★★★½
The Tillerman	★★★	Expensive	★★★½	★★½
The Broiler	★★½	Mod/Exp	★★★½	★★★½
STEAK				
Joe's Seafood, Prime Steak & Stone Crab	★★★★½	Expensive	★★★★½	★★★½

The Best Las Vegas Restaurants (continued)

NAME	OVERALL RATING	PRICE RATING	QUALITY RATING	VALUE RATING
STEAK (CONTINUED)				
Craftsteak	★★★★½	Expensive	★★★★½	★★★
Prime	★★★★	Expensive	★★★★½	★★½
Delmonico	★★★★	Expensive	★★★★	★★½
Samba Brazilian Steakhouse	★★★½	Mod/Exp	★★★★	★★★½
Kokomo's	★★★½	Very Exp	★★★★	★★½
The Steak House	★★★½	Expensive	★★★½	★★★½
A. J.'s Steakhouse	★★★	Expensive	★★★½	★★½
Alan Albert's	★★★	Expensive	★★★½	★★½
Rosewood Grille	★★★	Mod/Exp	★★★½	★★½
Billy Bob's Steakhouse	★★★	Mod/Exp	★★★	★★★½
The Broiler	★★½	Mod/Exp	★★★½	★★★½
SUSHI (SEE ALSO JAPANESE)				
Koto	★★★★	Inexp/Mod	★★★★½	★★★★★
Makino Sushi Restaurant	★★★½	Moderate	★★★★	★★★★½
Dragon Noodle Co. and Sushi Bar	★★★½	Inexp/Mod	★★★★	★★★★
Sapporo	★★★½	Mod/Exp	★★★★	★★★★
Little Buddha	★★★½	Mod/Exp	★★★★	★★★
Chinois	★★★	Moderate	★★★½	★★★½
Tokyo	★★½	Moderate	★★★	★★★½
THAI				
Lotus of Siam	★★★★	Moderate	★★★★	★★½
Noodles	★★★	Moderate	★★★★	★★★½
VIETNAMESE				
Noodles	★★★	Moderate	★★★★	★★★½
ROOMS WITH A VIEW				
Alizé	★★★★	Expensive	★★★★★	★★½
VooDoo Steak	★★★	Expensive	★★★½	★★½
Top of the World	★★★	Mod/Exp	★★★	★★½

COST Our expense description provides a comparative sense of how much a complete meal will cost. A complete meal for our purposes consists of an entree with vegetable or side dish, and choice of soup or salad. Appetizers, desserts, drinks, and tips are excluded.

Inexpensive	$14 or less per person
Moderate	$15–$30 per person
Expensive	$30–$45 per person
Very expensive	$46 or more per person

QUALITY RATING Beneath each heading appear a quality rating and a value rating. The quality rating is based expressly on the taste, freshness of ingredients, preparation, presentation, and creativity of food served. There is no consideration of price. If you are a person who wants the best food available, and cost is not an issue, you need look no further than the quality rating. The quality ratings are defined as:

★★★★★	Exceptional quality
★★★★	Good quality
★★★	Fair quality
★★	Somewhat-subpar quality
★	Subpar quality

VALUE RATING If, on the other hand, you are looking for both quality and value, then you should check the value rating. The value ratings are a function of the overall rating, the price rating, and the quality rating:

★★★★★	Exceptional value, a real bargain
★★★★	Good value
★★★	Fair value, you get exactly what you pay for
★★	Somewhat overpriced
★	Significantly overpriced

LOCATION Next to the value rating is an area designation. This designation will give you an idea of where the restaurant described is located. For ease of use, we divide Las Vegas into seven geographic areas:

South Strip and Environs	Mid-Strip and Environs
North Strip and Environs	East of Strip
West of Strip	Downtown
Southeast Las Vegas–Henderson	

OUR PICKS OF THE BEST LAS VEGAS RESTAURANTS

BECAUSE RESTAURANTS ARE OPENING AND CLOSING all the time in Las Vegas, we have tried to confine our list to establishments with a proven track record over a fairly long period of time. Newer restaurants (and older restaurants under new management) are listed but not profiled. Those newer or changed establishments that demonstrate staying power and consistency will be profiled in subsequent editions. Also, the list is highly selective. Exclusion of a particular place does not necessarily indicate that the restaurant is not good, only that it was not ranked among the best in its genre. Note that some restaurants appear in more than one category.

MORE RECOMMENDATIONS

The Best Bagels

- **Harrie's Bagelmania** 855 East Twain Avenue (at Swenson); ☎ 702-369-3322. Baked on the premises; garlic and onion among the choices. Locals' hangout.

The Best Bakeries

- **Albina's Italian Bakery** 3035 East Tropicana Avenue in the Wal-Mart Center; ☎ 702-433-5400. Classic Italian pastries; baba au rhum, with and without custard; Italian and American cheesecakes; wide variety of cookies.
- **Chocolate Swan** Mandalay Place, 3930 South Las Vegas Boulevard, Suite 121B; ☎ 702-632-9366.
  Chocolates, pastries, cheesecakes, and frozen custard, many of which come with a wine or cordial recommendation.
- **Great Buns** 8320 West Sahara Avenue; ☎ 702-676-2022
  Commercial and retail; fragrant rosemary bread, sticky buns, and apple loaf are good choices. More than 400 varieties of breads and pastries.
- **Tintoretto** Italian bakery, Canal Shops at The Venetian Hotel; ☎ 702-414-3400. International breads, cakes, and cookies. Charming European design and a patio perfect for people-watching.

The Best Brewpubs

- **Gordon Biersch Brewpub** 3987 Paradise Road (Hughes Center); ☎ 702-312-5247. Upbeat brewery restaurant with contemporary menu and surprisingly good food at reasonable prices.
- **Monte Carlo Pub and Brewery** Monte Carlo; ☎ 702-730-7777.
  Located adjacent to the pool area in a faux-warehouse setting, this new brewpub offers six different beers and affordable food options. The beer is brewed on the premises. Eighteen different pizzas are available, as well as sandwiches, pastas, and more.
- **Triple Seven Brewpub** 200 North Main Street (Main Street Station); ☎ 702-387-1896. Late-night happy hour with bargain brews and food specials. Open 24 hours.

The Best Burgers

- **Burger Bar** Mandalay Bay Place, 3930 Las Vegas Boulevard; ☎ 702-632-9364. Burgers of every description, some outrageous.
- **Champagnes Café** 3557 South Maryland Parkway; ☎ 702-737-1699. Classic half-pounder with creative toppings.
- **Kilroy's** 1021 South Buffalo Drive (at West Charleston); ☎ 702-363-4933. Half-pound burgers, choice of 15 toppings.

Las Vegas Restaurants by Area

SOUTH STRIP AND ENVIRONS
Alan Albert's
Andre's
Aureole
Bootlegger Bistro
China Grill
Craftsteak
Dragon Noodle Co. and Sushi Bar
Emeril's New Orleans Fish House
Fiamma Trattoria
Il Fornaio
Panevino Ristorante/ Gourmet Deli
Pearl
Red Square
Rosewood Grille
rumjungle
SeaBlue
Sir Galahad's
Trattoria del Lupo
Wolfgang Puck Bar & Grill

MID STRIP AND ENVIRONS
Ah Sin
Alizé
Antonio's

Bouchon
Bradley Ogden
Buzios
Chinois
Circo
David Burke
Delmonico
8-0-8
Garduño's at the Palms
Gaylord
Isla

Joe's Seafood, Prime Steak & Stone Crab
Kokomo's
Little Buddha
Michael's
Mon Ami Gabi
Neros
Noodles
Olives
Picasso
Pinot Brasserie
Prime
Samba Brazilian Steakhouse
Spago
Trevi
VooDoo Steak

NORTH STRIP AND ENVIRONS
Café Heidelberg
Fellini's
Florida Café
Garduño's of Mexico
Piero's
The Steak House
Top of the World

EAST OF STRIP
A. J.'s Steakhouse
Hofbräuhaus
La Scala
Lawry's The Prime Rib
Lotus of Siam
Marrakech
Pamplemousse
Simon Kitchen & Bar
Tokyo

WEST OF STRIP
Fellini's
Grape Street Café
Habib's
JR's Italian Kitchen

Makino Sushi Restaurant
Mama Jo's
Marché Bacchus/ Bacchus Bistro
Mayflower Cuisinier (relocating to the Venetian January 2008)
168 Shanghai Restaurant
Rosemary's Restaurant
Sam Woo Bar-B-Q
Sapporo
Sazio

DOWNTOWN
Andre's
Hugo's Cellar
Pasta Pirate
Redwood Bar & Grill

SOUTHEAST LAS VEGAS/HENDERSON
Anna Bella
Billy Bob's Steakhouse
Bonjour French Restaurant
The Broiler
China Spice
Fellini's
Fuji
Il Fornaio
Kathy's Southern Cooking
Koreana
Koto
Lindo Michoacan
Lucille's Smokehouse Bar-B-Que
Medici Café
Memphis Championship Barbecue
Table 34
The Tillerman
Ventano

The Best Burgers (continued)

- **Lone Star**   1290 East Flamingo Road; ☎ 702-893-0348.
  1611 South Decatur Boulevard; ☎ 702-259-0105.
  210 Nellis Boulevard; ☎ 702-453-7827.
  3131 North Rainbow; ☎ 702-656-7125.
  Cheese, Bubba, Texas, Mexi, or Willie half-pounders on a toasted
  onion bun.

The Best Delis

- **Canter's Delicatessen at Treasure Island**   3300 South Las Vegas Boulevard;
  ☎ 702-894-6390. Sandwiches served on legendary sourdough rye
  bread, soups including signature barley bean, New York cheesecake, and
  a world-famous chocolate chip racetrack cake.
- **Harrie's Bagelmania**   855 East Twain (at Swenson); ☎ 702-369-3322.
  Breakfast and lunch only. Full-service bagel bakery and deli. On Tuesdays,
  buy bagels by the dozen at half price as well as pastrami and corned beef
  by the pound at half price.
- **Siena Deli**   2250 East Tropicana Avenue (at Eastern); ☎ 702-736-8424.
  Italian spoken here: everything Italian and homemade. Excellent bread
  baked every morning. Siena bakes bread for many of the area's Italian
  restaurants. Local favorite for Italian grocery items.
- **Stage Deli**   The Forum Shops at Caesars; ☎ 702-893-4045. Las Vegas branch
  of New York's famous pastrami palace; enormous menu runs gamut of
  Jewish specialties, including triple-decker sandwiches named for celebrities, and 26 desserts. Open wide—the sandwiches are skyscrapers.
- **Weiss Family Deli**   2744 North Green Valley Parkway, Henderson;
  ☎ 702-454-0565. Full-service deli, bakery, and restaurant. Home cooking and giant matzo balls.

The Best Espresso and Dessert

- **Café Sensations**   4350 East Sunset Road (east of Green Valley Parkway);
  ☎ 702-456-7803. Scrumptious variety of baked goods, casual food,
  sandwiches, salads.
- **Chocolate Swan**   Mandalay Place, 3930 South Las Vegas Boulevard,
  Suite 201B; ☎ 702-632-9366.
  Pastries, frozen custard, and much more.
- **Coffee Bean and Tea Leaf**   4550 South Maryland Parkway;
  ☎ 702-944-5029. Many more locations around the city.
  California-based chain of speciality coffeehouses.
- **Coffee Pub**   2800 West Sahara Avenue, Suite 2A; ☎ 702-367-1913.
  Great breakfast and lunch location, imaginative menu.
- **Cypress Market**   Caesars Palace; ☎ 702-731-7110.
  Caesars' bakers create pies, cakes, and cookies.
- **Palio**   Bellagio; ☎ 702-693-8160. Cafeteria-style coffeehouse with
  scrumptious pastries and casual eats—quiche, salads, and sandwiches.

- **Spago** The Forum Shops at Caesars; ☎ 702-369-6300.
  Wolfgang Puck's pastry chef crafts imaginative and sinful creations.
  Available all day in the café and at dinner in the dining room.
- **Starbucks Coffeehouses** Many area locations.
- **Tintoretto at The Venetian** Canal Shops at The Venetian; ☎ 702-414-3400.

The Best Oyster and Clam Bars

- **Buzios** Rio; ☎ 702-252-7697. Oyster stews, cioppino, shellfish, and pan
  roasts. Table service or oyster bar.
- **Emeril's New Orleans Fish House** MGM Grand; ☎ 702-891-1111.
- **SeaBlue** MGM Grand; ☎ 702-891-3486. Superior tuna tartare.

The Best Pizza

- **Balboa Pizza** District at Green Valley Ranch; ☎ 702-407-5273.
  Good value, great pizzas and salads. Kids love it.
- **Bootlegger** 7700 South Las Vegas Boulevard; ☎ 702-736-4939.
  Great selection; crispy, tender, homemade crust.
- **Metro Pizza** 1395 East Tropicana Avenue; ☎ 702-736-1955. Fast service,
  generous with the cheese. Try the Old New York with thick-sliced moz-
  zarella, plum tomatoes, and basil. Thick ragù-style tomato sauce.
- **Spago** The Forum Shops at Caesars; ☎ 702-369-6300. Wolfgang Puck's
  regular specials include spicy shrimp, duck sausage, and smoked salmon
  with dill cream and golden caviar. Other toppings change frequently.

The Best Soup and Salad Bars

- **Souper Salad** 2051 North Rainbow; ☎ 702-631-2604.
  4022 South Maryland Parkway; ☎ 702-792-8555. Moderate prices, many
  combinations, shiny clean, and inexpensive.

Restaurants with a View

- **Alizé** Palms; ☎ 702-951-7000. At the top of the Palms, Alizé's
  panoramic view includes portions of the Strip.
- **Circo** Bellagio; ☎ 702-693-8150. Circo (full name Osteria Del Circo) is
  adjacent to its pricier sister, Le Cirque. Tuscan fare with a view of Lake
  Como and Paris's Eiffel tower.
- **Eiffel Tower Restaurant** Paris; ☎ 702-948-6937. Fancy French food in a
  drop-dead gorgeous setting that towers over the Strip. This is one spectacular view that encompasses the fountains at Bellagio.
- **Picasso** Bellagio; ☎ 702-693-7223. Highly original food and glorious
  original artwork by Picasso. As good as it gets (since you can't eat in
  the Louvre!).
- **VooDoo Café** Rio Hotel and Casino; ☎ 702-252-7777. At the top of the
  new Rio tower, VooDoo offers the mystique of New Orleans, a complete
  view of the city, Cajun/Creole cooking, and late-night lounge.

RESTAURANT PROFILES

A. J.'s Steakhouse   ★★★

| STEAK | EXPENSIVE | QUALITY ★★★½ | VALUE ★★½ |

Hard Rock Hotel, 4455 Paradise Road; East of Strip; ☎ 702-693-5500; 800-HRD-ROCK

Customers Visitors, locals. **Reservations** Recommended, especially during conventions. **When to go** Anytime. **Entree range** $30–$50. **Payment** AE, CB, DC, MC, V. **Service rating** ★★★½. **Friendliness rating** ★★½. **Parking** Shopping-center lot, garage, valet. **Bar** Attractive, full service. **Wine selection** Excellent. **Dress** Business casual. **Disabled access** Same level as parking lot. **Hours** Tuesday–Saturday, 6–11 p.m.; closed Sunday and Monday.

SETTING AND ATMOSPHERE   Men's club atmosphere, with paneled boardroom (for large parties), polished oak barroom, and comfortable booths.

HOUSE SPECIALTIES   Black-bean soup; whole onion bread; double-breasted chicken; New York sirloin steak; veal chop with mushroom sauce; double filet mignon; Alaskan salmon; seared ahi tuna; huge strawberries with sabayon sauce.

OTHER RECOMMENDATIONS   Appetizer of broiled sea scallops wrapped in bacon, apricot chutney; broccoli with hollandaise sauce; lemon-oregano chicken, crab cakes, banana cream pie.

ENTERTAINMENT AND AMENITIES   Storage lockers for regular guests' wines.

SUMMARY AND COMMENTS   Branch of Chicago-based steak house. Everything à la carte, including side dishes, and served in large portions. The dessert soufflés are a specialty but disappointing. Stick to selections from the pastry tray or the fresh berries. Cigar smoking is encouraged in the dining room. Prime steaks, but a less-than-prime attitude.

Ah Sin   ★★★½

| ASIAN/SUSHI | MODERATE | QUALITY ★★★★½ | VALUE ★★★½ |

Paris, 3655 South Las Vegas Boulevard; South Strip and Environs; ☎ 702-946-4593; www.parislasvegas.com

Customers Visitors, locals. **Reservations** Recommended. **When to go** Anytime. **Entree range** $15–$35. **Payment** All major credit cards. **Service rating** ★★★½. **Friendliness rating** ★★★★½. **Parking** Valet, garage. **Bar** Full service. **Wine selection** Good. **Dress** Casual chic. **Disabled access** Ground floor. **Hours** Wednesday–Sunday, 5:30–10:30 p.m.; closed Monday and Tuesday.

SETTING AND ATMOSPHERE   There are many parts to Ah Sin, all beautiful. Asian artifacts and artwork fill the room, cleverly dividing it, yet allowing open views. A sushi bar flows almost to the dining room. The Malaysian satay bar is another work of art and the first of its kind in Las Vegas.

HOUSE SPECIALTIES   Cantonese crêpes, the Ah Sin version of mu shu, freshly made on oversize French irons; barbecue from the Korean oven, including suckling pig, roast duck, chicken in the Ko Samet style, and Macau pork tenderloin; such appetizers as Malaysian lobster salad or Indochine foie gras; nigiri sushi and sashimi and the many special sushi rolls; seafood from live tanks; special teas.

OTHER RECOMMENDATIONS Dim sum, Sarawak roasted duck salad, the noodle and rice dishes, the Mongolian lamb chops topped with sweet curried onions.

SUMMARY AND COMMENTS Ah Sin offers an exceptional selection of Asian dishes. All menu items are available wherever you choose to sit, including at the sushi bar. Desserts are offered at Ah Sin, but it's more fun to have dessert at Risqué, a late-night spot right above the restaurant. The dessert bar is separated from the club by a translucent glass wall. The range of desserts includes everything from made-to-order soufflés to flambéed desserts to such homespun favorites as banana fritters and rice pudding. Work off the indulgence at Risqué's billiard table.

Alan Albert's ★★★

STEAK/LOBSTER	EXPENSIVE	QUALITY ★★★½	VALUE ★★½

3793 South Las Vegas Boulevard, Epicenter Plaza, North of the MGM Grand; South Strip and Environs; ☎ 702-795-4006

Customers Visitors, locals. **Reservations** Accepted. **When to go** Anytime. **Entree range** $25–$35. **Payment** All major credit cards. **Service rating** ★★★★½. **Friendliness rating** ★★★★½. **Parking** Lot. **Bar** Full service. **Wine selection** Excellent. **Dress** Business attire, informal. **Disabled access** Ground floor. **Hours** Daily, 5–11:30 p.m.

SETTING AND ATMOSPHERE This self-named "vintage steakhouse" features beveled glass, fine wood paneling, and photo walls showcasing celebrities and stars of the glory days of Old Las Vegas. The dining room has comfortable, easy-to-get-into booths and expert, flattering lighting.

HOUSE SPECIALTIES Prime Angus steaks and jumbo lobsters; a flavorful culotte steak seldom found elsewhere; crab cakes; osso buco; a 26-ounce rib eye; veal and lamb chops.

OTHER RECOMMENDATIONS Grilled salmon on garlic spinach; oysters Rockefeller; delectable desserts, especially the tiramisù.

SUMMARY AND COMMENTS Tucked away in the corner of a strip mall, Alan Albert's is a pleasant surprise. Lobsters are fairly priced—choose one from the live tank. Average weight is 2.5 pounds. Portions are generous. A meal could be made from appetizers. Lobster prices fluctuate; ask pound price before ordering.

Alizé ★★★★

FRENCH	EXPENSIVE	QUALITY ★★★★★	VALUE ★★½

Palms, 4321 West Flamingo Road; Mid-Strip and Environs; ☎ 702-951-7000; www.alizelv.com

Customers Visitors, locals. **Reservations** Requested. **When to go** Anytime. **Entree range** $30–$67. **Payment** All major credit cards. **Service rating** ★★★½.

dining and nightlife on the south strip

Friendliness rating ★★★★½. Parking Valet, garage, lot. **Bar** Full service. **Wine selection** Excellent. **Dress** Upscale business attire. **Disabled access** Elevator. **Hours** Nightly, 5:30–10 p.m.

SETTING AND ATMOSPHERE On the top floor of the Palms tower, Alizé offers a spectacular view from most tables. Elegantly furnished and appointed, Alizé is as romantic as it gets.

HOUSE SPECIALTIES Such daily specials as white tiger shrimp and bacon ravioli with grilled cuttlefish; Maine lobster civet; lobster Thermidor, truffle and cashew-crusted rack of lamb, sautéed veal sweetbreads with truffle; and sautéed Muscovy duck breast with walnut crêpe.

OTHER RECOMMENDATIONS Andre's duck foie gras with caramelized citrus fruit, the phyllo-wrapped baked pear salad and Roquefort cheese; the after-dinner cheese plate with imported and domestic cheeses (your choice) served from a trolley; the luscious desserts and soufflés.

SUMMARY AND COMMENTS There is a $45 food minimum per person (does not include beverages). Alizé is the dream-come-true for owners Andre Rochat and Mary Jane Jarvis, who also own two Andre's restaurants.

Andre's ★★★★

CONTINENTAL/FRENCH   EXPENSIVE   QUALITY ★★★★   VALUE ★★½

Monte Carlo Hotel; South Strip and Environs; ☎ 702-798-7151; 401 South Sixth Street; Downtown; ☎ 702-385-5016; www.andresfrenchrest.com

Customers Visitors, locals. **Reservations** Necessary. **When to go** Early or late. **Entree range** $36–$67. **Payment** AE, DC, MC, V. **Service rating** ★★★½. **Friendliness rating** ★★★½. **Parking** Street, valet. **Bar** Full service. **Wine selection** Excellent. **Dress** Sport coat, dressy. **Disabled access** Ramps. **Hours** Daily, 5:30 p.m.–close.

SETTING AND ATMOSPHERE Country-French decor in a converted former residence in a historic part of the city. Elegant European decor at the Monte Carlo location.

HOUSE SPECIALTIES Menu changes with the seasons. Sea scallops with duck foie gras, black truffle, and port wine en papillote; seafood ravioli with crab sauce; pan-seared duck breast and confit of duck leg; grilled pork chop with apricot sauce; sautéed filet of beef in Cognac cream sauce; chicken breast stuffed with crab meat; dover sole. Memorable sweetbreads, soufflés, and pastries.

OTHER RECOMMENDATIONS The daily specials, especially the fish. Ask if you can tour Andre's extensive wine cellar; vintages date back to 1830.

SUMMARY AND COMMENTS Chef-owner Andre Rochat is mostly in the kitchen of Alizé, his dining room at the top of the Palms (spectacular view). He honors special requests if given 24-hour notice. Spectacular winemaker dinners (Thursday nights) several times a year. Ask to be put on the mailing list. Downtown location is closed the month of July.

HONORS AND AWARDS AAA Four Diamond Award 2007; *Wine Spectator* Award of Excellence; *Travel/Holiday* magazine award for many years; Ambassador Award of Excellence through 1987 (discontinued); DiRoNA Award.

Anna Bella ★★★½

TRADITIONAL ITALIAN   MODERATE   QUALITY ★★★½   VALUE ★★★½

Pebble Marketplace, 1000 North Green Valley Parkway, Henderson; ☎ 702-434-2537

Customers Visitors, locals. **Reservations** Suggested. **When to go** Anytime. **Entree range** $14–$23. **Payment** Most major credit cards. **Service rating** ★★★★. **Friendliness rating** ★★★★. **Parking** Large lot. **Bar** Separate bar and lounge. **Wine**

selection Modest. **Dress** Casual. **Disabled access** Ramp. **Hours** Monday–Friday, 11:30 a.m.–2:30 p.m. and 4–10 p.m.; Saturday, 4–10 p.m.; Sunday, 4–9 p.m.

SETTING AND ATMOSPHERE Anna Bella's small neighborhood restaurant has moved up to Green Valley. These new digs are larger and more contemporary, with deep-green walls and booths and a cozy bar and lounge where smokers can drink and dine.

HOUSE SPECIALTIES Owners Janina and Tony are always creating new dishes and keeping the faves, so the menu is quite large. Vitello al limone, pan-seared veal scallops with fresh herbs and white wine–lemon butter sauce; fettuccine al salmone, Alaskan king salmon on pasta with garlic, vodka, and a light marinara sauce; a selection of risotti; and cannelloni, thin crêpes filled with chicken, mushrooms, ricotta, spinach, and marinara in a light cream sauce.

OTHER RECOMMENDATIONS Traditional veal Parmigiana; pollo al marsala; lasagna with a meat sauce made with ground sirloin; melanzane (eggplant) della chef; and zesty fried calamari.

SUMMARY AND COMMENTS It took awhile to move up to Green Valley, but Anna Bella took the move in stride, despite some skulduggery by the former landlord, who wouldn't allow a sign announcing the restaurant's new locale. Loyal followers have made the trek since Anna Bella opened.

Antonio's ★★★½

ITALIAN	MODERATE/EXPENSIVE	QUALITY ★★★★	VALUE ★★★½

Rio, 3700 West Flamingo Road; Mid-Strip and Environs; ☎ 702-777-7923; www.riolasvegas.com

Customers Visitors, locals. **Reservations** Suggested. **When to go** Anytime **Entree range** $15–$45. **Payment** AE, D, DC, MC, V. **Service rating** ★★★★½. **Friendliness rating** ★★★★½. **Parking** Lot, valet, garage. **Bar** Full service. **Wine selection** Excellent. **Dress** Informal slacks and collared shirts for men. **Disabled access** Through casino. **Hours** Sunday–Thursday, 5–10 p.m.; Friday and Saturday, 5–10:30 p.m.

SETTING AND ATMOSPHERE Marble accents, fresh flowers, elegant table appointments, and expert lighting highlight the comfortable dining room; domed ceiling replicates the sky. Enjoy drinks and Italian coffees before or after dinner in the comfortable lounge.

HOUSE SPECIALTIES The chef's appetizer of the day; scaloppine with porcini mushroom marsala; osso buco, the traditional braised veal shank, is presented à la the Rio chef.

OTHER RECOMMENDATIONS Seared sea scallops with foie gras ravioli. There's a small patio outside with its own moderately priced menu of soups, salads, and a dozen pastas. Cioppino. Tiramisù.

SUMMARY AND COMMENTS There are nice touches at Antonio's. A fruity olive oil for dunking is offered instead of butter—the imported breadsticks are habit-forming; a complimentary liqueur is offered "to thank you for dining at Antonio's." A small private dining room for up to 12 is available. This attractive restaurant is a local favorite.

dining and nightlife mid-strip

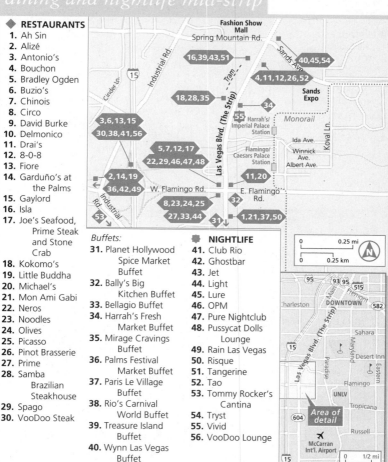

◆ **RESTAURANTS**
1. Ah Sin
2. Alizé
3. Antonio's
4. Bouchon
5. Bradley Ogden
6. Buzio's
7. Chinois
8. Circo
9. David Burke
10. Delmonico
11. Drai's
12. 8-0-8
13. Fiore
14. Garduño's at the Palms
15. Gaylord
16. Isla
17. Joe's Seafood, Prime Steak and Stone Crab
18. Kokomo's
19. Little Buddha
20. Michael's
21. Mon Ami Gabi
22. Neros
23. Noodles
24. Olives
25. Picasso
26. Pinot Brasserie
27. Prime
28. Samba Brazilian Steakhouse
29. Spago
30. VooDoo Steak

Buffets:
31. Planet Hollywood Spice Market Buffet
32. Bally's Big Kitchen Buffet
33. Bellagio Buffet
34. Harrah's Fresh Market Buffet
35. Mirage Cravings Buffet
36. Palms Festival Market Buffet
37. Paris Le Village Buffet
38. Rio's Carnival World Buffet
39. Treasure Island Buffet
40. Wynn Las Vegas Buffet

🍸 **NIGHTLIFE**
41. Club Rio
42. Ghostbar
43. Jet
44. Light
45. Lure
46. OPM
47. Pure Nightclub
48. Pussycat Dolls Lounge
49. Rain Las Vegas
50. Risque
51. Tangerine
52. Tao
53. Tommy Rocker's Cantina
54. Tryst
55. Vivid
56. VooDoo Lounge

Aureole ★★★★½

AMERICAN   VERY EXPENSIVE   QUALITY ★★★★½   VALUE ★★½

Mandalay Bay, 3950 South Las Vegas Boulevard; South Strip and Environs; ☎ 702-632-7401; www.aureolelv.com

Customers Visitors, locals. **Reservations** Required. **When to go** Anytime. **Entree range** $55–$75 prix fixe menus; 6-course tasting menu, $95; à la carte menu $10–$40 in lounge area only. **Payment** All major credit cards. **Service rating** ★★★★½. **Friendliness rating** ★★★★½. **Parking** Valet, garage. **Bar** Full service.

dining and nightlife on the north strip

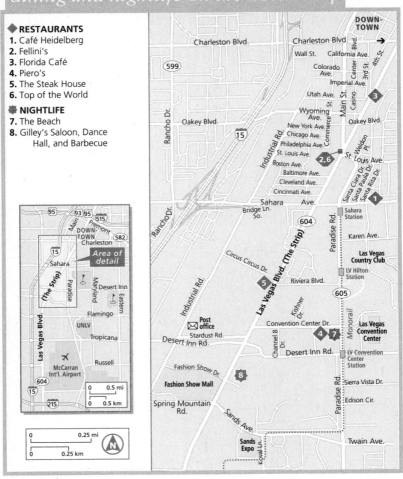

◆ RESTAURANTS
1. Café Heidelberg
2. Fellini's
3. Florida Café
4. Piero's
5. The Steak House
6. Top of the World

◼ NIGHTLIFE
7. The Beach
8. Gilley's Saloon, Dance Hall, and Barbecue

Wine selection Outstanding. **Dress** Upscale casual. **Disabled access** Elevator. **Hours** Daily, 6–11 p.m.; lounge open (serving food) 6 p.m–midnight.

SETTING AND ATMOSPHERE A one-of-a-kind, four-story wine tower dominates the entrance to this exceptional restaurant. There are three dining rooms and the separate Swan Court with just 14 tables—all have a view of the waterfall and live swans.

HOUSE SPECIALTIES Honey-spiced marinated duck; roast spring rack of lamb with sweet garlic; lobster chowder with grilled prawns; citrus-basted chicken; potato gnocchi with black truffles. (Some dishes are seasonal and may not be available.)

OTHER RECOMMENDATIONS Thyme-roasted filet mignon; curry-nut crusted ahi tuna. Scrumptious desserts; homemade chocolates served with coffee.

SUMMARY AND COMMENTS The wine tower is unique—the bottles are accessed by black-clad females who hoist themselves up to the various levels to remove the bottles. It's quite a show and a great photo op. Another wine first is Aureole's wine e-book, which enables patrons to order their favorite dinner wines in advance. All dining rooms offer prix fixe menus only, with an à la carte menu available in the lounge and bar area. Several multicourse tasting menus are available.

Billy Bob's Steakhouse & Saloon ★★★

STEAK	MODERATE/EXPENSIVE	QUALITY ★★★	VALUE ★★★½

Sam's Town, 5111 Boulder Highway; Southeast Las Vegas;
☎ **702-456-7777; www.samstownlv.com**

Customers Visitors, locals. **Reservations** Suggested. **When to go** Anytime. **Entree range** $18–$50. **Payment** AE, D, DC, MC, V. **Service rating** ★★★½. **Friendliness rating** ★★★½. **Parking** Valet, lot, garage. **Bar** Full service. **Wine selection** Good **Dress** Come as you are. **Disabled access** Through casino. **Hours** Sunday–Thursday, 5–10 p.m.; Friday and Saturday, 5–11 p.m.

SETTING AND ATMOSPHERE Stroll through the lovely climate-controlled park to Billy Bob's. The critters that chirp and peep are lifelike robotics; the trees and lush foliage are real. Mosey into the Western-themed Billy Bob's for a taste of the Old West and some mighty fine grub.

HOUSE SPECIALTIES Beef is king at Billy Bob's: steaks and prime rib. The 40-ounce rib eye is a huge favorite. Entree prices include soup or salad and a selection from the potato bar. Desserts serve four to six. The Grand Canyon chocolate cake could serve a small army. The foot-long éclair is a dessert lover's fantasy.

SUMMARY AND COMMENTS Prepare to eat as if you were heading out for a day on the range. The setting and the prices make Billy Bob's a popular choice. At prime times, even with a reservation, there might be a wait. Have a drink in the saloon. After dusk, enjoy the laser light show complete with original music and a lifelike wolf who shows up on the mountaintop.

Bonjour French Restaurant ★★★

FRENCH	MOD/EXP	QUALITY ★★★	VALUE ★★½	SOUTHEAST LAS VEGAS

8878 South Eastern Avenue (Colonnade movie center at Pebble);
☎ **702-270-2102; www.bonjourvegas.com**

Customers Locals. **Reservations** Weekends. **Entree range** $16–$24. **Payment** All major credit cards. **Service rating** ★★★½. **Friendliness rating** ★★½. **Parking** Large lot. **When to go** Anytime. **Bar** Full service. **Wine selection** Good. **Dress** Casual. **Disabled access** Ground floor. **Hours** Monday–Friday, 11 a.m.–2 p.m and 5–10 p.m.; Saturday and Sunday, 5–10 p.m.

SETTING AND ATMOSPHERE Typically French, with checked tablecloths, rustic chandeliers, candlelight, and French music.

HOUSE SPECIALTIES Rack of lamb with herb crust; salmon en croûte on a bed of spinach with tarragon sauce; bouillabaisse; mussels marinière.

OTHER RECOMMENDATIONS Potato-crusted sea bass on a bed of green lentils; rainbow trout with almonds in beurre blanc sauce; vegetable ravioli with wild mushrooms and artichokes.

SUMMARY AND COMMENTS This charming neighborhood eatery has a loyal local following who take advantage of the four-course prix fixe midweek special (Tuesday through Thursday). It's a fine value. Marie and Bernard Calatayud are the congenial owners. She is the chef; he oversees the friendly, relaxed dining room.

The Bootlegger Bistro ★★★

ITALIAN	MODERATE/EXPENSIVE	QUALITY ★★★½	VALUE ★★★★½

7700 South Las Vegas Boulevard; South Strip and Environs;
☎ **702-736-4939; www.bootleggerlasvegas.com**

Customers Locals, some visitors. **Reservations** Accepted. **When to go** Anytime. **Entree range** $12–$40. **Payment** AE, D, DC, MC, V. **Service rating** ★★★½. **Friendliness rating** ★★★★½. **Parking** Shopping-center lot. **Bar** Full service. **Wine selection** Large. **Dress** Informal. **Disabled access** Ground floor. **Hours** Full menu available 24 hours a day.

SETTING AND ATMOSPHERE Turn-of-the-20th-century decor, Italian-style. Wonderful ancestral portraits decorate the walls. The full bar overlooks an informal dining room with fireplace. Two additional dining rooms offer comfortable banquettes, which are original to the previous location. The booths were relocated in the new location at the request of sentimental longtime Bootlegger patrons. Twenty-two-hundred-square-foot tavern offers round-the-clock drinking opportunity and a late-night menu.

HOUSE SPECIALTIES Complimentary appetizer panettis (small bread puffs) tossed with garlic, oregano, and oil, served with tomato-basil sauce. Homemade breads. Seafood diavolo; New York steak topped with mushrooms and peppercorn wine sauce; veal Lorraine with fresh mushrooms in a cream and wine sauce, named for the owners. Varied pasta menu, vegetarian menu, pizzas, and calzones. Biscuit tortoni and tartufo.

OTHER RECOMMENDATIONS The seafood dishes are very good.

SUMMARY AND COMMENTS This venerable Italian restaurant is owned by Nevada's current lieutenant governor. The joint swings on the weekends with regular appearances by entertainers in the golden era of Old Las Vegas. The New Hip Era show up regularly. The menu offers all of the Bootlegger faves.

Bouchon ★★★★½

FRENCH BISTRO	MODERATE	QUALITY ★★★★	VALUE ★★★★

Venetian Hotel, 3355 Las Vegas Boulevard, Venezia Tower; Mid-Strip and Environs; ☎ **702-414-6200; www.venetian.com**

dining and nightlife east of strip

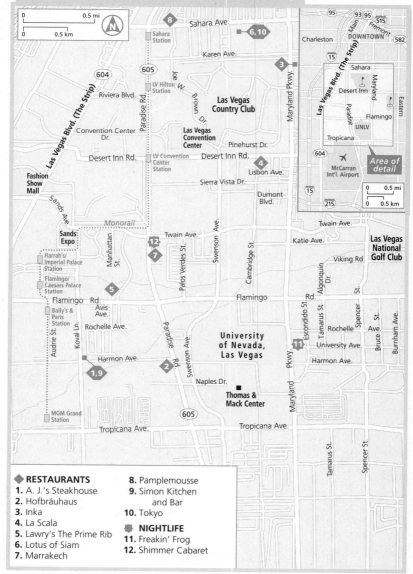

◆ **RESTAURANTS**
1. A. J.'s Steakhouse
2. Hofbräuhaus
3. Inka
4. La Scala
5. Lawry's The Prime Rib
6. Lotus of Siam
7. Marrakech
8. Pamplemousse
9. Simon Kitchen and Bar
10. Tokyo

🍸 **NIGHTLIFE**
11. Freakin' Frog
12. Shimmer Cabaret

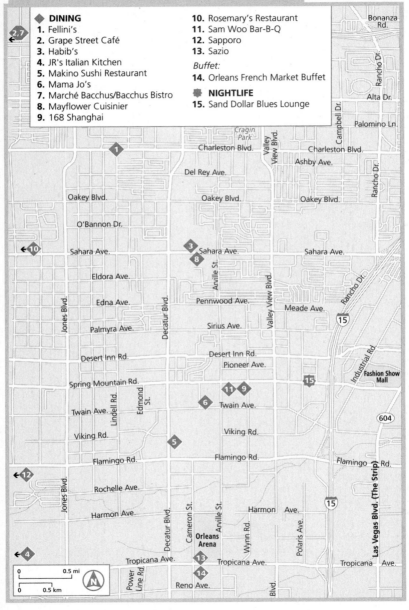

dining and nightlife west of strip

◆ **DINING**
1. Fellini's
2. Grape Street Café
3. Habib's
4. JR's Italian Kitchen
5. Makino Sushi Restaurant
6. Mama Jo's
7. Marché Bacchus/Bacchus Bistro
8. Mayflower Cuisinier
9. 168 Shanghai

10. Rosemary's Restaurant
11. Sam Woo Bar-B-Q
12. Sapporo
13. Sazio
Buffet:
14. Orleans French Market Buffet

🍸 **NIGHTLIFE**
15. Sand Dollar Blues Lounge

Customers Visitors, locals. **Reservations** A must on weekends. **When to go** Anytime. **Entree range** $16–$33. **Payment** All major credit cards. **Service rating** ★★★★½. **Friendliness rating** ★★★★½. **Parking** Valet, garage. **Bar** Full service. **Wine selection** Very good. **Dress** Upscale casual. **Disabled access** Elevator. **Hours** Daily, 7–10:30 a.m and 5–11 p.m.; Saturday and Sunday brunch, 8 a.m.– 2 p.m.; Oyster Bar & Lounge, 3–11 p.m.

SETTING AND ATMOSPHERE Designed to be the ultimate bistro, Bouchon is beautiful. Owner-chef Thomas Keller and renowned restaurant and hotel designer Adam Tihany have created a setting with great appeal. This is bistro as an art form.

HOUSE SPECIALTIES Fresh seafood plateaus, grand plates with an assortment of freshly shucked raw items and shrimp and lobster. The superb oysters— selection changes with the season. Country pâté served with cornichons and radishes. Roasted leg of lamb with flageolet beans in thyme jus. A raw-seafood bar.

OTHER RECOMMENDATIONS Bouchon mussels steamed in white wine, mustard, and saffron; steak frites, a pan-seared flatiron steak with a heap of French fries. Endive salad with Roquefort, apple, walnuts, and walnut vinaigrette. Blood sausage with potato puree and caramelized apples.

SUMMARY AND COMMENTS The most requested tables are on the outdoor terrace. Difficult to get, but worth a try. There are many à la carte options at moderate cost. Keller has added a hip new dimension to bistro dining.

Bradley Ogden   ★★★★

AMERICAN	EXPENSIVE	QUALITY ★★★★½	VALUE ★★½

Caesars Palace, 3570 South Las Vegas Boulevard; Mid-Strip and Environs;
☎ **702-731-7413; www.caesars.com**

Customers Visitors, locals. **Reservations** Suggested. **When to go** Anytime. **Entree range** $29–$48 (changes daily with menu). **Payment** All major credit cards. **Service rating** ★★★★½. **Friendliness rating** ★★★★½. **Parking** Valet, garage. **Bar** Full service. **Wine selection** Very good. **Dress** Upscale casual. **Disabled access** Ground floor. **Hours** Nightly, 5 p.m.–close; Bar & Lounge day menu, 2:30–5 p.m.; night menu, 5 p.m. until kitchen closes.

SETTING AND ATMOSPHERE Elegance and simplicity. Soft lighting, beautiful table appointments and comfortable seating in the restaurant and the adjacent bar and lounge. Relaxed and inviting surroundings.

HOUSE SPECIALTIES Menus change daily, but such signatures as the foie gras, Vintage Prime Summerfield Farms New York Steak, the seasonal oysters, the blue cheese soufflé appetizer (not to be missed), and the selection of artisan American cheeses are always in place. Noted chef-owner Bradley Ogden has dubbed his cooking "Farm Fresh American cuisine," buying exclusively from American producers and farmers.

OTHER RECOMMENDATIONS Any of the fish and seafood dishes. Selection varies with the season, but is always exciting. Wood-grilled yellowtail with Dungeness crab leg and green-onion pancake, roasted monkfish with mussels, grilled rack of lamb and barbecued lamb bacon, and clay-pot Guinea hen with Kara Kara orange sauce are typical. Whimsical, delicious desserts—Carnival Jubilee with a snow cone, mini–funnel cake, ice-cream sandwich, sweet hot pretzel with a trio of fondue sauces, cotton candy, rhubarb up-side-down cake with vanilla crème fraîche ice cream, and the intriguing chocolate childhood tasting.

SUMMARY AND COMMENTS Allow enough time to dine (at least two hours) if you plan to see the Celine show. A four-course, prix fixe pre-theater menu is available. Except for the signature dishes, foods mentioned here may not be available. Lunch and bar menus also change daily. Cooking with Ogden is his son Bryan, graduate of the Culinary Institute of America. In 2004, Bradley Ogden became the first Las Vegas restaurant to be named the nation's Best New Restaurant by James Beard Foundation.

The Broiler ★★½

STEAK/SEAFOOD	MOD/EXP	QUALITY ★★★½	VALUE ★★★½

Boulder Station, 4111 Boulder Highway; Southeast Las Vegas;
☎ 702-432-7777; www.boulderstation.com

Customers Visitors, locals. Reservations Suggested. When to go Anytime. Entree range $16–$56. Payment AE, D, DC, MC, V. Service rating ★★★½. Friendliness rating ★★★★½. Parking Valet, lot. Bar Full service. Wine selection Fair. Dress Casual. Disabled access Through casino. Hours Sunday–Thursday, 5–10 p.m.; Friday and Saturday, 5–11 p.m.; Sunday brunch, 10 a.m.–2:30 p.m.

SETTING AND ATMOSPHERE Comfortable, relaxed dining room with greenery, an exhibition kitchen, and a handsome soup and salad bar. Desert decor with style. A refrigerated showcase displays daily fresh fish and meat selections.

HOUSE SPECIALTIES Fresh seafood, steaks, and prime rib. All entrees include the soup and salad bar, a choice of potatoes or rice, and vegetable or coleslaw. Fish selections are mesquite-grilled or broiled, baked, or sautéed. Most earn the American Heart Association heart symbol for being low cholesterol. Nonfat dressings and sour cream are available, too. Chicken, marinated in herbs and garlic, is cooked on the rotisserie. Sunday brunch is a fine value. Included are the soup and salad bar, dessert, and table service for the entrees.

SUMMARY AND COMMENTS Reservations should be made for dinner and Sunday brunch.

Buzios ★★★½

SEAFOOD	MODERATE/EXPENSIVE	QUALITY ★★★★	VALUE ★★½

Rio, 3700 West Flamingo Road; Mid-Strip and Environs;
☎ 702-777-7923; www.riolasvegas.com

Customers Visitors, locals. Reservations Recommended for dinner. When to go Anytime. Entree range $11–$48. Payment AE, D, DC, MC, V. Service rating ★★★½. Friendliness rating ★★★½. Parking Valet, lot, covered garage. Bar Full service. Wine selection Very good. Dress Casual. Disabled access Through casino. Hours Daily, 5–11 p.m.

dining downtown

◆ **RESTAURANTS**
1. Andre's
2. Hugo's Cellar
3. Pasta Pirate
4. Redwood Bar and Grill

Fremont Street Experience

SETTING AND ATMOSPHERE This popular seafood restaurant is a magnet to local business types. The decor includes massive alabaster chandeliers and flowering plants suspended from the canvas-tented ceiling. Walls of glass allow a beautiful view of the sandy beach and pool. A comfortable counter à la Grand Central Station attracts diners who like to watch the seafood being prepared in the individual high-pressure steam kettles. The counter is a good choice for quick meals.

HOUSE SPECIALTIES Buzios offers a selection of fresh oysters from Canada, Maine, and Washington state; clams; shrimp; and many hot seafood appetizers. Fish soups and stews such as New England clam chowder and bouillabaisse; huge bowls filled with a savory assortment of denizens of the deep. Rockefeller-style prawns, clams, or oysters; lobsters from Japan, Australia, Finland, Great Britain, Germany, Iceland, and The Netherlands; a selection of fresh fish flown in daily. The irresistible Rio breads, baked in their own bakery in a European open-hearth oven, accompany all dishes. They're wonderful when used

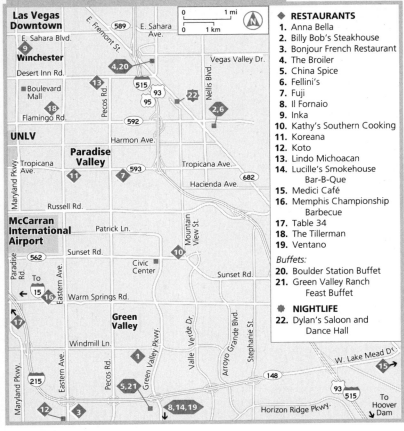

dining and nightlife in southeast las vegas–henderson

◆ RESTAURANTS
1. Anna Bella
2. Billy Bob's Steakhouse
3. Bonjour French Restaurant
4. The Broiler
5. China Spice
6. Fellini's
7. Fuji
8. Il Fornaio
9. Inka
10. Kathy's Southern Cooking
11. Koreana
12. Koto
13. Lindo Michoacan
14. Lucille's Smokehouse
    Bar-B-Que
15. Medici Café
16. Memphis Championship
    Barbecue
17. Table 34
18. The Tillerman
19. Ventano

Buffets:
20. Boulder Station Buffet
21. Green Valley Ranch
    Feast Buffet

❀ NIGHTLIFE
22. Dylan's Saloon and
    Dance Hall

to mop up the broth from the fish soups and stews. Endless baskets are provided.

OTHER RECOMMENDATIONS Seafood salads and pastas; filet of black-canyon beef with oven-roasted Australian lobster.

SUMMARY AND COMMENTS Buzios is named for a small Portuguese fishing village. All entrees include a choice of salad or soup. On weekends and during conventions, even with reservations, there is sometimes a short wait for a table. Don't fret. For seafood aficionados Buzios is worth a brief delay. Or sit at the oyster bar; the savory pan roasts are quickly prepared.

Café Heidelberg ★★★

GERMAN	MODERATE	QUALITY ★★½	VALUE ★★★½

610 East Sahara Avenue (behind Marie Callender's); North Strip and Environs; ☎ 702-731-5310

Customers Locals and German community. **Reservations** Recommended. **When to go** Anytime. **Entree range** $17–$24. **Payment** All major credit cards. **Service rating** ★★★½. **Friendliness rating** ★★★★½. **Parking** Lot. **Bar** No. **Wine selection** Limited. **Dress** Casual, neat. **Disabled access** Ground floor. **Hours** Daily, 10 a.m.–10 p.m.

SETTING AND ATMOSPHERE Simple, clean café setting with patio chairs and tables separated from the old-world booth-lined dining room.

HOUSE SPECIALTIES The generous hot schnitzel sandwich served only at lunch; jägerschnitzel pork cutlet sautéed in mushroom and onion wine sauce; the Bavarian plate, a sausage sampler of bratwurst, knockwurst, and Polish sausage.

OTHER RECOMMENDATIONS Rouladen, thin slices of beef filled with onion, smoked bacon, and pickles, then rolled; schnitzel Holstein with fried egg and capers.

SUMMARY AND COMMENTS Good intentions and generous portions have made Café Heidelberg a success for many years. The lunch specials are a good value; entrees include soup or salad and side dishes. When ordering the apple strudel, ask to have it warmed in the oven, not the microwave. A deli on the opposite side of the cafe sells all things German—meats, cheeses, groceries, and gift items.

China Grill ★★★½

ASIAN	MODERATE/EXPENSIVE	QUALITY ★★★½	VALUE ★★★½

Mandalay Bay, 3950 South Las Vegas Boulevard; South Strip and Environs; ☎ 702-632-7404; www.mandalaybay.com

Customers Visitors, locals. **Reservations** Accepted. **When to go** Anytime. **Entree range** $20–$45. **Payment** All major credit cards. **Service rating** ★★★½. **Friendliness rating** ★★★★½. **Parking** Valet, self. **Bar** Full service. **Wine selection** Excellent. **Dress** Casual. **Disabled access** Ground floor. **Hours** Daily, 5:30 p.m.–midnight.

SETTING AND ATMOSPHERE Highly original furnishings and lighting and contemporary art and accessories make a dramatic statement at China Grill.

HOUSE SPECIALTIES Lamb spareribs in a spiced plum sauce; duck pancakes; sake-cured salmon rolls; calamari salad; Shanghai lobster; sizzling whole fish; pan-seared spicy tuna. Kobe beef tartare; grilled dry-aged Szechuan beef; grilled garlic shrimp.

OTHER RECOMMENDATIONS Asian antipasto; crispy duck with caramelized black vinegar sauce; beef and scallion dumplings; China Grill banana split—enough for a crowd.

SUMMARY AND COMMENTS Unlike the New York original, Vegas's China Grill has a sound level that allows conversation. The comfy lounge is a fine place for relaxing. Food portions are sized to be shared.

China Spice ★★★½

| CHINESE/ASIAN | MODERATE | QUALITY ★★★★ | VALUE ★★★★½ |

Green Valley Ranch Resort & Spa, 2300 Paseo Verde Parkway, Henderson; ☎ 702-617-7002; www.greenvalleyranchresort.com

Customers Locals, hotel guests. **Reservations** Accepted. **When to go** Anytime. **Entree range** $9.95–market price. **Payment** All major credit cards. **Service rating** ★★★½. **Friendliness rating** ★★★½. **Parking** Valet, garage, lot. **Bar** Full service. **Wine selection** Good. **Dress** Casual. **Disabled access** Elevator, ground floor. **Hours** Sunday–Thursday, 5–10 p.m.; Friday and Saturday, 5–11 p.m.

SETTING AND ATMOSPHERE High-tech decor that surrounds the room like a spaceship, yet is hip and appealing. China Spice is small; the menu is large.

HOUSE SPECIALTIES Peking duck à la chef—scallion pancakes, cucumbers, scallions, and hoisin sauce, for a moderate price; heart-healthy dishes; minced chicken in lettuce wraps, Singapore chicken salad, vegetarian lettuce wraps, and soups and vegetable chow fun. Pan-fried pot stickers with a hot ginger-soy dipping sauce. Wok-fried fresh Dungeness crab.

OTHER RECOMMENDATIONS The combination seafood served in a crispy "bird's nest," a fried-potato basket. Crispy-fried garlic chicken; honey-glazed walnut prawns. Try something really different and sample one of the dishes from the menu designed for the hotel's Asian clientele. The pan-fried squid with shrimp paste is delish.

SUMMARY AND COMMENTS Adjacent to China Spice is Sushi+Sake. Ask nicely and the sushi master just might oblige by sending sushi to China Spice.

Chinois ★★★

| CHINESE/FRENCH | MODERATE | QUALITY ★★★½ | VALUE ★★★½ |

The Forum Shops at Caesars Palace; 3500 South Las Vegas Boulevard; Mid-Strip and Environs; ☎ 702-737-9700; www.wolfgangpuck.com

Customers Visitors, locals. **Reservations** Recommended. **When to go** Avoid conventions. **Entree range** Lunch $13–$16; dinner $13–$38; sushi $5–$30. **Payment** AE, D, DC, MC, V. **Service rating** ★★★★. **Friendliness rating** ★★★★½. **Parking** Valet, garage, lot. **Bar** Full service. **Wine selection** Excellent. **Dress** Casual. **Disabled access** Ground floor and elevator. **Hours** Sunday–Thursday, 11 a.m.–10 p.m.; Friday, 11 a.m.–11 p.m.; Saturday, 5–11 p.m.

SETTING AND ATMOSPHERE Enchanting Asian decor by Barbara Lazaroff, the former wife and still partner of Chinois owner Wolfgang Puck. All the Asian art and artifacts are from her own private collection. Steps on the dramatic staircase to the upstairs banquet and party room are emblazoned with bits of wisdom in English and Chinese. A waterfall trickles down the stone wall. Both the cafe and dining room blaze with ribbons of color that, according to Lazaroff, "energize the viewer."

HOUSE SPECIALTIES Firecracker shrimp; satays; noodles; steamed salmon; duck pancakes; lettuce wraps; pork pot stickers; and Szechuan flatiron steak. The sushi-bar area includes table seating—sushi selection is extensive and excellent. The menu includes many signature dishes from Puck's Chinois on Main in Santa Monica, California—Shanghai lobster, whole sizzling catfish, and roasted Cantonese duck. A small vegetarian menu is now available, and the chef will adapt other dishes upon request. Service is family-style. Entrees are sized to share. Asian-influenced desserts are by the award-winning Spago pastry chef. Have one of the cold premium sakes served in a wineglass, but sip slowly—this is heady stuff.

SUMMARY AND COMMENTS Chinois is another winner for Puck. The view is wonderful, but it can be noisy when the Trojan horse across the way at FAO Schwarz speaks his piece. The outdoor patio is a fine place for people-watching. OPM, a modern, late-night club on the second floor accessed by a bold staircase in Chinois, serves an after-hours menu.

Circo ★★★★

ITALIAN	MODERATE/EXPENSIVE	QUALITY ★★★★½	VALUE ★★½

Bellagio, 3600 South Las Vegas Boulevard; Mid-Strip and Environs; ☎ 702-693-8150; www.bellagio.com

Customers Visitors, locals. **Reservations** Recommended. **When to go** Anytime. **Entree range** $21–$44. **Payment** All major credit cards. **Service rating** ★★★½. **Friendliness rating** ★★★½. **Parking** Valet, garage. **Bar** Full service. **Wine selection** Excellent. **Dress** Upscale casual. **Disabled access** Through casino. **Hours** Nightly, 5:30–10:30 p.m.

SETTING AND ATMOSPHERE Circo is a delight. At once whimsical and vibrant, the circus decor is pure fun. Booths, tables, and hideaway corners with a view of the fountains are wonderful. Linger over an espresso and enjoy the action in this homespun-yet-chic haven.

HOUSE SPECIALTIES Pizzas and homemade focaccia breads; home-style Tuscan food inspired by Egidiana Maccioni, matriarch of the New York family that owns the adjacent popular Le Cirque; grilled filet mignon with pancetta; seared chicken breast stuffed with foie gras; Tuscan octopus and calamari stew. Half orders are a good starter.

OTHER RECOMMENDATIONS Rack of lamb crusted in herbs and potatoes; marinated wild boar chops in red wine. The sensational desserts.

SUMMARY AND COMMENTS This elegant Italian restaurant is not as grand as the adjacent Le Cirque, but it's every bit as inviting, and there are super views of the fountain from most tables. Mario Maccioni, son of the founders, directs both restaurants. Menus change seasonally.

Craftsteak ★★★★½

AMERICAN/STEAK	EXPENSIVE	QUALITY ★★★★½	VALUE ★★★

MGM Grand Studio Walk; South Strip and Environs; ☎ 702-891-7318; www.craftrestaurant.com

Customers Visitors, locals. **Reservations** Recommended. **When to go** Anytime. **Entree range** $26–$70; tasting menu, $80–$125. **Payment** All major credit cards. **Service rating** ★★★★½. **Friendliness rating** ★★★★½. **Parking** Valet, garage. **Bar** Full service. **Wine selection** Excellent. **Dress** Casual. **Disabled access** Ground floor. **Hours** Daily, 5:30–10:30 p.m.

SETTING AND ATMOSPHERE Smashing decor, almost a clone to chef-owner Tom Colicchio's acclaimed Craft eatery in New York City, but larger. Colicchio strives for simplicity and quality and can describe the reason for every design component, from the exotic-wood floor to the bronze-and-wood tables with butcher-block elements. The same approach defines the bar and lounge.

HOUSE SPECIALTIES Braised, roasted, and grilled foods; a terrific selection of seasonal side dishes and vegetables; roasted or smoked sweetbreads; grain-fed and grass-fed New York strip steaks; lobster braised in butter.

OTHER RECOMMENDATIONS Roasted pork loin, beef porterhouse for two, grilled leg of lamb, quail for an appetizer or main course, kobe beef tartare. Any of the nostalgic desserts, especially the liquid chocolate cake. The roasted peaches are divine and so are flourless chocolate Napoleons and the B52 parfait.

SUMMARY AND COMMENTS Smokers can dine in the lounge or at the bar. Menus change seasonally, so some of the dishes mentioned above may not be available. Valet service for Studio Walk restaurants is available nearby the MGM Grand Arena.

David Burke ★★★★

AMERICAN	EXPENSIVE	QUALITY ★★★★½	VALUE ★★★½

Venetian Hotel, 3355 South Las Vegas Boulevard; Mid-Strip and Environs; ☎ 702-414-7111; www.davidburkelasvegas.net

Customers Locals and visitors. **Reservations** not required but accepted. **Entree range** $24–$56. **Payment** All major credit cards. **Service rating** ★★★★. **Friendliness rating** ★★★★. **Parking** Lot, two valet locations, large parking garage. **When to go** Anytime. **Bar** Full service, with separate bar and lounge. **Wine selection** Excellent. **Dress** Upscale casual. **Disabled access** Ground floor. **Hours** Daily, 5–11 p.m.

SETTING AND ATMOSPHERE Creative casual with colorful fabrics, comfy booths, and beautiful table appointments. The private chef's table should be reserved.

HOUSE SPECIALTIES Burke-in-a-Box, an assortment of appetizer-sized Burke signatures, such as Millionaire's Meatloaf, is delicious. Kentucky's Creekstone Farms angus filets and rib-eye steaks are supplied by Burke's partner.

OTHER RECOMMENDATIONS Crispy and Angry (spicy) lobster cocktail; roasted day-boat scallops Benedict, layered with a potato cake; crispy chorizo-and-lobster aioli; salads tossed at the table; pretzel-crusted crab cakes.

SUMMARY AND COMMENTS Burke is usually on the scene, as is executive chef and overseer Troy Thompson. Burke collects eggs, so Humpty Dumpties are part of the decor. Come early if you don't like the din that comes with busy dining rooms.

Delmonico ★★★★

STEAK	EXPENSIVE	QUALITY ★★★★	VALUE ★★½

Venetian Hotel, 3355 South Las Vegas Boulevard; Mid-Strip and Environs; ☎ 702-414-3737; www.emerils.com or www.venetian.com

Customers Visitors, locals. **Reservations** A must. **When to go** Avoid conventions. **Entree range** $30–$60. **Payment** AE, D, DC, MC, V. **Service rating** ★★★★. **Friendliness rating** ★★★★½. **Parking** Valet, garage. **Bar** Full service. **Wine selection** Excellent. **Dress** Upscale resort wear. **Disabled access** Ground floor. **Hours** Sunday–Thursday, 11:30 a.m.–1:45 p.m. and 5–10 p.m.; Friday and Saturday, 11:30 a.m.–1:45 p.m. and 5–10:30 p.m.

SETTING AND ATMOSPHERE Expert lighting sets off the handsome decor highlighted with rich woods and fine fabrics. A separate cigar lounge and bar adjoins the dining room. A chef's table in a private room gives a full view of the kitchen, but must be reserved in advance.

HOUSE SPECIALTIES Dry-aged beefsteaks; lobsters from the live tank and fresh fish; grilled pork chop and bacon-wrapped shrimp bourbon; seared tenderloin and sea scallops-bacon-potato confit; the side dishes—especially the addictive truffle oil-and-Parmesan homemade potato chips.

OTHER RECOMMENDATIONS Grilled chicken and black pepper pasta; sautéed Gulf shrimp scampi; panfried Parmesan oysters; Caesar salad, served tableside for two; prime beef and beer cheese fondue.

SUMMARY AND COMMENTS It's not surprising that owner Emeril Lagasse has infused the menu with strong Creole influences. Getting a reservation for prime dinner hours is not easy, but if you're willing to dine late or early you may get lucky. (Even with a reservation, diners must confirm by 3 p.m. on reservation day.) A private kitchen table is open to those who order a tasting menu, with an optional wine-pairing offered.

Dragon Noodle Co. and Sushi Bar ★★★½

ASIAN/SUSHI   INEXPENSIVE/MODERATE   QUALITY ★★★★   VALUE ★★★★

Monte Carlo Resort, 3770 South Las Vegas Boulevard; South Strip and Environs; ☎ 702-730-7967; www.montecarlo.com or www.dragonnoodleco.com

Customers Visitors and locals. **Reservations** Suggested. **When to go** Anytime. **Entree range** Lunch from $6.95; dinner $12–$39. **Payment** All major credit cards. **Service rating** ★★★½. **Friendliness rating** ★★★★. **Parking** Valet and garage. **Bar** Jazzy cocktails and mixed drinks. **Wine selection** None. **Dress** Casual chic. **Disabled access** Ground floor. **Hours** Sunday–Thursday, 11 a.m.–10 p.m.; Friday and Saturday, 11 a.m.–11 p.m.; sushi bar open daily from 4:30 p.m.

SETTING AND ATMOSPHERE The lacquered-red feng shui door has made way for the sushi bar. This colorful cafe is a happy, busy place. A small outdoor patio offers some excellent people-watching.

HOUSE SPECIALTIES Premium shark fin soup with crabmeat or chicken; Dragon platter appetizer sampler for two or more diners; Dragon's version of pot stickers, steamed and crisped; Dragon fish, a whole fish steamed or served golden brown from the wok; Hong Kong–style roasted Peking duck—a whole duck or half.

OTHER RECOMMENDATIONS Dry-sautéed string beans; wok-tossed garlic eggplant in the chef's special sauce; the four clay pot offerings: seafood, assorted meat, duck with oyster, and flounder with ginger. Scallops with the chef's special X.O. sauce. Fixed-price multicourse dinners for two or more diners.

SUMMARY AND COMMENTS　A tea sampling bar features many different teas that can be purchased to take home. Taste the tea, order your favorite to drink in or take out.

8-0-8　★★★½

HAWAIIAN/FRENCH	EXPENSIVE	QUALITY ★★★★	VALUE ★★½

Caesars Palace, 3570 South Las Vegas Boulevard; Mid-Strip and Environs; ☎ 702-731-7731; www.caesars.com

Customers Locals, visitors. **Reservations** Accepted. **When to go** Anytime. **Entree range** $16–$60. **Payment** All major credit cards. **Service rating** ★★★½. **Friendliness rating** ★★½. **Parking** Valet, garage, lot. **Bar** Full service. **Wine selection** Good. **Dress** Casual. **Disabled access** Ground floor. **Hours** Daily, 5–11 p.m.

SETTING AND ATMOSPHERE　This newest Caesars dining gem was conceived by Hawaii's premier chef, French transplant Jean-Marie Josselin. The small dining room and bar glow with special lighting (flattering to everyone). The island influence is everywhere, in the furnishings and appointments. Yet it's not hokey—it's relaxing and lovely.

HOUSE SPECIALTIES　Josselin has created an à la carte menu of original specialties with his own island twist. A chilled-seafood platter includes seasonal fish and seafood—a typical variety includes Kumamoto oysters, sashimi, sesame poke, shrimp, lobster, and clams (market price). The deconstructed ahi roll is as gorgeous as it is delicious. Wok-stirred fried lobster, sesame-crusted mahimahi, miso-charred salmon; any of the terrific appetizers. Desserts are choice—more masterful fusion.

SUMMARY AND COMMENTS　Caesars continues to update and revamp this veteran hotel. It's trendy without being chichi.

Emeril's New Orleans Fish House　★★★½

SEAFOOD/NEW ORLEANS	EXPENSIVE	QUALITY ★★★½	VALUE ★★★½

MGM Grand, 3799 South Las Vegas Boulevard; South Strip and Environs; ☎ 702-891-7374; www.emerils.com or www.mgmgrand.com

Customers Visitors, locals. **Reservations** Always. **When to go** Avoid convention times. **Entree range** $25–$45; prix fixe, $70 (not including wine). **Payment** AE, D, DC, MC, V. **Service rating** ★★★★½. **Friendliness rating** ★★★★½. **Parking** Valet, lot, covered garage. **Bar** Full service. **Wine selection** Excellent. **Dress** Upscale casual. **Disabled access** Through casino. **Hours** Daily, 11:30 a.m.–2:30 p.m. and 5:30–10:30 p.m.; Oyster Bar/Café, daily, 11:30 a.m.–10:30 p.m.

SETTING AND ATMOSPHERE　"A bit of New Orleans" is the way award-winning chef-owner Emeril Lagasse describes his beautiful restaurant. The main restaurant is comfortable and handsome, with fine appointments and accessories. The separate courtyard dining room is French Quarter pretty with a faux balcony and louvered shutters. Masses of real plants and a stone floor complete the illusion.

HOUSE SPECIALTIES　The five- to eight-course "tasting" dinner is a fine way to sample small portions of many dishes, prix fixe at $70; some are special recipes being considered for the menu. Emeril's New Orleans barbecue shrimp; grilled and roasted pork chop with caramelized sweet potatoes; baked Maine lobster stuffed with mushrooms; sesame-crusted Gulf shrimp; Louisiana cedar-plank campfire steak served on a bed of country-style mashed potatoes and drizzled with warm rémoulade and Emeril's homemade Worcestershire sauce.

SUMMARY AND COMMENTS Emeril's is an exciting restaurant that personifies the "new Las Vegas." The faithful, drawn by Emeril's success on the Food Network, regularly fill his Las Vegas eateries.

HONORS AND AWARDS Emeril's is the recipient of many dining awards, including "Best Southeast Regional Chef"—The James Beard Foundation; "One of the Top 25 Chefs in the Country"—*Food & Wine* magazine; "American Express Fine Dining Hall of Fame"—*Nation's Restaurant News.*

Fellini's ★★★

ITALIAN	MODERATE	QUALITY ★★★½	VALUE ★★★★½

5555 West Charleston Boulevard; West of Strip; ☎ 702-870-9999;
Stratosphere, 2000 Las Vegas Boulevard; North Strip and Environs;
☎ 702-383-4859
Sam's Town, 5111 Boulder Highway; Southeast Las Vegas;
☎ 702-454-8041; www.fellinislv.com

Customers Visitors, locals. Reservations Suggested. When to go Anytime. Entree range $16–$30. Payment AE, D, MC, V. Service rating ★★★★. Friendliness rating ★★★★. Parking Lot. Bar Full service. Wine selection Good. Dress Upscale casual. Disabled access Ground floor. Hours Daily, 5–11 p.m.

SETTING AND ATMOSPHERE Inviting decor and lighting, comfortable seating, fresh flowers, a European-style dessert table, and congenial management that welcomes everyone as if they were longtime friends.

HOUSE SPECIALTIES Fellini salad; shrimp fra diavolo (jumbo shrimp sautéed in a hot and spicy sauce of garlic, white wine, tomatoes, and fresh herbs served on a bed of linguine); New Zealand and California mussels in a tomato and white-wine sauce; bistecca Fiorentina (the famous steak of Florence); Tuscan-style grilled chicken breast with little pillows of polenta.

OTHER RECOMMENDATIONS The breads and desserts (all made on the premises); homemade contuccini (small biscotti), served with a glass of Italian dessert wine, Vin Santo—dunk the hard cookies in the wine, as they do in Tuscany.

SUMMARY AND COMMENTS Fellini's chef-partner Chaz LaForte spent four years in Tuscany refining his skills. He frequently comes out of the kitchen to talk with diners. Live piano music is played at just the right level. Fellini's has a strong local following. The Stratosphere location offers a smaller menu and casual fare.

Fiamma Trattoria & Bar ★★★★

ITALIAN	MODERATE/EXPENSIVE	QUALITY ★★★★	VALUE ★★★½

MGM Grand, 3799 South Las Vegas Boulevard; South Strip and Environs;
☎ 702-891-7600; www.mgmgrand.com

Customers Visitors, locals. **Reservations** A must on weekends and holidays. **When to go** Avoid convention times. **Entree range** $22–$42. **Payment** All major credit cards. **Service rating** ★★½. **Friendliness rating** ★★★½. **Parking** Valet, garage. **Bar** Full service. **Wine selection** Very good. **Dress** Upscale casual. **Disabled access** Main valet, garage. **Hours** Sunday–Thursday, 5:30–10 p.m.; Friday and Saturday, 5:30–11 p.m.

SETTING AND ATMOSPHERE This first Las Vegas venture for New York restaurateur Stephen Hanson is a casual version of Fiamma New York. A cheerful fireplace near the bar adds a comforting touch. Separate dining rooms that flow together make this sizable Italian restaurant more intimate.

HOUSE SPECIALTIES Sage-roasted chicken with white-truffle potatoes; braised short rib–filled ravioli with just enough meat and a drizzle of wine sauce; thin-sliced cured beef tenderloin, with black truffle, arugula, and Parmigiano; wild king salmon with sweet-corn ragù; mozzarella with tomatoes, yellow-pepper crema, and basil oil.

OTHER RECOMMENDATIONS Any of the creamy risottos that change each day; the citrus-grilled octopus appetizer, seared diver scallops with pistachio. The wonderful selection of house-made pastas made on an Italian pasta machine as big as a small cottage. The irresistible pastries, especially the hot-from-the-fryer amaretti doughnuts served with dipping sauces.

SUMMARY AND COMMENTS Adventurers can order a multicourse tasting dinner. Pricey but wonderful.

Florida Café ★★★

CUBAN	INEXPENSIVE/MODERATE	QUALITY ★★★½	VALUE ★★★★½

Howard Johnson Hotel, 1401 South Las Vegas Boulevard; North Strip and Environs; ☎ 702-385-3013; www.floridacafecuban.com

Customers Cuban community, locals, HoJo guests. **Reservations** No. **When to go** Anytime. **Entree range** $7–$18. **Payment** AE, DC, MC, V. **Service rating** ★★★. **Friendliness rating** ★★★½. **Parking** Lot. **Bar** Wine and beer. **Wine selection** Small. **Dress** Casual. **Disabled access** Yes. **Hours** Daily, 8 a.m.–10 p.m.

SETTING AND ATMOSPHERE Colorful Cuban paintings adorn the walls, but it's still a coffee shop at heart.

HOUSE SPECIALTIES Cuban-American food at value prices; Cuban breakfast eggs, stuffed potatoes, sweet plantains, and toast; croquettes; corn tamales; fresh seafood; real Cuban sandwiches, pressed thin in a special grill. All entrees include side dishes.

OTHER RECOMMENDATIONS Classic arroz con pollo, chicken with yellow rice; marinated leg of pork; Cuban pizzas; the many Cuban desserts. A meal could be made from the à la carte side dishes.

SUMMARY AND COMMENTS Very little English is spoken here, but the staff is accommodating, and menu descriptions are clear. A favorite local eatery.

Fuji ★★½

JAPANESE	INEXPENSIVE/MODERATE	QUALITY ★★★½	VALUE ★★★½

3430 East Tropicana Avenue; Southeast Las Vegas; ☎ 702-435-8838

Customers Locals. **Reservations** Accepted, required on weekends. **When to go** Anytime. **Entree range** $8–$19. **Payment** AE, DC, JCB, MC, V. **Service rating** ★★★½. **Friendliness rating** ★★★½. **Parking** Large lot **Bar** Beer and wine only. **Wine selection** Fair. **Dress** Casual. **Disabled access** Ground floor. **Hours** Tuesday–Saturday, 4:30–10:30 p.m.; Sunday, 4:30–10 p.m.

SETTING AND ATMOSPHERE Small family-style restaurant with two teppan tables, booths, and traditional seating.

HOUSE SPECIALTIES All the basic Japanese fare is available: sushi, tempura, sukiyaki, teriyaki. Combination dinners also available.

OTHER RECOMMENDATIONS Tall or large diners will find a table more comfortable than the small booths.

SUMMARY AND COMMENTS Moderate prices, a caring staff, and good food make Fuji a popular local dining option. Children are treated like honored guests.

Garduño's at the Palms   ★★★

MEXICAN	INEXPENSIVE/MODERATE	QUALITY ★★★½	VALUE ★★★½

Palms, 4321 West Flamingo Road; Mid-Strip and Environs;
☎ 702-942-7777; www.palms.com

Customers Visitors, locals. **Reservations** No. **When to go** Anytime. **Entree range** $9–$24. **Payment** All major credit cards. **Service rating** ★★★½. **Friendliness rating** ★★★★½. **Parking** Valet, lot, parking garage. **Bar** Full service. **Wine selection** Good. **Dress** Casual. **Disabled access** Ramp. **Hours** Sunday–Thursday 11 a.m.–10 p.m. (except holidays); Friday and Saturday, 11 a.m.–11 p.m.; Sunday margarita brunch, 10 a.m.–3 p.m. ($14).

SETTING AND ATMOSPHERE Upscale Mexican chic. Two patios for outdoor dining, dining rooms on two levels, both with views. Garduño's casino perimeter is ringed with oversize, elegant planters. Mexican art and artifacts throughout. The Blue Agave oyster and chile bar gives diners a view of the chefs at work.

HOUSE SPECIALTIES The sizzling fajitas, including a vegetarian version; pastas with Mexican flair—green-chile Alfredo, Cajun shrimp and red-chipotle chicken. The award-winning Blue Agave pan roasts (voted best new dish by the National Restaurant Association), king crab, lobster, scallop, shrimp, or the house roast—lobster, crab, and shrimp.

OTHER RECOMMENDATIONS Homemade tamales, the relleno combo, green-chile Caesars salad, steak enchiladas, the chunky burritos and chimichangas, and the zesty guacamole prepared tableside. Each server has a unique version. Diners can add their own touches or eliminate any ingredient they don't want. Fun to watch and delicious.

SUMMARY AND COMMENTS Garduño's at the Palm offers more than tasty food. There's a seemingly endless selection of margaritas, tequilas, and "mockaritas." Have the fried ice cream for dessert.

Garduño's of Mexico ★★★½

Fiesta Hotel, 2400 North Rancho Drive; North Strip and Environs;
☎ **702-631-7000; rancho.fiestacasino.com**

Customers Visitors, locals. **Reservations** Not accepted. **When to go** Anytime.
Entree range $9–$22. **Payment** AE, D, DC, MC, V. **Service rating** ★★★½. **Friendliness
rating** ★★★½. **Parking** Valet, lot. **Bar** Full service. **Wine selection** Good. **Dress**
Informal. **Disabled access** Ground floor. **Hours** Sunday–Thursday, 4–9 p.m.; Friday
and Saturday, 4–10 p.m.

SETTING AND ATMOSPHERE Colorful, appealing Mexican decor with many
plants and beautiful artifacts. This large restaurant has been cleverly
divided, which makes it intimate.

HOUSE SPECIALTIES Hatch chiles, grown only in the Mesa Valley of New Mexico, are used exclusively. Baskets of fresh sopaipillas accompany entrees.
The honey on the table is for pouring over the puffy pillows of dough.
Spicy chili verde served in a huge bowl. Guacamole prepared tableside;
fresh avocados are mashed, then lime juice, spices, chiles, and seasonings
are added to your taste. Tortillas are handmade the old-fashioned way.
Posole soup rich with hominy, pork, and red chiles. Any of the fajitas.

SUMMARY AND COMMENTS The food is authentic and good. Daily lunch specials are large enough to be an early dinner. The Sunday margarita
brunch is a fine value and a good way to get to know the Garduño style
of Mexican cooking.

Gaylord ★★½

Rio, 3700 West Flamingo Road; Mid-Strip and Environs;
☎ **702-777-2277; www.riolasvegas.com**

Customers Visitors, locals. **Reservations** Weekends. **When to go** Anytime. **Entree
range** $16–$26. **Payment** All major credit cards. **Service rating** ★★★. **Friendliness rating** ★★★½. **Parking** Valet, garage, large lot. **Bar** Full service. **Wine selection** Small. **Dress** Casual chic. **Disabled access** Ground floor. **Hours** Daily, 11:30
a.m.–2:30 p.m and 5–11 p.m.; brunch buffet Friday–Sunday, 11:30 a.m.–3 p.m.

SETTING AND ATMOSPHERE Beautiful Indian art and artifacts, etched-glass windows designed to emulate lace. Splendid carved teakwood elephants
guard the entrance.

HOUSE SPECIALTIES Tandoori salmon; tandoori breads; vegetarian appetizers
(the samosas and pakoras are terrific); Bombay chicken wings (hot-hot);
Royal feast combination dinners; chicken or lamb curries.

OTHER RECOMMENDATIONS The large variety of meatless specialties; prawn
biryani (saffron-flavored basmati rice with prawns); chicken tikka masala
(mesquite-broiled chicken in a mild tomato-butter sauce) mattar paneer
(cubed farmer's cheese and peas in a spiced sauce).

SUMMARY AND COMMENTS Gaylord has the makings of a fine Indian restaurant, but has not yet found its way. Unlike at its San Francisco branch,

the service and food are uneven. On a good night, the food is what it's supposed to be. But hey, this is Las Vegas, so take a chance.

Grape Street Café ★★★

| AMERICAN | MODERATE | QUALITY ★★★½ | VALUE ★★★½ |

Summerhill Plaza, 7501 West Lake Mead Boulevard; North Strip and Environs; ☎ 702-228-9463; www.grapestreetcafe.com

Customers Locals. **Reservations** Accepted. **When to go** Anytime. **Entree range** $9–$32. **Payment** AE, MC, V. **Service rating** ★★★½. **Friendliness rating** ★★★★½. **Parking** Lot. **Bar** Wine and beer. **Wine selection** Excellent. **Dress** Informal. **Disabled access** Ground floor. **Hours** Sunday, Tuesday–Thursday, 11 a.m.–10 p.m.; Friday and Saturday, 11 a.m.–11 p.m. Dinner specials available from 4 p.m.

SETTING AND ATMOSPHERE The 90-seat dining room has brick walls, polished concrete floors, hand-forged wrought-iron tables and chairs (available for sale), a counter facing the kitchen, and a wine bar. Adjacent to the dining room is the wine-cellar sales room and a take-out counter. Grape Street is a very homey place with a San Francisco feel.

HOUSE SPECIALTIES Any of the daily specials; the grilled gouda and portobello mushroom "Philly" sandwich; the exceptional chopped salad; any of the entree-sized salads; linguine with Brie; the plate-sized pizzas with creative toppings, or make up your own; the tapas appetizer (roasted garlic and vegetables, Greek meatballs, olives, and goat cheese); the salmon burger.

OTHER RECOMMENDATIONS The reasonably priced dinner specials served after 4 p.m., which include a house salad and side dishes; honey-herbed lamb chops with cabernet sauce; chocolate fondue with fruit and cake for dipping, big enough for two.

SUMMARY AND COMMENTS Grape Street is a delightful, informal eatery with caring owners. An outdoor patio seats 50. It's always busy. At least 50 wines are always available by the glass. Wines from the cellar are available with meals for just $6 over the retail price. The take-out counter sells pâtés, imported cheeses, and a variety of prepared dishes that would be ideal for a picnic. Live music every Thursday night includes everything from flamenco to jazz to steel drums to folk and acoustic.

Habib's ★★★

| PERSIAN | MODERATE | QUALITY ★★★½ | VALUE ★★½ |

Sahara Pavilion, 4750 West Sahara Avenue; West of Strip; ☎ 702-870-0860; www.habibspersiancuisine.com

Customers Visitors, locals. **Reservations** Suggested. **When to go** Anytime. **Entree range** $11–$22. **Payment** AE, MC, V. **Service rating** ★★½. **Friendliness rating** ★★★½. **Parking** Shopping-center lot. **Bar** Beer and wine only. **Wine selection** Poor. **Dress** Casual. **Disabled access** Ground level. **Hours** Monday–Saturday, 11:30 a.m.–3 p.m. and 5:30–10 p.m.

SETTING AND ATMOSPHERE Located in the restaurant corridor of a popular neighborhood shopping center, this attractive, small restaurant has gained a loyal local following. A mist-controlled outdoor patio allows for alfresco dining even in warm weather. The area is filled with lovely plants.

HOUSE SPECIALTIES Middle Eastern appetizers and salads; chicken, ground beef, and beefsteak kabobs; many Persian specialties.

OTHER RECOMMENDATIONS Tabbouleh salad so fresh the parsley tastes just-picked; eggplant appetizer, borani; hummus; torshi, a mixture of pickled, aged vegetables; sereshk polo, a seasoned chicken-breast kabob prepared with barberries and fragrant spices that are then mixed with rice.

SUMMARY AND COMMENTS Habib's menu is not large, but it is filled with exotic, delicious dishes that, except for the Middle Eastern starters and salads, have unfamiliar names. The waitstaff is happy to explain the food to the best of their ability. At least two of the special Persian dishes listed separately on the menu are available each day. Habib's is the only Persian restaurant in Las Vegas; the Middle Eastern dishes are a concession to his sizable following of Middle Eastern customers. Photos of the dishes are included with the menu, enabling diners unfamiliar with the cuisine to see what the finished dish looks like. A selection of American dishes has been added as well as a Habib market offering exotic foods and gifts.

Hofbräuhaus ★★★

| GERMAN | MODERATE | QUALITY ★★★½ | VALUE ★★★★½ |

4510 Paradise Road; East of Strip; ☎ 702-853-2337; www.hofbrauhauslasvegas.com

Customers Visitors, local German community, beer enthusiasts. **Reservations** Requested for main dining room. **When to go** Anytime. **Entree range** $9–$26. **Payment** All major credit cards. **Service rating** ★★★½. **Friendliness rating** ★★★½. **Parking** Valet, large lot. **Bar** Limited. **Wine selection** Small. **Dress** Casual. **Disabled access** Ramp. **Hours** 11 a.m.–close; specials served until 5 p.m.

SETTING AND ATMOSPHERE A mini-replica of Munich's Hofbräuhaus that required permission from the German government. The main dining room is where the action is. Communal tables and oompah bands flown in monthly put the din in dinner, yet the crowds love it. Comely *frauleins* dressed in dirndls hoist as many as eight steins without a tray.

HOUSE SPECIALTIES Tennis-ball-sized dumplings that accompany the pork stew and a few other braised dishes; sauerbraten that can be on the dry side—the beer makes it easier to go down. Roasted chicken and potato pancakes. Pretzels baked throughout the day. The dough is shipped in containers from Germany, then shaped and baked in the kitchen.

OTHER RECOMMENDATIONS Crisp apple strudel, not too sweet, just delicious.

SUMMARY AND COMMENTS Take advantage of the discount coupons available in most hotels and taxis. Those seeking German food in more bucolic surroundings can request to sit in the faux gardens behind the main dining room.

Hugo's Cellar ★★★

| AMERICAN | EXPENSIVE | QUALITY ★★★½ | VALUE ★★★½ |

Four Queens Hotel, 202 Fremont Street; Downtown; ☎ 702-385-4011; www.hugoscellar.com

Customers Visitors, locals. **Reservations** Strongly recommended. **When to go** Anytime but Friday and Saturday. **Entree range** $29–$58. **Payment** AE, DC, MC, V. **Service rating** ★★★½. **Friendliness rating** ★★★★½. **Parking** Indoor garage, valet **Bar** Full service. **Wine selection** Very good. **Dress** Casually elegant, tie and jacket suggested. **Disabled access** Elevator to cellar. **Hours** Daily, 5:30–11 p.m.

SETTING AND ATMOSPHERE Unique cellar location, comfortable lounge, warm bar, and gracious hostess. Booths provide privacy; noise at minimum. Cozy cocktail lounge serves pâté, cheese, crackers, and very large drinks.

HOUSE SPECIALTIES Variety of breads, including lavosh crackers. Waiter creates salad of choice from selection on the cart wheeled to your table. Steaks and prime rib; duck flambé anise; snapper en papillote with shallots and white wine; medallions of lobster with white wine, crushed red pepper, sun-dried tomatoes, and mushrooms.

OTHER RECOMMENDATIONS Appetizer for two of beef tenderloin medallions, marinated swordfish, breast of chicken, and jumbo shrimp cooked at the table on a sizzling granite slab, accompanied by a selection of herbs, seasonings and special sauces. Imaginative preparations of veal and chicken; rack of lamb Indonesian.

ENTERTAINMENT AND AMENITIES Hostess presents a fresh rose to female guests. Chocolate-dipped fruits with whipped cream are presented before dessert order is taken.

SUMMARY AND COMMENTS A most popular downtown restaurant. On weekends the Cellar is packed. Expert wine steward to assist you with selection. Don't let the little cone of sherbet served between courses throw you—it's a house signature. A consistent local favorite, in spite of too-high prices.

Il Fornaio ★★★½

ITALIAN	MODERATE	QUALITY ★★★½	VALUE ★★★½

New York–New York, 3790 South Las Vegas Boulevard; South Strip and Environs; ☎ 702-650-6500
Green Valley Ranch Resort & Spa, 2300 Paseo Verde Drive, Henderson; ☎ 702-492-0054; www.ilfornaio.com

Customers Visitors, locals. **Reservations** Suggested for dinner. **When to go** Anytime. **Entree range** $8–$35. **Payment** AE, CB, JCB, MC, V. **Service rating** ★★★½. **Friendliness rating** ★★★★½. **Parking** Valet, garage. **Bar** Full service. **Wine selection** Small, but good. **Dress** Informal. **Disabled access** Ground floor. **Hours** New York–New York, daily, 7:30 a.m.–midnight; Green Valley, Sunday–Thursday, 11:30 a.m.–11 p.m., Friday and Saturday, 11:30 a.m.–midnight.

SETTING AND ATMOSPHERE Upscale, upbeat contemporary decor. Rich woods and natural stone and marble accents. Dine on the outdoor patio with a view of the flowing brook and people-watch as you dine. Faux trees add an almost real touch of nature.

HOUSE SPECIALTIES Carpaccio with shavings of Italian cheese, capers, and baby arugula; minestrone soup; spinach salad with ricotta, onions, applewood-smoked bacon, and champignon mushrooms; the selection of thin-crusted pizzas baked in the wood-fired oven. Eat at the bar and watch as they're assembled and baked. The herbed chicken roasted on the wood-burning rotisserie and served with vegetables and roasted potatoes; the 22-ounce certified Angus porterhouse marinated in olive oil and rosemary, served with Tuscan white beans and sautéed spinach; the remarkable breads, baked on the premises, served with all meals.

OTHER RECOMMENDATIONS Any of the homemade pastas, especially the ravioli filled with butternut squash and walnuts; grilled fresh salmon; veal scallopini with baby artichokes and lemon; shell pasta with chicken breast, broccoli, and sun-dried tomatoes.

SUMMARY AND COMMENTS The success of New York–New York has brought an enormous amount of business to Il Fornaio. Dine during off-hours for the most relaxing experience. Patio dining is the most requested. It can be noisy, so opt to dine in the lovely dining room. Take home the remarkable Il Fornaio European breads. They're sold at Il Fornaio's retail bakery–coffeehouse just a few doors from the restaurant. The new location at Green Valley Ranch in Henderson is more upscale and less crowded. Outdoor dining, handsome Tuscan decor. Same crusty breads!

Isla ★★★★½

CONTEMPORARY MEXICAN   INEXPENSIVE   QUALITY ★★★★   VALUE ★★★★½

T. I., 3300 South Las Vegas Boulevard; Mid-Strip and Environs;
☎ **702-894-7111; www.treasureisland.com**

Customers Visitors, locals. **Reservations** Suggested for weekends. **When to go** Anytime. **Entree range** $7–$15. **Payment** All major credit cards. **Service rating** ★★★★½. **Friendliness rating** ★★★★½. **Parking** Valet, garage. **Bar** Full service, excellent tequila list. **Wine selection** Interesting and good. **Dress** Casual. **Disabled access** Valet or elevator. **Hours** Sunday–Tuesday, Thursday, 4–11 p.m.; Wednesday, Friday, Saturday, 4 p.m.–midnight. Lounge: daily, 11 a.m.–2 a.m.

SETTING AND ATMOSPHERE Isla is a comfort zone just off the casino. Sophisticated decor without pretense. The patio bar is designed for those who want a bit of people-watching with their cocktails and light noshes.

HOUSE SPECIALTIES Made-from-scratch guacamole, including lobster guacamole studded with bits of lobster, achiote passion fruit, and serrano chiles. Pulled-pork tamale with sweet-and-spicy chipotle sauce; the Sandoval family dish—roast pork pipian, lean pork tenderloin marinated in tamarind sauce. Slices of the roast pork are arranged atop a bed of crushed sweet corn and encircled with a rich pumpkinseed puree.

OTHER RECOMMENDATIONS Crispy empanadas filled with shredded beef, toasted pine nuts, and dried cherries; the delicious trio of corn masa cakes with various toppings; crispy rock-shrimp tacos laced with chipotle rouille, a Mexican spin on the garlicky mayonnaise; the huitlacoche dumpling served with the spiced chicken breast.

SUMMARY AND COMMENTS Garbed in an eye-catching gown, the statuesque tequila goddess gives diners a crash course in tequila. The selection of original Mexican dishes is unique and outstanding. The names may be familiar, but the food is original and wonderful. Service is often slow. The food is worth the wait, but a reminder to the manager is not a bad idea.

Joe's Seafood, Prime Steak & Stone Crab ★★★★½

SEAFOOD AND STEAK	EXPENSIVE	QUALITY ★★★★½	VALUE ★★★½

Forum Shops at Caesars Palace, 3500 South Las Vegas Boulevard; Mid-Strip and Environs; ☎ 702-792-9222; www.icon.com/joes

Customers Visitors and locals. **Reservations** A must for dinner. **When to go** Avoid conventions and holidays. **Entree range** $13–$90. **Payment** All major credit cards. **Service rating** ★★★½. **Friendliness rating** ★★★★½. **Parking** Their own valet entrance. **Bar** Bar and lounge. **Wine selection** Very good. **Dress** Business or upscale casual. **Disabled access** Valet, Forum Shops. **Hours** Sunday–Thursday, 11:30 a.m.–10 p.m.; Friday and Saturday, 11:30 a.m.–11 p.m.

SETTING AND ATMOSPHERE Handsome Chicago-style decor that is a far cry from the original Miami Beach Joe's Stone Crab. The history of Joe's is chronicled in the artfully arranged photos that cover the dining-room walls. Joe's at the Forum Shops is fashioned after the Chicago Joe's.

HOUSE SPECIALTIES Stone crab as an appetizer or entree is available year-round. The-always-in-demand claws are shipped frozen when the season ends, yet are always wonderful. Jumbo lump crabmeat cakes; chilled or warm seafood platters priced per person; glazed black cod; prime steaks and chops.

OTHER RECOMMENDATIONS Signature bone-in steaks—the 22-ounce porterhouse is a terrific slab of beef. It's sliced in the kitchen and is perfect for sharing. Calf's liver with onions; superb hash-brown potatoes, crusty and golden brown with a creamy interior; outstanding side dishes—don't miss the fried green tomatoes or the signature grilled tomatoes with spinach and a cheddar-cheese topping.

SUMMARY AND COMMENTS Be prepared for noise—not overwhelming, but sometimes intrusive. Early dining is wise. Joe's reservation policy is peculiar: management prefers online reservations made well in advance. Walk-ins are not turned away but often have a wait at the bar. Joe's is a hot ticket, so be patient.

JR's Italian Kitchen ★★★½

ITALIAN	MODERATE	QUALITY ★★★½	VALUE ★★★★

5745 South Durango Drive; Southwest Las Vegas; ☎702-312-2180

Customers Locals, visitors. **Reservations** Weekends. **Entree range** $12.95–$17.95. **Payment** All major credit cards. **Service rating** ★★★★½. **Friendliness rating** ★★★★½. **Parking** Large lot. **When to go** Anytime. **Bar** Full service. **Wine selection** Small. **Dress** Casual. **Disabled access** Ground floor. **Hours** 24/7.

SETTING AND ATMOSPHERE Pleasant and simple, with burgundy-colored booths.

HOUSE SPECIALTIES Antipasto for two, large enough for four; very large, tender meatballs; Panini served with addictive house-made potato chips; Panini sandwich with Parma prosciutto, Fontina cheese, and arugula salad.

OTHER RECOMMENDATIONS A variety of hot and cold gyro sandwiches—the crusty Italian bread wraps around generous amounts of fillings: Braciole on a roll, Po' Boy with fried clams or shrimp; ten-ounce steak; black angus beef hamburgers with fries or homemade potato chips (the chips are better). Homespun, delicious eats.

SUMMARY AND COMMENTS JR's is a real find. Prices are down to earth. JR does the cooking. This small eatery is a local favorite, and the take-home boxes a way of life. Many fried foods, zero trans fat.

Kathy's Southern Cooking ★★½

AMERICAN	MODERATE	QUALITY ★★★½	VALUE ★★★★½

6407 Mountain Vista Street; Southeast Las Vegas; ☎ 702-433-1005

Customers Locals. **Reservations** Suggested, especially for groups of 6 or more. **When to go** Anytime. **Entree range** $12–$23. **Payment** AE, D, MC, V. **Service rating** ★★★½. **Friendliness rating** ★★★½. **Parking** Shopping-center lot. **Bar** Wine and beer only. **Wine selection** Limited (house wine). **Dress** Informal. **Disabled access** Ground floor. **Hours** Tuesday–Thursday, 11 a.m.–8:30 p.m.; Friday and Saturday, 11 a.m.–9:30 p.m.; Sunday, 1–7:30 p.m. Closed Monday.

SETTING AND ATMOSPHERE Casual, down-home dining room with 46 seats. One wall is painted with a mural of a paddlewheeler on the Mississippi River.

HOUSE SPECIALTIES Gumbo; catfish; "gravy dinners"—smothered pork chop, steak, or chicken with rice or mashed potatoes, slabs of corn bread, and a side dish from a selection of black-eyed peas, red beans and rice, greens, and more.

OTHER RECOMMENDATIONS Jambalaya; shrimp Creole; barbecued beef and spare-ribs; bread pudding. Kathy's spareribs are huge, with a zesty sauce that will make you tingle. Hearty, wholesome fare.

SUMMARY AND COMMENTS The owner of this family operation, Kathy Cook, presents authentic selections from Mississippi and Louisiana kitchens "like Mama used to make." Comfortable, with a "you all" kind of friendliness. Park in shopping center and walk through to Mountain Vista Street (no access from shopping center).

Kokomo's ★★★½

SEAFOOD/STEAK	VERY EXPENSIVE	QUALITY ★★★★	VALUE ★★½

The Mirage, 3400 South Las Vegas Boulevard; Mid-Strip and Environs; ☎ 702-791-7111; www.mirage.com

Customers Visitors. **Reservations** Required; high rollers and hotel guests get preference; reservations available 7 days in advance. **When to go** Anytime. **Entree range** $27–market price (à la carte). **Payment** AE, D, DC, MC, V. **Service rating**

★★★★½. **Friendliness rating** ★★★½. **Parking** Lot (long walk), valet. **Bar** Full service. **Wine selection** Good choices. **Dress** Casual. **Disabled access** Ramp. **Hours** Daily, 5–10:30 p.m.

SETTING AND ATMOSPHERE Magnificent tropical decor—waterfalls, streams, lush foliage, orchids, and other exotic flowers—brings the South Pacific to the Strip. Tables are well spaced for privacy.

HOUSE SPECIALTIES Red onion soup with Monterey Jack and Parmesan cheeses. Mashed sweet potatoes; steaks; chops and ribs; grilled rib eye with sautéed red onions and tricolor pepper sauce. Crème brûlée; peanut-butter cheesecake; chocolate mousse; bread pudding.

OTHER RECOMMENDATIONS Blackened Kansas City steak with spicy shrimp; veal and shrimp combo; double rib lamb chops; American kobe steak; crab cakes; oven-roasted, ginger-soy marinated Chilean sea bass; grilled mahimahi; wood-smoked Atlantic salmon; marshmallow brownie cheesecake; apple torte with cinnamon ice cream; taco shell delight; raspberries with Grand Marnier crème; chocolate sinful pâté with pecan brandy sauce.

SUMMARY AND COMMENTS Imaginative chefs and decor combine to create a memorable lunch or dinner in this romantic room. Peaceful and romantic, Kokomo's is a sleeper. One of the best-kept secrets in town.

Koreana ★★½

KOREAN	MODERATE	QUALITY ★★★★	VALUE ★★½

2447 East Tropicana Avenue; East of Strip; ☎ 702-458-6869

Customers Locals. **Reservations** Suggested weekends. **When to go** Anytime. **Entree range** $12–$20. **Payment** MC, V. **Service rating** ★★★½. **Friendliness rating** ★★★★½. **Parking** Lot. **Bar** Wine and beer. **Wine selection** No. **Dress** Casual. **Disabled access** Ground floor. **Hours** Sunday–Thursday, 11:30 a.m.–10:30 p.m.; Friday and Saturday, 11:30 a.m.–midnight.

SETTING AND ATMOSPHERE Minimalist decor (there isn't any) does not detract from the good food served in this neat and clean, small Korean eatery.

HOUSE SPECIALTIES Dinners cooked at the table, by the server, on an electric grill. Price includes a number of side dishes—cooked seaweed, not-too-fiery kimchi, spinach, cucumbers and seaweed, bean sprouts, a bowl of salad, and slightly vinegared rice. The marinated rib eye is a good choice.

OTHER RECOMMENDATIONS Selections from the à la carte menu: shredded beef brisket noodle soup, broiled fish, the casserole dishes.

SUMMARY AND COMMENTS Good, moderately priced food without any frills. Service is caring. English is limited, but somehow questions get answered.

Koto ★★★★

JAPANESE	INEXPENSIVE/MODERATE	QUALITY ★★★★½	VALUE ★★★★★

9400 South Eastern Avenue, Henderson; ☎ 702-221-1600; www.kotolasvegas.com

Customers Locals, visitors. **Reservations** A must on weekends. **When to go** Anytime. **Entree range** $5–$17. **Payment** All major credit cards. **Service rating** ★★★★. **Friendliness rating** ★★★★★. **Parking** Lot. **Bar** None. **Wine selection**

Small; sake and beer. **Dress** Casual. **Disabled access** Ramp. **Hours** Monday–Friday, noon–9:30 p.m.; Saturday, 4–9:30 p.m.; closed Sunday.

SETTING AND ATMOSPHERE Authentic Japanese restaurant in a strip mall with attractive decor designed and fabricated by chef-owner Toshiaki Horiai and his wife-partner, Mary Beth. The small, handsome sushi bar was also created by the owners.

HOUSE SPECIALTIES Excellent sushi, combination box dinners that include the bento box, soup, cucumber salad, rice, tea, and dessert. All-you-can-eat sushi—no restrictions on the amount, but ordering more than you can eat is a no-no. Noodle bowls.

OTHER RECOMMENDATIONS Broiled yellowtail collar, sweet and tender. "Little tasters" (tapas-size plates); beef tataki.

SUMMARY AND COMMENTS This modest restaurant is a terrific value. Many of the dishes served here are not found elsewhere. The owners are charming, personable people who have made the most of their limited space.

La Scala ★★★

ITALIAN	MODERATE	QUALITY ★★★	VALUE ★★½

1020 East Desert Inn Road; East of Strip;
☎ **702-699-9980; www.lascalarestaurant.net**

Customers Visitors, locals. **Reservations** Suggested weekends. **When to go** Anytime. **Entree range** $11–$28. **Payment** All major credit cards. **Service rating** ★★★★½. **Friendliness rating** ★★★½. **Parking** Lot. **Bar** Full service. **Wine selection** Good. **Dress** Upscale casual. **Disabled access** Ground level. **Hours** Daily, 11:30 a.m.–4 p.m. and 5–10 p.m.

SETTING AND ATMOSPHERE Recently refurbished, La Scala is a cheerful, pretty room that belies its history with many previous owners.

HOUSE SPECIALTIES The daily specials listed on a reader board (the fresh fish is the most expensive); any of the homemade pastas; the calamari or pescolini fritti—deep-fried squid or smelts with a spicy marinara sauce; peppered pan-sautéed whole Cornish hen; sautéed chicken breast filled with porcini mushroom and fontina cheese topped with bagna cauda (garlic, anchovy) sauce.

OTHER RECOMMENDATIONS The five-course tasting dinner (two-person minimum) that lets the chef show off his culinary talent. Lamb loin with balsamic vinegar and blueberry reduction; Melanzane alla Parmigiana, a more delicate take on the standard eggplant fave; linguine with lobster in tomato sauce.

SUMMARY AND COMMENTS The new owner is a chef with attitude. Food is good but overpriced, and the former owner's camaraderie is missing.

Lawry's The Prime Rib ★★★½

AMERICAN/PRIME RIB	EXPENSIVE	QUALITY ★★★½	VALUE ★★½

4043 Howard Hughes Parkway; East of Strip; ☎ **702-893-2223;**
www.lawrysonline.com

Customers Visitors, locals. **Reservations** Requested. **When to go** Anytime but convention times. **Entree range** $29–$42. **Payment** All major credit cards, JCB. **Service rating** ★★★★½. **Friendliness rating** ★★★★½. **Parking** Valet, lot. **Bar** Full service. **Wine selection** Good **Dress** Business attire. **Disabled access** Ground floor. **Hours** Sunday–Thursday, 5–10 p.m.; Friday and Saturday, 5–11 p.m.

SETTING AND ATMOSPHERE Elegant but not intimidating, Lawry's reflects the founder's philosophy that a restaurant should be "believable, understandable, and appeal to all." The dramatic "silver" carts brought to the table so the beef can be carved as you watch are actually made of hammered stainless steel. A handsome separate bar is a fine place for before- or after-dinner drinks.

HOUSE SPECIALTIES Prime rib, and not much else, has kept diners happy since the original Lawry's The Prime Rib opened in Beverly Hills, California, in 1938. All prime-rib dinners include a spinning salad bowl, Yorkshire pudding, mashed potatoes, and whipped cream horseradish. Five cuts of prime rib are offered. Add twin lobster tails to a prime-rib dinner for an additional $19.50.

OTHER RECOMMENDATIONS The fresh fish of the day—expertly prepared in the kitchen, accompanied by seasonal vegetables; the nostalgic creamed spinach or creamed corn. The selection of homespun desserts, especially the deep-dish apple pie with caramel sauce.

SUMMARY AND COMMENTS How can a restaurant survive that's devoted almost exclusively to prime rib in a town filled with inexpensive prime-rib deals? Very well, indeed. Lawry's Las Vegas opened with a rush that's never stopped. For prime-rib devotees, it's the ultimate luxurious temple of beefdom. Consistent food and service.

Lindo Michoacan ★★★½

MEXICAN INEXPENSIVE/MODERATE QUALITY ★★★★ VALUE ★★★★

2655 East Desert Inn Road; Southeast Las Vegas; ☎ 702-735-6828; www.lindomichoacan.com

Customers Locals and visitors. **Reservations** Suggested for dinner. **When to go** Anytime. **Entree range** $7.50–$17. **Payment** All major credit cards. **Service rating** ★★★½. **Friendliness rating** ★★★★. **Parking** Large lot. **Bar** Beer, cocktails, tequila. **Wine selection** None. **Dress** Casual. **Disabled access** Ground floor. **Hours** Monday–Wednesday, 11 a.m.–10 p.m.; Thursday and Friday, 11 a.m.–11 p.m.; Saturday and Sunday, 9:30 a.m.–11 p.m.; Sunday buffet brunch, 11 a.m.–2 p.m.; regular menu all day.

SETTING AND ATMOSPHERE A few years ago, a devastating fire destroyed Lindo Michoacan. Happily, the restaurant is back bigger and noisier, with flamboyant, colorful decor and an expanded menu of Mexican specialties.

HOUSE SPECIALTIES Lunch specials served from 11 a.m. to 5 p.m. Prices include a beverage and one refill, rice and beans, and, with most choices, thin flour tortillas. With such a large menu and so many offerings, try the à la carte tacos, enchiladas, and burritos smothered with salsa and Monterey cheese; tortas, Mexican sandwiches. On Saturdays and Sundays, Michoacan-style menudo (tripe soup) is served with fresh tortillas.

OTHER RECOMMENDATIONS Flan tío raul, traditional Mexican caramel custard; delicate sopaipillas drizzled with honey. Also try the sopitos, six hand-made gorditas topped with beef, chicken, or chorizo, plus lettuce, cheese, and tomatoes.

SUMMARY AND COMMENTS Lindo Michoacan is a popular party place. The din is deafening when the staff salutes the celebrants by beating on drums. Enjoy a late lunch if noise is not your thing. The beverage list is endless and much too tempting. Lunch is served until 5 p.m. and is a super value. Service is better and diners are spared the high decibels.

Little Buddha   ★★★½

CHINESE/SUSHI	MODERATE/EXPENSIVE	QUALITY ★★★★	VALUE ★★★

Palms, 4321 West Flamingo Road; Mid-Strip and Environs;
☎ **702-942-7778; www.littlebuddhalasvegas.com**

Customers Locals, celebs, visitors. **Reservations** Suggested weekends. **When to go** Anytime. **Entree range** $16–$45. **Payment** All major credit cards. **Service rating** ★★★½. **Friendliness rating** ★★★★½. **Parking** Valet, garage, lot. **Bar** Full service. **Wine selection** Small but good. **Dress** Casual chic. **Disabled access** Ground floor. **Hours** Daily, 5:30 p.m. until closing.

SETTING AND ATMOSPHERE Soft lighting and elegant, laid-back decor. A handsome sushi bar was recently added. Have a drink at the bar. It's the place for conversation and making new friends.

HOUSE SPECIALTIES Lettuce wraps with a generous amount of chicken, not minced, but sliced into chunks. Wok-fried salt-and-pepper calamari; crispy chicken spring rolls with a sweet chili sauce. Mochiko-crusted scallops with Asian pear–sake glaze; filet mignon cooked teppanyaki-style. Maui onion-crusted mahimahi with Thai chile–lime butter; grilled lobster tail with citrus butter sauce.

OTHER RECOMMENDATIONS Szechuan barbecue beef. The banana and mango phyllo roll, the caramelized lemon tart, or crème brûlée desserts.

SUMMARY AND COMMENTS The superb sushi is available at the sushi bar or at a table. The dinner menu is also offered at the sushi bar.

Lotus of Siam   ★★★★

THAI	MODERATE	QUALITY ★★★★	VALUE ★★½

Commercial Center, 953 East Sahara Avenue; East of Strip;
☎ **702-735-3033; www.saipinchutima.com**

Customers Locals, visitors. **Reservations** Not required. **When to go** Anytime. **Entree range** $8–$20; lunch buffet, $10. **Payment** MC, V. **Service rating** ★★½. **Friendliness rating** ★★★★½. **Parking** Lot. **Bar** No. **Wine selection** Good. **Dress** Casually elegant. **Disabled access** Ground floor. **Hours** Monday–Thursday (buffet and menu), 11:30 a.m.–2 p.m. and 5:30–9:30 p.m.; Friday, 11:30 a.m.–2 p.m. and 5:30–10 p.m.; Saturday, 5:30–10 p.m.; Sunday, 5–9 p.m.

SETTING AND ATMOSPHERE Attractive, though modest, decor; teak tables and comfortable chairs. Thai paintings and accessories.

HOUSE SPECIALTIES Beef jerky, Issan-style—crisp yet tender marinated beef served in a spicy sauce. Green papaya salad with or without crab; salmon Panang—charbroiled fresh salmon, served Thai-style with a creamy curry sauce.

OTHER RECOMMENDATIONS Long-grained sticky rice steamed and served in small bamboo baskets; the generously sized satays. Ask the owner to design a special menu of Isan dishes for your party. The seasonal soft-shell, crispy prawns are outstanding. Shells are edible—chew carefully.

SUMMARY AND COMMENTS The Isan specialties featured here come from the Northwestern corner of Thailand, bordering Laos. These dishes are both hotter and more highly seasoned than most Thai food, but the chef/owner will temper the heat to suit your taste. Gentle, caring service and exceptional, if little-known, Thai dishes make Lotus of Siam a fine choice when you've jostled through quite enough surf 'n' turf buffets, thank you.

Lucille's Smokehouse Bar-B-Que ★★★½

SOUTHERN/BARBECUE   MOD/EXP   QUALITY ★★★★   VALUE ★★★★½

The District at Green Valley Ranch, 2245 Village Walk Drive; Southeast Las Vegas; ☎ 702-257-7427; www.lucillesbbq.com

Customers Locals, visitors. **Reservations** No. **When to go** Anytime. **Entree range** $9.50–$25.50. **Payment** All major credit cards. **Service rating** ★★★. **Friendliness rating** ★★★★½. **Parking** Large lot. **Bar** Full service. **Wine selection** Modest. **Dress** Casual. **Disabled access** Ramp. **Hours** Sunday–Thursday, 11 a.m.–10 p.m.; Friday and Saturday, 11 a.m.–11 p.m.

SETTING AND ATMOSPHERE The legend of Lucille and her life with grandma "in a tiny little nothing of a place on a back road," is a fairy tale concocted by the California family who owns this funky barbecue restaurant and four more in California. It's designed to look like a roadside restaurant before fast food took over the country's landscape.

HOUSE SPECIALTIES Humongous portions of tasty appetizers, salads, Bunyan-sized barbecue dinners, and many specialities. The buttermilk biscuits are warm, tender, and like everything else at Lucille's—bigger than life. Sandwiches and burgers on homemade buns or baguettes. The dinosaur-sized beef ribs are awesome.

OTHER RECOMMENDATIONS The fried shrimp or barbecue-rib-tip appetizer large enough for two or three people; Lucille's onion straws. The best old-fashioned banana pudding ever, served in a pint-sized, wide-mouth Mason jar—the pudding is made from scratch and assembled when ordered; the peach cobbler with a biscuit crumb topping.

SUMMARY AND COMMENTS Live jazz and blues Friday and Saturday nights. Take-home boxes are a way of life at Lucille's. Order the full rack of ribs for just a few dollars more and share dinner. Kids love Lucille's. Call ahead and they'll tell you how long the wait is or come early and shop Las Vegas's newest mall. It's designed for walking and sightseeing.

Makino Sushi Restaurant ★★★½

JAPANESE   MODERATE   QUALITY ★★★★   VALUE ★★★★½

Renaissance Center, 3965 South Decatur Boulevard (near Flamingo); West of Strip; ☎ 702-889-4477

Customers Asian community, locals. **Reservations** Groups of 6 or more only. **When to go** Anytime. **Entree range** Fixed buffet price ($15–$24). **Payment** AE, MC, V. **Service rating** ★★★½. **Friendliness rating** ★★★½. **Parking** Large lot. **Bar** Wine and beer. **Dress** Casual. **Disabled access** Ground floor. **Hours** Monday–Friday, 11 a.m.–2:30 p.m. ($15); Friday–Sunday and holidays, 11:30 a.m.–3 p.m. ($16); Monday–Thursday, 5:30–9:30 p.m. ($23); Friday, 5:30–9:30 p.m.; Saturday, 5–10 p.m.; Sunday and holidays, 5–9 p.m. ($24). Seniors (65+) get 20% discount at dinner; kids under 5 feet tall eat for half-price; under 2 years of age eat free.

SETTING AND ATMOSPHERE   Simple, pleasant Japanese decor. The dining room is surrounded by food stations. The food stations are captivating, especially the sizable sushi, sashimi, and nigiri sushi area.

HOUSE SPECIALTIES   More than 40 varieties of sushi made as you watch (a supply is always ready) by a cadre of sushi chefs who work nonstop. More than 12,000 pieces of sushi are made most days. Hot and cold salads, some include seafood. A remarkable selection of hot seafood and Japanese specialties, including roast chicken, noodle dishes, sukiyaki, and much more. The food selections change daily. The largest selection is at dinner, when mountains of snow crab legs, shrimp, and other pricey seafood are added. Makino offers a spectacular selection of fresh fruits and desserts. The almond cookies, more like French sugar cookies, are exceptional.

SUMMARY AND COMMENTS   If you enjoy serving yourself, Makino is a fantastic deal. You'll not find a more appealing array of foods. Salads and desserts are presented on white porcelain platters. Everything is appealing and tasty. This is no ordinary buffet. Before making your choices, take the time to walk all of the stations. It would be nigh impossible to taste all of the foods, so hone in on your favorites. Except for the array of sushi, the food is put out in small amounts and replaced as needed. The sushi alone is worth more than what it costs for this no-limits Japanese feast.

Mama Jo's ★★½

ITALIAN   INEXPENSIVE/MODERATE   QUALITY ★★★   VALUE ★★½

3655 South Durango Drive; West of Strip; ☎ 702-869-8099

Customers Locals. **Reservations** Suggested. **When to go** Anytime. **Entree range** $10–$20. **Payment** All major credit cards. **Service rating** ★★★. **Friendliness rating** ★★★½. **Parking** Large lot. **Bar** Full service. **Wine selection** Small. **Dress** Casual. **Disabled access** Ramp. **Hours** Monday–Saturday, 11 a.m.–10 p.m.; Sunday, 3–9 p.m.

SETTING AND ATMOSPHERE   Spacious, simply furnished, a good old-fashioned family-style Italian restaurant with a separate bar for adults.

HOUSE SPECIALTIES   Mama's famous red sauce, on such standards as veal marsala, lasagna Bolognese, and eggplant Parmigiana. Fish soup bowls with a choice of flavored broth.

OTHER RECOMMENDATIONS Bruschetta, herb-crusted chicken salad, chicken cacciatore, mix-and-match pastas, subs and sandwiches (panini).

SUMMARY AND COMMENTS Good wholesome food in pleasant surroundings that will please those who like their Italian food familiar and plentiful. Low-carb menu available.

Marché Bacchus/Bacchus Bistro ★★★★

FRENCH BISTRO   MODERATE   QUALITY ★★★★   VALUE ★★★★

2620 Regatta Drive, # 106; West of Strip; ☎ 702-804-8008
www.marchebacchus.com

Customers Locals. **Reservations** Suggested weekends. **When to go** Anytime. **Entree range** Dinner $18–$27. **Payment** All major credit cards. **Service rating** ★★★★½. **Friendliness rating** ★★★★½. **Parking** Large lot. **Bar** Full service. **Wine selection** Extensive. **Dress** Casual. **Disabled access** Ground floor. **Hours** Daily, 10:30 a.m.–4 p.m. and 7–9 p.m.

SETTING AND ATMOSPHERE Walk through the wineshop to the adjacent bistro, or dine on the terrace with its gorgeous view of Regatta Lake (man-made). Simply furnished, this neighborhood eatery is an escape from the cares of the day. After one visit, you're welcomed by owners Agathe and Gregoire Verge as if you're members of the family.

HOUSE SPECIALTIES Bacchus clams sautéed with sausage, prosciutto, and pepper in white-wine cream sauce. Traditional cassoulet with duck confit, navy beans, and Toulouse and garlic sausages is served year-round, or the regulars get grumpy.

OTHER RECOMMENDATIONS This inviting Summerlin bistro and wineshop is favored by Strip chefs who come here to unwind.

SUMMARY AND COMMENTS Good wholesome food in pleasant surroundings that will please those who like their Italian food familiar and plentiful. Wheelchair access on lower level.

Marrakech ★★½

MOROCCAN   MODERATE   QUALITY ★★★½   VALUE ★★★½

3900 Paradise Road; East of Strip; ☎ 702-737-5611

Customers Visitors, locals. **Reservations** Suggested; required on weekends. **When to go** After 6:30 p.m. for belly dancers; busy during conventions. **Entree range** 6-course complete dinner, $30. **Payment** All major credit cards. **Service rating** ★★★½. **Friendliness rating** ★★★½. **Parking** Shopping-center lot. **Bar** Full service. **Wine selection** A Moroccan red and French white by the glass or bottle; Mondavi and Jordan, plus imported wines. **Dress** Informal, casual. **Disabled access** Ground floor. **Hours** Sunday–Thursday, 5:30–10 p.m.; Friday and Saturday, 5:30–11 p.m.

SETTING AND ATMOSPHERE Simulated desert tent with servers in native garb. Brass tables, floor pillows, and benches for seating maintain the illusion. Diners eat with their hands.

HOUSE SPECIALTIES Shrimp scampi; harira soup; Cornish hen in light lemon sauce; marinated lamb kabob. Multicourse fixed-price dinner, which does not include couscous. Bastila, a flaky chicken pie, normally a dinner course, is served for dessert at Marrakech.

ENTERTAINMENT AND AMENITIES Belly dancers undulate and undulate, pausing only to have greenbacks thrust into their costumes.

SUMMARY AND COMMENTS Las Vegas version of Moroccan food in an *Arabian Nights* setting. Belly dancing is competent but often intrusive. It's not authentic, but it's fun.

Mayflower Cuisinier ★★★★ *(relocating to the Venetian January 2008)*

| CHINESE/FRENCH | MODERATE | QUALITY ★★★★ | VALUE ★★★★½ |

4750 West Sahara Avenue; West of Strip; ☎ 702-870-8432; www.mayflowercuisinier.com

Customers Locals, some visitors. Reservations Suggested. When to go Anytime. Entree range $7–$23. Payment AE, D, DC, MC, V. Service rating ★★★½. Friendliness rating ★★★★. Parking Shopping-center lot. Bar Full service. Wine selection Upscale. Dress Casual to semidressy. Disabled access Ground floor. Hours Monday–Thursday, 11 a.m.–3 p.m. and 5–10 p.m.; Friday 11 a.m.–3 p.m. and 5–11 p.m.; Saturday, 5–11 p.m.; Sunday, closed.

SETTING AND ATMOSPHERE Two-level, 100-seat dining room; tastefully decorated in pink with contemporary black lacquer accents and handsome wall hangings. Choose from the main-level dining room or the more private mezzanine, or dine on the mist-cooled patio.

HOUSE SPECIALTIES Sake-miso–crusted sea bass; grilled rare ahi tuna salad; kung pao seafood medley of shrimp, scallops and salmon; stir-fried garlic mushrooms, asparagus, and spinach; chicken pot stickers with peanut-basil sauce; grilled lemongrass shrimp salad; grilled tenderloin of beef with Mongolian sauce.

OTHER RECOMMENDATIONS Ginger-basil seafood pasta; hot-and-sour soup; Mongolian grilled lamb chops with cilantro-mint sauce; seared ahi tuna with Dijon-lime sauce; stir-fried chicken in mushrooms and pineapples. Imaginative desserts that change seasonally.

SUMMARY AND COMMENTS Chef-owner Ming See Woo and manager Theresa, her daughter, created this fine cross-cultural restaurant. The new bar is ideal for a pre-dinner drink. An excellent fusion of Chinese and other cuisines.

Medici Café ★★★★

| ITALIAN | EXPENSIVE | QUALITY ★★★★½ | VALUE ★★★½ |

Ritz-Carlton, 1610 Lake Las Vegas Parkway, Henderson; ☎ 702-567-4700; www.ritzcarlton.com

Customers Visitors, locals. Reservations Recommended. When to go Anytime. Entree range $31–$50. Payment All major credit cards. Service rating ★★★★½. Friendliness rating ★★★★½. Parking Valet, lot. Bar Full service.

Wine selection Good. **Dress** Upscale casual. **Disabled access** Elevator. **Hours** Daily, 6:30 a.m.–2 p.m. and 6–10 p.m.

SETTING AND ATMOSPHERE Tuscan-themed, spacious dining room with elegant appointments and decor. Earthy and beautiful, Medici Café offers a view of the Florentine gardens, a favorite wedding setting.

HOUSE SPECIALTIES The portobello carpaccio appetizer with oven-cured tomatoes, with truffled vinaigrette and frisée salad; lobster two ways (a whole, split Maine lobster and potato-lobster potpie); bone-in New York steak with herbed French fries; seasonal daily specials.

OTHER RECOMMENDATIONS Roasted chicken with caramelized vegetables; red wine–braised short ribs; and pan-flashed striped sea bass with baby artichokes. The terrific selection of desserts: pineapple confit with mango ice cream and tapioca pudding, a martini glass filled with passion-fruit panna cotta, and lychee ice cream topped with a miniature savarin.

SUMMARY AND COMMENTS The Ritz-Carlton's Tuscan theme is a delight. Have a meal, and visit the gardens and the Ponte Vecchio bridge. Visit Monte Lago Village on Lake Como. Ideal for an after-meal walk and shopping.

Memphis Championship Barbecue ★★★

SOUTHERN BARBECUE   INEXPENSIVE   QUALITY ★★★½   VALUE ★★★★½

2250 East Warm Springs Road, Warm Springs; ☎ 702-260-6909
1401 South Rainbow Boulevard; Southeast Las Vegas; ☎ 702-254-0520;
4379 Las Vegas Boulevard; North Strip and Environs; ☎ 702-644-0000
www.memphis-bbq.com

Customers Visitors, locals. **Reservations** Advised on weekends and holidays. **When to go** Anytime. **Entree range** $7–$20 (includes sides). **Payment** All major credit cards. **Service rating** ★★★½. **Friendliness rating** ★★★★½. **Parking** Large lot. **Bar** Full service. **Wine selection** Modest; beer selection good. **Dress** Casual. **Disabled access** Ramp, ground floor. **Hours** Sunday–Thursday, 11 a.m.–10 p.m.; Friday and Saturday, 11 a.m.–10:30 p.m.

SETTING AND ATMOSPHERE Down-home comfort with ranch-house decor. Plenty of Southern memorabilia, including a street sign from the town where owner Mike Mills grew up.

HOUSE SPECIALTIES Real pit barbecue perfected by the owner. Mills is still using the family recipe that he continually tweaks. Southern-fried dill-pickle appetizer—much too good. It may sound crazy, but these pickles are addictive. Mama Faye's Down Home Supper, named for Mill's mother. A whopping platter for four that could easily feed more. Included are a rack of ribs, pork, beef brisket, hot links, one whole chicken, four sides, and rolls.

OTHER RECOMMENDATIONS Barbecued pork shoulder, blackened rib eye, charbroiled shrimp, the half-pound burgers, sandwiches from the pit. The Southern catfish dinner is a good choice.

SUMMARY AND COMMENTS Mike Mills is a legendary pit barbecue master. He's won four World Championship Cook-offs at the annual competition in Memphis and many more. Read the legend on the menu. Lunch prices are smaller and so are the portions. Dinner menu is available all day.

Michael's ★★★½

CONTINENTAL	VERY EXPENSIVE	QUALITY ★★★★	VALUE ★★½

South Point Hotel, 9777 South Las Vegas Boulevard; South Strip and Environs; ☎ 702-796-7111; www.southpointcasino.com

Customers Visitors, locals. **Reservations** Difficult, but starts taking reservations at 3:30 p.m. **When to go** Whenever you can get a reservation. **Entree range** $58–$148, à la carte. **Payment** All major credit cards. **Service rating** ★★★★½. **Friendliness rating** ★★★★½. **Parking. Parking** garage, valet. **Bar** Full service. **Wine selection** Excellent. **Dress** Sport coat, dressy. **Disabled access** Small staircase. **Hours** Daily, 2 seatings at 6 and 9 p.m.

SETTING AND ATMOSPHERE Comfortable chairs in intimate table settings. Deep carpeting and romantic lighting create a luxurious room in the rococo style of early Las Vegas.

HOUSE SPECIALTIES Rack of lamb bouquetière for two; live Maine lobster; veal saltimbocca, sautéed and topped with prosciutto; fresh Dover sole; the complimentary relish plate with humongous green and black olives.

OTHER RECOMMENDATIONS Shrimp cocktail served atop an igloo of ice, illuminated from within; bananas foster for two. All meats are prime.

ENTERTAINMENT AND AMENITIES Complimentary petits fours, chocolate-dipped fruits, and fancy fresh fruits are presented after dinner. Old Las Vegas lives at this opulent signature of the past.

SUMMARY AND COMMENTS If you're staying at a Strip hotel, the casino can help with a reservation. Early diners have a better chance of securing a table than those who like to dine at prime time. The menu (strictly à la carte) is a high-priced view of the Las Vegas of yesteryear.

Mon Ami Gabi ★★★½

CONTINENTAL/FRENCH	MOD/EXP	QUALITY ★★★★	VALUE ★★★½

Paris, 3655 South Las Vegas Boulevard; Mid-Strip and Environs; ☎ 702-944-GABI; www.parislasvegas.com

Customers Visitors, locals. **Reservations** Requested for dining room, not accepted for patio. **When to go** Anytime. **Entree range** $16–market price. **Payment** AE, DC, MC, V. **Service rating** ★★★½. **Friendliness rating** ★★★½. **Parking** Garage. **Bar** Full service. **Wine selection** All French wines. **Dress** Upscale casual. **Disabled access** Yes. **Hours** Sunday–Thursday, 11:30 a.m.–3 p.m. and 4–11 p.m.; Friday and Saturday, 11:30 a.m.–3 p.m. and 5 p.m.–midnight.

SETTING AND ATMOSPHERE Handsome brasserie with black-leather booths and tables. The main dining room leads to a wonderful, plant-filled patio and a marvelous sidewalk cafe with a view of the Strip.

HOUSE SPECIALTIES Steak frites, thin-sliced steak and French fries; an excellent selection of seafood and hors d'oeuvres; many hot seafood appetizers; the daily special listed on the blackboard; filet mignon and New York strip are among the regular steak selections.

OTHER RECOMMENDATIONS Crêpes; omelets and sandwiches served at lunch; plates of seafood, mussels gribiche (mussels with caper mayonnaise).

ENTERTAINMENT AND AMENITIES The restaurant is child-friendly, accepts take-out requests, and features banquet dining with fixed-price gourmet meals.

SUMMARY AND COMMENTS Mon Ami is a charming dining place. Everyone wants to dine at the sidewalk cafe, but you'll have to come early to get a table (there are no reservations for the cafe). The frites are curly fries, not steak fries, but they're crisp and good: so what if they're not authentic? Everything else is right on the mark. And for those whose dinner isn't complete without a good bottle of wine, there's a separate list of fine reserve wines.

Neros ★★★½

CONTEMPORARY AMERICAN   EXPENSIVE   QUALITY ★★★★   VALUE ★★½

Caesars Palace, 3570 South Las Vegas Boulevard; Mid-Strip and Environs; ☎ 702-731-7731; www.caesars.com

Customers Visitors, locals. Reservations Requested. When to go Anytime except convention times. Entree range $23–$65. Payment All major credit cards. Service rating ★★★★½. Friendliness rating ★★★★½. Parking Valet, garage, lot. Bar Full service. Wine selection Excellent. Dress Business attire. Disabled access Ground floor. Hours Daily, 5–11 p.m.

SETTING AND ATMOSPHERE Softly lit, with comfortable booths and tables, Neros is a fine example of understated elegance.

HOUSE SPECIALTIES Filet Châteaubriand for two; 28-ounce T-bone; pan-seared foie gras with 100-year-old balsamic vinegar; yellowfin tuna tartare; smoky Vidalia-onion soup with herbed goat-cheese croutons; Alaskan halibut with mushroom and bacon; sage-roasted chicken.

OTHER RECOMMENDATIONS Slow-baked salmon; wild mushroom fricassee; 20-ounce New York strip; the splendid desserts, especially the delectable fallen chocolate soufflé.

SUMMARY AND COMMENTS A prime steak house with a contemporary menu of upscale fare.

Noodles ★★★

CHINESE/JAPANESE/THAI   MODERATE   QUALITY ★★★★   VALUE ★★★½

Bellagio, 3600 South Las Vegas Boulevard; Mid-Strip and Environs; ☎ 702-693-7223; www.bellagio.com

Customers Visitors, locals. Reservations No. When to go Anytime. Entree range À la carte $12–$30. Payment All major credit cards. Service rating ★★★½. Friendliness rating ★★★½. Parking Valet, lot. Bar Full service. Wine selection Good. Dress Casual. Disabled access Ground floor. Hours Daily, 11 a.m.–2 a.m. Dim sum: Friday–Sunday, 11 a.m.–3 p.m.

SETTING AND ATMOSPHERE Follow the marble floor with Chinese brass inlays that represent bits of Asian wisdom into this wonderful eatery. There's an open kitchen, a wall of artifacts, and the hustle and bustle of an authentic noodle kitchen.

HOUSE SPECIALTIES Oodles of slurpy, authentic noodle dishes from China, Vietnam, Thailand, and Japan and authentic Hong Kong–style barbecue dishes. There's a long list of appetizers and many different teas.

SUMMARY AND COMMENTS Noodles is small, only 88 seats, so it's tough to get in at prime times, but it's open long hours so you're bound to get in sometime. This is a favorite stop for Bellagio's Asian clientele. Find the Baccarat bar, and you'll find Noodles.

Olives ★★★½

| AMERICAN/MEDITERRANEAN | MOD/EXP | QUALITY ★★★★ | VALUE ★★★½ |

Bellagio, 3600 South Las Vegas Boulevard; Mid-Strip and Environs; ☎ 702-693-8181; www.bellagio.com

Customers Visitors, locals. **Reservations** Accepted. **When to go** Anytime. **Entree range** Lunch, $15–$22; dinner, $20–$38. **Payment** All major credit cards. **Service rating** ★★★½. **Friendliness rating** ★★★★½. **Parking** Valet, garage. **Bar** Full service. **Wine selection** Eclectic. **Dress** Casual. **Disabled access** Ground floor. **Hours** Daily, 11 a.m.–3 p.m. and 5–10:30 p.m.

SETTING AND ATMOSPHERE Intricate mosaic tiling, a sculpted wood ceiling, an open kitchen, and an outdoor patio with a view of the lake.

HOUSE SPECIALTIES The menu changes regularly but always includes a lobster scampi; the signature butternut squash tortellini with brown butter, sage, and Parmesan cheese; the savory spit-roasted chicken on a crisp mashed-potato cake; individual pizzas with a flatbreadlike crust; and grilled pork chop in clam-chorizo broth. Typical of the daily specials is the slow-braised lamb chops.

OTHER RECOMMENDATIONS Beef carpaccio; grilled squid and octopus; pan-seared salmon; chocolate falling cake; roasted banana tiramisù; any of the wonderful sandwiches served only at lunch.

SUMMARY AND COMMENTS Recently remodeled, Olives is a sleeker version of the Boston original and has the same warmth and expert staff; many are from the Boston Olives. These Olives veterans have re-created the essence and spirit of the original. Everyone wants a terrace table but the terrace seating cannot be reserved.

168 Shanghai Restaurant ★★★½

| CHINESE | MODERATE | QUALITY ★★★½ | VALUE ★★★★ |

4215 Spring Mountain Road (China Town Plaza); West of the Strip; ☎ 702-889-8700

Customers Locals and adventurers. **Reservations** For parties of 6 or more. **Entree range** $6.95–$10.95. **Payment** MC, V. **Service rating** ★★★★. **Friendliness rating** ★★★½. **Parking** Large lot. **When to go** Anytime. **Bar** Beer. **Wine selection** None. **Dress** Casual. **Disabled access** Ramps, elevator. **Hours** Daily, 10:30 a.m.–10 p.m.

SETTING AND ATMOSPHERE Bustling, informal neighborhood diner.

HOUSE SPECIALTIES Honeyed pecan prawns; spicy General Tso Chicken; spicy eggplant and tofu.

OTHER RECOMMENDATIONS Best bets are the large bowls filled with won ton or dumplings. Slurp along with everyone and fit right in.

SUMMARY AND COMMENTS À la carte menu in Chinese with some attempts at fractured English. Very little English spoken. No frills, just good Chinese food at modest prices.

Pamplemousse ★★★

CONTINENTAL/FRENCH	MODERATE	QUALITY ★★★½	VALUE ★★½

400 East Sahara Avenue; East of Strip; ☎ 702-733-2066; www.pamplemousserestaurant.com

Customers Visitors, locals. Reservations Required. When to go Avoid conventions. Entree range $18–$24. Payment AE, D, DC, MC, V. Service rating ★★★½. Friendliness rating ★★★★½. Parking Street, lot. Bar Beer and wine only. Wine selection Excellent. Dress Upscale casual. Disabled access Ground floor. Hours Daily, 5:30–10:30 p.m.

SETTING AND ATMOSPHERE Country French. Attractive wine cellar at entrance to dining room. Restaurant has no menu; waiters recite the day's offerings and describe each dish.

HOUSE SPECIALTIES Duckling dishes; medallions of veal prepared with baked apples; special seafood dishes in season—mussels, monkfish, salmon; assorted desserts, all delicious.

OTHER RECOMMENDATIONS Dinner begins with a fine assortment of fresh vegetables (crudités) served from a handsome basket with an individual crock of house vinaigrette.

SUMMARY AND COMMENTS Waiters will give prices when reciting menu only if asked. Ask, so there are no surprises when the check arrives.

Panevino Ristorante/Gourmet Deli ★★★½

ITALIAN	MODERATE/EXPENSIVE	QUALITY ★★★★½	VALUE ★★★½

246 Via Antonio, east of Las Vegas Boulevard on Sunset; South Strip and Environs; ☎ 702-222-2400; www.panevinolasvegas.com

Customers Visitors, locals. Reservations Recommended. When to go Anytime. Entree range $14–$36. Payment All major credit cards. Service rating ★★★★½. Friendliness rating ★★★★½. Parking Large. Bar Full service. Wine selection Excellent Italian. Dress Business casual. Disabled access Ground floor. Hours Monday–Thursday, 11 a.m.–3 p.m. and 5–10 p.m.; Friday, 11 a.m.–3 p.m. and 5–11 p.m.; Saturday, 5–11 p.m.; Sunday, 5–10 p.m.

SETTING AND ATMOSPHERE Designed by owner Anthony Marnell, Panevino's red travertine walls were custom-quarried in Italy. A spectacular curved glass wall shapes the view of the Las Vegas skyline. Italy's finest artisans contributed their best to this gorgeous restaurant.

HOUSE SPECIALTIES Pastas, breads, and pastries baked daily. Farfalline Contadina, bow-tie pasta in a creamy pesto sauce with grilled chicken; risotto porcini, arborio rice slowly cooked with mushrooms, sausage, and cheese; pollo alla brace, grilled boneless chicken breast prepared with olive oil, garlic, red pepper, and rosemary and served with roasted potatoes; filetto di Manzo, a 10-ounce filet mignon with shallots, corn-mashed potatoes, and porcini-mushroom sauce.

OTHER RECOMMENDATIONS Pear and gorgonzola cheese salad; pappardelle pasta with lamb ragù, tomato, and mushroom sauce.

SUMMARY AND COMMENTS Panevino is located in Marnell's corporate office business complex. There is plenty of signage on Sunset Road, but the entrance is easy to miss, so stay alert. Adjacent to Panevino Ristorante is a delightful gourmet deli featuring homemade soups, sandwiches, salads, and other casual Italian eats. Eat in or take out. Prices are reasonable, the staff is congenial, and this is the prettiest deli outside of Italy.

Pasta Pirate ★★★

SEAFOOD/PASTA   MODERATE/EXPENSIVE   QUALITY ★★★½   VALUE ★★★★½

California Hotel, 12 East Ogden Avenue; Downtown; ☎ 702-385-1222; www.thecal.com

Customers Visitors, locals. Reservations Suggested. When to go Anytime. Entree range $12–$40. Payment AE, D, DC, MC, V. Service rating ★★★½. Friendliness rating ★★★½. Parking Garage, valet. Bar Full service. Wine selection Adequate. Dress Casual. Disabled access Ground floor. Hours Wednesday–Monday, 5–11 p.m.; closed Tuesday.

SETTING AND ATMOSPHERE Small restaurant with waterfront motif featuring tin walls, a brick floor, fishnets, neon signs, and an open kitchen.

HOUSE SPECIALTIES Pasta and seafood; Alaskan king crab legs; scampi; baby lobster tails; and marinated sesame lobster brochettes. A glass of wine is included with all entrees.

OTHER RECOMMENDATIONS Filet mignon with prawns; live Maine lobster; rigatoni Romano; cavatelli with broccoli; penne Diana; Cajun tuna.

ENTERTAINMENT AND AMENITIES Piano player entertains between bar and dining room entrances, 6 to 11 p.m.

SUMMARY AND COMMENTS The Pasta Pirate offers an imaginative menu at moderate prices. Consistently good food and prices.

Pearl ★★★★

CHINESE   EXPENSIVE   QUALITY ★★★★   VALUE ★★½

MGM Grand, 3799 South Las Vegas Boulevard; South Strip and Environs; ☎ 702-891-7380; www.mgmgrand.com

Customers Visitors, locals. Reservations Suggested. When to go Anytime. Entree range $12–market price. Payment All major credit cards. Service rating ★★★★½. Friendliness rating ★★★★½. Parking Valet, parking garage. Bar Full service. Wine selection Very good. Dress Business attire, casual chic. Disabled access Ramp. Hours Daily, 5:30–10:30 p.m.

SETTING AND ATMOSPHERE Arguably the most beautiful Chinese dining room in Las Vegas. Sleek and inviting, the tall booths offer privacy and a view of the dining room. A private dining area adjacent to the wine cellar is in great demand. Expert lighting and gorgeous appointments.

HOUSE SPECIALTIES Multicourse tasting menu; pricey, but worth it. Pearl's family-style menus for two or more—six or more courses for a fixed price. Spider-prawn dumplings, minced tiger prawns and pine nuts in lettuce petals; deep-fried shiitake mushrooms glazed with spicy black vinegar. The live fish and seafood selection; Dungeness crabmeat baked in the shell; wok-fried filet of venison and asparagus, Cantonese-style.

OTHER RECOMMENDATIONS The signature Asian bouillabaisse, spiced king crab legs with chili and garlic, the steamed Maine and Australian lobster tasting. Maine lobster fried rice, braised Thai eggplant with chili-plum sauce, star anise lamb chops with string beans. The tableside tea service.

SUMMARY AND COMMENTS Dining at Pearl is relaxing and satisfying. It's elegant, inviting, and a terrific departure from the usual Chinese restaurant.

Picasso ★★★½

FRENCH/SPANISH	VERY EXPENSIVE	QUALITY ★★★★	VALUE ★★½

Bellagio, 3600 South Las Vegas Boulevard; Mid-Strip and Environs;
☎ **702-693-8105; www.bellagio.com**

Customers Visitors, locals. Reservations A must. When to go Anytime you can get a reservation. Entree range Prix fixe only, $105 or $115. Payment All major credit cards. Service rating ★★★★½. Friendliness rating ★★★★½. Parking Valet, self. Bar Full service. Wine selection Excellent. Dress Casually elegant, jackets recommended. Disabled access Elevator. Hours Wednesday–Monday, 6–10 p.m.

SETTING AND ATMOSPHERE Arguably the most beautiful dining room in Las Vegas. A treasure of original Picasso artworks adorn the walls. The flower displays throughout the restaurant are exquisite. A wall of windows gives most tables a full view of the dancing fountains.

HOUSE SPECIALTIES Selections on both the five-course degustation and the four-course prix fixe menus change regularly according to the whim of the chef. The warm lobster salad, sautéed foie gras, sautéed medallions of swordfish, and aged lamb rôti with truffle crust appear often. The roasted pigeon (squab) is outstanding. Chef Julian Serrano, formerly of Masa's in San Francisco, sometimes offers a sensational *amuse-bouche*, a tiny potato pancake topped with crème fraîche and osetra caviar.

SUMMARY AND COMMENTS This exceptional restaurant is grand yet unpretentious. Allow enough time to enjoy the experience. After dinner have a drink on the terrace. Where else but in Las Vegas can you have a view of Lake Como as well as one of the Eiffel Tower? Chef Serrano was named the "Best Chef in the Southwest 2002" by the James Beard Foundation. Serrano is the first Las Vegas chef to win a Beard award.

Piero's ★★★★

ITALIAN	EXPENSIVE	QUALITY ★★★★	VALUE ★★½

355 Convention Center Drive; North Strip and Environs;
☎ **702-369-2305; www.pieroscuisine.com**

Customers Visitors, locals, conventioneers. Reservations Required. When to go Anytime. Entree range $26–$40 (higher for lobster). Payment AE, D, DC, MC, V.

Service rating ★★★★. Friendliness rating ★★★★. Parking Valet, lot. Bar Full service. Wine selection Excellent. Dress Business casual. Disabled access Ground floor. Hours Sunday–Thursday, 5:30–9 p.m.; Friday and Saturday, 5–10 p.m.

SETTING AND ATMOSPHERE Many softly lit booths and alcoves for guests desiring privacy. There are two private dining rooms for 12 to 20 people; a banquet room that can accommodate up to 250; a piano bar; and a much larger kitchen. The excellent waitstaff specializes in old-world-style service.

HOUSE SPECIALTIES Osso buco Piero; scaloppine Parmigiana; *verde e legumi inbrodo* (soup of fresh vegetables and pasta in broth); whole roasted kosher chicken as good or better than Mama used to make; any dish with Provimi veal; the Italian pastas with French-influenced sauces; the 25-ounce New York steak; stone crab claws or cakes of Maryland blue crab, in season.

SUMMARY AND COMMENTS Celebrities and sports figures always make their way to Piero's, as do Las Vegas power brokers, who consistently dine here. Dom Pérignon, Cristal, Grand Cordon Champagnes, and pricey bottles of Montrachet are the norm at Piero's.

Pinot Brasserie ★★★

FRENCH	MODERATE	QUALITY ★★★½	VALUE ★★½

**Venetian Hotel, 3355 South Las Vegas Boulevard; Mid-Strip and Environs;
☎ 702-414-8881; www.venetian.com**

Customers Visitors, locals. Reservations Requested at dinner. When to go Avoid conventions. Entree range $11–$18 (lunch); $21–market price (dinner). Payment AE, D, DC, MC, V. Service rating ★★★½. Friendliness rating ★★★★. Parking Valet, garage. Bar Full service. Wine selection Good. Dress Upscale casual (dinner). Disabled access Ground floor. Hours Daily, 7–10 a.m., 11:30 a.m.–3 p.m., and 5:30–10:30 p.m.

SETTING AND ATMOSPHERE Authentic French-brasserie decor, with comfortable booths and tables. The owners scoured flea markets and design centers in Paris to achieve this warm and inviting atmosphere. Everything from the lamps to the beautiful wood facade (rescued from an old hotel) are authentic.

HOUSE SPECIALTIES Fresh seafood—the shellfish platter for two is especially terrific, as are the steamed mussels with shallots, garlic, and wine; traditional French onion soup gratinée with a thick crust of melted cheese; rotisserie chicken with mushroom ragout; honey-glazed breast of duck; and cote du boeuf for two—a hearty grilled beef chop with roasted portobello mushrooms, roasted potatoes, onion rings, and red-wine shallot sauce.

OTHER RECOMMENDATIONS The daily *plat du jour,* which could be a classic cassoulet, lamb shank pot-au-feu, bouillabaisse, grilled veal chop, or a Sunday surprise, known only to the chef (for adventurous diners only). The desserts are scrumptious—order the chocolate soufflé when you order your entree.

SUMMARY AND COMMENTS A small cafe outside the Brasserie is a fine place to people-watch and enjoy a casual meal. They serve seafood, appetizers, sandwiches, salads, and some entrees—but it's plenty to choose from. Seafood is not inexpensive here, but this is a rare Las Vegas occurrence of truly getting what you pay for; just expect the higher tab. As in France, meals are leisurely at Pinot, especially so if the restaurant is busy. But with such carefully chosen decor and lush food, you might gladly while away an entire day here.

Prime ★★★★

STEAK	EXPENSIVE	QUALITY ★★★★½	VALUE ★★½

Bellagio, 3600 South Las Vegas Boulevard; Mid-Strip and Environs; ☎ 702-693-8484; www.bellagio.com

Customers Visitors, locals. **Reservations** Requested. **When to go** Avoid convention times. **Entree range** $25–$48. **Payment** All major credit cards. **Service rating** ★★★★½. **Friendliness rating** ★★★★½. **Parking** Valet, self. **Bar** Full service. **Wine selection** Excellent. **Dress** Casually elegant, jackets preferred. **Disabled access** Elevator. **Hours** Daily, 5–10 p.m.

SETTING AND ATMOSPHERE Dazzling powder-blue and chocolate carpets and wall hangings in a setting seldom seen for a steak house—it's gorgeous. In keeping with Bellagio's fine-arts policy, there's plenty of original art to view here. Have a drink at the elegant bar and take it all in.

HOUSE SPECIALTIES Prime, aged steaks and seafood; lamb chops in balsamic syrup; filet mignon with tomatoes; veal chop in pineapple chutney. A choice of a variety of sauces and excellent side dishes.

SUMMARY AND COMMENTS Prime is on the lower level of the shopping corridor beside Picasso. Both restaurants get their share of lookers, but the staff keeps them from disturbing diners. It's hard to resist this rare steak house with impeccable service.

Red Square ★★★

AMERICAN/RUSSIAN	MODERATE/EXPENSIVE	QUALITY ★★★½	VALUE ★★½

Mandalay Bay, 3950 South Las Vegas Boulevard; South Strip and Environs; ☎ 702-632-7407; www.mandalaybay.com

Customers Visitors, locals. **Reservations** Suggested on weekends. **When to go** Anytime. **Entree range** $19–$40. **Payment** AE, DC, MC, V. **Service rating** ★★★½. **Friendliness rating** ★★★½. **Parking** Valet, garage. **Bar** Full service. **Wine selection** Vodka's the drink here. **Dress** Casual. **Disabled access** Ground floor. **Hours** Daily, 5 p.m.–midnight; bar open Sunday–Thursday until 2 a.m., and until 4 a.m. Friday and Saturday.

SETTING AND ATMOSPHERE More American than Russian, this comfy dining room has Russian-inspired decor and a large bar with a top that's partly a slab of ice.

HOUSE SPECIALTIES Updated Russian classics: roasted lamb with sirniki; lobster and black truffle; smothered blini; apricot duck.

OTHER RECOMMENDATIONS The frozen-ice bar offers more than 100 frozen vodkas and infusions, plus martinis and Russian-inspired cocktails.

SUMMARY AND COMMENTS Another winning concept from the China Grill creators. There are some dining limits; ask when you make your reservation. Adventurers can don a provided coat and visit the chilly, glass-enclosed Walk-In Box, home to numerous vodkas—worth a nip of frostbite.

Redwood Bar & Grill ★★★½

AMERICAN/PRIME RIB	MODERATE	QUALITY ★★★½	VALUE ★★★★½

California Hotel, 12 East Ogden Avenue; Downtown; ☎ 702-385-1222; www.thecal.com

Customers Visitors, locals. **Reservations** Suggested. **When to go** Early evening. **Entree range** $13–$28. **Payment** AE, D, DC, MC, V. **Service rating** ★★★½. **Friendliness rating** ★★★★½. **Parking** Hotel lot and valet. **Bar** Full service. **Wine selection** Good. **Dress** Informal. **Disabled access** Ground floor. **Hours** Friday–Tuesday, 5:30–11 p.m.

SETTING AND ATMOSPHERE Country English furnishings and a fireplace make for comfortable dining. A quiet room where service is efficient and gracious.

HOUSE SPECIALTIES Caesar salad; steak Diane; chicken with apricot sauce. Porterhouse steak special: 18 ounces for $19.95 includes soup or salad, potatoes, vegetable, dessert.

OTHER RECOMMENDATIONS Soup du jour such as seafood chowder; Australian lobster tail; fresh fish; roast prime rib; veal Oscar; steak and lobster.

ENTERTAINMENT AND AMENITIES Piano music Friday through Tuesday.

SUMMARY AND COMMENTS Excellent value. Prime-rib portion is succulent, generous, and cooked as ordered. Although part of a locally owned group of five hotels, the Redwood Bar & Grill maintains its cozy individuality in both decor and service. Outstanding value.

Rosemary's Restaurant ★★★★

AMERICAN	EXPENSIVE	QUALITY ★★★★	VALUE ★★½

Summerlin, 8125 West Sahara Avenue; West of Strip; ☎ 702-869-2251; www.rosemarysrestaurant.com

Customers Visitors, locals. **Reservations** Recommended. **When to go** Anytime. **Entree range** $25–$45. **Payment** All major credit cards. **Service rating** ★★★★. **Friendliness rating** ★★★★½. **Parking** Large lot. **Bar** Full service. **Wine selection** Very good. **Dress** Upscale casual. **Disabled access** Ground level. **Hours** Monday–Friday, 11:30 a.m.–2:30 p.m. and 5:30–10 p.m.; Saturday and Sunday, 5:30–10 p.m.

SETTING AND ATMOSPHERE A comfortable bar separates the street side from the attractive dining room. Simple, effective decor with gauzy drapes and local artwork, all appealing. An open kitchen gives a view of the chefs.

HOUSE SPECIALTIES Roasted rack of lamb with black-olive mashed potatoes and arugula, crispy-skin striped bass, creole-spiced New York strip.

OTHER RECOMMENDATIONS Salmon tartare, sweet-corn soup, wilted spinach salad, brick chicken, seared scallops, any of the side dishes.

SUMMARY AND COMMENTS Chef-owner Michael Jordan was formerly the executive chef for Emeril's at MGM Grand. With the opening of Rosemary's on Sahara, he and his chef-wife, Wendy, are a peerless culinary team.

Rosewood Grille ★★★

| LOBSTER/STEAK | MODERATE/EXPENSIVE | QUALITY ★★★½ | VALUE ★★½ |

3763 South Las Vegas Boulevard; South Strip and Environs;
☎ **702-792-9099**

Customers Visitors. **Reservations** Strongly recommended. **When to go** Anytime. **Entree range** $21–$45, higher for lobster and stone crab. **Payment** All major credit cards. **Service rating** ★★★½. **Friendliness rating** ★★★½. **Parking** Lot behind restaurant. **Bar** Full service. **Wine selection** Excellent. **Dress** Informal. **Disabled access** Ground floor. **Hours** Daily, 5–11:30 p.m.

SETTING AND ATMOSPHERE Muted lighting, large booths, seating for 200. This always-busy restaurant still retains its old-world charm.

HOUSE SPECIALTIES Live Maine lobster in humongous sizes. Dinner includes salad and potatoes.

OTHER RECOMMENDATIONS Lobster and steak combination; beef chop; beef-eaters brochette; scampi; stone crabs; broiled salmon Charlotte; tournedos Scandia; lobster ravioli; chicken with strawberries in Cointreau. Strawberries with Dom Pérignon for two; café Mozart.

SUMMARY AND COMMENTS Restaurant stocks a week's supply of large and extra-large lobsters (up to 25 pounds). Price changes with the market. Ask the server for the day's price of lobsters before ordering.

rumjungle ★★★

| BRAZILIAN RODIZIO | MODERATE/EXPENSIVE | QUALITY ★★★½ | VALUE ★★½ |

Mandalay Bay, 3950 South Las Vegas Boulevard; South Strip and Environs; ☎ **702-632-7408; www.mandalaybay.com**

Customers Boomers and Gen-X–ers. **Reservations** Suggested for dinner. **When to go** Anytime. **Entree range** $22–$40 (rodizio, $36). **Payment** AE, D, DC, MC, V. **Service rating** ★★★. **Friendliness rating** ★★★★½. **Parking** Valet, garage. **Bar** Full service. **Wine selection** Small. **Dress** No overly funky clothes, no hats. A blazer or collared shirt must be worn with jeans. **Disabled access** No. **Hours** Daily, noon–4 p.m. and 5–10 p.m.

SETTING AND ATMOSPHERE Wild, junglelike setting, with soaring ceilings, an open fire pit, and a wall of fire. This place really rocks, though dinner hours are less frenetic.

HOUSE SPECIALTIES Unlimited quantities of meat, fish, and poultry with many accompaniments and sauces for a fixed price. The cost is about half the adult price for kids age 12 and under.

OTHER RECOMMENDATIONS À la carte appetizers—Jamaican-spiced chicken skewers; coconut shrimp; jerk-spiced chicken wings and Bahamian conch fritters; Honolulu Caesar salad; banana-leaf sea bass; baby back pork ribs.

SUMMARY AND COMMENTS There are so many rules and restrictions here, you need a guide to get you through without mishap. On weekends, parties of eight or more have two hours in which to dine. There is a cover charge after 11 p.m. Still, rumjungle is a cool spot for the younger (but over 21) set who find the dancing fire wall and pulsating dance floor a kick.

Sam Woo Bar-B-Q ★★★

CHINESE BARBECUE   INEXPENSIVE/MODERATE   QUALITY ★★★   VALUE ★★★★★

Chinatown Mall, 4215 Spring Mountain Road; West of Strip;
☎ **702-368-7628**

Customers Asian community, locals, tourists. **Reservations** No. **When to go** Anytime. **Entree range** $10–$20. **Payment** MC, V. **Service rating** ★★★½. **Friendliness rating** ★★★½. **Parking** Large lot. **Bar** None. **Wine selection** None. **Dress** Anything goes. **Disabled access** Ground floor. **Hours** Daily, 10 a.m.–11 p.m.

SETTING AND ATMOSPHERE Enter Sam Woo and enjoy the sights of meats and whole ducks hanging from hooks in the glass holding case. To the left is the popular take-out barbecue counter; to the right, a spacious good-sized restaurant. No frills, but pleasant.

HOUSE SPECIALTIES Any of the barbecued foods—roast pork, spare ribs, duck, and chicken; the Sam Woo combination plate is an exceptional value—the large platter is heaped high with roast and barbecued pork, roast duck, and chicken. Vegetable dishes are outstanding and inexpensive. The extensive menu is filled with an interesting selection of dishes, including hot pots that are cooked at the table.

SUMMARY AND COMMENTS Very little English is spoken here, but the menu is in English. Service is good, but can be brusque when the restaurant is busy. Take it in stride. Sam Woo is one of the best values in a town filled with them. Watch what other diners are eating for clues to what to order.

Samba Brazilian Steakhouse ★★★½

BRAZILIAN/STEAK   MODERATE/EXPENSIVE   QUALITY ★★★★   VALUE ★★★½

The Mirage, 3400 South Las Vegas Boulevard; Mid-Strip and Environs;
☎ **702-791-7111; www.mirage.com**

Customers Visitors, locals. **Reservations** Recommended. **When to go** Anytime. **Entree range** Rodizio, $35; à la carte, $19–$39. **Payment** All major credit cards. **Service rating** ★★★½. **Friendliness rating** ★★★★½. **Parking** Valet, garage. **Bar** Full. **Wine selection** Good. **Dress** Upscale casual. **Disabled access** Ground floor, ramp. **Hours** Daily, 5–10:30 p.m.

SETTING AND ATMOSPHERE Vibrant colors and colorful booths and appointments capture the theme of this Brazilian steak house. Remember Fiesta chinaware? The same palette of colors is found here.

HOUSE SPECIALTIES The Rodizio Experience: unlimited servings of marinated meats, poultry, and fish for a fixed price. Dinners include a bottomless bowl of Samba salad, side dishes of creamed spinach, black beans and rice, fried bananas, farofa carrots, and a basket of Brazilian breads. À la carte selections include the side dishes, but the meats are grilled, not cooked on a spit.

OTHER RECOMMENDATIONS À la carte appetizers, awesome coconut prawns; freshly made juices by the glass or pitcher—mango, passion fruit, grapefruit, and orange. The delectable rice pudding laced with fresh pineapple; a huge banana split for two that could easily serve four.

SUMMARY AND COMMENTS The jewel-like bar is a nice place for a drink and appetizers. Samba is a terrific restaurant with prices out of the past.

Sapporo ★★★½

ASIAN/SUSHI   **MODERATE/EXPENSIVE**   **QUALITY ★★★★**   **VALUE ★★★★**

Grand Flamingo Center at Flamingo and I-215, 9719 West Flamingo Road; West of Strip; ☎ 702-216-3080

Customers Locals, families, and visitors. **Reservations** Recommended. **When to go** Anytime. **Service rating** ★★★½. **Friendliness rating** ★★★★½. **Entree range** $12–$39. **Payment** All major credit cards. **Parking** Large lot. **Bar** Full service. **Wine selection** Small but good. **Dress** Casual chic. **Disabled access** Ground floor. **Hours** Sunday–Thursday, 4 p.m.–1 a.m.; Friday and Saturday, 4 p.m.–2 a.m.

SETTING AND ATMOSPHERE The sea is the setting. Shimmering shades of blue and silver dominate throughout. Flat-screen televisions along the sinuous wall display an array of fish. A soothing, tranquil effect. A freestanding portion of the bar opens to the patio. Strategically placed mirrors and lighting gives the restaurant its allure.

HOUSE SPECIALTIES Sizzling wok dishes, all value priced. Glazed Kabayaki scallops served with asparagus tips and shiitake mushrooms and scallions; Szechuan marinated beef and sweet and spicy chicken; blackened ahi in a savory soy-mustard sauce. A variety of small plates, including tuna or beef carpaccio, barbecued chicken egg rolls, lobster dumplings, and shrimp stuffed with lobster mousse.

OTHER RECOMMENDATIONS Tempura, the American Kobe beef burger with pepper Jack cheese, tomato, lettuce, and red onion with the house fries. Kung Pao Shanghai noodles. The teppan dinners that include soup, salad, fried rice, a shrimp appetizer, and teppanyaki vegetables. Tempura fried ice cream, Bananas Foster spring rolls, and the house signature chocolate cake with ginger cream.

SUMMARY AND COMMENTS Happy hour, daily from 4 to 7 p.m. features half-price martinis, cocktails, beer, wine, and sushi specials. Sapporo is the new kid on the block and is still tweaking the service, so be patient.

Sazio ★★★

ITALIAN   **MODERATE**   **QUALITY ★★★½**   **VALUE ★★★★½**

Orleans, 4500 West Tropicana Avenue; West of Strip; ☎ 702-948-9500; www.orleanscasino.com

Customers Visitors, locals. **Reservations** Accepted. **When to go** Anytime. **Service rating** ★★★½. **Friendliness rating** ★★★★½. **Entree range** $7–market price. **Payment** All major credit cards. **Parking** Valet, garage, lot. **Bar** Full service. **Wine selection** Limited. **Dress** Casual. **Disabled access** Ramp. **Hours** Sunday–Thursday, 11 a.m.–10 p.m.; Friday and Saturday, 11 a.m.–10:30 p.m. (dinner starts at 4 p.m.).

SETTING AND ATMOSPHERE Large framed artwork in the style of Andy Warhol dominate the various dining rooms. Featured are likenesses of local movers and shakers. Retro ceiling lights cast beams of color. Comfortable booths circle the rooms; sleek chairs and tables complete the design.

HOUSE SPECIALTIES Spit-roasted loin of pork, lightly seasoned with rosemary and garlic; spit-roasted chicken Diablo, brushed with hot mustard, herbed bread crumbs, and a peppercorn sauce. Walnut-crusted chicken salad; roasted tenderloin medallions; veal Sorrento; Mediterranean grilled shrimp. Crème brûleé and tiramisù for dessert (desserts are the only weakness on the menu).

SUMMARY AND COMMENTS Sazio is a terrific value. Portions are generous. Wines are priced right, too. This is Old Las Vegas revisited. Nothing fancy, just good, tasty food at affordable prices, in a most pleasant setting.

SeaBlue ★★★★

SEAFOOD	MODERATE/EXPENSIVE	QUALITY ★★★★	VALUE ★★★½

**MGM Grand, 3799 South Las Vegas Boulevard; South Strip and Environs;
☎ 702-891-3486; www.mgmgrand.com**

Customers Visitors, locals. Reservations Suggested weekends. When to go Anytime. Entree range Market price, but $24 average. Payment All major credit cards. Service rating ★★★½. Friendliness rating ★★★★½. Parking Valet, garage. Bar Full service. Wine selection Very good. Dress Upscale casual. Disabled access Main entrance. Hours Sunday–Thursday, 5:30–10 p.m.; Friday and Saturday, 5:30–10:30 p.m.

SETTING AND ATMOSPHERE A large circular aquarium filled with glimmering small fish captivates as diners approach SeaBlue, chef-owner Michael Mina's latest concept. A sizable raw bar almost fills one side of the dining room. There is booth seating here, too. SeaBlue puts into play a new Mina concept based on seafood. With cascading water walls and other special effects, SeaBlue's decor is magic.

HOUSE SPECIALTIES Small plates that can be a meal (think tapas). There are three choices in each category, mix and match as you will, marking off what you want on the list provided. Choose up to ten. The remarkable salad has a glorious mix of ingredients. The tuna kibbeh with pine nut crust.

OTHER RECOMMENDATIONS Orange-glazed chicken cooked in Moroccan clay casserole (tagine); no cream or butter is used in any of the dishes (excluding dessert). The fruit de mer is an abundance of seasonal shellfish nestled with hand-cut fettuccine. Apple-pomegranate cider à la mode, almond financier, cookies, ice creams, and fruits are refreshing and delicious.

SUMMARY AND COMMENTS Mina's passion for seafood was fired when he was part of the team that developed Aqua in San Francisco. Mina is also the managing chef of Michael Mina at Bellagio and Nobhill at MGM Grand.

Simon Kitchen and Bar ★★★★

AMERICAN	MODERATE	QUALITY ★★★★½	VALUE ★★½

**Hard Rock Hotel, 4455 Paradise Road; East of Strip; ☎ 702-693-4440
www.simonkitchen.com**

Customers Locals, celebs, visitors. Reservations Recommended. When to go Anytime. Entree range $14–market price. Payment All major credit cards. Service rating ★★★½. Friendliness rating ★★★★½. Parking Valet, garage, large lot. **Bar** Full service. **Wine selection** Good. **Dress** Upscale casual. **Disabled access** Ground level. **Hours** Sunday–Thursday, 6–10:30 p.m.; Friday and Saturday, 6–11 p.m.

SETTING AND ATMOSPHERE Casual and contemporary with eclectic decor and cool furnishings and appointments. Small intimate rooms that open to the dining room give privacy and a view of the patio and pool area.

HOUSE SPECIALTIES A colossal crab cake with young papaya Asian slaw; meat loaf with garlic mashed potatoes; the 20-ounce bone-in rib-eye steak. Shellfish platters with chilled oysters, clams, mussels, shrimp, crab claws, and Maine lobster can be ordered for dinner.

OTHER RECOMMENDATIONS Roasted sea bass with quinoa, currants, and pine nuts; Kerry's chicken curry; spit-roasted chicken with Tuscan fries. Warm-from-the-oven cookies and milk; a mountain of pink cotton candy; twice-baked banana bread with tempura bananas and brown sugar ice cream.

SUMMARY AND COMMENTS Chef-owner Kerry Simon has opened many acclaimed restaurants, including a few with über-chef Jean-Georges Vongerichten. This is the first on his own and he's put his heart into it. Restaurant consultant Elizabeth Blau is his partner. Some menu items change regularly, but the signatures remain.

Sir Galahad's ★★★

PRIME RIB	MODERATE/EXPENSIVE	QUALITY ★★★½	VALUE ★★★★½

Excalibur, 3850 South Las Vegas Boulevard; South Strip and Environs; ☎ 702-597-7448; www.excalibur.com

Customers Visitors, locals. **Reservations** Suggested. **When to go** Less crowded weekdays. **Entree range** $17–$40; prix fixe, $40. **Payment** AE, D, DC, MC, V. **Service rating** ★★★½. **Friendliness rating** ★★★½. **Parking** Large lot, valet, garage. **Bar** Full service. **Wine selection** Good. **Dress** Casual. **Disabled access** Elevators. **Hours** Sunday–Thursday, 5–10 p.m. (last seating); Friday and Saturday, 5–11 p.m. (last seating).

SETTING AND ATMOSPHERE English castle; waitstaff in costume of days of King Arthur. Prime rib served from large, gleaming steel and copper cart and sliced to order by skilled carvers tableside.

HOUSE SPECIALTIES Prime rib, prime rib, and prime rib served with beef barley soup or a garden salad, plus mashed potatoes, creamed spinach, and whipped cream horseradish.

OTHER RECOMMENDATIONS Appetizers such as mushrooms Cliffs of Dover. Chicken harlequin; fresh fish of the day.

SUMMARY AND COMMENTS Prime rib plus Yorkshire pudding, creamed spinach, mashed potatoes, and beef barley soup or green salad is a very hearty meal. Top it off, if you can, with English trifle or mud pie.

Spago ★★★★

AMERICAN	MODERATE/EXPENSIVE	QUALITY ★★★★½	VALUE ★★½

The Forum Shops at Caesars Palace; 3500 South Las Vegas Boulevard; Mid-Strip and Environs; ☎ 702-369-6300; www.wolfgangpuck.com

Customers Visitors, locals. **Reservations** Recommended for dinner. **When to go** Anytime except during busy conventions. **Entree range** $9–$25 café; $25–$45 dining room. **Payment** AE, D, DC, MC, V. **Service rating** ★★★½. **Friendliness rating** ★★★★½. **Parking** Garage, valet. **Bar** Full service. **Wine selection** Excellent. **Dress** Informal, casual. **Disabled access** Ground floor. **Hours** Café, Sunday–Thursday, 11 a.m.–11 p.m.; Friday and Saturday 11 a.m.–midnight; restaurant, daily, 5:30–10 p.m.

SETTING AND ATMOSPHERE There are two separate dining rooms. The casual cafe offers a fine bird's-eye view of The Forum Shops from the comfort of a European-styled sidewalk setting. The restaurant inside is an eclectic mix of modern art, wrought iron, and contemporary tables and chairs and booths. Each Sunday in the cafe from about 2:30 p.m. to 6:30 p.m., a jazz band entertains. A private banquet room is available for parties of up to 100. A small private room within the restaurant can seat up to 20.

HOUSE SPECIALTIES Café—Wolfgang Puck's signature pizzas; imaginative sandwiches salads; pastas; and frequently, a super-tasty meat loaf with port-wine sauce, grilled onions, and garlic-potato puree. Restaurant—exquisite appetizers; pastas; veal wiener schnitzel with potato salad and lemon-caper sauce; seared yellowfin tuna with jasmine rice, baby bok choy, and shiitakes; and grilled striped bass with artichoke ravioli and garlic nage. Menus in the cafe and restaurant change daily. Signature dishes always available.

SUMMARY AND COMMENTS Recently refurbished and updated, Spago has a new look. The cafe has been enlarged and the bar is a busy centerpiece. Locals, who've always considered Spago a favorite, now have their home parties catered by the restaurant. Owner Wolfgang Puck surrounds himself with the best staff, the best ingredients, the best of everything. One caveat—on very busy nights the dining room noise level can make conversation difficult. But the people-watching is terrific.

The Steak House   ★★★½

STEAK	EXPENSIVE	QUALITY ★★★½	VALUE ★★★½

Circus Circus, 2880 South Las Vegas Boulevard; North Strip and Environs; ☎ 702-794-3767; www.circuscircus.com

Customers Visitors, locals. **Reservations** Required. **When to go** Weekdays. **Entree range** $23–market price; brunch: $12 children, $35–$45 adults. **Payment** All major credit cards. **Service rating** ★★★½. **Friendliness rating** ★★★½. **Parking** Garage, lot, valet. **Bar** Full service. **Wine selection** Good. **Dress** Informal. **Disabled access** Ramps. **Hours** Sunday–Friday, 5–10 p.m.; Saturday, 5–11 p.m.; Sunday brunch, seatings at 9:30 a.m., 11:30 a.m., and 1:30 p.m.

SETTING AND ATMOSPHERE Wood-paneled rooms. The small dining room is decorated like a manor-house library. A mesquite-fired broiler in center of main room creates a cozy atmosphere. Glass refrigerator case displays over 3,000 pounds of aging meat.

HOUSE SPECIALTIES Thick steaks; black-bean soup; giant baked potato.

OTHER RECOMMENDATIONS Shrimp, crab, and lobster cocktails; Caesar salad; grilled chicken.

SUMMARY AND COMMENTS Consistently high quality and service. Don't be fooled by the children running around the lobby. Inside the Steak House, the atmosphere is adult, and the food is wonderful.

Table 34 ★★★½

CONTEMPORARY AMERICAN	MODERATE	QUALITY ★★★½	VALUE ★★★½

600 East Warm Springs Road; Southeast Las Vegas; ☎ 702-263-0034

Customers Locals, visitors. **Reservations** Suggested on weekends. **When to go** Anytime. **Entree range** $13.75–$28.50. **Payment** AE, MC, V. **Service rating** ★★★★. **Friendliness rating** ★★★★. **Parking** Large lot. **Bar** Full service. **Wine selection** Good; many wines by the glass. **Dress** Casual. **Disabled access** Ground floor. **Hours** Monday, 11 a.m.–3 p.m.; Tuesday–Friday, 11 a.m.–3 p.m. and 5 p.m.–close; Saturday, 5 p.m.–close; happy hour, Tuesday–Friday, 4–6 p.m.

SETTING AND ATMOSPHERE Formerly the location of Wild Sage Bistro, Table 34 has been completely refurbished. A freestanding bar has been added as well as another lavatory. The brilliant use of colors and a new floor have transformed Table 34 into a hip, appealing eatery.

HOUSE SPECIALTIES Menu changes with the seasons, but such favorites as chef Wes Kendrick's soups always remain. The apple-butternut squash (lunch only) is a joy, as is the cream of tomato with tarragon. Try the house-smoked salmon on a crisp potato galette (pancake); grilled Maine sea scallops with braised greens and Dijon barbecue sauce; gratinéed macaroni and cheese with smoked ham and English peas; or grilled shrimp with angel hair pasta. The all-beef meat loaf with mashed potatoes and onion gravy is like a taste of home.

OTHER RECOMMENDATIONS Grilled rack of pork with chipotle potatoes, asparagus, and hard cider glaze.; wild mushroom pizza with fresh herbs. There are sandwiches at lunch only—including hot pastrami with Swiss cheese on pumpernickel and the hearty corned beef Reuben with sauerkraut and Thousand Island dressing on light rye. Table 34's signature Key Lime pie. Note that menus change frequently; dishes listed here may not always be available.

SUMMARY AND COMMENTS Management is the same (the former owners), but Table 34, while a charming eatery, is missing a few of the touches that made the former bistro so special. Gone are the zesty, wafer-thin cracker breads and bountiful baskets of breads. Still, Table 34 is a fine place for bistro-style food at reasonable prices.

The Tillerman ★★★

SEAFOOD	EXPENSIVE	QUALITY ★★★½	VALUE ★★½

2245 East Flamingo Road; East of Strip; ☎ 702-731-4036; www.tillerman.com

Customers Visitors, locals. **Reservations** Requested. **When to go** Early evening. **Entree range** $18–$67. **Payment** AE, D, DC, MC, V. **Service rating** ★★★½. **Friendliness rating** ★★★½. **Parking** Lot. **Bar** Full service. **Wine selection** Excellent. **Dress** Informal, casual. **Disabled access** Ramp. **Hours** Daily, 11:30 a.m.–2:30 p.m. and 5–10 p.m.

SETTING AND ATMOSPHERE Attractive, airy main dining room with balcony seating. Hanging plants, wood paneling, beautiful live trees. Menu presented on scroll. Servers memorize orders without taking any notes. Ten to 15 fresh fish listed daily.

HOUSE SPECIALTIES Seafood fresh from California, the Gulf of Mexico, the Atlantic. Pacific salmon, Chilean sea bass, Alaskan halibut.

OTHER RECOMMENDATIONS Prime steaks; Tillerman pasta Portofino. Fresh homemade pastries.

SUMMARY AND COMMENTS One of the most popular Las Vegas seafood restaurants. Many improvements have been made to this family-run operation since the Tillerman came under new ownership.

HONORS AND AWARDS *Wine Spectator* Award of Excellence for many years.

Tokyo ★★½

JAPANESE/SUSHI	MODERATE	QUALITY ★★★	VALUE ★★★½

Commercial Center, 953 East Sahara Avenue; East of Strip;
☎ **702-735-7070**

Customers Visitors, locals. **Reservations** Recommended. **When to go** Anytime. **Entree range** $6–$20. **Payment** All major credit cards. **Service rating** ★★★½. **Friendliness rating** ★★★½. **Parking** Large lot. **Bar** Full service. **Wine selection** Fair. **Dress** Informal, casual. **Disabled access** Ground floor. **Hours** Thursday–Tuesday, 5–10:30 p.m. Closed Wednesdays.

SETTING AND ATMOSPHERE Attractive tatami room and sushi bar.

HOUSE SPECIALTIES Small hibachi grills for those who wish to cook their own dinner. Shabu shabu also available.

OTHER RECOMMENDATIONS Combination, special, and deluxe dinners, bento box dinners, all modestly priced; a wide selection is available.

SUMMARY AND COMMENTS This family-run restaurant, very popular with the locals, has had some personal problems recently, so be patient if the service is a bit slow. Tokyo is a terrific value.

Top of the World ★★★

AMERICAN	EXPENSIVE	QUALITY ★★★	VALUE ★★½

Stratosphere Tower, 2000 Las Vegas Boulevard; North Strip and Environs;
☎ **702-380-7711; www.stratospherehotel.com**

Customers Visitors, locals. **Reservations** Required. **When to go** Anytime. **Entree range** $32–market. **Payment** AE, D, DC, MC, V. **Service rating** ★★★★½. **Friendliness rating** ★★★½. **Parking** Valet, garage, and lot. **Bar** Full service. **Wine selection** Excellent. **Dress** Upscale casual. **Disabled access** Elevator. **Hours** Sunday–Thursday, 10 a.m.–3 p.m. and 5:30–10:30 p.m.; Friday and Saturday, 10 a.m.–3 p.m. and 5:30–11 p.m.

SETTING AND ATMOSPHERE Without question, Top of the World offers one of the most beautiful views of the city. The restaurant revolves as you dine, giving a panoramic spectacle of the surrounding mountains. The dining room is handsomely designed with inlaid tables, fine woods and brass, and copper accents. There are no bad tables.

HOUSE SPECIALTIES San Francisco–style cioppino; lobster bisque; charbroiled portobello mushrooms with Marsala demi-glace; Muscovy duck; Mediterranean chicken; seasonal specialties.

OTHER RECOMMENDATIONS Fresh Atlantic salmon encrusted with fresh sage and prosciutto di parma; lobster ravioli; the towering vacherin dessert; tiramisù or panna cotta.

SUMMARY AND COMMENTS The food is secondary to the view, which is simply spectacular, but the food is very good. Arrive before sunset and watch one of the best free shows. Be aware that there is a $15 food minimum. It's an easy amount to reach in this strictly à la carte room. The fine service and the view enhance any meal.

Trattoria del Lupo ★★★½

ITALIAN	MODERATE/EXPENSIVE	QUALITY ★★★★	VALUE ★★½

Mandalay Bay, 3950 South Las Vegas Boulevard; South Strip and Environs; ☎ 702-632-7410; www.mandalaybay.com

Customers Visitors, locals. Reservations Suggested. When to go Anytime. Entree range $20–$45 (dinner). Payment All major credit cards. Service rating ★★★½. Friendliness rating ★★★★½. Parking Valet, garage. Bar Full service. Wine selection Good. Dress Upscale casual. Disabled access Through casino. Hours Sunday–Thursday, 5–10 p.m.; Friday and Saturday, 5–11 p.m.

SETTING AND ATMOSPHERE Designed by renowned restaurant specialist Adam Tihany, Lupo features laid-back Italian-rustic decor, with vaulted ceilings, an open exhibition kitchen, and a handsome bar for imbibing or dining as the centerpiece of the dining room.

HOUSE SPECIALTIES Butternut squash soup with salsa verde; seared pork tenderloin with creamy sweet potatoes and watercress. The marvelous breads and pizzas; homemade charcuterie, pastas, and grilled fish. Heavenly desserts.

SUMMARY AND COMMENTS Yet another winner for Wolfgang Puck. Executive chef Mark Ferguson came to Lupo from Spago after a tour of Italy. His spin on such classic dishes as the Tuscan porterhouse is super. The bar attracts local power brokers who like nothing better than to observe the scene from the lofty barstools. Noisy and energetic, Lupo is a cool dining place. Menus change regularly.

Trevi ★★★

ITALIAN	MODERATE	QUALITY ★★★½	VALUE ★★★½

The Forum Shops at Caesars Palace; 3500 South Las Vegas Boulevard; Mid-Strip and Environs; ☎ 702-735-4663

Customers Visitors, locals. Reservations For large groups only. When to go Always busy, especially Friday and Saturday evenings. Entree range $14–$29. Payment AE, CB, DC, JCB, MC, V. Service rating ★★½. Friendliness rating ★★★½. Parking Hotel garage, valet. Bar Full service. Wine selection Good. Dress Informal, casual. Disabled access Ground floor. Hours Daily, 11 a.m.–11 p.m.

SETTING AND ATMOSPHERE The restaurant's beautifully decorated interior offers peaceful respite from the lively action of the dining patio. A colorful mural decorates one wall. There is a display of antipasto, a mesquite-fired pizza oven, an open kitchen, and a gelateria. Butcher paper–covered tables and crayons for doodling.

HOUSE SPECIALTIES Focaccia and pizza made in a wood-burning oven. Delmonico steak; insalata di pollo con pasta; Gorgonzola and fontina pizza with roasted potatoes and rosemary; rigatoni with sausage ragout, tomato sauce, and mozzarella; angel hair pomodoro. Homemade ice cream as well as cakes, espresso, and cappuccino in the gelateria.

OTHER RECOMMENDATIONS Salad with homemade mozzarella, tomatoes, and basil oil; prosciutto-crusted monkfish tournedo; roasted garlic, fresh spinach, béchamel, and mozzarella pizza; lasagna. Any of the new dishes, especially the herb-roasted lamb loin and the fazzoletto con funghi—a "handkerchief" of pasta enfolding spinach and ricotta cheese in a delicate wild mushroom sauce.

SUMMARY AND COMMENTS The Sidewalk Café outside Trevi overlooks the Forum's bustling scene and the Roman fountain. It's an ideal spot for photos. The fountain can be noisy, but no one seems to mind—it's so pretty.

Ventano ★★★½

ITALIAN	MODERATE	QUALITY ★★★½	VALUE ★★★★½

191 Arroyo Grande, Henderson; ☎ 702-944-4848; www.ventanoitalian.com

Customers Visitors, locals. Reservations Weekends. When to go Anytime; lunch hour is busy. Entree range $12–$28. Payment All major credit cards. Service rating ★★★★. Friendliness rating ★★★★½. Parking Large lot. Bar Full service. Wine selection Good. Dress Casual. Disabled access Ramp. Hours Daily, 11 a.m.–11 p.m. (dinner menu available all day); Oyster Bar, daily, 11 a.m.–11 p.m.; lounge open 24 hours.

SETTING AND ATMOSPHERE Rustic Italian with a spectacular view. The wraparound terrace for alfresco dining has an unobstructed view of the mountains and the surrounding area. Late-night dining is available in the comfy smoking lounge.

HOUSE SPECIALTIES Grilled shrimp (half pound) served on a hot "stone," redolent of garlic, herbs, and fresh lemon; this well-priced specialty is available all day. Lobster bisque served in a bread bowl; Sicilian rice balls; Rigatoni Portofino; fettuccine con funghi (shrimp and porcini mushrooms in pink sauce); osso buco agnello (a tasty spin on the usual veal shank); and costolette di Maiale (spareribs slowly cooked in honey and vinegar).

OTHER RECOMMENDATIONS Spiedini and scampi, the Italian version of surf and turf; scarpariello, roasted chicken with sausage and vegetables; the pizzas and sandwiches served at lunch; and the pan roasts at the oyster bar (some oyster bar specialties are offered in the dining room).

SUMMARY AND COMMENTS Ventano is a lively, friendly place with affable owners. No pretensions, just good food at reasonable prices.

VooDoo Steak   ★★★

CREOLE/CAJUN	EXPENSIVE	QUALITY ★★★½	VALUE ★★½

Rio, 3700 West Flamingo Road; Mid-Strip and Environs;
☎ **702-777-7923; www.riolasvegas.com**

Customers Visitors, locals. **Reservations** Suggested. **When to go** Anytime. **Entree range** $26–$45. **Payment** AE, D, DC, MC, V. **Service rating** ★★★½. **Friendliness rating** ★★★★½. **Parking** Valet, garage, lot. **Bar** Full service. **Wine selection** Excellent. **Dress** Sport coat or dress shirt with collar for men; no shorts, sneakers, T-shirts, or jeans. **Disabled access** Elevator. **Hours** Daily, 5–11 p.m.

SETTING AND ATMOSPHERE Voodoo decor, black walls accented with splashes of color, comfortable booths and tables, and a spectacular view from atop one of the city's tallest buildings. With its location west of the Strip, the view of the action is the absolute best.

HOUSE SPECIALTIES Crawfish and blue-crab cakes; frog legs d'Armond; baked oyster sampler with Rockefeller, Bienville, and tasso toppings; spicy, boiled Louisiana crawfish; VooDoo gumbo; the house salad with red-wine vinaigrette; seared ahi tuna; stuffed crabs gratin.

OTHER RECOMMENDATIONS Cajun rib eye; Chilean sea bass wrapped in bacon; a seafood plate of cornmeal-crusted fried oysters, shrimp, and crawfish.

SUMMARY AND COMMENTS It took a while for VooDoo to hit its stride, but now this colorful eatery and late-night hangout offers some very tasty food. The lounge features bartenders who do tricks while mixing drinks. In the past they performed flaming tricks, tossing the fiery libations from glass to glass, but those spoilsports at the fire department put out their fire.

Wolfgang Puck Bar & Grill   ★★★★

AMERICAN	MODERATE/EXPENSIVE	QUALITY ★★★★	VALUE ★★★★½

MGM Grand, 3799 South Las Vegas Boulevard; South Strip and Environs;
☎ **702-891-3000; www.wolfgangpuck.com or www.mgmgrand.com**

Customers Visitors, locals. **Reservations** Suggested. **When to go** Anytime. **Entree range** $14–$38. **Payment** All major credit cards. **Service rating** ★★★★½. **Friendliness rating** ★★★★½. **Parking** Valet, garage. **Bar** Full service. **Wine selection** Very good. **Dress** Casual. **Disabled access** Ground floor. **Hours** Monday–Thursday, 11:30 a.m.–10:30 p.m.; Friday–Sunday, 11:30 a.m.–11:30 p.m.

SETTING AND ATMOSPHERE A celebration of America, this restaurant takes us back to early California and its laid-back style. Relaxed and beautiful decor with a flavor reminiscent of Puck's first restaurant. It's lovely.

HOUSE SPECIALTIES The boneless rib eye, a succulent pleaser served with crushed red potatoes and onion rings; pizzas with newly created toppings.

OTHER RECOMMENDATIONS Starters and salads that could be a light meal; calf's liver with leeks and pancetta; the special fish of the day; ricotta gnocchi with sweet fennel sausage; grilled pork chop with goat cheese polenta and tomato sauce.

SUMMARY AND COMMENTS Menus change all the time, but the favorites always remain. Puck's is a hipster's hangout.

PART FIVE

SHOPPING *and* SEEING *the* SIGHTS

SHOPPING *in* LAS VEGAS

THE MOST INTERESTING AND DIVERSIFIED specialty shopping in Las Vegas is centered on the Strip at the **Fashion Show Mall** (☎ 702-369-0704), **Grand Canal Shoppes at the Venetian** (☎ 702-414-4500), and **The Forum and Appian Way Shops at Caesars Palace** (☎ 702-893-4800). These three venues, within walking distance of each other, collectively offer the most unusual, and arguably the most concentrated, aggregation of upscale retailers in the United States. In fairness, it should be noted that The Forum Shops and the Grand Canal Shoppes are not your average shopping centers. In fact, both are attractions in their own right and should be on your must-see list even if you don't like to shop. Both feature designer shops, exclusive boutiques, and specialty retailers. Fashion Show Mall, by comparison, is plain white-bread, with no discernible theme but a great lineup of big-name department stores.

unofficial **TIP**
The Fashion Show Mall is the place to go for that new sport coat, tie, blouse, or skirt at a reasonable price.

At the intersection of Las Vegas Boulevard and Spring Mountain Road, the Fashion Show Mall is anchored by **Saks Fifth Avenue, Neiman Marcus, Macy's, Nordstrom, Bloomingdale's, Ann Taylor, The Sharper Image,** and **Dillard's,** and contains more than 100 specialty shops, including four art galleries. There is no theme here—no Roman columns or canals with gondolas. At the Fashion Show Mall, shopping is king. And although there is no shortage of boutiques or designer shops, the presence of the big department stores defines the experience for most customers. The selection is immense, and most of the retailers are familiar and well known. To underscore its name, the mall stages free fashion shows most afternoons.

The Forum Shops is a *très chic (et très cher)* shopping complex situated between Caesars Palace and the Mirage. Connected to the

Forum Casino in Caesars Palace, The Forum Shops offers a Roman-market-themed shopping environment. Executed on a scale that is extraordinary even for Caesars, The Forum Shops replicate the grandeur of Rome at the height of its glory. Nearly 100 shops and restaurants line an ancient Roman street punctuated by plazas and fountains. Dozens of retailers and eateries populate the three-story, 175,000-square-foot Appian Way expansion. Though indoors, clouds, sky, and celestial bodies are projected on the vaulted ceilings to simulate the actual time of day outside. Statuary in The Forum is magnificent; some is even animatronic.

The Grand Canal Shoppes are similar to The Forum Shops in terms of the realistic theming, only this time the setting is the modern-day canals of Venice. Sixty-five shops, boutiques, restaurants, and cafes are arrayed along a quarter-mile-long Venetian street flanking a canal. A 70-foot ceiling (more than six stories high) with simulated sky enhances the openness and provides perspective. Meanwhile, gondolas navigating the canal add a heightened sense of commerce and activity. The centerpiece of the Grand Canal Shoppes is a replica of St. Mark's Square, without the pigeons.

A fourth major Strip shopping venue is **Miracle Mile Shops** (formerly Desert Passage), a 450,000-square-foot shopping and entertainment complex at the Planet Hollywood (☎ 888-800-8284). The venue re-creates street scenes from a boutique shopping concourse and stretches around the periphery of the hotel and casino. The shop facades sit beneath an arched ceiling painted and lighted to simulate the evening sky. Overall, although the replication is effective, it is bland compared to the Forum Shops and the Grand Canal Shoppes. Like the Grand Canal Shoppes, Miracle Mile Shops offers primarily upscale boutique shopping, but more of it, with 144 shops and restaurants compared with the Canal Shoppes' 65.

At Paris is **Rue de la Paix,** 31,000 square feet of upscale French boutique shopping. Modest in size by Las Vegas shopping standards, the Rue de la Paix re-creates a Paris street scene with cobblestone pavement and winding alleyways.

The Wynn Esplanade at Wynn Las Vegas (☎ 702-770-7000) is, as you'd expect, an insanely expensive array of upscale shops and boutiques, including **Brioni, Oscar de la Renta, Graff, Jean Paul Gaultier,** and **Manolo Blahnik.** Garnering the most attention is the **Penske-Wynn Ferrari Maserati** dealership, including a Ferrari merchandise store.

Mandalay Place, a mall with more than 40 boutiques and restaurants, also serves as the pedestrian connector linking Mandalay Bay and Luxor. The retailers seem more diverse and selectively chosen than at many other venues, making the shopping interesting even for those not hooked on shopping. There's a great wine shop with very affordable selections, a bookstore specializing in Las Vegas lore, a barber spa and retail shaving emporium for men, and a chocolate shop, among many others. Among the restaurants is the Burger Joint, featuring a $60 hamburger dressed with truffles. Fortunately, there are also less frou-frou burgers at reasonable prices.

Another Strip shopping venue is the **Showcase,** adjacent to the MGM Grand. Although most of the 190,000-square-foot shopping and entertainment complex is devoted to theme restaurants, a Sega electronic games arcade, and an eight-plex movie theater, space remains for a number of retail specialty shops. Practically next door is the **Hawaiian Marketplace** (☎ 702-795-2247), an 80,000-square-foot mall. Though the theme is Polynesian, the mall's restaurants and retailers are an eclectic lot ranging from **Café Capri** to **Zingers,** and from **Tropical Jewelers** to the **Las Vegas Tobacco Company.**

There are three large neighborhood malls in Las Vegas: the **Boulevard Mall** (☎ 702-732-8949), the **Meadows Mall** (☎ 702-878-3331), and the **Galleria at Sunset** (☎ 702-434-0202). The Boulevard Mall, with 122 stores anchored by **Sears, JC Penney, Marshalls, Dillard's,** and **Macy's,** is on Maryland Avenue, between Desert Inn Road and Flamingo Road. The Meadows, featuring the same department stores (except for Marshalls), has more than 100 stores spread over two levels. The Meadows is situated between West Charleston Boulevard and the Las Vegas Expressway (US 95) on Valley View. The third mall, Galleria at Sunset, at 1300 Sunset Road, offers 125 stores and restaurants with **Dillard's, JC Penney, Macy's,** and **Mervyns California** leading the lineup.

Because the neighborhood malls target locals, and because locals also have access to area discount shopping, these three malls offer lowball prices to stay competitive. You won't have the choice available at Fashion Show Mall, but if you can find what you're looking for, it will probably be cheaper.

unofficial **TIP**
For those without transportation, Las Vegas Citizen's Area Transit (CAT) operates a bus route that connects the various Strip and suburban shopping centers. Fare is $1.25 in residential areas and $2 on the Strip. Service is provided daily, 5:30 a.m.–1:30 a.m. For more information on CAT, call ☎ 702-228-7433.

Adjacent to the Green Valley Ranch Resort & Spa, **The District** is a 40-store shopping complex. The shops line a long pedestrian plaza with two smaller plazas intersecting. Resembling a Georgetown, Washington, D.C., commercial and residential street, The District's shopping mix includes restaurants, 14 apparel shops, and a couple dozen specialty stores, including **REI, Williams-Sonoma, Pottery Barn,** and **Mel Fisher's Treasures,** selling artifacts from shipwrecks. For further information, call ☎ 702-564-8595.

Downtown is **Las Vegas Premium Outlets** (☎ 702-474-7500), an $85-million, 120-store outlet mall. A clone of other Premium Outlet malls, featured brands include **AIX Armani Exchange, Dolce & Gabbana, Ann Taylor, Kenneth Cole, Lacoste,** and **Coach.** The mall is just west of downtown, between downtown and Interstate 15. It's a bit far from downtown to walk but is only a short cab ride away. From I-15, the mall entrance is off Charleston Boulevard.

Another large discount shopping venue has materialized about five miles south of Tropicana Avenue on Las Vegas Boulevard, near the Blue Diamond Road exit off I-15. Just north of Blue Diamond Road is a **Las Vegas Outlet Center** mall (☎ 702-896-5599), with 135 stores. Las Vegas Outlet Center, like The Forum Shops, doubled its size in 1998. Promotional literature listing the individual shops is available in almost all hotel-brochure racks. The easiest way to reach the outlets is to drive south on I-15 to Exit 33, Blue Diamond Road. Proceed east on Blue Diamond to the intersection with Las Vegas Boulevard. Turn left on Las Vegas Boulevard to the Las Vegas Outlet Center.

About an hour southwest on I-15 in Primm, Nevada, is **Fashion Outlets of Las Vegas Mall** (☎ 702-874-1400), offering themed dining and 100 outlet stores. You'll find **Williams-Sonoma, American Eagle Outfitters, Versace, Jones New York, Fossil, Tommy Hilfiger, Kenneth Cole, Banana Republic, Perry Ellis, Tommy Bahama,** and **Last Call from Neiman Marcus,** among others. The mall is adjacent to the Primm Valley Resort and Casino.

UNIQUE SHOPPING OPPORTUNITIES

WINE AND LIQUOR Though not centrally located, **Lee's Discount Liquors** (☎ 702-269-2400) on South Las Vegas Boulevard just south of Blue Diamond Road offers the best selection of wine, liquor, and beer within easy access of the Strip. Unless your hotel is south of Tropicana, take I-15 to the Blue Diamond Road exit and then head south on South Las Vegas Boulevard. If your hotel is south of Tropicana you're just as well off taking South Las Vegas Boulevard the whole way.

OUTDOOR GEAR Las Vegas went from famine to feast in the outdoor-retailer department with an **REI** store (☎ 702-896-7111) in the District shopping complex next to Green Valley Ranch, and a **Bass Pro Shops Outdoor World** (☎ 702-730-5200) at the Silverton Casino. Between the two stores you'll find everything you need to go fishing on Lake Mead or mount a safari to Tanzania. The Bass Pro Shop is a hoot, with dozens of stuffed critters placed strategically throughout the store.

ART Las Vegas is a great place to shop for contemporary and nontraditional art and sculpture, with galleries in the Fashion Show Mall, The Forum Shops, the Grand Canal Shoppes, and elsewhere around town. Do not, however, expect any bargains.

GAMBLING STUFF As you would expect, Las Vegas is a shopping mecca when it comes to anything gambling related. If you are in the market for a roulette wheel, a blackjack table, or some personalized chips, try the **Gamblers General Store** at 800 South Main (☎ 702-382-9903 or 800-322-CHIP outside Nevada; **www.gamblersgeneralstore.com**). For books and periodicals on gambling, we recommend the **Gamblers Book Club** store at 630 South 11th Street (☎ 702-382-7555 or 800-522-1777).

If you have always wanted a slot machine for your living room, you can buy one at Showcase Slot Machines, 4305 South Industrial Road (☎ 702-740-5722 or 888-522-7568; **www.showcaseslots.com**). Possession of a slot machine (including video poker and blackjack) for personal use is legal in the following states:

Alaska	Kentucky	Nevada	Texas	West Virginia
Arizona	Maine	Ohio	Utah	
Arkansas	Minnesota	Rhode Island	Virginia	

In all other states, the possession of any type of slot machine is illegal.

HEAD RUGS The next time you go to a Las Vegas production show, pay attention to the showgirls' hair. You will notice that the same woman will have a different hairdo for every number. Having made this observation, you will not be surprised that the largest wig and hairpiece retailer in the United States is in Las Vegas. At 953 East Sahara Avenue, about five minutes away from the Strip, **Serge's Showgirl Wigs** inventories over 7,000 hairpieces and wigs, made from both synthetic materials and human hair. In addition to serving the local showgirl population, Serge's Showgirl Wigs also specializes in assisting chemotherapy patients. A catalog and additional information can be obtained by calling ☎ 702-732-1015 or 800-947-9447 or visiting **www.showgirlwigs.com.**

ETHNIC SHOPPING At the southwest corner of Spring Mountain and Wynn Roads is **Las Vegas Chinatown Plaza** with 22 outlets (☎ 702-221-8448; **www.lvchinatown.com**). This location offers Asian theme shopping and restaurants.

For Native American art, crafts, books, music, and attire, try the **Las Vegas Indian Center** at 2300 West Bonanza Boulevard (☎ 702-647-5842; **www.lasvegasindiancenter.org**). And 25 minutes north of Las Vegas in Moapa, Nevada, you'll find the **Moapa Tribal Enterprises Casino and Gift Center** (☎ 702-864-2600). Take I-15 north to Exit 75.

ZOOT SUITS No kidding. For the coolest threads in town, try **Valentino's Zootsuit Collection: Vintage Apparel & Collectibles** at 906 South Sixth Street. If you only want to zoot up for a special occasion, rentals are available (☎ 702-383-9555).

COSTUMES Halloween Experience (☎ 800-811-4877) at 5800 South Valley View features thousands of costumes, masks, and accessories year-round. The showroom is open Monday through Friday to the public and on weekends by special arrangement (☎ 702-740-4224). For "sex-theme" apparel and costumes, try **Bare Essentials Fantasy Fashions** at 4029 West Sahara (☎ 702-247-4711). You'll find everything from dresses to G-strings. There's even a large selection of "bare essentials" for men. Some merchandise would be at home in suburbia, but some is strictly XXX. And speaking of XXX, that goes for sizes, too.

SHOES If you have feet a helicopter could land on, you might want to check out **Leonard's Wide Shoes,** 3999 South Las Vegas Boulevard

(☎ 702-895-9993; **www.leonardswideshoes.com**). Leonard's specializes in W-I-D-E sizes, 5 to 13EE for women, and 6 to 18 (6E) for men. If smoking stunted your growth, increase your height with custom-made platforms, boots, and high heels from **Red Shoes,** 4011 West Sahara, Unit 1 (☎ 702-889-4442). For a great selection of cowboy boots, try **Cowtown Boots,** 2989 Paradise Road (☎ 702-737-8469).

CONSIGNMENT SHOPPING The 1,700-square-foot, upscale consignment store, **It's Paradise Boutique,** located at 2029 Paradise Road (☎ 702-369-3300), offers a deep selection of designer business, casual, and evening attire, as well as shoes, accessories, and handbags.

WESTERN WEAR **Sheplers,** the world's largest Western-wear retailer, has three locations in Las Vegas: Sam's Town on Boulder Highway (☎ 702-454-5266); 4700 West Sahara Avenue (☎ 702-258-2000); and 3025 East Tropicana Avenue (☎ 702-898-3000).

GUNS Want to fire a machine gun? You can blast away at **The Gun Store**'s indoor range (2900 East Tropicana; ☎ 702-454-1110). Firearm brands include Uzi, Thompson, and Madsen, among others.

SEEING *the* SIGHTS

RESIDENTS OF LAS VEGAS ARE JUSTIFIABLY PROUD of their city and are quick to point out that it has much to offer besides gambling. Quality theater, college and professional sports, dance, concerts, art shows, museums, and film festivals contribute to making Las Vegas a truly great place to live. In addition, there is a diverse and colorful natural and historical heritage. What Las Vegas residents sometimes have a difficult time understanding, however, is that the average business and leisure traveler doesn't really give a big hoot. Las Vegas differs from Orlando and Southern California in that it does not have any bona fide tourist attractions except Hoover Dam. Nobody drives all the way to Las Vegas to take their children to visit the Liberace Museum. While there have always been some great places to detox from a long trade show or too many hours at the casino, they are totally peripheral in the minds of visitors. Las Vegas needs a legitimate, nongaming tourist draw, but the strange aggregation of little museums, factory tours, and mini–theme parks is not it.

In 1993, the opening of the MGM Grand Hotel and Casino and Grand Adventures Theme Park brought Las Vegas a little closer to penetrating the consciousness of the nongambling traveler, but, alas, the park was a dud. It limped along for eight years before shutting down in 2001. During the 1990s, Circus Circus opened a smaller theme park, Adventuredome, behind its main casino. For the most part, the new theme parks have made little impression on either the locals or the tourists. From 1997 through 2000, a number of Strip casinos, including Caesars Palace, the Stratosphere, New York–New

York, the Sahara, and the Las Vegas Hilton, opened new attractions. They are, by and large, imaginative, visually appealing, and high-tech. Some, like the Hilton's *Star Trek* attraction, would stand out as headliners in any theme park in the country. Others, while not up to Disney or Universal Studios standards, represent a giant leap forward for Las Vegas. Clearly, the competition learned a few things from MGM Grand's theme-park flop.

ADVENTUREDOME AT CIRCUS CIRCUS

TO FURTHER APPEAL TO THE FAMILY MARKET targeted by the MGM Grand Adventures Theme Park, Circus Circus opened a small but innovative amusement park in August of 1993. Situated directly behind the main hotel and casino, the park now goes by the name of Adventuredome. Architecturally compelling, the entire park is built two stories high atop the casino's parking structure and is totally enclosed by a huge glass dome. From the outside, the dome surface is reflective, mirroring its surroundings in hot tropical pink. Inside, however, the dome is transparent, allowing guests in the park to see out. Composed of a multilayer glass-and-plastic sandwich, the dome allows light in but blocks ultraviolet rays. The entire park is air-conditioned and climate-controlled 365 days a year.

Adventuredome is a fun way to escape the heat of a Vegas summer day.

The park is designed to resemble a classic Western desert canyon. From top to bottom, hand-painted artificial rock is sculpted into caverns, pinnacles, steep cliffs, and buttes. A stream runs through the stark landscape, cascading over a 90-foot falls into a rippling blue-green pool. Set among the rock structures are the attractions: a roller coaster, a flume ride, an inverter ride, and Chaos, a spinning amusement that hauls riders randomly through three dimensions. There are also some rides for small children. Embellishing the scene are several life-sized animatronic dinosaurs, a re-creation of an archeological dig, a fossil wall, and a replica of a Pueblo cliff dwelling. There is also a small theater featuring magic and illusion. Finally, and inevitably, there is an electronic games arcade.

Adventuredome's premier attractions are the **Canyon Blaster,** the only indoor, double-loop, corkscrew roller coaster in the United States; the **Rim Runner,** a three-and-a-half-minute water-flume ride, and **Chaos,** a vertical Tilt-A-Whirl on steroids. Canyon Blaster and Rim Runner wind in, around, and between the rocks and cliffs. The flume ride additionally passes under the snouts of the dinosaurs.

Guests can reach the theme park by proceeding through the rear of the main casino to the entrance and ticket plaza situated on the mezzanine level. Circus Circus has changed the admission policy so many times we have lost track. You can choose between paying for each attraction individually ($4 to $7) or opting for an all-inclusive day pass

($24.95 adults; $14.95 juniors). For exact admission prices on the day of your visit, call ☎ 702-794-3939 or visit **www.adventuredome.com.**

BELLAGIO ATTRACTIONS

THE BIG DRAW AT THE BELLAGIO is the **Gallery of Fine Art Exhibition,** which hosts temporary traveling exhibits. Tickets usually run about $15 for adults, $12 for children and seniors. For information, call ☎ 702-693-7871 or visit **www.bgfa.biz.**

A very worthwhile and free attraction is the **Bellagio Conservatory and Botanical Gardens.** Located adjacent to the hotel lobby, the display features more than 10,000 blooming flowers, a diverse variety of plants, and even trees. The flora is changed periodically to reflect the season of the year or the theme of upcoming holidays.

Bellagio's free outdoor spectacle is a choreographed **water-fountain show** presented on the lake in front of the hotel (which stretches the length of three football fields). At the bottom of the eight-acre lake over 1,000 "water expressions"—think jets—and 4,000-plus individually programmable white lights are harnessed in choreography to "dance," if you will, to classical, popular, operatic, holiday, and sacred music. The waters are capable of reaching 240 feet into the air (approaching a football field's length), undulating in graceful S-curves, or cascading open like a gigantic surrendering lotus. Realized by WetDesigns, the entire vision, including the music selections, is Steve Wynn's, who is famous for his involvement with every detail of every aspect of the properties he designs. The magical waters of the Bellagio are for all to enjoy on the half-hour every Saturday and Sunday from noon to 7 p.m. and every 15 minutes from 7 to 11 p.m. Weekdays the schedule begins at 3 p.m. The view from the street is assuredly wonderful, but many of the rooms at Caesars across the street can also offer a visual feast.

 Bellagio's dramatic three-story, glass-domed botanical garden provides a quiet oasis.

LAS VEGAS HILTON ATTRACTIONS

THE HILTON OFFERS AN ATTRACTION called *Star Trek: The Experience* (**www.startrekexp.com**). You enter through a museum of *Star Trek* TV/movie memorabilia and props en route to a 18-minute *Klingon Encounter* that culminates in a four-minute space-flight simulation ride. The Hilton ride differs from other simulation attractions in that the field of vision seemingly surrounds the guests. In 2004, a sister *Star Trek* attraction, *Borg Invasion 4-D,* was added. In this one, the Borg attack your spaceship and chase you to an escape spacecraft (actually a theater) where you see a 3-D movie in which your spacecraft helps defeat the Borg. The special effects are good, but the plot is a little fuzzy to anyone not already familiar with the Borg. All you need to know, really, is that the Borg drill out your

*un*official **TIP**
At *Star Trek: The Experience,* the entrance from "Deep Space Promenade" is free.

brain and inhabit your body. You can purchase tickets for each attraction individually or opt for a ticket that covers both.

Upon returning from your mission to far-flung reaches of the galaxy, you are welcomed back to this planet at the gift shop. **The History of the Future Museum** is a self-guided exhibit that you can enjoy at your own pace. Besides the museum, the *Klingon Encounter,* the *Borg Invasion,* and the gift shop, *Star Trek: The Experience* includes an electronic-games arcade, a restaurant, and a lounge.

unofficial **TIP**
The best times to see *Star Trek: The Experience* and *Borg Invasion 4-D* are on weekdays from 12:30 to 2 p.m. or after 4:30 p.m.

Although the visuals on the simulator ride are a little fuzzy by modern standards, the overall experience, including *Borg Invasion 4-D* (which offers several neat twists and surprises), earns *Star Trek* a first-place ranking among Las Vegas's attractions. Not wanting to detract from your enjoyment of *Star Trek,* we're not going to tell you what happens. Suffice it to say that it's extremely well done, and the total experience gives most Disney or Universal attractions a good run for their money. Both *Klingon Encounter* and *Borg Invasion 4-D* are approximately 18 minutes long. Each experience is complete with live interaction. If you happen to go when there is not much of a line, take time to check out the chronological history of the universe. The history show is open Sunday through Thursday, 11 a.m. to 10 p.m. and Friday and Saturday, 11 a.m. to 11 p.m. Admission is $38.99 for adults, $35.99 for seniors and children age 12 and under, including tax. You can purchase tickets three days in advance only at the Star Trek box office (at entrance). For information, call ☎ 888-462-6535.

LUXOR ATTRACTIONS

THE LUXOR OFFERS SEVERAL CONTINUOUSLY RUNNING gated (paid admission) attractions inside the pyramid on the level above the casino. Designed by Douglas Trumbull, creator of the *Back to the Future* ride at Universal Studios, **In Search of the Obelisk** (in the Egyptian ruins) consists of two motion simulators: a runaway freight elevator that gives you the unusual (and disconcerting!) sensation of plummeting a fair distance, and a runaway tour tram in the bowels of a subterranean world. Two other so-called "ride films" are **Dracula's Haunted Castle,** a sort of high-tech spookhouse, and **Reboot,** where you careen around "a metropolis set deep inside a computer." Yikes! In addition, a seven-story IMAX 3-D theater with a 30,000-watt sound system runs 24 hours a day and costs about $12 per show.

MANDALAY BAY ATTRACTIONS

THE BIG DRAW AT MANDALAY BAY is the **Shark Reef** aquarium featuring sharks, rays, sea turtles, venomous stonefish, and dozens of other denizens of the deep playing house in a 1.3-million-gallon tank. If you don't like fish, separate exhibits showcase rare golden crocodiles and pythons. Something for everybody, you might say. The Shark Reef audio tour is open daily from 10 a.m. until 11 p.m. Admission is about $16 for adults, $10 for children ages 12 and under, and ages 4 and under are free. Additional information is available at ☎ 702-632-4555.

MGM GRAND ATTRACTIONS

THE MGM GRAND HOSTS a **tri-story 5,000-square-foot lion habitat** that houses up to five of the big cats. The lions are on duty from 11 a.m. until 10 p.m. daily and admission is free. There is also, of course, an MGM Lion logo shop and the opportunity (for $20) to be photographed with a lion.

MIRAGE AND T. I. ATTRACTIONS

NOT ONLY ARE THE MIRAGE AND T. I. ATTRACTIONS of top quality, they are also free. The two biggies are the **Sirens of Treasure Island** and the **exploding volcano at the Mirage.** The disco naval battle takes place every 90 minutes, weather permitting, beginning at 7 p.m., with the last performance at 10 p.m. (11:30 p.m. during warm-weather months) nightly. In 2003, as part of an image makeover, T. I. wrote the British out of the script (they always lost anyway) and replaced them with "a group of sexy women" called the Sirens of T. I., who now fight the pirates. In the new production, the pirates are apparently so disconcerted by all the leg and cleavage that they do not put up a very robust fight. The best vantage points are along the rope rail on the entrance bridge to the casino. On weekdays, claim your spot 15 to 20 minutes before showtime. On weekends, make that 35 to 45 minutes. If you do not insist on having a *perfect* vantage point, you can see most everything just by joining the crowd at the last minute. If you are short, or have children in your party, it's probably worth the effort to arrive early and nail down a position by the rail.

The volcano at the Mirage goes off about every hour from 7 p.m. until midnight, if the weather is good and the winds are light. In the winter, when it gets dark earlier, the volcano starts popping off at 6 p.m. Usually, because of the frequency of performances (eruptions?), getting a good railside vantage point is not too difficult. If you want to combine the volcano with a meal, grab a window table at the second-floor restaurant in the Casino Royale across the street. Dinner here costs $10 to $20, though, so these are not cheap seats.

The Mirage has some of *Siegfried and Roy*'s white tigers on display in a well-executed, natural habitat exhibit. In addition to the tigers, the Mirage maintains a nice dolphin exhibit. Both are open daily, from 10 a.m. to 7 p.m. The exhibit costs $15 for adults and $10 for children ages 4 to 12. (Children ages 3 and under get in free.) For the price of admission you can also take in the **Secret Garden** next to the dolphin habitat, a small zoo with Siegfried and Roy's white and Bengal tigers, white lions, an Indian elephant, and more (the Secret Garden tigers retire at 3:30 p.m.). For more information about

unofficial **TIP**
If accessing Paris's observation platform seems like too much work, take the separate elevator that serves the restaurant and bar on the 11th floor of the tower. You don't need reservations to patronize the bar, but you must be nicely dressed (that is, jackets recommended for men and absolutely no jeans, T-shirts, tank tops, or sandals). The bar is open nightly from 5 p.m. until midnight.

Mirage, call ☎ 702-791-7111. For more information about Treasure Island, call ☎ 702-894-7111.

PARIS LAS VEGAS ATTRACTIONS

THE BIG DRAW AT PARIS IS, OF COURSE, the 540-foot-tall replica of the **Eiffel Tower.** Requiring 10 million pounds of steel and more than two years to erect, the Las Vegas version is a little more than half the size of the original. Just below the top (at 460 feet) is an observation deck accessible via two ten-passenger glass elevators. It costs a stiff nine bucks to ride, but that's just the beginning of the story. You must first line up to buy tickets. Your ticket will show a designated time to report to the escalator (that's right: *escalator*. You must take an escalator to reach the elevators). If you're late you'll be turned away, and there are no refunds. The escalator will deposit you in yet another line where you'll wait for the elevator. The elevators run from 10 a.m. until 1 a.m., except when it's raining.

Though all this hopping from line to line is supposed to take 5 to 20 minutes, we found 40 to 60 minutes more the norm. Here's the rub. The observation deck holds fewer than 100 persons, and once people get up there, they can stay as long as they want. Hence, when the observation deck is at max capacity, nobody can go up unless someone comes down. Because the tower affords such a great view of the Bellagio across the street, gridlock ensues several times nightly while people squeeze on the observation deck overlong to watch Bellagio's dancing-waters show.

SAHARA ATTRACTIONS

THE NEWLY RENOVATED AND EXPANDED Sahara has its own entry in the raging simulator-ride craze. Called **Cyber Speedway,** the attraction draws its inspiration from Indy car racing. You can elect to drive an Indy car in an interactive simulated race, or alternatively, you can strap in as a passive passenger for a 3-D, motion-simulator movie race. The interactive race cars respond exactly like a real race car to braking, acceleration, and steering control. You can even choose between driving a manual or automatic (recommended) transmission. Your race pits you against other drivers and lasts about eight minutes.

Once your race begins, driving the course at high speed demands intense concentration. If you have a simulated crash, you'll be directed to the simulated pits for repairs. The visuals on the screen in front of your car are reasonably good but come to you at numbing speed. If you are sensitive to motion sickness, the Indy car simulator will leave your stomach spinning.

In our opinion, you need to race once just to understand how everything works. After you get the hang of it, you will enjoy the experience more and also be more competitive. Start out on a simple course with an automatic transmission and work up to more demanding courses. After each race you will be given a computer-generated report that tells how you finished, and it provides some comparative information on your general performance. Each race you drive costs $10.

Speed, the roller coaster at the Sahara, opened in June 2000. You race down 1,350 feet of track, including one 360-degree loop and a harrowing 224-foot climb straight up a tower. From the tower's top, you'll roll *backwards* back to the starting point. The round-trip takes 48 seconds. Special electromagnetic fields slingshot riders from 0 to 40 miles per hour and again from 35 to 70 miles per hour in two seconds flat. Yikes! Speed is flat out the fastest roller coaster in town, and is open Sunday through Thursday, 11 a.m. to 10 p.m. and Friday and Saturday, 11 a.m. to midnight. Rides cost about $10 each or $21.95 all day, call ☎ 702-737-2111 on the day you go.

STRATOSPHERE ATTRACTIONS

THE STRATOSPHERE TOWER STANDS 1,149-FEET TALL and offers an unparalleled view of Las Vegas. You can watch aircraft take off simultaneously from McCarran International Airport and Nellis Air Force Base. To the south, the entire Las Vegas Strip is visible. To the west, Red Rock Canyon seems practically within spitting distance. North of the Tower, downtown glitters beneath the canopy of the Fremont Street Experience. By day, the rich geology of the Colorado Basin and Spring Mountains merge in an earth-tone and evergreen tapestry. At night, the dark desert circumscribes a blazing strand of twinkling neon.

A 12-level pod crowns the futuristic contours of three immense buttresses that form the Tower's base. Level 12, the highest level, serves as the boarding area for **X Scream,** a dangle-daddy; **Insanity,** a sort of Tilt-A-Whirl in the sky; and the **Big Shot,** an acceleration–free-fall thrill ride. Levels 11 and 10 are not open to the public. An outdoor observation deck is Level 9, with an indoor observation deck directly beneath it on Level 8. Level 7 features a 220-seat lounge, and Level 6 houses an upscale revolving restaurant. Levels 4 and 3 contain meeting rooms, and the remaining levels—1, 2, and 5—are not open to the public.

The view from the Tower is so magnificent that we recommend experiencing it at different times of the day and night. Sunset is particularly stunning, and a storm system rolling in over the mountains is a sight you won't quickly forget. Be sure to try both the indoor and outdoor observation decks.

The rides are a mixed bag. The Big Shot is cardiac arrest. Sixteen people at a time are seated at the base of the skyward-projecting needle that tops the pod. You are blasted 160 feet straight up in the air at 45 miles per hour and then allowed to partially free-fall back down. At the apex of the ascent, it feels as if your seat belt and restraint have mysteriously evaporated, leaving you momentarily hovering 100-plus stories up in the air. The ride lasts only about a half-minute, but unless you're accustomed to being shot from a cannon, that's more than enough.

If you're having difficulty forming a mental image of the Big Shot, picture the carnival game where macho guys swing a sledgehammer, propelling a metal sphere up a vertical shaft. At the top of the shaft is a bell. If the macho man drives the sphere high enough to ring the bell, he wins a prize. Got the picture? OK, on the Big Shot, you are the metal sphere.

In X Scream, you ride in a large gondola attached to a huge steel arm. The arm dangles the gondola over the edge of the Tower, then releases it to slide forward a few feet as if the gondola is coming unglued from the arm. All and all, it's pretty dull.

The third ride, Insanity, is a little harder to describe. It consists of an arm that extends 64 feet over the edge of the Tower. Passengers are suspended from the arm in beefed-up swing seats and spun at up to three g's. As the ride spins faster and faster, the riders are propelled up to an angle of 70 degrees, at which point they're pretty much looking straight down. The Stratosphere touts the ride as providing "a great view of historic Downtown Las Vegas."

unofficial **TIP**
If you must see the Tower on a weekend, go in the morning as soon as it opens.

The elevators to the Tower are at the end of the shopping arcade on the second floor of the Stratosphere, above the casino. Get tickets for the Tower at the ticket center in the elevator lobby on the second floor or at various places in the casino. Tower tickets cost about $10. Packages including the Tower and the rides run from $14 to $30, depending on the number of rides included. You can purchase individual tickets for the rides at a cost of $8, in addition to your Tower admission.

Expect big crowds at the Tower on weekends. Once up top, the observation levels are congested, as are the lounge, snack bar, restrooms, and gift shops. If you want to try the rides, expect to wait an additional 20 to 40 minutes for each on weekends. When you've had your fill of the Tower and are ready to descend, you'll have another long wait before boarding the elevator. However, if you walk down to the restaurant (you'll take the emergency staircase; ask an attendant where to find it), you can catch the down elevator with virtually no wait at all.

Another way to see the Tower without a long wait is to make a reservation for the **Top of the World** restaurant. To be safe, reservations should be made at least two weeks in advance. When you arrive, inform the greeter in the elevator lobby that you have a dinner reservation and give him your confirmation number. You will be ushered immediately into an express elevator. The restaurant is pricey, but the food is good and the view is a knockout, and you do not have to pay the Tower admission. If you want to try the Big Shot or the High Roller, purchase ride tickets before taking the elevator to the restaurant. Finally, be aware that most folks dress up to eat at the Top of the World.

On weekdays, it is much easier to visit the Stratosphere Tower. Monday through Thursday, except at sunset, the wait to ascend is usually short. Waits for the rides are also short. Tower hours are Sunday to Thursday, 10 a.m. to 1 a.m. and Friday and Saturday, 10 a.m. to 2 a.m. For more information, call ☎ 702-380-7711.

VENETIAN ATTRACTIONS

LIKE NEW YORK–NEW YORK DOWN THE STRIP, it can be argued that the entire Venetian is an attraction, and there's a lot to gawk at even if you limit your inspection to the streetside Italian icons and the Grand Canal Shoppes. But there's more. The Venetian is host to the first **Madame Tussaud's Wax Museum** in the United States. Covering two floors and 28,000 square feet, the museum is about half the size of the original London exhibit (☎ 702-862-7800; **www.mtvegas .com**). Approximately 100 wax figures are displayed in theme settings. Some, like Frank Sinatra and Tom Jones, were central to the development of the entertainment scene in Las Vegas. The museum opens daily at 10 a.m. Admission is $24 per adult and $14 per child.

The Venetian also hosts the **Guggenheim Hermitage Museum,** which presents rotating exhibits from the Guggenheim collection. In 2007, the museum showcased *Modern Masters Collection* with the works of Monet, Cezanne, and Picasso. Admission is $19.50 for adults, $15 for seniors and Nevada residents, $12.50 for students with ID, $9.50 for children ages 6 to 12; children 5 and under get in for free. Admission discount coupons are routinely available in the hotel lobby. A portable audio guide is included in the price of ticket. For additional information, call ☎ 702-414-2440 or visit **www.venetian.com** or **www.guggen heimlasvegas.org.** Museum hours are 9:30 a.m. to 7:30 p.m. daily.

A WORD ABOUT STRIP ROLLER COASTERS

THERE ARE NOW THREE ROLLER COASTERS on the Strip. After careful sampling, we have decided that, although shorter, the **Canyon Blaster** at **Adventuredome** offers a better ride than the more visually appealing **Manhattan Express** at **New York–New York.** The Canyon Blaster is tight and oh-so-smooth. The Manhattan Express, on the other hand, goes along in fits and starts, all of which are jerky and rough. It does, however, provide a great view of the Strip as it zips in and out of the various New York–New York buildings. **Speed,** at the Sahara, lives up to its name, but is overpriced at $10.

The Canyon Blaster at Adventuredome is the *Unofficial* favorite of the Vegas Strip coasters.

OTHER ATTRACTIONS

THERE ARE A GOODLY NUMBER of Las Vegas attractions, ranging from go-cart tracks to planetariums and aviation museums, that we don't have space to cover in the *Unofficial Guide.* All of them are listed and described at **www.nevadaattractions.com.** If you provide your name and address they'll mail you a free brochure. The site is sponsored by Museums and Attractions in Nevada (MAIN) in partnership with the Nevada Commission on Tourism.

FREE STUFF

TWO FREE "ATTRACTIONS" worthy of your consideration are the **Fremont Street Experience** and the Rio's **Masquerade in the Sky.** The Fremont Street Experience is an electric-light show produced on a futuristic canopy over the Fremont Street pedestrian concourse downtown. Shows begin at 4 p.m. and run about once an hour through 10 p.m. on weekdays, and 11 p.m. on weekends. The show at the Rio is a sort of musical Mardi Gras parade complete with floats, acrobats, musicians, and dancers, circling the casino suspended from a track on the ceiling (who thinks this stuff up?). Both shows are free. A third free attraction is the **water-and-laser show** at Caesars Palace at the Forum Shops. This production, staged on the hour daily beginning at 10 a.m., combines animatronic statues and fire drama. Outdoor productions at Bellagio, T. I., and the Mirage (all described earlier) are also free.

REALLY EXPENSIVE THRILLS

FOR $99 TO $3,000 YOU CAN FLY a foot off the ground at the **Richard Petty Driving Experience.** Here you can get behind the wheel of a 600-horsepower NASCAR Winston Cup–style stock car. The Driving Experience is located at the Las Vegas Motor Speedway. Call ☎ 702-643-4343 or visit **www.1800bepetty.com** for additional information.

OTHER AREA ATTRACTIONS

THE LOCAL VISITOR GUIDES DESCRIBE nearby attractions and sites pretty honestly. If you have children, try the **Lied Discovery Children's Museum,** ☎ 702-382-3445, for a truly rewarding afternoon of exploration and enjoyable education. Right across the street from the Lied is the **Las Vegas Natural History Museum,** ☎ 702-384-3466.

Near scenic Red Rock, a curious side trip just outside of Las Vegas is **Bonnie Springs Old Nevada.** This rustic recreation of an Old West town features trinket stores, a saloon, two museums, a restaurant, a petting zoo, and guided horse rides. The hoot, though, that goes with this holler is the low-budget melodrama. The kicker is the real, live Western hanging that takes place at noon, 2:30, and 5 p.m. "You can't hang me, sheriff!" "Why not?!" "Cause yer wife'll miss me!" Cost to get in—$10 per carload; ☎ 702-875-4191; **www.bonniesprings.com.** Real rope, real fun.

Adults who wax nostalgic over vintage automobiles should check out the **Auto Collection at the Imperial Palace,** ☎ 702-794-3174, where more than 200 antique and historically significant vehicles are on display. The collection is well worth the admission price of $6.95, $3.50 for seniors and children under age 12, though discount coupons are readily available in the local visitor guides and at the Imperial Palace casino.

The Liberace Foundation and Museum, ☎ 702-798-5595, **www .liberace.org,** on East Tropicana Avenue, is one of Las Vegas's most popular tourist attractions. The exhibit chronicles the music, life, and excesses of Liberace. Though possibly the most professionally organized and well-presented celebrity museum in the United States, it's definitely more fun if you are a Liberace fan ($12.50 adults; $8.50 seniors 65 and older and students with a valid ID; free for children ages 10 and under).

Unique to Las Vegas is the **Atomic Testing Museum,** which chronicles through exhibits and film the history of the Nevada Test Site, where atomic bombs were detonated only 65 miles from Las Vegas. When a vital sense of place, artifacts, and good storytelling come together, the result should be a powerful museum experience. This is the case at the Atomic Testing Museum, which presents the story of the development of nuclear weapons. In particular, the Nevada Test Site located just north of Las Vegas is featured, where as one Nevada governor put it, "atoms bloom(ed) in the desert."

This museum is cerebral, instructive, and entertaining. Laden with artifacts, there much to look at (and much to read for a full encounter). The strength of the experience is greatly enhanced by the overall design that recreates settings with fine attention to materials. For example, the entrance to the 8,000 square feet of exhibit space is a replica of the stainless-steel facade of the Wackenhut guard station located at the Nevada Test Site. A good balance of videos and interactive stations can engage anyone with a passing interest in this seemingly and sadly ever-important topic. Although varied, with metal and concrete dominating, in sum the exhibit spaces convey the sense of a bunker. This scheme sounds oppressive, but it deftly supports the power and secrecy of the nuclear program. In one of two small theaters, the brief, overpowering experience of a nuclear test explosion is alone nearly worth the price of admission. Near the end of the technology-based interpretations, a room of Native American artifacts and perspectives restores a balance to the mechanistic themes. It also provokes thought about the timeless power of the earth, the deathly horrors of humankind, and the need for nuclear weapons in an age of terrorism.

If you are looking for some brain stimulation to escape the mid-way atmosphere of the casinos, you can't do better than the Atomic Testing Museum, created in association with the Smithsonian Institution. Furthermore, the museum store might be a good place to look for a stimulating present for that eggheaded child you left at home. Open daily, the museum is located at 755 East Flamingo Road. Admission is $12 adults and $9 children. Call ☎ 702-794-5161 for more information, or see **www.atomictestingmuseum.org.**

Adjacent to the MGM Grand is the **Showcase,** a shopping, dining, and entertainment venue with a giant Sega arcade, an eight-screen movie complex, and the World of Coca-Cola—a 150-foot Coke bottle housing two elevators.

NATURAL ATTRACTIONS NEAR LAS VEGAS

IN THE MEXICAN PAVILION OF EPCOT at Walt Disney World, tourists rush obliviously past some of the most rare and valuable artifacts of the Spanish colonial period in order to take a short, uninspired boat ride. Many Las Vegas visitors, likewise, never look beyond the Strip. Like the Epcot tourists, they are missing something pretty special.

Las Vegas's geological and topographical diversity, in combination with its stellar outdoor resources, provides the best opportunities for worthwhile sightseeing. So different and varied are the flora, fauna, and geology at each distinct level of elevation that traveling from the banks of Lake Mead to the high, ponderosa pine forests of Mount Charleston encompasses (in 90 minutes) as much environmental change as driving from Mexico to Alaska.

Red Rock Canyon, the **Valley of Fire,** the **Mojave Desert,** and the **Black Canyon of the Colorado River** are world-class scenic attractions. In combination with the summits of the **Spring Mountains,** they comprise one of the most dramatically diversified natural areas on the North American continent. So excuse us if we leave coverage of the Guinness World of Records Museum to the local visitor's guides.

Driving Tours

For those who wish to sample the natural diversity of the Las Vegas area, we recommend the following driving tours. The trips begin and end in Las Vegas and take from two hours to all day, depending on the number of stops and side trips. The driving tours can conveniently be combined with picnicking, hiking, horseback riding, and sightseeing. If you have the bucks ($70 to $200 per person, depending on the package), we also recommend taking one of the air/ground tours of the Grand Canyon.

1. MOUNT CHARLESTON, KYLE CANYON, LEE CANYON, AND THE TOIYABE NATIONAL FOREST 4 to 6 hours
If you have had more than enough desert, this is the drive for you. Head north out of Las Vegas on US 95 and turn left on NV 157. Leave the desert and head into the pine and fir forest of the Spring Mountains. Continue up Kyle Canyon to the Mount Charleston Inn (a good place for lunch) and from there to the end of the canyon. Backtracking a few miles, take NV 158 over the Robbers Roost and into Lee Canyon. When you hit NV 156, turn left and proceed to the Lee Canyon Ski Area. For the return trip to Las Vegas, simply take NV 156 out of the mountains until it intersects US 95. Turn south (right) on US 95 to return to Las Vegas. If you start feeling your oats once you get into the mountains, there are some nice short hikes (less than a mile) to especially scenic overlooks. If you are so inclined, there is also horseback riding, and there are some great places for picnics.

las vegas–area driving tours

2. RED ROCK CANYON SCENIC LOOP 1½ to 3 hours

Red Rock Canyon is a stunningly beautiful desert canyonland only 20 minutes from Las Vegas. A scenic loop winds among imposing, rust-red Aztec sandstone towers. There is a visitor center, as well as hiking trails and picnic areas. With very little effort you can walk to popular rock-climbing sites and watch the action. From Las Vegas, head west on Charleston Boulevard (NV 159) directly to Red Rock Canyon. The scenic loop is 13 miles (all one-way), with numerous places to stop and enjoy the rugged vistas. The loop road brings you back to NV 159. Turn left and return to town via Charleston Boulevard.

3. LAKE MEAD AND THE VALLEY OF FIRE 5 to 8 hours

This drive takes you to the Lake Mead National Recreation Area and Valley of Fire State Park. How long the drive takes depends on how many side trips you make. If you plan to visit Hoover Dam during your visit, it will be convenient to work it into this itinerary. The same is true if you wish to tour the Ethel M (as in Mars bars) Chocolate Factory and Cactus Garden.

Head south out of Las Vegas on US 95/93 (detour west on Sunset Road to visit the Chocolate Factory and Cactus Garden), continuing straight on US 93 to Boulder City. From Boulder City continue to the Hoover Dam on US 93 (if desired) or turn left on the Lakeshore Scenic Drive (NV 166) to continue the drive. Travel through the washes and canyons above the lake until you reach the Northshore Scenic Drive (NV 147 and NV 167). Turn right, continuing to the right on NV 167 when the routes split. If you wish, you can descend to the lake at Callville Bay, Echo Bay, or Overton Beach. If you are hungry, Callville Bay and Echo Bay have restaurants and lounges. Overton Beach has a snack bar, but Echo Bay has the best beach.

Near Overton Beach, turn left to NV 169 and follow signs for Valley of Fire State Park. Bear left on NV 169 away from Overton. Valley of Fire features exceptional desert canyon scenery, panoramic vistas, unusual and colorful sandstone formations, and Indian petroglyphs. A short two-mile scenic loop makes it easy to see many of the valley's most interesting formations. If you have time, take the road past the visitor center and climb to the Rainbow Vista overlook. From here a new highway accesses some of the most extraordinary terrain in the American Southwest. After the loop (and any other detours that interest you), continue west on NV 169 until it intersects I-15. Head south to return to Las Vegas.

Hoover Dam

Hoover Dam is definitely worth seeing. There is a film, a guided tour, and a theater presentation on the Colorado River drainage, as well as some static exhibits. Try to go on a Monday, Thursday, or Friday. Arrive no later than 9 a.m., when the visitor area opens, and do the tour first ($11, $9 seniors, and $6 students). After 9:30 a.m. or so, long lines form for the tour, especially on Tuesdays, Wednesdays, Saturdays, and Sundays. The dam is closed to visitors at 6 p.m. A ban on visitors inside the dam, initiated following 9/11, was subsequently lifted, but there are security checkpoints on US 93 leading to the dam.

Other than chauffeured transportation, there is no advantage in going to Hoover Dam on a bus tour. You will still have to wait in line for the tour of the dam and to see the other presentations. If you are the sort of person who tours quickly, you probably will have a lot of time to kill waiting for the rest of the folks to return to the bus.

The Canyons of the Southwest

Las Vegas tourist magazines claim **Bryce Canyon** (400 miles round-trip; ☎ 435-834-5322) and **Zion Canyon, Utah** (350 miles round-trip; ☎ 435-772-3256), as well as the **Grand Canyon, Arizona** (☎ 928-638-7888) as local attractions. We recommend all of the canyons if you are on an extended drive through the Southwest. If your time is limited, however, you might consider taking one of the air day-tours that visit the canyons from Las Vegas. Running between $100 and $400 per passenger, the excursions follow one of two basic formats: air only, or air and ground combined. Some tour companies offer discounted fares for a second person if the first person pays full fare. Also, discount coupons are regularly available in *What's On* and *Today in Las Vegas,* distributed free of charge in most hotels.

Almost all canyon tours include a pass over **Lake Mead** and **Hoover Dam.** The trip involving the least commitment of time and money is a round-trip flyover of one or more of the canyons. A Grand Canyon fly-over, for example, takeoff to touchdown, takes about two hours. While flying over any of the canyons is an exhilarating experience, air traffic restrictions concerning the Grand Canyon severely limit what air passengers can see. Flying over the other canyons is somewhat less restricted.

If you want to get a real feel for the Grand Canyon particularly, go with one of the air/ground excursions. The Grand Canyon is many times more impressive from the ground than from the air.

The air/ground trips fly over the Grand Canyon and then land. Passengers are transferred to a bus that motors them along the rim of the canyon, stopping en route for lunch. Excursions sometimes additionally include boat and helicopter rides. These multifaceted tours last from seven to ten hours. Many flights offer multilingual translations of the tour narrative.

All of the aircraft used will feel very small to anyone accustomed to flying on big commercial jets. Most of the planes carry between 8 and 20 passengers. The captain often performs the duties of both flight attendant and pilot. Each passenger usually has a window, though some of the windows are pretty small. Cabin conditions for the most part are spartan, and there is usually no toilet on board.

Because small aircraft sometimes get bounced around and buffeted by air currents, we recommend taking an over-the-counter motion-sickness medication if you think you might be adversely affected. The other thing you want to do for sure is to relieve your bladder *immediately* before boarding.

Following are descriptions of the tours we consider to be the cream of the crop. Because they offer the most extensive introduction to the Grand Canyon, they rank among the most expensive (see chart on page 421).

GRAND CANYON RESERVATIONS One of Grand Canyon Reservations' most popular tours, and in our opinion the best package from the company, is the **Grand Canyon West Air, Boat, and Helicopter Tour.**
After the hotel pickup, you are shuttled to the North Las Vegas airport for the 45-minute air tour with views of the Hoover Dam and Lake Mead en route to the Grand Canyon West Rim. All planes are high wing, which means there's no chance you might get stuck in a seat overlooking the plane's wing. Once at the West Rim, guests board a helicopter for the seven-minute descent into the Canyon. Upon reaching

the bottom of the Grand Canyon, you climb onto a pontoon boat for a relaxing, scenic 20-minute ride down three calm miles of the Colorado River. For those mischievous or more adventurous types, we'll pass along the warning we received from the reservations agent: "Jumping or 'falling' into the river is heavily frowned upon!"

After the river ride, guests are helicoptered back up to the rim, bused over to Guano Point (nicer than it sounds) for a barbecue lunch, as well as to various lookout points along the West Rim. Opportunities are also provided to explore on foot. After the two-hour coach tour and lunch, you board the plane and head back to Las Vegas. If you are 18 or older, you must bring a photo ID.

BEST TOURS The **Grand Canyon West Rim Voyager** and **Grand Canyon #1 Best Adventure Airplane, Copter, and Boat Tours** carry the best bang for your buck from Best Tours. The only difference between the two tours is the transportation used to see Boulder City, Lake Mead, and the Hoover Dam, and to reach the Grand Canyon.

If you would prefer an aerial view of Boulder City, Lake Mead, and the Hoover Dam, then Grand Canyon #1 is your tour. All airplanes are high wing, and helicopters sport extra-large vista windows, allowing all passengers to have a spectacular view. If you wish for a more up-close and personal look at the attractions, and have an extra three and a half hours to allocate, the Grand Canyon West Rim Voyager tour incorporates the aforementioned sights into a three-hour relaxing motorcoach ride en route to the Canyon.

The tours are identical once you reach the Grand Canyon. You take a chopper to the Canyon floor (15 minutes), and shuffle onto a pontoon boat for a 25-minute ride down a flatwater section of the Colorado River. After the ride, you are airlifted back up to the West Canyon Rim to enjoy a barbecue lunch. Following lunch, you reboard the coach or plane and head back to Vegas.

GRAND CANYON HELICOPTER FLIGHTS **Grand Canyon Helicopter Below the Rim and Sunset Ranch Adventure** is the best package we reviewed for those wanting to combine a lengthy helicopter tour with other activities. Leaving from Las Vegas, the tour consists of a 45-minute helicopter flight with views of the Hoover Dam and Lake Mead, and flying through the Canyon at 1,500 feet below the rim.

Upon arrival at the Grand Canyon West Ranch, about 12 miles from the West Rim, you are shuttled in about ten minutes from the landing pad to the ranch in a horse-drawn wagon. At the ranch, horseback riding is available for an additional charge of $55 (1 hour) or $39 (30 minutes). A Western-style dinner along with songs and stories around a campfire complete the ranch experience. Alcohol is available at an additional charge, and the ranch buildings are air-conditioned if you need an escape from the heat. The return trip to Las Vegas is by bus and takes about two and a half hours.

Grand Canyon Tours

Grand Canyon West Air, Boat, and Helicopter ☎ 877-645-9380		**The Grand Canyon West Rim Voyage** ☎ 702-851-8436		**Grand Canyon #1 Best Adventure** ☎ 702-851-8436	
TRANSPORTATION	AIR, BOAT, AND HELICOPTER	TRANSPORTATION	BUS, HELICOPTER, BOAT	TRANSPORTATION	AIRPLANE, HELICOPTER, BOAT
SIGHTSEEING	HOOVER DAM, LAKE MEAD, COLORADO RIVER, CANYON WEST RIM	SIGHTSEEING	BOULDER CITY, HOOVER DAM, LAKE MEAD, WEST RIM, COLORADO RIVER	SIGHTSEEING	BOULDER CITY, HOOVER DAM, LAKE MEAD, WEST RIM, COLORADO RIVER
LENGTH	7 HOURS*	LENGTH	11 HOURS*	LENGTH	7½ HOURS*
COST	$285	COST	$240	COST	$286

Grand Canyon Helicopter Below the Rim and Sunset Ranch Adventure ☎ 800-359-8727		**North Rim Deluxe Air and Ground Tour** ☎ 702-380-1106		**Grand Canyon Picnic** ☎ 800-653-1881	
TRANSPORTATION	HELICOPTER, WAGON, BUS, HORSEBACK (ADDITIONAL CHARGE)	TRANSPORTATION	AIR, VAN, OR ATV (ADDITIONAL CHARGE)	TRANSPORTATION	HELICOPTER, WAGON, BUS, HORSEBACK (ADDITIONAL CHARGE
SIGHTSEEING	HOOVER DAM, LAKE MEAD, CANYON WEST RIM, RANCH	SIGHTSEEING	HOOVER DAM, LAKE MEAD, CANYON NORTH RIM, BAR 10	SIGHTSEEING	HOOVER DAM, LAKE MEAD, EXTINCT VOLCANOES, LAVA FLOWS, CANYON WEST RIM
LENGTH	8 HOURS*	LENGTH	8 HOURS*	LENGTH	3½ HOURS*
COST	$249	COST	$191	COST	$364 (DISCOUNTS AT LOOKTOURS.COM)

Length includes hotel pick-ups and drop-offs.

MAGIC TOURS We found the **North Rim Deluxe Air and Ground Tour** to be the most family friendly and best combination of activities if you don't have your heart set on a helicopter tour. Unlike the other tours reviewed in this section, Magic Tours takes you to the North Rim, rather than the popular West Rim.

The air-tour portion is 90 minutes round-trip, flying over the Hoover Dam, Lake Mead, and below the rim of the Grand Canyon. The company has both high- and low-winged planes ("low-winged" meaning there's a chance that you could be stuck sitting by a window viewing the plane wing rather than the dam or the Canyon). They claim that if you are thrown onto a low-winged plane going one direction, you'll be on a high winged plane going the other way. When you call to make reservations, just be firm about what type of plane or seat you wish to have.

The plane lands in the inner gorge of the Canyon at the working Bar 10 Ranch, where you're served a barbecue lunch and can participate in activities such as skeet shooting, horseshoes, and billiards. There are two options for reaching the inner gorge lookout: by van, or (for an additional charge) by ATV. After two and a half hours on the ground, you're loaded back onto the plane for the return flight to Las Vegas.

SUNDANCE HELICOPTERS If all you seek is a helicopter ride without the added bells and whistles of additional activities, then go with the **Sundance Grand Canyon Picnic Tour.** You will arrive at the launch pad in style by a ride in the complimentary limousine.

The helicopter tour is a round-trip one and a half hours spent in the air, viewing the Hoover Dam, Lake Mead, extinct volcanoes, lava formations, and the West Rim of the Grand Canyon. A maximum number of six people can fit in the helicopter. However, if a guest weighs over 275 pounds, he or she will have to purchase two seats. All guests have unobstructed views.

The helicopter lands on a plateau between the river and the ridge. A box lunch and Champagne are provided, and there is time to do a little exploring on foot before jumping back in the helicopter for the ride back to the Strip. Reserve the flight through **www.looktours.com** and save over $70 per person as opposed to reserving through the Sundance company directly.

IF YOU GO Grand Canyon tours are a perfect respite from the glitz and frenetic activity of the Strip. Whether you're looking for a fly-by, great photo ops, or a cowboy ranch experience, it can be found with one of the tours we describe.

All tours described above are geared toward families and people of all ages, from your 3-year-old nephew to your 75-year-old grandmother. The tours involving a boat ride use craft that guests of all ages can easily board, and the gentle, scenic section of the river featured contains no rapids. If you are seeking a whitewater thrill on the Colorado River, you won't find it in these tours.

SKYWALK Located 121 miles from Las Vegas over some primitive roads, Skywalk is horseshoe-shaped observation platform projecting from the remote western edge of the Grand Canyon on the Hualapai reservation. The ends of the horseshoe are anchored to the rim of the canyon while the rounded section, the observation platform, cantilevers into space 4,000 feet above the canyon floor. Both the sides and the floor of the platform are transparent. Though Skywalk is designed to withstand 100-mph winds and 8.0-magnitude earthquakes and to support 71 million pounds, it's flexible like a diving board. In other words, it wobbles and vibrates a little. The sensation is somewhat like walking on a cruise ship—not unpleasant at sea but disconcerting when you're hanging over the Grand Canyon. Add the fact that the walls are only about mid–chest high and Skywalk begins to seem as much a thrill ride as somewhere to go for a pretty view.

Speaking of the view, it's magnificent. From Skywalk you can see standing waves on the Colorado River to the left (they look like tiny ripples from this height) and Eagle Point to the right, where the configuration of the canyon looks like the outstretched wings of a bird.

To walk on the Skywalk you must purchase a Sky Tour package, which also includes a visit to the Hualapai Ranch, Guano Point, and Eagle Point, a Native American cultural performance, and an all-you-can-eat meal among other things (see **www.destinationgrand canyon.com** or call ☎ 877-716-9378). The package runs $81 (including taxes and fees) for adults and $61 for children ages 4 to 11. A wheelchair ramp will be completed by the end of 2007. There's no limit to the time you can spend on Skywalk and no maximum weight for visitors. You are not allowed to bring cameras or any personal belongings onto Skywalk. For additional information see **www.grand canyonskywalk.com.**

If you drive from Las Vegas but don't want to drive the final 14-mile unpaved, washboard road to the reservation (you need a high-clearance vehicle), make a reservation to use the Park & Ride service by calling ☎ 702-260-6506. Because the drive is a little over three hours one-way from Las Vegas, you'll have to get rolling pretty early to take advantage of all the elements of the tour package. If you want to drive over on the day prior to your tour, you can spend the night at the Hualapai Lodge in the hardscrabble town of Peach Springs (49 miles away), the center of the Hualapai Tribe; call ☎ 877-716-9378 for reservations.

If you don't want to drive, the following companies will fly you there:

Vision Holidays **www.visionholidays.com** | ☎ 702-647-7000

Maverick Helicopters **www.maverickhelicopter.com** | ☎ 702-261-0007

Sundance Helicopters **www.helicoptour.com** | ☎ 702-736-0606

Fares range from $250 to over $500 round-trip, although sometimes a discount can be found on the Internet. Fares sometimes include a tour but not the Skywalk so you're stuck with buying one of the Hualapai tours in addition to your airfare.

PART SIX

EXERCISE *and* RECREATION

■ WORKING OUT

MOST OF THE FOLKS ON OUR *UNOFFICIAL GUIDE* research team work out routinely. Some bike; some run; some lift weights or do aerobics. Staying in hotels on the Strip and downtown, it didn't take them long to discover that working out in Las Vegas presents its own peculiar challenges.

The best months for outdoor exercise are October through April. The rest of the year it is extremely hot, though mornings and evenings are generally pleasant in September and May. During the scorching summer, particularly for visitors, we recommend working out indoors or, for bikers and runners, very early in the morning.

If you do anything strenuous outside, any time of year, drink plenty of water. Dehydration and heat prostration can overtake you quickly and unexpectedly in Las Vegas's desert climate. For outdoor workouts in Las Vegas comparable to what you are used to at home, you will deplete your body's water at two to three times the usual rate.

WALKING

PRIMARILY FLAT, LAS VEGAS IS MADE FOR WALKING and great people-watching. Security is very good both downtown and on the Strip, making for a safe walking environment at practically all hours of the day and night. Downtown, everything is concentrated in such a small area that you might be inclined to venture away from the casino center. While this is no more perilous than walking in any other city, the areas surrounding downtown are not particularly interesting or aesthetically compelling. If the downtown casino center is not large enough to accommodate your exercise needs, you are better off busing or cabbing to the Strip and doing your walking there.

If you are walking the Strip, it is about four miles from Mandalay Bay on the south end to the Stratosphere on the north end. Because

las vegas strip walking map

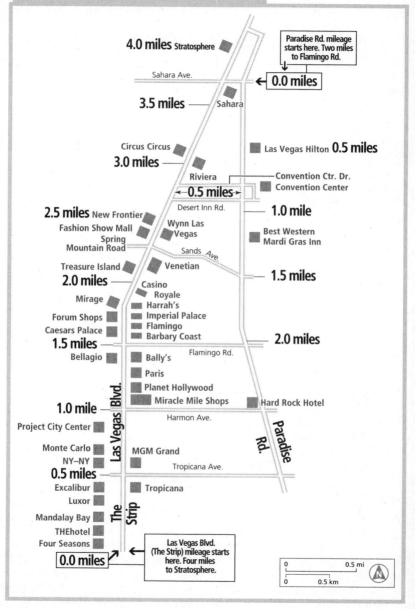

4.0 miles Stratosphere

Paradise Rd. mileage starts here. Two miles to Flamingo Rd.

Sahara Ave.

← 0.0 miles

3.5 miles — Sahara

Las Vegas Hilton 0.5 miles

Circus Circus
3.0 miles

Riviera

Convention Ctr. Dr.
Convention Center

← 0.5 miles →

Desert Inn Rd.

1.0 mile

2.5 miles New Frontier
Fashion Show Mall
Spring
Mountain Road

Wynn Las
Vegas

Best Western
Mardi Gras Inn

Sands Ave.

Treasure Island
2.0 miles — Venetian

1.5 miles

Casino
Royale

Mirage

Harrah's
Imperial Palace
Flamingo
Barbary Coast

Forum Shops
Caesars Palace
1.5 miles —

2.0 miles

Bellagio

Bally's

Flamingo Rd.

Paris

Las Vegas Blvd.

Planet Hollywood
Miracle Mile Shops

Hard Rock Hotel

1.0 mile —

Harmon Ave.

Project City Center

Paradise Rd.

Monte Carlo
NY–NY
0.5 miles

MGM Grand

Tropicana Ave.

Excalibur
Luxor

Tropicana

Mandalay Bay
THEhotel
Four Seasons

The Strip

0.0 miles

Las Vegas Blvd.
(The Strip) mileage starts here. Four miles to Stratosphere.

0   0.5 mi
0   0.5 km

the topography is so flat, however, it does not look that far. We met a number of people who set out on foot along the Strip and managed to overextend themselves. Check out our Strip walking distance map before you go, and bear in mind that even without hills, marching in the arid desert climate will take a lot out of you.

When walking the Strip, carry enough money to buy refreshments en route and to take a cab or bus back to your hotel if you poop out or develop a blister.

RUNNING

IF YOU STAY ON THE STRIP, you will have more options than if you stay downtown. Those of us who are used to running on pavement ran on the broad sidewalks of South Las Vegas Boulevard. These runs are great for people-watching also, but are frequently interrupted by long minutes of jogging in place at intersections, waiting for traffic lights to change. Our early risers would often run before 7:30 a.m. on a golf course. This was the best (and safest) running in town, with good footing, beautiful scenery, and no traffic. Suffice it to say, however, that course managers were less than overjoyed to see a small platoon of travel writers trotting off the 18th fairway. If you run on a golf course, stay off the greens and try to complete your run by 7:30 a.m. In addition to area golf courses, the Las Vegas Hilton and Mandalay Bay each have a jogging circuit.

If you stay downtown, you must either run on the sidewalks or drive to a more suitable venue. Sidewalks downtown are more congested than those on the Strip, and there are more intersections and traffic lights with which to contend. If you want to run downtown, particularly on Fremont Street, try to get your workout in before 10 a.m.

For those who dislike pounding the blacktop, sneaking onto golf courses, or exercising early in the morning, a convenient option is to run on the track at the university. Located about two miles east of the Strip on Harmon Avenue, **UNLV** offers both a regulation track and some large, grassy athletic fields. Park in the dirt lot near the tennis courts if you do not have a university parking sticker. For more information, call ☎ 702-895-3177.

If you have a car and a little time, two of the better off-road runs in the area are at **Red Rock Canyon,** out Charleston Avenue, 35 minutes west of town. Red Rock Canyon Conservation Area, managed by the U.S. Bureau of Land Management, is Western desert and canyon scenery at its best. Spectacular geology combined with the unique desert flora and fauna make Red Rock Canyon a truly memorable place. Maps and information can be obtained at the visitor center, on site.

A two-mile round trip, the **Moenkopi Loop,** begins and ends at the visitor center. A three-mile circuit, the **Willow Springs Trail,** begins at the Willow Springs Picnic Area and circles around to Lost Creek Canyon. Both routes are moderately hilly, with generally good footing. The Moenkopi Loop is characterized by open desert and expansive vistas, while the Willow Springs Trail ventures into the canyons. The Willow Springs Trail is also distinguished by numerous Indian petroglyphs and other artifacts. Both trails, of course, are great for hiking as well as for running.

Finally, if you want to hook up with local runners, you can join the Las Vegas Track Club for a weekly run to **Tule Springs** (north of downtown on US 95) or many other area locations. For a current schedule or additional information, call the Running Store at ☎ 702-898-7866 or the Runner's Hotline at ☎ 702-594-0970.

SWIMMING AND SUNBATHING

SWIMMING, DURING WARM-WEATHER MONTHS, is the most dependable and generally accessible form of exercise in Las Vegas. Most of the Strip hotels and a couple of the downtown hotels have nice pools. Sometimes the pools are too congested for swimming laps, but usually it is possible to stake out a lane.

If the pool at your hotel is a funny shape or too crowded for a workout, there are pools more conducive to serious swimming at the **Las Vegas Athletic Club** on Flamingo Road and in the **McDermott Physical Education Complex** of UNLV.

For those who want to work on their tans in style, the **Mirage, Tropicana, Wynn Las Vegas, Mandalay Bay, Venetian, Paris, Monte Carlo, MGM Grand, T. I., Caesars Palace, Rio, Las Vegas Hilton, Flamingo, Alexis Park Resort & Villas, Palms, Green Valley Ranch, Hard Rock Hotel, Bellagio, Aladdin/Planet Hollywood,** and **JW Marriott Las Vegas,** among others, have particularly elegant facilities. Hotels with above-average pools include **Luxor, New Frontier, Riviera, Harrah's, Imperial Palace,** and **Sahara.**

Be forewarned that sunbathing in Las Vegas can be dangerous. The climate is so arid that you will not feel yourself perspiring: perspiration evaporates as soon as it surfaces on your skin. If there is a breeze, particularly on a pleasant fall or spring day, you may never feel hot, sticky, or in any way uncomfortable until you come out of the sun and discover that you have been fried.

You can get sunburned in a hurry if you do not protect yourself properly, and even those who already have a good tan need to be extra careful. We recommend using twice the block you use in nondesert areas. Come out of the sun frequently to check yourself, and be careful not to fall asleep in the sun for an extended period.

HEALTH CLUBS

IF YOU CAN GET BY WITH A LIFECYCLE, a StairMaster, or a rowing machine, the fitness rooms of most major hotels should serve your needs. Fortunately, local health clubs welcome visitors for a daily ($15 to $20) or weekly ($30 to $50) fee. All of the clubs described here are coed.

The **Las Vegas Athletic Clubs,** with five locations, offer racquetball, tennis, basketball, exercise equipment, and aerobics, though not all features are provided at each location. The Las Vegas Athletic Clubs depend more on local patronage than on visitors; their facilities are commodious but not luxurious, and fees are at the lower end of the range. While reasonably convenient to the Strip, only the West Sahara club is within walking distance. For rates and additional information call:

Las Vegas Athletic Club
5200 W. Sahara Ave.
☎ 702-364-5822

Las Vegas Athletic Club
9065 S. Eastern Ave.
☎ 702-853-5822

Las Vegas Athletic Club
E. Flamingo at Sandhill Rd.
☎ 702-898-5822

Las Vegas Athletic Club
2655 S. Maryland Pkwy.
☎ 702-734-5822

Las Vegas Athletic Club
1725 N. Rainbow
☎ 702-835-5822

The **24 Hour Fitness** centers, with three locations, run an excellent aerobics program and have an extensive weight and exercise facility. While the facilities are good and the use fees midrange, the locations are a little remote for most visitors staying on the Strip or downtown.

24 Hour Fitness
S. Eastern near Sahara
☎ 702-641-2222

24 Hour Fitness
Cheyenne and Rainbow
☎ 702-656-7777

24 Hour Fitness
S. Valley View, half a
mile south of Sahara
☎ 702-368-1111

AEROBICS

A NUMBER OF HEALTH CLUBS offer coed aerobics on a daily basis. Daily or weekly rates are available. For additional information, see the preceding Health Clubs section.

FREE WEIGHTS AND NAUTILUS

ALMOST ALL OF THE MAJOR HOTELS have a spa or fitness room with weight-lifting equipment. Some properties have a single Universal machine, while others offer a wide range of free-weight and Nautilus equipment. Hotels with above-average facilities for pumping iron are the **Las Vegas Hilton, Bellagio, Venetian, Caesars Palace, Golden Nugget, Mirage, Paris, Wynn Las Vegas, Monte Carlo, MGM Grand, Luxor,** and **T. I.**

For hard-core power lifters and bodybuilders, try **Gold's Gym.** Gold's is coed and offers daily, weekly, and monthly rates for use of its Nautilus and free weights ($15, $35, and $75, respectively). Contact them at any one of their five locations: West, ☎ 702-877-6966; East, ☎ 702-451-4222; North, ☎ 702-646-4669; South, ☎ 702-914-5885; and Summerlin, ☎ 702-360-8205.

RACQUETBALL, SQUASH, AND HANDBALL

VISITORS ARE WELCOME AT MOST LOCAL racquet and health clubs. **Sports Club–Las Vegas** and the **Las Vegas Athletic Clubs,** among others, provide good court facilities. For additional information, see the preceding Health Club section.

GOLF

PEAK SEASON FOR GOLF IN LAS VEGAS is October through May. The other four months are considered prohibitively warm for most golfers, and greens fees are reduced substantially at most courses during the

GOLF COURSE RATINGS

Quality rating	★★★	Championship, challenging
	★★	Playable, suitable for all caliber golfers
	★	Preferred by beginners and casual golfers
Value rating	1	A good bargain
	2	A fair price
	3	Not a good bargain

Note: Quality and value ratings are abbreviated as QV rating in the following listings.

summer. Certain courses also have reduced rates for locals and for guests staying at hotels affiliated with the golf course. Also, almost all Las Vegas area courses offer discounted twilight rates, which, depending on time of year, often start as early as noon, one, or two o'clock. Beware that Stallion Mountain, a 27-hole facility regarded by many as poorly maintained, heavily played, and overpriced, has a friendly agreement with the concierge staffs of many top Vegas hotels and is often the first place recommended. Morning tee times are always more difficult to arrange than afternoons. Call the pro shop one day before you wish to play. Same-day phone calls are discouraged. In summer, most courses and driving ranges stay open until at least 7:30 p.m. A well-established company called **Stand-By Golf** offers unsold tee times from many of the city's best (and not so best) courses for the next day, or if you call early, for the same day, and can almost always accommodate last-minute requests at discounts of 30 to 50% (☎ 866-711-2665, **www .standbygolf.com**). In winter and early spring, temperatures drop rapidly near sundown, so always bring a sweater or jacket. It can also be very windy. Las Vegas has an elevation of 2,000 feet and is considered high desert. Take this into account when making club selections.

IMPORTANT NOTE Many top Las Vegas courses are private clubs that do not allow outside access, and thus are not listed. In addition, Las Vegas has created a unique sort of golf course that could be called "almost private." This started with **Shadow Creek Country Club,** which was built specifically for the highest of high rollers and originally had neither members nor allowed paying guests. Now privately owned by MGM/Mirage Resorts, Inc., the course is open to guests of its hotels, but on a very limited basis. Only a handful of "public" tee times are available each day (Monday through Thursday only) at a cost of $500 per person, which along with similar courses Cascata and Wynn's, constitute the nation's highest greens fees. In this sense Vegas has created its own category of courses that are open only to a handful of guests from specific hotels at extremely high prices. Not quite so extravagant is **The Tournament Players Club,** open only to guests of JW Marriott Las Vegas at Summerlin at high, but not sky-high, prices. The TPC has regularly hosted the Champions (Senior) Tour and is the venue for the Las Vegas Invitational, now called the Frys.com Classic;

this is where Tiger Woods won his very first PGA Tour event back in 1996. The Summerlin course was designed by architect Bobby Weed with assistance from player-consultant Fuzzy Zoeller and is rated by both *Golf Digest* and *Golfweek* magazines as the second-best course in Nevada, behind Shadow Creek. Many current professional athletes are members, including pitcher Greg Maddux (Chicago Cubs), and golfers Jim Colbert, Robert Gamez, and Bob May.

Despite the number of golf courses in the Las Vegas area, for serious golf travel fans there are only two choices that could accurately be called golf resorts. **Lake Las Vegas,** about half an hour from the Strip, has three hotels, numerous rental condos, and two excellent golf courses, Reflection Bay and the Falls. A third, Tom Fazio's Rainbow Canyon, is expected to open next year. In **Summerlin,** about 25 minutes from the Strip, the JW Marriott is surrounded by nine courses within ten minutes, and offers preferred tee times and free shuttles to all of them, making it a true destination golf resort. Both resorts have lavish spas, pools, and activities, but this still being Vegas, both also feature multiple restaurants, bars, and casinos.

Angel Park Golf Club

ESTABLISHED	1989	STATUS	MUNICIPAL	QV	RATING	★★	2

100 South Rampart Boulevard, Las Vegas, NV 89145; ☎ 702-254-4653; www.angelpark.com

Tees

PALM COURSE

- **Championship: 6,530 yards, par 70, USGA 72.6, slope 130**
- **Men's: 5,857 yards, par 70, USGA 69.8, slope 120**
- **Ladies': 5,438 yards, par 70, USGA 68.6, slope 112**

MOUNTAIN COURSE

- **Championship: 6,722 yards, par 71, slope 128**
- **Men's: 6,235 yards, par 71, slope 117**
- **Ladies': 5,751 yards, par 71, slope 116**

Fees Nonresidents: Monday–Thursday, $75–$135; Friday–Sunday and holidays, $90–$155. Residents: Monday–Thursday, $50–$65; Friday–Sunday and holidays, $50–$75.

Facilities Pro shop, night-lighted driving range, 12-hole par-3 course and 18-hole putting course, putting green, restaurant, snack bar, bar, tennis courts, golf club and shoe rentals.

Comments Angel Park, a good, functional golf complex, is rapidly becoming one of the most successful public golf facilities in the United States. Its courses are well designed—by Arnold Palmer, no less—and the sophisticated 18-hole putting course, complete with night lighting, sand traps, rough, and water hazards, is a popular attraction even for nongolfers. Its "Cloud Nine" short course is very unique and great for golfers needing a quick fix, with reproductions of 12 famous par-3 holes from throughout the world, 9 of which are lighted for night play. Angel Park has matured and become lush and attractive. Both courses are crowded year-round, as the facility is close to the Strip and popular with locals.

Bali Hai

ESTABLISHED	2000	STATUS	PUBLIC	QV	RATING	★★	3

5160 Las Vegas Boulevard, Las Vegas, NV 89119; ☎ 888-427-6678; www.balihaigolfclub.com

Tees

- **Championship: 7,002 yards, par 72, USGA 73.0, slope 130**
- **Men's: 6,619 yards, par 72, USGA 70.2, slope 125**
- **Ladies': 6,174 yards, par 72, USGA 68.6, slope 113**

Fees September–May: weekdays, $265; weekends, $325. June–August: weekdays, $175; weekends, $195.

Facilities Pro shop, tropical boutique, driving range, putting green, snack bar, restaurant, full locker facilities, caddies, fore-caddies, club rentals.

Comments In real estate, location is everything, and the only reason Bali Hai commands these outrageous greens fees is its location on the Strip next to Mandalay Bay. It is the only course besides the guest-only Wynn Golf Course that is located so close to the major casinos. It also strives for luxury, with caddies as well as a pro shop selling tropical plants. Designed in a tropical theme, Bali Hai features water everywhere, with an island green, endless tropical flora, and vast expanses of black "coral" and white sand. No island golf course, even in the South Pacific, looks anything like this, and for a reason: Bali Hai is undeniably beautiful, but that does not make it a great course, and better golf can be had for less, even with the taxi fares.

Bear's Best

ESTABLISHED	2002	STATUS	PUBLIC	QV	RATING	★★★	2

11111 West Flamingo Road, Las Vegas, NV 89135; ☎ 866-385-8500; www.bearsbest.com

Tees

- **Gold: 7,194 yards, par 72, USGA 74.0, slope 147**
- **Blue: 6,628 yards, par 72, USGA 71.3, slope 130**
- **White: 6,043 yards, par 72, USGA 68.3, slope 122**
- **Red: 5,043 yards, par 72, USGA 68.7, slope 116**

Fees High season, $205–$255. Caddies by request after noon. Low season, $120–$160 plus caddie gratuity (required). Caddies optional in low season for twilight play.

Facilities Pro shop, driving range, putting green, restaurant, full locker facilities, caddies, fore-caddies, club and shoe rentals.

Comments One of only two Bear's Best courses (the other is in Atlanta), this is a unique tribute by Jack Nicklaus, aka the Golden Bear, to himself. Here Nicklaus has re-created holes from his favorite original designs, but unlike most tribute or replica courses, including Vegas's Royal Links, the holes were specifically chosen to fit the desert setting. As a result, this is one of the best of these gimmicky layouts in the world, and all the holes are very good, giving fans an opportunity to play holes from Nicklaus's most acclaimed public courses, such as Cabo del Sol, Palmilla, and Castle Pines, along with very private ones from Desert Mountain, Desert Highlands, and PGA West. Since opening it has been ranked among the city's very best. It is also a very classy operation, and one of the few golf clubs anywhere to boast of its top-quality rental sets, sparing no expense right down to Scotty Cameron putters and choice of shaft stiffness.

Black Mountain Golf and Country Club

| ESTABLISHED | 1959 | STATUS | SEMIPRIVATE | QV | RATING | ★ | 1 |

500 Greenway Road, Henderson, NV 89015; ☎ 702-565-7933; www.golfblackmountain.com

Tees
- **Championship: 6,550 yards, par 72, USGA 71.2, slope 123**
- **Men's: 6,223 yards, par 72, USGA 69.8, slope 120**
- **Ladies': 5,518 yards, par 72, USGA 71.6, slope 120**

Fees   Nonresidents: high season, $95 (carts included and required on weekends only); low season, $75. Residents: high season, $50; low season, $45.

Facilities   Pro shop, clubhouse, driving range, putting green, restaurant, club rentals, snack bar, bar.

Comments   Black Mountain is set amidst the Henderson hills, 20 minutes from the Strip. Heavy discounts make it a local favorite, but even for visitors it's a bargain, especially in high season. Many who prefer walking to riding play here, as it's one of the few area courses that doesn't require electric carts during the week. Many bunkers and unimproved areas off fairways make for tough recovery shots, but nobody said the game was supposed to be easy. A good course for beginning and intermediate golfers and juniors. A third nine, the Desert, was added in 2002, making this a 27-hole course.

Cascata

| ESTABLISHED | 2000 | STATUS | PUBLIC | QV | RATING | ★★★ | 3 |

3654 Las Vegas Boulevard, Boulder City, NV 89142; ☎ 702-294-2000; www.cascatagolf.com

Tees
- **Green: 7,137 yards, par 72, USGA 74.6, slope 143**
- **Black: 7,030 yards, par 72, USGA 74.1, slope 132**
- **Blue: 6,664 yards, par 72, USGA 71.17, slope 138**
- **Gold: 6,206 yards, par 72, USGA 69.9, slope 135**
- **Red: 5,559 yards, par 72, USGA 67.2, slope 117**

Fees $500. Closed Tuesdays. Fees include round-trip limo transfer from hotel and caddie (recommended tip $50). Must be a guest of a Harrah's Entertainment Properties hotel to play.

Facilities   Pro shop, driving range, putting green, restaurant, full locker facilities, caddies.

Comments After the runaway success of Shadow Creek, another casino group built the even more expensive Cascata, said to have the highest golf course construction price tag ever, for its high rollers. Now owned by Harrah's, it is a truly unique design in golf. Acclaimed designer Rees Jones blasted the course out of a rocky mountain. The holes are built in a series of narrow, parallel finger canyons radiating from the summit and running up and down the rocky slopes. Sitting in the canyons, the lush green fairways are completely isolated from one another by sloped canyon walls. The par-3s are especially dramatic, often backed by amphitheater cliffs and waterfalls. Because its name is Italian for "waterfall," Jones built one 40 stories high that pours through the center of the marble Italian palazzo–style clubhouse. Thanks to competitors Shadow Creek and Wynn, Cascata no longer offers midweek discounts.

Desert Pines Golf Club

ESTABLISHED 1997 | STATUS PUBLIC | QV RATING ★ 2

3415 East Bonanza Road, Las Vegas, NV 89101; ☎ 702-366-1616; www.waltersgolf.com

Tees

- **Championship: 6,810 yards, par 71, USGA 70.4, slope 122**
- **Men's: 6,464 yards, par 71, USGA 66.8, slope 112**
- **Ladies': 5,873 yards, par 71, USGA 69.4, slope 116**

Fees Peak Season: $129 Monday-Thursday ($79 twilight); $154 Friday–Sunday ($99 twilight). Off-season: $69 Monday–Thursday ($29 twilight); $79 Friday–Sunday ($39 twilight).

Facilities Pro shop, driving range, putting green, snack bar, restaurant.

Comments Desert Pines is a 6,810-yard course on Bonanza Road between Mohave and Pecos roads. Inspired by the Pinehurst courses in North Carolina, its fairways and greens are flanked by trees, some already as tall as 40 feet. Instead of rough, developer Bill Walters laid down 45,000 bales of red-pine needles imported from South Carolina, making it hard to lose a ball here. Its very low off-season rates make it one of the best hot-weather choices in the region. The course was closed for three full months last year for renovations to fairways and putting surfaces and is in its best shape in years.

Desert Rose Golf Course

ESTABLISHED 1960 | STATUS MUNICIPAL | QV RATING ★ 2

5483 Club House Drive, Las Vegas, NV 89122; ☎ 702-431-4653

Tees

- **Championship: 6,511 yards, par 71, USGA 69.6, slope 117**
- **Men's: 6,135 yards, par 71, USGA 69, slope 114**
- **Ladies': 5,458 yards, par 71, USGA 69, slope 119**

Fees Nonresidents: $59 weekdays, $79 weekends and holidays. Twilight $30 daily. Cart included in all prices. Club rentals, $39.

Facilities Pro shop, driving range, 3 putting/chipping greens, restaurant, banquet room, snack bar, bar.

Comments With a name change (formerly Winterwood) and much moving of dirt, former PGA tour star Jim Colbert has created a functional public golf course that gets a lot of play year-round. A good course for recreational golfers, Desert Rose has fairly wide-open fairways with just a few out-of-bounds holes.

Highland Falls Golf Club

| ESTABLISHED | 1992 | STATUS | SEMIPRIVATE | QV | RATING | ★★★ | 2 |

10201 Sun City Boulevard, Las Vegas, NV 89134; ☎ 702-566-7618; www.golfsummerlin.com

Tees
- **Championship: 6,512 yards, par 72,** USGA **71.2, slope 12**
- **Men's: 6,017 yards, par 72,** USGA **68.6, slope 11**
- **Gold: 5,579 yards, par 72,** USGA **67.1, slope 112**
- **Ladies': 5,099 yards, par 72,** USGA **68.8, slope 115**

Fees Nonresidents: peak season, $100 weekends, $80 weekdays; off peak, $60 every day. Residents: peak season, $60 weekends, $50 weekdays; off peak, $45 every day.

Facilities Pro shop, driving range, putting green, restaurant, luncheon area, patio for outside dining, bar.

Comments A testing layout designed by Hall of Famer Billy Casper's company, Casper-Nash Associates. The unique design sits in the mountains at over 300 feet, and the cooler weather allows it to use superior quality bentgrass greens, unusual in this climate, and Bermuda fairways to combine the best of both worlds. More undulations than most desert courses, with several demanding holes. No one broke par for the first six months after opening. Schedule your tee time at least seven days in advance. It is a bargain for visitors but one of the few area courses with no twilight discount in peak season.

Lake Las Vegas

| ESTABLISHED | 1998 | STATUS | RESORT, | PUBLIC | QV | RATING | ★★★ | 2 |

75 MonteLago Boulevard, Henderson, NV 89011; ☎ 877-698-4653; www.lakelasvegas.com

Tees
REFLECTION BAY
- **Black: 7,261 yards, par 72,** USGA **74.8, slope 138**
- **Blue: 6,862 yards, par 72,** USGA **73.0, slope 134**
- **White: 6,391 yards, par 72,** USGA **71.2, slope 130**
- **Gold: 5,891 yards, par 72,** USGA **69.6, slope 128**
- **Red: 5,166 yards, par 72,** USGA **70.0, slope 127**

THE FALLS
- **Black: 7,250 yards, par 72,** USGA **74.8, slope 138**
- **Blue: 6,872 yards, par 72,** USGA **73.0, slope 134**
- **White: 6,336 yards, par 72,** USGA **71.2, slope 130**

- **Gold:** 5,634 yards, par 72, USGA 69.6, slope 128
- **Red:** 5,021 yards, par 72, USGA 70.0, slope 127

Fees Public: peak season, weekday $275, twilight $160; weekend $295, twilight $180; off peak, weekday $170, twilight $120; weekend $190, twilight $130. Resort guests: peak season, weekday $150–$215, twilight $135–$160; weekend $160–$235, twilight $150–$180; off season, weekday $140, twilight $120; weekend $150, twilight $130.

Facilities Pro shop, driving range, putting green, snack bar, restaurant, full locker facilities, Gary Knapp Golf Institute, resort hotel.

Comments Expensive but worth it. On *Golf Magazine*'s Top 100 You Can Play list shortly after opening, Refection Bay is simply one of the best public courses in the nation, and vies with the twice-as-expensive Shadow Creek as the top course in Nevada. This was the first public course in the Lake Las Vegas residential community, and along with the private South Shore Club, hosted the Wendy's Three Tour Challenge several times. A stunning combination of hilly desert fraught with ravines and boulders, and waterfront "coastal" holes on the state's largest man-made private lake, with gorgeous water features throughout, including streams and waterfalls. On one hole, golfers step across stones in the stream to putt out. Also on the property is the newer Falls Golf Club by acclaimed designer Tom Weiskopf. Its not quite as well balanced, but also an eye-popping beauty, with some of the most drastic elevation changes in the nation on its trademark canyon holes. This duo is now part of a full-service destination resort that includes Ritz-Carlton and Loews hotels, a faux Italian lakeside village with numerous shops, restaurants, another hotel, and a casino. If that is not enough, Tom Fazio just started work on a third public course, Rainbow Canyon. Off-peak golf and lodging packages with village hotel or condos can be bargains.

Las Vegas Golf Club

| ESTABLISHED | 1949 | STATUS | PUBLIC | QV | RATING | ★ | 1 |

4300 West Washington Avenue, Las Vegas, NV 89107; ☎ 702-646-3003; www.lasvegasgolfclub.reachlocal.net

Tees

- **Championship:** 6,319 yards, par 72, USGA 70, slope 112
- **Men's:** 5,917 yards, par 72, USGA 68.1, slope 105
- **Ladies':** 5,200 yards, par 72, USGA 69.9, slope 112

Fees Nonresidents: weekdays $69 before noon, $49 after noon. Weekends $89 before noon, $69 after noon.

Facilities Pro shop, night-lighted driving range, putting green, restaurant, snack bar, bar, and beverage-cart girls who patrol the course.

Comments The first golf course in Las Vegas, this one was laid out by the legendary William Bell in 1938. It has always remained a popular public course and a site of many local amateur tournaments. Formerly owned and managed by Senior PGA star Jim Colbert, it is now operated by American Golf. A good choice for recreational golfers, it offers fairly wide-open fairways and not a lot of trouble, so play should move briskly. Tee times are always in great demand.

Las Vegas National

ESTABLISHED 1961 | STATUS PUBLIC (PRIVATELY OWNED) | QV RATING ★ ★ 2

1911 East Desert Inn Road, Las Vegas NV 89109; ☎ 800-GO-TRY-18 or 702-734-1796 (tee-time service and other reservations); www.lasvegasnational.com

Tees

- **Championship: 6,815 yards, par 72, USGA 72.1, slope 130**
- **Men's: 6,418 yards, par 70, USGA 70.2, slope 121**
- **Ladies': 5,741 yards, par 72, USGA 72.9, slope 127**

Fees Peak season: weekdays $129, weekends $159; twilight (starting time varies) $89. Off peak: weekdays $89, weekends $109; twilight (starting time varies) $59.

Facilities Pro shop, night-lighted driving range, putting green, restaurant, bar.

Comments A championship course that has at one time cohosted the Tournament of Champions, the Sahara Invitational, and the Ladies' Sahara Classic. The PGA Tour's Las Vegas Invitational was held here several times. Excellent variety of holes, with good bunkering and elevation changes uncharacteristic of a desert course. Better for intermediate and advanced golfers. No longer has any affiliation with the Sahara Hotel. The house used by Sharon Stone and Robert DeNiro in the film *Casino* is located to the left of the first tee, between the first and eighteenth fairways.

Las Vegas Paiute Resort

ESTABLISHED 1995 | STATUS PUBLIC | QV RATING ★ ★ 2 (SNOW/SUN) ★ ★ ★ 2 (WOLF)

10325 Nu/Wav Kaiv Boulevard, Las Vegas, NV 89124 (US 95 between Kyle Canyon and Lee Canyon turn-off to Mount Charleston); ☎ 702-658-1400 or 866-284-2833; www.lvpaiutegolf.com

Tees

SNOW MOUNTAIN

- **Tournament: 7,158 yards, par 72, USGA 73.9, slope 125**
- **Championship: 6,665 yards, par 72, USGA 71.2, slope 120**
- **Ladies' (white): 6,035 yards, par 72, USGA 74.5, slope 129**
- **Ladies' (red): 5,341 yards, par 72, USGA 70.4, slope 117**

SUN MOUNTAIN

- **Tournament: 7,112 yards, par 72, USGA 73.3, slope 130**
- **Championship: 6,631 yards, par 72, USGA 70.9, slope 124**
- **Ladies' (white): 6,074 yards, par 72, USGA 74.8, slope 131**
- **Ladies' (red): 5,465 yards, par 72, USGA 71, slope 123**

WOLF

- **Tournament: 7,604 yards, par 72, USGA 76.3, slope 149**
- **Black: 7,009 yards, par 72, USGA 73.5, slope 134**
- **Yellow: 6,483 yards, par 72, USGA 71.4, slope 130**
- **Ladies' (white): 5,910 yards, par 72, USGA 76.5, slope 125**
- **Ladies' (red): 5,130 yards, par 72, USGA 68.6, slope 116**

Fees Snow Mountain and Sun Mountain: Monday–Thursday, $79–$169; twilight, $59–$110; Friday–Sunday, $89–$189; twilight, $59–$110; includes unlimited balls and cart. Wolf: Monday–Thursday, $105–$199; twilight, $75–$135; Friday–Sunday, $129–$220; twilight, $75–$135; includes unlimited balls and cart.

Facilities Pro shop, driving range, 2 putting greens, restaurant, snack bar, bar with gaming.

Comments The region's only 54-hole resort golf complex, all three courses are Pete Dye designs. Dye is infamous for creating difficult tests, but the original two layouts, Snow and Sun Mountain, are comfortable desert courses, beauty without brawn, and have remained among the public favorites in the region since opening. Not so for the newer Wolf, which is one of, if not the most, difficult courses in Las Vegas. From the tips it is 500 yards longer than any course most golfers have played, and strewn with hazards of the wet and dry variety. Still, it is as well-conditioned and thought out as its tamer siblings, and has a near re-creation of Dye's famous island hole par-3 he pioneered at the TPC Sawgrass. Despite its stiff challenge, it has quickly become the most demanded course here and is accordingly priced higher.

Legacy Golf Club

ESTABLISHED 1989 | STATUS PUBLIC (PRIVATELY OWNED) | QV RATING ★★ 2

130 Par Excellence Drive, Henderson, NV 89014; ☎ 702-897-2187; www.thelegacygc.com

Tees

- **Championship: 7,233 yards, par 72, USGA 74.9, slope 136**
- **Men's: 6,744 yards, par 72, USGA 72.1, slope 128**
- **Ladies': 5,340 yards, par 72, USGA 71, slope 120**
- **Resort: 6,211 yards, par 72, USGA 69.1, slope 118**

Fees 18 holes (no 9-hole rate): weekdays, $135; weekends, $155. Summer rates (June 1–October 2): weekdays, $75; weekends, $90. Twilight rates vary. All greens fees include mandatory carts. Club rentals, $50.

Facilities Clubhouse, pro shop, driving range, chipping facility, putting green, restaurant, snack bar, bar.

Comments Legacy is a mixture of rolling fairways and target golf. Championship tees require long carry on tee-ball to clear desert mounding. Located at the southeastern tip of Las Vegas, Legacy has quickly become a favorite of intermediate and advanced golfers. Course hosts a number of mini-tour professional events. This is the region's only course designed by the renowned Arthur Hills and often has aggressive online special deals.

Los Prados Country Club

ESTABLISHED   1985 | STATUS   SEMIPRIVATE | QV   RATING   ★   2

5150 Los Prados Circle, Las Vegas, NV 89130; ☎ 702-645-4523; pro shop, ☎ 702-645-5696; www.losprados-golf.com

Tees

- **Championship: 6,000 yards, par 70, USGA 64.8, slope 103**

- **Ladies': 4,474 yards, par 70, USGA 64.4, slope 104**

Fees Nonresidents, $60–$70; twilight, $40–$50. Club rentals, $30.

Facilities Pro shop, putting green, chipping green, restaurant, snack bar, bar.

Comments Los Prados is a short, executive course, making it a good choice for beginners, intermediates, and families. You will find many short par-4s. It is well maintained and resides in a gated community. Like most real-estate developments in which golf is secondary to property values, the emphasis of the builders was on homesites rather than the design of the course. Nearly a 25-minute drive from the Strip.

Painted Desert

| ESTABLISHED | 1987 | STATUS | PUBLIC | QV | RATING | ★★ | 2 |

5555 Painted Mirage Drive, Las Vegas, NV 89149; ☎ 702-645-2570; www.painteddesertgc.com

Tees

- **Championship: 6,840 yards, par 73, USGA 73.7, slope 136**
- **Men's: 6,323 yards, par 72, USGA 71, slope 128**
- **Ladies': 5,711 yards, par 72, USGA 73.0, slope 127**

Fees Peak season: Monday–Thursday, $109; twilight rate, $69; Friday–Sunday, $129; twilight rate, $69. Off-peak: Monday–Thursday, $65; twilight rate, $50; Friday–Sunday, $85; twilight rate, $50. Regular club rentals, $40; deluxe clubs, $50.

Facilities Pro shop, driving range, putting green, restaurant, bar.

Comments Target course designed by renowned architect Jay Morrish, Tom Weiskopf's partner. Lush fairway landing pads and well-manicured greens, but make certain you're on target. The rough is pure waste-area. Course gets heavy traffic, primarily from intermediate and advanced golfers.

Palm Valley Golf Club

| ESTABLISHED | 1989 | STATUS | SEMIPRIVATE | QV | RATING | ★ | 1 |

9201-B Del Webb Boulevard, Las Vegas, NV 89134; ☎ 702-363-4373; www.golfsummerlin.com

Tees

- **Championship: 6,849 yards, par 72, USGA 72.3, slope 127**
- **Gold: 5,757 yards, par 72, USGA 67.5, slope 119**
- **Men's: 6,341 yards, par 72, USGA 69.8, slope 124**
- **Ladies': 5,502 yards, par 72, USGA 70.7, slope 119**

Fees Nonresidents: before noon, $45; after noon and weekends, $35. Carts included. Club rentals, $40.

Facilities Pro shop, driving range, 2 putting greens, luncheon area, bar. Additional facilities for members.

Comments A demanding layout in a retirement community. Rolling, wide-open terrain, heavy bunkering, and bentgrass greens. The course will close to public play when membership fills from the 3,100 homeowners in the community.

The Revere at Anthem

| ESTABLISHED | 1999 | STATUS | PUBLIC | QV | RATING | ★★ | 2 |

2600 Hampton Road, Henderson, NV 89052; ☎ 702-259-GOLF or 877-273-8373; www.reveregolf.com

Tees

LEXINGTON

- **Black: 7,143 yards, par 72, USGA 73.6, slope 139**
- **Gold: 6,590 yards, par 72, USGA 70.8, slope 131**
- **Silver (Ladies'): 5,305 yards, par 72**
- **Bronze (Ladies'): 5,941 yards, par 72**

CONCORD

- **Black: 7,034 yards, par 72, USGA 72.8, slope 126**
- **Gold: 6,529 yards, par 72, USGA 69.8, slope 121**
- **Silver: 6,055 yards, par 72, USGA 67.6, slope 119**
- **Bronze (Ladies'): 5,306 yards, par 72, USGA 70, slope 119**

Fees Lexington: $95–$195 Monday–Thursday; $95–$245 Friday–Sunday. Concord: $95–$175 Monday–Thursday; $95–$205 Friday–Sunday.

Facilities Fully stocked clubhouse and snack bar, golf shop, restaurant.

Comments This 36-hole facility was named the nation's best facility operated by Troon Golf, a highly respected management company. Both courses were designed by Billy Casper and Greg Nash, and the club is consistently rated among the city's top ten. About 20 minutes from the Strip in the southeast Las Vegas Valley, Revere is built in a natural canyon, with a feel that is secluded and intimate. Lexington is the longer and more challenging layout, with numerous risk–reward opportunities, while the slightly shorter and newer Concord features wider fairways and larger greens. Concord is also less expensive. Tee times, which must be reserved by credit card, can be made up to a year in advance.

Rio Secco Golf Club

| ESTABLISHED | 1997 | STATUS | RESORT, SEMIPRIVATE | QV | RATING | ★★ | 3 |

2851 Grand Hills Drive, Henderson, NV 89052; ☎ 888-867-3226; www.riosecco.net

Tees

- **Championship: 7,332 yards, par 72, USGA 75.7, slope 147**
- **Blue: 6,946 yards, par 72, USGA 74.0, slope 138**
- **Middle: 6,375 yards, par 72, USGA 71.0, slope 125**
- **Forward: 5,778 yards, par 72, USGA 70.0, slope 127**

Fees Weekday, $100–$200; weekend, $125–$250. Lodging and golf packages with significant discounts are frequently offered by the Rio All-Suite Casino Hotel, especially through the hotel's Web site, at times of low room occupancy.

Facilities Pro shop, driving range, putting green, snack bar, restaurant, full locker facilities, Butch Harmon Golf School.

Comments The best and closest of Las Vegas's pure desert-style courses, Rio Secco is set amid 240 acres of dramatic canyons just 12 minutes from the Strip and features six holes down in the canyons, six on relatively level plateaus, and six that roller coaster through a rugged setting of desert dry washes. Variety, beauty, and strategic design highlighted by 88 bunkers make this a challenging but beautiful course. Unfortunately, its perimeter is heavily lined with homes, which spoils the setting, negates some of the desert feel, and doesn't live up to the high prices. Traditionally available only to guests of the Rio Casino, the course now accepts guests of all six Harrah's area hotels and limited outside play. It is also golf-school headquarters for celebrity instructor Butch Harmon, whose former pupil, Tiger Woods, holds the course record with a stunning 63. The front and back nines were recently reversed to create an imposing close with back to back par-5s.

Royal Links

ESTABLISHED	1999	STATUS	PUBLIC	QV	RATING	★ ★	3

5995 East Vegas Valley Road, Las Vegas, NV 89142; ☎ 888-427-6678; www.royallinksgolfclub.com

Tees

- **Royal: 7,029 yards, par 72, USGA 73.7, slope 135**
- **Gold: 6,602 yards, par 72, USGA 71.2, slope 131**
- **Ruby: 5,864 yards, par 72, USGA 68.4, slope 125**
- **Emerald: 5,142 yards, par 72, USGA 69.8, slope 115**

Fees September–April, weekdays $225, weekends $250. Twilight (after 2:30 p.m.) weekdays $135, weekends $155. 225, weekends $250. Twilight (after 2:30 p.m.) weekdays $135, weekends $155. Summer rates, $125–$155; $75–$125 twilight. Club rentals, $70.

Facilities Pro shop, driving range, putting green, restaurant, English pub, full locker facilities, fore-caddies.

Comments Royal Links sets out to emulate 18 holes from British Open venues in England and Scotland. In many ways the course succeeds, with excellent representations of links bunkering, exposure to fierce winds, and even authentic rough and gorse. But nearly every course represented is actually on the ocean, something that cannot be replicated in the desert, and the re-creations are far from exact. As a result, the course is more fun the less you know about the real thing. For instance, the famous Postage Stamp hole from Royal Troon, the shortest hole on the British Open rota, is copied here, but for some reason the elevation is way off, the bunkering is different, and architect Perry Dye saw fit to add a pond to the famously dry hole. The very expensive layout is mainly worth playing as a novelty if you've never been to the English courses.

Shadow Creek Golf Club

ESTABLISHED	1990	STATUS	RESORT	QV	RATING	★ ★	3

3 Shadow Creek Drive, Las Vegas, NV 89030; ☎ 866-260-0069; www.shadowcreek.com

Tees
- **Championship: 7,239 yards, par 72, USGA 71.0, slope 115**
- **Regular: 6,701 yards, par 72, USGA 68.9, slope 113**

Fees Monday–Thursday $500, includes caddie and round-trip limo transportation; must be a guest of a Mirage/MGM casino hotel to play, weekends invited guests only. With the recent acquisition of the Mandalay Bay hotel group, this expands the choices to include everything from the Bellagio and MGM Grand to Mandalay Bay, Excalibur and Luxor, and many others in between.

Facilities Pro shop, driving range, putting green, restaurant, full locker facilities, caddies.

Comments Shadow Creek is widely rated as not just the best course in Las Vegas, but among the best in the country. It is ranked 31st in the nation, including privates, by *Golf Magazine,* and in the top ten among public courses, deservedly. Shadow Creek is better considered barely "near public," with the nation's highest greens fees (tied), and those allowed only Monday through Thursday, with weekends reserved for VIPs and high-rolling gamblers. Nonetheless, when the required lodging and dining are thrown in, Shadow Creek falls in the same price range as Pebble Beach and Pinehurst Number Two, and offers a far more luxurious experience than either. The course is always empty and meticulously maintained, the caddies are excellent, and the layout is both gorgeous and fun to play. An engineering marvel that transported a classic, heavily wooded Carolina-style parkland layout to the desert, it is rumored to be the most expensive course ever built, having cost about $38 million in the 1980s. The finishing three holes are as memorable and dramatic a close as you will find in the golf world.

Siena Golf Club

| ESTABLISHED | 2000 | STATUS | SEMIPRIVATE | QV | RATING | ★★ | 1 |

10575 Siena Monte Avenue, Las Vegas, NV 89135; ☎ 888-689-6469; golf shop ☎ 702-341-9200; www.sienagolfclub.com

Tees
- **Gold: 6,843 yards, par 72, USGA 71.5, slope 129**
- **Black: 6,538 yards, par 72, USGA 70.2, slope 126**
- **Blue: 6,146 yards, par 72, USGA 68.5, slope 123**
- **White: 5,639 yards, par 72, USGA 66.3, slope 115**
- **Green: 4,978 yards, par 72, USGA 68.0, slope 112**

Fees Weekdays, $99; weekends, $119; special twilight rates available.

Facilities Pro shop, driving range, putting green, snack bar, restaurant, full locker facilities.

Comments A sleeper course in the Summerlin residential community, Siena welcomes outside play and is one of the region's best buys, especially with the bargain replay option. The course showcases extensive rock outcroppings and water features, including cascading waterfalls around the 18th green. All four par-3s are unique and notable, including "sunken treasure," a gorgeous island green. Well-separated tees offer the right challenge for every player.

TPC Canyons

ESTABLISHED **1996** | **STATUS** **PUBLIC** | **QV** **RATING** ★★★ **3**

9851 Canyon Run Drive, Las Vegas, NV 89145; ☎ 702-256-2000; www.tpc.com

Tees

- **TPC: 7,063 yards, par 71, USGA 73.0, slope 131**
- **Blue: 7,072 yards, par 71, USGA 73.0, slope 128**
- **White: 6,047 yards, par 71, USGA 67.7, slope 118**
- **Red: 5,039 yards, par 71, USGA 67.0, slope 109**

Fees January–May and September–December: weekdays, $225; weekends, $275; June–August: weekdays, $125; weekends, $150; special twilight and replay rates available.

Facilities Pro shop, driving range, putting green, snack bar, restaurant, full locker facilities.

Comments Few of the Tournament Players Clubs, or the TPC network, so-called "stadium courses," designed specifically to host and showcase tournaments and owned by the PGA Tour, are public, and this is one. Designed by Bobby Weed and Ray Floyd, it hosts the Las Vegas Invitational and has hosted the Michelob Championship. This is a tough desert course with plenty of opportunities to lose balls in the dry washed and cacti, but well designed and appealing to the better player. The facilities are first-rate, and the course has packages with the adjacent JW Marriott Summerlin resort.

Wynn Country Club

ESTABLISHED **2005** | **STATUS** **PUBLIC** | **QV** **RATING** ★★ **3**

3131 South Las Vegas Boulevard, Las Vegas, NV 89109; ☎ 702-770-GOLF; www.wynnlasvegas.com

Tees

- **Back: 6,938 yards, par 70, USGA 74, slope 124**
- **Black: 6,464 yards, par 70, USGA 72.5, slope 120**

Fees $500. Fees include caddie. Must be a guest of Wynn Las Vegas hotel to play.

Facilities Pro shop, driving net, putting green, restaurant, full locker facilities, caddies.

Comments Steve Wynn collaborated with Tom Fazio, widely considered the top golf architect in the world, to build Shadow Creek when Wynn owned Mirage Resorts. Now the duo is back at work for this course on the former site of the Desert Inn Country Club. Nothing of the old layout is recognizable, as Fazio moved 800,000 cubic yards of earth and changed the flat course to one with rolling elevation changes, boulder-strewn creeks, a huge four-story waterfall you drive carts behind, and endless flowerbeds.

The fairways and greens are immaculate, and the devotion to maintenance and aesthetics are obvious, making Wynn CC a very attractive and
playable course, but frankly it is not on par with its $500 brethren, Cascata
and Shadow Creek, as once-in-a-lifetime experiences. Anywhere else this
course would be lucky to command $250, but as the old real estate adage
goes, location is everything, and this is the only hotel course on the Strip
where guests can walk to the first tee rather than face daunting cab rides.
Still, the location comes at a cost: the new Las Vegas Monorail runs along
the perimeter and instead of majestic trees, skyline views are of the Eiffel
Tower, Stratosphere, and myriad new condo high-rises. Lack of space explains the par-70 design, and even at that length it remains a bit crowded.

OUTDOOR RECREATION

LAS VEGAS AND THE SURROUNDING AREA offer a host of outdoor
and adventure activities. The following section provides information on
the activities available. A local tour operator, **Thanks Babs The Day Trip-
per** (☎ 702-370-6961; **www.thanksbabs.com**), specializes in adventure
tours. If you want to sit back and let someone else handle the arrangements, she'll put together a custom tour that includes all the adventure
activities for which you have energy.

BICYCLING

ASK ANY CYCLIST IN LAS VEGAS about the on- and off-road riding
nearby and you'll probably hear two kinds of comments. First, why
pedaling in the desert is such a treat: excellent surface conditions; the
option of pancake-flat or hilly riding; starkly beautiful scenery any
time of year, and cactus blossoms in March and April; the possibility
of spying raptors or jack rabbits or wild burros as you pedal; the
unbelievably colorful limestone and sandstone formations.

Unfortunately, newcomers to desert and high-elevation biking
often recall only these comments and not the "Be sure to carry—"
warnings, which fellow riders usually provide after they've gotten you
all revved up. So read the following and remember that bikers are
subject to those very same conditions—heat and aridity—that make
the desert so breathtaking.

Biking Essentials

1. TIME OF DAY Desert biking in late spring, summer, and early fall is
best done early or late in the day. Know your seasons, listen to weather
reports, and don't overestimate your speed and ability.

2. CLOTHING Ever see someone perched on a camel? What was he
wearing? Right, it wasn't a tank top and Lycra shorts. The point is
protection—from the sun during the day, from the cold in the morning and evening. And if you don't use a helmet, wear a hat.

3. SUNSCREEN In the desert, even well-tanned riders need this stuff.

4. SUNGLASSES The glare will blind you without them.

5. WATER The first time we rode in the desert, we carried as much water as we would have used on a ride of comparable distance in the eastern United States. Big mistake. Our need for water was at least twice what it normally would be in New York or Alabama. We were thirsty the entire trip and might have gotten into serious trouble had we not cut our ride short.

You already know that you will need extra water, but how much? Well, a human working hard in 90°F temperature requires ten quarts of fluid replenishment every day. Ten *quarts*. That's two and a half gallons—12 large water bottles, or 16 small ones. And with water weighing in at eight pounds per gallon, a one-day supply comes to a whopping 20 pounds.

Pack along two or three bottles even for the shortest rides. For longer rides, we carry a large Camelback water carrier along with two bottles of water on the bike frame and a third stuffed inside the mesh of the Camelback.

In the desert, the heat is dry, and you do not notice much perspiration because your sweat evaporates as quickly as it surfaces. Combine the dry heat with a little wind, and you can become extremely dehydrated before realizing it. Folks from the East (like us) tend to regard sweating as a barometer of our level of exertion (if you are not sweating much, in other words, you must not be exercising very hard). In the desert, it doesn't work that way. You may never notice that you are sweating. In the desert you need to stay ahead of dehydration by drinking more frequently and more regularly and by consuming much more than the same amount of exercise would warrant in other climates. Desert days literally suck the water right out of you, even during the cooler times of the year.

6. TOOLS Each rider has a personal "absolute minimum list," which usually includes most of the following:

tire levers	spoke wrench
chain rivet tool	allen wrenches (3, 4, 5, and 6 mm)
spare tube patch kit	6-inch crescent (adjustable-end)
spare chain link	wrench
air pump or CO_2 cartridges	small flat-blade screwdriver

7. FIRST-AID KIT This, too, is a personal matter, usually including those items a rider has needed due to past mishaps. So, with the desert in mind, add a pair of tweezers (for close encounters of the cactus kind) and a snakebite kit. Most Las Vegas bikers have only seen snakes at the zoo or squashed on the highway, but you'll feel better if you pack one (the kit, that is) along.

Road Biking

Road biking on the Strip, downtown, or in any of Las Vegas's high-traffic areas is suicidal. Each year an astoundingly high number of bikers are injured or killed playing Russian roulette with Las Vegas motorists. If you want to bike, either confine yourself to sleepy subdivisions or get way out of town on a road with wide shoulders and little traffic.

There are a number of superb rides within a 30- to 40-minute drive from downtown or the Strip. The best is the **Red Rock Canyon Scenic Loop ride,** due west of town, which carves a 15.4-mile circuit through the canyon's massive, rust-colored, sandstone cliffs. The route is arduous, with a 1,000-foot elevation gain in the first six miles, followed by eight miles of downhill and flats with one more steep hill. One-way traffic on the scenic loop applies to cyclists and motorists alike. Although there is a fair amount of traffic on weekends, the road is wide and the speed limit is a conservative 35 miles per hour. If you park your car at the Red Rock Canyon Visitor Center, take careful note of when the area closes. If you are delayed on your ride and get back late, your car might be trapped behind locked gates.

A second ride in the same area follows NV 159 from the town of Blue Diamond to the entrance of Red Rock Canyon Scenic Loop Drive and back again, approximately eight miles. From Blue Diamond the highway traverses undulating hills, with a net elevation gain of 193 feet on the outbound leg. In general, the ride offers gentle, long grades alternating with relatively flat stretches. Cliff walls and desert flora provide stunning vistas throughout. Traffic on NV 159 is a little heavy on weekends, but the road is plenty wide, with a good surface and wide shoulders. In the village of Blue Diamond there is a small store.

Another good out-and-back begins at Overton Beach on Lake Mead, northeast of Las Vegas, and ascends 867 feet in eight miles to the visitor center at the Valley of Fire State Park. (You can, of course, begin your round trip at the visitor center, but we always prefer to tackle the uphill leg first.) Geology in the park is spectacular, with the same red sandstone found in the cliffs and formations of the Grand Canyon. There are no shoulders, but traffic is light and the road surface is good. Since the route runs pretty much east–west, we like to schedule our ride in the afternoon so that we will have the setting sun at our back as we coast down to the lake on the return leg. Another good option is an early-morning ride with the sun at your back as you ascend and high in the sky as you return.

Dressing for a bike ride in the canyons and high country around Las Vegas is a challenge. In early December, when we rode the Red Rock loop, it was about 62°F in town and about 10°F cooler in the canyon. We started out in Lycra bike shorts and polypro long-sleeve windbreakers. By the time we completed the six-mile uphill, we were about to die of heat prostration. On the long, fast downhill, we froze.

Our recommendation is to layer on cooler days so that you can add or shuck clothing as conditions warrant. On warm days, try to bike early in the morning or late in the afternoon and wear light clothing. Always wear a helmet and always, always carry lots of water. If you are not used to biking in arid climates, take twice as much water as you would carry at home, and drink *before* you get thirsty.

There is no place on any of these routes to get help with a broken bike. You should bring an extra tube and a pump and know how to fix flats and make other necessary repairs. Water is available at Blue Diamond and at the Red Rock and Valley of Fire visitor centers, but no place else. Always replenish when you have the opportunity.

Mountain Biking

Las Vegas, most unexpectedly, has become a mountain-biking destination. Southwest of Las Vegas on NV 160 is Cottonwood Valley, with more than 200 miles of single track and double track for all skill levels. There are five named loop trails, two named out-and-backs, and miles of unnamed trails and unpaved roads. Trail surface is mostly packed sand (good traction) with loose rock and a little soft sand. Trails on the north side of NV 160 are mellower in general, though there's some advanced riding below the east face of Wilson Cliffs. If it's your first time in the area, start with the figure-8 Mustang Trail. Almost all single track on good surface, this trail over rolling high desert offers moderate climbs, gradual descents, and great views of the Red Rock cliffs and valleys. A number of trails branch off Mustang if you want to lengthen your ride or opt for more advanced terrain.

On the south side of NV 160, the rides require more climbing. The showcase trail is the Dead Horse Loop, 14 miles of intermediate to advanced single track. Site of NORBA races, the route climbs to an overlook, with a stunning view of Las Vegas in the distance, and then drops off the mountain in a blue-cruiser known locally as the three-mile smile. Out-and-backs and additional loops connecting to Dead Horse serve up more technical climbs and descents.

There are two ways to reach Cottonwood Valley. The fastest is to go south on I-15, exit onto NV 160, and head west 16 miles to the Mustang Trailhead parking lot (on the right) or 17 miles to the Cottonwood Valley Trailhead on the left. You can also go west out of town on Charleston Boulevard, which becomes NV 159. Take NV 159 until it intersects NV 160 south of Blue Diamond. Turn right on NV 160 for five to six miles to the parking lots.

Try riding Cottonwood Valley first. If Cottonwood doesn't offer enough challenge, try Bootleg Canyon.

Southeast of Las Vegas near Boulder City, Hoover Dam, and Lake Mead is Bootleg Canyon, primarily an advanced skill level mountain-bike park. Though it is mostly known for its full-body-armor downhills and jumps, the park also serves up some technical cross-country, great views of Boulder City, and, on the backside, Lake Mead. Though hard to get really lost, the layout, with lots of criss-crossing trails, is confusing to many bikers riding there for the first time. A lot, if not most, of the riding is hard core, as are the riders who hang here. Surface is packed dirt or sand and a lot of rock, much of it loose. Trails, carved into the side of the hill, are frequently off-camber. To get there from Las Vegas, take NV 93 to Boulder City. Turn left at the light onto Buchanan Boulevard, and then left onto Canyon Road. Continue beyond where the pavement gives way to dirt to the Bootleg Canyon parking lot situated between two hills. Usually there are freebie maps of the park in a box at the parking lot, but if possible, team up with locals who know the area and terrain.

If you're not used to riding in the high desert, you won't believe how much water you consume. We recommend a full Camelback plus as many water bottles as you can carry on the frame. Rental bikes, unfortunately, generally come with only one water holder. If you can jam an extra water bottle into the deep pouch on your Camelback, you'll be glad you did. Wind, almost always howling out of the west, is a factor at both biking destinations, so much so that trails are generally laid out on a north/south axis with as little east–west as possible. Even so, tackling a tough climb into a headwind will probably be part of your Nevada biking baptism. Finally, almost all of the riding is exposed. If you want shade, bring an umbrella.

Other area rides include the Bristlecone Pine Trail in Lee Canyon on Mount Charleston, about an hour northwest of Las Vegas. Though just under six miles in length, this loop trail is at altitude (above 7,500 feet) with a 700-foot rise and fall in elevation. Take US 95 north and then follow NV 157 for 17 miles up into the mountains until you see a dirt road where you can turn off and park.

Good bikes are available for rent at **Escape Adventures,** 8221 West Charleston Boulevard (☎ 702-596-2953 or **www.escapeadventures .com**). Helmets, bike racks, water bottles, Cottonwood Valley trail maps, and other gear are likewise available for rent or sale. Escape also offers guided mountain-bike tours daily, with trails chosen based on the skill level of the group. If you book a tour, Escape will pick you up at your hotel or one close by.

Another option is to rent a bike from **McGhie's Bike Outpost** (☎ 702-875-4820 or **www.bikeoutpost.com**), in the little desert town of Blue Diamond. Blue Diamond is off NV 159 about three miles north of the intersection with NV 160. Located on the east end of Cottonwood Valley, you can actually get on the trail outside the back door of the shop. That said, you have to bike quite a way uphill and west to access the popular loop trails.

In addition to the forgoing, many mountain bikers ride the paved scenic loop at Red Rock Canyon (described under "Road Biking," page 444). Call ☎ 702-875-4820; **www.redrockcanyonlv.org.**

HIKING AND BACKPACKING

HIKING OR BACKPACKING IN THE DESERT can be a very enjoyable experience. It can also be a hazardous adventure if you travel unprepared. Lake Mead ranger Debbie Savage suggests the following:

The best months for hiking are the cooler months of November through March. Hiking is not recommended in the summer, when temperatures reach 120°F in the shade. Never hike alone and always tell someone where you are going and when you plan to return. Carry plenty of water (at least a half gallon per person) and drink often.

Know your limits. Hiking the canyons and washes in the desert often means traveling over rough, steep terrain with frequent elevation changes. Try to pick a route that best suits your abilities. Distances in the desert are often deceiving. Be sure to check the weather forecast before departure. Sudden storms can cause flash flooding. Seek higher ground if thunderstorms threaten.

Essential equipment includes sturdy walking shoes and proper clothing. Long pants are suggested for protection from rocks and cactus. A hat, sunscreen, and sunglasses are also recommended. Carry a small daypack to hold such items as a first-aid kit, lunch, water, a light jacket, and a flashlight.

Canyons and washes often contain an impressive diversity of plant life, most easily observed during the spring wildflower season. Desert springs are located in some of the canyons and support a unique community of plants and animals. They are often the only source of water for many miles around. Take care not to contaminate them with trash or other human wastes. Along similar lines, understand that desert soils are often very fragile and take a long time to recover if disturbed. These surfaces are recognizable by their comparatively darker appearance and should be avoided whenever possible.

Poisonous animals such as snakes, spiders, and scorpions are most active after dark and are not often seen during daylight hours by hikers. Speckled rattlesnakes are common but are not aggressive. Scorpion stings are no more harmful than a bee sting, unless you are allergic. Black widow spiders are shy and secretive and are most often found around man-made structures. Watch where you place your hands and feet and don't disturb obvious hiding places.

The Las Vegas area offers quite a diversity of hiking options. Trips that include a choice of canyons, lakes, desert, mountains, or ponderosa pine forest can be found within an hour's drive of Las Vegas.

The Lake Mead National Recreation Area, an hour southeast of Las Vegas, offers a wide variety of hiking experiences, although there are few designated trails. Included within the NRA are Lakes Mead and Mohave, and part of the Mojave Desert. Ranger-guided hikes are offered during the winter months. The outings cover six to eight miles and are moderate to strenuous in difficulty. If you prefer to explore on your own, detailed maps and instructions to the most popular areas are available at the visitor centers. An admission fee of $5 per vehicle is good for five days. For information, call ☎ 702-293-8990.

The Red Rock Canyon National Conservation Area contains some of the most rugged rock formations in the West. Only 40 minutes from Las Vegas, Red Rock Canyon offers loop as well as out-and-back trails of varying lengths. (See map on page 451.) The short Moenkopi Loop originates at the visitor center, and it takes a little more than an hour to walk over undulating terrain in a broad desert valley. Other popular short hikes include out-and-backs to Lost Creek (three-tenths of a mile, one-way), Icebox Canyon (one and three-tenths miles, one-way), and Pine Creek Canyon (one mile, one-way), leading to the ruins of a historic homestead near a running creek surrounded by large ponderosa pine trees. Our favorite trail, and certainly one of the most scenic, is the out-and-back Calico Tanks Trail (two and a half miles, round-trip), which winds up through a narrow canyon to a *tinaja*, a circular canyon, or "tank," that forms a natural lake. The hike is a stunner, even in hot dry months when there's little or no water in the tank, and ends at the top of the canyon with a knockout view of Las Vegas on the distant valley floor.

Altogether there are 19 trails: 4 rated easy, 5 rated easy to moderate, 9 rated moderate, and 1 classified as difficult. Distances range from three-fourths of a mile to six miles. Estimated hiking times are one to two hours for most trails (30 minutes for the shortest and three hours for the longest). Most of the easy and easy-to-moderate trails are pretty level. Elevation gain for moderate and difficult trails ranges from 300 feet to 1,700 feet. Maps and hiking information are available free when you pay your entrance fee and for sale in the visitor center. For more information about Red Rock trails, see **www.sunsetcities.com/ redrock.html**. If you'd like to spend a few days here and camp, Red Rock offers a good campground (see profile below). For more information, call ☎ 702-515-5350, or check out **www.desertusa.com/ redrock** or **www.sunsetcities.com/redrock.html**.

Red Rock Canyon Campground

RV ★★★   TENT ★★   BEAUTY ★★★   SITE PRIVACY ★   QUIET ★★★½
SPACIOUSNESS ★★½ SECURITY ★★ CLEANLINESS ★★★ INSECT CONTROL ★★★★

Rock National Conservation Area, HCR 33, Box 5500, Las Vegas, NV 89124; ☎ 702-515-5350; www.nv.blm.gov/redrockcanyon

FACILITIES
Acres 60. **Number of RV sites** 5. **Number of tent-only sites** 71. **Number of multi-purpose sites** 52. **Site to acreage ratio** 1:0.8. **Hookups** None. **Each site** Table, fire pit. **Dump station** No. **Laundry** No. **Pay phone** No. **Restrooms and showers** Restrooms, no showers. **Fuel** No. **Propane** No. **Internal roads** Dirt. **RV service** No. **Market** No. **Restaurant** No. **General store** No. **Vending** No. **Swimming** No. **Playground** No. **Nearby attractions** Red Rock Canyon National Conservation Area.

KEY INFORMATION
Operated by Bureau of Land Management. **Open** September–May. **Site assignment** First come, first served. **Registration** At ranger station. **Fee** $10 per day per site. **Parking** Maximum 2 vehicles per site.

RESTRICTIONS
Pets On leash only. **Fires** Not allowed. **Alcoholic beverages** Not allowed. **Vehicle maximum length** 16'.

TO GET THERE From Las Vegas, drive west on Charleston Boulevard/NV 159 for six miles. Two miles before the Red Rock Canyon scenic drive, turn left on Moenkopi Drive. Pass the fire station on the right, the group campground on the left, then drive down the hill to the campground.

DESCRIPTION It's the desert, and nothing but. Set in a low hollow just below the Calico Hills, Red Rock Canyon Campground offers the bare minimum: a place to pitch your tent, and little else. The campground's compact main loop is bisected by two spoke roads, with sites feathering off at regular angles. Pit toilets are set at the corners. There's no foliage to screen your site from neighbors, who are not that far off in any case. A small RV loop and a similar-sized walk-in tent-only loop dangle off to the south, near the campground host. Five large group sites are set out near the entrance. The low setting makes views of the hills problematic, but it's extremely serene and quiet—and even with the lights of the Strip a few miles away, the clear night sky makes for great stargazing.

The Humboldt-Toiyabe National Forest, high in the mountains 40 minutes northwest of Las Vegas, provides a totally different outdoor experience. The air is cool, and the trails run among stately forests of ponderosa pine, quaking aspen, white fir, and mountain mahogany. Hikes range in distance from one-tenth of a mile to 21 miles, and in difficulty from easy to very difficult. Most popular are the Cathedral Rock Trail (two miles round-trip), which climbs 900 feet to a stark summit overlooking Kyle Canyon, and Bristlecone, a five-mile loop that traverses the ridges above the Lee Canyon Ski Area. Though the distances of these loops are not great, the terrain is exceedingly rugged, and the hikes are not recommended for one-day outings unless you begin very early in the morning and are used to strenuous exercise at high elevations. For more information, call ☎ 775-738-5171.

The Valley of Fire State Park, 45 minutes northeast of Las Vegas, rounds out the hiking picture. This park features rock formations similar to those found in the Grand Canyon, as well as a number of Indian petroglyphs. The *Las Vegas Advisor* compares hiking the Valley of Fire with being "beamed" onto another planet. Trails traverse desert terrain and vary from a half-mile to seven miles in length. Visitors should check in at the visitor center before they begin hiking. The park fee is $6; for more information, call ☎ 702-397-2088.

Guided Hikes and Tours

Rocky Trails (☎ 866-867-6259 or **www.rockytrails.com**) offers guided tours to the natural sites described above as well as to Death Valley, the Grand Canyon, Bryce Canyon, and Zion National Park. Guests are picked up at their hotel and transported in modern Suburbans or vans. Lunch or dinner is included. Expeditions to the Valley of Fire, Red Rock Canyon, Death Valley, and the Grand Canyon last six to ten hours and cost $89 to $499 per adult.

red rock canyon

White Rock

Willow Springs

Icebox Canyon

Red Rock
Canyon Visitor Ctr.

Pine Creek
Canyon

Oak Creek
Canyon

First Creek Canyon

Spring Mtn.
Ranch State Park

La Madre Mtn.
7000'
6000'

Turtlehead
△ Mtn.
5000'

Sandstone
Quarry

Calico
Hills

Moenkopi
Trail

White Rock Hills

6000'

Red Rock Canyon

Red Rock Wash

4000'

△
North
Peak

Bridge
△
Mtn.

159

Loop
Entrance

Wilson
7000'

SPRING MOUNTAINS

△ Rainbow
Mtn.

Loop Exit

Bonnie Springs/
Old Nevada

Cliffs
7000'

5000'

△ Mt.
Wilson

4000'

Blue
Diamond

Lovell Canyon Rd.

△ Indecision
Peak

Sandstone Mtn. △

6000' 4000'

159

Black Velvet
Peak △

4000'

6000'

△ Windy Peak

Mountain Springs ◎

5000'

160

Cottonwood Valley

To 15

0 _____ 2 mi
0 _____ 2 km

Primary roads
Secondary roads
4WD roads
• • • • • Hiking trails

Rest rooms .... 🛉	Telephone .... ✆	Groceries .... 🛒
Drinking water .... 🚰	Gasoline .... ⛽	Primitive camping .... ⛺
Picnic area .... 🛆	Restaurant .... 🍽	Hiking/photography .... 🥾
Group facilities .... 🏠	Riding stables .... 🐎	Natural history .... 🔗

ROCK CLIMBING AND BOULDERING

THE RED ROCK CANYON NATIONAL CONSERVATION AREA is one of the top rock-climbing resources in the United States. With more than 1,000 routes, abundant holds, and approaches ranging from roadside to remote wilderness, the area rivals Yosemite in scope and variety for climbers. Offering amazing diversity for every skill level amidst desert canyon scenery second to none, the area is less than a 40-minute drive from Las Vegas.

Though there is some granite and limestone, almost all of the climbing is done on sandstone. Overall, the rock is pretty solid, although there are some places where the sandstone gets a little crumbly, especially after a rain. Bolting is allowed but discouraged (local climbers have been systematically replacing bolts on some of the older routes with more modern bolts that blend with the rock). There are some great spots for bouldering, some of the best top-roping in the United States, a lifetime supply of big walls, and even some bivouac routes. Climbs range in difficulty from nonbelayed scrambles to 5.13 big-wall overhangs. You can climb year-round at Red Rock. Wind can be a problem, as can most of the other conditions that make a desert environment challenging. Having enough water can be a logistical nightmare on a long climb.

Red Rock Guide by Joanne Urioste describes a number of the older routes. Newer route descriptions can be obtained from **Desert Rock Sports** in Las Vegas (☎ 702-254-1143; **www.desertrocksports lv.com**). Desert Rock Sports can also help you find camping and showers and tell you where the loose rock is. Offering climbing-shoe rentals, the store is at 8221 West Charleston, conveniently on the way to the canyon from Las Vegas. The **Red Rock Climbing Center** (☎ 702-254-5604; **www.redrockclimbingcenter.com**) is next to Desert Rock Sports and offers excellent indoor climbing and showers. Guides and/ or instruction are available from Desert Rock Sports.

RIVER RUNNING

THE BLACK CANYON OF THE COLORADO RIVER can be run year-round below Hoover Dam. The most popular trip is from the tailwaters of the dam to Willow Beach. In this 11-mile section, canyon walls rise almost vertically from the water's edge, with scenery and wildlife very similar to that of the Colorado River in the Grand Canyon above Lake Mead. There are numerous warm springs and waterfalls on feeder streams, presenting the opportunity for good side-trip hikes. Small beaches provide good rest and lunch sites. Bighorn sheep roam the bluffs, and wild burros can often be seen up the canyons. The water in the river, about 53°F year-round, is drawn from the bottom of Lake Mead and released downstream through the Hoover Dam hydroelectric generators.

Under normal conditions, the Black Canyon is a nice flatwater float trip with a steady current to help you along. There are places along the river such as Ringbolt Rapids and the Chute that are named for falls and rapids long since covered up and flattened out by the voluminous discharge of water from the dam. There is nothing remaining on the run in the way of paddling challenges beyond a few swells and ripples. The Black Canyon is suitable for canoes, kayaks, and rafts. Motorized craft cannot be launched below the dam but can come upstream to the dam from Willow Beach or from other marinas farther downstream. The trip takes about six hours, including side trips and lunch, for a canoe or kayak, and about three and one half hours for a commercial motorized raft.

There are several ways you can get into serious trouble. The put-in below the dam is rocky and slippery. More than a few boaters have accidentally launched their boat before they climbed aboard, while others have managed to arrive in the river ahead of their boat. Once you're under way, it's important to keep your group close together. With the water temperature at 53°F, you want to pluck people our of the river post haste in the event of a capsize. When you go ashore to explore, pull your boat way up out of the water and tie it to something sturdy. If at the dam they happen to crank up an extra generator or two while you're off hiking in a side canyon, it's possible for the river to rise several feet, sweeping any unsecured boats and equipment downstream.

If the weather service predicts headwinds in excess of 18 miles an hour, cancel your paddling trip, even if it means losing your permit fee.

For the most part, the 11-mile run from the dam to Willow Beach does not require any prior paddling experience. On most days, you could practically float to the take out, with breaks for lunch and exploring, in five hours. The exception, and it's a big one, is when headwinds blow up the canyon from the west. Though headwinds of less than ten miles an hour won't affect the paddling situation much, winds of 10 to 18 miles an hour require more experience and advanced boat-handling skills. When the wind is high, it can blow you upstream, making forward progress grueling or impossible, and can whip up crosscurrents as well as waves up to three feet high. Chances of capsize grow exponentially with wind speed, and rescue efforts become correspondingly more difficult.

Private (noncommercial) parties must obtain a launch permit from:

Black Canyon/Willow Beach River Adventures
☎ 702-294-1414
fax 702-294-4464
www.blackcanyonadventures.com

The launch permit costs $13 per person and is required to launch from below Hoover Dam. A $3 per person National Park Service entrance fee is also required. Only 30 boats are allowed to launch from below the dam each day, so weekends sell out well in advance. On weekdays, it's sometimes possible to get a permit on short notice. Permits can be obtained on a first-come, first-serve basis six months in advance. The permits and fees apply to a specific date and are non-refundable, though if there's space available, the permitting authority will try to assign you an alternate date in the event of bad weather, high winds, or other mitigating circumstances.

The application can be downloaded from the above Web site; alternatively, you can phone and request that the application be faxed or mailed to you. Completed applications can be submitted by e-mail or fax. When your permit is approved, it will be e-mailed, faxed, or mailed to you along with directions, put-in/take-out instructions, and salient information about the river. Also included is information on canoe and kayak rentals, transportation of rented boats, and shuttle arrangements.

The best time to run the Canyon is in the fall through December. The spring is prettiest, with new green foliage seen on the beaches and in the side canyons. The spring, along with January and February, tend to be the windiest times of year, however. Summers are hot, and the canyons tend to hold the heat. The water, however, provides some natural cooling. Canoers and kayakers can make the run in one day or alternatively camp overnight in the canyon en route. Commercial raft trips are one-day affairs.

If you don't have your own equipment, you can rent canoes as well as one- and two-person kayaks from **Down River Outfitters** in nearby Boulder City (☎ 702-293-1190 or **www.downriveroutfitters.com**). The kayaks are the preferred craft but unfortunately don't come with spray skirts. This means essentially that every time you take a paddle stroke, 53°F water drips off the paddle into your lap. Canoes are drier, but slower, and more affected by wind. In addition to providing equipment, Down River Outfitters also transports you and your boat to the river. At the end of the run, they pick you up at Willow Beach and drive you back to your car. Canoe and two-person kayaks run $45 per person for one-day trips; one-person kayaks, $55. Call or visit the outfitter's Web site for booking procedures and rates for multiday trips. In addition to granting permits, Black Canyon/Willow Beach River Adventures also operates guided, motorized raft trips, with guest transportation provided from the Strip and downtown. No permit is required for these trips.

The raft outing is unlike most commercial river trips. First, the rafts are huge, accommodating more than two dozen guests. Secondly, the trip is entirely passive—no paddling or anything else required. The rafts motor up from Willow Beach in the morning and pick up their passengers at the put-in below the dam. From there, it's a scenic, narrated three-hour or so float back to Willow Beach, where guests are loaded up and transported back to their cars or delivered to their Las Vegas hotel. The trips run $83 for adults, $80 for children ages 13 to 15, and $51 for children ages 5 to 12. For transportation from your Las Vegas hotel, add $33.

There is little protection from the sun in the Black Canyon, and temperatures can surpass 110°F in the warmer months.

Long-sleeve shirts, long pants, tennis shoes, and a hat are recommended minimum attire year-round. Be sure to take sunscreen and lots of drinking water.

SNOW SKIING

THE LAS VEGAS SKI AND SNOWBOARD RESORT AT LEE CANYON is a 45-minute drive from Las Vegas. Situated in a granite canyon in the Spring Mountain range, the resort provides three double chair lifts servicing ten runs. Though the mountain is small and the runs short by Western standards, the skiing is solid intermediate. Of the ten runs, seven are blue, two are black, and there is one short green. Base elevation of 8,510 feet notwithstanding, snow conditions are usually dependable only during January. Because of its southerly location and the proximity of the hot, arid desert, there is a lot of thawing and refreezing in Lee Canyon, and hence, frequently icy skiing conditions. If the snow is good, a day at Lee Canyon is a great outing. If the mountain is icy, do something else.

Snowmaking equipment allows the resort to operate from Thanksgiving to Easter. There is no lodging on-site and only a modest coffee shop and lounge. The parking lot is a fairly good hike from the base facility.

Skis can be rented at the ski area. For information on lift tickets or snow conditions, call the ski area office at ☎ 702-385-2754 or see **www.skilasvegas.com.** For summer event info at Lee Canyon, call ☎ 702-593-9500.

HORSEBACK RIDING

THE CLOSEST HORSEBACK RIDING OUTFITTERS are in the Red Rock Canyon area half an hour west of Las Vegas. Riding is allowed on only a couple of trails in the Red Rock National Conservation Area, but there's a lot of riding to be found just outside the Conservation Area. **Bonnie Springs,** ☎ 702-875-4191; **Old West Tours,** ☎ 702-798-7788; and **Cowboy Trail Ride,** ☎ 702-387-2457, are all located within a four- to ten-minute drive from Red Rock Canyon.

A great place for horseback riding is Kyle Canyon in the Toiyabe National Forest northwest of Las Vegas. Quarter horses with Western saddles can be rented spring through fall for one-and-a-half- to two-hour daytime rides at $69 to $89. The scenery is spectacular, with mountain vistas, ponderosa pine forests, and 300,000 acres to explore. Guides are available. Advance payment and reservations are required. For information or reservations, call **Mount Charleston Riding Stables** at ☎ 702-387-2457.

FISHING

THE LAKE MEAD NATIONAL RECREATION AREA offers some of the best fishing in the United States. Lake Mead is the largest lake, with

LAKE MEAD BAIT AND TACKLE, BOAT RENTAL, FUEL, AND SUPPLIES	
Callville Bay Resort	☎ 702-565-8958
Cottonwood Cove Resort	☎ 702-297-1464
Echo Bay Resort	☎ 702-394-4000
Lake Mead Resort	☎ 702-293-2074 or 800-752-9669
Lake Mohave Resort (AZ)	☎ 928-754-3245
Temple Bar Resort (AZ)	☎ 928-767-3211

Lake Mohave, downstream on the Colorado River, offering the most diverse fishery. Largemouth bass, striped bass, channel catfish, crappie, and bluegill are found in both lakes. Rainbow and cutthroat trout are present only in Lake Mohave. Remote and beautiful in its upmost reaches, Lake Mohave is farther from Las Vegas but provides truly exceptional fishing. Bass and trout often run three pounds, and some trout weigh ten pounds or more. Willow Beach, near where the Colorado River enters the pool waters of Lake Mohave, is where many of the larger trout are taken.

Lake Mead, broader, more open, and much closer to Las Vegas, has become famous for its stripers, with an occasional catch weighing in at over 40 pounds. Bass fishing is consistently good throughout Lake Mead. The Overton Arm (accessed from Echo Bay or Overton Beach) offers the best panfish and catfish action.

Because lakes Mead and Mohave form the Arizona/Nevada state line, fishing license regulations are a little strange. If you are bank fishing, all you need is a license from the state you are in. If you fish from a boat, however, you need a fishing license from one state and a special-use stamp from the other. Fortunately, all required stamps and licenses can be obtained from marinas and local bait and tackle shops in either state.

Nonresidents have the option of purchasing one- to ten-day fishing permits in lieu of a license. Permits are $18 for one day and $69 for annual, and apply to the reciprocal waters of Lake Mead and Lake Mohave only. In addition to the permit, a special-use stamp costing $3 is required for those fishing from a boat, and a $10 trout stamp is necessary to take trout. In addition, a $10 stamp is available for fishing with two rods. Youngsters age 12 years and under in the company of a properly licensed, permitted, and stamped adult can fish without any sort of documentation.

Sixteen-foot, aluminum fishing boats (that seat five) can be rented on both lakes by the hour (about $40 with a two-hour minimum), by the half-day (four hours for about $50), or by the day (about $100). Bass boats, houseboats, and pontoon craft are also available. Rods and reels rent for about $5 for four hours or less and about $12 a day.

PLEASURE BOATING, SAILING, WATER SKIING, AND JET SKIING

LAKE MEAD AND LAKE MOHAVE are both excellent sites for pleasure boating, water skiing, and other activities. Both lakes are so large that it is easy to find a secluded spot for your favorite boating or swimming activity. Rock formations on the lakes are spectacular, and boaters can visit scenic canyons and coves that are inaccessible to those traveling by car. Boats, for example, can travel into the narrow, steep-walled gorge of Iceberg Canyon in Lake Mead or upstream into the Black Canyon from Lake Mohave.

First-timers, particularly on Lake Mead, frequently underestimate its vast size. It is not difficult to get lost on the open waters of Lake Mead or to get caught in bad weather. Winds can be severe on the lake, and waves of six feet sometimes arise during storms. In general, there is no shade on the lakes, and the steep rock formations along the shore do not make very hospitable emergency landing sites. When you boat on either lake, take plenty of water, be properly dressed and equipped, and be sure to tell someone where you are going and when you expect to return.

Most of the resorts listed under "Fishing" rent various types of pleasure craft and water-skiing equipment, and two of them, the Overton Beach Resort on Lake Mead and the Callville Bay Resort, rent personal watercraft. In addition, at Callville Bay on Lake Mead and Cottonwood Cove on Lake Mohave, luxury houseboats are available for rental. The boats sleep up to ten adults and have fully equipped galleys and heads. For rates and other information concerning houseboats, call ☎ 800-255-5561 or 800-752-9669.

RELAXATION *and* REJUVENATION

FOLLOWING A VIGOROUS DAY'S EXERCISE, Las Vegas offers numerous ways to relax, including a wide choice of health spas. The spas offer everything from massage to exotic body wraps. Each spa is different but, in addition to workout equipment, these spas generally have tanning facilities, skin treatments, and steam rooms.

Most spas are open to the public, but some cater only to hotel guests. A tourist staying in one of the larger hotel-casinos should have access to on-site spa facilities. Check the listing on the following page for phone numbers and access information.

Las Vegas Health Spas

SPAS OPEN TO THE PUBLIC

Planet Hollywood	Mandara Spa	☎ 702-785-5772
Alexis Park Resort & Villas	Alexis Park Health Spa	☎ 702-796-3364
Caesars Palace	Spa at Caesars Palace *(Sun.–Thurs.)*	☎ 702-731-7776
Excalibur	Royal Treatment Spa	☎ 702-597-7772
Flamingo	The Spa at Flamingo	☎ 702-733-3535
Four Seasons	The Spa at Four Seasons	☎ 702-632-5302
Green Valley Ranch Resort and Spa	The Spa at Green Valley Ranch	☎ 702-617-7570
Hard Rock Hotel	The Rock Spa	☎ 702-693-5000
Harrah's	The Spa at Harrah's	☎ 702-369-5189
Hyatt Regency at Lake Las Vegas	Spa Moulay	☎ 702-567-6049
Imperial Palace	The Spa at I. P.	☎ 702-794-3242
Las Vegas Hilton	The Spa at the Las Vegas Hilton	☎ 702-732-5648
Luxor	Oasis Spa	☎ 702-730-5721
Mandalay Bay	Spa Mandalay	☎ 702-632-7220
MGM Grand	The MGM Grand Spa *(Mon.–Thurs.)*	☎ 702-891-1111
Monte Carlo	The Spa at Monte Carlo	☎ 702-730-7777
New York–New York	The Spa at New York–New York	☎ 702-740-6955
Paris Las Vegas	Spa by Mandara	☎ 702-946-4366
Red Rock Resort	The Spa at Red Rock	☎ 702-797-7878
Rio	Rio Spa	☎ 702-777-7779
Riviera	Executive Fitness at the Riviera	☎ 702-794-9441
T. I.	Salon & Spa at T. I. *(undergoing renovation at press time)*	☎ 702-894-7474
Tropicana	Spa Tropicana	☎ 702-739-2680
The Venetian	Canyon Ranch SpaClub	☎ 702-414-3610

SPAS FOR HOTEL GUESTS ONLY

Bally's	The Spa at Bally's	☎ 702-967-4366
Bellagio	Spa Bellagio	☎ 702-693-7111
Caesars Palace	Spa at Caesars Palace *(Fri. and Sat.)*	☎ 702-731-7776
Golden Nugget	The Spa at Golden Nugget	☎ 702-386-8186
MGM Grand	MGM Grand Spa *(Fri. and Sat.)*	☎ 702-891-1111
Mirage	The Spa at the Mirage	☎ 702-891-5511
Wynn Las Vegas	The Spa at Wynn Las Vegas	☎ 702-770-3900

RESTAURANT INDEX

Note: Page numbers of restaurant profiles are in **boldface** type.

SUBJECT INDEX

If you would like to express your opinion in writing about Las Vegas or this guidebook, complete the following survey and mail it to:

> *Unofficial Guide* Reader Survey
> P.O. Box 43673
> Birmingham, AL 35243

Inclusive dates of your visit:_____

Members of your party:

	Person 1	Person 2	Person 3	Person 4	Person 5
Gender:	M F	M F	M F	M F	M F
Age:					

How many times have you been to Las Vegas? _____
On your most recent trip, where did you stay? _____

Concerning your accommodations, on a scale of 100 as best and 0 as worst, how would you rate:

The quality of your room?   The value of your room?
The quietness of your room?   Check-in/check-out efficiency?
Shuttle service to the airport?   Swimming pool facilities?

Did you rent a car?_____   From whom?_____

Concerning your rental car, on a scale of 100 as best and 0 as worst, how would you rate:

Pick-up processing efficiency?____ Return processing efficiency?___
Condition of the car?____   Cleanliness of the car?____
Airport shuttle efficiency?____

Concerning your dining experiences:

Estimate your meals in restaurants per day? _____
Approximately how much did your party spend on meals per day? ____
_____

Favorite restaurants in Las Vegas: _____
_____

Did you buy this guide before leaving? _____ While on your trip?_____

How did you hear about this guide? (check all that apply)

Loaned or recommended by a friend ☐   Radio or TV ☐
Newspaper or magazine ☐   Bookstore salesperson ☐
Just picked it out on my own ☐   Library ☐
Internet ☐

What other guidebooks did you use on this trip? _____
_____
_____
_____

On a scale of 100 as best and 0 as worst, how would you rate them?
_____
_____
_____

Using the same scale, how would you rate the *Unofficial Guide*(s)?

_____

Are *Unofficial Guides* readily available at bookstores in your area? _____

Have you used other *Unofficial Guides*? _____

Which one(s)? _____
_____
_____

Comments about your Las Vegas trip or the *Unofficial Guide*(s):
_____
_____
_____
_____
_____
_____
_____
_____
_____
_____
_____
_____
_____
_____
_____
_____
_____
_____